# Lecture Notes in Computer Science    11028

*Commenced Publication in 1973*
Founding and Former Series Editors:
Gerhard Goos, Juris Hartmanis, and Jan van Leeuwen

More information about this series at http://www.springer.com/series/7411

Andreas Podelski · François Taïani (Eds.)

# Networked Systems

6th International Conference, NETYS 2018
Essaouira, Morocco, May 9–11, 2018
Revised Selected Papers

 Springer

*Editors*
Andreas Podelski
Universität Freiburg
Freiburg, Germany

François Taïani 🄳
University of Rennes 1
Rennes, France

ISSN 0302-9743                ISSN 1611-3349   (electronic)
Lecture Notes in Computer Science
ISBN 978-3-030-05528-8        ISBN 978-3-030-05529-5   (eBook)
https://doi.org/10.1007/978-3-030-05529-5

Library of Congress Control Number: 2018963973

LNCS Sublibrary: SL5 – Computer Communication Networks and Telecommunications

This Springer imprint is published by the registered company Springer Nature Switzerland AG
The registered company address is: Gewerbestrasse 11, 6330 Cham, Switzerland

# Preface

In May 2018, the 6th edition of the International Conference on Networked Systems (NETYS) took place in Essaouira (Morocco). For this edition, we received 85 submissions, which were reviewed by a Program Committee of 39 international experts in various fields related to the design and verification of networked and distributed computing systems. Out of these submissions, the Program Committee decided to accept 22 regular papers and six short papers. In addition, several renowned researchers accepted to give keynote presentations:

- Nicolas Bjorner (Microsoft Research)
- Christophe Diot (Google)
- Bryon Ford (EPFL, Lausanne)
- Maurice Herlihy (Brown University, Providence)
- Ranjit Jhala (UC San Diego)
- Anne-Marie Kermarrec (Mediego and EPFL)
- Marta Kwiatkowska (Oxford University)
- Rupak Majumdar (MPI SWS, Kaiserslautern)
- Thomas Reps (University of Wisconsin-Madison)
- Liuba Shrira (Brandeis University)
- Renata Teixeira (Google)

As program chairs of NETYS 2018 and editors of these proceedings, we want to warmly thank again all the authors for their high-quality contributions and all the Program Committee members and external reviewers for their invaluable hard work. We also sincerely thank our keynote speakers for sharing their precious insights and expertise. Last but not least, our special thanks go to the Organizing Committee and to all the local arrangements coordinators, and the conference general chairs, Ahmed Bouajjani (Université Paris Diderot, France), Mohammed Erradi (ENSIAS, Rabat, Morocco), and Rachid Guerraoui (EPFL, Lausanne, Switzerland), without whom NETYS would simply not exist.

October 2018

Andreas Podelski
François Taïani

# Organization

## Executive Committee

### General Chair

Mohammed Erradi             ENSIAS, Mohammed V University in Rabat, Morocco

### General Co-chairs

Rachid Guerraoui          EPFL, Switzerland
Ahmed Bouajjani          IRIF, University of Paris Diderot, France

### Program Co-chairs

Andreas Podelski          University of Freiburg, Germany
François Taïani            Univ Rennes, CNRS, Inria, IRISA, France

### Organizing Committee

Khadija Bakkouch        IRFC, Rabat, Morocco
Yahya Benkaouz          FS, Mohammed V University, Rabat, Morocco
Abdellah Boulouz         FS, Ibn zohr University, Agadir, Morocco
Zahi Jarir                  FS, Cadi Ayyad University, Marrakech, Morocco
Abdellatif Kobbane       ENSIAS, Mohammed V University, Rabat, Morocco
Mohammed Ouzzif       EST, Hassan II University, Casablanca, Morocco

### Students Committee

Maryem Ait El Hadj      ENSIAS, UM5 Rabat, Morocco
Meryeme Ayache         ENSIAS, UM5 Rabat, Morocco
Rachid Zennou           ENSIAS, UM5 Rabat, Morocco

## Steering Committee

Parosh Aziz Abdulah     Uppsala University, Sweden
Ahmed Bouajjani          IRIF, University of Paris Diderot, France
Carole Delporte           IRIF, University of Paris Diderot, France
Mohammed Erradi        ENSIAS, UM5R, Morocco
Hugues Fauconnier      IRIF, University of Paris Diderot, France
Vincent Gramoli          University of Sydney, Australia
Rachid Guerraoui         EPFL, Switzerland
Guevara Noubir           Northeastern University, USA
Michel Raynal             Univ Rennes, CNRS, Inria, IRISA, France

## Program Committee

| | |
|---|---|
| Parosh Aziz Abdulla | Uppsala University, Sweden |
| Nadjib Badache | USTHB, CERIST, Algeria |
| Slimane Bah | EMI - Mohammed V University in Rabat, Morocco |
| Yahya Benkaouz | FS, Mohammed V University in Rabat, Morocco |
| Ismail Berrada | FS, Sidi Mohamed Ben Abdellah University, Fez, Morocco |
| Annette Bieniusa | Technische Universität Kaiserslautern, Germany |
| Borzoo Bonakdarpour | Iowa State University, USA |
| Ahmed Bouajjani | IRIF, University of Paris Diderot, France |
| David Bromberg | Univ Rennes, CNRS, Inria, IRISA, France |
| Deepak D'Souza | Indian Institute of Science, Bangalore, India |
| Xavier Défago | Tokyo Institute of Technology, Japan |
| Carole Delporte | IRIF, University of Paris Diderot, France |
| Cezara Dragoi | Ecole Normale Supérieure and Inria, France |
| Amr El Abbadi | University of California, Santa Barbara, USA |
| Mohamed El Kamili | FS, Sidi Mohamed Ben Abdellah University, Fez, Morocco |
| Michael Emmi | SRI International, USA |
| Constantin Enea | IRIF, University of Paris Diderot, France |
| Javier Esparza | Technical University of Munich, Germany |
| Bernd Freisleben | University of Marburg, Germany |
| Yassine Hadjadj-Aoul | Univ Rennes, CNRS, Inria, IRISA, France |
| Moumen Hamouma | Bejaia University, Algeria |
| Maurice Herlihy | Brown University, USA |
| Zahi Jarir | FS, Cadi Ayyad University, Marrakech, Morocco |
| Mohamed Jmaiel | Digital Research Center of Sfax, Tunisia |
| Fabian Kuhn | University of Freiburg, Germany |
| Akash Lal | Microsoft Research, India |
| Rupak Majumdar | MPI-SWS, Germany |
| Achour Mostéfaoui | University of Nantes, France |
| Markus Müller-Olm | Westfälische Wilhelms-Universität Münster, Germany |
| Christoph Neumann | Technicolor, France |
| Guevara Noubir | Northeastern University, USA |
| Mohammed Ouzzif | EST, Hassan II University, Casablanca, Morocco |
| Barry Porter | Lancaster University, UK |
| Michel Raynal | Univ Rennes, CNRS, Inria, IRISA, France and Polytechnic University of Hong Kong, SAR China |
| Etienne Rivière | UCLouvain, Belgium |
| Romain Rouvoy | University of Lille/Inria/IUF, France |
| Alexander Schwarzmann | Augusta University, USA |
| Liuba Shrira | Brandeis University, USA |
| Ennan Zhai | Yale University, USA |

# Additional Reviewers

Arora, Vaibhav
Chabot-Weingart, James
Charbit, Pierre
Cheikhrouhou, Saoussen
Devismes, Stéphane
El Ouadrhiri, Ahmed
Faghih, Fathiyeh
Fauconnier, Hugues
Golab, Wojciech
Gutsfeld, Jens Oliver
H. V., Kumar Swamy

Hadjistasi, Theophanis
Johnen, Colette
Kenter, Sebastian
Lakrami, Fatima
Maiyya, Sujaya
Nordhoff, Benedikt
Phi Diep, Bui
Rezine, Othmane
Siddique, Umair
Torjmen, Mouna
Zakhary, Victor

# Keynotes

# Scaling Z3 in Azure

Nikolaj Bjorner

Microsoft Research Redmond, USA
nbjorner@microsoft.com

Z3 is an efficient satisfiability modulo theories solver. It is widely used for program analysis, verification and testing, and selectively in other areas, such as product configuration and scheduling. We describe uses of Z3 and associated architectures in cloud based services, where depending on the application, response times are expected in milli-seconds or acceptable within hours, but not days or years. To verify network configurations in Azure, Z3 runs in a service that checks thousands of router configurations every day. The checks take milliseconds and provide immediate feedback to network changes. In the opposite end of the spectrum, for hard combinatorial constraints, we extended Z3 with a cube and conquer solver to run as a distributed service.

# Networks at Work in the Aerospace Industry

Chritophe Diot

Safran Analytics, France

This presentation will cover the main two aspects in networks and communication in aerospace industry. On one hand the challenge of digitizing the supply chain poses important challenges to this industry. On the other hand, aircrafts have tens of networks, all physically isolated, that represent an important source of complexity and weight, and also threads in terms of robustness, security, and availability. In both cases, we will describe the context, challenges and technologies that are involved in the transformation of networks in aeropsace industry.

# Clubs, Coins, and Crowds:
# Fairness and Decentralization in Blockchains and Cryptocurrencies

Bryan Ford

EPFL, Switzerland
bryan.ford@epfl.ch

Building secure systems from independent, mutually distrustful parties is an old topic in computer science. But despite its attendant hype and misinformation, today's "blockchain bandwagon" has successfully brought the gospel of decentralization – both a realization of its possibility and an appreciation for its value – to mainstream society. Currently-deployed blockchains, however, are slow, unscalable, weakly consistent, profligate in energy use, and have effectively re-centralized due to market pressures. We will explore ongoing challenges and progress in rethinking blockchain architecture to improve scalability, efficiency, functionality, privacy, and decentralization. We will explore how decentralized building blocks such as collective signatures and scalable distributed randomness enable architecturally modular solutions to challenges such as sharding, proof-of-stake, and blockchain-managed secrets. Finally, we explore challenges in fairness and democratization in decentralized systems, how "proof-of-personhood" blockchains could enable information forums and anonymous reputation systems resistant to propaganda campaigns, and how democratic cryptocurrencies could offer a permissionless analog of universal basic income.

# Blockchains and the Future
# of Distributed Computing

Maurice Herlihy

Brown University, Providence RI, USA
mph@cs.brown.edu

There has been a recent explosion of interest in blockchain-based distributed ledger systems such as Bitcoin, Ethereum, and many others. Much of this work originated outside the distributed computing community, but the questions raised, such as consensus, replication, fault-tolerance, privacy, and security, and so on, are all issues familiar to our community.

This talk surveys the theory and practice of blockchain-based distributed systems from the point of view of classical distributed computing, along with reckless speculation about promising future research directions for our community.

## References

1. Buterin, V.: On sharding blockchains
2. Eyal, I., Sirer, E.G.: Majority is not enough: bitcoin mining is vulnerable. In: Financial Cryptography and Data Security - 18th International Conference, FC 2014, Christ Church, Barbados, 3–7 March 2014, Revised Selected Papers, pp. 436–454 (2014)
3. Hearn, M.: The resolution of the bitcoin experiment
4. Herlihy, M.: Atomic cross-chain swaps. *CoRR*, abs/1801.09515, PODC 2018 (2018, to appear)
5. Nakamoto, S.: Bitcoin: a peer-to-peer electronic cash system, May 2009
6. Poon, J., Dryja, T.: The bitcoin lightning network: Scalable off-chain instant payments, January 2016. As of 29 December 2017

# Pretend Synchrony: Synchronous Verification of Asynchronous Programs

Ranjit Jhala

UC San Diego, USA
rjhala@eng.ucsd.edu

We present pretend synchrony, a new approach to verifying distributed systems. Our approach is based on the observation that while distributed programs must execute asynchronously, we can often soundly treat them as if they were synchronous when verifying their correctness. To do so, we compute a synchronization, a semantically equivalent program where all sends, receives, and buffers, have been replaced by simple assignments, yielding a program that can be verified using Floyd-Hoare style Verification Conditions and SMT. We have implemented our approach and use four challenging case studies — the classic two phase commit protocol, a distributed key-value store, the Raft leader election protocol and single decree Paxos — to demonstrate that pretend synchrony makes verification of functional correctness simpler by reducing the manually specified invariants by a factor of 6, and faster by three orders of magnitude.

# Recommenders: From the Lab to the Wild

Anne-Marie Kermarrec

Mediego/Inria France, EPFL, Switzerland
anne-marie.kermarrec@mediego.com

Recommenders are ubiquitous on the Internet today: they tell you which book to read, which movie you should watch, predict your next holiday destination, give you advices on restaurants and hotels, they are even responsible for the posts that you see on your favorite social media and potentially greatly influence your friendship on social networks.

While many approaches exist, collaborative filtering is one of the most popular approaches to build online recommenders that provide users with content that matches their interest. Interestingly, the very notion of users can be general and span actual humans or software applications. Recommenders come with many challenges beyond the quality of the recommendations. One of the most prominent ones is their ability to scale to a large number of users and a growing volume of data to provide real-time recommendations introducing many system challenges. Another challenge is related to privacy awareness: while recommenders rely on the very fact that users give away information about themselves, this potentially raises some privacy concerns.

In this talk, I will focus on the challenges associated to building efficient, scalable and privacy-aware recommenders.

# Safety Verification of Deep Neural Networks

Marta Kwiatkowska

University of Oxford, UK
Marta.Kwiatkowska@cs.ox.ac.uk

Deep neural networks have achieved impressive experimental results in image classification, but can surprisingly be unstable with respect to adversarial perturbations, that is, minimal changes to the input image that cause the network to misclassify it. With potential applications including perception modules and end-to-end controllers for self-driving cars, this raises concerns about their safety. This lecture will describe progress with developing a novel automated verification framework for deep neural networks to ensure safety of their classification decisions with respect to image manipulations, for example scratches or changes to camera angle or lighting conditions, that should not affect the classification. The techniques work directly with the network code and, in contrast to existing methods, can offer guarantees that adversarial examples are found if they exist. We implement the techniques using Z3 and evaluate them on state-of-the-art networks, including regularised and deep learning networks. We also compare against existing techniques to search for adversarial examples.

# Effective Random Testing for Concurrent and Distributed Programs

Rupak Majumdar

MPI-SWS Kaiserslautern, Germany
rupak@mpi-sws.org

Random testing has proven to be an effective way to catch bugs in distributed systems. This is surprising, as the space of executions is enormous. We provide a theoretical justification of the effectiveness of random testing under various "small depth" hypotheses. First, we show a general construction, using the probabilistic method from combinatorics, that shows that whenever a random test covers a fixed coverage goal with sufficiently high probability, a small randomly-chosen set of tests achieves full coverage with high probability. In particular, we show that our construction can give test sets exponentially smaller than systematic enumeration. Second, based on an empirical study of many bugs found by random testing in production distributed systems, we introduce notions of test coverage which capture the "small depth" hypothesis and are empirically effective in finding bugs. Finally, we show using combinatorial arguments that for these notions of test coverage we introduce, we can find a lower bound on the probability that a random test covers a given goal. Our general construction then explains why random testing tools achieve good coverage— and hence, find bugs—quickly.

# Program Analyses Using Newton's Method

Thomas Reps

University of Wisconsin, GrammaTech, Inc., USA
reps@cs.wisc.edu

Esparza et al. generalized Newton's method – a numerical-analysis algorithm for finding roots of real-valued functions – to a method for finding fixed-points of systems of equations over semirings. Their method provides a new way to solve interprocedural dataflow-analysis problems. As in its real-valued counterpart, each iteration of their method solves a simpler "linearized" problem.

Because essentially all fast iterative numerical methods are forms of Newton's method, this advance is exciting because it may provide the key to creating faster program-analysis algorithms. However, there is an important difference between the dataflow-analysis and numerical-analysis contexts: when Newton's method is used in numerical problems, commutativity of multiplication is relied on to rearrange an expression of the form "a * X * b + c * X * d" into "(a * b + c *d) * X."

Equations with such expressions correspond to path problems described by regular languages. In contrast, when Newton's method is used for interprocedural dataflow analysis, the "multiplication" operation involves function composition, and hence is non-commutative: "a * X * b + c * X * d" cannot be rearranged into "(a * b + c * d) * X." Equations with the former expressions correspond to path problems described by linear context-free languages (LCFLs).

This talk will present a surprising method for solving the LCFL sub-problems produced during successive rounds of Newton's method. The method applies to predicate abstraction, on which most of today's software model checkers rely, as well as to other abstract domains used in program analysis. Joint work with Emma Turetsky and Prathmesh Prabhu.

# Optimistic and Pessimistic Synchronization for Transactional Data Structures for In-memory Stores

Liuba Shrira

Brandei University, USA
liuba@cs.brandeis.edu

Dumb code and clever data structures work better than the other way around. A concurrent system's performance can often be improved if we understand the semantics of its data types. Type-specific concurrency control is particularly helpful in memory transaction systems where the penalty of false conflicts can be high. The talk focuses on memory transaction system implementation techniques that exploit type-specific knowledge to avoid false conflicts under both optimistic and pessimistic concurrency control schemes, and presents new approaches that allow to combine the benefits of both.

We start by examining the scalability limitations of software transactional memory systems [3] due to conflict tracking at the granularity of memory words. We then consider two existing approaches to overcome these scalability limitations, exploiting data structure semantics in an ad-hoc way at the cost of increased complexity of the code [1, 2, 5, 7], and exploiting highly concurrent data structures using a black box approach [4], and explain where these approaches come short. We then describe a recent approach that co-designs the concurrent data structure and the transactions system [6, 8], avoiding the limitations of the prior approaches, and allowing to combine the benefits. The software system implementing the approach is available at github.com/nathanielherman/sto.

## References

1. Nathan, G., Bronson, J.C., Chafi, H., Olukotun, K.: Transactional predication: high-performance concurrent sets and maps for STM. In: Proceedings of PODC 2010, 29th ACM SIGACT-SIGOPS Symposium on Principles of Distributed Computing, pp. 6–15. ACM (2010)
2. Felber, P., Gramoli, V., Guerraoui, R.: Elastic Transactions. In: Keidar, I. (eds.) Distributed Computing, DISC 2009, LNCS, vol. 5805, pp. 93–107. Springer, Heidelberg (2009)
3. Harris, T., Larus, J., Rajwar, R.: Transactional Memory. 2nd edn. Morgan and Claypool Publishers (2010)
4. Herlihy, M., Koskinen, E.: Transactional boosting: a methodology for highly-concurrent transactional objects. In: Proceedings of PPoPP 2008, 13th ACM SIGPLAN Symposium on Principles and Practice of Parallel Programming, pp. 207–216. ACM (2008)

5. Herlihy, M., Luchangco, V., Moir, M., Scherer III, W.N.: Software transactional memory for dynamic-sized data structures. In: Proceedings of PODC 2003, 22nd Annual Symposium on Principles of Distributed Computing, pp. 92–101. ACM (2003)
6. Herman, N., Inala, J.P., Huang, Y., Tsai, L., Kohler, E., Liskov, B., Shrira, L.: Type-aware transactions for faster concurrent code. In: Proceedings of the Eleventh European Conference on Computer Systems, EuroSys 2016, New York, NY, USA, pp. 31:1–31:16. ACM (2016)
7. Ni, Y., et al.: Open nesting in software transactional memory. In: Proceedings of PPoPP 2007, 12th ACM SIGPLAN Symposium on Principles and Practice of Parallel Programming, San Jose, CA, pp. 68–78. ACM (2007)
8. Spiegelman, A., Golan-Gueta, G., Keidar, I.: Transactional data structure libraries. In: Proceedings of the 37th ACM SIGPLAN Conference on Programming Language Design and Implementation, PLDI 2016. ACM (2016)

# Diagnosis of Internet Quality of Experience in Home Networks

Renata Teixeira

Inria Paris, France
renata.teixeira@inria.fr

With the availability of cheap broadband connectivity, Internet access from the home has become a ubiquity and the home network has become an important part of the "Internet experience", or Quality of Experience (QoE). In conventional networks, expert administrators are responsible for managing the network and to identify the root-cause of any problems affecting users. In contrast, most home networks have no technically skilled network administrator. Home users often simply blame their Internet Service Provider (ISP) when QoE degrades. Our research provides tools to assist home users and ISPs in diagnosing QoE degradation. This talk will discuss the challenges of conducting research in home network diagnosis. It will then present results of our research leveraging the home router as a monitoring point within the home. For example, our analysis of 2,652 homes across the United States shows that wireless bottlenecks are more common than access-link bottlenecks (particularly for home networks with downstream throughput greater than 20 Mbps). We also study the effects of the home wireless on QoE of four popular applications: Web, YouTube, and audio/video RTC. Our analysis of Wi-Fi metrics collected from 832 homes customers of a large residential ISP shows that QoE is good in most cases, still we find 9% of poor QoE samples. Worse, approximately 10% of stations have more than 25% poor QoE samples.

# Invited Papers

# Diagnosis of Internet Quality of Experience in Home Networks

Renata Teixeira

Inria Paris, France
renata.teixeira@inria.fr

**Abstract.** This paper presents the abstract of the presentation on diagnosing Internet Quality of Experience (QoE) in home networks.

**Keywords:** Internet measurements · Internet Quality of Experience Home networks

## 1 Introduction

With the availability of cheap broadband connectivity, Internet access from the home has become a ubiquity. Typical home communication and entertainment services such as telephony, television, and gaming are converging to operate over IP and users constantly access Internet services and applications from home. Modern households host a multitude of networked devices, ranging from personal devices such as laptops and smartphones to Internet of Things devices (such as printers, body scales, smart meters). These devices connect among themselves and to the Internet via a local-area network—a *home network*— that has become an important part of the "Internet experience", or Quality of Experience (QoE). In conventional networks, expert administrators are responsible for managing the network and to identify the root-cause of any problems affecting users. In contrast, most home networks have no technically skilled network administrator. Home users often simply blame their Internet Service Provider (ISP) when QoE degrades.

Our research provides tools to assist home users and ISPs in diagnosing QoE degradation. The development of home network diagnosis tools brings a number of challenges. First, home networks are heterogenous. The set of devices, configurations, and applications in home networks vary significantly from one home to another. We must develop sophisticated techniques that can learn and adapt to any home network as well as to the level of expertise of the user. Second, there are numerous ways in which applications can fail or experience poor performance in home networks. Often there are a number of explanations for a given symptom. We must devise techniques that can identify the most likely cause(s) for a given problem from a set of possible causes. Third, even if we can identify the cause of the problem, we must then be able to identify a solution. It is important that the output of the diagnosis tools we build is "actionable". Users should understand the output and know what to do.

The talk presented results of our research leveraging the home router as a monitoring point within the home. The home router is the ideal vantage point to diagnose Internet QoE from homes as it sits between the home network and the access link. We presented results of two research projects. First, our research in collaboration with the BISmark Project[1] has developed an algorithm to detect when the access link or the home Wi-Fi. Our results show that wireless bottlenecks are more common than access-link bottlenecks (particularly for home networks with downstream throughput greater than 20 Mbps). Then, we study in collaboration with Technicolor the effects of the home wireless on QoE of four popular applications: Web, YouTube, and audio/video RTC.

## 2  Home Network or Access Link? Locating Last-mile Downstream Throughput Bottlenecks

In this work [3], we asked whether downstream throughput bottlenecks occur more frequently in the home networks or in the access ISPs. We identified lightweight metrics that can accurately identify whether a throughput bottleneck lies inside or outside a user's home network. We developed an algorithm that passively observes home network traffic when it traverses the home router to locate these bottlenecks. We validated this algorithm in controlled settings and reported on results from two deployments, one of which included 2,652 homes across the United States, deployed by the Federal Communication Commission (FCC). We found that wireless bottlenecks are more common than access link bottlenecks–particularly for home networks with downstream throughput greater than 20 Mbps, where access-link bottlenecks are relatively rare.

This work was in collaboration with Nick Feamster (Princeton University) and Srikanth Sundaresan (ICSI) and was published at PAM 2016.

## 3  Predicting the Effect of Home Wi-Fi Quality on QoE

Poor Wi-Fi quality can disrupt home users' internet experience, or the Quality of Experience (QoE). Detecting when Wi-Fi degrades QoE is extremely valuable for residential Internet Service Providers (ISPs) as home users often hold the ISP responsible whenever QoE degrades. Yet, ISPs have little visibility within the home to assist users. Our goal is to develop a system that runs on commodity access points (APs) to assist ISPs in detecting when Wi-Fi degrades QoE. The first contribution of our work [1, 2] was to develop a method to detect instances of poor QoE based on the passive observation of Wi-Fi quality metrics available in commodity APs (e.g., PHY

---

[1] The BISmark Project (http://projectbismark.net), based at Princeton University, provides customized home routers running a measurement-instrumented version of the OpenWRT firmware to interested individuals at no cost.

rate). We used support vector regression to build predictors of QoE given Wi-Fi quality for popular internet applications. We then used K-means clustering to combine per-application predictors to identify regions of Wi-Fi quality where QoE is poor across applications. We call samples in these regions as poor QoE samples. Our second contribution was to apply our predictors to Wi-Fi metrics collected over one month from 3479 APs of customers of a large residential ISP. Our results showed that QoE is good on the vast majority of samples of the deployment, still we found 11.6% of poor QoE samples. Worse, approximately 21% of stations had more than 25% poor QoE samples. In some cases, we estimated that Wi-Fi quality causes poor QoE for many hours, though in most cases poor QoE events are short.

This work was in collaboration with Diego Da Hora (Inria/Technicolor), Karel Van Doorselaer (Technicolor), and Koen Van Oost (Technicolor) and was published at the ACM SIGCOMM Internet QoE workshop 2016 and IEEE INFOCOM 2018.

# References

1. Da Hora, D., Van Doorselaer, K., Van Oost, K., Teixeira, R.: Predicting the effect of home Wi-Fi quality on QoE. In: Proceedings of IEEE INFOCOM (2018)
2. da Hora, D.N., Teixeira, R., Van Doorselaer, K., Van Oost, K.: Predicting the effect of home Wi-Fi quality on web QoE. In: Proceedings of the 2016 Workshop on QoE-based Analysis and Management of Data Communication Networks (2016)
3. Sundaresan, S., Feamster, N., Teixeira, R.: Home network or access link? Locating last-mile downstream throughput bottlenecks. In: Proceedings of PAM (2016)

# Program Analyses Using Newton's Method

Thomas Reps[1]

University of Wisconsin, Madison, WI, USA
GrammaTech, Inc., Ithaca, NY, USA
reps@cs.wisc.edu

**Abstract.** Esparza et al. generalized Newton's method—a numerical-analysis algorithm for finding roots of real-valued functions—to a method for finding fixed-points of systems of equations over semirings. Their method provides a new way to solve interprocedural dataflow-analysis problems. As in its real-valued counterpart, each iteration of their method solves a simpler "linearized" problem.

Because essentially all fast iterative numerical methods are forms of Newton's method, this advance is exciting because it may provide the key to creating faster program-analysis algorithms. However, there is an important difference between the dataflow-analysis and numerical-analysis contexts: when Newton's method is used in numerical problems, commutativity of multiplication is relied on to rearrange an expression of the form "$a * Y * b + c * Y * d$" into "$(a * b + c * d) * Y$." Equations with such expressions correspond to path problems described by regular languages. In contrast, when Newton's method is used for interprocedural dataflow analysis, the "multiplication" operation involves function composition, and hence is non-commutative: "$a * Y * b + c * Y * d$" cannot be rearranged into "$(a * b + c * d) * Y$." Equations with the former expressions correspond to path problems described by linear context-free languages (LCFLs).

The invited talk that this paper accompanies presented a method that we developed in 2015 for solving the LCFL sub-problems produced during successive rounds of Newton's method. It uses some algebraic slight-of-hand to turn a class of LCFL path problems into regular-language path problems. This result is surprising because a reasonable sanity check—formal-language theory—suggests that it should be impossible: after all, the LCFL languages are a strict superset of the regular languages.

The talk summarized several concepts and prior results on which that result is based. The method described applies to predicate abstraction, on which most of today's software model checkers rely, as well as to other abstract domains used in program analysis.

---

[1] T. Reps has an ownership interest in GrammaTech, Inc., which has licensed elements of the technology discussed in this publication.

# Contents

**Verification**

**Networking**

**Self-Stabilization**

# Invited Paper

# Program Analyses Using Newton's Method (Invited Paper)

Thomas Reps[1,2(✉)]

[1] University of Wisconsin, Madison, WI, USA
reps@cs.wisc.edu
[2] GrammaTech, Inc., Ithaca, NY, USA

**Abstract.** Esparza et al. generalized Newton's method—a numerical-analysis algorithm for finding roots of real-valued functions—to a method for finding fixed-points of systems of equations over semirings. Their method provides a new way to solve interprocedural dataflow-analysis problems. As in its real-valued counterpart, each iteration of their method solves a simpler "linearized" problem.

Because essentially all fast iterative numerical methods are forms of Newton's method, this advance is exciting because it may provide the key to creating faster program-analysis algorithms. However, there is an important difference between the dataflow-analysis and numerical-analysis contexts: when Newton's method is used in numerical problems, commutativity of multiplication is relied on to rearrange an expression of the form "$a * Y * b + c * Y * d$" into "$(a * b + c * d) * Y$." Equations with such expressions correspond to path problems described by regular languages. In contrast, when Newton's method is used for interprocedural dataflow analysis, the "multiplication" operation involves function composition, and hence is non-commutative: "$a * Y * b + c * Y * d$" cannot be rearranged into "$(a * b + c * d) * Y$." Equations with the former expressions correspond to path problems described by linear context-free languages (LCFLs).

The invited talk that this paper accompanies presented a method that we developed in 2015 for solving the LCFL sub-problems produced during successive rounds of Newton's method. It uses some algebraic slight-of-hand to turn a class of LCFL path problems into regular-language path problems. This result is surprising because a reasonable sanity check—formal-language theory—suggests that it should be impossible: after all, the LCFL languages are a strict superset of the regular languages.

The talk summarized several concepts and prior results on which that result is based. The method described applies to predicate abstraction, on which most of today's software model checkers rely, as well as to other abstract domains used in program analysis.

Portions of this work are excerpted from [12].

T. Reps has an ownership interest in GrammaTech, Inc., which has licensed elements of the technology discussed in this publication.

© Springer Nature Switzerland AG 2019
A. Podelski and F. Taïani (Eds.): NETYS 2018, LNCS 11028, pp. 3–16, 2019.
https://doi.org/10.1007/978-3-030-05529-5_1

# 1   Introduction

Static program analysis provides a way to obtain information about the possible states that a program reaches during execution, but without actually running the program on specific inputs. Instead, static-analysis techniques explore a program's behavior for all possible inputs and all possible states that the program can reach. To make this approach feasible, the program is "run in the aggregate"—i.e., on descriptors that represent collections of many states.

This paper briefly reviews the conventional approach to interprocedural dataflow analysis, and then summarizes a line of work from the last ten years in which Newton's method—a numerical-analysis algorithm for finding roots of real-valued functions—has been generalized so that it can be used as a method for finding solutions to the systems of equations that arise in interprocedural dataflow-analysis problems.

# 2   Interprocedural Dataflow Analysis

*Example 1.* Consider the following program scheme, where $X_1$ represents the main procedure, $X_2$ represents a subroutine, and $s_a$, $s_b$, $s_c$, and $s_d$ represent four program statements:

$$
\begin{array}{ll}
& X_2() \ \{ \\
& \quad \text{if } (\star) \ \ s_d \\
X_1() \ \{ & \quad \text{else } \{ \\
\quad s_a; & \\
\quad X_2() & \quad\quad s_b; \ X_2(); \ X_2(); \ s_c \\
\} & \quad \} \\
& \}
\end{array}
$$

Suppose that we have a domain of functions whose elements correspond to some abstraction of the state-transformers of the programming language. (An example of such a domain is the domain of relations used to formulate an analysis based on predicate abstraction [6].) Let $a$, $b$, $c$, and $d$ denote the elements that abstract the actions of statements $s_a$, $s_b$, $s_c$, and $s_d$, respectively. The (abstract) actions of procedures $X_1$ and $X_2$ can be expressed as the following set of recursive equations:

$$X_1 = a \otimes X_2 \qquad\qquad X_2 = d \oplus b \otimes X_2 \otimes X_2 \otimes c, \qquad\qquad (1)$$

where $\oplus$ (*combine*) denotes the operation used to combine (or "join") information that flows along different paths to some variable, and $\otimes$ (*extend*) is an abstraction of (the reversal of) function composition. Such an equation system can also be viewed as a representation of a program's interprocedural control-flow graph (CFG). (See Fig. 1(a)).

Each unknown in an equation system represents an abstract transformer that serves as a *procedure summary*, in the sense of Sharir and Pnueli [13] and Reps et al. [11]. A summary for procedure $X_i$ overapproximates the behavior of $X_i$, including all procedures called transitively from $X_i$. Once procedure summaries have been obtained, one can use them to analyze each procedure $X_j$ to obtain

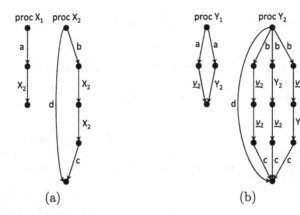

**Fig. 1.** (a) Graphical depiction of the equation system given in Eq. (1) as an interprocedural control-flow graph. The three edges labeled "$X_2$" represent calls to procedure $X_2$. (b) Linearized equation system over $\{Y_1, Y_2\}$ obtained from Eq. (1) via Eq. (6); see Example 3.

an abstract value $V_{j,p}$ for each program point $p$ in $X_j$ [13]. $V_{j,p}$ represents a superset of the states that can arise at $p$. To find potential bugs, for instance, one needs to determine if any bad states can arise at $p$, which can be done by checking whether any bad states are contained within the meaning of $V_{j,p}$—in abstract-interpretation terminology, by checking whether $(\gamma(V_{j,p}) \cap \text{Bad}) \neq \emptyset$. $\square$

A key goal of an interprocedural analyzer is to obtain a procedure summary for each procedure of the program. The reason is that with a summary function in hand for each procedure, one can reduce the problem of solving an interprocedural dataflow-analysis problem to that of solving a collection of intraprocedural dataflow-analysis problems.[1]

> **Problem Statement:**
> Given a set of possibly recursive procedures $\mathcal{P} = \{P_i\}$, and an abstract semantics, i.e.,
>
> - a transformer $f[m_i, n_i]$ on each edge $(m_i, n_i)$ in the control-flow graph of each procedure $P_i$,
> - extend ($\otimes$) and combine ($\oplus$) operators,
>
> find a procedure summary $\varphi[s_i, x_i]$ for each $P_i \in \mathcal{P}$, where $s_i$ and $x_i$ denote the start node and exit node of $P_i$, respectively.

---

[1] See [2, Sect. 5.1] for an interprocedural dataflow-analysis method that uses a somewhat similar approach.

The conventional approach to computing procedure-summary functions is to work with the set of variables

$$\Phi \overset{\text{def}}{=} \{\varphi[s_i, n_i] \mid 1 \le i \le |\mathcal{P}|, \ s_i \text{ the start node of } P_i, \text{ and } n_i \text{ a node of } P_i\},$$

and set up the following equation system over $\Phi$:

$$\varphi[s, s] = Id \qquad \text{for all } s \in StartNodes$$

$$\varphi[s_i, n_i] = \bigoplus_{(m_j, n_i) \in Edges_i} \varphi[s_i, m_j] \otimes f[m_j, n_i] \qquad \text{for all } \begin{cases} s_i \in StartNodes \\ \wedge \ n_i \notin StartNodes \\ \wedge \ s_i, m_j, n_i \in Nodes_i \end{cases}$$

$$\varphi[s_i, r_i] = \varphi[s_i, c_i] \otimes In_{c_i, s'} \otimes \varphi[s', x'] \otimes Out_{x', r_i} \quad \text{for all } \begin{cases} (c_i, r_i) \in CallSites \\ \wedge \ (c_i, s') \in Calls \\ \wedge \ (s', x') \in StartExitPairs \\ \wedge \ s_i, c_i, r_i \in Nodes_i \end{cases}$$

$$(2)$$

Equation (2) is then solved using a successive-approximation method (i.e., Kleene evaluation or chaotic iteration). Essentially this approach was proposed independently and contemporaneously by Cousot and Cousot [3] and Sharir and Pnueli [13].[2] Note that by solving Eq. (2), one obtains values for the set of functions $\Phi = \{\varphi[s_i, n_i]\}$, which contains more than just the set of summary functions $\{\varphi[s_i, x_i] \mid (s, x) \in StartExitPairs\}$ (which were referred to as the variables $\{X_i\}$ in Example 1).

It is useful to formalize these concepts by introducing the notion of a semiring.

**Definition 1.** *A **semiring** $\mathcal{S} = (D, \oplus, \otimes, \underline{0}, \underline{1})$ consists of a set of **elements** $D$ equipped with two binary operations: **combine** $(\oplus)$ and **extend** $(\otimes)$. $\oplus$ and $\otimes$ are associative, and have identity elements $\underline{0}$ and $\underline{1}$, respectively. $\oplus$ is commutative, and $\otimes$ distributes over $\oplus$. (A semiring is sometimes called a **weight domain**, in which case elements are called **weights**.)*

**Definition 2.** *If $A$ is a finite set, the relational weight domain on $A$ is defined as $(\mathcal{P}(A \times A), \cup, ;, \emptyset, id)$. A weight $R \subseteq A \times A$ is a binary relation on $A$,[3] $\oplus$ is union $(\cup)$, $\otimes$ is relational composition $(;)$, $\underline{0}$ is the empty relation, and $\underline{1}$ is the identity relation on $A$.*

*Example 2.* Definition 2 gives us a way to formalize each predicate-abstraction domain as a semiring. A Boolean program is a program whose only datatype is Boolean. A Boolean program $P$ can be used as an abstraction of a real-world program [1] via predicate abstraction. For each predicate $p$, there is a variable $v_p \in Var$ in the Boolean program, which holds the value of $p$ in states of the program being modeled. A state of the Boolean program is an assignment in $Var \to Bool$.

---

[2] Extensions for handling local variables are given by Knoop and Steffen [8], Müller-Olm and Seidl [10], and Lal et al. [9].

[3] A weight can also be thought of as a Boolean matrix with dimensions $|A| \times |A|$.

By instantiating $A$ in Definition 2 to be the set of assignments $Var \to$ Bool, we obtain a semiring whose values can encode the state-transformers of $P$: the semiring value associated with an assignment statement or assume statement st of $P$ is the binary relation on $A$ that represents the effect of st on the state of $P$. □

In this paper, the focus is on semirings in which $\oplus$ is *idempotent* (i.e., for all $a \in D$, $a \oplus a = a$). In an idempotent semiring, the order on elements is defined by $a \sqsubseteq b$ iff $a \oplus b = b$. (Idempotence would be expected in the context of dataflow analysis because an idempotent semiring is a join semilattice $(D, \oplus)$ in which the join operation is $\oplus$.)

A semiring is *commutative* if for all $a, b \in D$, $a \otimes b = b \otimes a$. In dataflow analysis, we typically work with *non-commutative* semirings: the $\otimes$ operation used in Eq. (2) is an abstraction of (the reversal of) function composition, and hence, in general, is not commutative.

## 3   Newtonian Program Analysis

Newtonian Program Analysis (NPA) provides an alternative to Kleene iteration or chaotic iteration for solving an equation system such as Eq. (2). The first step in the story of its development was a method developed for analyzing properties of Recursive Markov Chains (RMCs), which are a modeling formalism for probabilistic programs with possibly recursive procedures. To determine termination probabilities for vertices in a model, Etessami and Yannakakis [5] generate a set of equations that are, in general, non-linear. Answers can be irrational numbers, so one cannot hope to compute them exactly. Instead, their goal is to approximate the probabilities, or to answer decision questions (such as whether the probability is greater than or equal to a specific rational value). They developed an algorithm that uses a multivariate Newton's method for approximating probabilities. Moreover, they showed that, in the limit, when their method is started from the zero vector, it always converges to the correct answer. (In contrast, for general nonlinear polynomial equations over the reals, Newton's method is not guaranteed to converge.)

Etessami and Yannakakis worked with the probability semiring (namely, $(\mathbb{R}_0 \cup \{+\infty\}, +, \times, 0, 1)$), which has numeric values and a commutative $\otimes$ operation. Their work inspired Esparza et al. [4] to investigate whether a generalization of the approach could be applied to other kinds of program analyses—in particular, when control-flow graph edges are labeled with values from a semiring other than the probability semiring. The attempt was successful, and they developed a method for finding the least fixed-point of a system of equations over a semiring, which works for both commutative and *non-commutative* semirings, and does not require that the values be totally ordered. The fact that it applies when $\otimes$ is not commutative makes the work applicable to the problem of finding procedure-summary functions.

In general, let $\mathcal{S} = (D, \oplus, \otimes, \underline{0}, \underline{1})$ be a semiring and $a_1, \ldots, a_{k+1} \in D$ be semiring elements. Let $\mathcal{X}$ be a finite set of variables $X_1, \ldots, X_k$. A *monomial* is a finite expression $a_1X_1a_2\ldots a_kX_ka_{k+1}$, where $k \geq 0$. Monomials of the form $X_1a_2$, $a_1X_1$, and $a_1X_1a_2$ are *left-linear*, *right-linear*, and *linear*, respectively. (A monomial that consists of a single semiring constant $a_1$ is considered to be left-linear, right-linear, and linear.) A *polynomial* is a finite expression of the form $m_1 \oplus \ldots \oplus m_p$, where $p \geq 1$ and $m_1,\ldots,m_p$ are monomials. A polynomial is linear if all of its monomials are linear. A system of polynomial equations has the form

$$X_1 = f_1(X_1,\ldots,X_n)$$
$$\ldots$$
$$X_n = f_n(X_1,\ldots,X_n),$$

or, equivalently, $\overrightarrow{X} = \overrightarrow{f}(\overrightarrow{X})$, where $\overrightarrow{X} = \langle X_1,\ldots,X_n\rangle$ and $\overrightarrow{f} = \lambda\overrightarrow{X}.\langle f_1(\overrightarrow{X}),\ldots,f_n(\overrightarrow{X})\rangle$. For instance, for Eq. (1),

$$\overrightarrow{f} \overset{\text{def}}{=} \lambda\overrightarrow{X}.\langle a \otimes X_2, d \oplus b \otimes X_2 \otimes X_2 \otimes c\rangle.$$

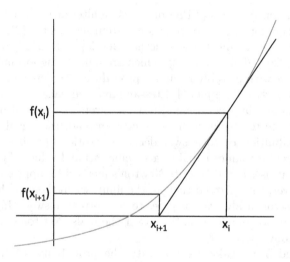

**Fig. 2.** The principle behind Newton's method for finding roots of real-valued functions.

In numerical problems, the workhorse for successive-approximation algorithms is Newton's method. Figure 2 illustrates how Newton's method can (sometimes) help identify where a root of a function lies. (Newton's method is not guaranteed to converge to a root.) The general principle is to create a *linear model* of the function—in this case the tangent line—and solve the problem for the linear model to obtain the next approximation to the root of the original function.

Compared to the numerical setting, Esparza et al. had two issues that they needed to finesse:

1. With numerical functions, the linear model is defined using derivatives, which are defined in terms of limits. We have no analogue of a limit in a semiring.
2. Newton's method is for root-finding (i.e., find $x$ such that $f(x) = 0$), whereas in program analysis we are interested in finding a fixed-point (i.e., find $x$ such that $f(x) = x$). Although one can easily convert a fixed-point problem into a root-finding problem—find $x$ such that $f(x) - x = 0$—this approach creates a new problem because there is no analogue of a subtraction operation in a semiring.

Kleene iteration is the well-known technique for finding the least fixed-point of $\vec{X} = \vec{f}(\vec{X})$ via the successive-approximation method

$$\boxed{\begin{aligned} \vec{\kappa}^{(0)} &= \vec{\perp} \\ \vec{\kappa}^{(i+i)} &= \vec{f}(\vec{\kappa}^{(i)}) \end{aligned}} \tag{3}$$

The NPA method of Esparza et al. [4] provides an alternative method for finding the least fixed-point of $\vec{X} = \vec{f}(\vec{X})$. NPA is also a successive-approximation method, but uses the following iterative scheme:[4]

$$\boxed{\begin{aligned} \vec{\nu}^{(0)} &= \vec{\perp} \\ \vec{\nu}^{(i+1)} &= \vec{f}(\vec{\nu}^{(i)}) \sqcup \text{LinearCorrectionTerm}(\vec{f}, \vec{\nu}^{(i)}) \end{aligned}} \tag{4}$$

where $\text{LinearCorrectionTerm}(\vec{f}, \vec{\nu}^{(i)})$ is a correction term—a function of $\vec{f}$ and the current approximation $\vec{\nu}^{(i)}$—that nudges the next approximation $\vec{\nu}^{(i+1)}$ in the right direction at each step. In essence, the insight behind the work of Esparza et al. is that the high-level principle of Newton's method, namely,

repeatedly, create a linear model of the function and use it to find a better approximation of the solution

can be applied to programs, too. The sense in which the correction term in Eq. (4) is "linear" is what makes it proper to say that Eq. (4) is a form of Newton's method.

More precisely, NPA solves the following sequence of problems for $\vec{\nu}$:

$$\boxed{\begin{aligned} \vec{\nu}^{(0)} &= \vec{f}(\vec{0}) \\ \vec{\nu}^{(i+1)} &= \vec{Y}^{(i)} \end{aligned}} \tag{5}$$

where $\vec{Y}^{(i)}$ is the value of $\vec{Y}$ in the least solution of

$$\boxed{\vec{Y} = \vec{f}(\vec{\nu}^{(i)}) \oplus \mathcal{D}\vec{f}\,|_{\vec{\nu}^{(i)}}(\vec{Y})} \tag{6}$$

---

[4] For reasons that are immaterial to this discussion, Esparza et al. start the iteration via $\vec{\nu}^{(0)} = \vec{f}(\vec{\perp})$, rather than $\vec{\nu}^{(0)} = \vec{\perp}$. Our goal here is to bring out the essential similarities between Eqs. (3) and (4).

and $\mathcal{D}\overrightarrow{f}|_{\overrightarrow{\nu}^{(i)}}(\overrightarrow{Y})$ is the *multivariate differential* of $\overrightarrow{f}$ at $\overrightarrow{\nu}^{(i)}$, defined below (see Definition 3). Equations (5) and (6) resemble Kleene iteration, except that on each iteration $\overrightarrow{f}(\overrightarrow{\nu}^{(i)})$ is "corrected" by the amount $\mathcal{D}\overrightarrow{f}|_{\overrightarrow{\nu}^{(i)}}(\overrightarrow{Y})$.

There is a close analogy between NPA and the use of Newton's method in numerical analysis to solve a system of polynomial equations $\overrightarrow{f}(\overrightarrow{X}) = \overrightarrow{0}$. In both cases, one creates a linear approximation of $\overrightarrow{f}$ around the point $(\overrightarrow{\nu}^{(i)}, \overrightarrow{f}(\overrightarrow{\nu}^{(i)}))$, and then uses the solution of the linear system in the next approximation of $\overrightarrow{X}$. The sequence $\overrightarrow{\nu}^{(0)}, \overrightarrow{\nu}^{(1)}, \ldots, \overrightarrow{\nu}^{(i)}, \ldots$ is called the *Newton sequence* for $\overrightarrow{X} = \overrightarrow{f}(\overrightarrow{X})$. The process of solving Eqs. (5) and (6) for $\overrightarrow{\nu}^{(i+1)}$, given $\overrightarrow{\nu}^{(i)}$, is called a *Newton step* or one *Newton round*.

For polynomial equations over a semiring, the linear approximation of $\overrightarrow{f}$ is created by the transformation given in Definition 3. It converts a system of equations with polynomial right-hand sides into a new equation system in which each equation's right-hand side is linear.

**Definition 3.** *[4] Let $f_i(\overrightarrow{X})$ be a component function of $\overrightarrow{f}(\overrightarrow{X})$. The **differential** of $f_i(\overrightarrow{X})$ with respect to $X_j$ at $\underline{\nu}$, denoted by $\mathcal{D}_{X_j}f_i|_{\underline{\nu}}(\overrightarrow{Y})$, is defined as follows:*

$$\mathcal{D}_{X_j}f_i|_{\underline{\nu}}(\overrightarrow{Y}) \overset{\text{def}}{=} \begin{cases} 0 & \text{if } f_i = s \in \mathcal{S} \\ 0 & \text{if } f_i = X_k \text{ and } k \neq j \\ Y_j & \text{if } f_i = X_j \\ \bigoplus_{k \in K} \mathcal{D}_{X_j}g_k|_{\underline{\nu}}(\overrightarrow{Y}) & \text{if } f_i = \bigoplus_{k \in K} g_k \\ \left( \begin{array}{c} \mathcal{D}_{X_j}g|_{\underline{\nu}}(\overrightarrow{Y}) \otimes h(\underline{\nu}) \\ \oplus\ g(\underline{\nu}) \otimes \mathcal{D}_{X_j}h|_{\underline{\nu}}(\overrightarrow{Y}) \end{array} \right) & \text{if } f_i = g \otimes h \end{cases} \quad (7)$$

*where $K \subseteq \mathbb{N}$ is some finite or infinite index set. Let $\overrightarrow{f}$ be a multivariate polynomial function defined by $\overrightarrow{f} \overset{\text{def}}{=} \lambda\overrightarrow{X}.\langle f_1(\overrightarrow{X}), \ldots, f_n(\overrightarrow{X})\rangle$. The **multivariate differential** of $\overrightarrow{f}$ at $\underline{\nu}$, denoted by $\mathcal{D}\overrightarrow{f}|_{\underline{\nu}}(\overrightarrow{Y})$, is defined as follows:*

$$\mathcal{D}\overrightarrow{f}|_{\underline{\nu}}(\overrightarrow{Y}) \overset{\text{def}}{=} \left\langle \begin{array}{c} \mathcal{D}_{X_1}f_1|_{\underline{\nu}}(\overrightarrow{Y}) \oplus \ldots \oplus \mathcal{D}_{X_n}f_1|_{\underline{\nu}}(\overrightarrow{Y}), \\ \vdots \\ \mathcal{D}_{X_1}f_n|_{\underline{\nu}}(\overrightarrow{Y}) \oplus \ldots \oplus \mathcal{D}_{X_n}f_n|_{\underline{\nu}}(\overrightarrow{Y}) \end{array} \right\rangle$$

$\mathcal{D}f_i|_{\underline{\nu}}(\overrightarrow{Y}) \overset{\text{def}}{=} \bigoplus_{k=1}^{n} \mathcal{D}_{X_k}f_i|_{\underline{\nu}}(\overrightarrow{Y})$ *denotes the $i^{th}$ component of $\mathcal{D}\overrightarrow{f}|_{\underline{\nu}}(\overrightarrow{Y})$.*

The fourth case in Eq. (7) generalizes the differential of a binary combine, i.e.,

$$\mathcal{D}_{X_j}g_1|_{\underline{\nu}}(\overrightarrow{Y}) \oplus \mathcal{D}_{X_j}g_2|_{\underline{\nu}}(\overrightarrow{Y}) \qquad \text{if } f_i = g_1 \oplus g_2,$$

to infinite combines. Note how the fifth case, for "$g \otimes h$", resembles the product rule from differential calculus

$$\frac{d}{dx}(g * h) = \frac{dg}{dx} * h + g * \frac{dg}{dx},$$

and in particular the differential form of the product rule:

$$d(g * h) = dg * h + g * dh.$$

The multivariate differential defined in Definition 3 is how Esparza et al. addressed the issue raised in item (1) above: the multivariate differential is a *formal operator* on a polynomial expression over a semiring, and does not involve any notion of "the limit as $\Delta X$ approaches 0." Here Esparza et al. [4] were inspired by a formal differentiation operation defined by Hopkins and Kozen [7] for *commutative* Kleene algebra. Esparza et al. generalized that notion to one for creating a formal differential for an equation system defined over a *non-commutative* semiring.

*Example 3.* For Eq. (1), the multivariate differential of $\overrightarrow{f}$ at the value $\overrightarrow{\underline{\nu}} = \langle \underline{\nu}_1, \underline{\nu}_2 \rangle$ is

$$\mathcal{D}\overrightarrow{f}|_{\langle \underline{\nu}_1, \underline{\nu}_2 \rangle}(\overrightarrow{Y}) = \left\langle \begin{array}{c} \mathcal{D}_{X_1} f_1|_{\langle \underline{\nu}_1, \underline{\nu}_2 \rangle}(\overrightarrow{Y}) \oplus \mathcal{D}_{X_2} f_1|_{\langle \underline{\nu}_1, \underline{\nu}_2 \rangle}(\overrightarrow{Y}), \\ \mathcal{D}_{X_1} f_2|_{\langle \underline{\nu}_1, \underline{\nu}_2 \rangle}(\overrightarrow{Y}) \oplus \mathcal{D}_{X_2} f_2|_{\langle \underline{\nu}_1, \underline{\nu}_2 \rangle}(\overrightarrow{Y}) \end{array} \right\rangle$$

$$= \left\langle \underline{0} \oplus a \otimes Y_2, \underline{0} \oplus \left( \begin{array}{c} \underline{0} \\ \oplus\ b \otimes Y_2 \otimes \underline{\nu}_2 \otimes c \\ \oplus\ b \otimes \underline{\nu}_2 \otimes Y_2 \otimes c \end{array} \right) \right\rangle$$

$$= \left\langle a \otimes Y_2, \left( \begin{array}{c} b \otimes Y_2 \otimes \underline{\nu}_2 \otimes c \\ \oplus\ b \otimes \underline{\nu}_2 \otimes Y_2 \otimes c \end{array} \right) \right\rangle \tag{8}$$

From Eq. (6), we then obtain the following linearized system of equations, which is also depicted graphically in Fig. 1(b):

$$\langle Y_1, Y_2 \rangle = \left\langle \left( \begin{array}{c} a \otimes \underline{\nu}_2 \\ \oplus\ a \otimes Y_2 \end{array} \right), \left( \begin{array}{c} d \\ \oplus\ b \otimes \underline{\nu}_2 \otimes \underline{\nu}_2 \otimes c \\ \oplus\ b \otimes Y_2 \otimes \underline{\nu}_2 \otimes c \\ \oplus\ b \otimes \underline{\nu}_2 \otimes Y_2 \otimes c \end{array} \right) \right\rangle \tag{9}$$

On the $i + 1^{st}$ Newton round, we need to solve Eq. (9) for $\langle Y_1, Y_2 \rangle$ with $\langle \underline{\nu}_1, \underline{\nu}_2 \rangle$ set to the value $\langle \nu_1^{(i)}, \nu_2^{(i)} \rangle$ obtained on the $i^{th}$ round, and then perform the assignment $\langle \nu_1^{(i+1)}, \nu_2^{(i+1)} \rangle \leftarrow \langle Y_1, Y_2 \rangle$.

NPA can also be thought of as a kind of sampling method for the state space of the program. For instance, in Example 1, procedure $X_2$ has two call-sites. In the corresponding linearized program in Fig. 1(b), each path through $Y_2$ has at most one call site: the NPA linearizing transformation inserted the value $\underline{\nu}_2$ at various call-sites, and left at most one variable in each summand. In essence, during a given Newton round the analyzer samples the state space of $Y_2$ by taking the $\oplus$ of various paths through $Y_2$. Along each such path, the abstract values for the call-sites encountered are held fixed at $\underline{\nu}_2$, except for possibly one call-site on the path, which is explored by visiting (the linearized version of) the called procedure. The abstract values for $\underline{\nu}_1$ and $\underline{\nu}_2$ are updated according to the results of this state-space exploration, and the algorithm proceeds to the next Newton round.                                                                                □

## 4   Newtonian Program Analysis via Tensor Product (NPA-TP)

Consider the (recursive) equation for $Y_2$:

$$Y_2 = \begin{pmatrix} d \\ \oplus\ b \otimes \underline{\nu}_2 \otimes \underline{\nu}_2 \otimes c \\ \oplus\ b \otimes Y_2 \otimes \underline{\nu}_2 \otimes c \\ \oplus\ b \otimes \underline{\nu}_2 \otimes Y_2 \otimes c \end{pmatrix} \tag{10}$$

Each monomial in Eq. (10) is *linear*. In contrast, the equation for $X_2$ in the original equation system (Eq. (1)), $X_2 = d \oplus b \otimes X_2 \otimes X_2 \otimes c$, involves a monomial that is *quadratic*. In general, as in the example above, NPA reduces the problem of solving an equation system that involves polynomial right-hand sides to the problem of solving a sequence of equation systems, each of which has only linear right-hand sides.

At first blush, one might think (as the author did at one point) that NPA reduces the problem of solving a polynomial equation system for an *inter*procedural dataflow-analysis problem to a sequence of *intra*procedural dataflow-analysis problems. That would be desirable because there exist fast methods to solve an intraprocedural dataflow-analysis problem. For instance, Tarjan [15] introduced the idea of using regular expressions as a kind of "most-general dataflow-analysis method." Specific dataflow-analysis problems are solved by first solving the *path-expression problem*: a program's CFG is considered to be a finite-state machine in which CFG nodes are states, and each edge is labeled by an alphabet symbol unique to that edge. Tarjan's path-expression method [14] creates for each node $n$ a regular expression $R_n$ whose language, $L(R_n)$, is (exactly) the set of all paths from the CFG's start node to $n$. The "client" dataflow-analysis problem is then solved by evaluating each regular expression $R_n$, bottom up, using a suitable interpretation, in which the regular-expression operators $+$, $\cdot$, and $*$—now treated as syntactic operators—are interpreted as some suitable (sound) operations, $\oplus$, $\otimes$, and $*$, respectively, in the analysis domain [15].

Because both the regular languages (Reg) and the linear context-free languages (LCFLs) will play a role in what follows, it is worth recalling a few facts.

- $L(FSM) = L(RegExp) = \text{Reg}$
- For a *left-linear* context-free grammar, e.g., $W ::= Wc \mid Wd \mid \epsilon$, $L(W) \in \text{Reg}$. For instance, $L(W) = (c + d)^* \in \text{Reg}$.
- For the *linear* context-free grammar $W ::= aWb \mid \epsilon$, $L(W) = \{a^i b^i\} \notin \text{Reg}$.
- For the *linear* context-free grammar $W ::= a_1 W b_1 \mid a_2 W b_2 \mid \epsilon$,

$$L(W) = \{\ldots, a_1\,\underbrace{a_2 b_2}\,b_1, a_2\,\underbrace{a_1 b_1}\,b_2, a_2\,a_1\,\underbrace{a_2 b_2}\,b_1\,b_2, \ldots\} \notin \text{Reg}.$$

In particular, note the "mirrored symmetry" of each word in $L(W)$, as shown above by the underbraces.

Returning to Eq. (10), note that the third and fourth monomials each extend $Y_2$ by nontrivial quantities on both the left and the right. Thus, we are truly working with a linear equation system—*not one that is left-linear or right-linear.* In other words, there is a mismatch:

- Tarjan's method solves a left-linear (or right-linear) system of equations.
- The NPA method of Esparza et al. repeatedly creates a linear system that needs to be solved.
- However, in general, one cannot apply Tarjan's method to the linear systems created by NPA.

One can also consider Eq. (10) as defining the following linear context-free grammar over the set of nonterminals $\{Y_2\}$ and the set of terminals $\{b, c, d, \underline{\nu_2}\}$:

$$Y_2 ::= d \mid b \, \underline{\nu_2} \, \underline{\nu_2} \, c \mid b \, Y_2 \, \underline{\nu_2} \, c \mid b \, \underline{\nu_2} \, Y_2 \, c \qquad (11)$$

**Definition 4.** *An equation system over semiring $S$ is an **LCFL equation system** if each equation has the form*

$$Y_j = c_j \oplus \bigoplus_{i,k} (a_{i,j,k} \otimes Y_i \otimes b_{i,j,k}),$$

*where $a_{i,j,k}, b_{i,j,k}, c_j \in S$.*

As mentioned earlier, NPA performs a Kleene-like iteration, during which a linear correction is applied on each round. Definition 4 allows us to be more precise: the correction value used on each round is the solution to an LCFL equation system. The contribution of NPA-TP to NPA is to address the following problem:

> Given an LCFL equation system $\mathcal{L}$, devise an efficient method for finding the least solution of $\mathcal{L}$.

**Definition 5.** *An LCFL equation system over semiring $S$ is a **left-linear equation system** if each equation has the form*

$$Z_j = c_j \oplus \bigoplus_{i,k} (Z_i \otimes b_{i,j,k}),$$

*where $b_{i,j,k}, c_j \in S$.*

In contrast to a general LCFL equation system (Definition 4), with a left-linear equation system one can always collect coefficients for a given $Z_i$—i.e., $d_{i,j} = \bigoplus_k b_{i,j,k}$—so that equations can always be put in a form in which $Z_j$ has a single dependence on each $Z_i$:

$$Z_j = c_j \oplus \bigoplus_i (Z_i \otimes d_{i,j}),$$

where $c_j, d_{i,j} \in S$.

A left-linear equation system corresponds to a left-linear grammar, and hence a regular language. The fact that Tarjan's path-expression method provides a fast method for solving left-linear equation systems led us to pose the following question:

Is it possible to "regularize" the LCFL equation system $\mathcal{L}$ that arises on each Newton round—i.e., transform $\mathcal{L}$ into a left-linear equation system $\mathcal{L}_{\text{Reg}}$?

If the extend ($\otimes$) operation of the semiring is commutative, it is trivial to turn an LCFL equation system into a left-linear equation system. However, in dataflow-analysis problems, we rarely have a commutative extend operation; thus, our goal was to find a way to regularize a *non-commutative* LCFL equation system.

On the face of it, this line of attack seems unlikely to pan out; after all, Eq. (11) resembles the *linear* grammar $\overrightarrow{Y} ::= a_1 \overrightarrow{Y} b_1 \mid a_2 \overrightarrow{Y} b_2 \mid \epsilon$, whose simpler cousin $\overrightarrow{Y} ::= a \overrightarrow{Y} b \mid \epsilon$, which is also a linear grammar, generates the language $L(\overrightarrow{Y}) = \{a^i b^i \mid i \in \mathbb{N}\}$—the canonical example of an LCFL that is not regular! For the linear context-free grammar $\overrightarrow{Y} ::= a_1 \overrightarrow{Y} b_1 \mid a_2 \overrightarrow{Y} b_2 \mid \epsilon$,

$$L(\overrightarrow{Y}) = \{\ldots, a_1 \underbrace{a_2 b_2} b_1, a_2 \underbrace{a_1 b_1} b_2, a_2 a_1 \underbrace{a_2 b_2} b_1 b_2, \ldots\} \notin \text{Reg}, \tag{12}$$

In particular, note the "mirrored symmetry" of each word in $L(\overrightarrow{Y})$, as shown above by the underbraces. Any solution to the problem of regularizing a non-commutative LCFL equation system has to accommodate such mirrored correlation patterns.

The challenge is to devise a way to accumulate matching quantities on both the left and right sides, whereas in a regular language, we can only accumulate values on one side. What we contributed in [12] is a way, under certain conditions, to convert each LCFL equation system into a left-linear (and hence regular-language) equation system. The result is surprising because a reasonable sanity check—formal-language theory—suggests that it should be impossible: the LCFLs are strictly more expressive than the regular languages.

The secret is that we are not working with words: the combine ($\oplus$) and extend ($\otimes$) operators of the semiring do not denote alternation and concatenation, as in formal-language theory; on the contrary, $\oplus$ and $\otimes$ are interpreted operators. In [12], we used some algebraic slight-of-hand to turn a class of LCFL equation systems into left-linear equation systems. To accomplish such a transformation, we require the semiring to support a few additional operations (which we call "transpose," "tensor product," and "detensor"—denoted by $^t$, $\odot$, and $\oint$, respectively) that one does not have with words. However, one does have such operations for the so-called "predicate-abstraction problems" (an important family of dataflow-analysis problems used in essentially all modern-day software model checkers). In predicate-abstraction problems,

- a semiring value is a square Boolean matrix

- the extend operation is Boolean matrix multiplication
- the combine operation is pointwise "or"
- transpose is matrix transpose, and
- tensor product is Kronecker product of square Boolean matrices

The key step is to take each equation of the form "$Y = a \otimes Y \otimes b$" and turn it into "$Z = Z \otimes_T (a^t \odot b)$," where $\otimes_T$ denotes the extend operation in the domain of tensored values. (For predicate abstraction, $\otimes_T$ is Boolean matrix multiplication of tensored matrices.) When this transformation is performed on all equation right-hand sides, the resulting equation system over $Z$ is left-linear, and hence describes a set of paths in a regular language. Consequently, it can be solved by means of Tarjan's path-expression method.

What is not immediately obvious is that from the least-fixed point of the $Z$ system one can obtain the least-fixed point of the $Y$ system—i.e., the $Z$ system can be used to solve the $Y$ system with no loss of precision. The intuition behind the transformation is that linear paths in the $Z$ system mimic derivation trees in the linear context-free grammar of the $Y$ system; as we follow a path in the $Z$ system along edges labeled with, e.g., first $(a_1^t \odot b_1)$ and then $(a_2^t \odot b_2)$, we obtain

$$(a_1^t \odot b_1) \otimes_T (a_2^t \odot b_2) = (a_1^t \otimes a_2^t) \odot (b_2 \otimes b_1)$$
$$= (a_1 \otimes a_2)^t \odot \underbrace{(b_2 \otimes b_1)}$$

which produces the kind of mirrored symmetry that we need to track properly the values that arise in the $Y$ system, which have such symmetric correlations (cf. Eq. (12)). More precisely, the detensor operation performs

$$\not\downarrow (a^t \odot b) = a \otimes b,$$

so that when $\not\downarrow$ is applied to the path's value, we obtain

$$\not\downarrow ((a_1 \otimes a_2)^t \odot (b_2 \otimes b_1)) = a_1 \otimes \underbrace{a_2 \otimes b_2} \otimes b_1,$$

which has the mirrored symmetry found in the values of derivation trees in the $Y$ system. The $Z$ system's paths encode all and only the derivation trees of the $Y$ system.

To use this idea to solve an LCFL equation system precisely, there is one further requirement: the $\not\downarrow$ operation must distribute over the tensored-sum operation. This property causes the detensor of the sum-over-all-$Z$-paths to equal the desired sum-over-all-$Y$-tree-valuations. It turns out that such a distributive detensor operation exists for Kronecker products of Boolean matrices, and thus all the pieces fit together for the predicate-abstraction problems. Full details can be found in [12].

**Acknowledgments.** This work was supported, in part, by a gift from Rajiv and Ritu Batra; DARPA MUSE award FA8750-14-2-0270 and DARPA STAC award FA8750-15-C-0082; and by the UW-Madison Office of the Vice Chancellor for Research and

Graduate Education with funding from the Wisconsin Alumni Research Foundation. Any opinions, findings, and conclusions or recommendations expressed in this publication are those of the authors, and do not necessarily reflect the views of the sponsoring agencies.

# References

1. Ball, T., Rajamani, S.K.: Bebop: a symbolic model checker for boolean programs. In: Havelund, K., Penix, J., Visser, W. (eds.) SPIN 2000. LNCS, vol. 1885, pp. 113–130. Springer, Heidelberg (2000). https://doi.org/10.1007/10722468_7
2. Bouajjani, A., Esparza, J., Touili, T.: A generic approach to the static analysis of concurrent programs with procedures. In: POPL (2003)
3. Cousot, P., Cousot, R.: Static determination of dynamic properties of recursive procedures. In: Neuhold, E. (ed.) Formal Descriptions of Programming Concepts, IFIP WG 2.2, St. Andrews, Canada, August 1977, pp. 237–277. North-Holland (1978)
4. Esparza, J., Kiefer, S., Luttenberger, M.: Newtonian program analysis. J. ACM 57(6), 33 (2010)
5. Etessami, K., Yannakakis, M.: Recursive Markov chains, stochastic grammars, and monotone systems of nonlinear equations. J. ACM 56(1), 1 (2009)
6. Graf, S., Saidi, H.: Construction of abstract state graphs with PVS. In: Grumberg, O. (ed.) CAV 1997. LNCS, vol. 1254, pp. 72–83. Springer, Heidelberg (1997). https://doi.org/10.1007/3-540-63166-6_10
7. Hopkins, M., Kozen, D.: Parikh's theorem in commutative Kleene algebra. In: LICS (1999)
8. Knoop, J., Steffen, B.: The interprocedural coincidence theorem. In: Kastens, U., Pfahler, P. (eds.) CC 1992. LNCS, vol. 641, pp. 125–140. Springer, Heidelberg (1992). https://doi.org/10.1007/3-540-55984-1_13
9. Lal, A., Reps, T., Balakrishnan, G.: Extended weighted pushdown systems. In: Etessami, K., Rajamani, S.K. (eds.) CAV 2005. LNCS, vol. 3576, pp. 434–448. Springer, Heidelberg (2005). https://doi.org/10.1007/11513988_44
10. Müller-Olm, M., Seidl, H.: Precise interprocedural analysis through linear algebra. In: POPL (2004)
11. Reps, T., Horwitz, S., Sagiv, M.: Precise interprocedural dataflow analysis via graph reachability. In: POPL (1995)
12. Reps, T., Turetsky, E., Prabhu, P.: Newtonian program analysis via tensor product. TOPLAS 39(2), 9 (2017)
13. Sharir, M., Pnueli, A.: Two Approaches to Interprocedural Data Flow Analysis. In: Program Flow Analysis: Theory and Applications. Prentice-Hall (1981)
14. Tarjan, R.: Fast algorithms for solving path problems. J. ACM 28(3), 594–614 (1981)
15. Tarjan, R.: A unified approach to path problems. J. ACM 28(3), 577–593 (1981)

# Distribution

# Formalizing and Implementing
# Distributed Ledger Objects

Antonio Fernández Anta[1], Chryssis Georgiou[2], Kishori Konwar[3],
and Nicolas Nicolaou[4,5(✉)]

[1] IMDEA Networks Institute, Madrid, Spain
antonio.fernandez@imdea.org
[2] Department of Computer Science, University of Cyprus, Nicosia, Cyprus
chryssis@cs.ucy.ac.cy
[3] MIT, Cambridge, USA
kishori@mit.edu
[4] KIOS Research and Innovation Center of Excellence,
University of Cyprus, Nicosia, Cyprus
nicolasn@ucy.ac.cy
[5] Algolysis Ltd., Nicosia, Cyprus

**Abstract.** Despite the hype about blockchains and distributed ledgers, no formal abstraction of these objects has been proposed (This observation was also pointed out by Maurice Herlihy in his PODC2017 keynote talk). To face this issue, in this paper we provide a proper formulation of a *distributed ledger object*. In brief, we define a *ledger* object as a sequence of *records*, and we provide the operations and the properties that such an object should support. Implementation of a ledger object on top of multiple (possibly geographically dispersed) computing devices gives rise to the *distributed ledger object*. In contrast to the centralized object, distribution allows operations to be applied concurrently on the ledger, introducing challenges on the *consistency* of the ledger in each participant. We provide the definitions of three well known consistency guarantees in terms of the operations supported by the ledger object: (1) *atomic consistency (linearizability)*, (2) *sequential consistency*, and (3) *eventual consistency*. We then provide implementations of distributed ledgers on asynchronous message passing crash-prone systems using an Atomic Broadcast service, and show that they provide eventual, sequential or atomic consistency semantics. We conclude with a variation of the ledger – the *validated ledger* – which requires that each record in the ledger satisfies a particular *validation rule*.

## 1 Introduction

We are living a huge hype of the so-called crypto-currencies, and their technological support, the blockchain [20]. It is claimed that using crypto-currencies and

Partially supported by the Spanish Ministry of Science, Innovation and Universities grant DiscoEdge (TIN2017-88749-R), the Regional Government of Madrid (CM) grant Cloud4BigData (S2013/ICE-2894) co-funded by FSE & FEDER, the NSF of China grant 61520106005, and by funds for the promotion of research at the University of Cyprus. We would like to thank Paul Rimba and Neha Narula for helpful discussions.

© Springer Nature Switzerland AG 2019
A. Podelski and F. Taïani (Eds.): NETYS 2018, LNCS 11028, pp. 19–35, 2019.
https://doi.org/10.1007/978-3-030-05529-5_2

public distributed ledgers (i.e., public blockchains) will liberate stakeholder own-
ers from centralized trusted authorities [23]. Moreover, it is believed that there
is the opportunity of becoming rich by mining coins, speculating with them, or
even launching your own coin (i.e. with an initial coin offering, ICO).

Cryptocurrencies were first introduced in 2009 by Nakamoto [20]. In his
paper, Nakamoto introduced the first algorithm that allowed economic transactions to be accomplished between peers without the need of a central authority.
An initial analysis of the security of the protocol was presented in [20], although
a more formal and thorough analysis was developed by Garay, Kiayias, and
Leonardos in [10]. In that paper the authors define and prove two fundamental
properties of the blockchain implementation behind bitcoin: (i) *common-prefix*,
and (ii) *quality of chain*.

Although the recent popularity of distributed ledger technology (DLT), or
blockchain, is primarily due to the explosive growth of numerous cryptocurrencies, there are many applications of this core technology that are outside
the financial industry. These applications arise from leveraging various useful
features provided by distributed ledgers such as a decentralized information
management, immutable record keeping for possible audit trail, a robust and
available system, and a system that provides security and privacy. For example,
an emerging area is the use of DLT in medical and health care applications. At
a high level, the distributed ledger can be used as a platform to store health
care data for sharing, recording, analysis, research, etc. One of the most widely
discussed approaches in adopting DLT is to implement a Health Information
Exchange (HIE) system, for sharing transactions among the participants such
as patients, caregivers and other relevant parties [16]. Another interesting open-
source initiative is Namecoin that uses DLT to improve the registration and
ownership transfer of internet components such as DNS [21].

In the light of these works indeed crypto-currencies and (public and private)
distributed ledgers[1] have the potential to impact our society deeply. However
most experts, often do not clearly differentiate between the coin, the ledger that
supports it, and the service they provide. Instead, they get very technical, talking
about the cryptography involved, the mining used to maintain the ledger, or the
smart contract technology used. Moreover, when asked for details it is often the
case that there is no formal specification of the protocols, algorithms, and service
provided, with a few exceptions [26]. In many cases "the code is the spec".

From the theoretical point of view there are many fundamental questions
with the current distributed ledger (and crypto-currency) systems that are very
often not properly answered: What is the service that must be provided by a distributed ledger? What properties a distributed ledger must satisfy? What are the
assumptions made by the protocols and algorithms on the underlying system?
Does a distributed ledger require a linked crypto-currency? In his PODC'2017
keynote address, Herlihy pointed out that, despite the hype about blockchains
and distributed ledgers, no formal abstraction of these objects has been proposed [14]. He stated that there is a need for the formalization of the distributed

---

[1] We will use distributed ledger from now on, instead of blockchain.

systems that are at the heart of most cryptocurrency implementations, and leverage the decades of experience in the distributed computing community in formal specification when designing and proving various properties of such systems. In particular, he noted that the distributed ledger can be formally described by its sequential specification, and be implemented using a universal construction, based on well-known concurrent objects, like consensus objects.

| **Code 1.** Ledger Object $\mathcal{L}$ | **Code 2.** Validated Ledger Object $\mathcal{VL}$ (only append) |
|---|---|

```
Code 1. Ledger Object L

1: Init: S ← ∅
2: function L.get( )
3:      return S
4: function L.append(r)
5:      S ← S‖r
6:      return
```

```
Code 2. Validated Ledger Object VL
(only append)

1: function VL.append(r)
2:      if Valid(S‖r) then
3:          S ← S‖r
4:          return ACK
5:      else return NACK
```

In this paper we provide a proper formulation of a family of *ledger objects*, starting from a centralized, non replicated ledger object, and moving to distributed, concurrent implementations of ledger objects, subject to validation rules. In particular, we provide definitions and sample implementations for the following types of ledger objects:

**Ledger Object (LO):** We begin with a formal definition of a *ledger object* as a sequence of *records*, supporting two basic operations: get and append. In brief, the ledger object is captured by Code 1 (in which ‖ is the concatenation operator), where the get operation returns the ledger as a sequence $S$ of records, and the append operation inserts a new record at the end of the sequence. The *sequential specification* of the object is then presented, to explicitly define the expected behavior of the object when accessed sequentially by get and append operations.

**Distributed Ledger Object (DLO):** With the ledger object implemented on top of multiple (possibly geographically dispersed) *computing devices* or *servers* we obtain *distributed ledgers* – the main focus of this paper. Distribution allows a (potentially very large) set of distributed *client processes* to access the distributed ledger, by issuing get and append operations concurrently. To explain the behavior of the operations during concurrency we define three consistency semantics: ($i$) eventual consistency, ($ii$) sequential consistency, and ($iii$) atomic consistency. The definitions provided are independent of the properties of the underlying system and the failure model.

**Implementations of DLO:** In light of our semantic definitions, we provide a number of algorithms that implement DLO satisfying the above mentioned consistency semantics, in asynchronous crash-prone systems, using an Atomic Broadcast service.

**Validated (Distributed) Ledger Object (V[D]LO):** We then provide a variation of the ledger object – the *validated ledger object* – which requires that each record in the ledger satisfies a particular *validation rule*, expressed as a predicate *Valid*(). To this end, the basic append operation of this type of ledger filters each record through the *Valid*() predicate before is appended to the ledger (see Code 2).

**Other Related Work.** A distributed ledger can be used to implement a replicated state machine [17,25]. Paxos [19] is one the first proposals of a replicated state machine implemented with repeated consensus instances. The Practical Byzantine Fault Tolerance solution of Castro and Liskov [6] is proposed to be used in Byzantine-tolerant blockchains. In fact, it is used by them to implement an asynchronous replicated state machine [5]. The recent work of Abraham and Malkhi [1] discusses in depth the relation between BFT protocols and blockchains consensus protocols. All these suggest that at the heart of implementing a distributed ledger object there is a version of a consensus mechanism, which directly impacts the efficiency of the implemented DLO. In a later section, we show that an eventual consistent DLO can be used to implement consensus, and consensus can be used to implement a DLO; this reinforces the relationship identified in the above-mentioned works.

Among the proposals for distributed ledgers, Algorand [12] is an algorithm for blockchain that boasts much higher throughput than Bitcoin and Ethereum. This work is a new resilient optimal Byzantine consensus algorithm targeting consortium blockchains. To this end, it first revisits the consensus validity property by requiring that the decided value satisfies a predefined predicate, which does not systematically exclude a value proposed only by Byzantine processes, thereby generalizing the validity properties found in the literature. Gramoli et al. [8,13] propose blockchains implemented using Byzantine consensus algorithms that also relax the validity property of the commonly defined consensus problem.

One of the closest works to ours is the one by Anceaume et al. [2], which like our work, attempts to connect the concept of distributed ledgers with distributed objects, although they concentrate in Bitcoin. In particular, they first show that read-write registers do not capture Bitcoin's behavior. To this end, they introduce the Distributed Ledger Register (DLR), a register that builds on read-write registers for mimicking the behavior of Bitcoin. In fact, they show the conditions under which the Bitcoin blockchain algorithm satisfies the DLR properties. Our work, although it shares the same spirit of formulating and connecting ledgers with concurrent objects (in the spirit of [22]), it differs in many aspects. For example, our formulation does not focus on a specific blockchain (such as Bitcoin), but aims to be more general, and beyond crypto-currencies. Hence, for example, instead of using sequences of blocks (as in [2]) we talk about sequences of records. Furthermore, following the concurrent object literature, we define the ledger object on new primitives (**get** and **append**), instead on building on multi-writer, multi-reader R/W register primitives. We pay particular attention on formulating the consistency semantics of the distributed ledger object and demonstrate their versatility by presenting implementations. Nevertheless, both works, although taking different approaches, contribute to the better understanding of the basic underlying principles of distributed ledgers from the theoretical distributed computing point of view.

# 2    The Ledger Object

## 2.1    Concurrent Objects and the Ledger Object

An *object type* $T$ specifies ($i$) the set of *values* (or states) that any object $O$ of type $T$ can take, and ($ii$) the set of *operations* that a process can use to modify or access the value of $O$. An object $O$ of type $T$ is a *concurrent object* if it is a shared object accessed by multiple processes [24]. Each operation on an object $O$ consists of an *invocation* event and a *response* event, that must occur in this order. A *history* of operations on $O$, denoted by $H_O$, is a sequence of invocation and response events, starting with an invocation event. (The sequence order of a history reflects the real time ordering of the events.) An operation $\pi$ is *complete* in a history $H_O$, if $H_O$ contains both the invocation and the matching response of $\pi$, in this order. A history $H_O$ is *complete* if it contains only complete operations; otherwise it is *partial* [24]. An operation $\pi_1$ *precedes* an operation $\pi_2$ (or $\pi_2$ *succeeds* $\pi_1$), denoted by $\pi_1 \rightarrow \pi_2$, in $H_O$, if the response event of $\pi_1$ appears before the invocation event of $\pi_2$ in $H_O$. Two operations are *concurrent* if none precedes the other.

A complete history $H_O$ is *sequential* if it contains no concurrent operations, i.e., it is an alternative sequence of matching invocation and response events, starting with an invocation and ending with a response event. A partial history is sequential, if removing its last event (that must be an invocation) makes it a complete sequential history. A *sequential specification* of an object $O$, describes the behavior of $O$ when accessed sequentially. In particular, the sequential specification of $O$ is the set of all possible sequential histories involving solely object $O$ [24].

A *ledger* $\mathcal{L}$ is a concurrent object that stores a totally ordered sequence $\mathcal{L}.S$ of *records* and supports two operations (available to any process $p$): (i) $\mathcal{L}.\mathsf{get}_p()$, and (ii) $\mathcal{L}.\mathsf{append}_p(r)$. A *record* is a triple $r = \langle \tau, p, v \rangle$, where $\tau$ is a *unique* record identifier from a set $\mathcal{T}$, $p \in \mathcal{P}$ is the identifier of the process that created record $r$, and $v$ is the data of the record drawn from an alphabet $A$. We will use $r.p$ to denote the id of the process that created record $r$; similarly we define $r.\tau$ and $r.v$. A process $p$ invokes a $\mathcal{L}.\mathsf{get}_p()$ operation[2] to obtain the sequence $\mathcal{L}.S$ of records stored in the ledger object $\mathcal{L}$, and $p$ invokes a $\mathcal{L}.\mathsf{append}_p(r)$ operation to extend $\mathcal{L}.S$ with a new record $r$. Initially, the sequence $\mathcal{L}.S$ is empty.

**Definition 1.** *The* sequential specification *of a ledger $\mathcal{L}$ over the sequential history $H_{\mathcal{L}}$ is defined as follows. The value of the sequence $\mathcal{L}.S$ of the ledger is initially the empty sequence. If at the invocation event of an operation $\pi$ in $H_{\mathcal{L}}$ the value of the sequence in ledger $\mathcal{L}$ is $\mathcal{L}.S = V$, then:*

1. *if $\pi$ is a $\mathcal{L}.\mathsf{get}_p()$ operation, then the response event of $\pi$ returns $V$, and*
2. *if $\pi$ is a $\mathcal{L}.\mathsf{append}_p(r)$ operation, then at the response event of $\pi$, the value of the sequence in ledger $\mathcal{L}$ is $\mathcal{L}.S = V\|r$ (where $\|$ is the concatenation operator).*

---

[2] We define only one operation to access the value of the ledger for simplicity. In practice, other operations, like those to access individual records in the sequence, will also be available.

## 2.2  Implementation of Ledgers

Processes execute operations and instructions sequentially (i.e., we make the usual well-formedness assumption where a process invokes one operation at a time). A process $p$ interacts with a ledger $\mathcal{L}$ by invoking an operation ($\mathcal{L}.\text{get}_p()$ or $\mathcal{L}.\text{append}_p(r)$), which causes a request to be sent from $p$ to $\mathcal{L}$, and a response from $\mathcal{L}$ to $p$. The response marks the end of the operation and carries the result of the operation.[3] The result for a get operation is a sequence of records, while the result for an append operation is a confirmation (ACK). This interaction (from the point of view of $p$) is depicted in Code 3. A possible centralized implementation of the ledger that processes requests sequentially is presented in Code 4 (each block **receive** is assumed to be executed in mutual exclusion). Figure 1 (left) abstracts the interaction between the processes and the ledger.

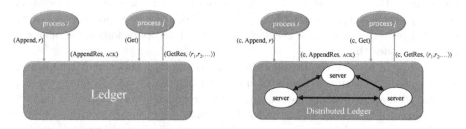

**Fig. 1.** The interaction between processes and the ledger, where $r, r_1, r_2, \ldots$ are records. Left: General abstraction; Right: Distributed ledger implemented by servers

---

**Code 3.** External Interface (Executed by a Process $p$) of a Ledger Object $\mathcal{L}$

```
1: function L.get( )
2:     send request (GET) to ledger L
3:     wait response (GETRES, V) from L
4:     return V
5: function L.append(r)
6:     send request (APPEND, r) to ledger L
7:     wait response (APPENDRES, res) from L
8:     return res
```

**Code 4.** Ledger $\mathcal{L}$ (centralized)

```
1: Init: S ← ∅
2: receive (GET) from process p
3:     send response (GETRES, S) to p

4: receive (APPEND, r) from process p
5:     S ← S‖r
6:     send resp (APPENDRES, ACK) to p
```

# 3  Distributed Ledger Objects

In this section we define distributed ledger objects, and some of the levels of consistency guarantees that can be provided. These definitions are general and do not rely on the properties of the underlying distributed system, unless otherwise stated. In particular, they do not make any assumption on the types of failures

---

[3] We make explicit the exchange of request and responses between the process and the ledger to reveal the fact that the ledger is concurrent, i.e., accessed by several processes.

that may occur. Then, we show how to implement distributed ledger objects that satisfy these consistency levels using an atomic broadcast [9] service on an asynchronous system with *crash* failures.

## 3.1 Distributed Ledgers and Consistency

**Distributed Ledgers.** A *distributed ledger object* (distributed ledger for short) is a concurrent ledger object that is implemented in a distributed manner. In particular, the ledger object is *implemented* by (and possibly replicated among) a set of (possibly distinct and geographically dispersed) computing devices, that we refer as *servers*. We refer to the processes that invoke the get() and append() operations of the distributed ledger as *clients*. Figure 1 (right) depicts the interaction between the clients and the distributed ledger, implemented by servers.

In general, servers can fail. This leads to introducing mechanisms in the algorithm that implements the distributed ledger to achieve fault tolerance, like replicating the ledger. Additionally, the interaction of the clients with the servers will have to take into account the faulty nature of individual servers, as we discuss later in the section.

**Consistency of Distributed Ledgers.** Distribution and replication intend to ensure availability and survivability of the ledger, in case a subset of the servers fails. At the same time, they raise the challenge of maintaining *consistency* among the different views that different clients get of the distributed ledger: what is the latest value of the ledger when multiple clients may send operation requests at different servers concurrently? Consistency semantics need to be in place to precisely describe the allowed values that a get() operation may return when it is executed concurrently with other get() or append() operations. Here, as examples, we provide the properties that operations must satisfy in order to guarantee *atomic consistency* (linearizability) [15], *sequential consistency* [18] and *eventual consistency* [11] semantics. In a similar way, other consistency guarantees, such as session and causal consistencies could be formally defined [11].

Atomicity (aka, linearizability) [4,15] provides the illusion that the distributed ledger is accessed sequentially respecting the real time order, even when operations are invoked concurrently. I.e., the distributed ledger seems to be a centralized ledger like the one implemented by Code 4. Formally[4],

**Definition 2.** *A distributed ledger $\mathcal{L}$ is atomic if, given any complete history $H_{\mathcal{L}}$, there exists a permutation $\sigma$ of the operations in $H_{\mathcal{L}}$ such that:*

1. *$\sigma$ follows the sequential specification of $\mathcal{L}$, and*
2. *for every pair of operations $\pi_1, \pi_2$, if $\pi_1 \to \pi_2$ in $H_{\mathcal{L}}$, then $\pi_1$ appears before $\pi_2$ in $\sigma$.*

---

[4] Our formal definitions of linearizability and sequential consistency are adapted from [4].

Sequential consistency [4,18] is weaker than atomicity in the sense that it only requires that operations respect the local ordering at each process, not the real time ordering. Formally,

**Definition 3.** *A distributed ledger $\mathcal{L}$ is* sequentially consistent *if, given any complete history $H_{\mathcal{L}}$, there exists a permutation $\sigma$ of the operations in $H_{\mathcal{L}}$ such that:*

1. *$\sigma$ follows the sequential specification of $\mathcal{L}$, and*
2. *for every pair of operations $\pi_1, \pi_2$ invoked by a process $p$, if $\pi_1 \rightarrow \pi_2$ in $H_{\mathcal{L}}$, then $\pi_1$ appears before $\pi_2$ in $\sigma$.*

Let us finally give a definition of eventually consistent distributed ledgers. Informally speaking, a distributed ledger is eventual consistent, if for every append($r$) operation that completes, *eventually* all get() operations return sequences that contain record $r$, and in the same position. Formally,

**Definition 4.** *A distributed ledger $\mathcal{L}$ is* eventually consistent *if, given any complete history $H_{\mathcal{L}}$, there exists a permutation $\sigma$ of the operations in $H_{\mathcal{L}}$ such that:*

(a) *$\sigma$ follows the sequential specification of $\mathcal{L}$, and*
(b) *for every $\mathcal{L}$.append($r$) $\in H_{\mathcal{L}}$, there exists a complete history $H'_{\mathcal{L}}$ that extends[5] $H_{\mathcal{L}}$ such that, for every complete history $H''_{\mathcal{L}}$ that extends $H'_{\mathcal{L}}$, every complete operation $\mathcal{L}$.get() in $H''_{\mathcal{L}} \setminus H'_{\mathcal{L}}$ returns a sequence that contains $r$.*

*Remark:* Observe that in the above definitions we consider $H_{\mathcal{L}}$ to be complete. As argued in [24], the definitions can be extended to sequences that are not complete by reducing the problem of determining whether a complete sequence extracted by the non complete one is consistent. That is, given a partial history $H_{\mathcal{L}}$, if $H_{\mathcal{L}}$ can be modified in such a way that every invocation of a non complete operation is either removed or completed with a response event, and the resulting, complete, sequence $H'_{\mathcal{L}}$ checks for consistency, then $H_{\mathcal{L}}$ also checks for consistency. Alternatively, following [4], a liveness assumption can be made where every invocation event has a matching response event (and hence all histories are complete).

### 3.2   Distributed Ledger Implementations in a System with Crash Failures

In this section we provide implementations of distributed ledgers with different levels of consistency in an asynchronous distributed system with crash failures, as a mean of illustrating the generality and versatility of our ledger formulation. These implementations build on a generic deterministic atomic broadcast service [9].

---

[5] A sequence $X$ extends a sequence $Y$ when $Y$ is a prefix of $X$.

**Distributed Setting.** We consider an asynchronous message-passing distributed system. There is an unbounded number of clients accessing the distributed ledger. There is a set $S$ of $n$ servers, that emulate a ledger (c.f., Code 4) in a distributed manner. Both clients and servers might fail by crashing. However, no more than $f < n$ of servers might crash[6]. Processes (clients and servers) interact by message passing communication over asynchronous reliable channels.

We assume that clients are aware of the faulty nature of servers and know (an upper bound on) the maximum number of faulty servers $f$. Hence, we assume they use a modified version of the interface presented in Code 3 to deal with server unreliability. The new interface is presented in Code 5. As can be seen there, every operation request is sent to a set $L$ of at least $f + 1$

**Code 5.** External Interface of a Distributed Ledger Object $\mathcal{L}$ Executed by a Process $p$

```
1:  c ← 0
2:  Let L ⊆ S : |L| ≥ f + 1
3:  function L.get( )
4:      c ← c + 1
5:      send request (c, GET) to the servers in L
6:      wait response (c, GETRES, V) from some i ∈ L
7:      return V
8:  function L.append(r)
9:      c ← c + 1
10:     send request (c, APPEND, r) to the servers in L
11:     wait response (c, APPENDRES, res) from some i ∈ L
12:     return res
```

servers, to guarantee that at least one correct server receives and processes the request (if an upper bound on $f$ is not known, then the clients contact all servers). Moreover, at least one such correct server will send a response which guarantees the termination of the operations. For formalization purposes, the first response received for an operation will be considered as the response event of the operation. In order to differentiate from different responses, all operations (and their requests and responses) are uniquely numbered with counter $c$, so duplicated responses will be identified and ignored (i.e., only the first one will be processed by the client).

In the remainder of the section we focus on providing the code run by the servers, i.e., the distributed ledger emulation. The servers will take into account Code 5, and in particular the fact that clients send the same request to multiple servers. This is important, for instance, to make sure that the same record $r$ is not included in the sequence of records of the ledger multiple times. As already mentioned, our algorithms will use as a building block an atomic broadcast service. Consequently, our algorithms' correctness depends on the modeling assumptions of the specific atomic broadcast implementation used. We now give the guarantees that our atomic broadcast service need to provide.

**Atomic Broadcast Service.** The Atomic Broadcast service (aka, total order broadcast service) [9] has two operations: ABroadcast($m$) used by a server to broadcast a message $m$ to all servers $s \in S$, and ADeliver($m$) used by the atomic broadcast service to deliver a message $m$ to a server. The following properties are guaranteed (adopted from [9]):

---

[6] The atomic broadcast service used in the algorithms may internally have more restrictive requirements.

- *Validity*: if a correct server broadcasts a message, then it will eventually deliver it.
- *Uniform Agreement*: if a server delivers a message, then all correct servers will eventually deliver that message.
- *Uniform Integrity*: a message is delivered by each server at most once, and only if it was previously broadcast.
- *Uniform Total Order*: the messages are totally ordered; that is, if any server delivers message $m$ before message $m'$, then every server that delivers them, must do it in that order.

**Eventual Consistency and Relation with Consensus.** We now use the Atomic Broadcast service to implement distributed ledgers in our set of servers $\mathcal{S}$ guaranteeing different consistency semantics. We start by showing that the algorithm presented in Code 6 implements an eventually consistent ledger, as specified in Definition 4.

| **Code 6** . Eventually Consistent Distributed Ledger $\mathcal{L}$; Code for Server $i \in \mathcal{S}$ |
|---|
| 1: **Init:** $S_i \leftarrow \emptyset$ |
| 2: **receive** (c, GET) from process $p$ |
| 3:     **send** response (c, GETRES, $S_i$) to $p$ |
| 4: **receive** (c, APPEND, $r$) from process $p$ |
| 5:     ABroadcast($r$) |
| 6:     **send** response (c, APPENDRES, ACK) to $p$ |
| 7: **upon** (ADeliver($r$)) do |
| 8:     **if** $r \notin S_i$ **then** $S_i \leftarrow S_i \| r$ |

| **Code 7.** Consensus Algorithm Using an Eventually Consistent Ledger $\mathcal{L}$ |
|---|
| 1: **function** propose (v) |
| 2:     $\mathcal{L}$.append(v) |
| 3:     $V_i \leftarrow \mathcal{L}$.get() |
| 4:     **while** $V_i = \emptyset$ **do** |
| 5:         $V_i \leftarrow \mathcal{L}$.get() |
| 6:     **decide** the first value in $V_i$ |

**Lemma 1.** *The combination of the algorithms presented in Codes 5 and 6 implements an eventually consistent distributed ledger.*

**Proof Sketch.** The lemma follows from the properties of atomic broadcast. Considering any complete history $H_{\mathcal{L}}$, a permutation $\sigma$ that follows the sequential specification can be constructed by ordering: (i) an append($r$) operation according to the order the atomic broadcast service delivers the first copy of $r$, and (ii) a get operation that returns $V$ immediately after the append($r$) operation, such that $r$ is the last record in $V$. Moreover, by Code 5, when an append($r$) operation is invoked, at least one correct server receives and atomically broadcasts $r$. By uniform agreement and uniform total order properties, all the correct servers receive the first copy of $r$ in the same order, and hence all add $r$ in the same position in their local sequences. Therefore, eventually all get operations will return a sequence that will contain $r$.     □

Let us now explore the power of any eventually consistent distributed ledger. It is known that atomic broadcast is equivalent to consensus in a crash-prone system like the one considered here [7]. Then, the algorithm presented in Code 6 can be implemented as soon as a consensus object is available. What we show now is that a distributed ledger that provides the eventual consistency can be used to solve the consensus problem, defined as follows.

*Consensus Problem:* Consider a system with at least one non-faulty process and in which each process $p_i$ proposes a value $v_i$ from the set $V$ (calling a propose($v_i$) function), and then decides a value $o_i \in V$, called the *decision.* Any decision is irreversible, and the following conditions are satisfied: (*i*) *Agreement:* All decision values are identical. (*ii*) *Validity:* If all calls to the propose function that occur contain the same value $v$, then $v$ is the only possible decision value. and (*iii*) *Termination:* In any fair execution every non-faulty process decides a value.

**Lemma 2.** *The algorithm presented in Code 7 solves the consensus problem if the ledger $\mathcal{L}$ guarantees eventual consistency.*

**Proof Sketch.** A correct process $p$ that invokes propose$_p(v)$ will complete its $\mathcal{L}$.append$_p(v)$ operation. By eventual consistency, some server will eventually deliver $v$ and the $\mathcal{L}$.get$_p()$ will return a non-empty sequence. Condition (a) of Definition 4 guarantees that, given any two sequences returned by $\mathcal{L}$.get() operations, one is a prefix of the other, hence guaranteeing agreement. Finally, from the same condition, the sequences returned by $\mathcal{L}$.get() operations can only contain values appended with $\mathcal{L}$.append$_p(v)$, hence guaranteeing validity.    □

Combining the above arguments and lemmas we have the following theorem.

**Theorem 1.** *Consensus and eventually consistent distributed ledgers are equivalent in a crash-prone distributed system.*

**Atomic Consistency.** Observe that the eventual consistent implementation does not guarantee that record $r$ has been added to the ledger before a response APPENDRES is received by the client $p$ issuing the append($r$). This may lead to situations in which a client may complete an append() operation, and a succeeding get() may not contain the appended record. This behavior is also apparent in Definition 4, that allows any get() operation, that is invoked and completed in $H'_{\mathcal{L}}$, to return a sequence that does not include a record $r$ which was appended by an append($r$) operation that appears in $H_{\mathcal{L}}$.

An *atomic distributed ledger* avoids this problem and requires that a record $r$ appended by an append($r$) operation, is received by any succeeding get() operation, even if the two operations were invoked at different processes. Code 8, describes the algorithm at the servers in order to implement an atomic consistent distributed ledger. The algorithm of each client is depicted from Code 5. Briefly, when a server receives a *get* or an *append* request, it adds the request in a pending set and atomically broadcasts the request to all other servers. When an append or get message is delivered, then the server replies to the requesting process (if it did not reply yet).

**Theorem 2.** *The combination of the algorithms presented in Codes 8 and 5 implements an atomic distributed ledger.*

**Proof.** To show that atomic consistency is preserved, we need to prove that our algorithm satisfies the properties presented in Definition 2. The underlying atomic broadcast defines the order of events when operations are concurrent. It remains to show that operations that are separate in time can be ordered with respect to their real time ordering. The following properties capture the necessary conditions that must be satisfied by non-concurrent operations that appear in a history $H_{\mathcal{L}}$:

---

**Code 8 .** Atomic Distributed Ledger; Code for Server $i$

```
 1: Init: S_i ← ∅; pending_i ← ∅; g_pending_i ← ∅
 2: receive (c, GET) from process p
 3:     ABroadcast(get, p, c)
 4:     add (p, c) to g_pending_i
 5: receive (c, APPEND, r) from process p
 6:     ABroadcast(append, r)
 7:     add (c, r) to pending_i
 8: upon (ADeliver(append, r)) do
 9:     if r ∉ S_i then
10:         S_i ← S_i‖r
11:         if ∃(c, r) ∈ pending_i then
12:             send response (c, APPENDRES, ACK) to r.p
13:             remove (c, r) from pending_i
14: upon (ADeliver(get, p, c)) do
15:         if (p, c) ∈ g_pending_i then
16:             send response (c, GETRES, S_i) to p
17:             remove (p, c) from g_pending_i
```

---

**A1** if $\mathsf{append}_{p_1}(r_1) \rightarrow \mathsf{append}_{p_2}(r_2)$ from processes $p_1$ and $p_2$, then $r_1$ must appear before $r_2$ in any sequence returned by the ledger

**A2** if $\mathsf{append}_{p_1}(r_1) \rightarrow \mathsf{get}_{p_2}()$, then $r_1$ appears in the sequence returned by $\mathsf{get}_{p_2}()$

**A3** if $\pi_1$ and $\pi_2$ are two $\mathsf{get}()$ operations from $p_1$ and $p_2$, s.t. $\pi_1 \rightarrow \pi_2$, that return sequences $S_1$ and $S_2$ respectively, then $S_1$ must be a prefix of $S_2$

**A4** if $\mathsf{get}_{p_1}() \rightarrow \mathsf{append}_{p_2}(r_2)$, then $p_1$ returns a sequence $S_1$ that does not contain $r_2$.

Property, **A1** is preserved from the fact that record $r_1$ is atomically broadcasted and delivered before $r_2$ is broadcasted among the servers. In particular, let $p_1$ be the process that invokes $\pi_1 = \mathsf{append}_{p_1}(r_1)$, and $p_2$ the process that invokes $\pi_2 = \mathsf{append}_{p_2}(r_2)$ ($p_1$ and $p_2$ may be the same process). Since $\pi_1 \rightarrow \pi_2$, then $p_1$ receives a response to the $\pi_1$ operation, before $p_2$ invokes the $\pi_2$ operation. Let server $s$ be the first to respond to $p_1$ for $\pi_1$. Server $s$ sends a response only if the procedure $\mathsf{ADeliver}(append, r_1)$ occurs at $s$. This means that the atomic broadcast service delivers $(append, r_1)$ to $s$. Since $\pi_1 \rightarrow \pi_2$ then no server received the append request for $\pi_2$, and thus $r_2$ was not broadcasted before the $\mathsf{ADeliver}(append, r_1)$ at $s$. Hence, by the *Uniform Total Order* of the atomic broadcast, every server delivers $(append, r_1)$ before delivering $(append, r_2)$. Thus, the $\mathsf{ADeliver}(append, r_2)$ occurs in any server $s'$ after the appearance of $\mathsf{ADeliver}(append, r_1)$ at $s'$. Therefore, if $s'$ is the first server to reply to $p_2$ for $\pi_2$, it must be the case that $s'$ added $r_1$ in his ledger sequence before adding $r_2$.

In similar manner we can show that property **A2** is also satisfied. In particular let processes $p_1$ and $p_2$ (not necessarily different), invoke operations $\pi_1 = \mathsf{append}_{p_1}(r_1)$ and $\pi_2 = \mathsf{get}_{p_2}()$, s.t. $\pi_1 \rightarrow \pi_2$. Since $\pi_1$ completes before $\pi_2$ is invoked then there exists some server $s$ in which $\mathsf{ADeliver}(append, r_1)$ occurs before responding to $p_1$. Also, since the GET request from $p_2$ is sent, after $\pi_1$ has completed, then it follows that is sent after ADeliver$(append, r_1)$ occurred in $s$. Therefore, $(get, p_2, c)$ is broadcasted after ADeliver$(append, r_1)$ as well. Hence by *Uniform Total Order* atomic broadcast, every server delivers $(append, r_1)$ before delivering $(get, p_2, c)$. So if $s'$ is the first server to reply to $p_2$, it must be the case that $s'$ received $(append, r_1)$ before receiving $(get, p_2, c)$ and hence replies with an $S_i$ to $p_2$ that contains $r_1$.

The proof of property **A3** is slightly different. Let $\pi_1 = \text{get}_{p1}()$ and $\pi_2 = \text{get}_{p2}()$, s.t. $\pi_1 \to \pi_2$. Since $\pi_1$ completes before $\pi_2$ is invoked then the $(get, p_1, c_1)$ must be delivered to at least a server $s$ that responds to $p_1$, before the invocation of $\pi_2$, and thus the broadcast of $(get, p_2, c_2)$. By *Uniform Total Order* again, all servers deliver $(get, p_1, c_1)$ before delivering $(get, p_2, c_2)$. Let $S_1$ be the sequence sent by $s$ to $p_1$. Notice that $S_1$ contains all the records $r$ such that $(append, r)$ delivered to $s$ before the delivery of $(get, p_1, c_1)$ to $s$. Thus, for every $r$ in $S_1$, ADeliver$(append, r)$ occurs in $s$ before ADeliver$(get, p_1, c)$. Let $s'$ be the first server that responds for $\pi_2$. By *Uniform Agreement*, since $s'$ has not crashed before responding to $p_2$, then every $r$ in $S_1$ that was delivered in $s$, was also delivered in $s'$. Also, by *Uniform Total Order*, it must be the case that all records in $S_1$ will be delivered to $s'$ in the same order that have been delivered to $s$. Furthermore all the records will be delivered to $s'$ before the delivery of $(get, p_1, c1)$. Thus, all records are delivered at server $s'$ before $(get, p_2, c_2)$ as well, and hence the sequence $S_2$ sent by $s'$ to $p_2$ is a suffix of $S_1$.

Finally, if $\text{get}_{p_1}() \to \text{append}_{p_2}(r_2)$ as in property **A4**, then trivially $p_1$ cannot return $r_2$, since it has not yet been broadcasted (*Uniform Integrity* of the atomic broadcast). $\qquad\square$

**Sequential Consistency.** An atomic distributed ledger also satisfies sequential consistency. As sequential consistency is weaker than atomic consistency, one may wonder whether a sequentially consistent ledger can be implemented in a simpler way.

We propose here an implementation, depicted in Code 9, that avoids the atomic broadcast of the get requests. Instead, it applies some changes to the client code to achieve sequential consistency, as presented in Code 10. This implementation provides both sequential (cf. Definition 3) and eventual consistency (cf. Definition 4).

**Theorem 3.** *The combination of the algorithms presented in Codes 9 and 10 implements a sequentially consistent distributed ledger.*

**Proof Sketch.** Due to lack of space the detailed proof can be found in [3]. In brief, a permutation $\sigma$ (as required in Definition 3) can be constructed by placing the concurrent operations in an order that satisfies the sequential specification of the ledger. The ordering of operations at each process is captured by the following properties:

**S1** if $append_p(r_1) \to append_p(r_2)$ then $r_1$ must appear before $r_2$ in the ledger.
**S2** if $get_p() \to append_p(r_1)$, then $get_p$ returns a sequence $V_p$ that does not contain $r_1$
**S3** if $append_p(r_1) \to get_p()$, then $get_p$ returns a sequence $V_p$ that contains $r_1$
**S4** if $\pi_1$ and $\pi_2$ are two $get_p()$ operations, such that $\pi_1 \to \pi_2$, and that return sequences $V_1$ and $V_2$ respectively, then $V_1$ must be a prefix of $V_2$.

We can show that Codes 9 and 10 satisfy the above properties, following claims similar to the ones we used in the case of an atomic distributed ledger.☐

---

**Code 9.** Sequentially Consistent Distributed Ledger; Code for Server $i \in \mathcal{S}$

```
 1: Init: S_i ← ∅; pending_i ← ∅; g_pending_i ← ∅
 2: receive (c, GET, ℓ) from process p
 3:     if |S_i| ≥ ℓ then
 4:         send response (c, GETRES, S_i) to p
 5:     else
 6:         add (c, p, ℓ) to g_pending_i
 7: receive (c, APPEND, r) from process p
 8:     ABroadcast(c, r)
 9:     add (c, r) to pending_i
10: upon (ADeliver(c, r)) do
11:     if r ∉ S_i then S_i ← S_i‖r
12:     if (c, r) ∈ pending_i then
13:         send resp. (c, APPENDRES, ACK, |S_i|) to r.p
14:         remove (c, r) from pending_i
15:     if ∃(c', p, ℓ) ∈ g_pending_i : |S_i| ≥ ℓ then
16:         send response (c', GETRES, S_i) to p
17:         remove (c', p, ℓ) from g_pending_i
```

**Code 10.** External Interface for Sequential Consistency Executed by a Process $p$

```
 1: c ← 0; ℓ_last ← 0
 2: Let L ⊆ S : |L| ≥ f + 1
 3: function L.get( )
 4:     c ← c + 1
 5:     send request (c, GET, ℓ_last) to the servers in L
 6:     wait response (c, GETRES, V) from some i ∈ L
 7:     ℓ_last ← |V|
 8:     return V
 9: function L.append(r)
10:     c ← c + 1
11:     send request (c, APPEND, r) to the servers in L
12:     wait response (c, APPENDRES, res, pos) from some
            i ∈ L
13:     ℓ_last ← pos
14:     return res
```

---

## 4  Validated Ledgers

A *validated ledger* $\mathcal{VL}$ is a ledger in which specific semantics are imposed on the contents of the records stored in the ledger. For instance, if the records are (bitcoin-like) financial transactions,

**Code 11.** Validated Ledger $\mathcal{VL}$ (centralized)

```
 1: Init: S ← ∅
 2: receive (GET) from process p
 3:         send response (GETRES, S) to p
 4: receive (APPEND, r) from process p
 5:     if Valid(S‖r) then
 6:         S ← S‖r
 7:         send response (APPENDRES, ACK) to p
 8:     else send response (APPENDRES, NACK) to p
```

the semantics should, for example, prevent double spending, or apply other transaction validation used as part of the Bitcoin protocol [20]. The ledger preserves the semantics with a validity check in the form of a Boolean function $Valid()$ that takes as an input a sequence of records $S$ and returns *true* if and only if the semantics are preserved. In a validated ledger the result of an $append_p(r)$ operation may be NACK if the validity check fails. Code 11 presents a centralized implementation of a validated ledger $\mathcal{VL}$.

The sequential specification of a validated ledger must take into account the possibility that an append returns NACK. To this respect, property (2) of Definition 1 must be revised as follows:

**Definition 5.** *The sequential specification of a* **validated** *ledger* $\mathcal{VL}$ *over the sequential history* $H_{\mathcal{VL}}$ *is defined as follows. The value of the sequence* $\mathcal{VL}.S$ *is initially the empty sequence. If at the invocation event of an operation* $\pi$ *in* $H_{\mathcal{VL}}$ *the value of the sequence in ledger* $\mathcal{VL}$ *is* $\mathcal{VL}.S = V$, *then:*

*1. if* $\pi$ *is a* $\mathcal{VL}$.get$_p()$ *operation, then the response event of* $\pi$ *returns* $V$,

*2(a). if* $\pi$ *is an* $\mathcal{VL}$.append$_p(r)$ *operation that returns* ACK, *then* $Valid(V\|r) = true$ *and at the response event of* $\pi$, *the value of the sequence in ledger* $\mathcal{VL}$ *is* $\mathcal{VL}.S = V\|r$, *and*

*2(b). if* $\pi$ *is a* $\mathcal{VL}$.append$_p(r)$ *operation that returns* NACK, *then* $Valid(V\|r) = false$ *and at the response event of* $\pi$, *the value of the sequence in ledger* $\mathcal{VL}$ *is* $\mathcal{VL}.S = V$.

Based on this revised notion of sequential specification, one can define the eventual, sequential and atomic consistent validated distributed ledger and design implementations in a similar manner as in Sect. 3.

It is interesting to observe that a validated ledger $\mathcal{VL}$ can be implemented with a regular ledger $\mathcal{L}$ if we are willing to waste some resources and accuracy (e.g., not rejecting invalid records). In particular, processes can use a ledger $\mathcal{L}$ to store *all* the records appended, even if they make the validity to be broken. Then, when the function get() is invoked, the records that make the validity to be violated are removed, and only the valid records are returned. This algorithm does not check validity in a $\pi = $ append$(r)$ operation which returns ACK, because it is not possible to know when $\pi$ is processed the final position $r$ will take in the ledger (and hence to check its validity).

## 5   Conclusions

In this paper we formally define the concept of a distributed ledger object with and without validation. We have focused on the definition of the basic operational properties that a distributed ledger must satisfy, and their consistency semantics, independently of the underlying system characteristics and the failure model. Finally, we have explored implementations of fault-tolerant distributed ledger objects with different types of consistency in crash-prone systems augmented with an atomic broadcast service. Comparing the distributed ledger object and its consistency models with popular existing blockchain implementations, like Bitcoin or Ethereum, we must note that these do not satisfy even eventual consistency. Observe that their blockchain may (temporarily) fork, and hence two clients may see (with an operation analogous to our get) two conflicting sequences, in which neither one is a prefix of the other. This violates the sequential specification of the ledger. The main issue with these blockchains is that they use probabilistic consensus, with a recovery mechanism when it fails.

As mentioned, this paper is only an attempt to formally address the many questions that were posed in the introduction. In that sense we have only scratched the surface. There is a large list of pending issues that can be explored. For instance, we believe that the implementations we have can be adapted to deal with Byzantine failures if the appropriate atomic broadcast service is used. However, dealing with Byzantine failures will require to use cryptographic tools. Cryptography was not needed in the implementations presented in this paper because we assumed benign crash failures. Another extension worth exploring is how to deal with highly dynamic sets of possibly anonymous servers in order to implement distributed ledgers, to get closer to the Bitcoin-like ecosystem. In a more ambitious but possibly related tone, we would like to fully explore the properties of validated ledgers and their relation with cryptocurrencies.

# References

1. Abraham, I., Malkhi, D.: The blockchain consensus layer and BFT. Bull. EATCS **3**(123), 74–95 (2017)
2. Anceaume, E., Ludinard, R., Potop-Butucaru, M., Tronel, F.: Bitcoin a distributed shared register. In: Spirakis, P., Tsigas, P. (eds.) SSS 2017. LNCS, vol. 10616, pp. 456–468. Springer, Cham (2017). https://doi.org/10.1007/978-3-319-69084-1_34
3. Fernández Anta, A., Georgiou, C., Konwar, K.M., Nicolaou, N.C.: Formalizing and implementing distributed ledger objects. CoRR, abs/1802.07817 (2018)
4. Attiya, H., Welch, J.L.: Sequential consistency versus linearizability. ACM Trans. Comput. Syst. **12**(2), 91–122 (1994)
5. Castro, M., Liskov, B.: Proactive recovery in a Byzantine-fault-tolerant system. In: Proceedings of the 4th conference on Symposium on Operating System Design & Implementation, vol. 4, p. 19. USENIX Association (2000)
6. Castro, M., Liskov, B.: Practical Byzantine fault tolerance and proactive recovery. ACM Trans. Comput. Syst. (TOCS) **20**(4), 398–461 (2002)
7. Chandra, T.D., Toueg, S.: Unreliable failure detectors for reliable distributed systems. J. ACM **43**(2), 225–267 (1996)
8. Crain, T., Gramoli, V., Larrea, M., Raynal, M.: (Leader/randomization/signature)-free Byzantine consensus for consortium blockchains. CoRR, abs/1702.03068 (2017)
9. Défago, X., Schiper, A., Urbán, P.: Total order broadcast and multicast algorithms: taxonomy and survey. ACM Comput. Surv. **36**(4), 372–421 (2004)
10. Garay, J., Kiayias, A., Leonardos, N.: The bitcoin backbone protocol: analysis and applications. In: Oswald, E., Fischlin, M. (eds.) EUROCRYPT 2015. LNCS, vol. 9057, pp. 281–310. Springer, Heidelberg (2015). https://doi.org/10.1007/978-3-662-46803-6_10
11. Gentz, M., Dude, J.: Tunable data consistency levels in Microsoft Azure Cosmos DB, June 2017
12. Gilad, Y., Hemo, R., Micali, S., Vlachos, G., Zeldovich, N.: Algorand: scaling Byzantine agreements for cryptocurrencies. In: Proceedings of the 26th Symposium on Operating Systems Principles, pp. 51–68. ACM (2017)
13. Gramoli, V.: From blockchain consensus back to Byzantine consensus. Future Generation Computer Systems (2017, in press)
14. Herlihy, M.: Blockchains and the future of distributed computing. In: Schiller, E.M., Schwarzmann, A.A. (eds.) Proceedings of the ACM Symposium on Principles of Distributed Computing, PODC 2017, Washington, DC, USA, 25–27 July 2017, p. 155. ACM (2017)
15. Herlihy, M.P., Wing, J.M.: Linearizability: a correctness condition for concurrent objects. ACM Trans. Program. Lang. Syst. **12**(3), 463–492 (1990)

16. Kuo, T.-T., Kim, H.-E., Ohno-Machado, L.: Blockchain distributed ledger technologies for biomedical and health care applications. J. Am. Med. Inform. Assoc. **24**(6), 1211–1220 (2017)

17. Lamport, L.: Time, clocks, and the ordering of events in a distributed system. Commun. ACM **21**(7), 558–565 (1978)

18. Lamport, L.: How to make a multiprocessor computer that correctly executes multiprocess programs. IEEE Trans. Comput. **C–28**(9), 690–691 (1979)

19. Lamport, L.: The part-time parliament. ACM Trans. Comput. Syst. **16**(2), 133–169 (1998)

20. Nakamoto, S.: Bitcoin: a peer-to-peer electronic cash system (2008). https://bitcoin.org/en/bitcoin-paper. Accessed 3 Apr 2018

21. Namecoin. https://www.namecoin.org. Accessed 3 Apr 2018

22. Nicolaou, N., Fernández Anta, A., Georgiou, C.: CoVer-ability: consistent versioning in asynchronous, fail-prone, message-passing environments. In: 2016 IEEE 15th International Symposium on Network Computing and Applications, NCA, pp. 224–231 (2016)

23. Popper, N., Lohr, S.: Blockchain: a better way to track pork chops, bonds, bad peanut butter? New York Times, March 2017

24. Raynal, M.: Concurrent Programming: Algorithms, Principles, and Foundations. Springer, Heidelberg (2013). https://doi.org/10.1007/978-3-642-32027-9

25. Schneider, F.B.: Implementing fault-tolerant services using the state machine approach: a tutorial. ACM Comput. Surv. (CSUR) **22**(4), 299–319 (1990)

26. Wood, G.: Ethereum: a secure decentralised generalised transaction ledger (2014)

# On the Unfairness of Blockchain

Rachid Guerraoui and Jingjing Wang$^{(\boxtimes)}$

École Polytechnique Fédérale de Lausanne, IC, Lausanne, Switzerland
{rachid.guerraoui,jingjing.wang}@epfl.ch

**Abstract.** The success of *Bitcoin* relies on the perception of a *fair* underlying peer-to-peer protocol: *blockchain*. Fairness here means that the reward (in bitcoins) given to any participant that helps maintain the consistency of the protocol by *mining*, is proportional to the computational power devoted by that participant to the mining task. Without such perception of fairness, honest miners might be disincentivized to maintain the protocol, leaving the space for dishonest miners to reach a majority and jeopardize the consistency of the entire system.

We prove that blockchain is *unfair*, even in a distributed system of only *two honest miners*. In a realistic setting where message delivery is not instantaneous, the ratio between the (expected) number of blocks committed by two miners is actually lower bounded by a term *exponential* in the product of the message delay and the difference between the two miners' hashrates. To obtain our result, we model the growth of blockchain, which may be of independent interest. We also apply our result to explain recent empirical observations and vulnerabilities.

## 1   Introduction

At the heart of the celebrated *Bitcoin* currency and payment system [1–3] lies a distributed protocol called *blockchain*, now considered of independent interest [4]. Essentially, this protocol maintains a distributed data structure, also called *the blockchain*, made of a series of transaction *blocks*, and updated by specific nodes called *miners*. To update a blockchain, a miner $\mathcal{M}$ devotes computational resources into a task called "proof-of-work" [5] in order to *mine* a block. Each block mined by $\mathcal{M}$ includes an extra *coinbase* transaction to reward $\mathcal{M}$'s computational effort with bitcoins [6]. The computational power of any miner is characterized by a *hashrate*, $\lambda$, meaning that, on average, it takes $\frac{1}{\lambda}$ units of time to mine a block. Once a block is mined, the block is propagated to the other miners. Roughly speaking, the block is said to be *committed* when it is delivered to all miners.

The success of Bitcoin relies on the perception of *fairness* [7]: in short, the reward of a given honest miner $\mathcal{M}$ is proportional to $\mathcal{M}$'s hashrate [8,9]. Fairness in this sense is crucial, for otherwise (i.e., if the reward of an honest miner were lower than its fair proportion), honest miners could be disincentivized and stop maintaining the blockchain, leaving the space for dishonest miners (the proportion of which could then grow to a majority) to jeopardize the correct functioning of the entire system [10].

© Springer Nature Switzerland AG 2019
A. Podelski and F. Taïani (Eds.): NETYS 2018, LNCS 11028, pp. 36–50, 2019.
https://doi.org/10.1007/978-3-030-05529-5_3

We prove in this paper that Bitcoin blockchain is actually *unfair*. The fundamental reason is simple: blockchain is a distributed protocol, meaning that message delivery is not instantaneous. We show that with non-nil message delays, in a distributed system of *two honest miners*, $\mathcal{M}_1$ and $\mathcal{M}_2$ with hashrates $\lambda_1$ and $\lambda_2$, respectively, and message delay $u$ between them, if $\lambda_1 > \lambda_2$, then $\mathcal{M}_1$ can commit many more blocks than $\mathcal{M}_2$ in expectation. The ratio between the expected number of blocks committed by $\mathcal{M}_1$ and $\mathcal{M}_2$ is lower bounded by $\frac{e^{\lambda_1 u}\lambda_1}{e^{\lambda_2 u}\lambda_2}$, which is *exponential* in the product of the message delay and the difference between the hashrates of $\mathcal{M}_1$ and $\mathcal{M}_2$.

To establish our lower bound, we go beyond most previous theoretical analyses of blockchain that take communication delays into account, typically assuming a delay rate (the percentage of miners receiving a certain message) [11], or dividing time into discrete steps (which may be viewed as an approximation of continuous time) [8,12]. We rather model time in a *continuous way* to relate hashrates to communication delays, and model exactly how the blockchain grows in time (which may be of independent interest). We construct our proof of the lower bound in two steps: we first establish (1) the unfairness per se, and then (2) the exponential advantage. The key to our proof is the probability distribution of when the blockchain grows so that the blockchain includes $k$ blocks for any $k \in \mathbb{Z}^+$. We show that the miner with a higher hashrate can grow its chain earlier for any $k$ with a higher probability, implying unfairness, as the first step. In the second step, we extract the exponential term from the fact that no block is mined during some message delay $u$.

Our result on unfairness of blockchain among honest miners has several applications. For instance, our result explains disproportionate rewards reported via empirical experiments on blockchain [13,14]. It also implies a trade-off between the speed to mine a block and the fairness of committed blocks in blockchain as well as its variants (such as Bitcoin-NG [13], and GHOST [15][1]): namely, the legitimate temptation to increase the throughput of blockchain by reducing its mining time can however cause even more unfairness. Our result can also help extend previous results on the benefits of selfish miners (which are dishonest, deviating from the mining algorithm to maximize their rewards). Indeed, Eyal and Sirer [11] (and follow-up work [9,16]) showed that a *selfish* miner $\mathcal{M}$'s reward can be more than its fair share if the proportion $\alpha$ of $\mathcal{M}$'s hashrate, among all hashrates, passes the threshold $th = \frac{1}{3}$ (which is a sufficient condition). Their result assumed, however, no message delay. In a setting with message delays, we show a lower bound $\mathcal{L}$ such that the threshold $th > \mathcal{L}$, where $\mathcal{L}$ is a function of $u$, $\lambda_1$ and $\lambda_2$. (For reasonable message delays measured for the Bitcoin blockchain implementation [17], $\mathcal{L} > \frac{1}{3}$.) Another application of our result is the unfairness of blockchain in the context of two clusters of miners with some negligible message delay within each cluster and a larger message delay between the two clusters. In this case, we show that even between two miners with the same hashrate, blockchain can favor a miner $\mathcal{M}$ with an advantage that is expo-

---

[1] In the case of two honest miners, GHOST is equivalent to Bitcoin blockchain [15].

nential in the product of $\mathcal{M}$'s hashrate and the message delay, if $\mathcal{M}$ is closer to the cluster of miners with higher hashrates.

The rest of the paper is organized as follows. Section 2 recalls the basic blockchain mining scheme. Section 3 presents our main result. Sections 4 and 5 present applications of our result. Section 6 discusses related work. For space limitation, we defer proofs to our technical report [18].

# 2    Model

## 2.1    Miners

We establish our main result in a system of 2 processes, called *miners*, denoted $\mathcal{M}_1$ and $\mathcal{M}_2$. (A miner is sometimes also denoted $\mathcal{M}$ or $\mathcal{M}^*$.) Both follow the algorithm assigned, and none crashes. The two miners interact by exchanging messages. Communication channels do not modify, inject, duplicate or lose messages. Between two miners, the delay on message transmission is denoted $u$.

---

**Algorithm 1.** Mining algorithm

---

1: Upon an update of $\mathcal{C}$: (1) fetch a block $B$; (2) create a special string $tx$ that includes an identifier of $\mathcal{M}$; (3) run task **SolvePuzzle**$(\mathcal{C}, B, tx)$ (and stop previous **SolvePuzzle** task if any).

2: Task **SolvePuzzle**$(\mathcal{C}, B, tx)$:
  - Increment a counter $\mathcal{N}$ until $\mathcal{N}$ satisfies $\mathcal{H}(h_\mathcal{C}||B||tx||\mathcal{N}) < d$.
  - Assign $CB := h_\mathcal{C}||B||tx||\mathcal{N}$ and $\mathcal{C} := \mathcal{C}, CB$.
  - Send $\mathcal{C}$ to every other miner.

3: Upon receiving an alternative chain $\mathcal{C}^*$: if $\mathcal{C}^*$ is longer than $\mathcal{C}$, then assign $\mathcal{C} := \mathcal{C}^*$, and send $\mathcal{C}$ to every other miner.

---

We consider the classical mining scheme of [6,19] in which a *(block) chain* is a series of blocks starting from a *genesis* block $G$ (the initial block in any chain). Let $\mathcal{C} = CB_0(= G), CB_1, CB_2, \ldots, CB_l, l \geq 1$ be any chain of length $l$. As in Garay et al.'s analysis of the Bitcoin backbone algorithm [8], as well as Eyal and Sirer's analysis of selfish mining [11], we define the length of $\mathcal{C}$ as the total number $l$ of blocks. For each $j \in \{1, 2, \ldots, l\}$, $CB_j$ has reference $h_{\mathcal{C},j-1} = \mathcal{H}(CB_{j-1})$ to $CB_{j-1}$, where $\mathcal{H}$ is a hash function agreed by all miners. The hash $h_{\mathcal{C},l}$ of the last block is sometimes called the hash of $\mathcal{C}$, and denoted $h_\mathcal{C}$. Every miner stores a chain as a local variable. Two miners might have two different chains. For each miner $\mathcal{M}$, a chain different from its local one is called an *alternative* chain. The mining scheme maintains and updates $\mathcal{M}$'s local chain. Algorithm 1 depicts the basic mining scheme[2] Before Algorithm 1 starts, every

---

[2] Algorithm 1 is a simplified variant of the algorithm of [6,19]. After a chain is updated, while the original mining algorithm exchanges the data and inventories of newly created blocks [20] for performance reasons, Algorithm 1 sends the whole new chain. The two algorithms are equivalent for the purpose of establishing our results.

miner assigns $C$ to a chain of length 0 containing only $G$, and all miners agree on a *difficulty level* $d$ for finding a *preimage* of $H$ (which we explain later). In addition, we assume that $M$ has access to an infinite number of blocks so that at any point in time, $M$ has a block to append.

If task **SolvePuzzle** in Algorithm 1 returns a chain $C$ of length $l$ at $M$, then $M$ ignores any alternative chain $C^*$ of length $l$ received later. If $M$ *extends* $M$'s chain $C$ to $l$, then we mean that $C$ is updated such that its length becomes $l$. If $M$ updates $C$ after the return of task **SolvePuzzle**, we say that $M$ *creates* a new block on $C_{old}$, the old chain of length $l - 1$; we also index this new block by $l$ and say that $M$ creates the $l$th block. If $M$ updates $C$, due to the reception of an alternative chain $C^*$ from some miner $M^*$, we say that $M$ *adopts* $M^*$'s chain $C^*$. When $M$ creates a new block $CB$, $CB$ includes a string $tx$ (denoting coinbase transaction) that identifies $M$, and a reference $h_C$ to $M$'s chain $C$; thus each block is unique. We say that $CB$ is *committed* when every miner's chain includes $CB$; and $M$ commits $CB$ if $M$ has created $CB$ and $CB$ is committed.

## 2.2  Mining as a Poisson Process

Task **SolvePuzzle**$(C, *, *)$ is the proof-of-work used in the classic Bitcoin implementation [5]. Performing such task is called *mining* (on chain $C$). We model mining as a Poisson process.[3] For any miner $M_i$, for any string $s$, the time to find $N$ such that $H(s||N) < d$ can be modelled as a continuous random variable $X_{i,s}$. Let $X_i$ be the random variable for the common distribution of $X_{i,s}, \forall s$ which has an exponential distribution. The probability density function is $f_i(x) = \lambda_i e^{-\lambda_i x}, x \geq 0$, where parameter $\lambda_i$ is called the *hashrate* of $M_i$. We assume that compared with the time spent on mining and communication, other tasks take negligible time. Rate $\lambda$ depends on the difficulty level $d$. In the classic Bitcoin implementation [6,19], $d$ is selected such that $\frac{1}{\lambda} = 600$ s.

# 3   Unfairness of Blockchain

We establish here our main result, Theorem 1. Consider any $a \in \mathbb{Z}^+$, let $C_{i,a}$ be $M_i$'s chain when $M_i$ extends $M_i$'s chain to length $a$ for $i \in \{1,2\}$. Denoted by $N_{i,a}$, the random variable for the number of blocks committed by $M_i$ in $C_{1,a}$ and $C_{2,a}$, i.e., the number of blocks created by $M_i$ which both $C_{1,a}$ and $C_{2,a}$ include.

**Theorem 1 (Ratio of committed blocks).** *If $\lambda_1 > \lambda_2$, then*

$$\frac{E(N_{1,a})}{E(N_{2,a})} \geq \frac{e^{\lambda_1 u}}{e^{\lambda_2 u}} \cdot \frac{\lambda_1}{\lambda_2} > \frac{\lambda_1}{\lambda_2}.$$

---

[3] Decker and Wattenhofer's experiment [17] on blockchain supported such model, which was also adopted in the analysis of selfish mining [9,11].

*Proof Outline of Theorem* 1. To prove Theorem 1, by the linearity of expectation, we examine the expectation of the event that $\mathcal{M}_i$ creates $CB$ as $\mathcal{M}_i$'s $k$th block for $k \in \mathbb{Z}^+$ (and later commits $CB$) for each $i \in \{1,2\}$, the probability of which depends on when the two miners' chains grow to $k-1$. To this end, we show a fundamental unfairness property on the growth of the blockchain (Sect. 3.2). We then show unfairness on the success probability in committing $CB$ as the $k$th block and hence unfairness on the expected number of committed blocks (Sect. 3.3). To formalize the growth of the blockchain and the success probability, we first introduce some definitions and terminologies in Sect. 3.1 below.

## 3.1  Definitions and Terminologies

We model here with random variables the growth (in length) of the blockchain as well as the events of success of both miners.

**Definition 1 (Growth in length of the blockchain.** *For each miner* $\mathcal{M}_i, i \in \{1,2\}$, *let* $\{\tau_{k,i}|k = 1,2,\ldots\}$ *be the sequence of time instants such that at* $\tau_{k,i}$, $\mathcal{M}_i$ *extends* $\mathcal{M}_i$'s *chain to length* $k$. *W.l.o.g., we define* $\tau_{0,i} = 0$ *(i.e., the two miners start at the same time 0).*

As defined in Definition 1, each of the two miners maintains a local chain which grows in length by one. When a miner has a chain of length $k-1$, we say that the miner starts its $k$th round. For $\mathcal{M}_i$, the $k$th round is thus $[\tau_{k-1,i}, \tau_{k,i}]$. At $\tau_{k-1,i}$, $\mathcal{M}_i$ starts mining a new block. We denote by $X_{k-1,i}$ the random variable of the time which $\mathcal{M}_i$ spends on mining when $\mathcal{M}_i$ is alone (without a second miner sending an alternative chain). Two miners can have different chains. Given length $a$, it is unknown whether two miners have the same chain or not. However, if they have the same $k$th block $CB$ in their chains respectively when $a \geq k$, the $k$th block remains there. We define this event and its probability $p_{k,i,a}$ in Definition 2. A prerequisite of $p_{k,i,a} > 0$ is that $\mathcal{M}_i$ completes its mining at the $k$th round (even with the other miner), which we denote by $W_k \in \{0,i\}$. When $W_k = 0$, both miners complete their mining at the $k$th round, as defined in Definition 3, and can commit one of the two blocks mined later, illustrated in Fig. 1. Notations (except for $W_k$) are summarized in Table 1.

**Table 1.** Summary of notations

| | |
|---|---|
| $M_i$ | A miner with hashrate $\lambda_i$ |
| $C_{i,a}$ | $M_i$'s local chain when it grows to length $a$ |
| $\tau_{k,i}$ | When $M_i$'s local chain grows to length $k$ |
| $X_{k,i}$ | The time spent on mining by $M_i$ if $M_i$ mines alone |
| $N_{i,a}$ | The number of blocks committed by $M_i$ in the blockchain of length $a$ |
| $p_{k,i,a}$ | The probability of $M_i$ committing the $k$th block in the blockchain of length $a$ |

**Definition 2 (Success of the $k$th block).** *For any $k \in \mathbb{Z}^+, a \geq k$, we define $p_{k,i,a}$, the probability of the event that (1) $\mathcal{M}_i$ creates $CB$ at the $k$th round, and (2) both $\mathcal{C}_{1,a}$ and $\mathcal{C}_{2,a}$ have $CB$.*

**Definition 3 (Creation of the $k$th block).** *For each miner $\mathcal{M}_i, i \in \{1,2\}$, let $W_k = i$ if $\mathcal{M}_{3-i}$ adopts the alternative chain (in $\mathcal{M}_{3-i}$'s perspective) from $\mathcal{M}_i$ at the end of the $k$th round, and $W_k = 0$ when both miners create their $k$th blocks respectively and fork the blockchain.*

### 3.2    Unfairness on the Growth of the Blockchain

We first determine the probability distribution of when the $k$th round ends (i.e., the blockchain grows to length $k$) in Lemma 1 and then present a property of this probability distribution in Lemma 2.

It is important to know when the blockchain grows to a certain length $k$ at the two miners, since the difference (in time) at the two miners can give one of them a head start. The calculation of probability distribution is actually straightforward. For each $k = 1, 2, \ldots$, consider $\tau_k = (\tau_{k,1}, \tau_{k,2})$. Suppose that the probability distribution of $\tau_{k-1}$ is known. As illustrated in Fig. 1, there are three possibilities of how the blockchain grows to $k$: (a) that the blockchain forks; (b) that $\mathcal{M}_1$ mines a block and $\mathcal{M}_2$ receives this block before mining one; (c) that $\mathcal{M}_2$ mines a block and $\mathcal{M}_1$ receives this block before mining one. Since the probability distribution of $X_{k-1,1}, X_{k-1,2}$ is known, the probability distribution of $\delta_k = \tau_{k+1} - \tau_k$ can be calculated as well as $\tau_{k+1}$. The base case where $k = 0$ is simpler: $\tau_0 = (0,0)$ is assumed and thus $\tau_1 = \delta_0$. As a result, the probability distribution of $\tau_k$ includes a recursive equation $D_k$, which can be evaluated to a function of $s, t$ alone if $\lambda_1, \lambda_2, u$ are specified. The expression $Pr(\tau_k = (s,t))$ in Lemma 1 represents the following probability: $Pr(s \leq \tau_{k,1} \leq s + ds, t \leq \tau_{k,2} \leq t + dt)$ where $ds$ and $dt$ are the infinitesimals.[4] The full proofs of Lemmas 1 and 2 follow from the calculation above and are deferred to our technical report [18].

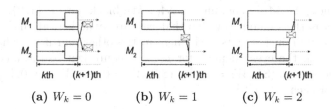

(a) $W_k = 0$      (b) $W_k = 1$      (c) $W_k = 2$

**Fig. 1.** Three possibilities of round $k$

---

[4] The probability distribution of $\tau_k$ cannot be expressed by a cumulative distribution function because $\tau_k - \tau_{k-1}$ is neither continuous nor discrete.

**Lemma 1 (The growth of the blockchain).** *For $s > 0, t > 0$, let $D_0(s,t) = 1$ and for each $k = 1, 2, \ldots$, let*

$$D_k(s,t) = \lambda_1\lambda_2 \int_{\substack{|y-z|<u, \\ 0<y<s, \\ 0<z<t}} D_{k-1}(y,z)dydz + \lambda_1 \int_{\substack{y-z=-u, \\ 0<y<s, \\ 0<z<t}} D_{k-1}(y,z)dy$$

$$+ \lambda_2 \int_{\substack{y-z=u, \\ 0<y<s, \\ 0<z<t}} D_{k-1}(y,z)dz.$$

*Then the probability of $\tau_k$ is*

$$Pr(\tau_k = (s,t)) = \begin{cases} 0 & |s-t| > u; \\ \lambda_1\lambda_2 e^{-\lambda_1 s - \lambda_2 t} D_{k-1}(s,t)dsdt & |s-t| < u; \\ \lambda_1 e^{-\lambda_1 s - \lambda_2 t} D_{k-1}(s,t)ds & s - t = -u; \\ \lambda_2 e^{-\lambda_1 s - \lambda_2 t} D_{k-1}(s,t)dt & s - t = u. \end{cases}$$

**Lemma 2.** *For $s > 0, t > 0, |s-t| \le u$ and $u > 0$, if $\lambda_1 > \lambda_2$ and $s > t, s > u$, then $D_k(s,t) < D_k(t,s), \forall k \in \mathbb{Z}^+$; if $u > s > t$, then $D_k(s,t) = D_k(t,s), \forall k \in \mathbb{Z}^+$.*

Lemma 2 implies a property of $\tau_k$: for any length $k$, the probability that the miner with a higher hashrate has a chain of length $k$ earlier than the other is higher, which is the intuition behind the proof of inequality in Theorem 1. Lemma 1 can be easily extended to any number of miners. A result similar to Lemma 2 follows: for any number of miners, between any two miners, for any length $k$, the probability that the miner with a higher computational power has a chain of length $k$ earlier than the other is higher.

### 3.3 Unfairness on the Success of the $k$th Block

We prove Theorem 1 by showing a lower bound on the ratio between the success probability $p_{k,i,a}$ of $\mathcal{M}_i$ in committing $\mathcal{M}_i$'s $k$th block, for $i \in \{1, 2\}$.

Since $W_k$ is the random variable that captures whether, at the end of the $k$th round, some miner adopts a chain from the other and if so, whose chain is adopted, then the event defined for $p_{k,i,a}$ is equivalent to the union of the following two events: (S1) $W_k = i$, and (S2) $W_k = 0, \ldots, W_{j-1} = 0, W_j = i$. We thus have, for each $i \in \{1, 2\}$,

$$p_{k,i,a} = Pr(W_k = i) + \sum_{j=k+1}^{a} Pr(W_k = 0, \ldots, W_{j-1} = 0, W_j = i).$$

In Lemma 3, we determine a lower bound for each of the two possibilities (S1) and (S2) by (1) determining $Pr(W_k = i)$ and $Pr(W_k = 0, \ldots, W_{j-1} = 0, W_j = i)$ based on Lemma 1 and (2) applying the inequality in Lemma 2. The intuition behind the exponential term in Lemma 3 is that (1) at round $k$ when a block is committed, there is a gap of $u$ (the message delay) between $\tau_{k,1}$ and $\tau_{k,2}$ (i.e., when the two miners end round $k$ respectively) and (2) by the Poisson process, the probability of a block created during the gap is exponential in $u$. The full proof of Lemma 3 is deferred to our technical report [18].

**Lemma 3.** *For any* $j, k, a \in \mathbb{Z}^+$ *and* $a \geq k + 1$, *if* $\lambda_1 > \lambda_2$, *then*

$$\frac{Pr(W_k = 1)}{Pr(W_k = 2)} > \frac{e^{\lambda_1 u}}{e^{\lambda_2 u}} \cdot \frac{\lambda_1}{\lambda_2}, \quad \forall k \geq 2; \quad \frac{Pr(W_k = 1)}{Pr(W_k = 2)} = \frac{e^{\lambda_1 u}}{e^{\lambda_2 u}} \cdot \frac{\lambda_1}{\lambda_2}, \quad k = 1; \quad (1)$$

$$\frac{Pr(W_k = 0, \ldots, W_{j-1} = 0, W_j = 1)}{Pr(W_k = 0, \ldots, W_{j-1} = 0, W_j = 2)} \geq \frac{e^{\lambda_1 u}}{e^{\lambda_2 u}} \cdot \frac{\lambda_1}{\lambda_2}, \forall j, k + 1 \leq j \leq a. \quad (2)$$

The proof of Theorem 1 follows Lemma 3. First, $E(N_{i,a}) = \sum_{k=1}^{a} p_{k,i,a}$. Then by Lemma 3, $\forall k \in \mathbb{Z}^+, a \geq k$, $\frac{p_{k,1,a}}{p_{k,2,a}}$ is lower bounded by $\frac{e^{\lambda_1 u}}{e^{\lambda_2 u}} \cdot \frac{\lambda_1}{\lambda_2}$; therefore, $\frac{E(N_{1,a})}{E(N_{2,a})}$ is lower bounded by the same. We remark that the lower bound is supported by the inequality between $D_k(s,t)$ and $D_k(t,s)$ in Lemma 2, implying that the lower bound $\frac{e^{\lambda_1 u}}{e^{\lambda_2 u}} \cdot \frac{\lambda_1}{\lambda_2}$ is not yet tight.

*Trade-Off Between the Mining Speed and Fairness.* Theorem 1 highlights the fragility of tentative implementations that would reduce the time spent on mining (today set to 600 s on average) to improve the throughput of transactions [21,22]. Recall from Sect. 2 that this would reduce the difficulty level, which would in turn increase every miner's hashrate proportionally. As a result, fairness could be further undermined: the proportional increase of $\lambda_1$ and $\lambda_2$ results in a larger gap in the exponential factor $\frac{e^{\lambda_1 u}}{e^{\lambda_2 u}}$, which highlights a trade-off between the speed to mine a block and the fairness of blockchain.

*Extension to Any Number of Miners.* Similar to Lemmas 1 and 2, Eq. 1 in Lemma 3 can be easily extended to any number of miners. In other words, among any number $N$ of miners, if we only compare the probability of a miner committing its block immediately between two out of $N$ miners, then the ratio between the two probabilities is also greater than the ratio between hashrates and at least exponential in delay $u$. Yet it is unclear whether Eq. 2 can be extended to any number of miners, which can be a future direction of our work.

## 4   Application to Selfish Mining

We show here how our result can be used to generalize one of the main results in selfish mining [11]. Selfish mining is an attack for a minority of miners to commit more blocks in expectation than its fair share. In a model of two miners, one selfish and one honest, with message delay $u = 0$, Eyal and Sirer [11] showed that, it is sufficient for $\alpha > \frac{1}{3} \triangleq th$ to launch selfish mining.[5] We generalize the threshold $th$ to a realistic setting with $u > 0$.[6] We first recall below the selfish mining algorithm and some of its results from [11]. For the classic Bitcoin blockchain implementation, we show that blockchain is not as vulnerable as previously believed against selfish mining.

### 4.1   Selfish Mining

We recall the main idea underlying the selfish mining algorithm below, assuming a selfish miner $\mathcal{M}_2$ and an honest miner $\mathcal{M}_1$. (More details can be found in [11].) When both $\mathcal{M}_1$ and $\mathcal{M}_2$ mine on chain $\mathcal{C}$ and $\mathcal{M}_2$ succeeds in creating a block $CB$ on $\mathcal{C}$, $\mathcal{M}_2$ continues to mine on $\mathcal{C}_{mi} = \mathcal{C}, CB$ (instead of sending $\mathcal{C}_{mi}$ to $\mathcal{M}_1$ as in Algorithm 1). Then $\mathcal{M}_2$ maintains two chains $\mathcal{C}_{mi}$ and $\mathcal{C}_{ma}$ locally. The latter is initialized to $\mathcal{C}$. Miner $\mathcal{M}_2$ updates $\mathcal{C}_{mi}$ when it creates a new block on $\mathcal{C}_{mi}$; $\mathcal{M}_2$ updates $\mathcal{C}_{ma}$ when $\mathcal{M}_1$ sends an alternative chain. The goal of $\mathcal{M}_2$ is to commit all blocks created by $\mathcal{M}_2$ on $\mathcal{C}_{mi}$ (those blocks of $\mathcal{C}_{mi}$ after prefix $\mathcal{C}$). There are two scenarios where $\mathcal{M}_2$ commits by sending $\mathcal{C}_{mi}$ to $\mathcal{M}_1$:

1. After an update of $\mathcal{C}_{ma}$, $\mathcal{C}_{mi}$ and $\mathcal{C}_{ma}$ have the same length but differ at the last block (event $E_1$), and $\mathcal{M}_2$ creates a new block on $\mathcal{C}_{mi}$;
2. After an update of $\mathcal{C}_{ma}$, $\mathcal{C}_{mi}$ has one more block than $\mathcal{C}_{ma}$ (event $E_2$).

   The state machine of selfish mining is illustrated in Fig. 2, where $k, k \geq 0, k \in \mathbb{Z}$ in each state represents that $\mathcal{C}_{mi}$ is $k$-block longer than $\mathcal{C}_{ma}$ at $\mathcal{M}_2$ and $0'$ is the resulting state of commit in $E_2$. Then $N_2$ and $N_1$, the expected numbers of blocks which $\mathcal{M}_2$ and $\mathcal{M}_1$ commit respectively, can be calculated from the state machine in terms of $\alpha$. Let $R_0 = N_2/(N_1 + N_2)$. The threshold $th$ is the solution $\alpha^*$ to $R_0(\alpha) = \alpha$.

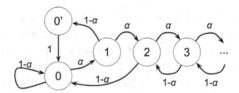

**Fig. 2.** State machine of selfish mining without message delay

---

[5] Eyal and Sirer [11] showed a lower bound $\mathcal{L}$ (on $\alpha$) as a function of parameter $\gamma$ which represents the percentage of miners in the honest majority $\mathcal{M}_1$ that adopt the selfish minority $\mathcal{M}_2$'s chain, and did not consider exact message delay $u$. The sufficient condition (i.e., an upper bound on $\mathcal{L}$) in [11] is obtained when $\gamma = 0$, which implies $u = 0$.

[6] If we consider $\gamma$ and $u$ as two parameters of the lower bound, then when $u > 0$, for all $\gamma$, the case where $\gamma = 0$ requires the highest computational power $th$ from the selfish minority. As a result, we consider here parameter $\gamma = 0$ for $u > 0$, and $\alpha > th$ is still a sufficient condition.

## 4.2  Upper Bound on the Number of Committed Blocks

Let $R$ be the proportion of the expected number of blocks committed by $\mathcal{M}_2$. We show that $R$ is upper bounded in Theorem 2 in a realistic setting where $u > 0$. The key is that due to non-zero message delays, when $E_j, j \in \{1, 2\}$ occurs, $\mathcal{M}_2$ only *tries* to commit by sending $\mathcal{C}_{mi}$. There are several possibilities following $\mathcal{M}_2$'s sending $\mathcal{C}_{mi}$: $\mathcal{M}_2$ commits and then $\mathcal{M}_2$ has additional $2u$ units of time as a head start, or $\mathcal{M}_2$ fails. The state machine of selfish mining thus changes. In Fig. 3, $N_{2u}$ represents how many blocks $\mathcal{M}_2$ can find during $2u$, $\rho_1$ and $\rho_2$ represent upper bounds on the probability of $\mathcal{M}_2$ committing $\mathcal{C}_{mi}$. The full proof of Theorem 2 is deferred to our technical report [18] for space limitation.

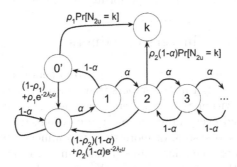

**Fig. 3.** State machine of selfish mining with message delay ($k \in \mathbb{Z}^+$)

**Theorem 2.** *Let $\mathcal{M}_1$ and $\mathcal{M}_2$ be two miners with hashrates $\lambda_1$ and $\lambda_2$ respectively. Let*

$$\mathcal{U} = \frac{2P_1\rho_1(1-\alpha) + 2P_2\rho_2(1-\alpha) + P_{k>2}\rho_2(1-\alpha)}{2P_1(1-\alpha) + 2P_2(1-\alpha) + P_0(1-\alpha) + P_{k>2}(1-\alpha) + P_2(1-\rho_2)(1-\alpha)}$$

*where $\rho_1 = \alpha e^{-2\lambda_1 u} + \alpha(1 - e^{-2\lambda_1 u})r_2$, $\rho_2 = e^{-2\lambda_1 u} + (1 - e^{-2\lambda_1 u})[\alpha + (1 - \alpha)(1 - e^{-2\lambda_2 u})r_2]$ and $r_2 = \frac{1}{r+1}, r = \frac{e^{\lambda_1 u}}{e^{\lambda_2 u}} \cdot \frac{\lambda_1}{\lambda_2}$ and $P_{0'}$ and $P_k, k \geq 0, k \in \mathbb{Z}$ are the probabilities of each state in the state machine of Fig. 3.*
*If $\lambda_1 > \lambda_2$ and $\mathcal{U} > \alpha$, then $R \leq \mathcal{U}$.*

## 4.3  Lower Bound on the Threshold

We are now ready to find a lower bound on the threshold assuming message delay $u > 0$. Recall that the threshold should be the solution to $R(\alpha) = \alpha$. According to Theorem 2, since the relative number of blocks committed by the selfish miner is upper bounded by $\mathcal{U}$, the solution $\mathcal{L}$ to $\mathcal{U}(\alpha) = \alpha$ is a lower bound on the threshold.

Assuming $\lambda = \frac{1}{600}$, and $u = 1, 10, 20, 100$ (where the units of time are seconds), which are taken from the classic Bitcoin implementation [6,17,19], we

**Table 2.** Lower bound on the threshold

| $u$ | 1 | 10 | 20 | 100 |
|---|---|---|---|---|
| $\mathcal{L}$ | 0.334 | 0.339 | 0.343 | 0.371 |
| $\mathcal{U}(\mathcal{L})$ | 0.33418 | 0.33999 | 0.34361 | 0.37087 |

show the numeric calculation of $\mathcal{L}$ in Table 2, which is greater than $\frac{1}{3}$. In addition, for small $u > 0$ such that $Pr[N_{2u} = k], \forall k \in \mathbb{Z}^+$ is negligible, $\mathcal{L} > \frac{1}{3}$ is always true in theory. In either way, we obtain that $\mathcal{L} > \frac{1}{3} = th$, suggesting that with reasonable message delay $u > 0$, blockchain is not as *unfair* as previously believed when some dishonest miner performs selfish mining.

## 5   Application to Clusters of Miners

We consider in our main result (Theorem 1) two miners with message delay $u$. We now consider a model of $m > 2$ miners that can be divided into two sets $S_1$ and $S_2$ such that (1) within $S_1$ or $S_2$, there is no message delay, and (2) between every miner in $S_1$ and every miner in $S_2$, there is message delay $u$. Corollary 1 below shows that in a system of more than two miners, between two miners with the same hashrate, one miner can still have an exponential advantage over the other as long as the former one is very close (such that the message delay is 0) to some other miner with a high hashrate.

**Corollary 1 (Lower bound with more than two miners).** *Let $\mathcal{M}_1 \in S_1$ and $\mathcal{M}_2 \in S_2$ be any two miners with the same hashrate $\lambda_0$. Assume message delay $u$ between $S_1$ and $S_2$. Suppose that the sum of all miners' hashrates in $S_1$ is $m_1\lambda_0$ and that of $S_2$ is $m_2\lambda_0$. Recall that for $i \in \{1,2\}$, $N_{i,a}$ denotes the number of blocks committed by $\mathcal{M}_i$ before the end of round $a$. Assuming $\mathcal{M}_1$ and $\mathcal{M}_2$ start with the same chain at the same time, if $m_1 > m_2$, then*

$$\frac{E(N_{1,a})}{E(N_{2,a})} \geq \frac{e^{m_1\lambda_0 u}}{e^{m_2\lambda_0 u}} > 1.$$

## 6   Related Work

### 6.1   Theoretical Analyses of Blockchain

Satoshi Nakamoto [19] was credited for the proposal of Bitcoin and its underlying distributed protocol, blockchain. With the popularity of Bitcoin, a lot of work has been devoted to formalizing blockchain and verifying its claimed properties [8,12,23,24]. We discuss below some approaches, and contrast our main result with the properties obtained from previous theoretical analyses.

Garay et al. [8] proposed the *q-bounded synchronous setting* to model blockchain. Given that the mining algorithm increments a counter to find the preimage of some hash function, this $q$-bounded synchronous setting assumes that, in each round, any miner can increment at most $q$ times the counter [8].[7] Pass et al. [12] studied blockchain in an asynchronous network where message delays can be arbitrary. Both Garay et al. [8], as well as Pass et al. [12] verified the *chain quality* property, in their models respectively, considering dishonest miners. The $(\mu, \ell)$-chain quality property identifies an upper bound on the proportion of dishonest miners' committed blocks among any $\ell$ consecutive blocks for some $\ell$ [8,12]. This property differs from our notion of fairness, in that ours considers the proportion of the expected number of committed blocks. (Later Pass and Shi [24] strengthened chain quality property as fairness and used the term, eventual fairness, for our notion of fairness.) Pass et al. [8], as well as Garay et al. [12], derived chain quality property with $\mu$ higher than the proportion of dishonest miners' hashrates, which thus does not imply the (un)fairness of blockchain (as considered in this paper). Kosba et al. [23] proposed a cryptographic model of blockchain, assuming ideal functionality; i.e., they assumed that blockchain satisfies certain idealized properties, which do not fit our analysis here.

## 6.2  Unfairness of Blockchain

Lewenberg et al. [14], as well as Eyal et al. [13], simulated blockchain (among honest miners), and observed indeed that some miner's reward can be lower than its fair share; yet neither work provided a theoretical explanation of such unfairness. Both presented an exponentially descending curve for the proportion of the victim's committed blocks with increasing speed to mine a block [13,14], which our Theorem 1 explains. To mitigate the fairness issue, Lewenberg et al. [14] and Eyal et al. [13] proposed alternatives. However, both alternatives rely on blockchain and thus still suffer from the unfairness we highlight in this paper.[8] Lewenberg et al. [25] presented a formula on the proportion of one miner's committed blocks between two miners and omitted the proof. To compare with, we model the growth of blockchain, which can be extended to any number of miners and may be of independent interest, and prove our result based on the model of growth, independently from [25].

Eyal and Sirer [11] proposed a very interesting attack, called *selfish mining*, for a minority of miners to commit more blocks in expectation than its fair share. (Sapirshtein et al. [9], as well as Gervais et al. [16] and Nayak et al. [26], optimized selfish mining.) Such unfairness resulting from selfish (dishonest) miners does not imply our result. Assuming no message delay, Eyal and Sirer [11] determined a threshold $th$ on the proportion $\alpha$ of the minority's hashrate for selfish mining,

---

[7] This setting neglects the variable relation between mining and time, e.g., when a message is delayed, a miner may have more time (more increments) to mine a block.

[8] Lewenberg et al. [14] proposed *inclusive blockchain* as an alternative, which stores all possible blockchains in a directed acyclic graph, and then still observed disproportionate rewards among honest miners. Eyal et al. [13] proposed *Bitcoin-NG*, where a leader (a special miner that is entitled to include transaction blocks) is elected based on blockchain (and its companion mining algorithm); the leader election could still suffer from the unfairness of blockchain as shown in this paper.

while Sapirshtein et al. [9] established a lower threshold by optimizing selfish mining for each value of $\alpha$. As an application of our main result, we extend Eyal and Sirer's threshold in a model with message delays. In Sect. 4, we show that the classic Bitcoin blockchain implementation can tolerate selfish mining more than previously believed: under reasonable message delays, a threshold for selfish mining is greater than $th$. Sapirshtein et al. [9] additionally showed that, assuming message delays, any miner can commit more blocks by being dishonest, but did not study the effect of message delays on selfish mining. Unlike previous work, Gervais et al. [16] modelled selfish mining with Markov Decision Processes parameterized by the stale block rate (which intuitively captures message delays as well as hashrates) yet did not provide a threshold. Nayak et al. [26] composed network-level attacks (eclipse attacks) with generalized selfish mining, which however focused on isolating miners instead of concrete message delays.

Heilman et al. [27] presented *eclipse attacks* on Bitcoin, which enforce some miners to connect only to an attacker (which may control multiple miners). As these honest miners are fed with selected transactions and blocks, a dishonest miner's reward can be higher than its fair proportion [27]. Eclipse attacks can also increase message delays [17,27], and can then transform Theorem 1 into an attack against the miner with a low hashrate.

In addition, to address unfairness resulting from dishonest miners, Pass and Shi [24] proposed fruitchain, which mines another data structure called fruits, as well as blocks. They proved that the proportion of dishonest miners' committed fruits is upper bounded by their proportional hashrate and in this sense, is fair [24]. Since fruitchain takes a different approach from the blockchain considered in this paper, our result and theirs are incomparable.

### 6.3   Message Delays in Blockchain

Our assumptions on message delays (level of seconds in Sect. 4) as well as our model of mining (as a Poisson process throughout the paper) have already been discussed in the literature.

Our assumptions on message delays are justified by the study of Decker and Wattenhofer [17], as well as Croman et al. [21], on block propagation delays in Bitcoin network. Decker and Wattenhofer [17] showed that in 2013, the median time for a node (not necessarily a miner) to receive a block is 6.5 s, whilst the mean is 12.6 s [17]. Croman et al. [21] repeated the measurement of block propagation in 2014 and 2015, and found a median time of 8.7 s. Our model of mining is justified by Decker and Wattenhofer [17]'s measurement on the probability of the time to create a block in the Bitcoin network. The measured distribution fits the exponential distribution [17], which justifies the mining Poisson process widely used in this paper and in the literature [2,9,11].

Assuming message delays, Natoli and Gramoli [28] observed a *blockchain anomaly*, which can be considered as an extreme case of our Theorem 1. The classic Bitcoin implementation stipulates a value $k = 6$ such that, if an honest miner $\mathcal{M}$'s chain has at least $k$ blocks after a certain block $CB$, then $\mathcal{M}$ considers $CB$ confirmed. Natoli and Gramoli [28] exhibited an attack that only delays messages (arbitrarily) in a system of two miners, against any $k$: as long as the attacker's hashrate is higher than $\mathcal{M}$, for any $k$, a confirmed block can be later removed from $\mathcal{M}$'s chain. Theorem 1 explains such anomaly: with the message delay approaching infinity, an attacker commits almost all blocks with a high probability, while $\mathcal{M}$ commits (or confirms) nearly none. In this sense, our unfairness result can be viewed as a generalization of the observation of [28].

## 7 Concluding Remarks

We show that blockchain is unfair by proving a lower bound on the expected number of committed blocks in a distributed system of two honest miners. Possible future work includes quantifying the unfairness in a distributed system of more than two honest miners, which as suggested by Lemmas 1 and 2, may also be unfair.

**Acknowledgement.** This work has been supported in part by the European ERC Grant 339539 - AOC.

## References

1. 100+ companies that accept bitcoins as payment. Online (2015). http://www.ebay.com/gds/100-Companies-That-Accept-Bitcoins-As-Payment-/10000000206483242/g.html
2. Bitcoin community: "Bitcoin", Januray 2016. https://en.bitcoin.it/wiki/Bitcoin
3. Davidson, J.: No, big companies aren't really accepting bitcoin. Online (2015). http://time.com/money/3658361/dell-microsoft-expedia-bitcoin/
4. McMillan, R.: IBM bets on bitcoin ledger", February 2016. https://www.wsj.com/articles/ibm-bets-on-bitcoin-ledger-1455598864
5. Bitcoin community: "Proof of work", May 2016. https://en.bitcoin.it/wiki/Proof_of_work
6. Bitcoin community: "Protocol rules", October 2016. https://en.bitcoin.it/wiki/Protocol_rules
7. Felten, E.: Bitcoin research in princeton cs, Online, November 2013. https://freedom-to-tinker.com/2013/11/29/bitcoin-research-in-princeton-cs/
8. Garay, J., Kiayias, A., Leonardos, N.: The bitcoin backbone protocol: analysis and applications. In: Oswald, E., Fischlin, M. (eds.) EUROCRYPT 2015. LNCS, vol. 9057, pp. 281–310. Springer, Heidelberg (2015). https://doi.org/10.1007/978-3-662-46803-6_10
9. Sapirshtein, A., Sompolinsky, Y., Zohar, A.: Optimal selfish mining strategies in bitcoin. CoRR, vol. abs/1507.06183 (2015). [Online]. https://arxiv.org/abs/1507.06183
10. Bitcoin community: "Majority attack", July 2015. https://en.bitcoin.it/wiki/Majority_attack
11. Eyal, I., Sirer, E.G.: Majority is not enough: bitcoin mining is vulnerable. In: Christin, N., Safavi-Naini, R. (eds.) FC 2014. LNCS, vol. 8437, pp. 436–454. Springer, Heidelberg (2014). https://doi.org/10.1007/978-3-662-45472-5_28

12. Pass, R., Seeman, L., Shelat, A.: Analysis of the blockchain protocol in asynchronous networks. Cryptology ePrint Archive, Report 2016/454 (2016). http://eprint.iacr.org/2016/454
13. Eyal, I., Gencer, A.E., Sirer, E.G., Renesse, R.V.: Bitcoin-NG: a scalable blockchain protocol. In: NSDI 2016, pp. 45–59. USENIX Association (2016)
14. Lewenberg, Y., Sompolinsky, Y., Zohar, A.: Inclusive block chain protocols. In: Böhme, R., Okamoto, T. (eds.) FC 2015. LNCS, vol. 8975, pp. 528–547. Springer, Heidelberg (2015). https://doi.org/10.1007/978-3-662-47854-7_33
15. Sompolinsky, Y., Zohar, A.: Secure high-rate transaction processing in bitcoin. In: Böhme, R., Okamoto, T. (eds.) FC 2015. LNCS, vol. 8975, pp. 507–527. Springer, Heidelberg (2015). https://doi.org/10.1007/978-3-662-47854-7_32
16. Gervais, A., Karame, G.O., Wüst, K., Glykantzis, V., Ritzdorf, H., Capkun, S.: On the security and performance of proof of work blockchains. In: CCS 2016, pp. 3-16. ACM, New York (2016)
17. Decker, C., Wattenhofer, R.: Information propagation in the bitcoin network. In: IEEE P2P2013, pp. 1–10 (2013)
18. Guerraoui, R., Wang, J.: On the unfairness of blockchain. Ecole Polytechnique Federale de Lausanne, Switzerland, Technical report (2018). https://infoscience.ep.ch/record/252950/
19. Nakamoto, S.: Bitcoin: A peer-to-peer electronic cash system. (2008). https://bitcoin.org/bitcoin.pdf
20. Bitcoin community: "Block chain download", January 2016. https://en.bitcoin.it/wiki/Block_chain_download
21. Croman, K., et al.: On scaling decentralized blockchains. In: Clark, J., Meiklejohn, S., Ryan, P.Y.A., Wallach, D., Brenner, M., Rohloff, K. (eds.) FC 2016. LNCS, vol. 9604, pp. 106–125. Springer, Heidelberg (2016). https://doi.org/10.1007/978-3-662-53357-4_8
22. Vukolić, M.: The quest for scalable blockchain fabric: proof-of-work vs. BFT replication. In: Camenisch, J., Kesdoğan, D. (eds.) iNetSec 2015. LNCS, vol. 9591, pp. 112–125. Springer, Cham (2016). https://doi.org/10.1007/978-3-319-39028-4_9
23. Kosba, A., Miller, A., Shi, E., Wen, Z., Papamanthou, C.: Hawk: the blockchain model of cryptography and privacy-preserving smart contracts. In: SP 2016, pp. 839–858 (2016)
24. Pass, R., Shi, E.: Fruitchains: A fair blockchain, Cryptology ePrintArchive, Report 2016/916 (2016). http://eprint.iacr.org/2016/916
25. Lewenberg, Y., Bachrach, Y., Sompolinsky, Y., Zohar, A., Rosenschein, J.S.: Bitcoin mining pools: a cooperative game theoretic analysis. In: AAMAS 2015, pp. 919–927 (2015). International Foundation for Autonomous Agents and Multiagent Systems, Richland (2015)
26. Nayak, K., Kumar, S., Miller, A., Shi, E.: Stubborn mining: generalizing selfish mining and combining with an eclipse attack. In: EuroS&P 2016, pp. 305–320 (2016)
27. Heilman, E., Kendler, A., Zohar, A., Goldberg, S.: Eclipse attacks on bitcoin's peer-to-peer network. In: SEC 2015, pp. 129-144. USENIX Association, Berkeley (2015)
28. Natoli, C., Gramoli, V.: The blockchain anomaly. In: NCA 2016, pp. 310–317 (2016)

# Weak Failures: Definitions, Algorithms and Impossibility Results

Gadi Taubenfeld[✉]

The Interdisciplinary Center, P.O.Box 167, 46150 Herzliya, Israel
tgadi@idc.ac.il

**Abstract.** The notion of weak failures, which should be viewed as *fractions* of traditional failures, is introduced and studied. It is known that there is no consensus algorithm using registers that can tolerate even a single crash failure. Is there a consensus algorithm using registers that can tolerate a "fraction" of a crash failure, i.e., a weak failure? It is known that there is no $k$-set consensus algorithm for $n > k$ processes using registers that can tolerate $k$ crash failures. How many weak failures can a $k$-set consensus algorithm which uses registers tolerate? Answers to these questions follow from our general possibility and impossibility results regarding the ability to tolerate weak failures.

**Keywords:** Weak failures · Shared memory · Consensus
$k$-set consensus · Contention

## 1 Introduction

Fractions were studied by Egyptians mathematicians around 1600 B.C. However, fractions, as we use them today, didn't exist in Europe until the 17th century. It seems natural that we consider fractions also in the context of fault tolerance. Below we define, motivate and explore the new notion of weak failures. Weak failures should be viewed as *fractions* of traditional failures.

Tolerating traditional failures is always defined with respect to *all* possible executions of a given system. A system is said to tolerate $t$ failures w.r.t. some property $\phi$, if in *all* possible executions of the system in which at most $t$ processes fails, $\phi$ is satisfied. When tolerating weak failures, also called fractional failures, it is only required that in *some* executions, and not necessarily in all executions, $\phi$ is satisfied. There are several ways for identifying the subset of executions in which $\phi$ should be satisfied. Below, we provide two possible definitions of weak failures.

### 1.1 Defining Weak Failures

A process is participating in an algorithm if it has executed at least one statement of that algorithm. The *point contention* of an algorithm at a given time is the maximal number of (correct and faulty) processes simultaneously participating in the algorithm. The point contention is bounded by the total number of processes.

© Springer Nature Switzerland AG 2019
A. Podelski and F. Taïani (Eds.): NETYS 2018, LNCS 11028, pp. 51–66, 2019.
https://doi.org/10.1007/978-3-030-05529-5_4

1. An *m-failure* of *type* 1 is a failure of a process that (1) after it has failed the process executes no more steps, and (2) the failure may occur only while the point contention is *at most m*. That is, such weak failures are assumed *not to occur* once a certain predefined threshold on the level of point contention is reached.
2. An *m-failure type* 2 is a failure of a process that (1) after it has failed the process executes no more steps, and (2) the failure may occur only while the point contention is *at least m*. That is, such weak failures are assumed to happen once a certain predefined threshold on the level of point contention is reached.

When designing an algorithm for $n$ processes, $n$-failures of type 1 and 1-failures of type 2 are the traditional crash failures. Thus, $m$-failures of type 1 where $m < n$, and $m$-failures of type 2 where $m > 1$, can be referred to as weak crash failures. Other types of weak failures, weak Byzantine failures, for example, can be defined similarly (but are not studied in this paper).

Considering weak failures of type 1, at first sight, it seems counterintuitive to tolerate failures in low contention environments, as the probability that a process crashes seems more likely to increase as system load increases. Below we provide motivating examples why weak failures, regardless of their type, are interesting.

We emphasize that *nothing* is preventing a process from failing. However, in the case of algorithms that tolerate weak failures of type 1 (resp. of type 2), when a process fails after (resp. before) the predefined threshold is reached, no correctness guarantees are given. It would be nice to be able to give guarantees for all the cases; unfortunately, this is not always possible.

## 1.2  Motivation

As already mentioned, weak failures should be viewed as *fractions* of traditional failures. This will enable us to design algorithms that can tolerate several traditional failures plus several additional weak failures. More precisely, assume that a problem can be solved in the presence of $t$ traditional failures, but cannot be solved in the presence of $t + 1$ such failures. Yet, the problem might be solvable in the presence of $t$ failures plus $t' > 0$ weak failures (of some type).

Adding the ability to tolerate weak failures to algorithms that are already designed to circumvent various impossibility results, such as the Paxos algorithm [13] and indulgent algorithms in general [10,11], would make such algorithms even more robust against possible failures. An indulgent algorithm never violates its safety property, and eventually satisfies its liveness property when the synchrony assumptions it relies on are satisfied. An indulgent algorithm which in addition (to being indulgent) tolerates weak failures may, in many cases, satisfy its liveness property even before the synchrony assumptions it relies on are satisfied.

When facing a failure related impossibility result, such as the impossibility of consensus in the presence of a single faulty process [9], one is often tempted to use a solution which guarantees no resiliency at all. We point out that there is a middle ground: tolerating weak failures (of some type) enables to tolerate failures some of the time. Also, traditional $t$-resilient algorithms tolerate failures only some of the time (i.e., as long as the number of failures is at most $t$). Afterall, something is better than nothing.

The first type of weak failures is in particular useful in systems in which contention is usually low. The second type of weak failures may correspond to a situation where, when there is high contention, processes are slowed down and as a result give up and abort.

Finally, the new failure model establishes a link between contention and failures, which enables us to better understand various known impossibility results, like the impossibility result for consensus [9] and its generalizations [4,12,18].

## 1.3   Contributions

We have identified new types of weak failures, where failures are assumed to occur only before (type 1) or after (type 2) a specific predefined threshold on the level of contention is reached. All our technical results are for weak failures of type 1 only. From the rest of the paper, whenever we use the term weak failures, we mean weak failures of type 1, and whenever we use the term *crash m-failures*, we mean $m$-failures of type 1.

To illustrate the utility of the new definitions, we derive possibility and impossibility results for solving the well-known problems of consensus and $k$-set consensus in the presence of weak failures. The $k$-set consensus problem is to design an algorithm for $n$ processes, where each process starts with an input value from some domain and must choose some participating process' input as its output. All $n$ processes together may choose no more than $k$ distinct output values. The 1-set consensus problem is the familiar consensus problem.

It is known that, in asynchronous systems, there is no consensus algorithm for $n$ processes using registers that can tolerate even a single crash $n$-failure [9,14]. We show that, in asynchronous systems, there is a consensus algorithm for $n$ processes, using registers, that can tolerate a single crash $(n-1)$-failure, for every $n > 1$. The above bound is tight. We show that there is no consensus algorithm for $n$ processes, using registers, that can tolerate *two* crash $(n-1)$-failures, for every $n > 2$.

It is known that, in asynchronous systems, there is no $k$-set consensus algorithm for $n > k$ processes using registers that can tolerate $k$ crash $n$-failures [4,12,18]. We show that, in asynchronous systems, for every $\ell \geq 1$, $k \geq 1$ and $n \geq 2\ell + k - 2$, there is a $k$-set consensus algorithm for $n$ processes, using registers, that can tolerate $\ell + k - 2$ crash $(n-\ell)$-failures. We show that there is no $k$-set consensus algorithm that can tolerate $\ell + k$ crash $(n-\ell)$-failures.

Solving consensus with a single crash $(n-1)$-failure using only registers is a deceptive problem. Once you are told that it is solvable, at first glance, it may seem simple to solve. The only way to understand its tricky nature is by trying to solve it. For that reason, we suggest the readers to try to solve the problem themselves.

## 2    Computational Model

Our model of computation consists of an asynchronous collection of $n$ deterministic processes that communicate via atomic read/write registers. The processes have unique identifiers. Asynchrony means that there is no assumption on the relative speeds of the processes.

A register can be atomic or non-atomic. With an *atomic* register, it is assumed that operations on the register occur in some definite order. That is, reading or writing an atomic register is an indivisible action. We will consider only atomic registers. In the sequel, by *registers*, we mean *atomic* registers.

A process executes its algorithm correctly until it possibly crashes. After it has crashed, it executes no more steps. A process that crashes is said to be *faulty*; otherwise, it is *correct*. In an asynchronous system, there is no way to distinguish between a faulty and a very slow process.

In a model where participation is required, every correct process must eventually become active and execute its code. Another situation is one in which participation is not required, as is usually assumed when solving the mutual exclusion or $k$-exclusion problems. All the known impossibility results for consensus and $k$-set consensus hold even when participating is required (and hence, of course, also when participating is not required). Unless explicitly stated otherwise (i.e., when we use a known solution for $k$-exclusion) we will assume that *participation is required*.

## 3    Possibility of Consensus with a Single Crash $(n-1)$-Failure

The consensus problem is defined as follows: There are $n$ processes where each process $i \in \{1, ..., n\}$ has an input value $in_i$. The requirements of the consensus problem are that there exists a decision value $v$ such that: (1) [*Agreement & termination*] each non-faulty process eventually decides on $v$, and (2) [*Validity*] $v \in \{in_1, ..., in_n\}$.

A fundamental result in distributed computing is that it is impossible to solve consensus with a single crash failure (i.e., a single crash $n$-failure) [9,14]. We consider the strongest failure type which is strictly weaker than the traditional crash failure, namely $(n-1)$-failure, and show that it is possible to solve consensus with a single crash $(n-1)$-failure.

**Theorem 1.** *There is a consensus algorithm for $n$ processes, using registers, that can tolerate a single crash $(n-1)$-failure, for every $n \geq 1$.*

The above bound on the number of crash $(n-1)$-failures is tight. In Sect. 5, it is shown that there does not exist a consensus algorithm for $n$ processes, using registers, that can tolerate *two* crash $(n-1)$-failures, for any $n > 2$.

Final remark before presenting the algorithm. Assume that you know how to solve consensus for two processes with a single crash 1-failure. A common approach for solving consensus for many processes in the presence of a single fault is as follows: Choose the two processes with the smallest identifiers, have them run the two-process solution, and write the result into a register. The remaining processes keep reading the register until the result appears there. We notice that such a solution for many processes guarantees to tolerate only a single crash 1-failure, but not a single crash 2-failure.

## 3.1   The Algorithm

The code of the algorithm appears in Fig. 1. In the algorithm, each process can be in one of four states, 0, 1, 2 or 3, as recorded in its *state* register. A process participates in three rounds (lines 2–15). At each round $round \in \{1, 2, 3\}$, the process first checks whether all the other $n-1$ processes have already written the round number *round* into their *state* registers (lines 4–6). In case of a positive answer, the process sets the *decision* register to the maximum input value among the input values of the other $n-1$ processes, decides on that maximum value and terminates (line 7). Otherwise, it writes the value of *round* into its *state* register (line 8) and waits until either a decision is made or at least $n - 1$ processes, including itself, have written the round number *round* into their single-writer *state* registers, whatever comes first (lines 9–13). In the former case, it adopts the decision value (line 14), in the latter case it completes the current round and moves on.

After completing three rounds, the process checks if there exists a process, say process $j$, that has not written the value 2 into its state register (lines 16–19). In case of a positive answer, it concludes that process $j$ will never be able to reach round three, and thus, $j$ will never set its state register to 3. This is so because $j$ will notice that $n - 1$ other processes have already set their state registers to 3, and will decide (line 7) before incrementing its state register (line 8). Thus, the process sets the *decision* register to the maximum input value among all the processes, excluding process $j$, decides on that maximum value and terminates (line 20).

Otherwise, if all the $n$ processes have written the value 2 into their state registers, the process concludes that all the $n$ processes are still active and are guaranteed not to fail. It waits until either a decision is made or until all the processes complete round three, whatever comes first (lines 21–24). In the former case, it adopts the decision value (line 23), in the latter case it decides on maximum input value among the input values of all the $n$ processes and terminates (line 25).

## 3.2   Correctness Proof

We say that process $i$ is in round $r$ if its local variable *round* equals to $r$.

**Lemma 1.** *For every $i \in \{1, ..., n\}$, when process $i$ sets state$[i]$ to 2 (in line 8), either the point contention is already $n$ or for some $j \neq i$, state$[j]$ will always be 0.*

A CONSENSUS ALGORITHM WHICH CAN TOLERATE A SINGLE CRASH $(n-1)$-FAILURE:
Program for process $i \in \{1, ..., n\}$ with a non-negative input $in_i$.

**Shared**: $state[1..n]$: array of registers, ranges over $\{0, 1, 2, 3\}$, initially all entries are 0
$input[1..n]$: arrays of registers, initial values immaterial          // input values
$decision$: register, initially $\bot$          // final decision value
**Local**: $counter, max, round, j$: local variables, initial values immaterial

```
1    input[i] := in_i;
2    for round = 1 to 3 do
3      counter := 0; max := 0;                              // state[i] = round − 1
4      for j = 1 to n do                                    // Am I last in this round?
5        if state[j] ≥ round then counter := counter + 1;   // notice: state[i] = round − 1
6          if max < input[j] then max := input[j] fi fi od;
7      if counter = n − 1 then                              // I'm last
           decision := max; decide(max) fi;                 // decide & terminate
8      state[i] := round;                                   // counter < n − 1, increment state
9      repeat                                               // wait until n − 1 processes arrive
10       counter := 0;
11       for j = 1 to n do
12         if state[j] ≥ round then counter := counter + 1 fi od   // i counts also itself
13       until (counter ≥ n − 1 or decision ≠ ⊥)
14       if decision ≠ ⊥ then decide(decision) fi           // decide & terminate
15    od;
                                                            // 3 rounds have been completed
16   if counter = n − 1 then counter := 0; max := 0;        // if counter ≠ n, revisit round 2
17     for j = 1 to n do                                    // is some process missing from round 2?
18       if state[j] ≥ 2 then counter := counter + 1;
19         if max < input[j] then max := input[j] fi fi od;
20       if counter = n − 1 then decision := max; decide(max) fi fi;   //decide&terminate
                                                            // at this point it must be that counter = n
21   for j = 1 to n do                                      // wait until all n processes arrive to round 3
22     await (state[j] = 3 or decision ≠ ⊥);                // or wait for a decision to be made
23     if decision ≠ ⊥ then decide(decision) fi;            // decide & terminate
24     if max < input[j] then max := input[j] fi od;
25   decision := max; decide(max).                          // all have arrived; decide & terminate
```

**Fig. 1.** A consensus algorithm which can tolerate a single crash $(n-1)$-failure.

*Proof.* If the point contention is not $n$ when $i$ sets $state[i]$ to 2 (in line 8), it follows that (1) by definition, some process, say $j$, hasn't taken any steps yet, and (2) except for process $j$, all the other $n-1$ processes have already incremented their $state$ registers. If $j$ is a correct process, it will reach line 7 at which point its counter register will become equal to $n-1$. Thus, $j$ will decide and terminate without ever incrementing its state register.     □

**Lemma 2.** *If at some point in time, for every $i \in \{1, ..., n\}$ state$[i] \geq 2$, then all the $n$ processes are active, no process has failed before that point, and no process will fail after that point.*

*Proof.* Assume that for every $i \in \{1, ..., n\}$, state$[i] \geq 2$. It follows from this assumption and Lemma 1 that, for every $i \in \{1, ..., n\}$, when process $i$ has set state$[i]$ to 2 (in line 8), the point contention was already $n$. Thus, process $i$ will never fail since it is assumed that no process fails once the point contention is $n$. □

**Lemma 3.** *For every process $i \in \{1, ..., n\}$,*

1. *if process $i$ writes into the decision register in line 7, then no other process writes into the decision register in line 7;*
2. *if process $i$ writes into the decision register in line 7, then no other process writes into the decision register in line 25;*
3. *if process $i$ writes into the decision register in line 20, then no other process writes into the decision register in line 25.*

*Proof.* Suppose process $i$ writes into *decision* in line 7 in round $r \in \{1, 2, 3\}$. This means that all the other $n - 1$ processes have already written $r$ into their state registers, and hence have not written into *decision* in line 7 in round $r$ or in previous rounds. After $i$ writes into *decision*, it immediately terminates. Thus, $i$ will never write a value $r' \geq r$ into its state register. Thus, for every other process, after executing the for loop in lines 4–6, the value of *counter* will be at most $n - 2$, and the test in line 7 will fail. Also, since state$[i]$ will never equal 3, no process will ever reach line 25.

Suppose process $i$ writes into *decision* in line 20. This means that there exists a process, say process $j$, that has not written the value 2 into its state register, at the time when process $i$ checked state$[j]$ in line 18. Although process $j$ may still set state$[j]$ to 2 at a later time, it will never be able to set state$[j]$ to 3 at a later time, because, in round 3, the counter of $j$ will reach $n - 1$ when $j$ will execute the for-loop in lines 4–6, and if continues it will terminate at line 7. For that reason when some other process executes line 22 "**await** (state$[j] = 3$ or *decision* $\neq \perp$)", the waiting may terminate only because *decision* $\neq \perp$. Thus, no process will ever reach and execute line 25. □

**Lemma 4.** *For every two processes $i$ and $j$,*

1. *if $i$ writes the value $v$ into the decision register in line 7, and $j$ writes the value $v'$ into the decision register in line 20, then $v = v'$.*
2. *if $i$ writes the value $v$ into the decision register in line 20, and $j$ writes the value $v'$ into the decision register also in line 20, then $v = v'$.*
3. *if $i$ writes the value $v$ into the decision register in line 25, and $j$ writes the value $v'$ into the decision register also in line 25, then $v = v'$.*

*Proof.*

1. Assume that $i$ writes the value $v$ into the decision register in line 7, and $j$ writes the value $v'$ into the decision register in line 20. When $i$ terminates, the value of its state register is either 0, 1 or 2. In the first two cases (0 and 1), the value of $max$ that $j$ computes in line 19, does not depend on the input value of $i$, and hence $v = v'$. Consider the case that when $i$ terminates (line 7), the value of its state register is 2. Thus, when $i$ terminates, the values of all the other $n - 1$ state registers must be 3. When $j$ starts executing the for-loop in line 17, the value of the state registers of $n - 1$ processes must be 3. Thus, $i$ and $j$ set their $max$ registers (in lines 6 and 19, respectively) to the same value since they both choose the maximum input value from the set of $n - 1$ input values which does not include the input value of process $i$. Thus, $v = v'$.
2. Assume that $i$ writes the value $v$ into the decision register in line 20, and $j$ writes the value $v'$ into the decision register also in line 20. When $i$ started executed the for-loop in line 17, the value of the state register of *exactly* one process, say process $k$, was less than 2. Similarly, when $j$ started executed the for-loop in line 17, the value of the state register of *exactly* one process, say process $k'$, was less than 2. Since the value of a state register never decreases, it follows that $k = k'$. Thus, $i$ and $j$ set their $max$ registers (in line 19) to the same value, since they choose the maximum input value from the same $n - 1$ input values. Thus, $v = v'$.
3. Assume that $i$ writes the value $v$ into the decision register in line 25, and $j$ writes the value $v'$ into the decision register in line 25. Both $i$ and $j$ set their $max$ registers (line 24) to the same value, since they choose the maximum input value from the set of all $n$ input values. Thus, $v = v'$.    □

**Theorem 2 (agreement & validity).** *All the participating processes decide on the same value, and this decision value is the input of a participating process.*

*Proof.* It follows from Lemmas 3 and 4, that whenever two processes write into the decision register, they write the same value. Also, whenever a process writes into the decision register, this written value is the input of a participating process. Each correct process decides only on a value written into the decision register.    □

**Theorem 3 (termination).** *In the presence of at most a single crash $(n - 1)$-failure, every correct process eventually terminates.*

*Proof.* There are exactly two places in the algorithm where a process may need to wait for some other process to take a step: (1) in the repeat-until loop in lines 9–13, and (2) in the await statement in line 22. In both places, whenever a process needs to wait, it continuously examines the value of the decision register, and if it finds out that $decision \neq \bot$ it decides on the value written in $decision$ and terminates. Thus, we can conclude that: if some process terminates then every correct process will eventually terminate.

So, let us assume, by contradiction, that no correct process ever terminates. There are at least $n - 1$ correct processes. At least $n - 1$ correct process will execute the for loop in lines 1–15 with $round = 1$. They all will eventually execute the assignment in line 8, setting their state registers to 1. Thus, each correct process with $round = 1$, will eventually exit the repeat loop in lines 9–14, and will move to round two. By a similar argument, each correct process will eventually complete rounds two and three (i.e., will complete the for loop in lines 2–15).

A process reaches the for loop in lines 21–24, only if its local *counter* register equals $n$, which implies that for every $i \in \{1, ..., n\}$ $state[i] \geq 2$. Thus, by Lemma 2, if some process executes the for loop in lines 21–24 all the $n$ processes are active and will never fail. Since, by contradiction, no process terminates, all the $n$ processes must eventually get stuck in the await statement on line 22. However, this is not possible since the value of the state register of each process which reaches line 22 must be 3. Thus, all the waiting processes in line 22, will be able to proceed beyond the await statement and terminate. A contradiction. □

**Remark:** It is tempting to simplify the algorithm by deleting the shared register *decision*, and removing all the read and write accesses to it. In such an algorithm a process decides only on the maximum value it has computed. Such a simplification would make the algorithm incorrect, as a process in round 2 may get stuck forever in the repeat-until loop in lines 9–13. This will happen if some process decides in round 1 (and terminates) while another process fails in round 1.

## 4   Possibility of $k$-Set Consensus with $l+k-2$ Crash $(n-l)$-Failures

The $k$-set consensus problem is to design an algorithm for $n$ processes, where each process starts with an input value from some domain and must choose some participating process' input as its output. All $n$ processes together may choose no more than $k$ distinct output values. The 1-set consensus problem is the familiar consensus problem.

Another fundamental result in distributed computing is that for $1 \leq k \leq n - 1$, it is impossible to solve $k$-set consensus in the presence of $k$ crash failures (i.e., $k$ crash $n$-failures) for $n$ processes [4, 12, 18]. We show that it is possible to solve $k$-set consensus in the presence of $\ell + k - 2$ crash $(n - \ell)$-failures. In particular, it is possible to solve $k$-set consensus in the presence of $k$ crash $(n-2)$-failures. The possibility result presented below *does not* imply the result stated in Theorem 1.

**Theorem 4.** *For every $\ell \geq 1$, $k \geq 1$ and $n \geq 2\ell + k - 2$, there is a $k$-set consensus algorithm for $n$ processes, using registers, that can tolerate $\ell + k - 2$ crash $(n - \ell)$-failures.*

The following algorithm solves $k$-set consensus and tolerates $\ell + k - 2$ crash $(n - \ell)$-failures. In Sect. 5, we show that there is no $k$-set consensus algorithm that can tolerate $\ell + k$ crash $(n - \ell)$-failures. The question whether it is possible to solve $k$-set consensus in the presence of $\ell + k - 1$ crash $(n - \ell)$-failures, is an interesting open problem.

## 4.1   The Algorithm

In the implementation below we use a shared object called *atomic snapshot* which can be wait-free implemented from registers [1,3]. A snapshot object consists of a set of $m > 1$ components, each capable of storing value. Processes can perform two different types of operations: UPDATE any individual component or instantaneously (atomically) SCAN the entire collection to obtain the values of all the components. So, for an atomic snapshot object $S$, $S.update(i, v)$ writes $v$ to the $i^{th}$ component, and $S.scan$ returns a snapshot of all $m$ components.

A *single-writer* atomic snapshot object is a restricted version in which there are the same number of processes as components and only process $i \in \{1, ..., n\}$ can UPDATE the $i^{th}$ component. Let $A[1...n]$ be an array of $n$ registers and $S$ be a single-writer atomic snapshot object. Then, the assignment $A := S.scan$ atomically sets $A[i]$ to the value of the $i^{th}$ component of $S$, for each $i \in \{1, ..., n\}$. It is often easier to design fault-tolerant algorithms for asynchronous systems and prove them correct if one can think of the shared memory as a snapshot object, rather than as a collection of individual registers.

The algorithm also makes use of a single one-shot mutual exclusion object and a single one-shot $(k - 1)$-exclusion object. The $k$-*exclusion* problem, which is a natural generalization of the mutual exclusion problem, is to design an algorithm which guarantees that up to $k$ processes and no more are permitted to be in their critical sections simultaneously. A solution is required to withstand the slow-down or even the crash (fail by stopping) of up to $k - 1$ of processes. For $k = 1$, the 1-exclusion problem is exactly the mutual exclusion problem. The simpler *one-shot* version assumes that a process may try to access its critical section at most once. It is well known that, for any $k \geq 1$, $k$-exclusion can be solved using registers only, even when it is assumed that participation is *not* required [2,16]. We assume that the reader is familiar with the definition of the $k$-exclusion problem. A formal definition of the $k$-exclusion problem is given in the Appendix.

The code of the algorithm appears in Fig. 2. The first step of each process $i$ is to set the $i^{th}$ component *Flag* to 1 (line 1). Then, process $i$ repeatedly takes a snapshot of the *Flag* object (line 3) and each time it takes a snapshot, it sets *counter* to the number of Flag components which are set to 1 (line 4). Processes $i$ continues to take snapshots until *counter* $\geq n - \ell - k + 2$ (line 5). Since at most $\ell + k - 2$ processes may fail, each correct process must eventually notice that *counter* $\geq n - \ell - k + 2$. Next, process $i$ participates in either $EX[1]$ or $EX[2]$ depending on the current value of *group* (line 7). If, at any point, process $i$ notices that *decision* $\neq \perp$ it decides on the value of *decision* (line 8). If it enters its critical section, it sets *decision* to its input value and decides on that value.

A $k$-SET CONSENSUS ALGORITHM WHICH CAN TOLERATE $\ell+k-2$ CRASH $(n-\ell)$-FAILURES:
Program for process $i \in \{1, ..., n\}$ with a non-negative input $in_i$.

**Constants**: $\ell$, $k$: positive integers
**Shared**:   $Flag$: single-writer atomic snapshot object, ranges over $\{0, 1\}$, initially all entries are 0
           $decision$: register, initially $\perp$                 // final decision value
           $EX[1]$: one-shot mutual exclusion object        // used for election
           $EX[2]$: one-shot $(k-1)$-exclusion object
**Local**:   $lflag[1..n]$: array of variables, ranges over $\{0, 1\}$, initial values immaterial
          $counter, group, j$: variables, initial values immaterial

```
1    Flag.update(i, 1);                                    // announce participation
2    repeat                    // wait until at least n − ℓ − k + 2 processes participate
3        lflag := Flag.scan; counter := 0;
4        for j = 1 to n do if lflag[j] = 1 then counter := counter + 1 fi od    // counting
5    until counter ≥ n − ℓ − k + 2;
6    if counter ≤ n − ℓ then group := 2 else group := 1 fi
7    participate in EX[group] and in parallel continuously check if decision ≠ ⊥
8        if at any point decision ≠ ⊥ then decide(decision) fi;    // decide & terminate
9        if you enter the critical section of EX[group]
10       then decision := in_i; decide(in_i) fi.                   // decide & terminate
```

**Fig. 2.** A $k$-set consensus algorithm which can tolerate $\ell + k - 2$ crash $(n - \ell)$-failures.

## 4.2 Correctness Proof

We notice that the *maximum* value of the *counter* of a process is when the process exits the repeat-loop, and at that point, this value is at least $n - \ell - k + 2$. We use the notation $counter.p$ to denote the local counter variable of process $p$. As stated in Theorem 4, it is assumed below that: $\ell \geq 1$, $k \geq 1$ and $n \geq 2\ell + k - 2$.

**Lemma 5.** *For every* $m \in \{n - \ell - k + 2, ..., n\}$, *the maximum value of the counter of at most $m$ processes is at most $m$.*

*Proof.* Assume to the contrary that for some $m \in \{n - \ell - k + 2, ..., n\}$, the maximum value of the counter of more than $m$ processes is at most $m$. Let $P$ denote the set of these processes. Let $p \in P$ be the last process, among the processes in $P$, to update $Flag$ in line 1. Since $|P| > m$, when $p$ takes a snapshot it must notice that at least $m + 1$ components of $Flag$ are already set to 1. A contradiction.      □

**Lemma 6.** *At least $\ell$ processes do not participate in $EX[2]$. Thus, at least $\ell$ processes participate in $EX[1]$ or fail.*

*Proof.* A process, say $p$, may participate in $EX[2]$, only if on exit of the repeat-loop, $counter.p \leq n - \ell$. Thus, by Lemma 5, at most $n - l$ processes participate in $EX[2]$, which implies that at least $\ell$ processes do not participate in $EX[2]$. This implies that, at least $\ell$ processes participate in $EX[1]$ or fail.      □

**Lemma 7.** *If a process participates in $EX[1]$ then this process cannot fail.*

*Proof.* For a process, say $p$, to participate in $EX[1]$, it must be that on exit of the repeat-loop, $counter.p > n - \ell$. This implies that when $p$ exits the repeat-loop, the point contention is at least $n - \ell + 1$. Since the only type of failures is crash $(n - \ell)$-failures, $p$ will not fail once it exits the repeat-loop and starts participating in $EX[1]$. □

**Lemma 8.** *There is at least one correct process.*

*Proof.* Since at most $\ell + k - 2$ processes may fail, the number of correct processes is at least $n - (\ell + k - 2)$. It is assumed (in the statement of Theorem 4) that $n \geq 2\ell + k - 2$. Thus, the number of correct processes is at least $(2\ell + k - 2) - (\ell + k - 2) = \ell$. Since it is assumed that $\ell \geq 1$, there is at least one correct process. □

**Theorem 5 (termination).** *In the presence of at most $\ell + k - 2$ crash $(n - \ell)$-failures, every correct process eventually terminates.*

*Proof.* First we notice that no correct process will get stuck forever in the repeat-loop (lines 2–5). Since at most $\ell + k - 2$ processes may fail, each correct process must eventually notice that at least $n - \ell - k + 2$ of the components of *Flag* are set to 1 and will exit the repeat-loop (lines 2–5).

By Lemma 7, if a process participates in $EX[1]$ then this process *cannot* fail. Thus, if some process participates in $EX[1]$, eventually some process will write its input value into *decision* letting all the other correct processes terminate.

So, let's assume that no process participates in $EX[1]$. This means that each one of the $n$ processes either participates in $EX[2]$ or fails. Thus, by Lemma 8, at least one correct process participates in $EX[2]$. Also, by Lemma 6, at least $\ell$ processes which do not participate in $EX[2]$ fail, and since at most $\ell + k - 2$ processes may fail, we conclude that at most $k - 2$ of the processes that participate in $EX[2]$ may fail.

Since (1) $EX[2]$ is a one-shot $(k - 1)$-exclusion object (that, by definition, can tolerate $k - 2$ crash $n$-failures), (2) there exists a correct process which participates in $EX[2]$ (i.e., this process never fails), and (3) at most $k - 2$ of the processes which participate in $EX[2]$ fail, it follows that some correct process which participates in $EX[2]$, will eventually enter its critical section write its input value into *decision*, letting all the other correct processes terminate. □

**Theorem 6 ($k$-agreement & validity).** *All the participating processes decide on at most $k$ different values, and each one of these decision values is the input of a participating process.*

*Proof.* There are exactly one one-shot mutual exclusion object and one one-shot $(k - 1)$-exclusion object. In $EX[1]$ at most one process enters its critical section, and writes its input value into the decision register. In $EX[2]$ at most $k - 1$ processes enter their critical sections and write their input value into the decision register. Thus, at most $k$ different values are written into *decision*. Also, whenever a process writes into the decision register, this written value is its input. Each correct process decides only on a value written into the decision register. □

# 5    Impossibility Results

A natural question to ask next is, for a given $k$ and $\ell$, what is the maximum number of crash $(n - \ell)$-failures that can be tolerated by a $k$-set consensus algorithm? An *initial failure* of a given process is a failure which happens before the process has taken any steps.

**Theorem 7.** *For every $\ell \geq 0$, $k \geq 1$ and $n > \ell + k$, there is no $k$-set consensus algorithm for $n$ processes, using registers, that can tolerate $k$ crash $(n-\ell)$-failures and $\ell$ initial failures.*

*Proof.* Assume to the contrary that for some $\ell \geq 0$, $k \geq 1$ and $n > \ell + k$, there is an algorithm that can tolerate $k$ crash $(n - \ell)$-failures and $\ell$ initial failures. Let $m = n - \ell$. Since we can always remove $\ell$ processes assuming that they always fail initially, it implies that there is a $k$-set consensus algorithm for $m$ processes, where $m > k$, using registers, that can tolerate $k$ crash $m$-failures. However, this is known to be impossible [4,12,18].                                                   □

Since, for $m \geq 1$ a crash $m$-failure is strictly stronger (i.e., more severe) type of a failure than initial failure, an immediate corollary of Theorem 7 is that:

**Corollary 1.** *For every $\ell \geq 0$, $k \geq 1$ and $n > 2\ell + k$, there is no $k$-set consensus algorithm for $n$ processes, using registers, that can tolerate $\ell + k$ crash $(n - \ell)$-failures.*

In the statement of Corollary 1, it is assumed that $n > 2\ell + k$, since in the context of $\ell + k$ crash $(n - \ell)$-failures, it makes sense to assume that $\ell + k$ is at most $n - \ell$. For the special case of consensus (i.e., 1-set consensus), we get that:

**Corollary 2.** *For every $0 \leq \ell < n/2$, there is no consensus algorithm for $n$ processes, using registers, that can tolerate $\ell + 1$ crash $(n - \ell)$-failures.*

We have shown earlier (Theorem 1) that there is a consensus algorithm for $n$ processes, using registers, that can tolerate a *single* crash $(n - 1)$-failure. It follows from Corollary 2 that, there is no consensus algorithm that can tolerate *two* crash $(n - 1)$-failures.

# 6    Related Work

Extensions of the notion of fault tolerance, which are different from those considered in this paper, were proposed in [5]. In [5], a precise way is presented to characterize adversaries by introducing the notion of disagreement power: the biggest integer $k$ for which the adversary can prevent processes from agreeing on $k$ values when using registers only; and it is shown how to compute the disagreement power of an adversary.

In [20], the traditional notion of fault tolerance is generalized by allowing a limited number of participating correct processes not to terminate in the presence of faults. Every process that does terminate is required to return a correct result. Thus, the new definition guarantees safety but may sacrifice liveness (termination), for a limited number of processes, in the presence of faults. Initial failures were investigated in [21].

The consensus problem was formally defined in [15]. The impossibility result that there is no consensus algorithm that can tolerate even a single crash failure was first proved for the asynchronous message-passing model in [9], and later has been extended for the shared memory model with atomic registers in [14]. The impossibility result that, for $1 \leq k \leq n-1$ there is no $k$-resilient $k$-set-consensus algorithm for $n$ processes using atomic registers is from [4,12,18].

The mutual exclusion problem was first stated and solved for $n$ processes by Dijkstra in [6]. Numerous solutions for the problem have been proposed since it was first introduced in 1965. Dozens of interesting mutual exclusion algorithms and lower bounds are described in details in [17,19]. The $\ell$-exclusion problem, which generalizes the mutual exclusion problem, was first defined and solved in [7,8]. Several papers have proposed $\ell$-exclusion algorithms for solving the problem using atomic read/write registers satisfying various progress properties (see for example, [2,16]).

## 7   Discussion

We have provided a new perspective on the relationship between failures and contention. From the computability point of view, this new perspective allows us to derive "fine-grained" analysis of the limit in computability for consensus and set consensus. That is, to illustrate the utility of the new definitions of weak failures, we have derived possibility and impossibility results for the well-known basic problems of consensus and $k$-set consensus. The definitions together with our technical results indicate that there is an interesting area of fault tolerance that deserves further investigation.

Two specific interesting open problems are: (1) Is the following generalization of Theorem 1 correct: There is a $k$-set consensus algorithm for $n$ processes, using registers, that can tolerate $k$ crash $(n-1)$-failures, for every $n > k \geq 1$; (2) Is the following generalization of Theorem 4 correct: For every $\ell \geq 0$, $k \geq 1$ and $n \geq 2\ell+k-1$, there is a $k$-set consensus algorithm for $n$ processes, using registers, that can tolerate $\ell + k - 1$ crash $(n-\ell)$-failures.

All our results are presented in the context of weakening the notion of crash failures in asynchronous systems. It would be interesting to consider also other types of weak failures such as weak omission failures or weak Byzantine failures and to consider synchronous systems. Another interesting direction would be to extend the results to objects other than atomic registers and to consider problems other than consensus and set-consensus. We have assumed that the number of processes is finite and known, it would be interesting to consider also the case of unbounded concurrency. Considering failure detectors in the context of the new definitions is another interesting direction.

# A    A Formal Definition of the $k$-Exclusion Problem

The $k$-*exclusion* problem, which is a natural generalization of the mutual exclusion problem is to design a protocol which guarantees that up to $k$ processes and no more may simultaneously access identical copies of the same non-sharable resource when there are several competing processes. That is, $k$ processes are permitted to be in their critical section simultaneously. A solution is required to withstand the slow-down or even the crash (fail by stopping) of up to $k - 1$ of processes. For $k = 1$, the 1-exclusion problem is the exactly mutual exclusion problem.

To illustrate the $k$-exclusion problem, consider the case of buying a ticket for a bus ride. Here a resource is a seat on the bus, and the parameter $k$ is the number of available seats. In the $k$-exclusion problem, a passenger needs only to make sure that there is some free seat on the bus, but not to reserve a particular seat.

More formally, it is assumed that each process is executing a sequence of instructions in an infinite loop. The instructions are divided into four continuous sections of code: the *remainder, entry, critical section* and *exit*. The $k$-exclusion problem is to write the code for the *entry code* and the *exit code* in such a way that the following basic requirements are satisfied.

- $k$-*exclusion:* No more than $k$ processes are at their critical section at the same time.
- $k$-*deadlock-freedom:* If strictly fewer than $k$ processes fail (are delayed forever) then if a process is trying to enter its critical section, then some process, not necessarily the same one, eventually enters its critical section.

The $k$-deadlock-freedom requirement may still allow "starvation" of individual processes. It is possible to consider stronger progress requirements which do not allow starvation.

# References

1. Afek, Y., Attiya, H., Dolev, D., Gafni, E., Merritt, M., Shavit, N.: Atomic snapshots of shared memory. J. ACM **40**(4), 873–890 (1993)
2. Afek, Y., Dolev, D., Gafni, E., Merritt, M., Shavit, N.: A bounded first-in, first-enabled solution to the $\ell$-exclusion problem. ACM Trans. Program. Lang. Syst. **16**(3), 939–953 (1994)
3. Anderson, J.H.: Composite registers. Distrib. Comput. **6**(3), 141–154 (1993)
4. Borowsky, E., Gafni, E.: Generalizecl FLP impossibility result for $t$-resilient asynchronous computations. In: Proceedings of 25th ACM Symposium on Theory of Computing, pp. 91–100 (1993)
5. Delporte-Gallet, C., Fauconnier, H., Guerraoui, R., Tielmanns, A.: The disagreement power of an adversary. Distrib. Comput. **24**(3), 137–147 (2011)
6. Dijkstra, E.W.: Solution of a problem in concurrent programming control. Commun. ACM **8**(9), 569 (1965)

7. Fischer, M.J., Lynch, N.A., Burns, J.E., Borodin, A.: Distributed FIFO allocation of identical resources using small shared space. ACM Trans. Program. Lang. Syst. **11**(1), 90–114 (1989)

8. Fischer, M.J., Lynch, N.A., Burns, J.E., Borodin, A.: Resource allocation with immunity to limited process failure. In: Proceedings of 20th IEEE Symposium on Foundations of Computer Science, pp. 234–254, October 1979

9. Fischer, M.J., Lynch, N.A., Paterson, M.S.: Impossibility of distributed consensus with one faulty process. J. ACM **32**(2), 374–382 (1985)

10. Guerraoui, R.: Indulgent algorithms. In: Proceedings of 19th ACM Symposium on Principles of Distributed Computing, pp. 289–298 (2000)

11. Guerraoui, R., Raynal, M.: The information structure of indulgent consensus. IEEE Trans. Comput. **53**(4), 453–466 (2004)

12. Herlihy, M.P., Shavit, N.: The topological structure of asynchronous computability. J. ACM **46**(6), 858–923 (1999)

13. Lamport, L.: The part-time parliament. ACM Trans. Comput. Syst. **16**(2), 133–169 (1998)

14. Loui, M.C., Abu-Amara, H.: Memory requirements for agreement among unreliable asynchronous processes. Adv. Comput. Res. **4**, 163–183 (1987)

15. Pease, M., Shostak, R., Lamport, L.: Reaching agreement in the presence of faults. J. ACM **27**(2), 228–234 (1980)

16. Peterson, G.L.: Observations on $\ell$-exclusion. In: 28th Annual Allerton Conference on Communication, Control and Computing, pp. 568–577, October 1990

17. Raynal, M.: Algorithms for Mutual Exclusion. The MIT Press, Cambridge (1986). Translation of: Algorithmique du parallélisme (1984)

18. Saks, M., Zaharoglou, F.: Wait-free $k$-set agreement is impossible: the topology of public knowledge. SIAM J. Comput. **29**, 1449–1483 (2000)

19. Taubenfeld, G.: Synchronization Algorithms and Concurrent Programming, p. 423. Pearson/Prentice-Hall, London/Upper Saddle River (2006). ISBN 0-131-97259-6

20. Taubenfeld, G.: A closer look at fault tolerance. In: Proceedings of 31st ACM Symposium on Principles of Distributed Computing, pp. 261–270 (2012)

21. Taubenfeld, G., Katz, S., Moran, S.: Initial failures in distributed computations. Int. J. Parallel Program. **18**(4), 255–276 (1989)

# Complete Visibility for Oblivious Robots in $\mathcal{O}(N)$ Time

Gokarna Sharma[1]([✉]), Costas Busch[2], and Supratik Mukhopadhyay[2]

[1] Department of Computer Science, Kent State University, Kent, OH 44242, USA
sharma@cs.kent.edu
[2] School of Electrical Engineering and Computer Science, Louisiana State University, Baton Rouge, LA 70803, USA
{busch,supratik}@csc.lsu.edu

**Abstract.** We consider the distributed setting of $N$ autonomous mobile robots that operate in *Look-Compute-Move* cycles following the *classic oblivious robots* model. We study the fundamental problem where starting from an arbitrary initial configuration, $N$ autonomous robots reposition themselves to a convex hull formation on the plane where each robot is visible to all others (the COMPLETE VISIBILITY problem). We assume *obstructed visibility*, where a robot cannot see another robot if a third robot is positioned between them on the straight line connecting them. We provide the first $\mathcal{O}(N)$ time algorithm for this problem in the fully synchronous setting. Our contribution is a significant improvement over the runtime of the only previously known algorithm for this problem which has a lower bound of $\Omega(N^2)$ in the fully synchronous setting. The proposed algorithm is *collision-free* – robots do not share positions and their paths do not cross.

## 1 Introduction

The well-celebrated *classic oblivious model* of distributed computing by a finite team of autonomous mobile robots enjoys a long history of research [14]. In this model, the robots are points in a plane, which is also what we assume here. In a large spatial extent, robots can be seen as points relative to the spatial extent in which they operate and the solutions obtained for point robots form the building blocks for the robots that are not points (i.e., robots that occupy certain space such as an unit disk area). Moreover, many robot motion planning algorithms in $\mathbb{R}^2$ (such as bug algorithms [4]) have been studied for the point robots. Point robots are also interesting for exploring the computational efficiency of solving basic robot coordination tasks.

In this classic model, the point robots are: *autonomous* (no external control), *anonymous* (no unique identifiers), *indistinguishable* (no external identifiers), *oblivious* (do not remember their previous actions or the previous positions of the other robots), *silent* (no direct means of communication), and *disoriented* (no common coordinate system or unit of measure for the distances) [14]. Each

© Springer Nature Switzerland AG 2019
A. Podelski and F. Taïani (Eds.): NETYS 2018, LNCS 11028, pp. 67–84, 2019.
https://doi.org/10.1007/978-3-030-05529-5_5

robot executes the same algorithm and they all perform their actions following *Look-Compute-Move* (LCM) cycles, i.e., when a robot becomes active, it first observes the positions of other robots (*Look*), then computes a destination point based on that observation (*Compute*), and finally moves towards the destination (*Move*). Many fundamental distributed coordination problems, such as pattern formation, gathering, scattering, etc., were solved in this model [14].

However, this model makes one important assumption of *unobstructed visibility*: Each robot is visible to all others at all times [14]. This assumption can be easily refuted because the view of the robots that are collinear is blocked in a real setting. Therefore, we remove this assumption which leads to the scenario of *obstructed visibility* under which a robot $r_i$ can see another robot $r_j$ if and only if there is no third robot in the line segment joining their positions. Except the presence of robots, there is no other obstacle for any two robots to see each other.

Di Luna *et al.* [1] gave the first algorithm for classic oblivious robots to solve the fundamental COMPLETE VISIBILITY problem with obstructed visibility: Given a team of $N$ mobile robots in arbitrary distinct positions in the Euclidean plane $\mathbb{R}^2$, all the robots reach a convex hull configuration in which each robot is in a distinct corner position from which it can see all other robots. The importance of solving the COMPLETE VISIBILITY problem is that it makes it possible to solve many other robot coordination problems, including gathering, shape formation, and leader election, under obstructed visibility. This problem is also called MUTUAL VISIBILITY in some papers [13,20].

Di Luna *et al.* [1] proved the correctness of their algorithm but gave no runtime analysis (except a proof of finite time termination). The goal of this work is to develop a fast runtime algorithm for COMPLETE VISIBILITY by classic oblivious robots in the same model of [1]. Similar to [1], in our solution the robots are arranged on corners of a convex polygon. Although there might be other ways to arrange robots to have mutual unobstructed visibility, we focus on a convex hull solution since in addition to guaranteeing that each robot sees all others, it often provides extra benefits for solving additional coordination problems [13,20].

**Contributions.** We consider autonomous, anonymous, indistinguishable, oblivious, silent, and disoriented point robots as in the classic oblivious robots model [14]. Visibility could be obstructed by other robots in the line of sight. Following Di Luna *et al.* [1], we assume that the number of robots $N$ is known to the robots (which is solely for the termination detection of the algorithm) and a robot in motion cannot be stopped by an adversary, i.e., a robot stops only after it reaches to its destination point (also called *rigid* moves). Moreover, as in [1], we assume that two robots cannot head to the same destination point and also the paths of robots cannot cross (this would constitute a *collision*). Furthermore, we assume that the robot setting is *fully synchronous*, i.e., there is a notion of common time and all robots perform their LCM cycles simultaneously in each round. In this paper, we prove the following result which, to our knowledge, is the first algorithm for COMPLETE VISIBILITY that achieves linear runtime for classic oblivious robots with obstructed visibility.

**Theorem 1.** *For any initial configuration of $N \geq 3$ classic oblivious robots being in distinct positions in a plane, there is a collision-free algorithm that solves* COMPLETE VISIBILITY *in $\mathcal{O}(N)$ time in the fully synchronous setting under rigid movements.*

The proof of Theorem 1 is constructive since we provide a deterministic algorithm satisfying Theorem 1. This is a significant improvement since it can be shown that the algorithm of Di Luna *et al.* [1] has the time lower bound of $\Omega(N^2)$ in the fully synchronous setting. The lower bound proof idea is to use an initial configuration where all $N$ robots are on the points of two concentric circles, big and small, with distance between each robot and its two neighbors the same. Moreover, the robots in the small circle are collinear with the robots in the big circle. Since the algorithm of [1] only moves the robots in the big circle inward, it can be shown, with appropriately chosen number of robots in the big and small circle, that the big circle does not coincide with the small circle even after $c \cdot N^2$ rounds, for some constant $c$. Moreover, collinear robots stay collinear during these rounds. The formal proof will be similar to [19, Theorem 4].

**Technique.** The main idea is to make robots move autonomously based on their local views (and without communicating with other robots) to become corners of a $N$-vertex convex hull. When all $N$ robots become corners of a convex hull, the configuration naturally solves COMPLETE VISIBILITY. Let **H** be a convex hull of the given $N$ robots. Initially, the robots are either in the perimeter of **H** (i.e., corners and sides of **H**) or in its interior. The only previous algorithm [1] asks robots in the corners of **H** to move inward to shrink the hull so that the existing corners of **H** remain as corners and the internal robots of **H** become new corners of **H**. The corners of **H** do not need to know completely **H** to move inward. It is sufficient for a corner robot $r$ of **H** to determine all $N$ robots are in a plane with angle $< 180°$ formed by $r$ with the leftmost and the rightmost robot it sees. When a robot that was in the interior of **H** becomes a new corner of **H**, it also starts moving inward causing other interior robots new corners of **H**. Since the robots know $N$, they eventually recognize the situation of all robots being in the corners of **H** and terminate. However, this approach has the time lower bound of $\Omega(N^2)$. In contrast, the algorithm we present runs in $\mathcal{O}(N)$ time.

Our technique is to move internal robots in **H** outward towards the perimeter of **H** in addition to the moves of the corners of **H** inward used in [1]. This is challenging since internal robots in **H** may not know which direction is outward and which direction is inward (since they do not have direction information). We indeed address this challenge and able to show that, in each round, at least one internal robot in **H** can correctly move outward towards the perimeter of **H** and becomes a new corner of **H**. Our technique might be of independent interest. We also show that our technique achieves this progress avoiding collisions.

**Paper Organization.** We discuss related work in Sect. 2. We then present the robot model and some preliminaries in Sect. 3. After that, we present our algorithm in Sect. 4 and analyze it in Sect. 5. We finally conclude in Sect. 6. Pseudocode of the algorithm and many proofs are omitted due to space constraints.

## 2  Related Work

Sharma *et al.* [21] presented the brief announcement of the results of this paper in SPAA'17. Besides [21], the only previous work for this problem is Di Luna *et al.* [1] which has time lower bound of $\Omega(N^2)$. Recently, [13,20] provided solutions to COMPLETE VISIBILITY minimizing the number of colors in the *robots with lights* model [17], where each robot is provided with a local externally visible light which can assume (different) colors from a fixed set (of constant size). The lights are *persistent*, i.e., the color assumed by a light is not erased at the end of a round. Trivially, the robots with lights model falls back to the classic model when the number of colors is 1.

Vaidyanathan *et al.* [25] considered runtime for the very first time for COMPLETE VISIBILITY in the robots with lights model. They provided an algorithm that runs in $\mathcal{O}(\log N)$ time using $\mathcal{O}(1)$ colors in the fully synchronous setting. Later, Sharma *et al.* [23] provided an $\mathcal{O}(1)$ time algorithm using $\mathcal{O}(1)$ colors in the semi-synchronous setting. Recently, Sharma *et al.* [22,24] provided an $\mathcal{O}(1)$ time algorithm using $\mathcal{O}(1)$ colors in the asynchronous setting. However, the techniques of [22–25] cannot be applied to the classic model as the robots in the lights model are not completely oblivious as in the classic model due to lights.

The obstructed visibility, in general, is considered in the problem of uniformly spreading robots operating in a line [6]. The work of Pagli *et al.* [16] considers a problem where collisions must be avoided among robots. However, they do not provide runtime analysis. The obstructed visibility is also considered in the so-called *fat robots* model [2,7,10] in which robots are not points, but non-transparent unit discs, and hence they can obstruct visibility of collinear robots. However, no work in the fat robots model has studied runtime. Recently, Sharma *et al.* [18] provided an $\mathcal{O}(N)$ algorithm for COMPLETE VISIBILITY for fat robots enhanced with lights which also cannot be applied to the oblivious model due to lights.

Similarly, much work on the classic model [3,5,15,26] showed that GATHERING – robots come together to be in a not predefined point – is achieved in finite time without a full runtime analysis, except [5,9,11,12]. However, these work do not consider obstructed visibility. Finally, there is a line of work that removes unobstructed visibility from the classic model by considering *limited visibility*, where the robots have a limit on their visibility range [3,11]. However, our study of obstructed visibility is different since, under limited visibility, the collinear robots within the pre-specified radius of a robot are still assumed to be visible to each other.

# 3    Model and Preliminaries

**Robots.** We consider a distributed system of $N$ robots (agents) from a set $Q = \{r_1, \ldots, r_N\}$. Each robot is a (dimensionless) point that can move in an infinite 2-dimensional real plane $\mathbb{R}^2$ following the classic oblivious robots model [14]. Throughout the paper, we will use a point to refer to a robot as well as its position. A robot $r_i$ can see, and be visible to, another robot $r_j$ if there is no third robot $r_k$ in the line segment joining $r_i$ and $r_j$. Following Di Luna *et al.* [1], we assume that $N$ is known to robots (used only for termination detection of the algorithm).

**Look-Compute-Move.** Each robot $r_i$ is either active or inactive. When a robot $r_i$ becomes active, it performs the "Look-Compute-Move" cycle described below.

- *Look:* For each robot $r_j$ that is visible to it, $r_i$ can observe the position of $r_j$ on the plane. Robot $r_i$ can also observe its own position; i.e., $r_i$ is visible to itself. Each robot observes position on its own frame of reference, i.e., two different robots observing the position of the same point may produce different coordinates. However, a robot observes the positions of points accurately within its own reference frame.
- *Compute:* In any cycle, robot $r_i$ may perform an arbitrary computation using only the positions observed during the "look" portion of that cycle. This computation includes determination of a (possibly) new position for $r_i$ for the start of next cycle.
- *Move:* At the end of the cycle, robot $r_i$ moves to its new position.

In the fully synchronous setting (FSYNC), every robot is active in every LCM cycle. In the semi-synchronous setting (SSYNC), at least one robot is active, and over an infinite number of LCM cycles, every robot is active infinitely often. In the asynchronous setting (ASYNC), there is no common notion of time and no assumption is made on the number and frequency of LCM cycles in which a robot can be active. The only guarantee is that every robot is active infinitely often. We assume that the moves of robots are *rigid*, i.e., during the *Move* phase a robot stops only after it reaches its destination point computed during the *Compute* phase.

**Time.** Time is measured in rounds. A *round* is the smallest number of LCM cycles within which each robot is guaranteed to be active at least once [8]. Since we assume the FSYNC setting, a round is a LCM cycle.

**Convex Polygon.** For $M \geq 3$, a *convex polygon* (or convex hull) can be represented as a sequence $\mathbf{H} = (c_0, c_1, \cdots, c_{M-1})$ of *corner points*, which are centers of robots, in a plane that enumerates the polygon vertices in clockwise order. Figure 1 shows a 5-corner convex polygon $(c_0, c_1, c_2, c_3, c_4)$. A point $s$ on the plane is a *side point* of $\mathbf{H}$ iff there exists $0 \leq i < M$ such that $c_i, s, c_{(i+1)(\bmod\ M)}$ are collinear. Figure 1 shows six side points $s_1 - s_6$. A side $S = (c_i, s_1, s_2, \cdots, s_m, c_{i+1})$ is a sequence of collinear points whose beginning and end are adjacent corner points and whose remaining points are side points. For a given polygon **H**, the plane can be divided into the interior and exterior parts. Figure 1 shows the interior of the polygon (the rest of the plane is the exterior).

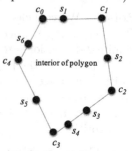

For any pair of points $a, b$, we denote the line segment connecting them by $\overline{ab}$ and the length of $\overline{ab}$ by length($\overline{ab}$). Moreover, for any three points $a, b, c$, we denote the angle formed by sides $\overline{ab}$ and $\overline{bc}$ by $\angle abc$ (the angle is formed at $b$) and the triangle formed by lines $\overline{ab}, \overline{bc}$, and $\overline{ac}$ by $\triangle abc$. Furthermore, we denote the perpendicular distance from $a$ to $\overline{bc}$ by dist($a, \overline{bc}$).

**Fig. 1.** An illustration of a convex polygon (hull).

**Configuration and Local Convex Polygon.** A *configuration* $\mathbf{C}_t = \{r_1^t, \ldots, r_N^t\}$ defines the positions of the robots in $\mathcal{Q}$ any time $t \geq 0$. A configuration for a robot $r_i \in \mathcal{Q}$, $\mathbf{C}_t(r_i)$, defines the positions of the robots in $\mathcal{Q}$ that are visible to $r_i$ (including $r_i$), i.e., $\mathbf{C}_t(r_i) \subseteq \mathbf{C}_t$, at any time $t \geq 0$. The convex polygon formed by $\mathbf{C}_t(r_i)$, $\mathbf{H}_t(r_i)$, is *local* to $r_i$ since $\mathbf{H}_t(r_i)$ depends on the points that are visible to $r_i$ at time $t$, i.e., $\mathbf{H}_t(r_i)$ is formed from the robots that $r_i$ sees at time $t$. We sometime write $\mathbf{C}, \mathbf{H}, \mathbf{C}(r_i), \mathbf{H}(r_i)$ to denote $\mathbf{C}_t, \mathbf{H}_t, \mathbf{C}_t(r_i), \mathbf{H}_t(r_i)$, respectively.

**Convex Hull Layers.** The robots in $\mathcal{Q}$ can be partitioned into layers of convex hulls: $\mathcal{L}_0, \mathcal{L}_1, \ldots$; $\mathcal{L}_0$ is **H** and all the robots in $\mathcal{Q}$ are either in the boundary of $\mathcal{L}_0$ or in its interior. Denote by $\mathcal{Q}_0$ the robots in the boundary of $\mathcal{L}_0$ (the corner and side robots of $\mathcal{L}_0$). Let $\widehat{\mathcal{Q}} := \mathcal{Q} \backslash \mathcal{Q}_0$, i.e., the robots in $\mathcal{Q}$ without considering the robots in the boundary of $\mathcal{L}_0$. Note that the robots in $\widehat{\mathcal{Q}}$ are the *interior robots* of **H**. $\mathcal{L}_i, i \geq 1$, is the convex polygon **H** formed by the robots in $\mathcal{Q} \backslash \sum_{j=0}^{i-1} \mathcal{Q}_j$, i.e., the robots that are not in the boundaries of $\mathcal{L}_0$ up to $\mathcal{L}_{i-1}$. Figure 2 illustrates the convex hull layers.

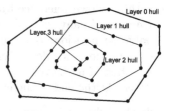

**Fig. 2.** An illustration of convex hull layers $\mathcal{L}_0$ up to $\mathcal{L}_3$.

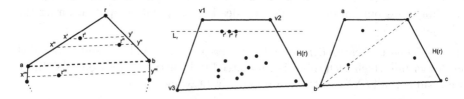

**Fig. 3.** An illustration of (left) the closest internal robot, where $r'$ is the closest internal robot to the corner $r$ of **H**, (center) the closest edge robot, where edge $\overline{v_1 v_2}$ is the closest edge robot to $r$ and $r'$ but not to $r''$, and (right) the external and behind robots, where $r$ is the external robot for $r'$ and $b$ is the behind robot for $r'$.

**Closest Internal Robot.** Let $r$ be a corner robot of **H** and $a, b$ be its neighbors in the boundary of **H**. Let $r'$ be a robot in the interior of **H** and $L_{r'}$ be a line parallel to line segment $\overline{ab}$ passing through $r'$. Robot $r'$ is said to be *closest internal robot* to $r$ if there is no other robot in the interior of $\mathbf{H}$ divided by line $L_{r'}$ towards $r$ (the top of Fig. 3).

**Closest Edge.** Let $r$ be a robot in the interior of $\mathbf{H}(r)$ and $\overline{v_1 v_2}$ be an edge in $\mathbf{H}(r)$ between two consecutive corners $v_1, v_2$ of $\mathbf{H}(r)$. Let $L_r$ be a line parallel to $\overline{v_1 v_2}$ passing through $r$. Edge $\overline{v_1 v_2}$ is said to be *closest* to $r$ (or vice-versa) if

  (i) there is no side robot on $\overline{v_1 v_2}$,
 (ii) there is no other robot in the interior of $\mathbf{H}(r)$ divided by line $L_r$ towards $\overline{v_1 v_2}$, and
(iii) there are no two robots $r', r''$ such that $\mathsf{dist}(r', \overline{v_1 v_2}) = \mathsf{dist}(r'', \overline{v_1 v_2}) = \mathsf{dist}(r, \overline{v_1 v_2})$, and one of $r', r''$ is appearing in the left and the other is appearing in the right of $r$.

The middle of Fig. 3 illustrates a closest edge to $r$.

**External and Behind Robots.** Let $r$ be a robot in the interior of $\mathbf{H}$ with its local hull $\mathbf{H}(r)$ and let $r'$ be a corner of $\mathbf{H}(r)$. Let $a, b, c$ be any three consecutive corners of $\mathbf{H}(r)$. Robot $r$ is said to be *external robot* for $r'$ if $r$ is inside triangle $\Delta abc$ and robots $b, r, r'$ are collinear. Moreover, robot $b$ (that is collinear with $r, r'$) is called the *behind robot* for $r'$ (the bottom of Fig. 3). We can prove the following two basic results.

**Lemma 1.** *Let $r$ be an internal robot in $\mathbf{H}(r)$ and $r'$ be its corner. If $r$ is the external robot for $r'$ then there exists a behind robot for $r'$ and, $\forall r''$ behind $r$, $r'$ cannot see $r''$.*

**Lemma 2.** *If $r$ is the only internal robot in $\mathbf{H}(r)$, there exists at most one corner $r'$ in $\mathbf{H}(r)$ such that $r$ is its external robot.*

**Triangle and Corner Line Segments.** Let $a, r, b$ be three consecutive corners in $\mathbf{H}(r)$ and let $\Delta arb$ be the triangle formed by these corners. Let $\overline{xy}$ be a line parallel to $\overline{ab}$ passing through points $x = \mathsf{length}(\overline{ra})/8$ and $y = \mathsf{length}(\overline{rb})/8$ from $r$ in lines $\overline{ra}$ and $\overline{rb}$, respectively. We say line $\overline{xy}$ is the *triangle line segment* and denote it by $TLS_r$.

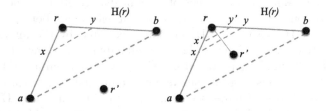

**Fig. 4.** An illustration of (left) triangle line segment, where $\overline{xy}$ is $TLS_r$ and (right) corner line segment, where $\overline{x'y'}$ is $CLS_r$.

Let $r'$ be a robot inside $\Delta arb$. Let $z$ be the point in $\overline{rr'}$ at distance length$(\overline{rr'})/8$ from $r$. Let $\overline{x'y'}$ be a line parallel to $\overline{ab}$ (or $\overline{xy}$) passing through point $z$. We say line $\overline{x'y'}$ is the *corner line segment* and denote it by $CLS_r$. If there are many robots inside $\Delta arb$, let $r'$ and $r''$ be the robots inside $\Delta arb$ that are closest to $\overline{ra}$ and $\overline{rb}$, respectively. $CLS_r$ is computed based on $r'$ or $r''$ that is closest to $r$. According to the definition of $CLS_r$ and $TLS_r$, $CLS_r$ is parallel to $TLS_r$ and $CLS_r$ is closer to $r$ than $TLS_r$ (Fig. 4).

## 4   Algorithm

In this section, we outline our $\mathcal{O}(N)$ time algorithm for Complete Visibility; the pseudocode is omitted due to space constraints. The algorithm consists of interior depletion (ID) and corner depletion (CD) procedures which work together to make robots positioned on the corners of a $N$-vertex convex hull (polygon) **H** and terminate. A special case in our algorithm is when initially all robots in $\mathcal{Q}$ are collinear. This situation can be detected when a robot $r_i$ sees at most two other robots $r_j, r_k$, and $r_i, r_j, r_k$ are collinear. If $r_i$ sees two other robots $r_j, r_k$, then $r_i$ is not an endpoint robot of that line. Robot $r_i$ moves a small distance $\delta > 0$ directly perpendicular to line $\overline{r_j r_k}$. For $N \geq 3$, this move of $r_i$ ensures that in the resulting configuration not all robots in $\mathcal{Q}$ are collinear. (We omit the case of $N \leq 2$ since the problem becomes trivial when $N \leq 2$.)

**Overview of the Algorithm.** The ID procedure makes the robots in $\mathcal{L}_1$ (the interior of **H**) move outward toward the perimeter of **H** (i.e., $\mathcal{L}_0$), and the CD procedure makes the corner robots of **H** move inward (toward $\mathcal{L}_1$). The robots in $\mathcal{Q}$ can easily determine whether they are corners of **H** or in its interior. If a robot $r_i$ sees all robots in $\mathbf{C}(r_i)$ are within an angle of $< 180°$, $r_i$ realizes that it is a corner robot of **H** and executes the CD procedure to move inward. If $r_i$ does not see all robots in $\mathbf{C}(r_i)$ within an angle of $< 180°$, it realizes that it is an interior robot and executes the ID procedure to move outward toward the perimeter of **H**. The robots which are already on the edges of **H** (angle exactly $= 180°$) perform no action until they become corners of **H**.

The CD procedure for the corner robots of **H** is executed in such a way that they remain as corners of **H** and at least one robot that is not the corner of **H** (edge or interior) becomes a new corner of **H**. If there is at least one edge robot in **H**, it becomes a new corner of **H** immediately after all the corners of **H** move inward once. If there is no edge robot, at least one robot in $\mathcal{L}_1$ becomes a new corner of **H** due to the ID procedure executed by the interior robots (simultaneously with the corners of **H**). This all happens in a single round $\kappa$ due to the FSYNC setting. This is crucial since it allows us to guarantee the claimed runtime of $\mathcal{O}(N)$ rounds. Figure 5 shows how an internal robot $r'$ in $\mathcal{L}_1$ become a new corner of **H** after $r'$ moves to a point $z'$ and the corner $v_1$ in **H** moves to point $z''$. A robot $r_i$ terminates as soon as it sees $N$ corners in $\mathbf{H}(r_i)$, i.e., all $N$ robots in $\mathcal{Q}$ are in the corners of $\mathbf{H}(r_i)$ ($r_i$ can do this as it knows $N$).

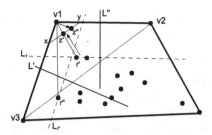

**Fig. 5.** An illustration of how a corner robot $v_1 \in \mathbf{H}$ moves inward and an internal robot $r' \in \mathcal{L}_1$ moves outward toward $v_1$. Both $v_1$ and $r'$ move to $CLS_{v_1}$ (shown as $\overline{xy}$ in the figure) where the position of $r'$ is the point $z'$ at $\mathsf{length}(\overline{v_1 r'})/8$ from $v_1$ in line $\overline{v_1 r'}$ and the position of $v_1$ is the point $z''$ that is midpoint of $\overline{z'y}$ with $y$ being the point of intersection of $CLS_{v_1}$ and $\overline{v_1 v_2}$.

Formally, let $v_1$ be a corner robot of $\mathbf{H}$ and $a, b$ be its left and right neighbors in the boundary of $\mathbf{H}$, respectively. Robot $v_1$ executes the CD procedure as follows.

- **No robot inside $\Delta a v_1 b$:** Robot $v_1$ moves to a position in $TLS_{v_1}$.
- **Robots inside $\Delta a v_1 b$:** Robot $v_1$ moves to a position in $CLS_{v_1}$.

Simultaneously at the same round, an internal robot $r'$ in $\mathcal{L}_1$ executes the ID procedure as follows.

- **Robot $r'$ is not inside $\Delta a v_1 b$:** Robot $r'$ moves to a position in the triangle line segment $TLS_{v_1}$ (different than the one that will be occupied by $v_1$).
- **Robot $r'$ is inside $\Delta a v_1 b$:** Robot $r'$ moves to a position in the corner line segment $CLS_{v_1}$ (different than the one that will be occupied by $v_1$).

We then prove that when both $v_1$ and $r'$ move to either $TLS_r$ or $CLS_r$, $v_1$ remains as a corner of $\mathbf{H}$ and $r'$ becomes a new corner of $\mathbf{H}$. This provides the progress guarantee of our algorithm.

For $r'$ to move outward toward $v_1$, $\overline{v_1 a}$ and/or $\overline{v_1 b}$ must be the closest edge to $r'$ and $r'$ is closest to $v_1$ than $a$ and/or $b$. In situations where there are robots inside the triangular area divided by $TLS_{v_1}$ or $CLS_{v_1}$ towards $v_1$, $r'$ may not become a new corner of $\mathbf{H}$ even after it moves to $TLS_{v_1}$ or $CLS_{v_1}$. In this situation, we are able to show that some robot $\widehat{r'}$ inside that triangular area will become a new corner of $\mathbf{H}$. Furthermore, $r'$ may not be able to compute $CLS_{v_1}$ when $r'$ does not see $b$ (or $a$). But, what we are able to guarantee is that $CLS_{v_1}$ passes through the point that $r'$ moves to and this is sufficient for our algorithm. Figure 5 shows how a corner robot $v_1$ of $\mathbf{H}$ moves inward and a robot $r'$ in $\mathcal{L}_1$ inside triangle $\Delta v_2 v_1 v_3$ moves outward toward $v_1$ and both get positioned in two distinct positions of $CLS_{v_1}$ (shown as line segment $\overline{xy}$ in the figure). The figure also shows the positions $z'$ and $z''$ that $r'$ and $v_1$ occupy, respectively, in $CLS_{v_1}$. The point $z'$ is at distance $\mathsf{length}(\overline{v_1 r'})/8$ from $v_1$ in line $\overline{v_1 r'}$ and the point $z''$ is the midpoint of $\overline{z'y}$ with $y$ being the intersection point of $CLS_{v_1}$ and $\overline{v_1 v_2}$.

Note also that if two internal robots $r', r''$ closest to $\overline{v_1 a}$ and $\overline{v_1 b}$ move toward corner $v_1$, then our technique guarantees that at least one of $r', r''$ and $v_1$ are positioned in $CLS_{v_1}$.

Note here that, if there is a side robot on an edge $\overline{v_1 v_2}$ in $\mathbf{H}(r)$ of a robot $r$ that is in the interior of $\mathbf{H}(r)$, then $\overline{v_1 v_2}$ is not considered as the closest edge (even if it is closest to $r$ among the other edges of $\mathbf{H}(r)$). I.e., $r$ does not move towards $v_1$ or $v_2$. This is to handle the situations similar to the one shown in Fig. 6 so that robots do not move towards each other and collide. In Fig. 6, robots $a, b$ are interior robots in their local hulls $\mathbf{H}(a) = (1, 2, 3, b)$ and $\mathbf{H}(b) = (a, 4, 5, 6)$. Since edge $\overline{1b}$ and $\overline{3b}$ are the closest edges for $a$, and $\overline{a6}$ and $\overline{a4}$ are the closest edges for $b$, if these edges are considered, $a, b$ move towards each other and collide. Therefore, our definition of the closest edge (Sect. 3) excludes these edges while computing the closest edges for an interior robot to move to. The intuition is that if $a, b$ can not move then side robots first become corners and then $a, b$ will get chance to move.

Each robot $r_i \in Q$ works autonomously having only the information about $\mathbf{C}(r_i)$. If $\mathbf{H}(r_i)$ is not a line segment for each $r_i \in Q$, then the ID and CD procedures start immediately. However, if $\mathbf{H}(r_i)$ is a line segment, then in one round, the procedure we use for a collinear $\mathbf{C}_0$ transforms $\mathbf{C}_0$ into a non-collinear configuration and the ID and CD procedures start in the second round. The ID and CD procedures then run until all robots of $Q$ become corners of $\mathbf{H}$. The algorithm then terminates. We provide formal details on how the ID and CD procedures work separately below.

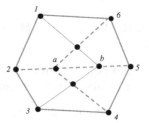

**Fig. 6.** Interior robots do not move toward edges having side robots.

**The Interior Depletion (ID) Procedure.** Let $r'$ be an interior robot in $\mathbf{H}(r')$. The main idea is to determine a corner robot in $\mathbf{H}(r')$ that $r'$ can move closer to without colliding with other robots. Robot $r'$ may not be the robot in $\mathcal{L}_1$ when it executes the ID procedure. However, in the analysis we will only consider the moves of the robots in $\mathcal{L}_1$ outward toward $\mathcal{L}_0$ and this is sufficient to prove the runtime claim for our algorithm.

Robot $r'$ finds whether such a corner robot exists in $\mathbf{H}(r')$ by computing the edge set $Q(r')$ and the corner robot set $X(r')$. $Q(r')$ is the set of edges of $\mathbf{H}(r')$ which is computed first. $X(r')$ is the set of corners of $\mathbf{H}(r')$ which is computed if and only if $Q(r')$ is non-empty. Note that if $r'$ finds $Q(r')$ empty at some round $\kappa \geq 0$, it does not move at that round.

**Computing the Edge Set $Q(r')$.** $Q(r')$ is essentially the set of closest edges of $r'$ in $\mathbf{H}(r')$. Robot $r'$ computes $Q(r')$ as follows: If any edge of $\mathbf{H}(r')$ satisfies the closest edge definition for $r'$ (Sect. 3), $r'$ includes that edge in the set $Q(r')$. Therefore, $Q(r')$ includes all the edges of $\mathbf{H}(r')$ that $r'$ is closest to. Note that the edges with side robots are not considered in $Q(r')$. Note also that if $r'$ satisfies the closest edge definition for (at least) one edge in $\mathbf{H}(r')$, $Q(r')$ is non-empty. For example, in Fig. 8, the edges $\overline{v_1 v_2}$ and $\overline{v_2 v_4}$ are in $Q(r)$ for the robot $r$.

**Computing the Corner Set** $X(r')$. $X(r')$ is essentially the set of corners of $\mathbf{H}(r')$ that are collinear with $r'$ in line $\overleftrightarrow{br'}$ when $r'$ is inside $\triangle abc$ formed by three consecutive corners $a, b, c$ of $\mathbf{H}(r')$. According to this computation, corners $a, b, c$ of $\mathbf{H}(r')$ will not be the members of $X(r')$. Robot $r'$ now have the following two cases based on $X(r')$.

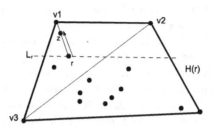

**Fig. 7.** An illustration of Case I2.1.1 in which an internal robot $r$ with only one edge $\overline{v_1 v_2}$ in $Q(r)$ moves toward the closest corner $v_1$ at point $z = \mathsf{length}(\overline{v_1 r})/8$ from $v_1$ in $\overline{v_1 r}$.

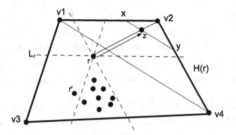

**Fig. 8.** An illustration of Case I2.1.2 in which an internal robot $r$ with two edges $\overline{v_1 v_2}, \overline{v_2 v_4}$ in $Q(r)$ moves toward the common corner $v_2$ at the intersection point $z$ of $TLS_{v_2}$ and $\overline{v_2 r}$ when it is outside $\triangle v_1 v_2 v_4$.

**Case I1:** $X(r')$ **is non-empty.** Robot $r'$ picks an arbitrary robot $r_x$ in $X(r')$; according to the computation of $X(r')$, $r_x$ is a corner of $\mathbf{H}(r')$. It then finds a corner robot $r_d$ in $\mathbf{H}(r')$ that is collinear with $r'$ and $r_x$, and moves toward $r_d$ (note that when $X(r')$ is non-empty, $r_d$ exists for any $r_x \in X(r')$). According to the computation of $X(r')$, $r'$ is inside $\triangle ar_db$ of the corner $r_d$ of $\mathbf{H}(r')$, where $a, b$ are left and right neighbor corners of $r_d$ in $\mathbf{H}(r')$. Specifically, $r'$ computes as destination the point $z$ at distance $\mathsf{length}(\overline{r_d r'})/8$ from $r_d$ in $\overline{r_d r'}$ and moves to $z$. The bottom of Fig. 3 illustrates these ideas, where an internal robot $r$ in $\mathbf{H}(r)$ moves toward $b$ since $r' \in X(r)$.

**Case I2:** $X(r')$ **is empty.** There are two sub-cases based on whether $r'$ sees (at least) one other robot in the interior of $\mathbf{H}(r')$. We assume that $r'$ is the only closest robot to each edge in $Q(r')$. We consider later when two or more robots are equally closest to any edge of $Q(r')$.

– **Case I2.1:** $r'$ **sees at least one other robot in the interior of** $\mathbf{H}(r')$. Robot $r'$ has three sub-cases to consider based on the size of $Q(r')$. We denote size by $|Q(r_i)|$.
  - **Case I2.1.1:** $|Q(r')| = 1$. Let $\overline{v_1 v_2}$ be the only edge in $Q(r')$ and let $r'$ be closest to $v_1$ than $v_2$. Robot $r'$ draws a line $\overline{v_1 r'}$ from it to corner $v_1$ and moves to point $z$ at distance $\mathsf{length}(\overline{v_1 r'})/8$ from $v_1$ in $\overline{v_1 r'}$.
    Figure 7 illustrates this move for an internal robot $r$ with $|Q(r)| = 1$ to point $z$ towards $v_1$ in edge $\overline{v_1 r}$.
  - **Case I2.1.2:** $|Q(r')| = 2$. Let $b$ be the common endpoint of the two edges $\overline{ab}, \overline{bc}$ in $Q(r')$; robot $b$ exists since the edges in $Q(r')$ are the consecutive edges of $\mathbf{H}$ when $|Q(r')| \geq 2$. Robot $r'$ moves toward $b$ as follows: If $r'$ is inside the triangle $\triangle abc$, it moves to a point $z$ at distance $\mathsf{length}(\overline{br'})/8$ from $b$ in $\overline{br'}$. If it is outside $\triangle abc$, it moves to the intersection point $z$ of lines $TLS_b$ and $\overline{br'}$. Figure 8 provides an illustration of this move for an internal robot $r$ in $\mathbf{H}(r)$ (when $|Q(r)| = 2$ and $r$ is outside $\triangle v_1 v_2 v_4$) towards the common endpoint $v_2$.
  - **Case I2.1.3:** $|Q(r')| \geq 3$. Robot $r'$ chooses an interior robot in $\mathbf{H}(r')$ arbitrarily. Let $r_j$ be that robot. We have that $r_j \neq r'$. Robot $r'$ then draws a line $\overleftrightarrow{r_j r'}$. Let $e$ be an edge of $\mathbf{H}(r')$ that $\overleftrightarrow{r_j r'}$ intersects. Let the intersection point be $z$. If $e \in Q(r')$, $r'$ finds the endpoint of $e$ that is closest from $z$ and moves closer to that endpoint similar to Case I2.1.2.
– **Case I2.2: Robot** $r'$ **sees no other robot in the interior of** $\mathbf{H}(r')$. In this case, $Q(r')$ has all the edges of $\mathbf{H}(r')$. Therefore, $r'$ picks an arbitrary corner of $\mathbf{H}(r')$ and moves closer to that robot similar to Case I2.1.2.

There are situations in Case I2.1 where more than one robot is equally closest to an edge $\overline{v_1 v_2} \in Q(r')$. In this case, $r'$ draws a line that connects it to the midpoint $m$ of $\overline{v_1 v_2}$. It then checks in which half-plane the other equally closest robot to $\overline{v_1 v_2}$ belongs to. After that, $r'$ chooses the endpoint of $\overline{v_1 v_2}$ in the another half-plane and moves closer to that endpoint. Figure 9 illustrates the move of the internal robot $r$ towards $v_2$ (although it is closer to $v_1$) due to the presence of the other equidistant robot $r'$ in the half-plane divided by line $\overline{rm}$ towards $v_1$.

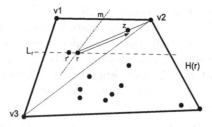

**Fig. 9.** An illustration of a special situation in Case I2.1 where the internal robot $r$ moves towards $v_2$ (although it is closer to $v_1$) due to the presence of the other equidistant robot $r'$ towards $v_1$.

**The Corner Depletion (CD) Procedure.** Let $v_1$ be a corner robot in **H** (or $\mathcal{L}_0$). The main idea is to determine a point in the interior of **H** such that when $v_1$ moves to that point in some round $\kappa$, it remains as a corner robot of $\mathcal{L}_0$ and either a robot in an edge of $\mathcal{L}_0$ (if there exists one) or a robot in the interior of **H** (that moves toward $\mathcal{L}_0$ due to the ID procedure) becomes a new corner of **H** at the same round $\kappa$.

A corner robot $v_1$ of $\mathcal{L}_0$ (or **H**) moves inward as follows. Let $a, b$ be the left and right neighbors of $v_1$, respectively, in the perimeter of $\mathcal{L}_0$. Robot $v_1$ moves inside the triangle $\Delta a v_1 b$ in the corner line segment $CLS_{v_1}$ or triangle line segment $TLS_{v_1}$ depending on whether there is (at least) one robot inside $\Delta a v_1 b$ or not.

To compute the exact point $z''$ in $CLS_{v_1}$ or $TLS_{v_1}$ to move to, $v_1$ finds two robots $r', r''$ in the interior of $\mathcal{L}_0$, one closest to the edge $\overline{v_1 a}$ and the other closest to the edge $\overline{v_1 b}$. It then draws two lines $L', L''$, one perpendicular to $\overline{v_1 a}$ and another perpendicular to $\overline{v_1 b}$, passing through the midpoints of $\overline{v_1 a}$ and $\overline{v_1 b}$, respectively. Let $HP', HP''$ be two half-planes divided by lines $L', L''$, respectively, such that $v_1$ is in those half-planes. We have three different cases for $r_i$ for the computation of the point $z''$ based on whether $r' \in HP'$ and $r'' \in HP''$, or not.

- **Case C1: Robot $r' \in HP'$ and $r'' \in HP''$.** There are three different sub-cases for $v_1$ based on whether $r', r''$ are inside triangle $\Delta a v_1 b$ or not.
    - **Case C1.1: Both $r', r''$ are inside $\Delta a v_1 b$.** Robot $r_i$ chooses the closest robot between $r'$ and $r''$ (the closest internal robot definition). Let $r'$ be that robot. Robot $v_1$ computes $CLS_{v_1}$. Let $z'$ be the intersection point of $\overline{v_1 r'}$ and $CLS_{v_1}$. Moreover, let $y$ be the intersection point of $CLS_{v_1}$ and $\overline{v_1 b}$. Robot $v_1$ then moves to the midpoint $z''$ of line segment $\overline{z' y}$. Figure 5 shows how the corner $v_1$ of $\mathcal{L}_0$ moves to point $z''$ inside $\Delta v_3 v_1 v_2$ in the corner line segment $CLS_{v_1}$ (shown as $\overline{xy}$ in the figure) when $r'$ is inside $\Delta v_3 v_1 v_2$.
    - **Case C1.2: Either of $r', r''$ is inside $\Delta a v_1 b$.** Let $r'$ be the robot inside $\Delta a v_1 b$. Robot $v_1$ moves as in Case C1.1 to point $z''$.
    - **Case C1.3: Neither of $r', r''$ is inside $\Delta a v_1 b$.** Robot $v_1$ computes the triangle line segment $TLS_{v_1}$. It then finds point $z'$ as the intersection point of the line segment $\overline{v_1 r''}$ (that connects $v_1$ to the robot $r''$ that is closest to the edge $\overline{v_1 b}$) and $TLS_{v_1}$, and moves to the midpoint $z''$ of $\overline{z' y}$.
- **Case C2: Robot $r' \in HP'$ or $r'' \in HP''$.** Say $r' \in HP'$ and $r'' \notin HP''$. There are two different sub-cases for $v_1$ based on whether $r'$ is inside $\Delta a v_1 b$ or not (similar to Case C1).
    - **Case C2.1: Robot $r'$ is inside $\Delta a v_1 b$.** Robot $v_1$ moves similarly as in Case C1.2. Figure 5 depicts this case where $r'$ is inside $\Delta v_3 v_1 v_2$ and $r'' \notin HP''$.
    - **Case C2.2: $r'$ is not inside $\Delta a v_1 b$.** Robot $v_1$ moves similar to Case C1.3.
- **Case C3: Robot $r' \notin HP'$ and $r'' \notin HP''$.** Robot $v_1$ moves similar to Case C1.3.

In some situations, $> 1$ robots may be closest to $\overline{v_1 a}$ and/or $\overline{v_1 b}$. In this case, $v_1$ chooses as $r'$ the internal robot that is closest to it among all the robots that are closest to $\overline{v_1 a}$. This applies analogously for $r''$ that is closest to $\overline{v_1 b}$. E.g., in Fig. 5, $v_1$ chooses $r'$ as the closest to it since $r'$ is closest to it than the other equidistant robot $r$ to $\overline{v_1 v_2}$.

## 5   Analysis of the Algorithm

**Overview of the Analysis.** The main goal is to show that in each round $\kappa \geq 0$, at least one robot either on any side of $\mathcal{L}_0$ or on corners and sides of $\mathcal{L}_1$ becomes a new corner of $\mathcal{L}_0$. This will immediately give the claimed runtime of $\mathcal{O}(N)$ for our algorithm. Since robots know $N$, after all robots in $\mathcal{Q}$ become corners of $\mathcal{L}_0$, each robot can decide on its own (without communicating with other robots) COMPLETE VISIBILITY is solved and terminate its computation. To prove the above claim, we first show that at least one robot in $\mathcal{L}_1$ moves outward toward $\mathcal{L}_0$ in each round $\kappa \geq 0$ (Lemma 11). We then prove that in the same round $\kappa$ due to the moves of corner robots of $\mathcal{L}_0$ inward toward $\mathcal{L}_1$, a robot in any side of $\mathcal{L}_0$ or in the corners or sides of $\mathcal{L}_1$ becomes a new corner of $\mathcal{L}_0$ (Theorem 2). We also show that the corner robots of $\mathcal{L}_0$ remain as corners of $\mathcal{L}_0$ even after they have moved toward $\mathcal{L}_1$ (Lemma 13). We then prove that this indeed happens without collisions in every round $\kappa$ (Theorem 3). This altogether provides the $\mathcal{O}(N)$ runtime for our algorithm avoiding collisions (Theorem 1).

**Detailed Analysis of the Algorithm.** We start with the following lemmas. Recall that $\widehat{\mathcal{Q}}$ denotes the interior robots of $\mathbf{H}$.

**Lemma 3.** *If $|\widehat{\mathcal{Q}}| \geq 2$ in any round $\kappa$, then there are at least 2 corner robots in $\mathcal{L}_1$.*

**Lemma 4.** *If $|\mathcal{Q}_1| \geq 2$ in any round $\kappa$, then at least 2 corner robots in $\mathcal{L}_1$ must find at least one edge in $\mathcal{L}_0$ the closest to them.*

Let $r'$ be a corner in $\mathcal{L}_1$ that satisfies Lemma 4. We show that $r'$ includes in $Q(r')$ the edge of $\mathcal{L}_0$ that it finds closest to. Note that $r'$ computes $Q(r')$ based only on $\mathbf{H}(r')$.

**Lemma 5.** *If $|\widehat{\mathcal{Q}}| \geq 2$ at any round $\kappa$, at least 2 corner robots of $\mathcal{L}_1$ have at least one edge of $\mathcal{L}_0$ in their edge set $Q(*)$.*

We have the following observation when $|Q(r_i)| \geq 2$.

**Observation 1.** *For any round $\kappa$, if $|Q(r')| \geq 2$ for a robot $r' \in \widehat{\mathcal{Q}}$, then all the edges of $Q(r')$ are the consecutive edges in $\mathbf{H}(r')$.*

**Definition 1.** *A corner robot $r' \in \mathcal{L}_1$ is called* eligible-layer-1-corner *robot if at least one edge of $\mathcal{L}_0$ is in $Q(r')$.*

We have from Definition 1 and Lemma 5 that, when $|\widehat{Q}| \geq 2$, there are at least 2 eligible-layer-1-corner robots in $\mathcal{L}_1$.

We now focus on the eligible-layer-1-corner robots. We show that, in any round $\kappa$, at least one eligible-layer-1-corner robot moves toward $\mathcal{L}_0$. We differentiate the cases of $|Q(r')| = 1$, $|Q(r')| = 2$, and $|Q(r')| \geq 3$ for an eligible-layer-1-corner robot $r'$.

**Lemma 6.** *In any round $\kappa$, if $|Q(r')| = 1$ for an eligible-layer-1-corner $r'$, then the only edge of $Q(r')$ is an edge of $\mathcal{L}_0$.*

**Lemma 7.** *In any round $\kappa$, if $|Q(r')| \geq 2$ for an eligible-layer-1-corner $r'$, then at least one edge of $Q(r')$ is an edge of $\mathcal{L}_0$.*

We are now ready to prove Lemma 8. We will need this lemma to prove Lemma 11.

**Lemma 8.** *If $|\widehat{Q}| \geq 3$ in any round $\kappa$, then there is an eligible-layer-1-corner robot $r' \in \mathcal{L}_1$ that sees a robot $r \in \widehat{Q}$ as internal in $\mathbf{H}(r')$, where $r' \neq r$.*

We now consider the case of $|\widehat{Q}| = 2$. Both the robots $r_i, r_j \in \widehat{Q}$ are eligible-layer-1-corner robots (Lemma 5). Moreover, both $r_i, r_j \in \mathcal{L}_1$. Therefore, if $r_i$ sees $r_j$ (or $r_j$ sees $r_i$) as internal in $\mathbf{H}(r_i)$ (or $\mathbf{H}(r_j)$), then we have Lemma 8. We prove the following lemma if $r_i$ does not see $r_j$ as internal in $\mathbf{H}(r_i)$ (or vice-versa).

**Lemma 9.** *If $|\widehat{Q}| = 2$ in any round $\kappa$ and $r_i \in \widehat{Q}$ does not see $r_j \in \widehat{Q}$ as internal in $\mathbf{H}(r_i)$ (and vice-versa), then both $r_i, r_j$ are collinear with two corner robots, say $v_3, v_4$, of $\mathcal{L}_0$. Moreover, $r_i$ (or $r_j$) is inside triangle $\triangle av_3b$ and $r_j$ (or $r_i$) is inside triangle $\triangle a'v_4b'$, where $a, b, a', b'$ are the left and right neighbors of $v_3, v_4$, respectively, in the boundary of $\mathcal{L}_0$.*

The following lemma bounds the size of the corner set $X(r_i)$.

**Lemma 10.** *In any round $\kappa$, for any eligible-layer-1-corner $r_i$, $|X(r_i)| \leq 1$ and if $|X(r_i)| = 1$, $r_i$ is inside triangle $\triangle av_3b$ of a corner $v_3$ of $\mathcal{L}_0$, where $a, b$ are the left and right neighbors of $v_3$ in the boundary of $\mathcal{L}_0$.*

We are now ready to prove the crucial lemma for the progress guarantee.

**Lemma 11.** *If $\widehat{Q} \neq \emptyset$ in any round $\kappa$, at least one eligible-layer-1-corner robot $r_i$ moves toward $\mathcal{L}_0$ at that round.*

We prove the following on the positions of robots in $\mathcal{L}_1$ after they move toward $\mathcal{L}_0$.

**Lemma 12.** *In any round $\kappa$, let all the robots in $\mathcal{L}_0$ be corners (i.e., there are no side robots in $\mathcal{L}_0$). Let $v_1$ be a corner in $\mathcal{L}_0$, and $a, b$ be its left and right neighbors, respectively, in the boundary of $\mathcal{L}_0$. Let $r', r''$ be the robots in $\mathcal{L}_1$ that are closest to $\overline{v_1 a}, \overline{v_1 b}$, respectively, with $r'$ being closer to $v_1$ than $r''$. Let $TLS_{v_1}$ (or $CLS_{v_1}$) be a line parallel to $\overline{ab}$ depending on whether $r'$ is outside*

$\Delta av_1 b$ (or inside $\Delta av_1 b$). Let $w, w'$ be the intersection points of lines $TLS_{v_1}$ (or $CLS_{v_1}$), $\overline{v_1 r'}$ and $TLS_{v_1}$ (or $CLS_{v_1}$), $\overline{v_1 r''}$, respectively, and let $PL', PL''$ be the lines parallel to $\overline{v_1 a}, \overline{v_1 b}$ passing through $w, w'$, respectively. The robots in $\mathcal{L}_1$ moving toward corner $v_1$ do not cross lines $PL', PL''$.

Each corner robot $v_1$ in $\mathcal{L}_0$ also moves inward in round $\kappa$ of the algorithm simultaneously with the robots of $\mathcal{L}_1$ moving outward toward $\mathcal{L}_0$ at that round $\kappa$. We prove that any corner $v_1$ in $\mathcal{L}_0$ always remains as a corner of $\mathcal{L}_0$ during the execution.

**Lemma 13.** *In any round $\kappa$, a corner robot $v_1$ of $\mathcal{L}_0$ remains as a corner of $\mathcal{L}_0$.*

The following theorem provides the progress guarantee for our algorithm.

**Theorem 2.** *In each round $\kappa$, either an edge robot in $\mathcal{L}_0$ or a robot in $\mathcal{L}_1$ becomes a new corner of $\mathcal{L}_0$.*

We now prove that the algorithm is collision-free. Note that the initial configuration $\mathbf{C}_0$ is collision-free since each robot in $\mathcal{Q}$ is in distinct positions of $\mathbb{R}^2$.

**Theorem 3.** *The algorithm is collision-free.*

We are now ready to prove our main result, Theorem 1.

**Proof of Theorem 1.** Starting from any non-collinear initial configuration $\mathbf{C}_0$, we have from Theorem 2 that, in every round $\kappa$, at least one robot in the interior of $\mathcal{L}_0$ becomes a new corner of $\mathcal{L}_0$ while executing the algorithm. Therefore, since we have $N$ robots in $\mathcal{Q}$, the algorithm solves COMPLETE VISIBILITY in at most $N$ rounds. The execution is collision-free (Theorem 3).

We now show that starting from any initial collinear configuration $\mathbf{C}_0$, $\mathbf{C}_0$ converts to a non-collinear configuration in a single round. Consider $N \geq 3$; the case of $N \leq 2$ is trivial. Given $\mathbf{C}_0$, $\mathbf{H}_0$ is a line for each robot $r_i \in \mathcal{Q}$, two endpoint robots of $\mathbf{H}_0$ see only one other robot, and the remaining robots of $\mathbf{H}_0$ see exactly two other robots (one on their left and one on their right). All the robots except the two endpoint robots move perpendicular to $\mathbf{H}_0$ by a small distance $\delta > 0$ simultaneously in the first round. As the endpoints of $\mathbf{H}_0$ do not move, when $N \geq 3$, the robots now do not see a line segment $\mathbf{H}_0$ anymore. Therefore, the configuration $\mathbf{C}_1$ after the first round does not revert back to a collinear configuration. The first round is collision-free since robots move perpendicularly to $\mathbf{H}_0$ and the line segment $\mathbf{H}_0$ is the same for each robot.    $\square$

## 6  Concluding Remarks

We have presented the first algorithm with runtime $\mathcal{O}(N)$ for the COMPLETE VISIBILITY problem for classic oblivious robots in the FSYNC setting. This is a significant improvement over the runtime lower bound of $\Omega(N^2)$ of the only previous algorithm [1]. For the future work, it will be interesting to extend our algorithm to handle non-rigid moves and also to the SSYNC and ASYNC settings. Moreover, it will be interesting to prove a generic lower bound that applies to any COMPLETE VISIBILITY algorithm. Furthermore, it will be interesting to combine both obstructed and limited visibility for classic oblivious robots, which might lead to more difficult technical problems.

# References

1. Di Luna, G.A., Flocchini, P., Poloni, F., Santoro, N., Viglietta, G.: The mutual visibility problem for oblivious robots. In: CCCG (2014)
2. Agathangelou, C., Georgiou, C., Mavronicolas, M.: A distributed algorithm for gathering many fat mobile robots in the plane. In: PODC, pp. 250–259 (2013)
3. Ando, H., Suzuki, I., Yamashita, M.: Formation and agreement problems for synchronous mobile robots with limited visibility. In: ISIC, pp. 453–460, August 1995
4. Choset, H., et al.: Principles of Robot Motion: Theory, Algorithms, and Implementations. MIT Press, Cambridge (2005)
5. Cohen, R., Peleg, D.: Robot convergence via center-of-gravity algorithms. In: Královič, R., Sýkora, O. (eds.) SIROCCO 2004. LNCS, vol. 3104, pp. 79–88. Springer, Heidelberg (2004). https://doi.org/10.1007/978-3-540-27796-5_8
6. Cohen, R., Peleg, D.: Local spreading algorithms for autonomous robot systems. Theor. Comput. Sci. **399**(1–2), 71–82 (2008)
7. Cord-Landwehr, A., et al.: Collisionless gathering of robots with an extent. In: Černá, I., et al. (eds.) SOFSEM 2011. LNCS, vol. 6543, pp. 178–189. Springer, Heidelberg (2011). https://doi.org/10.1007/978-3-642-18381-2_15
8. Cord-Landwehr, A., et al.: A new approach for analyzing convergence algorithms for mobile robots. In: Aceto, L., Henzinger, M., Sgall, J. (eds.) ICALP 2011. LNCS, vol. 6756, pp. 650–661. Springer, Heidelberg (2011). https://doi.org/10.1007/978-3-642-22012-8_52
9. Cord-Landwehr, A., Fischer, M., Jung, D., Meyer auf der Heide, F.: Asymptotically optimal gathering on a grid. In: SPAA, pp. 301–312 (2016)
10. Czyzowicz, J., Gasieniec, L., Pelc, A.: Gathering few fat mobile robots in the plane. Theor. Comput. Sci. **410**(6–7), 481–499 (2009)
11. Degener, B., Kempkes, B., Langner, T., Meyer auf der Heide, F., Pietrzyk, P., Wattenhofer, R.: A tight runtime bound for synchronous gathering of autonomous robots with limited visibility. In: SPAA, pp. 139–148 (2011)
12. Degener, B., Kempkes, B., Meyer auf der Heide, F.: A local o($n^2$) gathering algorithm. In: SPAA, pp. 217–223 (2010)
13. Di Luna, G.A., Flocchini, P., Chaudhuri, S.G., Poloni, F., Santoro, N., Viglietta, G.: Mutual visibility by luminous robots without collisions. Inf. Comput. **254**, 392–418 (2017)
14. Flocchini, P., Prencipe, G., Santoro, N.: Distributed computing by oblivious mobile robots. Synth. Lect. Distrib. Comput. Theory **3**(2), 1–185 (2012)
15. Izumi, T., Izumi, T., Kamei, S., Ooshita, F.: Feasibility of polynomial-time randomized gathering for oblivious mobile robots. IEEE Trans. Parallel Distrib. Syst. **24**(4), 716–723 (2013)
16. Pagli, L., Prencipe, G., Viglietta, G.: Getting close without touching: near-gathering for autonomous mobile robots. Distrib. Comput. **28**(5), 333–349 (2015)

17. Peleg, D.: Distributed coordination algorithms for mobile robot swarms: new directions and challenges. In: Pal, A., Kshemkalyani, A.D., Kumar, R., Gupta, A. (eds.) IWDC 2005. LNCS, vol. 3741, pp. 1–12. Springer, Heidelberg (2005). https://doi.org/10.1007/11603771_1

18. Sharma, G., Alsaedi, R., Busch, C., Mukhopadhyay, S.: The complete visibility problem for fat robots with lights. In: ICDCN, pp. 21:1–21:4 (2018)

19. Sharma, G., Busch, C., Mukhopadhyay, S.: Bounds on mutual visibility algorithms. In: CCCG, pp. 268–274 (2015)

20. Sharma, Gokarna, Busch, Costas, Mukhopadhyay, Supratik: Mutual visibility with an optimal number of colors. In: Bose, Prosenjit, Gasieniec, L., Römer, K., Wattenhofer, R. (eds.) ALGOSENSORS 2015. LNCS, vol. 9536, pp. 196–210. Springer, Cham (2015). https://doi.org/10.1007/978-3-319-28472-9_15

21. Sharma, G., Busch, C., Mukhopadhyay, S.: Brief announcement: complete visibility for oblivious robots in linear time. In: SPAA, pp. 325–327 (2017)

22. Sharma, G., Vaidyanathan, R., Trahan, J.L.: Constant-time complete visibility for asynchronous robots with lights. In: Spirakis, P., Tsigas, P. (eds.) SSS 2017. LNCS, vol. 10616, pp. 265–281. Springer, Cham (2017). https://doi.org/10.1007/978-3-319-69084-1_18

23. Sharma, G., Vaidyanathan, R., Trahan, J.L., Busch, C., Rai, S.: Complete visibility for robots with lights in $O(1)$ time. In: Bonakdarpour, B., Petit, F. (eds.) SSS 2016. LNCS, vol. 10083, pp. 327–345. Springer, Cham (2016). https://doi.org/10.1007/978-3-319-49259-9_26

24. Sharma, G., Vaidyanathan, R., Trahan, J.L., Busch, C., Rai, S.: Logarithmic-time complete visibility for asynchronous robots with lights. In: IPDPS, pp. 513–522 (2017)

25. Vaidyanathan, R., Busch, C., Trahan, J.L., Sharma, G., Rai, S.: Logarithmic-time complete visibility for robots with lights. In: IPDPS.,pp. 375–384 (2015)

26. Yamashita, M., Suzuki, I.: Characterizing geometric patterns formable by oblivious anonymous mobile robots. Theor. Comput. Sci. 411(26–28), 2433–2453 (2010)

# Gathering of Mobile Agents
# in Asynchronous Byzantine Environments
# with Authenticated Whiteboards

Masashi Tsuchida[✉], Fukuhito Ooshita, and Michiko Inoue

Nara Institute of Science and Technology, Ikoma, Japan
tsuchida.masashi.td8@is.naist.jp

**Abstract.** We propose two algorithms for the gathering problem of $k$ mobile agents in asynchronous Byzantine environments. For both algorithms, we assume that graph topology is arbitrary, each node is equipped with an authenticated whiteboard, agents have unique IDs, and at most $f$ weakly Byzantine agents exist. Under these assumptions, the first algorithm achieves the gathering without termination in $O(m + fn)$ moves per agent ($m$ is the number of edges and $n$ is the number of nodes). The second algorithm achieves the gathering with termination in $O(m + fn)$ moves per agent by additionally assuming that agents on the same node are synchronized, $f < \lceil \frac{1}{3}k \rceil$ holds, and agents know $k$. To the best of our knowledge, this is the first work to address the gathering problem of mobile agents for arbitrary topology networks in asynchronous Byzantine environments.

## 1 Introduction

Distributed systems, which are composed of multiple computers (nodes) that can communicate with each other, have become larger in scale recently. This makes it complicated to design distributed systems because developers must maintain a huge number of nodes and treat massive data communication among them. As a way to mitigate the difficulty, (mobile) agents have attracted a lot of attention [2]. Agents are software programs that can autonomously move from a node to a node and execute various tasks in distributed systems. In systems with agents, nodes do not need to communicate with other nodes because agents themselves can collect and analyze data by moving around the network, which simplifies design of distributed systems. In addition, agents can efficiently execute tasks by cooperating with other agents. Hence many works study algorithms to realize cooperation among multiple agents.

The gathering problem is a fundamental task to realize cooperation among multiple agents. The goal of the gathering problem is to make all agents meet at a single node. By achieving gathering, all agents can communicate with each other at the single node.

This work was supported by JSPS KAKENHI Grant Number 26330084. The full version of this paper is provided in [20].

A. Podelski and F. Taïani (Eds.): NETYS 2018, LNCS 11028, pp. 85–99, 2019.
https://doi.org/10.1007/978-3-030-05529-5_6

However, since agents themselves move on the distributed system and might be affected by several nodes that they visit, some of agents might be cracked and do not follow the algorithm. We call such agents Byzantine agents. An Byzantine agent is supposed to execute arbitrary operations without following an algorithm. In this paper, we propose two algorithms that can make all correct agents meet at a single node regardless of the behavior of Byzantine agents.

## 1.1  Related Works

The gathering problem has been widely studied in literature [13,16]. Table 1 summarizes some of the results. In this table, we show the number of moves for an agent as the time complexity for asynchronous models. These works aim to clarify solvability of the gathering problem in various environments, and, if it is solvable, they aim to clarify optimal costs (e.g., time, number of moves, and memory space) required to achieve the gathering. To clarify solvability and optimal costs, many studies have been conducted under various environments with different assumptions on synchronization, anonymity, randomized behavior, topology, and presence of node memory (whiteboard).

**Table 1.** Gathering of agents with unique IDs in graphs ($n$ is the number of nodes, $l$ is the length of the smallest ID of agents, $\tau$ is the maximum difference among activation times of agents, $m$ is the number of edges, $\lambda$ is the length of the longest ID of agents, $f_u$ is the upper bound of the number of Byzantine agents, $D$ is the diameter of the graph, $f$ is the number of Byzantine agents).

| | Synchronicity | Graph | Byzantine | Whiteboard | Termination | Time complexity |
|---|---|---|---|---|---|---|
| [8][a] | Synchronous | Arbitrary | Absence | None | Possible | $\tilde{O}(n^5\sqrt{\tau l}+n^{10}l)$ |
| [12][a] | Synchronous | Arbitrary | Absence | None | Possible | $\tilde{O}(n^{15}+l^3)$ |
| [18][a] | Synchronous | Arbitrary | Absence | None | Possible | $\tilde{O}(n^5 l)$ |
| [9] | Synchronous | Arbitrary | Presence | None | Possible | $\tilde{O}(n^9 \lambda)$ |
| [19] | Synchronous | Arbitrary | Presence | Authenticated | Possible | $O(f_u m)$ |
| [7][a] | Asynchronous | Infinite lines | Absence | None | Possible | $O((D+\lambda)^3)$ |
| [7][a] | Asynchronous | Rings | Absence | None | Possible | $O((n\lambda))$ |
| [10][a] | Asynchronous | Arbitrary | Absence | None | Possible | $poly(n,l)$ |
| Trivial | Asynchronous | Arbitrary | Absence | Existence | Possible | $O(m)$ |
| Proposed 1 | Asynchronous | Arbitrary | Presence | Authenticated | Impossible | $O(m+fn)$ |
| Proposed 2 | Asynchronous[b] | Arbitrary | Presence | Authenticated | Possible | $O(m+fn)$ |

[a]This algorithm is originally proposed for a rendezvous problem (i.e., gathering of two agents). However, it can be easily extended to the gathering problem by a technique in [12] and its time complexity is not changed.
[b]Agents on a single node are synchronized.

For synchronous networks, many deterministic algorithms to achieve the gathering have been proposed [1,8,12,18]. If agents do not have unique IDs, they cannot gather in symmetric graphs such as rings because they cannot break symmetry. Therefore, some works [8,12,18] assume unique IDs to achieve the gathering for any graph. Dessmark et al. [8] proposed an algorithm that realizes gathering in $\tilde{O}(n^5\sqrt{\tau l}+n^{10}l)$ unit times for any graph, where $n$ is the number of nodes, $l$ is the length of the smallest ID of agents, and $\tau$ is the maximum difference between activation times of two agents. Kowalski et al. [12] and Ta-Shma et al. [18] improved the time complexity to $\tilde{O}(n^{15}+l^3)$ and $\tilde{O}(n^5l)$ respectively, which are independent of $\tau$. On the other hand, some works [4,5,11] studied the case that agents have no unique IDs. In this case, gathering is not solvable for some graphs and initial positions of agents. So the works proposed algorithms only for solvable graphs and initial positions. They proposed memory-efficient gathering algorithms for trees [5,11] and arbitrary graphs [4].

If a whiteboard exists on each node, the time required for gathering can be significantly reduced. Whiteboards are areas prepared on each node, and agents can leave information to them. For example, when agents have unique IDs, they can write their IDs into whiteboards on their initial nodes. Agents can collect all the IDs by traversing the network [14], and they can achieve the gathering by moving to the initial node of the agent with the smallest ID. This trivial algorithm achieves the gathering in $O(m)$ unit times, where $m$ is the number of edges. On the other hand, when agents have no unique IDs, gathering is not trivial even if they use whiteboards and randomization. Ooshita et al. [15] clarified the relationship between solvability of randomized gathering and termination detection in ring networks with whiteboards.

Recently, some works have considered gathering in the presence of Byzantine agents in synchronous networks [1,9,19]. Byzantine agents can make an arbitrary behavior without following the algorithm due to system errors, cracking, and so on. Dieudonné et al. [9] proposed an algorithm to achieve the gathering in Byzantine environments in $\tilde{O}(n^9\lambda)$ unit times, where $\lambda$ is the length of the longest ID of agents. Bouchard et al. [1] minimized the number of correct agents required to achieve the gathering, but the time required for gathering is exponential of the number of nodes and labels of agents. Tsuchida et al. [19] reduced the time complexity to $O(f_um)$ unit times by using authenticated whiteboards, where $f_u$ is the upper bound of the number of Byzantine agents and $m$ is the number of edges. They used authenticated whiteboards for each node, in which each agent is given a dedicated area to write information and it can write information with its signature.

For asynchronous networks, many works consider the gathering problem with additional assumptions. De Marco et al. [7] proposed an algorithm to achieve the gathering of two agents in asynchronous networks without considering Byzantine agents. They considered infinite lines and rings under the assumption that agents have unique IDs and can meet inside an edge. In infinite lines, their algorithm can achieve the gathering in $O((D+\lambda)^3)$ moves, where $D$ is the distance between two agents in the initial configuration. In rings, they proposed an algorithm to achieve the gathering in $O(n\lambda)$ moves. Dieudonné et al. [10] considered a gathering problem for arbitrary graphs under the same assumptions as [7]. They realized a gathering in polynomial moves of the number of nodes and the length of the minimum ID of agents.

Das et al. [6] assumed the ability of Byzantine agents different from works in [1,9,19], and they realized the gathering in asynchronous ring and mesh networks with Byzantine agents. In their model, correct agents can distinguish Byzantine agents. In addition, correct agents and Byzantine agents can neither meet on the same node nor pass each other on edges. Das et al. proposed an algorithm to achieve the gathering in $O(n)$ moves in this model.

Pelc [17] considered the gathering problem with crash faults under a weak synchronization model. Pelc considered a model in which each agent moves at a constant speed, but the moving speed is different. That is, although each agent has the same rate clock, the agent cannot know the number of clocks required for movement of other agents. In this work, some agents may become crashed, that is, they may fail and stop at a node or an edge. Under this assumption, Pelc proposed algorithms to achieve the gathering in polynomial time for two cases: agents stop with or without keeping their memory contents.

In other failure models, Chalopin et al. [3] considered a gathering problem with an asynchronous model in which not agents but edges of the networks become faulty. Chalopin et al. considered the case that some of the edges in the network are dangerous or faulty such that any agent travelling along one of these edges would disappear. They proposed an algorithm to achieve the gathering in $O(m(m + k))$ moves in this model and they proved that this cost is optimal, where $k$ is the number of agents.

## 1.2   Our Contributions

In this work, we propose two algorithms to achieve the gathering in asynchronous networks with Byzantine agents. In the first algorithm, we adopt the same model as Tsuchida et al. [19] except synchronicity. That is, Byzantine agents exist in an asynchronous network, and an authenticated whiteboard is equipped on each node. Since most of recent distributed systems are asynchronous, we can apply the proposed algorithm to many systems compared to previous algorithms for synchronous networks. To the best of our knowledge, there are no previous works for asynchronous networks with Byzantine agents. If Byzantine agents do not exist, we can use the trivial algorithm with whiteboards in asynchronous networks. That is, agent can achieve the gathering in $O(m)$ moves by using whiteboards in asynchronous networks. However, this trivial algorithm does not work when Byzantine agents exist. The first algorithm achieves the gathering without termination in at most $2m + 4n + 10fn = O(m + fn)$ moves per agent by using authenticated whiteboards even if Byzantine agents exist in asynchronous networks. Note that this algorithm can also work in synchronous environments, and achieve the gathering earlier than the algorithm in [19]. On the other hand, the algorithm in [19] achieves the gathering with termination. This means the first algorithm reduces the time complexity by sacrificing termination detection.

The second algorithm realizes gathering with termination by putting additional assumptions. By realizing termination, it is possible to notify the upper layer application of the terminating, which simplifies design of distributed systems. In order to realize this, we assume that agents on the same node are synchronized. This assumption is practical and easy to implement because, in many mobile agent systems, each node can control activation times of agents on the node. In addition, we assume $f < \lceil \frac{1}{3}k \rceil$ holds and agents know $k$. Under these assumptions, this algorithm achieves the gathering with termination in $O(m + fn)$ moves per agent. Compared to the first algorithm, this algorithm realizes termination detection without additional moves. When we apply the second algorithm to synchronous networks, the algorithm achieves the gathering with termination earlier than the algorithm in [19]. This means, by putting additional assumptions ($f < \lceil \frac{1}{3}k \rceil$ and each agent knows $k$), we can improve the time complexity for the gathering with termination in synchronous networks.

## 2 Preliminaries

### 2.1 A Distributed System

A distributed system is modeled by a connected undirected graph $G = (V, E)$, where $V$ is a set of nodes and $E$ is a set of edges. The number of nodes is denoted by $n = |V|$. When $(u, v) \in E$ holds, $u$ and $v$ are adjacent. A set of adjacent nodes of node $v$ is denoted by $N_v = \{u|(u,v) \in E\}$. The degree of node $v$ is defined as $d(v) = |N_v|$. Each edge is labeled locally by function $\lambda_v : \{(v, u)|u \in N_v\} \to \{1, 2, \cdots, d(v)\}$ such that $\lambda_v(v, u) \neq \lambda_v(v, w)$ holds for $u \neq w$. We say $\lambda_v(v, u)$ is a port number (or port) of edge $(v, u)$ on node $v$.

Each node does not have a unique ID. Each node has an (authenticated) whiteboard where agents can leave information. Each agent is assigned a dedicated writable area in the whiteboard, and the agent can write information only to that area. On the other hand, each agent can read information from all areas (including areas of other agents) in the whiteboard.

### 2.2 A Mobile Agent

Multiple agents exist in a distributed system. The number of agents is denoted by $k$, and a set of agents is denoted by $A = \{a_1, a_2, \cdots, a_k\}$. Each agent has a unique ID, and the ID of agent $a_i$ is denoted by $ID_i$. In the first algorithm (Sect. 3), each agent knows neither $n$ nor $k$. In the second algorithm (Sect. 4), each agent knows $k$ but does not know $n$.

Each agent is modeled as a state machine $(S, \delta)$. The first element $S$ is a set of agent states, where each agent state is determined by values of variables in its memory. The second element $\delta$ is the state transition function that decides the behavior of an agent. The input of $\delta$ is the states of all agents on the current node, the content of the whiteboard in the current node, and the incoming port number. The output of $\delta$ is the next agent state, the next content of the whiteboard, whether the agent stays or leaves, and the outgoing port number if the agent leaves.

We assume activations of agents are scheduled by an adversary. The adversary chooses one or more agents at one time, and each selected agent executes an atomic operation at the same time. The atomic operation of an agent selected by the adversary is shown below.

- If agent is selected at node $v$, $a_i$ executes the following operations as an atomic operation. First, $a_i$ takes a snapshot, that is, $a_i$ gets states of all agents at $v$ and contents of the whiteboard at $v$. After that, $a_i$ changes its own state and the content of the dedicated writable area in the whiteboard at $v$. Moreover, if $a_i$ decides move to an edge as a result of the local computation, it leaves $v$.
- If agent $a_j$ is selected at edge $e$, $a_j$ arrives at the destination node as an atomic operation. That is, $a_j$ arrive at node.

In the first algorithm (Sect. 3), we assume that agents operate in an asynchronous manner. To guarantee a progress, we assume that for any agent $a$, the adversary chooses $a$ infinitely many times. In the second algorithm (Sect. 4), we assume that agents on the same node are synchronized. That is in addition to the above assumption, we assume that, if the adversary selects an agent $a$ at a node $v$, it selects all agents at the node $v$ at the same time.

In the initial configuration, each agent stays at an arbitrary different node. We assume that each agent makes an operation on its starting node earlier than other agents. That is, we assume that the adversary selects all agents at the same time in the beginning of an execution.

## 2.3    Signature

Each agent $a_i$ can make a signed information that guarantees its ID $ID_i$ and its current node $v$ by a signature function $Sign_{i,v}()$. That is, any agent identifies an ID of the signed agent and whether it is signed at the current node or not from the signature. We assume $a_i$ can use signature function $Sign_{i,v}()$ at only $v$. We call the output of signature function a *marker*, and denote a marker signed by $a_i$ at node $v$ by $marker_{i,v}$. The marker's signature cannot be counterfeited, that is, an agent $a_i$ can use a signature function $Sign_{i,v}()$ at $v$ but cannot compute $Sign_{j,u}()$ for either $i \neq j$ or $v \neq u$ when $a_i$ stay at $v$. Any agents can copy the marker and can paste any whiteboard, but cannot modify it while keeping its validity.

In this paper, when algorithms treats a marker, it first checks the validity of signatures and ignores the marker if it includes wrong signatures. We omit this behavior from descriptions, and assume all signatures of every marker are valid.

When $a_i$ creates the signed marker at node $v$, the marker contains $ID_i$ and information of the node $v$. That is, when an agent finds a signed marker, it can identify (1) the ID of the agent that created it and (2) whether it is created at the current node or not. Therefore, it is guaranteed that signed marker $marker_{i,v}$ is created by $a_i$ at $v$. When the agent $a_j$ stays at node $v$, $a_j$ can recognize that

$marker_{i,v}$ was created at $v$, and when $a_j$ stays at node $u(\neq v)$, $a_j$ can recognize that it was created at another node.

## 2.4  Byzantine Agents

Byzantine agents may exist in a distributed system. Each Byzantine agent behaves arbitrarily without following the algorithm. However, each Byzantine agent cannot change its ID. In addition, even if agent $a_i$ is Byzantine, $a_i$ cannot compute $Sign_{j,u}()(i \neq j$ or $v \neq u)$ at node $v$, and therefore $a_i$ cannot create $marker_{j,u}(i \neq j$ or $v \neq u)$. In this paper, we assume that each agent do not know number of Byzantine agents exist. We assume $f$ Byzantine agents exist. In the second algorithm, we assume $f < \lceil \frac{1}{3}k \rceil$ holds.

## 2.5  The Gathering Problem

We consider two types of gathering problems, gathering without termination and gathering with termination. We say an algorithm solves gathering without termination if all correct agents meet at a single node and continue to stay at the node after a certain point of time. In the second problem, we require agents to declare termination. Once an agent declares termination, it can neither change its state nor move to another node after that. We say an algorithm solves gathering with termination if all correct agents meet at a single node and declare termination at the node. We assume that, in the initial configuration, each agent stays at an arbitrary different node. To evaluate the performance of the algorithm, we consider the maximum number of moves required for an agent to achieve the gathering.

## 2.6  Procedure DFS

In this subsection, we introduce a procedure depth-first search (DFS) used in our algorithm. The DFS is a well-known technique to explore a graph. In the DFS, an agent continues to explore an unexplored port as long as it visits a new node. If the agent visits an already visited node, it backtracks to the previous node and explores another unexplored port. If no unexplored port exists, the agent backtracks to the node from which it enters the current node for the first time. By repeating this behavior, each agent can visit all nodes in $2m$ moves, where $m$ is the number of edges. Note that, since each agent can realize the DFS by using only its dedicated area on whiteboard, Byzantine agents cannot disturb the DFS of correct agents. In this paper, when algorithms executes DFS, each agent use only its dedicated area on whiteboard. We omit this area on whiteboard.

# 3    Gathering Algorithm Without Declaring Termination

In this section, we propose an algorithm that solves gathering without termination. Here, we assume agents operate in an asynchronous manner. In addition, $f$ Byzantine agents exist and each agent does not know $n$, $k$ or $f$.

## 3.1    Our Algorithm

**Overview.** First, we give an overview of our algorithm. This algorithm achieves the gathering of all correct agents in asynchronous networks even if Byzantine agents exist. The basic strategy of the algorithm is as follows.

When agent $a_i$ starts the execution on node $v_{start}$, $a_i$ creates a marker $makrer_{i,v_{start}}$ indicating that $a_i$ starts from node $v_{start}$. We call this marker a starting marker. This marker contains information on the ID of the agent and the node where $a_i$ creates the marker. In this algorithm, all agents share their starting markers and then meet at the node where the agent with the minimum ID creates the starting marker.

To share the starting marker, $a_i$ executes DFS and leaves a copy of the marker to all nodes. When agent $a_i$ sees other agents' markers, $a_i$ stores the markers to its own local variable. After agent $a_i$ finishes the DFS and returns to $v_{start}$, $a_i$ has all markers of correct agents and may have some markers of Byzantine agents. After that, $a_i$ selects the marker $marker_{min,v_{min}}$ which was made by the agent $a_{min}$ with the minimum ID. If Byzantine agents do not exist, agent $a_i$ can achieve the gathering by moving to node $v_{min}$ where the marker $marker_{min,v_{min}}$ is created.

However, if Byzantine agents exist, they may interfere with the gathering in various ways. For example, Byzantine agents might not make their own starting markers, they might write and delete starting markers so that only some correct agents can see the markers, or they might create multiple starting markers. By these operations, agents may calculate different gathering nodes. To overcome this problem, in this algorithm, each agent shares information on the starting marker created by the agent with the minimum ID with all agents to get a common marker. If all correct agents get a common marker of the minimum ID agent, they can calculate the same gathering node. However, while agents share the markers, Byzantine agents may make new markers to interfere with sharing. If agent share all markers of Byzantine agents, they may move infinite times to share the markers because Byzantine agents can create markers infinite times. To prevent from such interference, each agent also shares an blacklist. The blacklist is a list of Byzantine agents' IDs. If the markers and the blacklists are shared, correct agents can identify the common marker that is created by the agent with the minimum ID among the agents not in the blacklist. We explain how agents identify Byzantine agents. When $a_i$ calculates a gathering node and moves to that node for the first time, $a_i$ refers the marker $marker_{min,v}$ created by the agent $a_{min}$ with minimum ID. If other agents copy marker $marker_{min,u}(v \neq u)$ and paste it to the node $v$, $a_i$ can judge that the two markers $marker_{min,v}$ and $marker_{min,u}$ were created by the same ID agent.

---

**Algorithm 1.** Algorithm code of agent $a_i$. The node $v$ indicates the node which $a_i$ is staying.

---

1:  $marker_{i,v} = Sign_{i,v}()$, $a_i.marker = marker_{i,v}$, $a_i.All = \emptyset$, $a_i.state = \mathtt{explore}$
2:  **while** $a_i$ *is executing DFS* **do**
3:      $v.wb[ID_i] = \{a_i.marker\}$
4:      $a_i.All = a_i.All \cup \bigcup_{id} v.wb[id]$
5:      *Store network topology*
6:      *Move to the next node by DFS*
7:  **end while**
8:  $a_i.t_{min} = null$, $a_i.min = \infty$, $a_i.Byz = \emptyset$, $a_i.T_{Byz} = \emptyset$
9:  **while** $True$ **do**
10:     $a_i.All = a_i.All \cup \bigcup_{id} v.wb[id]$
11:     $min\_tmp = min\{writer(t) : t \in a_i.All \wedge writer(t) \notin a_i.Byz\}$
12:     **if** $a_i.min > min\_tmp$ **then**
13:         $a_i.state = \mathtt{explore}$
14:         $a_i.t_{min} = t$ *s.t.* $t \in a_i.All \wedge writer(t) == min\_tmp$
15:         $a_i.min = min\_tmp$
16:         **while** $a_i$ *goes around the network* **do**
17:             $v.wb[ID_i] = v.wb[ID_i] \cup \{a_i.t_{min}\}$
18:             *Move to the next node*
19:         **end while**
20:         *Move to the node where $a_i.t_{min}$ is created*
21:     **else**
22:         **if** $\exists x : x \in a_i.All \wedge writer(x) == a_i.min \wedge node\_check(x) == false$ **then**
23:             $a_i.state = \mathtt{explore}$
24:             $a_i.T_{Byz} = \{x, a_i.t_{min}\}$
25:             **while** $a_i$ *goes around the network* **do**
26:                 $v.wb[ID_i] = v.wb[ID_i] \cup a_i.T_{Byz}$
27:                 *Move to the next node*
28:             **end while**
29:             $a_i.Byz = a_i.Byz \cup a_i.min$
30:             $a_i.min = \infty$
31:         **else**
32:             $a_i.state = \mathtt{gather}$
33:             *Stay at the node $v$*
34:         **end if**
35:     **end if**
36: **end while**

---

Since the starting marker has been signed, each agent cannot camouflage the starting marker of other agents. In addition, correct agents create the markers only once when they start the algorithms. Therefore, when there are two starting markers $marker_{min,v}$ and $marker_{min,u}(v \neq u)$ created by single agent $a_{min}$, $a_i$ can distinguish that $a_{min}$ is a Byzantine agent. When $a_i$ understands that $a_{min}$ is a Byzantine agent, $a_i$ adds $ID_{min}$ to the blacklist and shares $ID_{min}$ with all agents as a member of the blacklist. To share $ID_{min}$, agent $a_i$ shares two starting markers created by the Byzantine agent $a_{min}$. That is, $a_i$ copies $a_{min}$'s two markers and paste them to all the nodes so that all other agents also judge that $a_{min}$ is a Byzantine agent. After that, all correct agents ignore all markers of $a_{min}$ and identify the marker created by the agent with the minimum ID among the agents not in the blacklist. By these operations, all agents can select the node with the marker as the common gathering node.

Since we consider an asynchronous network, agent $a_i$ does not know when other agents write starting marker on the whiteboard. For this reason, after $a_i$ moves to the gathering node, $a_i$ continues to monitor the whiteboard and check the presence of new markers. When $a_i$ finds a new agent with the minimum ID or Byzantine agents, $a_i$ repeats the above operation.

**Details of the Algorithm.** The pseudo-code of the algorithm is given in Algorithm 1. We denote by $v.wb[ID_i]$ the dedicated writable area of agent $a_i$ in the whiteboard on node $v$. Agent $a_i$ manages the local variables $a_i.All$, $a_i.state$, $a_i.min$, $a_i.t_{min}$ and $a_i.Byz$. Variable $a_i.All$ stores all the markers observed by $a_i$. Variable $a_i.state$ stores explore or gather. When $a_i.state =$ gather holds, $a_i$ arrives at the current gathering node and waits for other agents. When $a_i.state =$ explore holds, $a_i$ is currently computing the gathering node or moving to the node. Variable $a_i.t_{min}$ stores the marker created by agent with minimum ID except Byzantine agents' ID that $a_i$ has observed so far. Variable $a_i.min$ stores the ID of the agent that created $a_i.t_{min}$. Variable $a_i.Byz$ is a blacklist, that is, it stores Byzantine agent IDs that $a_i$ has confirmed so far. The initial values of these variables are $a_i.All = \emptyset$, $a_i.state =$ explore, $a_i.min = \infty$, $a_i, t_{min} = null$ and $a_i.Byz = \emptyset$. In addition, function $writer(marker_{i,v})$ returns $i$, that is, the ID of the agent that creates $marker_{i,v}$. Function $node\_check(marker_{i,v})$ returns true if $marker_{i,v}$ was created on the current node, and otherwise returns false.

Recall that, in an atomic operation, an agent obtains the snapshot, updates its state and the whiteboard, and then, possibly leaves the node. In the pseudo-code, each agent executes the operations as an atomic operation until it leaves (lines 6, 18, 20 and 27) or it decides to stay (line 33). When an agent reads from the whiteboard, it uses the snapshot taken at the beginning of an atomic operation.

When $a_i$ starts the algorithm, it makes starting marker $marker_{i,v} = Sign_{i,v}()$ and becomes explore (line 1). After $a_i$ creates the starting marker, in order to inform other agents about the marker, $a_i$ executes DFS and copies the marker and pastes it to all nodes (line 2 to 7). On every node, $a_i$ adds other agent's marker to $a_i.All$ (line 4). In order to obtain the network topology, $a_i$ memorizes the connection relation between all nodes and all edges during the DFS. Consequently, $a_i$ can traverse the network with at most $2n$ moves after it finishes DFS.

After $a_i$ finishes DFS, $a_i$ checks the markers collected in $a_i.All$ and calculates a gathering node (lines 9 to 36). First, $a_i$ stores markers of the current node in $a_i.All$ to check new markers. After that, $a_i$ selects the ID $ID_{min}$ such that $ID_{min} = min\{writer(t) : t \in a_i.All \land writer(t) \notin a_i.Byz\}$ holds (line 11). If $a_i.min > ID_{min}$, $a_i$ executes an update operation of a gathering node (lines 12 to 20). Otherwise, $a_i$ executes a detection operation of Byzantine agents (lines 22 to 30).

In the update operation of a gathering node, $a_i$ calculates a new gathering node. In this step, $a_i$ stores marker $t$ satisfying $writer(t) == min\{writer(t) : t \in a_i.All \land writer(t) \notin a_i.Byz\}$ to $a_i.t_{min}$ and stores $writer(a_i.t_{min})$ to $a_i.min$. After that, $a_i$ copies $a_i.t_{min}$ and $a_i$ pastes it to all nodes in order to inform other agents of that minimum ID agent's marker (lines 16 to 19). Note that, since $a_i$ knows the graph topology, it can visit all nodes in at most $2n$ moves. In addition, since $a_i$ visits all nodes, $a_i$ can know at which node $a_i.t_{min}$ was created. Therefore, after $a_i$ copies $a_i.t_{min}$ and $a_i$ pastes it to all nodes, $a_i$ can move to the node where $a_i.t_{min}$ was created. If there are two or more markers created by an agent with the minimum ID, $a_i$ refers to one of the markers and calculates a gathering node. Then, in the detection operation of the next while-loop, $a_i$ determines an agent with the minimum ID as a Byzantine agent.

In detection operation of Byzantine agents, $a_i$ determines whether the minimum ID agent is a Byzantine agent. If there is a marker $x$ that satisfies $x \in a_i.All \land writer(x) == a_i.min \land node\_check(x) == false$, $a_i$ determines that $writer(x)$ is a Byzantine agent. This is because, since correct agents create markers only once, only Byzantine agents can create markers on two nodes. In this case, $a_i$ informs other agents of the ID of the Byzantine agent and executes the update operation in a next while-loop. In order to realize this, $a_i$ copies the starting markers of the Byzantine agent and pastes them to all nodes, and then $a_i$ initializes $a_i.min = \infty$.

Finally, if $a_i$ executes local computation and decides the current node as a gathering node, $a_i$ changes the $a_i.state$ to **gather** state. After that, if $a_i$ decides to change the gathering node, $a_i$ changes $a_i.state$ to **explore** again (lines 13 and 23).

By repeating the above operation, eventually all the correct agents refer to the starting markers created by the same minimum ID agent and gather at the same node.

For Algorithm 1, we have the following lemma and theorem. Due to limitation of space, the proof is given in the full version of this paper [20].

**Lemma 1.** *Correct agents $a_i$ never adds correct agent $a_j$'s ID $ID_j$ to $a_i.Byz$.*

**Lemma 2.** *For any correct agent $a_i$, after $a_i$ finishes DFS, there exists at least one marker $marker_{x,v}$ that satisfies $marker_{x,v} \in a_i.All \land writer(marker_{x,v}) \notin a_i.Byz$.*

**Lemma 3.** *After correct agent $a_i$ calculates a gathering node for the first time, $a_i$ updates $a_i.min$ at most $2f$ times.*

**Lemma 4.** *For any correct agents $a_i$ and $a_j$, after the last updates of $a_i.min$ and $a_j.min$, $a_i.min$ and $a_j.min$ are equal.*

**Lemma 5.** *All correct agents gather at one node with **gather** state within a finite time.*

**Theorem 1.** *Algorithm 1 solves gathering with termination. In the algorithm, each agent moves at most $2m + 4n + 10fn$ times.*

# 4    Gathering Algorithm with Declaring Termination

In this section, we propose an algorithm that solves gathering with termination. To realize the algorithm we add assumptions that agents on a single node are synchronized, $f < \lceil \frac{1}{3}k \rceil$ holds, and agents know $k$. In addition, we define $f_u = \lfloor \frac{k-1}{3} \rfloor$. Note that, since $f_u$ is the maximum integer less than $\lceil \frac{1}{3}k \rceil$, $f_u$ is an upper bound of $f$.

## 4.1    Our Algorithm

**Overview.** First, we give an overview of our algorithm. This algorithm achieves the gathering with termination in asynchronous networks even if Byzantine agents exist. Agents execute the same operations as Algorithm 1 until $k - f_u$ agents gather at the same node and enter **gather** state. After at least $k - f_u$ agents of **gather** state gather at one node $v$, all correct agents at $v$ terminate. Note that, since the $k - f_u$ agents execute the algorithm in synchronously at $v$ and at most $f_u$ Byzantine agents exist, at least $k - 2f_u \geq f_u + 1$ correct agents terminate at $v$ from $f_u = \lfloor \frac{k-1}{3} \rfloor$. As we show in Lemma 8, correct agents that have not terminated yet eventually visit $v$. When correct agents visit $v$, they can see that at least $f_u + 1$ agents have terminated, and then they also terminate at $v$. In addition, we show in Lemma 7 that there is only one node $v$ where at least $f_u + 1$ agents have terminated. Thus, all correct agents gather at one node and terminate.

**Details of the Algorithm.** The pseudo-code of the algorithm is given in Algorithm 2. It is basically the same as Algorithm 1, but differences are additional lines 10 to 12 and 21 to 23. Recall that, in an atomic operation, an agent obtains the snapshot, updates its state and the whiteboard, and then, possibly leaves the node. In the pseudo-code, each agent executes the operations as an atomic operation until it leaves (lines 6, 26, 28 and 35) or it decides to stay (line 41) or it declare termination (lines 12 and 23). When an agent reads from the whiteboard, it uses the snapshot taken at the beginning of an atomic operation.

In Algorithm 2, agents execute the same operations as Algorithm reffig:alg1 until at least $k - f_u$ agents of **gather** state gather at its current node $v$. After at least $k - f_u$ agents of **gather** state gather at node $v$, correct agents terminate at the node $v$ (lines 10 to 12). If agent $a_i$ sees at least $k - f_u$ agents of **gather** state or at least $f_u + 1$ agents of **terminate** state at node $v$, $a_i$ terminates at $v$ (lines 21 to 23). Agent $a_i$ executes the above operation while $a_i$ visits all nodes to paste marker $a_i.t_{min}$ for updating the gathering node. Note that $a_i$ does not execute the operation while $a_i$ visits nodes to paste $a_i.t_{Biz}$ for updating the blacklist of Byzantine agents (lines 30 to 38). This is because $a_i$ executes an update operation of the gathering node after an update operation of the blacklist.

By repeating the above operation, eventually all the correct agents refer to the starting marker created by the minimum ID agent and gather at the same node with declaring termination.

**Algorithm 2.** $main()$ Algorithm code of agent $a_i$. The node $v$ indicates the node which $a_i$ is staying.

1:   $marker_{i,v} = Sign_{i,v}()$, $a_i.marker = marker_{i,v}$, $a_i.All = \emptyset$, $a_i.state = \texttt{explore}$
2: **while** $a_i$ is executing DFS **do**
3:     $v.wb[ID_i] = \{a_i.marker\}$
4:     $a_i.All = a_i.All \cup \bigcup_{id} v.wb[id]$
5:     *Store network topology*
6:     *Move to the next node by DFS*
7: **end while**
8: $a_i.t_{min} = null$, $A_i.min = \infty$, $a_i.Byz = \emptyset$, $a_i.T_{Byz} = \emptyset$
9: **while** $true$ **do**
10:     **if** *There exist at least* $k - f_u$ *agents of* $\texttt{gather}$ *state at node* $v$ **then**
11:       $a_i.state = \texttt{terminate}$
12:       *declare termination*
13:     **else**
14:       $a_i.All = a_i.All \cup \bigcup_{id} v.wb[id]$
15:       $min\_tmp = min\{writer(t) : t \in a_i.All \wedge writer(t) \notin a_i.Byz\}$
16:       **if** $a_i.min > min\_tmp$ **then**
17:         $a_i.state = \texttt{explore}$
18:         $a_i.t_{min} = t$ *s.t.* $t \in a_i.All \wedge writer(t) == min\_tmp$
19:         $a_i.min = min\_tmp$
20:         **while** $a_i$ *goes around the network* **do**
21:           **if** *There are at least* $k - f_u$ *agents of* $\texttt{gather}$ *state or at least* $f_u +$ $1$ *agents of* $\texttt{terminate}$ *state at node* $v$ **then**
22:             $a_i.state = \texttt{terminate}$
23:             *declare termination*
24:           **end if**
25:           $v.wb[ID_i] = v.wb[ID_i] \cup \{a_i.t_{min}\}$
26:           *Move to the next node*
27:         **end while**
28:         *Move to the node where $a_i.t_{min}$ is created*
29:       **else**
30:         **if** $\exists x : x \in a_i.All \wedge writer(x) == a_i.min \wedge node\_check(x) == false$ **then**
31:           $a_i.state = \texttt{explore}$
32:           $a_i.T_{Byz} = \{x, a_i.t_{min}\}$
33:           **while** $a_i$ *goes around the network* **do**
34:             $v.wb[ID_i] = v.wb[ID_i] \cup a_i.T_{Byz}$
35:             *Move to the next node*
36:           **end while**
37:           $a_i.Byz = a_i.Byz \cup a_i.min$
38:           $a_i.min = \infty$
39:         **else**
40:           $a_i.state = \texttt{gather}$
41:           *stay at the node* $v$
42:         **end if**
43:       **end if**
44:     **end if**
45: **end while**

For Algorithm 2, we have the following lemma and theorem. Due to limitation of space, the proof is given in the full version of this paper [20].

**Lemma 6.** *If a correct agent of* terminate *state exists at a node $v$, at least $f_u + 1$ correct agents of* terminate *state exist at $v$.*

**Lemma 7.** *At least one correct agent eventually terminates.*

We define $a_f$ as the correct agent that terminates earliest among all agents. Let $t_f$ be the time at which $a_f$ terminates and $v_f$ be the node where $a_f$ terminates.

**Lemma 8.** *Each agent moves at most $O(m + fn)$ times before time $t_f$.*

**Lemma 9.** *No correct agent terminates at node $v'$ $(v' \neq v_f)$.*

**Corollary 1.** *After time $t_f$, $f_u + 1$ agents of* terminate *state exist at $v_f$. For any node $v'$ $(v' \neq v_f)$, the number of agents of* terminate *state at $v'$ is at most $f_u$.*

**Lemma 10.** *Each correct agent not in $v_f$ at time $t_f$ terminates at $v_f$ after moving $O(m)$ times.*

**Theorem 2.** *Algorithm 2 achieves the gathering with termination within a finite time. In the algorithm, each agent moves at most $O(m + fn)$.*

## 5   Conclusions

In this work, we have proposed two gathering algorithms for mobile agents in asynchronous Byzantine environments with authenticated whiteboards. Each algorithm achieves the gathering in $O(m + fn)$ moves per an agent. In the Algorithm 1 achieves the gathering without termination. In the Algorithm 2 realizes termination by putting additional assumptions. The additional assumptions are that agents on a single node are synchronized, each agent knows $f$ and $k$ where $f$ is number of Byzantine agents and $k$ is number of total agents.

## References

1. Bouchard, S., Dieudonné, Y., Ducourthial, B.: Byzantine gathering in networks. Distrib. Comput. **29**(6), 435–457 (2016)
2. Cao, J., Das, S.K.: Mobile Agents in Networking and Distributed Computing. Wiley, Hoboken (2012)
3. Chalopin, J., Das, S., Santoro, N.: Rendezvous of mobile agents in unknown graphs with faulty links. In: Pelc, A. (ed.) DISC 2007. LNCS, vol. 4731, pp. 108–122. Springer, Heidelberg (2007). https://doi.org/10.1007/978-3-540-75142-7_11
4. Czyzowicz, J., Kosowski, A., Pelc, A.: How to meet when you forget: log-space rendezvous in arbitrary graphs. Distrib. Comput. **25**(2), 165–178 (2012)

5. Czyzowicz, J., Kosowski, A., Pelc, A.: Time versus space trade-offs for rendezvous in trees. Distrib. Comput. **27**(2), 95–109 (2014)
6. Das, S., Luccio, F.L., Markou, E.: Mobile agents rendezvous in spite of a malicious agent. In: Bose, P., Gąsieniec, L.A., Römer, K., Wattenhofer, R. (eds.) ALGO-SENSORS 2015. LNCS, vol. 9536, pp. 211–224. Springer, Cham (2015). https://doi.org/10.1007/978-3-319-28472-9_16
7. De Marco, G., Gargano, L., Kranakis, E., Krizanc, D., Pelc, A., Vaccaro, U.: Asynchronous deterministic rendezvous in graphs. Theor. Comput. Sci. **355**(3), 315–326 (2006)
8. Dessmark, A., Fraigniaud, P., Kowalski, D.R., Pelc, A.: Deterministic rendezvous in graphs. Algorithmica **46**(1), 69–96 (2006)
9. Dieudonné, Y., Pelc, A., Peleg, D.: Gathering despite mischief. ACM Trans. Algorithms (TALG) **11**(1), 1:1–1:28 (2014)
10. Dieudonné, Y., Pelc, A., Villain, V.: How to meet asynchronously at polynomial cost. SIAM J. Comput. **44**(3), 844–867 (2015)
11. Fraigniaud, P., Pelc, A.: Delays induce an exponential memory gap for rendezvous in trees. ACM Trans. Algorithms (TALG) **9**(2), 17:1–17:24 (2013)
12. Kowalski, D.R., Malinowski, A.: How to meet in anonymous network. Theor. Comput. Sci. **399**(1–2), 141–156 (2008)
13. Kranakis, E., Krizanc, D., Markou, E.: The mobile agent rendezvous problem in the ring. Synth. Lect. Distrib. Comput. Theory **1**(1), 1–122 (2010)
14. Nakamura, J., Ooshita, F., Kakugawa, H., Masuzawa, T.: A single agent exploration in unknown undirected graphs with whiteboards. IEICE Trans. Fundam. Electron., Commun. Comput. Sci. **98**(10), 2117–2128 (2015)
15. Ooshita, F., Kawai, S., Kakugawa, H., Masuzawa, T.: Randomized gathering of mobile agents in anonymous unidirectional ring networks. IEEE Trans. Parallel Distrib. Syst. **25**(5), 1289–1296 (2014)
16. Pelc, A.: Deterministic rendezvous in networks: a comprehensive survey. Networks **59**(3), 331–347 (2012)
17. Pelc, A.: Deterministic gathering with crash faults. Networks **72**, 182–199 (2018)
18. Ta-Shma, A., Zwick, U.: Deterministic rendezvous, treasure hunts, and stronglyuniversal exploration sequences. ACM Trans. Algorithms (TALG) **10**(3), 12:1–12:15 (2014)
19. Tsuchida, M., Ooshita, F., Inoue, M.: Byzantine gathering in networks with authenticated whiteboards. In: Poon, S.-H., Rahman, M.S., Yen, H.-C. (eds.) WALCOM 2017. LNCS, vol. 10167, pp. 106–118. Springer, Cham (2017). https://doi.org/10.1007/978-3-319-53925-6_9
20. Tsuchida, M., Ooshita, F., Inoue, M.: Byzantine gathering in networks with authenticated whiteboards. NAIST Information Science Technical Report (NAIST-IS-TR2018001) (2018)

# Short Paper: BPMN Process Analysis: A Formal Validation and Verification Eclipse Plugin for BPMN Process Models

Anass Rachdi[✉], Abdeslam En-Nouaary, and Mohamed Dahchour

Institut National des Postes et Télécommunications (INPT), Rabat, Morocco
anass.rach@gmail.com

**Abstract.** Process models analysis is a critical step in Business Process Management life cycle. Its main goal is to detect technical and functional errors made in the process models. Since the latter are widely used for the software specification, the quality of the produced software will depend on the soundness and correctness of these process models. In this paper we present the "BPMN Process Analysis": a formal Validation and Verification Eclipse Plugin for BPMN Process Models. It allows us to perform three types of formal analyses, namely, the control flow, the data flow and the business rules analyses. Each analysis generates a certain amount of errors and violations. These anomalies are diagnosed and corrected in order to get the BPMN model free of certain control flow errors, data flow anomalies, as well as Business rules violations.

**Keywords:** BPMN · Business Process Modeling
Software engineering · Eclipse plugin · Information systems

## 1 Introduction

Business process model is considered as one of the most important components that contributes in developing companies software. The latter constitute the core of a business information system whose role is to help the company achieve its goals in effective and efficient way. However, these process models may contain different types of errors that lead to an incorrect implementation of the modeled process in information System.

The presented Eclipse plugin in this contribution, called "BPMN Process Analysis", detects formally some of these errors. It allows us to perform three types of analyses. Each analysis generates a certain amount of errors and violations. These anomalies are diagnosed and corrected in order to get the BPMN model free of control flow errors [1], data flow anomalies, [9] as well as Business rules violations. BPMN has been chosen as a modeling language for its status and success in both industrial and academic world.

The remainder of this paper is structured as follows: The next section introduces notations, approaches and concepts supported by "BPMN Process Analysis" Eclipse Plugin. Section 3 presents the different editors and analyses proposed

© Springer Nature Switzerland AG 2019
A. Podelski and F. Taïani (Eds.): NETYS 2018, LNCS 11028, pp. 100–104, 2019.
https://doi.org/10.1007/978-3-030-05529-5_7

by our BPMN Eclipse Plugin. Section 4 concludes the paper and presents future work.

## 2   Notations, Concepts and Approaches

"BPMN Process Analysis" plugin allows modelers and users to verify formally their models according to the three previously mentioned axes. We present here the main notations, approaches and concepts currently supported by this Eclipse plugin.

### 2.1   BPMN

BPMN stands for Business Process Modeling and Notation and is a public standard maintained by OMG and BPMI [4]. It has received a great success and support from academia and industrial world since it provides users with a range of diverse components, which are divided into four sets: flow objects (activities, events and gateways), connection objects (control flow, message flow and associations), artifact objects (data stores, data objects, data input and data output) and swim lanes (pools and lanes within pools).

### 2.2   BPMN-Time Petri Net Mapping

This approach covers the control flow analysis axis. It proposes a method for the verification of BPMN models by defining formal semantics of BPMN in terms of a mapping to Time Petri Nets (TPN) [6], which are equipped with very efficient analytical techniques. After the translation of BPMN models to TPN, verification is done to ensure that some functional properties are satisfied by the model under investigation, namely liveness and reachability properties (deadlock, dead activities...). The main advantage of this approach [6] over existing ones is that it takes into account the time components in modeling Business process models.

### 2.3   Data Record

This approach covers the data flow analysis axis. It proposes the data record concept [3] that helps us locate formally the stage where the data flow anomaly (missing, redundant, lost and inconsistent data) has taken place as well as the source of data flow problem. Therefore the designer can easily correct the anomaly in order to get the BPMN model free of data flow errors. The model's data flow problems are detected using an algorithm specific for the BPMN standard [7].

### 2.4  BPMN-Business Rule Language

This approach covers the business rules analysis axis: It introduces a method that can analyze business rules related to the internal business process's execution. The proposed approach includes the most important dimensions that have to be found in a business analysis which are: Resources, Tasks, Agents and Time. These dimensions constitute a process schema based on, we express common business rules using Business Rule Language (BRL) [10]. These rules could be verified by a Depth First Search algorithm adapted for the BPMN standard [5].

# 3  Components of "BPMN Process Analysis" Plugin

The BPMN plugin (implemented as an Eclipse menu) is composed of a BPMN 2.0 modeler, a business rule editor and three submenus to perform the control flow, the data flow and the business rules analyses (see Fig. 1).

### 3.1  BPMN 2.0 Modeler

The Eclipse BPMN 2.0 Modeler [2] (See Fig. 1- Window 1) allows us as to author business processes, collaboration diagrams and choreographies using the BPMN 2.0 XML syntax. It supports almost all BPMN 2.0 components and attributes (artifacts, swimlanes and flow objects except some compensation mechanisms). The goal of the Eclipse BPMN 2.0 Modeler is to not only provide a graphical modeling tool, but also to allow plug-in developers to easily customize the behavior and appearance of the editor for specific BPM workflow engines such as jBoss jBPM.

### 3.2  Business Rules Editor

This graphical editorallows us to create, update and delete business rules respecting the Business Rule Language semantics [5]. Business Rule Language is the language in which we specify conceived business rules. A business rule expresses a property of the traces (a sequence of BPMN events and tasks) of the process schema. The latter is composed of tasks (BPMN tasks and events), resources (BPMN data objects and flow objects properties), Agents (BPMN pools or/and lanes) and states of resources (Data objects states). Generally, every common business rule is composed of two clauses namely "IF" and "THEN" (see Fig. 1- Window 2). Each clause can be composed of one or several expressions (equalities or inequalities). These expressions are connected through logical operators (AND or OR). Since the business rules created by the users are dynamic and cannot be inserted in advance in the source code of the plugin, we used JEXL (Java Expression Language), which is a library intended to facilitate the implementation of dynamic and scripting features in applications and frameworks written in Java.

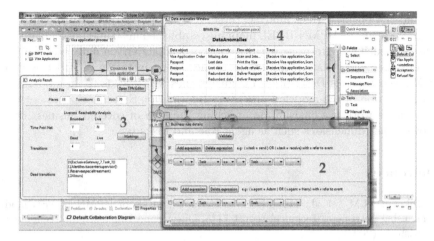

**Fig. 1.** "BPMN Process Analysis" eclipse plugin overview

### 3.3   Business Rules Analysis

Once the process is modeled and the business rules are edited, we can run the "Business Rules analysis" component [5]. The latter generates the business rules violations as well as the business rules whose conditions ("IF" clauses) are not verified. Detected violations can be a disorder of tasks, incompatibility between input data state and task...

### 3.4   Control Flow Analysis

The "Control Flow analysis" component implements the approach (BPMN-TPN mapping) cited in [6]. It allows us to detect the dead BPMN tasks and events. It also gives us other information related to the Time Petri Net components generated after the BPMN-TPN transformation such as number of places, number of transitions, boundness of the TPN (see Fig. 1- Window 3).

### 3.5   Data Flow Analysis

The "Data Flow analysis" component implemented the DataRecord approach cited in [7]. It allows us to detect the different data-flow anti-patterns (missing, redundant, lost and inconsistent data). It also gives us other information related to the flow object as well as to the trace where the data anomaly has taken place (see Fig. 1- Window 4)

## 4   Conclusion

In conclusion, we proposed in this paper a new "BPMN Process Analysis" plugin that gathers all necessary types of analysis, namely, the control flow, the data flow and the business rules analysis these analyses prove their utility when we take profit from the BPMN-BPEL mapping established in [4] and implemented in some tools such as Enterprise Architect [8]. A dead activity, a dataflow anomaly or a business rule violation can cause an incorrect generation of BPEL and/or WSDL(Web Services Description Language) files which leads to an inoperative implementation of the modeled process in Information System.

In future work, we envision on enriching the area of covered business rules to cover other dimensions such as agent role and tasks type.

# References

1. Dijkman, R.M., et al.: Formal semantics and analysis of BPMN process models using petri nets. Technical report 7115, Queensland University of Technology, Brisbane (2007)
2. Eclipse: BPMN2 Modeler, January 2018. http://www.eclipse.org/bpmn2-modeler/
3. Kabbaj, M.I., et al.: Towards an active help on detecting data flow errors in business process models. Int. J. Comput. Sci. Appl. **12**, 16–25 (2015)
4. OMG: Business Process Management and Notation (BPMN 2.0), Needham, USA(2011)
5. Rachdi, A., En-Nouaary, A., Dahchour, M.: Analysis of common business rules in BPMN process models using business rule language. In: 2016 11th International Conference on Intelligent Systems: Theories and Applications (SITA), pp. 1–6. IEEE (2016)
6. Rachdi, A., En-Nouaary, A., Dahchour, M.: Liveness and reachability analysis of BPMN process models. J. Comput. Inf. Technol. **24**(2), 195–207 (2016)
7. Rachdi, A., En-Nouaary, A., Dahchour, M.: Dataflow analysis in BPMN models. In: ICEIS 2017 - Proceedings of the 19th International Conference on Enterprise Information Systems, Porto, Portugal, 26–29 April 2017, vol. 2, pp. 229–237 (2017)
8. Sparx Systems: Enterprise Architect "EA", January 2018. http://www.sparxsystems.com/products/ea/index.html
9. Stackelberg, S.V., et al.: Detecting data-flow errors in BPMN 2.0. Open J. Inform. Syst. **1**, 1–19 (2014)
10. Van Hee, K., Hidders, J., Houben, G.J., Paredaens, J., Thiran, P.: Abstracting common business rules to petri nets. Enterp. Inf. Syst. **2010**, 113 (2010)

# Concurency

# On Helping and Stacks

Vitaly Aksenov[1,2(✉)], Petr Kuznetsov[3], and Anatoly Shalyto[1]

[1] ITMO University, Saint Petersburg, Russia
aksenov.vitaly@gmail.com
[2] Inria Paris, Paris, France
[3] LTCI, Télécom ParisTech, Université Paris-Saclay, Paris, France

**Abstract.** A concurrent algorithm exhibits *helping* when one process performs work on behalf of other processes. More formally, helping is observed when the order of some operation in a linearization is *fixed* by a step of another process. In this paper, we show that no wait-free linearizable implementation of a *stack* using read, write, compare&swap and fetch&add operations can be *help-free*, correcting a mistake in an earlier proof by Censor-Hillel et al.

## 1 Introduction

In a *wait-free* data structure, every process is guaranteed to make progress in its own speed, regardless of the behavior of other processes [8]. It has been observed, however, that achieving wait-freedom typically involves some *helping* mechanism (e.g., [6,7,13,14]). Informally, helping means that a process may perform additional work on behalf of other processes.

Censor-Hillel et al. [5] proposed a natural formalization of the concept of helping, based on the notion of *linearization*: a process $p$ helps an operation of a process $q$ in a given execution if a step of $p$ determines that an operation of $q$ takes effect, or *linearizes*, before some other operation in any possible extension. It was claimed in [5] that helping is required for any wait-free linearizable implementation of an *exact order* data type in a system provided with read, write, compare&swap and fetch&add shared memory primitives. Informally, a sequential data type is exact order if for some operation sequence every change in the relative order of two operations affects the result of some other operations. As examples of exact order data types, Censor-Hillel et al. gave (FIFO) queue and (LIFO) stack.

However, we observe that the stack data type is not exact order. As we show, in any sequential execution on stack, we can reorder any two operations $op$ and $op'$ in such a way that no other operation will see the difference. Hence, the proof of help-free impossibility for exact order types given in [5] does not apply to stack.

In this paper, we propose a direct proof that stack does not have a wait-free and help-free implementation. At first, we show the result for implementations using read, write and compare&swap operations in systems with at least three

A. Podelski and F. Taïani (Eds.): NETYS 2018, LNCS 11028, pp. 107–121, 2019.
https://doi.org/10.1007/978-3-030-05529-5_8

processes, and, then, extend the proof to those additionally using fetch&add in systems with at least four processes. The structure of these two proofs resembles the structure of the proofs from the paper by Censor-Hillel et al. [5], but the underlying reasoning is novel. Unlike their approach our proofs argue about the order of operations given their responses *only* after we empty the data structure. As a result, certain steps of the proof become more technically involved.

The paper is organized as follows. In Sect. 2 we present a computational model and necessary definitions. In Sect. 3 we recall the definition of helping and highlight the mistake in [5]. In Sect. 4 we give our direct proof. In Sect. 5 we discuss the related work. And, finally, we conclude in Sect. 6.

## 2    Model and Definitions

We consider a system of $n$ processes $p_1, \ldots, p_n$ communicating via invocations of *primitives* on a shared memory. We assume that primitives are *read*, *write* and *compare&swap*. In our second technical contribution, we consider one more primitive *fetch&add*.

A compare&swap primitive takes a target location, an expected value and a new value. The value stored in the location is compared to the expected value. If they are equal, then the value in the location is replaced with the new value and **true** is returned (we say that the operation is *successful*). Otherwise, the operation *fails* (i.e., the operation is *failed*) and returns **false**.

A fetch&add primitive takes a target location and an integer value. The primitive augments the value in the location by the provided value and returns the original value.

A high-level concurrent object or a data type is a tuple $(\Phi, \Gamma, Q, q_0, \theta)$, where $\Phi$ is a set of operations, $\Gamma$ is a set of responses, $Q$ is a set of states, $q_0$ is an initial state and a transition function $\theta \subset Q \times \Phi \times Q \times \Gamma$, that determines, for each state and each operation, the set of possible resulting states and produced responses.

In this paper, we concentrate on a stack data type (further, we omit "data type" and simply refer to it as "stack"). It exports two methods push($\cdot$) and pop(). A push($x$) adds a new element into the set. A pop() operations withdraws and returns the most recently added element, or returns $\perp$, if the stack is empty.

An implementation (or, simple object) of a high-level object $O$ is a distributed algorithm $A$ consisting of local state machines $A_1, \ldots, A_n$. $A_i$ specifies the primitives $p_i$ needs to execute to return a response to an invoked operation on $O$. For simplicity, all implementations considered in this paper are deterministic. The provided proofs can be easily extended to randomized implementations. For the rest of the section we fix some implementation of stack.

A *program* of a process specifies a sequence of operations calls on an object. The program may include local computations and can choose which operation to execute depending on the results of the previous operations.

A *history* is a finite or infinite sequence of primitive steps. Each step is coupled with a specific operation that is being executed by the process performing this step. The first step of an operation always comes with the input parameters of the operation, and the last step of an operation is associated with the return of the operation. Given two histories $h_1$ and $h_2$ we denote by $h_1 \circ h_2$ the concatenation of $h_1$ and $h_2$.

A *schedule* is a finite or infinite sequence of process identifiers. Given a schedule, an implementation and programs provided to the processes, one can unambiguously determine the corresponding history. And vice versa, given a history one can always build a schedule by substituting the steps of history to the process that performed it. Assuming a fixed program for each process (these programs will be clear from the context), and a history $h$, we denote by $h \circ p_i$ the history derived from scheduling process $p_i$ to take the next step (if any) following its program immediately after $h$.

The set of histories $H$ induced by an implementation consists of all possible histories induced by all possible processes' programs with all possible schedules. Note that, by the definition, $H$ is prefix- and limit-closed [10].

A history defines a partial order on the operations: $op_1$ precedes $op_2$ in a history $h$ (denoted: $op_1 \prec_h op_2$) if $op_1$ is completed before $op_2$ begins. A *linearization* $L$ of a history $h$ is a sequence of operations such that: (1) $L$ consists of all the completed operations and, possibly, some started but incompleted in $h$; (2) the operations have the same input and same output as corresponding operations in $h$; (3) $L$ consistent with the data type; (4) for every two operations $op_1 \prec_h op_2$ if $op_2$ is included in $L$, then $op_1$ preceds $op_2$ in $L$ ($op_1 \prec_L op_2$).

An implementation of a data type is linearizable if each history from the set of histories has a linearization. A *linearization function* defined over a set of linearizable histories $H$ maps every history in $H$ to a linearization. Note that a linearizable implementations may have multiple linearization functions defined on the set of its histories.

An implementation is *wait-free* if every process completes its operation in a finite number of steps.

## 3 Helping and Exact Order Types

In this section, we recall the definitions of helping and exact order type in [5], and show that stack is *not* exact order.

**Definition 1 (Decided before).** *For a history $h$ in a set of histories $H$, a linearization function $f$ over $H$, and two operations $op_1$ and $op_2$, we say that $op_1$ is decided before $op_2$ in $h$ with respect to $f$ and $H$, if there exists no extension $s \in H$ of $h$ such that $op_2 \prec_{f(s)} op_1$.*

**Definition 2 (Helping).** *A set of histories $H$ with a linearization function $f$ over $H$ is help-free if for every $h \in H$, every two operations $op_1$, $op_2$, and a single computation step $\gamma$ such that $h \circ \gamma \in H$ it holds that if $op_1$ is decided before $op_2$ in $h \circ \gamma$ and $op_1$ is not decided before $op_2$ in $h$ then $\gamma$ is a step in the execution of $op_1$.*

*An implementation is help-free, if there exists a linearization function $f$ such that the set of histories of this implementation with $f$ is help-free.*

Following the formalism of [5], if $S$ is a sequence of operations, we denote by $S(n)$ the first $n$ operations in $S$, and by $S_n$ the $n$-th operation of $S$. We denote by $(S + op?)$ the set of sequences that contains $S$ and all sequences that are similar to $S$, except that a single operation $op$ is inserted somewhere between (or before, or after) the operations of $S$.

**Definition 3 (Exact Order Types).** *An* exact order type *is a data type for which there exists an operation op, an infinite sequence of operations $W$, and a (finite or infinite) sequence of operations $R$, such that for every integer $n \geq 0$ there exists an integer $m \geq 1$, such that for any sequence $A$ from $W(n + 1) \circ (R(m) + op?)$ and any sequence $B$ from $W(n) \circ op \circ (R(m) + W_{n+1}?)$ at least one operation in $R(m)$ has different results in $A$ and $B$, where $\circ$ is a concatenation of sequences.*

It is shown in [5] that the implementations of exact order types require helping if they use only read, write, and compare&swap primitives. The paper also sketches the proof of a more general result for implementations that, additionally, use fetch&add. Further, it is claimed in [5] that stack and queue are exact order types. Indeed, at first glance, if you swap two subsequent operations, further operations have to acknowledge this difference. However, the definition of an exact order type is slightly more complicated, as it allows not only to swap operations but also move them. This relaxation does not affect queue, but, unfortunately, it affects stack.

**Theorem 1.** *Stack is not an exact order type.*

*Proof.* We prove that for any fixed $op$, $W$, $R$ and $n$ there does not exist $m$ that satisfies Definition 3. Note that the claim is stronger than what is needed to prove the theorem: it would be sufficient to prove that for all $op$, $W$ and $R$, the condition does not hold *for some* $n$. In a sense, this suggests that stack is *far* from being exact order.

Suppose, by contradiction, that there exists $m$ that satisfies Definition 3 for fixed $op$, $W$, $R$ and $n$. There are four cases for $op$ and $W_{n+1}$: pop-pop, push-pop, pop-push or push-push. For each of these cases, we find two sequences from $W(n + 1) \circ (R(m) + op?)$ and $W(n) \circ op \circ (R(m) + W_{n+1}?)$ for which all operations in $R(m)$ return the same results.

- $op = $ pop, $W_{n+1} = $ pop. Then, $W(n+1) \circ op \circ R(m)$ and $W(n) \circ op \circ W_{n+1} \circ R(m)$ satisfy, since $W_{n+1} \circ op$ and $op \circ W_{n+1}$ perform two pop operations.
- $op = $ push$(a)$, $W_{n+1} = $ pop. For the first sequence we take $A = W(n + 1) \circ op \circ R(m)$. Now, we choose the second sequence $B$ from $W(n) \circ op \circ (R(m) + W_{n+1}?)$. Let $W_{n+1}$ pop in $A$ the $x$-th element from the bottom of the stack. We extend $W(n) \circ op$ in $B$ with operations from $R(m)$ until some operation $op'$ tries to pop the $x$-th element from the bottom. Note that all operations $R(m)$ up to $op'$ (not including $op'$) return the same results in $A$ and $B$. If such $op'$ does not exist then we are done. Otherwise, we insert $W_{n+1}$ right before $op'$, i.e., pop this element. Subsequent operations in $R(m)$ are not affected, i.e., results of operations in $R(m)$ are the same in $A$ and $B$.

- $op = \text{pop}$, $W_{n+1} = \text{push}(b)$. This case is symmetric to the previous one.
- $op = \text{push}(a)$, $W_{n+1} = \text{push}(b)$. For the first sequence, we take $A = W(n+1) \circ op \circ R(m)$. Now, we build the second sequence $B$ from $W(n) \circ op \circ (R(m) + W_{n+1}?)$. Let $W_{n+1}$ push in $A$ the $x$-th element from the bottom of the stack. Let us perform $W(n) \circ op$ in $B$ and start performing operations from $R(m)$ until some operation $op'$ pops the $x$-th element (again, this should eventually happen, otherwise a contradiction is established). Note that all operations $R(m)$ up to $op'$ (including $op'$) return the same results in $A$ and $B$. If such $op'$ does not exist then we are done. Otherwise, right after $op'$ we perform $W_{n+1}$, i.e., push the element $b$ in its proper position. Subsequent operations in $R(m)$ are not affected and, thus, the results of all operations in $R(m)$ are the same in $A$ and $B$.

The contradiction implies that stack is not an exact order type.

# 4  Wait-Free Stack Cannot Be Help-Free

In this section, we prove that there does not exist a help-free wait-free implementation of stack in a system with reads, writes, and compare&swaps. We then extend the proof to the case when a system has one more primitive fetch&add.

## 4.1  Help-Free Stacks Using Reads, Writes and Compare&swap

Suppose that there exists such a help-free stack implementation $Q$ using read, write, and compare&swap primitives. We establish a contradiction by presenting a history $h$ in which some operation takes infinitely many steps without completing.

We start with three observations that immediately follow from the definition of linearizability.

**Observation 1** *In any history $h$:*

1. *Once an operation is completed it must be decided before all operations that have not yet started;*
2. *If an operation is not started it cannot be decided before any operation of a different process.*

**Lemma 1 (Transitivity).** *For any linearization function $f$ and finite history $h$, if an operation $op_2$ is completed in $h$, an operation $op_1$ is decided before $op_2$ in $h$ and $op_2$ is decided before an operation $op_3$ in $h$ then $op_1$ is decided before $op_3$ in $h$.*

*Proof.* Suppose that $op_1$ is not decided before $op_3$ in $h$ then there exists a extension $s$ of $h$ for which $op_3 \prec_{f(s)} op_1$. Since $op_2$ is linearized in $f(s)$ and $op_1$ is decided before $op_2$ then $op_1 \prec_{f(s)} op_2$. Together, $op_3 \prec_{f(s)} op_1 \prec_{f(s)} op_2$ contradicting with $op_2$ being decided before $op_3$ in $h$.

**Lemma 2.** *For any linearization function $f$ and finite history $h$, if an operation $op_1$ of a process $p_1$ is decided before an operation $op_2$ of a process $p_2$, then $op_1$ must be decided before any operation $op$ that has not started in $h$.*

*Proof.* Consider $h'$, the extension of $h$, in which $p_2$ runs solo until $op_2$ completes. Such an extension exists, as $Q$ is wait-free. By Observation 1 (1), $op_2$ is decided before $op$ in $h'$, and, consequently, by Transitivity Lemma 1, $op_1$ is decided before $op$ in $h'$.

Since in $h'$, only $p_2$ takes steps starting from $h$, $op_1$ must be decided before $op$ in $h$—otherwise, $h'$ has a prefix $h''$ such that $op_1$ is not decided before $op$ in $h''$ and $op_1$ is decided before $op$ in $h'' \circ p_2$—a contradiction with the assumption that $Q$ is help-free.

Now we build an *infinite* history $h$ in which $p_1$ executes infinitely many failed compare&swap steps, yet it never completes its operation. We assume that $p_1, p_2$ and $p_3$ are assigned the following programs: $p_1$ tries to perform $op_1 = \mathtt{push}(1)$; $p_2$ applies an infinite sequence of operations $\mathtt{push}(2), \mathtt{push}(3), \mathtt{push}(4), \ldots$; and $p_3$ is about to perform an infinite sequence of $\mathtt{pop}()$ operations.

The algorithm for constructing this "contradiction" history is given in Listing 1.1. Initially, $p_1$ invokes $op_1 = \mathtt{push}(1)$ and, concurrently, $p_2$ invokes $op_2 = \mathtt{push}(2)$. Then we interleave steps of $p_1$ and $p_2$ until a *critical* history $h$ is located: $op_1$ is decided before $op_2$ in $h \circ p_1$ and $op_2$ is decided before $op_1$ in $h \circ p_2$. We let $p_2$ and $p_1$ take the next step and, then, run $op_2$ after $h \circ p_2 \circ p_1$ until it completes. We will show that $op_1$ cannot complete and that we can reiterate the construction by allowing $p_2$ to invoke concurrent operations $\mathtt{push}(3), \mathtt{push}(4)$, etc. In the resulting infinite history, $p_1$ takes infinitely many steps without completing $op_1$.

```
1  h ← ε
2  op1 ← push(1)
3  id2 ← 2
4  while true:                 // outer loop
5     op2 ← push(id2)
6     while true:              // inner loop
7        if op1 is not decided before op2 in h ∘ p1:
8           h ← h ∘ p1
9           continue
10       if op2 is not decided before op1 in h ∘ p2:
11          h ← h ∘ p2
12          continue
13       break
14    h ← h ∘ p2
15    h ← h ∘ p1
16    while op2 is not completed:
17       h ← h ∘ p2
18    id2 ← id2 + 1
```

**Listing 1.1.** Constructing the history for the proof of Theorem 2

To ensure that at each iteration $op_1$ is not completed, we show that, at the start of each iteration of the outer loop (Line 6), the constructed history satisfies the following two invariants:

- $op_1$ is not decided before $op_2$ or before any operation of $p_3$;
- the operations of $p_2$ prior to $op_2$ are decided before $op_1$.

At the first iteration, the invariants trivially hold, since neither $op_1$ nor $op_2$ is started.

**Observation 2.** *The order between $op_1$ and $op_2$ cannot be decided during (and right after) the inner loop (Lines 6–13).*

**Lemma 3.** *During (and right after) the execution of the inner loop (Lines 6–13) $op_1$ and $op_2$ cannot be decided before any operation of $p_3$.*

*Proof.* Suppose that during an execution of the inner loop $op_1$ or $op_2$ is decided before some operation of $p_3$.

Before entering the inner loop, neither $op_1$ nor $op_2$ is decided before any operation of $p_3$: $op_1$ is not decided because of the first invariant, while $op_2$ is not started (Observation 1 (2)). Thus, at least one step is performed by $p_1$ or $p_2$ during the execution of the inner loop.

Let us execute the inner loop until the first point in time when $op_1$ or $op_2$ is decided before an operation of $p_3$. Let this history be $h$. Note, that because $Q$ is help-free only one of $op_1$ and $op_2$ is decided before an operation of $p_3$ in $h$. Suppose, that $op_1$ is decided before some $op_3$ of $p_3$, while $op_2$ is not decided before any operation of $p_3$. (The case when $op_2$ is decided before some $op_3$ is symmetric).

Now, $p_3$ runs **pop** operations until it completes operation $op_3$ and then, further, until the first **pop** operation returns $\perp$, i.e., the stack becomes empty. Let the resulting extension of $h$ be $h'$.

Recall that $op_2$ is not decided before any operation of $p_3$ in $h$ and, since $Q$ is help-free and only $p_3$ takes steps after $h$, $op_2$ cannot be decided before any operation of $p_3$ in $h'$. Hence, none of the completed operations of $p_3$ can return $id_2$, the argument of $op_2$, due to the fact that all **push** operations have different arguments. Since the operations of $p_3$ empty the stack, $op_2$ has to linearize after them, making $op_3$ to be decided before $op_2$ in $h'$. By Transitivity Lemma 1, $op_1$ is decided before $op_2$ in $h'$. Finally, since $Q$ is help-free and only $p_3$ takes steps after $h$ $op_1$ has to be decided before $op_2$ in $h$, contradicting Observation 2.

**Lemma 4.** *$op_1$ and $op_2$ cannot be completed after the inner loop (Lines 6–13).*

*Proof.* Suppose the contrary. By Observation 1 (1), $op_1$ has to be decided before all operations of $p_3$, contradicting Lemma 3.

**Lemma 5.** *The execution of the inner loop (Lines 6–13) is finite.*

*Proof.* Suppose that the execution is infinite. By Lemma 4, neither of $op_1$ and $op_2$ is completed in $h$. Thus, in our infinite execution either $op_1$ or $op_2$ takes infinite number of steps, contradicting wait-freedom of $Q$.

**Lemma 6.** *Just before Line 14 the following holds:*

1. *The next primitive step by $p_1$ and $p_2$ is to the same memory location.*
2. *The next primitive step by $p_1$ and $p_2$ is a compare&swap.*
3. *The expected value of the compare&swap steps of $p_1$ and $p_2$ is the value that appears in the designated address.*
4. *The new values of the compare&swap steps of $p_1$ and $p_2$ are different from the expected value.*

*Proof.* Suppose that the next primitive steps by $p_1$ and $p_2$ are to different locations. Consider two histories: $h' = h \circ p_1 \circ p_2 \circ \text{complete } op_1 \circ \text{complete } op_2$ and $h'' = h \circ p_2 \circ p_1 \circ \text{complete } op_1 \circ \text{complete } op_2$. Let us look at the first two $\text{pop}()$ operations by $p_3$. Executed after $h'$ they have to return $id_2$ then 1, since $op_1$ is decided before $op_2$ in $h'$ and both of them are completed. While executed after $h''$ they have to return 1 then $id_2$. But the local states of $p_3$ and shared memory states after $h'$ and $h''$ are identical and, thus, two $\text{pops}$ of $p_3$ must return the same values—a contradiction. The same argument will apply when both steps by $p_1$ and $p_2$ are reads.

Suppose that the next operation of $p_1$ is a write. (The case when the next operation of $p_2$ is write is symmetric) Consider two histories: $h' = h \circ p_2 \circ p_1 \circ \text{complete } op_1$ and $h'' = h \circ p_1 \circ \text{complete } op_1$. Let the process $p_1$ perform two $\text{pop}()$ operations ($op_1'$ and $op_1''$) and $p_2$ complete its operation after $h'$: $op_1'$ and $op_1''$ have to return 1 and $id_2$, correspondingly, since $op_1$ and $op_2$ are completed and $op_2$ is decided before $op_1$ in $h'$. Again, since the local states of $p_1$ and the shared memory states after $h'$ and $h''$ are identical, $op_1'$ and $op_1''$ performed by $p_1$ after $h''$ must return 1 and $id_2$. Hence, $op_2$ has to be decided before $op_1''$ in $\tilde{h} = h'' \circ \text{perform } op_1' \circ \text{perform } op_1''$ and, by Lemma 2, $op_2$ has to be decided before any operation of $p_3$ in $\tilde{h}$. Since only $p_1$ performs steps after $h$ in $\tilde{h}$ and $Q$ is help-free, $op_2$ has to be decided before any operation of $p_3$ at $h$, contradicting Lemma 3. Thus, both primitives have to be compare&swap.

By the same argument both compare&swap steps by $p_1$ and $p_2$ have the expected value that is equal to the current value in the designated memory location, and the new value is different from the expected. If it does not hold, either the local states of $p_1$ and the shared memory states after $h \circ p_1$ and $h \circ p_2 \circ p_1$ are identical or the local state of $p_2$ and the shared memory states after $h \circ p_2$ and $h \circ p_1 \circ p_2$ are identical.

**Observation 3.** *The primitive step of $p_2$ in Line 14 is a successful compare&swap, and the primitive step of $p_1$ in Line 15 is a failed compare&swap.*

**Observation 4.** *Immediately after Line 14 $op_2$ is decided before $op_1$.*

**Lemma 7.** *Immediately after Line 15 the order between $op_1$ and any operation of $p_3$ is not decided.*

*Proof.* By Lemma 3, the order between $op_1$ and any operation of $p_3$ is not decided before Line 14. Since $Q$ is help-free, the steps by $p_2$ cannot fix the order between

$op_1$ and any operation of $p_3$. Thus, the only step that can fix the order of $op_1$ and some operation of $p_3$ is a step by $p_1$ at Line 15, i.e., a failed compare&swap.

Suppose that $op_1$ is decided before some operation $op'_3$ of $p_3$ after Line 15. Let $h$ be the history right before Line 14. Consider two histories $h' = h \circ p_2 \circ p_1$ and $h'' = h \circ p_2$. Let $p_3$ solo run pop operations after $h'$ until it completes operation $op'_3$ and then, further, until pop operation returns $\perp$, i.e., the stack is empty. Since $op_1$ is decided before $op'_3$, some completed operation $op''_3$ of $p_3$ has to return 1: if we now complete $op_1$ it should be linearized before $op'_3$. Now, let $p_3$ to perform after $h''$ the same number of operations as it did after $h'$. Since the local states of $p_3$ and the shared memory states after $h'$ and $h''$ are identical ($p_1$ makes the failed compare&swap), $op''_3$ after $h''$ has to return 1 as after $h'$. Thus, $op_1$ is decided before $op''_3$ in $h''$. Since $Q$ is help-free and $p_1$ does not take steps after $h$ in $h''$, $op_1$ has to be decided before $op''_3$ before Line 14, contradicting Lemma 3.

**Lemma 8.** *At the end of the outer loop (Line 18) the order between $op_1$ and next $op_2 = push(id_2 + 1)$ is not yet decided.*

*Proof.* The operation $op_2$ is not started, thus, it cannot be decided before $op_1$ by Observation 1 (2).

Suppose that $op_1$ is decided before $op_2$. By Lemma 2 $op_1$ has to be decided before all operations of $p_3$, contradicting Lemma 7.

Thus after this iteration of the loop the two invariants hold (Observation 4 and Lemmas 7 and 8), and $p_1$ took at least one primitive step.

This way we build a history in which $p_1$ takes infinitely many steps, but $op_1$ is never completed. This contradicts the assumption that $Q$ is wait-free.

**Theorem 2.** *In a system with at least three processes and primitives read, write and compare&swap there does not exist a wait-free and help-free stack implementation.*

## 4.2 Adding Fetch&Add

Now, suppose that the implementation is allowed to additionally use fetch&add primitives. We prove that there is no wait-free and help-free stack implementation in a system with at least *four* processes.

Again, by contradiction, suppose that such an implementation $Q$ exists. We build an infinite history $h$ in which either $p_1$ or $p_2$ executes infinitely many failed compare&swap steps, yet it never completes its operation, contradicting wait-freedom. In $h$, processes $p_1$, $p_2$, $p_3$ and $p_4$ follow the following programs: for $1 \leq i \leq 2$, $p_i$ tries to perform $op_i = push(i)$; $p_3$ applies an infinite sequence of operations $push(3), push(4), push(5), \ldots$; and $p_4$ is about to perform an infinite sequence of pop() operations. The algorithm for constructing this "contradiction" history is given in Listing 1.2.

```
1  h ← ε
2  for i in 1..2:
3      op_i ← push(i)
4  id_3 ← 3
5  while true:                // outer loop
6      op_3 ← push(id_3)
7      while true:            // inner loop
8          moved ← False
9          for i in 1..3:
10             if op_i is not decided before any op_j in h ∘ p_i:
11                 h ← h ∘ p_i
12                 moved ← True
13         if not moved:
14             break
15
16     h ← h ∘ p_3
17     // let p_k be the process whose next primitive is compare&swap
18     h ← h ∘ p_k
19     while op_3 is not completed:
20         h ← h ∘ p_3
21     id_3 ← id_3 + 1
```

**Listing 1.2.** Constructing the history for the proof of Theorem 3

Similar to the proof of Theorem 2, we show that the following three invariants hold at the beginning of each iteration of the outer loop (Line 6):

– the order between any two operations among $op_1$, $op_2$ and $op_3$ is not decided;
– $op_1$ and $op_2$ are not decided before any operation of $p_4$;
– all the operations of $p_3$ prior to $op_3$ are decided before $op_1$ and $op_2$.

At the beginning of the first iteration, the invariants hold trivially, since none of $op_i$ is started.

**Observation 5.** *The order between $op_i$ and $op_j$ for $1 \leq i \neq j \leq 3$ cannot be decided during (and right after) the inner loop (Lines 7–14).*

*Proof.* From the first invariant, $op_i$ cannot be decided before $op_j$ prior to the inner loop (Lines 7–14). Since $Q$ is help-free, during the inner loop $op_i$ can become decided before $op_j$ only after a step by $p_i$ which is impossible due to the check in Line 10.

**Lemma 9.** *During (and right after) an execution of the inner loop (Lines 7–14) $op_1$, $op_2$ and $op_3$ cannot be decided before any operation of $p_4$.*

*Proof.* Suppose that during an execution of the inner loop $op_1$, $op_2$ or $op_3$ is decided before some operation of $p_4$.

At the beginning of the loop, none of $op_1$, $op_2$ and $op_3$ is decided before any operation of $p_4$: $op_1$ and $op_2$ are not decided because of the second invariant, while $op_3$ is not yet started. Suppose that during the execution of the inner loop some $op_i$ becomes decided before some operations of $p_4$.

Let us look at the execution and find the first point in time when some $op_k$ of $p_k$ is decided before some operation $op_4$ of $p_4$. Using the same argument as in the proof of Lemma 3, we can show that $op_k$ has to be decided before any other $op_j$ contradicting Observation 5: we let $p_4$ run until the operation $op_4$ is completed and, further, while stack is not empty; $op_4$ becomes decided before $op_j$; by Transitivity Lemma 1, $op_k$ is decided before $op_j$.

The proofs of the following two lemmas are identical to those of Lemmas 4 and 5.

**Lemma 10.** *For each $i$, $1 \leq i \leq 3$, $op_i$ cannot be completed after the inner loop (Lines 7–14).*

**Lemma 11.** *The execution of the inner loop (Lines 7–14) is finite.*

**Lemma 12.** *For all $i, j$, $1 \leq i \neq j \leq 3$, $op_i$ is decided before $op_j$ in $h \circ p_i$.*

*Proof.* Consider an operation of process $i$. At the end of the inner loop $op_i$ should be decided before some $op_k$ in $h \circ p_i$, otherwise, $p_i$ can make at least one more step during the inner loop. Thus, by Lemma 2 $op_i$ should be decided before $op_4$, the first operation of $p_4$. Let $p_4$ run **pop** operations after $h \circ p_i$ until one of them returns $\perp$, i.e., the stack is empty. Let this history be $h'$.

By Lemma 9, $op_j$ is not decided before any operation of $p_4$ in $h$. Since $Q$ is help-free and only $p_i$ and $p_4$ takes steps in $h'$ after $h$, $op_j$ cannot be decided before any operation of $p_4$ in $h'$, and, consequently, operations of $p_4$ cannot pop an argument of $op_j$. Since the operations of $p_4$ empty the stack, $op_j$ must be linearized after them. Thus, $op_4$ is decided before $op_j$ in $h'$. By Transitivity Lemma 1, $op_i$ is decided before $op_j$ in $h'$. Finally, since $Q$ is help-free and only $p_4$ takes steps in $h'$ after $h \circ p_i$, $op_i$ is decided before $op_j$ in $h \circ p_i$.

**Lemma 13.** *Immediately before Line 16 the following holds:*

1. *The next primitive step by $p_i$ for $1 \leq i \leq 3$ is to the same memory location.*
2. *The next primitive step by $p_i$ for $1 \leq i \leq 3$ is fetch&add with a non-zero argument or compare&swap for which the expected value is the value that appears in the designated location and the new value is different from the expected one.*

*Proof.* Suppose that for some pair $p_i$ and $p_j$ the next steps are to different memory locations. We consider two histories $h' = h \circ p_i \circ p_j \circ$ complete $op_i \circ$ complete $op_j$ and $h'' = h \circ p_j \circ p_i \circ$ complete $op_i \circ$ complete $op_j$. By Lemma 12, after $h'$, the two subsequent **pop** operations by $p_4$ should return first the argument of $op_j$ and then the argument of $op_i$, while after $h''$ they should return the two values in the opposite order. This is impossible, since the local states of $p_4$ and the shared memory states after $h'$ and $h''$ are identical. The same argument will apply if the next steps of some pair of processes are read primitives.

Suppose that the next primitive step of some $p_i$ is a write. We take any other process $p_j$ and build two histories: $h' = h \circ p_j \circ p_i \circ$ complete $op_i$ and $h'' =$

$h \circ p_i \circ$ complete $op_i$. As in the proof of Lemma 6, $p_i$ performs two pop() operations ($op'_i$ and $op''_i$) and $p_j$ completes its operation after $h'$: by Lemmas 1 and 12 $op'_i$ and $op''_i$ have to return the argument of $op_i$ and the argument of $op_j$, respectively. The local states of $p_i$ and the shared memory states after $h'$ and $h''$ are identical, thus, $op'_i$ and $op''_i$ after $h''$ should also return the arguments of $op_i$ and $op_j$. Hence, $op_j$ has to be decided before $op''_i$ in $\tilde{h} = h'' \circ$ perform $op'_i \circ$ perform $op''_i$. By Lemma 2, $op_j$ is decided before any operation of $p_4$ in $\tilde{h}$. And, finally, since $Q$ is help-free and $p_j$ does not take steps in $\tilde{h}$ after $h$, $op_j$ has to be decided before any operation of $p_4$ in $h$, contradicting Lemma 9.

A similar argument applies to the case when the next primitive step of some $p_i$ is fetch&add with argument zero, or compare&swap which expected value differs from the value in the designated location or the new value is equal to the expected. We take any other process $p_j$ ($1 \leq j \leq 3$) and build two histories $h' = h \circ p_i \circ p_j \circ$ complete $p_j$ and $h'' = h \circ p_j \circ$ complete $p_j$. The proof for the previous case applies except that now the roles of $p_i$ and $p_j$ are swapped.

**Lemma 14.** *At most one out of $p_1$ and $p_2$ can have fetch&add as their next primitive step.*

*Proof.* Suppose that $p_1$ and $p_2$ have fetch&add as their next primitive step. Consider two histories $h' = h \circ p_1 \circ p_2$ and $h'' = h \circ p_2 \circ p_1$. From Lemma 12 $op_1$ is decided before $op_2$ in $h'$, thus, by Lemma 2 $op_1$ is decided before the first operation $op_4$ of $p_4$. After $h'$ $p_4$ performs $k'$ pop operations until one of them returns $\bot$, i.e., the stack is empty. One pop has to return 1, because if we now complete $op_1$ it has to be linearized before $op_4$. The same with $h''$: $p_4$ performs $k''$ pops until one of them returns $\bot$, and one of these pop's return 2. Since the local states of $p_4$ and the shared memory states after $h'$ and $h''$ are the same: two pop operations $pop_1()$ and $pop_2()$ of $k'(= k'')$ operations of $p_4$ after $h'$ and $h''$ return 1 and 2.

Now, we show that $op_1$ and $op_2$ are decided before $op_3$ in $h'$. The same can be shown for $h''$. Consider a history $\tilde{h}$: $h'$ continued with $k'$ pop operations by $p_4$. By Lemma 12 $op_1$ is decided before $op_3$ in $h'$. From Lemma 9 and two facts that $Q$ is help-free and $op_3$ does not make any steps after $h$ in $\tilde{h}$, it follows that $op_3$ cannot be decided before any operation of $p_4$ in $\tilde{h}$ and, consequently, the operations of $p_4$ cannot pop an argument of $op_3$. Since $k'$ pops of $op_4$ empty the stack, $op_3$ has to linearize after them, making operation $pop_2()$ to be decided before $op_3$. Since $pop_2()$ returns 2 it has to be decided after $op_2$. By Transitivity Lemma 1, $op_2$ is decided before $op_3$ in $\tilde{h}$. $Q$ is help-free and only $p_4$ takes steps after $h'$, thus, $op_2$ is decided before $op_3$ in $h'$.

Now consider two histories $h' \circ$ complete $op_3$ and $h'' \circ$ complete $op_3$. In both of these histories, $op_1$ and $op_2$ are decided before $op_3$. After the first history let $p_4$ perform three pop operations and $p_1$ and $p_2$ complete push(1) and push(2): the three pops return $id_3$, 2 and 1, respectively. Analougously, after the second history three pop return $id_3$, 1 and 2. This is impossible, since the local states of $p_4$ and the memory states after these two histories are identical.

**Observation 6.** *From the previous lemma we know that the next primitive step of at least one process $p_1$ or $p_2$ is compare&swap. Let it be process $p_k$. By algorithm, $p_3$ takes a step at Line 16 changing the memory location either by fetch&add or by a successful compare&swap, thus, the next step of $p_k$ at Line 18 should be a failed compare&swap.*

**Observation 7.** *Immediately after Line 16, $op_3$ is decided before $op_1$ and $op_2$.*

**Lemma 15.** *Immediately after Line 18, $op_1$ and $op_2$ are not decided before any operation of $p_4$.*

*Proof.* We prove the claim for $op_1$, the case of $op_2$ is similar.

If $p_2$ took a step at Line 18, then by Lemma 9 and the fact that the steps by $p_2$ or $p_3$ cannot fix the order between $op_1$ and any operation of $p_4$ due to help-freedom, $op_1$ is not decided before any operation of $p_4$.

If $p_1$ took a step at Line 18, then by Lemma 9 and the fact that the steps by $p_3$ cannot fix the order between $op_1$ and any operation of $p_4$ due to help-freedom, the only step that could fix the order is a step by $p_1$ at Line 18, i.e., a failed compare&swap. Suppose that $op_1$ is decided before some $op'_4$ of $p_4$ after Line 18. We consider two histories $h' = h \circ p_3 \circ p_1$ and $h'' = h \circ p_3$. Let $p_4$ run solo after $h'$ until it completes $op'_4$, and then further until some **pop** returns $\bot$, i.e., the stack becomes empty. Since $op_1$ is decided before $op'_4$, some completed operation $op''_4$ of $p_4$ has to return 1: if we now complete $op_1$ it has to be linearized before $op'_4$. Now, let $p_4$ to run the same number of **pop** operations after $h''$. Since the local states of $p_4$ and the shared memory states after $h'$ and $h''$ are identical, $op''_4$ returns 1. Thus, $op_1$ is decided before $op''_4$ in $h''$. As $Q$ is help-free and $p_1$ does not take steps after $h$ in $h''$, $op_1$ has to be decided before $op''_4$ in $h$, contradicting Lemma 9.

**Lemma 16.** *At the end of the outer loop (Line 21), the order between any two operations among $op_1$, $op_2$ and the next $op_3 = push(id_3 + 1)$ is not yet decided.*

*Proof.* The operation $op_3$ is not yet started, thus, it cannot be decided before $op_i$, $i = 1, 2$, by Observation 1 (2).

Suppose that $op_i$, $i = 1, 2$, is decided before $op_j$, then by Lemma 2 $op_i$ has to be decided before all operations of $p_4$, contradicting Lemma 15.

We started with three invariants that hold before any iteration of the loop. By Observation 7 and Lemmas 15 and 16 the invariants hold after the iteration, and at least one of $p_1$ and $p_2$ made at least one primitive step.

This way we build a history in which one of $op_1$ and $op_2$ never completes its operation, even though it takes infinitely many steps. This contradicts the assumption that $Q$ is wait-free.

**Theorem 3.** *In a system with at least four processes and primitives read, write, compare&swap and fetch&add, there does not exist a wait-free and help-free stack implementation.*

## 5    Related Work

Helping is often observed in wait-free (e.g., [6,7,13,14]) and lock-free implementations (e.g., [3,9,11,12]): operations of a slow or crashed process may be finished by other processes. Typically, to benefit from helping, an operation should register a *descriptor* (either in a dedicated "announce" array or attached in the data items) that can be used by concurrent processes to help completing it.

We are aware of three alternative definitions of helping: (1) *linearization-based* by Censor-Hillel et al. [5] considered in this paper, (2) *valency-based* by Attiya et al. [4] and (3) *universal* by Attiya et al. [4].

Valency-based helping [4] captures helping through the values returned by the operations, which makes it quite restrictive. In particular, for stack, the definition cannot capture helping relation between two **push** operations. They distinguish *trivial* and *non-trivial* helping: for non-trivial helping, the operation that is being helped should return a data-structure-specific *non-trivial* (e.g., non-empty for stacks and queues) value. It is shown in [4] that any wait-free implementation of queue has non-trivial helping, while there exists a wait-free implementation of stack without non-trivial helping. This is an interesting result, given notorious attempts of showing that queue is in Common2 [2], i.e., that they can be implemented using reads, writes and 2-consensus objects, while stack has been shown to be in Common2 [1].

Attiya et al. [4] also introduce a very strong notion of helping—*universal helping*—which essentially boils down to requiring that every invoked operation eventually takes effect. This property is typically satisfied in universal constructions parameterized with object types. But most algorithms that involve helping in a more conventional (weaker) sense do not meet it, which makes the use of universal helping very limited.

Linearization-based helping [5] considered in this paper is based on the order between two operations in a possible linearization. Compared to valency-based definitions, this notion of helping operates on the linearization order and, thus, can be applied to all operations, not only to those that return (non-trivial) values. By relating "helping" to fixing positions in the linearization, this definition appears to be more intuitive: one process helps another make a "progress", i.e., linearize earlier. Censor-Hillel et al. [5] also introduce two classes of data types: exact order types (queue as an example) and global view types (snapshot and counter as examples). They showed that no wait-free implementation of data types from these two classes can be help-free. By assuming stack to be exact order, they deduced that this kind of helping is required for wait-free stack implementations. In this paper, we show that stack is in fact not an exact order type, and give a direct proof of their claim.

## 6    Concluding Remarks

In this paper, we give a direct proof that any wait-free implementation of stack in a system with read, write, comare&swap and fetch&add primitives is subject to linearization-based helping. This corrects a mistake in the indirect proof via exact order types in [5].

Let us come back to the original intuition of *helping* as a process performing work on behalf of other processes. One may say that linearization-based helping introduced by Censor-Hillel et al. and used in our paper does not adequately capture this intuition. For example, by examining the wait-free stack implementation by Afek et al. [1], we find out that none of the processes *explicitly* performs work for the others: to perform pop() a process goes down the stack from the current top until it reaches some value or the bottom of the stack; while to perform push($x$) a process simply increments the top of the stack and deposits $x$ there. But we just showed that any wait-free stack implementation has linearization-based helping, and indeed this algorithm has it. So we might think that valency-based helping is superior to linearization-based one, since the algorithm by Afek et al. does not have *non-trivial* valency-based helping. Nevertheless, the aforementioned algorithm has *trivial* valency-based helping, and, thus, the (quite unnatural) distinction between trivial and non-trivial helping seems to be chosen specifically to allow the algorithm by Afek et al. to be help-free.

A very interesting challenge is therefore to find a definition of linearization-based helping that would naturally reflect help-freedom of the algorithm by Afek et al., while queue does not have a wait-free and help-free implementation.

# References

1. Afek, Y., Gafni, E., Morrison, A.: Common2 extended to stacks and unbounded concurrency. Distrib. Comput. **20**(4), 239–252 (2007)
2. Afek, Y., Weisberger, E., Weisman, H.: A completeness theorem for a class of synchronization objects. In: PODC, pp. 159–170 (1993)
3. Arbel-Raviv, M., Brown, T.: Reuse, don't recycle: transforming lock-free algorithms that throw away descriptors. In: DISC, vol. 91, pp. 4:1–4:16 (2017)
4. Attiya, H., Castañeda, A., Hendler, D.: Nontrivial and universal helping for wait-free queues and stacks. In: OPODIS, vol. 46 (2016)
5. Censor-Hillel, K., Petrank, E., Timnat, S.: Help! In: PODC, pp. 241–250 (2015)
6. Fatourou, P., Kallimanis, N.D.: A highly-efficient wait-free universal construction. In: SPAA, pp. 325–334. ACM (2011)
7. Feldman, S., Laborde, P., Dechev, D.: A wait-free multi-word compare-and-swap operation. IJPP **43**(4), 572–596 (2015)
8. Herlihy, M.: Wait-free synchronization. ACM Trans. Program. Lang. Syst. **13**(1), 123–149 (1991)
9. Howley, S.V., Jones, J.: A non-blocking internal binary search tree. In: SPAA, pp. 161–171. ACM (2012)
10. Lynch, N.A.: Distributed Algorithms. Morgan Kaufmann, Burlington (1996)
11. Michael, M.M.: High performance dynamic lock-free hash tables and list-based sets. In: SPAA, pp. 73–82. ACM (2002)
12. Natarajan, A., Mittal, N.: Fast concurrent lock-free binary search trees. In: ACM SIGPLAN Notices, vol. 49, pp. 317–328. ACM (2014)
13. Peng, Y., Hao, Z.: FA-Stack: a fast array-based stack with wait-free progress guarantee. IEEE Trans. Parallel Distrib. Syst. (4), 843–857 (2018)
14. Timnat, S., Braginsky, A., Kogan, A., Petrank, E.: Wait-free linked-lists. In: Baldoni, R., Flocchini, P., Binoy, R. (eds.) OPODIS 2012. LNCS, vol. 7702, pp. 330–344. Springer, Heidelberg (2012). https://doi.org/10.1007/978-3-642-35476-2_23

# Anonymity in Distributed Read/Write Systems: An Introductory Survey

Michel Raynal[1,2(✉)] and Jiannong Cao[2]

[1] Institut Universitaire de France and Univ Rennes, IRISA CNRS INRIA,
Rennes, France
`raynal@irisa.fr`
[2] Department of Computing, Polytechnic University, Hung Hom, Hong Kong
`csjcao@comp.polyu.edu.hk`

**Abstract.** This paper is an algorithmic introduction to anonymity in asynchronous systems where processes communicate by reading and writing atomic read/write registers. Two types of anonymity are investigated: *process-anonymity* and *memory-anonymity*. Process-anonymity is when the processes cannot be distinguished the ones from the others (among other features, they do not have identifiers). Memory-anonymity is when the same memory locations can have different names at different processes (e.g., the location name $A$ used by process $p_i$ and the location name $B$ used by another process $p_j$ can correspond to the very same memory location $X$, and similarly for the names $B$ at $p_i$ and $A$ at $p_j$ which correspond to the same memory location $Y \neq X$). The paper shows how algorithms can cope with the uncertainty created by these two types of anonymity. To this end, taking examples from the literature, it presents anonymity-tolerant implementations of several concurrent objects, such as snapshot, consensus, and lock, each implementation satisfying a well-defined progress condition (obstruction-freedom, non-blocking, or wait-freedom). This paper must be considered as a short example-driven introductory tutorial on anonymous asynchronous read/write systems.

**Keywords:** Agreement problem · Anonymity
Anonymous processes · Anonymous shared memory
Consensus · Impossibility · Linearization point · Lower bound
Mutual exclusindon · Non-blocking · Obstruction-freedom
Progress condition · Snapshot · Wait-freedom

## 1 Introduction

### 1.1 Concurrent Objects and Their Progress Conditions

*Concurrent Objects.* An object type is defined by a finite set of operations and a specification describing the correct behaviors of the objects of that type. The internal representation of an object is hidden to the processes (and several

© Springer Nature Switzerland AG 2019
A. Podelski and F. Taïani (Eds.): NETYS 2018, LNCS 11028, pp. 122–140, 2019.
https://doi.org/10.1007/978-3-030-05529-5_9

objects of the same type can have different implementations). The only way for a process to access an object of a given type is by invoking one of its operations.

A *concurrent object* is an object that can be accessed by several processes (concurrently or not). The specification of such an object can be sequential or not. *Sequential* means that all correct behaviors of the object can be described with sequences (traces) of invocations of its operations. We consider such objects in the following. (Let us nevertheless remark that not all concurrent objects can be defined from sequential specifications. As an example, this is the case of a rendezvous object.)

*Progress Conditions.* Given an object $O$ and an invocation of an operation on $O$ by a process, the weakest non-trivial progress condition (which is always implicitly assumed) states that, if the process does not crash and its invocation occurs in a concurrency-free context (no other process has a pending invocation on $O$), then the invocation terminates.

Two progress conditions for object operations have been considered in failure-free systems, namely *deadlock-freedom* (DF), and *starvation-freedom* (SF). The first states that, if one or more processes concurrently invoke operations on an object, at least one process terminates its operation. The second one is *starvation-freedom*, which states that any invocation of an operation terminates. (Let us notice that, if we consider an object as a service offered to clients, starvation-freedom is client-oriented, while deadlock-freedom is service-oriented.) A classical way to implement a concurrent object in a failure-free system is to use locks. A lock allows the operations on an object to be executed sequentially, thereby eliminating concurrency.

As far as failure-prone systems are concerned (where a failure is a process crash), locks can no longer be used [29,30]. This is due to the fact that, if a process obtains a lock and crashes before releasing it, no other process can access the object. Hence, failure-prone systems requires the statement of progress conditions suited to the fact that, in the presence of asynchrony, no process can distinguish if another process crashed or is only very slow. Three progress conditions have been proposed to cope with asynchrony and process crashes. They are presented below in increasing order (from the weaker to the stronger).

- *Obstruction-freedom* (OB) was introduced in [20]. It requires that, if a process $p$ invokes an operation on an object $O$, and all other processes that have pending operations on $O$ pause during a long enough period, then process $p$ terminates its operation.

  (Let us notice that, at the implementation level, nothing prevents the processes that have pending operations to have modified parts of the internal representation of the object $O$ before pausing.)
- *Non-blocking* (NB) was introduced in [22]. It requires that, if several processes have concurrent invocations on an object $O$, and one of them does not crash, then one of these invocations terminates.
- *Wait-freedom* (WF) was introduced in [18]. It is the strongest progress condition. It requires that, if a process invokes an operation on an object $O$

and does not crash, it terminates its operation. This means that operation termination is guaranteed if the invoking process does not crash, whatever the behavior of the other processes. (Let us notice that, in some settings, obstruction-free algorithms are practically wait-free [13]).

Let us notice that, none of these progress conditions prevents processes that have pending operations from accessing and modifying parts of the internal representation of the object $O$. (Other "hybrid" progress conditions have been investigated in [24,31].)

The definition of the obstruction-freedom and non-blocking progress conditions involves the concurrency pattern in which operations are invoked. This is no longer the case for wait-freedom. Let us also observe that, while it has initially been defined in the context of failure-prone systems, obstruction-freedom is meaningful in failure-free systems.

## 1.2   Anonymous Systems

*Anonymous Processes.* For privacy reasons, some applications must hide the identities of the processes they involve. On another side, some applications (e.g., sensor networks) are made up of tiny computing entities that have no identifiers. These applications define the *process-anonymous* model, which is characterized by the fact there is no way for a process to distinguish any two other processes $p$ and $q$. In such a model, not only the processes have no identity, but they have the same code and the same initialization of their local variables (otherwise, some processes could be distinguished from the others).

Process-anonymous failure-free shared memory systems have been studied in [5], where is presented a characterization of problems solvable despite process-anonymity, but where each process knows the number of processes $n$. Relations between the broadcast communication abstraction and reliable process-anonymous shared memory systems have been studied in [4].

Anonymous failure-prone shared-memory systems have been studied in [16], where is presented an answer to the question "What can be deterministically implemented in the process-anonymous crash-prone model?" (deterministically means here that randomized algorithms cannot be used).

Process-anonymous systems has been studied since 1980 in the context of message-passing systems in [3], where are established several impossibility results in process-anonymous systems (e.g., the impossibility to deterministically elect a leader). Characterizations of problems that can be solved in asynchronous reliable message-passing, despite process anonymity, can be found in [6,34]. Failure detectors suited to crash-prone asynchronous process-anonymous systems have been introduced and investigated in [7,8].

*Notations and Assumptions.* The following notations and assumptions are used in the present article.

- The system is composed of $n$ processes $p_1$, ..., $p_n$. When considering process $p_i$, the integer $i$ is its index, and no two processes have the same index. If the processes are anonymous, the indexes are not known by the processes; they can be used only by an external observer in order to distinguish distinct processes.

Moreover, as we will see in the algorithms that are presented, some of them assume $n$ is known by the processes (i.e., appear in their code), while other algorithms do not.

- The shared variables are seen as a single array of read/write memory locations denoted with uppercase letters, namely $SM[1..m]$ if there are $m$ registers.

  The variables local to a process $p_i$ are denoted with lowercase letters, the corresponding identifiers being subscripted by the index $i$.

- As soon as the processes are anonymous, it is not possible to associate a subset of read/write registers to a given process so that they can be written only by this process. Hence, when considering process-anonymous systems, all atomic read/write registers are multi-writer/multi-reader (MWMR) registers.

*Anonymous memory* systems have been implicitly used in some works in the early eighties (e.g., [28]), but the notion of *memory-anonymity* has been explicitly defined and investigated as a concept in [32]. More precisely, this paper considers the case where "there is no a priori agreement between processes on the names of shared memory locations". Considering a shared memory defined as an array $SM[1..m]$ of memory locations, memory-anonymity means that, while the same location identifier $SM[x]$ always denotes the same memory location for a process $p_i$, it does not necessarily denote the same memory location for two different processes $p_i$ and $p_j$.

An example of memory-anonymous configuration is depicted in the table that appears below. The shared memory is an is an array of three atomic read/write registers denoted $SM[1..3]$ from an external global observer point of view. The first line (and similarly for the other lines) states that the location denoted $SM[1]$ from the global observer point of view, is known as $SM[2]$ by process $p_i$, and as $SM[3]$ by process $p_j$. Of course, no process knows this table.

| Names for the global observer | Local names for process $p_i$ | Local names for process $p_j$ |
| --- | --- | --- |
| $SM[1]$ | $SM[2]$ | $SM[3]$ |
| $SM[2]$ | $SM[3]$ | $SM[1]$ |
| $SM[3]$ | $SM[1]$ | $SM[2]$ |

## 1.3   Spirit, Content, and Roadmap of the Article

First lectures on sequential algorithms usually start with algorithms solving basic problems (such as sorting, simple graph problems, text analysis) and algorithms implementing simple data structures such stacks, queues, and trees. The aim is to give students basic notions and principles on what is called *algorithmic thinking* (or *computational thinking*) [17, 26, 33].

The goal of this paper is similar. Assuming readers know basic synchronization notions, concepts, and algorithms, its first aim is to give them an intuition of the difficulties generated by process-anonymity and memory-anonymity. A second aim is to present them a few example-based principles and techniques which can help them better understand which progress condition must be considered when one has to address process-anonymity or memory-anonymity.

As literature books, which presents "selected pieces" related to a novelist, a given period, or a thematic area, to attain its goal, this paper presents a few selected algorithms related to anonymous systems. More specifically, it presents algorithms implementing basic objects encountered in a lot of concurrent applications, namely, a snapshot object, a consensus object, and a lock (mutex) object. Each of these algorithms considers a type of anonymity (process-anonymity or memory-anonymity), and some of them tolerates any number of process crash failures.

As already said, all these algorithms presented in this article consider the basic asynchronous distributed read/write model. *Asynchronous* means that each process proceeds to its own speed, which can vary with time and remains always unknown to the other processes. *Read/write* means that the processes can communicate only by reading and writing atomic registers. Moreover, a process executes correctly its algorithm (until it possibly crashes). The selected algorithms are from [9, 10, 16, 32]. They are the following.

- Selected piece 1 (Sect. 2) is a snapshot algorithm whose adversaries are asynchrony, process-anonymity, and (any number of) process failures. This algorithm satisfies the non-blocking progress condition.
- Selected piece 2 (Sect. 3) is a binary consensus algorithm whose adversaries are the same as in the previous item. This algorithm satisfies the obstruction-freedom progress condition.
- Selected piece 3 (Sect. 4) concerns computability issues when considering the obstruction-freedom progress condition and any object defined by a sequential specification. It discusses an associated universal construction for asynchronous process-anonymous systems, in which any number of processes may crash.
- Selected piece 4 (Sect. 5) is a mutual exclusion algorithm whose adversaries are asynchrony and memory-anonymity. This algorithm satisfies the deadlock-freedom progress condition.
- Selected piece 5 (Sect. 6) is a consensus algorithm whose adversaries are asynchrony, memory-anonymity, and (any number of) process failures. It satisfies the obstruction-freedom progress condition.

# 2   Process-Anonymity and Any Number of Process Crashes: Non-blocking Snapshot

The first selected piece is a non-blocking snapshot algorithm suited to asynchronous process-anonymous read/write systems, in which any number of processes may crash. This algorithm is due to Guerraoui and Ruppert [16].

## 2.1   Snapshot Object

The concept of a *snapshot* object was introduced independently in [1] and [2]. Such an object, say $S$, can be seen as an array of $m$ multi-writer/multi-reader (MWMR) atomic registers, which provides the processes with an abstraction level higher than a simple array of $m$ independent read/write registers. More precisely, it is defined by two operations denoted write() and snapshot(). When a process $p_i$ invokes write($x, v$) (where $1 \leq x \leq m$), it writes the value $v$ at entry $x$ of the array. When it invokes snapshot(), it obtains the value of the whole array, as if the read on all its entries were done simultaneously and at the very same time. In other words, the operations write() and snapshot() are atomic, and the execution of a snapshot object is linearizable [22] (namely, the operations appear as if they have been executed one after the other, this total order being such that, if an operation op1() terminated before an operation op2() started, op1() appears before op2() in this total order).

In systems where processes have distinct names, it is possible to implement such a snapshot object, with the wait-freedom progress condition, on top of atomic read/write registers, despite asynchrony, and any number of process crashes [1, 2, 23, 29, 30].

## 2.2   Non-blocking Snapshot Despite Process-Anonymity and Crash Failures

The algorithm implementing a non-blocking snapshot object is presented in Fig. 1.

*Internal Representation of the Snapshot Object.* At the implementation level, the snapshot object is represented by an array $SM[1..m]$ of $m$ MWMR atomic read/write registers. Each register is initialized to the pair $\langle -, \perp \rangle$ (where $\perp$ is default initial value). Hence, a register $SM[x]$ is a pair $SM[x] = \langle SM[x].ts, SM[x].value \rangle$ (such that only $SM[i].value$ can be made visible outside).

Each anonymous process $p_i$ manages a local counter variable $ts_i$, initialized to 0, that it uses to associate a sequence number to its successive write operations into any atomic register $SM[x]$. Let us notice that two processes can associate the same sequence number to different write operations. A process $p_i$ manages also three auxiliary variables denoted $count_i$, $sm1_i[1..m]$, and $sm2_i[1..m]$.

```
operation write(x, v) is
(1)   SM[x] ← ⟨ts_i, v⟩; ts_i ← ts_i + 1; return().

operation snapshot() is
(2)   count_i ← 1; for each x ∈ {1, ..., m} do sm1_i[x] ← SM[x] end for;
(3)   repeat forever
(4)       for each y ∈ {1, ..., m} do sm2_i[y] ← SM[y] end for;
(5)       if (∀ x ∈ {1, ···, m} : sm1_i[x] = sm2_i[x])
(6)           then count_i ← count_i + 1;
(7)                   if (count_i = m(n − 1) + 2) then return(sm1_i[1..m].value) end if
(8)           else  count_i ← 1
(9)       end if;
(10)      sm1_i[1..m] ← sm2_i[1..m]
(11) end repeat.
```

**Fig. 1.** Non-blocking snapshot object [16] (code for $p_i$)

*Algorithm.* The algorithm implementing the operation write(), is self-explanatory. When a process $p_i$ invokes snapshot(), it repeatedly reads the array $SM[1..m]$ until it obtains an array value $sm[1..m]$ that does not change during $(m(n-1)+2)$ consecutive readings of $SM[1..m]$. When this occurs, the invoking process returns the corresponding array value $sm[1..m]$.

*Properties.* Trivially, any write operation terminates (it the invoking process does not crash during the invocation). As far the snapshot operation is concerned, it is easy to see that, if there is a time after which a process (that does not crash) executes alone it terminates its snapshot operation, hence the implementation is obstruction-free.

Assuming now each process invokes repeatedly $S$.write() (whatever $x$) followed by $S$.snapshot() (as done in nearly all uses of a snapshot object), let us show that the operation $S$.snapshot() is non-blocking. To this end, let us first observe that an invocation of $S$.snapshot() can be prevented from terminating only if processes issue permanently invocations of write(). The proof is by contradiction. Let us assume that no invocation of $S$.snapshot() terminates. This means that there are processes that permanently issue write operations. But this contradicts the assumption that each process alternates invocations of $S[x]$.write() (whatever $x$) and $REG$.snapshot(). This is because, between two writes issued by a same process, this process invoked $S$.snapshot(), and consequently this snapshot invocation terminated, which proves the non-blocking progress condition.

As far the linearization of the operations write() and snapshot() invoked by the processes is concerned we have the following [16]. Let us consider an invocation of snapshot() that terminates. It has seen $m(n - 1) + 2$ times the same vector $sm[1..m]$ in the array $SM[1..m]$. Since a given pair $\langle ts, v \rangle$ can be written at most once by a process, it can be written at most $(n - 1)$ times during a snapshot (once by each process, except the one invoking the snapshot). It follows that, among the $m(n-1)+2$ times where the same vector $sm[1..m]$ was read from $SM[1..m]$, there are least two consecutive reads during which no process wrote a register. The snapshot invocation is consequently linearized between these two sequential reads on the array $SM[1..m]$.

*Does Process-Anonymity Limit Snapshot Implementations?* A snapshot implementation, which ensures the strongest progress condition (wait-freedom) for both the operations write() and snapshot(), despite process-anonymity and any number of process crashes, is presented in [16]. This means that, for snapshot objects, process-anonymity does not create a *computability threshold* as far as progress conditions are concerned.

# 3    Process-Anonymity and Any Number of Process Crashes: Obstruction-Free Binary Consensus

The second selected piece is an obstruction-free consensus algorithm suited to asynchronous process-anonymous read/write systems, in which any number of processes may crash. This algorithm is due to Guerraoui and Ruppert [16].

## 3.1    Consensus Object

The *consensus* object is one of the most important objects of fault-tolerant distributed computing. A consensus object is a one-shot concurrent object that has a single operation, denoted propose() (one-shot means that a process invokes propose() at most once). When a process $p_i$ invokes propose($v$), we say "$p_i$ proposes value $v$". When its invocation terminates, $p_i$ obtains a value $w$, and we say "$p_i$ decides $w$". If only two values (e.g., 0 and 1) can be proposed, the consensus is *binary*. Otherwise, it is *multivalued*. The safety property of a consensus object is captured by the two following properties.

– Validity. If a process decides a value, this value was proposed by a process.
– Agreement. No two processes decide different values.

One of the most important results of distributed computing is the impossibility to implement a consensus object satisfying the wait-freedom progress condition in non-anonymous asynchronous systems, be the communication medium message-passing [14], or read/write registers [27], and even if only one process may crash. This impossibility extends trivially to process-anonymous systems.

## 3.2    Obstruction-Free Consensus Despite Process-Anonymity and Crash Failures

Figure 2 presents a relatively simple binary consensus algorithm (from the same authors) which guarantees the (weak) obstruction-freedom progress condition, in the presence of process-anonymity and any number of process crashes. This algorithm is a de-randomized version (due to Guerraoui and Ruppert [16]) of an anonymous randomized consensus algorithm due to Chandra [10].

*Internal Representation of the Binary Consensus Object.* At the implementation level, the consensus object is represented by a two-dimensional array $SM[0..1, 1..]$ (whose second dimension is unbounded) of MWMR atomic read/write registers. Each entry $SM[x, y]$ is initialized to the default value **down**, and it can then takes the value **up**. $SM[x, y]$ can be seen as flag which is raised by a process (and remains then raised forever) when some condition is satisfied.

A process $p_i$ locally manages a current estimate of the decision value ($est_i$) and an iteration number $k_i$.

---

**operation** propose($v_i$) **is**
(1)    $est_i \leftarrow v; k_i \leftarrow 0;$
(2)    **repeat forever**
(3)        $k_i \leftarrow k_i + 1;$ **let** $\overline{est_i} = 1 - est_i;$
(4)        **if** $(SM[\overline{est_i}, k_i] = $ **down**$)$
(5)            **then** $SM[est_i, k_i] \leftarrow$ **up**;
(6)                **if** $(k_i > 1) \wedge (SM[\overline{est_i}, k_i - 1] = $ **down**$)$ **then** return($est_i$) **end if**
(7)            **else** $est_i \leftarrow \overline{est_i}$
(8)        **end if**
(9)    **end repeat**.

---

**Fig. 2.** Obstruction-free binary consensus object [16] (code for $p_i$)

*Algorithm.* To understand the behavior of the algorithm, the reader is encouraged to execute it first when a single value is proposed, and then when both values are proposed.

As stated in [16], the algorithm can be seen as ruling a competition between two teams of processes, the team of the processes that champion 0, and the team of the processes that champion 1.

A process $p_i$ first progresses to its next iteration (line 3). Iteration numbers $k$ can be seen as defining a sequence of rounds executed asynchronously by the processes. Hence, the state of the flags $SM[0, k]$ and $SM[1, k]$ (which are up or down) describes the state of the competition at round $k$. When a process $p_i$ enters round $k$, there are two cases.

- If the flag associated with this round and the other value is up ($SM[\overline{est_i}, k] = $ up, i.e., the predicate of line 4 is not satisfied), $p_i$ changes its mind passing from the group of processes that champion $est_i$ to the group of processes that champion $\overline{est_i}$ (line 7). It then proceeds to the next round.
- If the flag associated with this round and the other value is down (the predicate of line 4 is then satisfied), maybe $est_i$ can be decided. To this end, $p_i$ indicates first that $est_i$ is competing to be the decided value by raising the round $k$ flag $SM[est_i, k]$ (line 5). The decision involves the two last rounds, namely $(k - 1)$ and $k$, attained by $p_i$ (hence, the sub-predicate $k > 1$ at line 6). If $p_i$ sees both the flags measuring the progress of $\overline{est_i}$ equal to down

at round $(k-1)$ and round $k$ (predicate $SM\,\overline{[est_i,k]}$ at line 4, and predicate $SM\,[\overline{est_i},k]$ at line 6), $\overline{est_i}$ is defeated, and $p_i$ consequently decides $est_i$.

To show this is correct, let us consider the smallest round $k$ during which a process decides. Moreover, let $p_i$ be a process that decides during this round, $v$ the value it decides, and $\tau$ the time at which $p_i$ reads $SM\,[\overline{v},k-1]$ before deciding (line 6 of round $k$). As $p_i$ decides, at time $\tau$ we have $SM\,[\overline{v},k-1] = \text{down}$. This means that, before time $\tau$, no process changed its mind from $v$ to $\overline{v}$ at line 6. The rest of the proof consists in showing that no process $p_j$ started round $k$ before time $\tau$ with $est_j = \overline{v}$. A full proof of this algorithm ensures the consensus is given in [16].

### 3.3 Computability Despite Process-Anonymity and Any Number of Crashes Failures

While it is impossible to implement a consensus object satisfying the wait-freedom progress condition, it is possible to implement a consensus object satisfying the non-blocking progress condition, despite process-anonymity. This shows that the consensus object reveals *computability threshold* separating the obstruction-freedom and wait-freedom progress conditions in crash-prone read/write asynchronous systems.

## 4 Process-Anonymity and Any Number of Process Crashes: Obstruction-Freedom-Compliant Universal Construction

The third selected piece is a universal construction which builds an obstruction-free implementation of any object defined by a sequential specification for asynchronous process-anonymous read/write systems, in which any number of processes may crash. This universal construction is due to due to Bouzid, Raynal, and Sutra [9].

### 4.1 Process-Anonymous $k$-Set Agreement

The notion of a $k$-set agreement object generalizes the consensus object. In both, each process proposes a value and decides a value. $k$-Set agreement is defined by the following safety properties:

- Validity. If a process decides a value, this value was proposed by a process.
- Agreement. At most $k$ different values are decided.

Hence, 1-set agreement is consensus, and $k$-set agreement is strictly stronger than $(k+1)$-set agreement.

The implementation of a $k$-set agreement object satisfying the obstruction-freedom progress condition in a system made up of $n$ asynchronous anonymous processes communicating through atomic read/write registers has recently been proposed in [9]. This algorithm uses $(n-k+1)$ atomic read/write registers only. From a shared memory cost point of view, this is the best algorithm known so far. When considering $k = 1$ (consensus), it is up to an addictive factor of 1 close to the best known lower bound [36].

## 4.2  On the Power of Repeated Anonymous Consensus

Using a sequence of repeated anonymous consensus instances, a universal construction for process-anonymous systems, is described [9], which provides the constructed objects with the obstruction-freedom progress condition.

In addition to such a universal construction, the previous article presents the following results for $n$-process anonymous systems.

*Universality of $n$ Atomic Read/Write Registers in Anonymous $n$-Process Systems.* Let $O$ be an object that can be obstruction-free implemented by $n$ anonymous processes and any number of MWMR atomic read/write registers. $O$ can be obstruction-free implemented by $n$ anonymous processes and $n$ MWMR atomic read/write registers.

Said differently, in an anonymous system, $n$ registers are sufficient to obstruction-free implement any object $O$ implemented with more registers.

*Anonymity and Distributed Task.* A distributed task $T()$ is made up of $n$ processes $p_1$, ..., $p_n$, such that each process has its own input (let $in_i$ denote the input of $p_i$) and must compute its own output (let $out_i$ denote the output of $p_i$) [19,21]. Let $I = [in_1, \cdots, in_n]$ be an input vector (let us notice that a process knows only its local input, it does not know the whole input vector). Let $O = [out_1, \cdots, out_n]$ be an output vector (similarly, even if a process is required to cooperate with the other processes, it has to compute its local output $out_i$, and not the whole output vector). A task $T$ is defined by a set $\mathcal{I}$ of input vectors, a set $\mathcal{O}$ of output vectors, and a mapping $T$ from $\mathcal{I}$ to $\mathcal{O}$, such that, given any input vector $I \in \mathcal{I}$, the output vector $O$ (cooperatively computed by processes) is such that $O \in T(I)$. The case $n = 1$ corresponds to sequential computing, and, in this case, a task boils down to a function.

A colorless task is a task such that if the input value of a process is $in$, any other process can have $in$ as input value, and similarly, if the output value of a process is $out$, any other process can have $out$ as output value. Expressed as a task, consensus is a colored task. The following theorems are proved in [9].

- If a task $T = (\Delta, \mathcal{I}, \mathcal{O})$ is obstruction-free solvable by $n$ anonymous processes and any number of MWMR atomic read/write registers, then it is obstruction-free solvable by $n$ anonymous processes with no more than $n$ MWMR atomic read/write registers.
- If a colorless task $T = (\Delta, \mathcal{I}, \mathcal{O})$ is obstruction-free solvable in a non-anonymous $n$-process system using any number of single-writer/multi-reader (SWMR) registers, it is also obstruction-free solvable in an anonymous $n$-process system with $n$ MWMR atomic registers.

Wait-free solvability of colorless tasks in $n$-process anonymous systems has also been investigated in [35].

# 5   Memory-Anonymity in a Failure-Free System: Mutex

As indicated in the introduction, the notion of *memory-anonymity* was recently introduced by Taubenfeld in [32]. The fourth selected piece is a deadlock-free mutex algorithm suited to asynchronous process-anonymous read/write crash-free systems. This algorithm is due to Taubenfeld [32].

## 5.1   Deadlock-Free Mutual Exclusion

Mutual exclusion is the oldest (and most important) synchronization problem. Formalized by Dijkstra in the late sixties [11,12], it consists in building what is called a lock (or mutex) object, defined by two operations, denoted acquire() and release().

The invocation of these operations by a process $p_i$ always follows the following pattern: "acquire(); *critical section*; release()", where "critical section" is any sequence of code. The mutex object satisfying the deadlock-freedom progress condition is defined by the following two properties.

- Mutual exclusion. No two processes are simultaneously in their critical section.
- Deadlock-freedom progress condition. If a process $p_i$ has a pending operation acquire(), a process $p_j$ (maybe $p_j \neq p_i$) eventually executes its critical section.

## 5.2   Symmetric Algorithm

An algorithm is *symmetric* if all the processes execute the same code. If the system in not process-anonymous (as it is the case here), the processes differs only in their identifier, which are all different. (Here, the identifier of $p_i$ is its index $i$). Moreover, to have an algorithm as general as possible, it is assumed that there is no order on the identifiers, they can only be compared. (Symmetry notions have been investigated since long time, in message-passing systems, e.g., [15,25].)

## 5.3   Deadlock-Free Mutex Object for Two Processes

*Internal Representation of the Mutex Object.* The process cooperates through a memory-anonymous array of atomic read/write registers $SM[1..m]$, where $m$ is an odd integer greater than 2. As $SM[1..m]$ is memory-anonymous, $SM[x]$ does not necessarily refers to the same register for two different processes $p_i$ and $p_j$. Hence, we use the notation $SM_i[x]$ to denote the register of $SM[1..m]$ accessed by $p_i$ with the array index $x$, and $SM_j[x]$ the register $SM[1..m]$ accessed by $p_j$ with the same array index $x$, which can be different registers of $SM[1..m]$.

Each process $p_i$ has two local variables. An integer variable $k_i$, whose domain is the set $\{1, \cdots, n\}$ (where $n = 2$), and a local array $sm_i[1..m]$.

*Algorithm of the Operation* acquire(). The algorithm is described in Fig. 3. Let us remember that $n = 2$, and $m$ is assumed to be an odd integer $\geq 3$.

When a process $p_i$ invokes acquire(), it first (asynchronously) sets to its identity $i$ all entries of $SM[1..m]$ it sees equal to 0, which is a neutral value (line 2). Then (line 3), $p_i$ asynchronously scans the "current state" of the mutex object, as defined by $SM[1..m]$. There are then two cases.

```
operation acquire() is
(1)    repeat
(2)        for ki ∈ {1, · · · , m} do if (SMi[ki] = 0) then SMi[ki] ← i end if end for;
(3)        for ki ∈ {1, · · · , m} do smi[ki] ← SMi[ki] end for;
(4)        if (|{x such that smi[x] = i}| < ⌈m/2⌉)
(5)            then for ki ∈ {1, · · · , m} do if (SMi[ki] = i) then SMi[ki] ← 0 end if end for;
(6)                repeat for ki ∈ {1, · · · , m} do smi[ki] ← SMi[ki] end for
(7)                until smi[1..m] = [0, . . . , 0] end repeat
(8)        end if
(9)    until smi[1..m] = [i, . . . , i] end repeat;
(10) return().

operation release() is
(11) for each ki ∈ {1, · · · , m} do SMi[ki] ← 0 end for;
(12) return().
```

**Fig. 3.** Deadlock-free 2-process mutex object [32] (code for $p_i$, $i \in \{1, 2\}$)

- If $p_i$ sees its identity in a majority of entries $SM[1..m]$ (the predicate of line 4 is then false), it considers it is on the "winning path", and starts another iteration. These iterations stop when $p_i$ sees its identity in all the entries of $SM[1..m]$ (predicate of line 9). When this occurs, $p_i$ is the winner of the competition and is allowed to enter its critical section code.

  It is easy to see that, if only $p_i$ invokes acquire(), we have $SM[1..m] = [i, \cdots, i]$ when it terminates line 2. In this case, both the predicates of line 4 and 9 are satisfied, and the invocation of acquire() by $p_i$ terminates.

- If the predicate of line 4 is satisfied, $p_i$ and $p_j$ are competing, and $p_i$ is losing the competition (let us recall that, as $m$ is odd, $p_i$ does not see a majority of entries of $SM$ with its identity). In this case, $p_i$ withdraws momentarily from the competition (line 5), and waits until it sees that $SM[1..m]$ has been reset to its initial value (lines 6–7). When this occurs, $p_i$ restarts competing by executing a new iteration of the external loop.

*Algorithm of the Operation* release(). This operation is a simple (non-atomic) reset of the array $SM[1..m]$ to its initial value $[0, \cdots, 0]$ (line 11).

*Proof.* We give here only a sketch of the mutual exclusion property. (The reader can consult [32] for a full proof including the deadlock-freedom property.) As the reads and the writes of the underlying registers $SM[1..M]$ are atomic, the time instants defined below are well-defined.

Let us assume that process $p_i$ is inside its critical section. When its invocation of acquire() terminated, $p_i$ was such that $sm_i[1..m] = [i, \cdots, i]$ (line 9); this constitutes Observation $O_i$. Let $\tau_i^1$ be the time of $p_i$'s last write in the array $SM$ at line 2, and $\tau_i^2 > \tau_i^1$ the time of its first read of an entry of the array $SM$ at line 3. It follows from Observation $O_i$ that $p_i$ read $sm_i[1..m] = [i, \cdots, i]$ at line 3. It follows that during the time interval $[\tau_i^1..\tau_i^2]$ $SM[1..m]$ has not been modified and was equal to $[i, \cdots, i]$.

After time $\tau_i^2$, it is possible that the other process $p_j$ assign $j$ to some entry $SM[k]$ (because, before time $\tau_i^1$, it read 0 from this entry at line 2), and this write overwrites the value $i$ previously written by $p_i$ in $SM[k]$. Then, when $p_j$ executes line 4, it finds that $j$ appears in only one entry, which it resets to 0 (line 5). There are then $(m - 1)$ entries of $SM$ equal to $i$, and $p_j$ loops in the internal loop (lines 6-7) until $p_i$ invokes release() (line 11). The mutex property follows.

### 5.4    On the Computability Side: Results and Open Problems

Several impossibility results are stated and proved in [32]. We state here one of them, and present an open problem.

- There is a memory-anonymous symmetric mutex algorithm for $n = 2$ processes, satisfying the deadlock-freedom progress condition, and using $m \geq 2$ atomic registers, if and only if $m$ is odd.
  When considering a classical (i.e., not memory-anonymous) system, there is an $n$-process deadlock-free mutex algorithm, based on identity comparison only, which uses $n$ atomic read/write registers. It follows that, when considering a mutex object and the deadlock-freedom progress condition, memory-anonymity entails a *computability threshold*: $n$ atomic read/write registers are sufficient when processes have identities (which can only be compared), while an odd number $\geq 3$ of registers is necessary when $n = 2$ and the ssytem is memory-anonymous.
- For $\geq 3$, the existence of a memory-anonymous symmetric mutex algorithm (and its design if it exists) satisfying the deadlock-freedom progress condition, is an open problem.
  Let us notice that there are algorithms that reduce $n$-process mutex to 2-process mutex [29,30]. Such algorithms are based on a tournament-tree, of size $\log(n)$, in which each node is a mutex algorithm for two processes. This technique cannot be applied here because, while no two nodes of the tree cannot be confused in a classical memory system, this is no longer true in a memory-anonymous system (the tree structure "collapses" in such a system because it has a linear memory $SM[1..m]$ where the same register name $SM[k]$ can be associated with different entries of $SM[1..m]$ at distinct processes).

## 5.5   Hybrid Memory-Anonymous System

A possible generalization of the pure memory-anonymous system consists in considering an hybrid version defined as follows. The memory, now denoted $HSM[1..k]$, is made up of $k$ partitions such that:

- The $k$ memory partitions $HSM[1]$, ..., $HSM[k]$ are not anonymous, which means that each $HSM[x]$, $1 \leq x \leq k$, refers to the same array of atomic read/write registers for all the processes.
- Each partition $HSM[x]$, $1 \leq x \leq k$, is a memory-anonymous array of size $s_x$.

It follows that, if for any $x$ we have $s_x = 1$, $HSM[1..k]$ is a classical non-anonymous array of read/write registers, and if $k = 1$, $HSM[1][1..s_1]$ is a memory-anonymous shared memory composed of $s_1$ read/write registers (i.e., $SM[1..s_1]$ in the previous parlance).

It is easy to see that such a hybrid memory-anonymous system allows us to use any algorithm that reduces $n$-process mutex to 2-process mutex. The lock associated with each node of the tournament tree can be implemented with the algorithm of Fig. 3, while each lock is non-anonymous. The hybrid memory is then $LOCK[1..k][1..2]$, where $k$ is the number of locks of the tournament tree. (Unfortunately, this does not answer the question of a mutex algorithm in a pure memory-anonymous system for $n \geq 3$ processes.)

# 6   Memory-Anonymity and Any Number of Process Crashes: Obstruction-Free Consensus

Consensus objects have been defined in Sect. 3.1. The fifth (and last) selected piece is an algorithm, due to Taubenfeld [32], which implements an obstruction-free consensus object in memory-anonymous systems made up of $n$ non-anonymous processes $p_1$, ..., $p_n$, and where any number of processes may crash.

*Internal Representation of the Consensus Object.* The consensus object is represented by an array $SM[1..2n-1]$ of atomic read/write registers. Each $SM[x]$ is composed of two fields: $SM[x].id$ which contains a process identity, and $SM[x].val$ which contains a value proposed by a process. Each $SM[x]$ is initialized to $\langle -, \perp \rangle$.

As in Sect. 5.3, given a process $p_i$, $SM_i[x]$ is used to locally denote the entry of $SM[1..2n-1]$ accessed with the index $x$ used by $p_i$. Due to memory-anonymity, for two different processes $p_i$ and $p_j$, $SM_i[x]$ and $SM_j[x]$ can be different registers of $SM[1..2n-1]$.

Each process $p_i$ manages three local variables. One is the array $sm_i[1..2n-1]$ (in which $p_i$ saves its reading of $SM_i[1..2n-1]$). The variable $est_i$ contains the current estimate of the decision value, as known by $p_i$. Finally, $k_i$ is a local index.

*Obstruction-Free Memory-Anonymous Consensus Algorithm.* When a process $p_i$ invokes propose($v_i$), where $v_i$ is the value it proposes, it first assigns $v_i$ to $est_i$ (line 1). Then $p_i$ enters a loop, in which it first reads asynchronously the shared array $SM_i[1..2n-1]$ (line 3). If it sees a majority value $v$ (line 4), $p_i$ adopts it as new estimate (line 5). Then, if it sees an entry $sm_i[x]$ that does not contain the pair $\langle i, est_i \rangle$, $p_i$ writes this pair in $SM_i[x]$ (lines 7–8). Finally, if all entries of $sm_i[1..2n-1]$ contain the pair $\langle i, est_i \rangle$, $p_i$ decides the value saved in $est_i$ (predicate of line 10 and line 11) (Fig. 4).

```
operation propose(v_i) is
(1)   est_i ← v;
(2)   repeat
(3)       for each k_i ∈ {1, ⋯ , 2n − 1} do sm_i[k_i] ← SM_i[k_i] end for;
(4)       if (∃v ≠ ⊥ : |{k such that sm_i[k].val = v}| ≥ n)
(5)           then est_i ← v
(6)       end if;
(7)       if (∃ x ∈ {1, ⋯ , 2n − 1} such that sm_i[x] ≠ ⟨i, est_i⟩)
(8)           then SM_i[x] ← ⟨i, est_i⟩
(9)       end if
(10)  until sm_i[1..2n − 1] = [⟨i, est_i⟩, ⋯ , ⟨i, est_i⟩] end repeat;
(11)  return(est_i).
```

**Fig. 4.** Obstruction-free multivalued memory-anonymous consensus object [16] (code for $p_i$)

*Sketch of a Proof* (from [32]). Let us first consider the agreement property. Let $p_i$ be the first process that decides, and let $v$ be the value it decides. It follows from line 10 that, before deciding, $p_i$ was such that $sm_i[1..2n-1] = [\langle i, est_i \rangle, \cdots, \langle i, est_i \rangle]$, i.e., $p_i$ has seen all entries of $SM[1..2n-1]$ equal to $\langle i, est_i \rangle$. Each other process $p_j$ may write into one of the shared registers at line 8, overwriting the pair $\langle i, est_i \rangle$. It follows that at most $(n-1)$ entries of $SM[1..2n-1]$ can be overwritten to a value different from $\langle i, est_i \rangle$. Consequently, when, after it read the shared array $SM[1..2n-1]$ at line 3, any other process $p_j$ will find that $v$ satisfies the predicate of line 4, and consequently adopts $v$ as new estimate (line 4). If follows that no value different from $v$ can be decided. The proof that the implementation is obstruction-free is left to the reader.

A more general obstruction-free algorithm solving $k$-set agreement with only $(n - k + 1)$ MWMR atomic read/write registers is described in [9].

# 7   Conclusion

Using as "selected pieces" recent algorithmic results in the domain of anonymous systems, where processes cooperate through atomic read/write registers, the aim of this article was to be an example-driven introduction to anonymity in distributed systems. Two types of "orthogonal" anonymities have been presented, namely, process-anonymity and memory-anonymity. A few algorithms illustrating the difficulty to cope with the uncertainty created by anonymity have been presented. This is summarized in the following table.

| Object | Anonymity | Failure | Progress condition | References |
|---|---|---|---|---|
| Snapshot | Processes | Crash | WF | [16] |
| Binary consensus | Processes | Crash | OB | [10,16] |
| $k$-set agreement | Processes | Crash | OB | [9] |
| Consensus | Memory | Crash | OB | [32] |
| Mutex | Memory | No failure | DF | [32] |

Be it due to privacy-based motivation or the manufacturing of identity-less anonymous tiny computing devices, the design of anonymous algorithms is becoming pervasive in more and more distributed applications. It follows that a theory of what can be computed in the presence of process/memory-anonymity seems to be a promising research domain.

**Acknowledgments.** The first author was supported by the Franco-German DFG-ANR Project 14-CE35-0010-02 DISCMAT (devoted to connections between mathematics and distributed computing), the French ANR project 16-CE40-0023-03 DESCARTES (devoted to layered and modular structures in distributed computing), and Hong Kong Polytechnic University. The first author wants also to thank G. Taubenfeld for discussions on anonymous systems, and F. Taïani for his encouragement to write this article. A special thanks to the authors of the presented algorithms, without them this article would not exist!

# References

1. Afek, Y., Attiya, H., Dolev, D., Gafni, E., Merritt, M., Shavit, N.: Atomic snapshots of shared memory. J. ACM **40**(4), 873–890 (1993)
2. Anderson, J.: Multi-writer composite registers. Distrib. Comput. **7**(4), 175–195 (1994)
3. Angluin, D., Local and global properties in networks of processes. In: Proceedings 12th Symposium on Theory of Computing (STOC 2080), pp. 82–93. ACM Press (1980)
4. Aspnes, J., Fich, F.E., Ruppert, E.: Relationship between broadcast and shared memory in reliable anonymous distributed systems. Distrib. Comput. **18**(3), 209–219 (2006)
5. Attiya, H., Gorbach, A., Moran, S.: Computing in totally anonymous asynchronous shared-memory systems. Inf. Comput. **173**(2), 162–183 (2002)
6. Attiya, H., Snir, M., Warmuth, M.K.: Computing on an anonymous ring. J. ACM **35**(4), 845–875 (1988)

7. Bonnet, F., Raynal, M.: The price of anonymity: optimal consensus despite asynchrony, crash and anonymity. ACM Trans. Auton. Adapt. Syst. **6**(4), 28 pages (2011)
8. Bonnet, F., Raynal, M.: Anonymous asynchronous systems: the case of failure detectors. Distrib. Comput. **26**(3), 141–158 (2013)
9. Bouzid, Z., Raynal, M., Sutra, P.: Anonymous obstruction-free $(n, k)$-set agreement with $(n-k+1)$ atomic read/write registers. Distrib. Comput. **31**(2), 99–117 (2018)
10. Chandra, T.D., Polylog randomized wait-free consensus. In: Proceedings 15th ACM Symposium on Principles of Distributed Computing (PODC 1996), pp. 166–175. ACM Press (1996)
11. Dijkstra, E.W.: Solution of a problem in concurrent programming control. Commun. ACM **8**(9), 569 (1965)
12. Dijkstra, E.W.: Hierarchical ordering of sequential processes. Acta Inf. **1**(1), 115–138 (1971)
13. Fich, F.E., Luchangco, V., Moir, M., Shavit, N.: Obstruction-free algorithms can be practically wait-free. In: Fraigniaud, P. (ed.) DISC 2005. LNCS, vol. 3724, pp. 78–92. Springer, Heidelberg (2005). https://doi.org/10.1007/11561927_8
14. Fischer, M.J., Lynch, N.A., Paterson, M.S.: Impossibility of distributed consensus with one faulty process. J. ACM **32**(2), 374–382 (1985)
15. Garg, V.K., Ghosh, J., Symmetry in spite of hierarchy. In: Proceeding 10th International Conference on Distributed Computing Systems (ICDCS 1990), pp. 4–11. IEEE Computer Press (1990)
16. Guerraoui, R., Ruppert, E.: Anonymous and fault-tolerant shared-memory computations. Distrib. Comput. **20**, 165–177 (2007)
17. Harel, D., Feldman, Y.: Algorithmics: The Spirit of Computing, p. 572. Springer, Heidelberg (2012)
18. Herlihy, M.: Wait-free synchronization. ACM Trans. Program. Lang. Syst. **13**(1), 124–149 (1991)
19. Herlihy, M., Rajsbaum, S., Raynal, M.: Power and limits of distributed computing shared memory models. Theor. Comput. Sci. **509**, 3–24 (2013)
20. Herlihy, M.P., Luchangco, V., Moir, M.: Obstruction-free synchronization: double-ended queues as an example. In: Proceedings 23th International IEEE Conference on Distributed Computing Systems (ICDCS 2003), pp. 522–529. IEEE Press (2003)
21. Herlihy, M.P., Shavit, N.: The topological structure of asynchronous computability. J. ACM **46**(6), 858–923 (1999)
22. Herlihy, M.P., Wing, J.M.: Linearizability: a correctness condition for concurrent objects. ACM Trans. Program. Lang. Syst. **12**(3), 463–492 (1990)
23. Imbs, D., Raynal, M.: Help when needed, but no more: an efficient partial snapshot algorithm. J. Parallel Distrib. Comput. **72**(1), 1–12 (2012)
24. Imbs, D., Raynal, M., Taubenfeld, G.: On asymmetric progress conditions. In: Proceedings 29th ACM Symposium on Principles of Distributed Computing (PODC 2010), pp. 55–64. ACM Press (2010)
25. Johnson, R.E., Schneider, F.B.: Symmetry and similarity in distributed systems. In: Proceedings 4th ACM Symposium on Principles of Distributed Computing (PODC 1985), pp. 13–22, ACM Press (1985)
26. Knuth, D.E.: Algorithmic thinking and mathematical thinking. Am. Math. Mon. **92**(3), 170–181 (1985)
27. Loui, M.C., Abu-Amara, H.H.: Memory requirements for agreement among unreliable asynchronous processes. Adv. Comput. Res. **4**, 163–183 (1987). Parallel and Distributed Computing

28. Rabin, M.: The choice coordination problem. Acta Inf. **17**(2), 121–134 (1982)
29. Raynal, M.: Concurrent Programming: Algorithms, Principles and Foundations. Springer, Heidelberg (2013). https://doi.org/10.1007/978-3-642-32027-9. ISBN 978-3-642-32026-2
30. Taubenfeld, G.: Synchronization algorithms and concurrent programming, p. 243. Pearson Education/Prentice Hall, London (2006). ISBN 0-131-97259-6
31. Taubenfeld, G.: The computational structure of progress conditions. In: Lynch, N.A., Shvartsman, A.A. (eds.) DISC 2010. LNCS, vol. 6343, pp. 221–235. Springer, Heidelberg (2010). https://doi.org/10.1007/978-3-642-15763-9_23
32. Taubenfeld G.: Coordination without prior agreement. In: Proceedings 36th ACM Symposium on Principles of Distributed Computing (PODC 2017), pp. 325–334 (2017)
33. Wing, J.: Computational thinking. Commun. ACM **49**(3), 33–35 (2006)
34. Yamashita, M., Kameda, T.: Computing on anonymous networks: part I - characterizing the solvable cases. IEEE Trans. Parallel Distrib. Syst. **7**(1), 69–89 (1996)
35. Yanagisawa, N.: Wait-Free solvability of colorless tasks in anonymous shared-memory model. In: Bonakdarpour, B., Petit, F. (eds.) SSS 2016. Lecture Notes in Computer Science, vol. 10083, pp. 415–429. Springer, Cham (2016). https://doi.org/10.1007/978-3-319-49259-9_32
36. Zhu L.: A tight space bound for consensus. In: Proceedings 48th Annual ACM Symposium on Theory of Computing (STOC 2016), pp. 345–350. ACM Press (2016)

# An Anonymous Wait-Free Weak-Set Object Implementation

Carole Delporte-Gallet[1], Hugues Fauconnier[1], Sergio Rajsbaum[2(✉)], and Nayuta Yanagisawa[3]

[1] IRIF-GANG-Université Paris-Diderot, Paris, France
{cd,hf}@irif.fr
[2] Instituto de Matemáticas, UNAM, Mexico City, Mexico
rajsbaum@math.unam.mx
[3] Department of Mathematics, Graduate School of Science, Kyoto University, Kyoto, Japan
nayuta87@math.kyoto-u.ac.jp

**Abstract.** We consider a system of $n$ anonymous processes communicating through multi-writer/multi-reader (MWMR) registers. A *weak-set* object is a particularly interesting communication abstraction for anonymous processes; it may be seen as the equivalent of an atomic snapshot object in an anonymous system. It can be accessed through two operations: ADD() and GET(). Intuitively, an ADD($v$) operation puts value $v$ in the set represented by the object, while a GET() operation returns the contents of the set. The paper describes a wait-free atomic implementation of a weak-set object shared by $n$ anonymous processes using $3n$ MWMR registers. The description of the algorithm is incremental. The paper first presents an implementation that is wait-free only for the GET() operations, using $2n$ MWMR registers. Then it describes an implementation that is wait-free for the GET() and the ADD() operations, using $3n + 1$ MWMR registers, and finally it is improved to an implementation using $3n$ MWMR registers. In addition, a lower-bound of $n$ registers for the implementation of a wait-free atomic weak-set is proved.

**Keywords:** Shared memory · Anonymous processes · Wait-free

## 1 Introduction

Distributed computing has long studied what can be computed by a system composed of $n$ failure-prone asynchronous processes communicating through shared-memory. Most papers consider a shared memory consisting of $n$ single-writer/multi-reader (SWMR) atomic registers. In such a model, each process has a unique identifier, which is used to identify the registers to which the process

C. Delporte-Gallet and H. Fauconnier—Supported by LiDiCo.
S. Rajsbaum—Supported by UNAM-PAPIIT project IN109917.

A. Podelski and F. Taïani (Eds.): NETYS 2018, LNCS 11028, pp. 141–156, 2019.
https://doi.org/10.1007/978-3-030-05529-5_10

can write. All registers can be read by all processes. Indeed, most algorithms use directly the assumption of unique identifiers, or indirectly to know which register is owned by which process.

In this paper, we are interested in *anonymous* systems. Anonymous systems are encountered in situations where processes do not have unique identifiers, like some sensor networks, or in situations where for privacy concerns, algorithms cannot use the process' identifiers, like in a peer-to-peer file sharing system. In addition to such practical motivations, studying anonymous computation is of theoretical importance, to better understand the nature of distributed computability.

Anonymous processes are programmed to run the same code (e.g. [2,4,20, 25]), and are indistinguishable from each other. Hence, when processes are anonymous, they cannot communicate through SWMR registers; a process has no means to identify its own register to which to write. Instead, in an anonymous system, processes communicate through multi-writer/multi-reader (MWMR) registers. Each register is completely symmetric, in that it can be read or written by any process.

Programming an anonymous system is very challenging. For example, even if a process writes a value $v$ to a register infinitely often, there is no way to ensure that the value will ever be visible by other processes: each time it writes the value, another process may immediately overwrite it. The problem does not come from the use of MWMR registers but from the anonymity. Indeed, when processes have identifiers, it is possible to simulate a system in which each process is assumed to have its own SWMR register using (enough) MWMR registers [15]. A value written in such a simulated register may only be erased by the owner of the register.

In this paper, we consider a completely symmetric shared object, that can be implemented on top of MWMR registers, that is still very useful to program an anonymous system: the *weak-set* object introduced in [12]. A weak-set object has two operations ADD($v$) and GET() to access a set of values. Informally, operation ADD($v$) adds the value $v$ to that set, and operation GET() returns the current value of the set. The object is called a "weak" set, because values can be added to the set, but there is no operation to remove values from the set.

Notice that, in contrast to a MWMR register, when a process executes an ADD($v$) operation, $v$ will forever be in the set, and it will always be included in the set returned by a subsequent GET() operation. However, among the set of values returned by a GET(), a process does not know in which order they have been added. In contrast, when using registers, the last value written to the register is well defined. It is possible to use shared timestamps [18] for anonymous processes, to define an order between ADD() operations, and then to distinguish the last value added. In this way, weak-set objects can emulate MWMR registers.

In the non-anonymous setting, the *atomic snapshot object* has been proposed to facilitate distributed programming [1], and many implementations have been designed (see for example the survey [19]), some on top of MWMR registers e.g. [23,24]. In a sense, a weak-set can be considered an atomic snapshot for anonymous systems. In the classic, one-shot atomic-snapshot, each process $p$ writes (also called update) at most once a shared SWMR register $T[p]$ and performs a scan that returns $C_p$, a copy of the current state of array $T$. Notice that (1) no value is lost and any scan performed after an update will contain this value (because each process writes its own register $T[p]$); (2) either $S_1 \subseteq S_2$ or $S_2 \subseteq S_1$, where $S_1$ and $S_2$ are the set of values (and not which process has written which value) returned by two consecutive scan operations. Properties (1) and (2) are properties that do not depend on the process identities, although atomic-snapshots are defined in the non-anonymous system (each process has its own SWMR register). A weak-set is an object guaranteeing property (1) and (2) in an anonymous context. In this sense, a weak-set may be considered as an atomic snapshot in the anonymous setting.

Weak-sets have already proved to be useful in previous research. They are used in [16] and [27] to characterize the computational power of anonymous processes concerning *colorless tasks*. Recall that colorless tasks [7] are defined only in terms of an input/output relation on sets of values, without referring to which process gets which input and which one should produce which output. Also, in [12], a weak-set is the primitive used to design a consensus algorithm with failure detector $\Omega$. Additional references and discussion about set objects can be found in [5].

In this paper, we prove that atomic weak-set objects can be implemented in a wait-free way using $3n$ MWMR registers with $n$ anonymous processes. Our interest is in computability rather than efficiency; further work is needed to obtain more efficient weak-set object implementations.

The paper is organized as follows. In Sect. 2, we describe the anonymous MWMR shared-memory system used in the paper, and discuss the weak-set object definition and its properties. In Sect. 3, we present a weak-set object implementation that is non-blocking. In Sect. 4, we show how to extend the algorithm to be wait-free. Section 5 discusses the space complexity of our algorithms and shows that at least $n$ registers are needed to implement an atomic weak-set object. The conclusions are in Sect. 6.

## 2    Model and Weak-Set

We first describe the anonymous MWMR shared-memory system used in the paper, and then we discuss weak-set objects.

### 2.1    Model

We assume a standard *anonymous asynchronous shared-memory model* [20] consisting of $n$ sequential processes that have no identifiers and execute an identical code. We sometimes refer to the processes by unique names $p_0, \ldots, p_{n-1}$ for notational convenience, but processes themselves have no means to access these names. Let $\Pi = \{p_0, \ldots, p_{n-1}\}$. Processes are asynchronous, i.e., they run at arbitrary speeds, independent from each other. Any process can stop running its code at any time, and *crash*. We assume that at least one process does not crash.

The processes communicate via multi-writer/multi-reader (MWMR) registers. Let $R[0 \dots m-1]$ denote an array of $m$ such registers. The read operation, denoted by READ($i$), returns the state of $R[i]$. The write operation, denoted by WRITE($i, v$), changes the state of $R[i]$ to $v$ and returns *ack*. The registers are assumed to be *atomic* [26]. We assume that the registers are initialized to some default value.

An *object* is a distributed data structure that can be accessed via a set of operations. It is defined by a *sequential specification* that specifies the effect of an operation on the object's state, and the value the operation returns, when operations are invoked sequentially. The behavior of the object on concurrent invocations is defined by the linearizability condition, ensuring the object is atomic. Roughly speaking, linearizability states that it is possible to associate to any concurrent execution a sequential execution, by identifying *linearization* points to each operation. More precise definitions can be found in Herlihy and Wing [22].

An implementation of an object is *wait-free* if each invocation of an operation performed by a process that does not crash terminates. An implementation of an object is *non-blocking* if when there is an infinite number of operation invocations then an infinite number of operations terminate.

A *timestamp* object provides one operation GETTS() that returns an integer value called a *timestamp*, such that if a GETTS() returning $t_1$ terminates before the beginning of a GETTS() returning $t_2$, then $t_1 < t_2$. A timestamp object enables to order non-concurrent events. Notice that a timestamp object is not an atomic object; concurrent invocations of GETTS() may return integers in any order. However, it can be specified formally using set-linearizability or interval-linearizability [9,10].

An implementation of a timestamp object using $n$ MWMR registers can be found in [18].

An *m-snapshot* represents an array $R$ of $m$ MWMR registers, indexed from 0 to $m-1$. It can be accessed with two operations, UPDATE($r, v$) ($r$ is the index of a register in $R$, and $v$ is a value) and SCAN() defined by the following sequential specification[1]:

- UPDATE($r, v$) sets the register $R[r]$ to value $v$,
- SCAN() returns a copy of $R$.

The $m$-snapshot object is atomic in the sense that SCAN() returns a view of the array $R$ with $m$ values that were *simultaneously* present at some point in time in $R$.

---

[1] The One-shot atomic-snapshot described in the introduction corresponds to a $n$ atomic-snapshot such that (1) each register is a SWMR register and each process is the writer of exactly one of these registers, and (2) each process may perform at most one UPDATE.

Guerrraoui and Ruppert present in [20] a wait-free implementation of an $m$-snapshot object for anonymous processes using $n + m$ MWMR registers (among them, $n$ registers are devoted to provide a timestamp).

Note that when using an $m$-snapshot object, even if a process $p$ infinitely often performs an UPDATE$(r, v)$, this value $v$ may never be "visible" if immediately after each UPDATE$(r, v)$ of $p$ another process performs an UPDATE$(r, v')$ with $v \neq v'$.

## 2.2  Weak-Set

An atomic *weak-set* object [12] guarantees that a value added will ever be "visible" for all processes. This object is used for maintaining a set of values taken from some universe of possible values $V$. It can be accessed using two operations ADD$(v)$ and GET$()$. The sequential specification is the following:

- the state of the object is defined by a set $S$ of values initially empty;
- an operation ADD$(v)$ adds $v$ to the set $S$, i.e., $S \leftarrow S \cup \{v\}$, and returns $ACK$;
- an operation GET$()$ returns the set $S$ without modifying it.

Two remarks concerning the computational power of a weak-set object:

1. It is easy to simulate a MWMR atomic register using timestamp and weak-set objects:
   - The values in the weak-set are pairs $(t, v)$ where $t$ is a timestamp obtained by a GETTS$()$.
   - To perform a WRITE$(v)$, a process performs an ADD$(v,$GETTS$())$.
   - To perform a READ$()$ a process performs a GET$()$ and returns the value associated with the largest $(t, v)$ in lexicographical order.
   
   Consider a WRITE$(v)$ that performs an ADD$(t, v)$ and a WRITE$(v')$ that performs an ADD$(t', v')$. If $(t, v) \leq (t', v')$ then the properties of timestamps ensure that WRITE$(v)$ is either concurrent with WRITE$(v')$ or WRITE$(v)$ terminates before the beginning of WRITE$(v')$. From this, it is not hard to deduce the atomicity of the simulated register.
2. From the previous remark, using timestamps, it is possible to know the last value added. However, there is no way to know the first value added to the set. Indeed, if it were possible, then consensus could be easily implemented, contradicting the consensus impossibility of [21]. Namely, each process adds its initial value, then performs a GET$()$, and decides the value returned by the GET$()$ that has been added first.

To conclude this section, notice that when the set of values $V$ is finite, a weak set object can be implemented with $card(|V|)$ MWMR registers. For this, consider an array $R$ of $card(|V|)$ MWMR boolean registers, each element of the array being indexed by a value $v \in V$. Array $R$ is initialized by *false* and:

- to perform an ADD$(v)$ a process simply does $R[v] = true$, and
- a GET$()$ returns a SCAN$()$ of $R$.

Shared variable :

    $n$-snapshot object : $R$ init $\emptyset$

CODE FOR A PROCESS

Local variable:

    **array of** $n$ **set of triples** $Snap[0 \ldots n-1]$
    **set of triples** $View$ init $\emptyset$
    **integer** $next$

Macro:

$vals(Snap) = \cup Snap[i]$

$values(View) = \{v| < v, -, - > \text{ in } View\}$

ADD($w$):

```
1   next = 0
2   t = GETTS()
3   g = GET()
4   v =< w, t, g >
5   Snap = R.SCAN()
6   View = View ∪ vals(Snap) ∪ {v}
7   while (#{r|v in Snap[r]} < n)
8       R.UPDATE(next, View)
9       next = (next + 1) mod n
10      Snap = R.SCAN()
11      View = View ∪ vals(Snap)
12  return ACK
```

GET:

```
13  next = 0
14  t = GETTS()
15  Snap = R.SCAN()
16  View = View ∪ vals(Snap)
17  while (#{r|View = Snap[r]} < n) and (∄ t' > t  < −, t', − >∈ View)
18      R.UPDATE(next, View)
19      next = (next + 1) mod n
20      Snap = R.SCAN()
21      View = View ∪ vals(Snap)
22  if (#{r|View = Snap[r]} = n) return values(View)
23  let < w, t', g > such that (t' > t and < w, t', g >∈ View) return g
```

**Fig. 1.** Non-blocking implementation of atomic weak set for $n$ processes. GET is wait-free

## 3   A Non-blocking Weak Set Object Implementation

In this section, we describe the atomic weak-set algorithm of Fig. 1. In what follows, we explain the algorithm and – for lack of space in this proceedings version – we give an informal explanation of why it is correct.

The implementation of the atomic weak-set presented in this section is non-blocking, i.e., if there are operations concurrently executed on the object by non-faulty processes, then at least one of them succeeds. However, the implementation is wait-free for all GET() operation invocations. That is, a GET() operation that is invoked by a non-faulty process always terminates regardless of other processes' behavior.

In an anonymous setting, it is impossible to allocate one register to each process, and guarantee that the process owning a register is the only one that can write to it. Hence, in an anonymous system, if a process writes a value to a register, the value may be over-written by another process. Thus, to ensure that a value added by a process will be visible after the end of the ADD() operation, we use techniques similar to those in [13,15] or in [8,14]. However, processes have unique identifiers in these papers, so we need to adapt the ideas to the anonymous case. In those papers, the processes have identifiers coming from a large space, and SWMR registers (for each process) are constructed using a linear number of MWMR registers. The goal of the papers is to implement a $k$-set agreement object [11] with fewer registers than the number of processes, in a way that each process is not the owner of a register.

In the algorithm of Fig. 1, the processes share $n$ MWMR registers. Each process maintains a variable $View$ that contains all the values that the process has seen in the registers. To execute ADD($v$), a process inserts $v$ in $View$ and repeatedly reads all the registers using a snapshot operation, and updates its variable $View$ by adding all the values it has just read. The process then writes $View$ in a register. In this algorithm, the process writes circularly the registers from 0 to $n-1$. The ADD($v$) operation ends when the value $v$ is in all the registers. The value is then in $n$ registers and in the variable $View$ of the writer. It may happen that some process writes its own $View$ in some register and its $View$ does not contain $v$, but at most $n-1$ processes may do that. After each write, the process performs a scan of the registers. As it remains at least one register containing value $v$, the process updates its $View$ with $v$, and $View$ forever contains $v$.

In this way, when the ADD($v$) ends, $v$ is in all the $n$ registers. After that, $v$ may be in fewer registers, but it remains in at least one register. If the number of registers that contains $v$ decreases, the number of processes that have $v$ in their $View$ increases. After at most $O(n^2)$ writes, $v$ is again in all registers and remains forever in all registers.

One may think that a GET() operation can be implemented by simply returning the values of all registers. However, it could happen that a value $v$ is written in some register by a process and the process takes no more steps. Then, this value $v$ could be returned by the GET() operation but, after that, the register could be over-written by another process with a $View$ that does not contain $v$, and then the value $v$ will not be returned by any following GET(). In this case, the weak-set is not atomic. Similar to the implementation of a register [3] in a message passing system, the GET() operation also has to write in the memory to obtain atomicity.

So far the implementation is non-blocking, the write of a register by a process during the ADD() or the GET() may be over-written by another process. Furthermore, the GET() may not terminate because there is an infinity of ADD(). To prevent this, at the beginning of an ADD($v$) operation, the process executes a GET() operation, and then it will write in the registers value $v$ with the result of that GET(). When a process executes a GET(), it ends either: (1) if all the values in the registers are the same or (2) if it can adopt one of the get values contained in the register, if this get value is "fresh" enough. To choose a fresh value we use a timestamp as defined in [18]. The timestamp has a GETTS() operation that returns an integer such that if two GETTS() are not concurrent the value returned by the first one is smaller than the value returned by the second one.

At the beginning of an ADD($v$) operation, the process takes a timestamp $t$ performing a GETTS(), executes a GET() operation and updates its *View*. The update of its *View* is by a triple containing the value $v$, the timestamp $t$, and the result of the GET(). Then, the process repeatedly reads all registers (by a snapshot), updates *View* and writes *View* in all registers circularly until it finds that triple in all the registers. At the first time the snapshot of Line 5 or Line 10 contains $v$ in all the registers, we can consider that ADD($v$) has taken effect (that defines the linearization point of ADD($v$)).

To perform a GET(), the process takes a timestamp, $t$, performing a GETTS(). Then it repeatedly reads all the registers (by a snapshot), updates *View* and writes *View* in registers circularly until it finds the same set in all registers, or it finds a value associated with a timestamp greater than $t$. If it finds the same set in all registers, each value of this set will remain forever in the register. In this case, the first time the snapshot of Line 15 or Line 15 finds the same value in all the registers, we can consider that GET() has taken effect (that defines the linearization point of GET()). Else, if the while loop Line 17 stops because it finds a triple associated with a timestamp greater than $t$, then the process may adopt the associated get part of the triple and return it. We can consider that at the time of the GET() operation that has written the get part of the triple, the GET() has taken effect (that defines the linearization point of GET()).

Using the linearization points that have been defined above, one can show that the sequential specification of the weak-set is ensured.

**Theorem 1.** *The algorithm in Fig. 1 implements a non-blocking atomic weak-set. Furthermore, the GET() operations are wait-free.*

## 4    A Wait-Free Atomic Weak-Set

In the previous algorithm, it may happen that a non-faulty process never succeed to complete an ADD($v$) operation. Each time the process writes in some register, the register may be over-written by another process, and if the value written is different, the first value written is lost. Note that the value is lost only in case of overwriting a value $v$ by a *different* value $v'$. Hence, with a finite number of values, we allocate a register for each value, and in order to write value $v$ a

Shared variable :
      $(2n+1)$-snapshot object : $R$ init $\emptyset$

CODE FOR A PROCESS

Local variable:
      **array of** $n$ **set of triple** $Snap[0\dots 2n]$
      **set of triple** $View$ init $\emptyset$
      **integer** $next$
      **integer** $ind$
      **sequence of values** $name$ init $\epsilon$
      **set of sequence of values** $Proc$ init $\emptyset$

Macro:

$vals(Snap) = \cup Snap[i]$
$values(View) = \{v | \exists \alpha, \beta\ <\alpha.v.\beta, -, - > \text{ in } View\}$
$proc(S) = \{w | \exists \tau, \gamma\ <w, \tau, \gamma > \in S \text{ and } (\not\exists <w', \tau', \gamma' > \in S \text{ such that } w \neq w' \text{ and } w \text{ prefix of } w')\}$

ADD($w$):

1   $next = 0$
2   $name = name.w$
3   $t = \text{GETTS}()$
4   $g = \text{GET}()$
5   $v =< name, t, g >$
6   $Snap = R.\text{SCAN}()$
7   $View = View \cup vals(Snap) \cup \{v\}$
8   $Proc = proc(View)$
9   **while** $(\#\{r | 0 \leq r \leq n-1\ \exists \beta < name.\beta, -, - > \text{ in } Snap[r]\} < n)$
10    **if** $(Snap[\#Proc + n] = \emptyset)$ **then**
11      $ind=$ index of $name$ in $Proc$
12      $R.\text{UPDATE}(\#Proc + n, View)$
13    **else**
14      **if** $(next = n)$ **then**
15         $R.\text{UPDATE}(ind + n - 1, View)$
16      **else** $R.\text{UPDATE}(next, View)$
17    $next = (next + 1) \bmod n + 1$
18    $Snap = R.\text{SCAN}()$
19    $View = View \cup vals(Snap)$
20    $Proc = proc(View)$
21  **return** $ACK$

GET:

22  $next = 0$
23  $t = \text{GETTS}()$
24  $Snap = R.\text{SCAN}()$
25  $View = vals(Snap) \cup View$
26  **while** $((\#\{r | 0 \leq r \leq n-1\ View = Snap[r]\} < n) \text{ and } (\not\exists\ t' > t\ <-, t', -> \in View)$
27    $R.\text{UPDATE}(next, View)$
28    $next = (next + 1) \bmod n$
29    $Snap = R.\text{SCAN}()$
30    $View = View \cup vals(Snap)$
31  **if** $(\#\{r | View = Snap[r]\} = n)$ **return** $values(View)$
32  **let** $< w, t', g >$ such that $(t' > t$ and $< w, t', g > \in View)$ **return** $g$

**Fig. 2.** Wait-free implementation of atomic weak-set for $n$ processes.

process writes only in the register allocated to value $v$; only processes writing the same value will over-write it. But of course the number of registers depends on the number of possible values. A possible way to avoid that overwriting is to force processes writing different values to write in different registers. For the weak-set, the solution we propose here is, roughly speaking, to force processes that add different sequences of values to write in (at least) one different register. In this way the number of register needed depends on $n$ the number of processes and not on the number of values.

In the algorithm of Fig. 2, among the $2n+1$ registers in $R$, $n+1$ registers will be used to ensure that processes performing different sequence of ADD write in different registers (the $n$ other registers are used to avoid a covering of registers by $n$ processes).

In a similar way as in [17], to attribute a register to a process that has performed a sequence of ADD operations, we give as "name" to that process the sequence of values it has added. Then, the techniques used in [15] ensure that eventually the process will be alone to write this register.

More precisely, the "name" of a process that executes an ADD($v$) operation is the sequence of values that it has added to the weak-set followed by $v$, the value that it try to add. For example if a process has added first 2, then 4, and 7 is the value that it tries to add, its name is 2.4.7.

As in the previous algorithm, a process that executes ADD($v$) maintains a variable $View$. To perform an ADD($v$), a process executes GETTS() that returns a timestamp $t$, GET() that returns $g$, and inserts the triple $<name, t, gt>$ in $View$. It repeatedly reads all registers using a snapshot operation, and updates its variable $View$ by adding all it has just read to $View$.

If $<2, -, ->, <2.4, -, ->, <2.4.7, -, ->$ is in $View$, it may have only one process that has added these three values, or it may have some processes that try to add 2, some processes that have already added 2 and try to add 4, and some processes that have already added 2 and 4 and try to add 7, and some processes that have already added 2,4 and 7. And there are also all the intermediate possibilities. Only one register among the additional $n + 1$ registers is allocated to these processes.

$proc(View)$ gives the set of different "names" of processes that are using the weak-set (Line 8 and Line 20) by removing all "names" that are strict prefixes of others. For example if $View$ contains $< 1, -, - > < 1.2, -, - > < 1.2.3, -, -> <2, -, -> <2.4, -, -> <2.4.7, -, -> <4, -, ->$, then $proc(View)$ is $\{1.2.3, 2.4.7, 4\}$. From $proc(View)$ a process determines the index (variable $ind$) of its "name" inside its current view of the set of actual names (variable $Proc$). More precisely, the set of name $Proc$ is ordered lexicographically. If $Proc = \{s_1, s_2, \ldots, s_k\}$, the index of $name$ is the first $i$ such that $name$ is a prefix of $s_i$. In our example, the processes with name 2, 2.4 or 2.4.7 have 2 as its index. When the process writes circularly to the registers from 0 to $n - 1$, it writes also in the $ind + n - 1$th register. The $ind$-th register in $R[n, \ldots, 2n + 1]$, namely register $R[n + ind - 1]$, will be the register assigned to processes with the same name.

The process uses two of the $n + 1$ additional registers: one to register the number of participants, and one, shared with the processes that have the same index, to make visible its value.

The $\#Proc + n$th register is used to store the processes that have been seen. It is written only if the process has seen no value in it. In particular, the process writes in this register only if it is the fist time that it finds as many processes.

The value of $ind$ may change during an ADD($v$) operation, when a process is added in $Proc$. But there is a time $\tau$ after which on each process that takes steps and tries to add a value the set $Proc$ keeps the same cardinality. The value of $Proc$ at some process is equivalent to the value of $Proc$ on another process (see Lemma 3 below).

Consider a process that takes steps and tries to ADD some value. We show that it succeeds; proving thus that the implementation is wait-free for the ADD operations:

If it has finished its ADD() at time $\tau$, we are done.

Else after time $\tau$, the value of $ind$ never changes. So after some time, during this ADD(), it is possible that several processes update the same register $ind + n - 1$ in the set of an additional register. There is a time after which, if the register $ind + n - 1$ is written by two processes, then the value of $name$ of the first process is a prefix or a continuation of the value of $name$ of the second process. Consider the process $p$ with the smallest $name$, $h$. Each time a process takes a snapshot, it sees the value of register $ind + n - 1$ and adds it in its $View$. So after a write of each register from 0 to $n - 1$ by $p$ (or another process), $h$ or a continuation of $h$ is written in each register from 0 to $n - 1$. This allows the process $p$ to terminate the while loop (Line 26). Thus, each ADD() operation executed by a process that does not crash, finishes.

The behavior of the processes concerning the registers from 0 to $n - 1$ is the same as in the first algorithm. Hence the algorithm implements an atomic weak-set, and the GET() operations remain wait-free.

**Theorem 2.** *The algorithm in Fig. 2 is an implementation of a wait-free atomic weak set.*

*Properties on ind and Proc.* We prove here some properties $ind$ and $Proc$ that are used in the previous explanation.

**Lemma 1.** *There exists a time after which, on each process that takes steps and tries to add a value, the set Proc keeps the same cardinality.*

*Proof.* The cardinality of $Proc$ is increasing and bounded by $n$ (the number of processes). So eventually the cardinality of $Proc$ never changes.

Let $\tau$ be the time after which, on each process that takes steps and tries to add a value the set $Proc$, keeps the same cardinality.

**Lemma 2.** *After time $\tau$, two processes that take steps and try to add a value have the same cardinality for Proc.*

*Proof.* Otherwise, consider a process with the largest *Proc*, it writes *View* in the $\#Proc + n$-th register, and this register can only be written by a process with the same cardinality for *Proc*. So when a process with a smaller set *Proc* executes a snapshot, this value is included in its View and it updates *Proc*.

Furthermore, after $\tau$, processes that take steps and try to add a value have an equivalent value of *Proc*. A process may have $\{1.2.3.6, 2.4.7.13, 4.3.2\}$ and another $\{1.2.3.6.5, 2.4.7, 4.3.2\}$. To be more precise:

**Definition 1.** *A set of processes $P$ is equivalent to a set $P'$ ($P' \equiv P$), if $P$ and $P'$ have the same cardinality, and in addition, for each process name in $P$, there is one process name in $P'$ such that name is a prefix of name' (including name = name') or name' is a prefix of name.*

**Lemma 3.** *After $\tau$, two processes that take steps and try to add a value have two equivalent sets Proc.*

*Proof.* A process updates only once the $\#Proc + n$- th register with *View*. This register is updated by at most $n$ processes (all processes have the same cardinality for their *Proc*). Consider the latest write by *View* such that $Proc(View) = P$. Any process, with $P'$ has a value of *Proc* that it tries to add, takes a snapshot and sees this value. If there is a name in $P$ that is not a prefix or a continuation of a name in $P'$ (or the reverse), the set *Proc* at this process increases, contradicting Lemma 2. After $\tau$, two processes that take steps and try to add a value have two equivalent sets *Proc*.

## 5　Space Complexity

Here we analyze the complexity of our algorithm in terms of the number of registers, and then prove a lower bound on the number of registers needed by any implementation of a weak-set object.

Our algorithms use $O(n)$ registers. To be more precise, the timestamp implementation uses $n$ registers. The $n$-snapshot implementation is implemented with a timestamp and an array of $n$ registers. Therefore, the algorithm of Fig. 1 uses $2n$ registers: $n$ for the timestamp implementation and $n$ for the array.

The algorithm of Fig. 2 uses a timestamp and a $(2n + 1)$-snapshot object. Therefore, the algorithm of Fig. 2 uses $3n + 1$ registers. In fact, it is possible to reduce a little this number of registers to $3n$ registers. For that, we may use a $2n$-snapshot object instead of a $(2n + 1)$-snapshot object. In our algorithm, we store in $R[2n + 1]$ a *View* such that $Proc(View) = n$ and in $R[2n]$ the current value of *View*. But when a process has seen $n$ different names for the processes, it cannot see more. So there is no need to have a specific register, the information is already contained in $R[2n]$. Therefore, the algorithm of Fig. 1, where Lines 10 to 17 16 are changed by the code of Fig. 3 uses $3n$ registers:

We show below that at least $n$ registers are needed to implement an atomic weak-set object.

Shared variable :
      $2n$-snapshot object: $R$ init $\emptyset$

Replace Lines 10 to 17 of algorithm Figure 2 by these:

```
1       if (#Proc = n) then
2           ind= index of name in Proc
3           if (next = n) then
4               R.UPDATE(ind + n − 1, View)
5           else R.UPDATE(next, View)
6       else
7           if (Snap[#Proc + n] = ∅) then
8               ind= index of name in Proc
9               R.UPDATE(#Proc + n, View)
10          else
11              if (next = n) then
12                  R.UPDATE(ind + n − 1, View)
13              else R.UPDATE(next, View)
```

**Fig. 3.** Wait-free implementation of atomic weak-set for $n$ processes in $3n$ registers.

**Theorem 3.** *If the set of values is greater than $n$, at least $n$ MWMR registers are necessary to implement a wait-free weak-set object shared by $n$ processes.*

The proof is a standard covering argument. Given a value $v$, a register $r$ is *covered* by a process $p$ for value $v$ if $p$ is in the middle of an ADD(W) operation for $v \neq w$ and the next step of $p$ is a WRITE into register $r$. If $r$ is covered by $p$: the current value of $r$ is about to be overwritten by $p$. Given a value $v$, a set $P$ of *processes covers* a set $R$ of registers, if every $r \in R$ is covered for $v$ by a process $p \in P$.

**Lemma 4.** *Consider a state in which a set of registers $R$ is covered for $v$ by a set of processes $P$, and no process has already performed an ADD(V), then if some process $p_0$ performs an ADD(V), $p_0$ has to write registers not in $R$.*

Assume for contradiction that $p_0$ writes only variables in $R$. Let $s$ be the state of the shared memory in the covering state. If each process $q \in P$ performs its next step, all registers in $R$ are written, getting a new state $s_0$ of the shared memory. For this state, if a process performs a GET(), the set returned by this get cannot contain value $v$.

Assume that $p_0$ performs ADD($v$) in the covering state. As the implementation is wait-free, $p_0$ terminates its ADD($v$) in some state $s_0$. Then each process in $P$ performs its next step and the new state of the shared memory is $s_0$ (in $s_0$ all traces of $p_0$ on the shared memory have disappeared). If some process performs a GET(), the set returned cannot contain value $v$. A contradiction to the specification of a weak-set object.

From Lemma 4, $n$ processes that perform ADD($v$) for $n$ different values have to write at least $n$ registers, proving Theorem 3.

# 6   Conclusion

In this paper, we have described a wait-free implementation of an atomic weak-set object in an anonymous setting. We have proceeded in an incremental way. First, we presented an implementation that is wait-free only for the GET() operations. Then, we presented another implementation that is wait-free for the GET() and the ADD() operations. We hope that the existence of a wait-free weak-set implementation in an anonymous setting helps to get a better understanding of anonymous distributed computability.

It is worth noting that the technique used for the second implementation consists in a way of giving names to anonymous processes, dynamically. Two processes having distinct behaviors (concerning the ADD() operation) get distinct names. This is a useful technique for programming anonymous processes, already noticed in [13,15,17].

Concerning the space complexity, our wait-free implementation uses a number of register that is linear to the number of processes (namely, $3n$ registers). In addition, we prove a lower-bound of $n$ registers for the implementation of a wait-free atomic weak-set.

For some applications, it is sufficient to have weak-set implementations that are non-blocking, notably, when the weak-set is used to solve a *task* [6]. We have presented in [16] an implementation of a weak-set that is non-blocking, that uses $n$ MWMR registers. The lower bound we prove here shows that the implementation in [16] is optimal. The non-blocking implementation presented here uses $2n$ MWMR registers, but the GET() is wait-free. To make the GET() wait-free we use a timestamp mechanism that uses $n$ MWMR registers. It would be interesting to find and algorithm that uses only $n$ MWMR registers where the GET() is wait-free, or to prove a lower bound that separates the non-blocking case from the wait-free case.

Concerning time complexity, we have not made any efforts in making our algorithms efficient. Our interest was in proving that it is possible to obtain linear number of registers weak-set implementations. Further work is needed to obtain more efficient implementations of a weak-set object.

# References

1. Afek, Y., Attiya, H., Dolev, D., Gafni, E., Merritt, M., Shavit, N.: Atomic snapshots of shared memory. J. ACM **40**(4), 873–890 (1993)
2. Aspnes, J., Fich, F.E., Ruppert, E.: Relationships between broadcast and shared memory in reliable anonymous distributed systems. Distrib. Comput. **18**(3), 209–219 (2006)
3. Attiya, H., Bar-Noy, A., Dolev, D.: Sharing memory robustly in message passing systems. J. ACM **42**(2), 124–142 (1995)
4. Attiya, H., Gorbach, A., Moran, S.: Computing in totally anonymous asynchronous shared memory systems. Inf. Comput. **173**(2), 162–183 (2002)
5. Baldoni, R., Bonomi, S., Raynal, M.: Implementing set objects in dynamic distributed systems. J. Comput. Syst. Sci. **82**(5), 654–689 (2016)

6. Biran, O., Moran, S., Zaks, S.: A combinatorial characterization of the distributed 1-solvable tasks. J. Algorithms **11**(3), 420–440 (1990)
7. Borowsky, E., Gafni, E., Lynch, N., Rajsbaum, S.: The BG distributed simulation algorithm. Distrib. Comput. **14**(3), 127–146 (2001)
8. Bouzid, Z., Raynal, M., Sutra, P.: Anonymous obstruction-free (n, k)-set agreement with n-k+1 atomic read/write registers. In: 19th International Conference on Principles of Distributed Systems, OPODIS 2015, Rennes, France, 14–17 December 2015, pp. 18:1–18:17 (2015)
9. Castañeda, A., Rajsbaum, S., Raynal, M.: Specifying concurrent problems: beyond linearizability and up to tasks. In: Moses, Y. (ed.) DISC 2015. LNCS, vol. 9363, pp. 420–435. Springer, Heidelberg (2015). https://doi.org/10.1007/978-3-662-48653-5_28
10. Castañeda, A., Rajsbaum, S., Raynal, M.: Long-lived tasks. In: El Abbadi, A., Garbinato, B. (eds.) NETYS 2017. LNCS, vol. 10299, pp. 439–454. Springer, Cham (2017). https://doi.org/10.1007/978-3-319-59647-1_32
11. Chaudhuri, S.: More choices allow more faults: set consensus problems in totally asynchronous systems. Inf. Comput. **105**(1), 132–158 (1993)
12. Delporte-Gallet, C., Fauconnier, H.: Two consensus algorithms with atomic registers and failure detector $\Omega$. In: Garg, V., Wattenhofer, R., Kothapalli, K. (eds.) ICDCN 2009. LNCS, vol. 5408, pp. 251–262. Springer, Heidelberg (2008). https://doi.org/10.1007/978-3-540-92295-7_31
13. Delporte-Gallet, C., Fauconnier, H., Gafni, E., Lamport, L.: Adaptive register allocation with a linear number of registers. In: Afek, Y. (ed.) DISC 2013. LNCS, vol. 8205, pp. 269–283. Springer, Heidelberg (2013). https://doi.org/10.1007/978-3-642-41527-2_19
14. Delporte-Gallet, C., Fauconnier, H., Gafni, E., Rajsbaum, S.: Black art: obstruction-free k-set agreement with |MWMR registers| < |proccesses|. In: Gramoli, V., Guerraoui, R. (eds.) NETYS 2013. LNCS, vol. 7853, pp. 28–41. Springer, Heidelberg (2013). https://doi.org/10.1007/978-3-642-40148-0_3
15. Delporte-Gallet, C., Fauconnier, H., Gafni, E., Rajsbaum, S.: Linear space bootstrap communication schemes. Theor. Comput. Sci. **561**(Part B), 122–133 (2015). Special Issue on Distributed Computing and Networking
16. Delporte-Gallet, C., Fauconnier, H., Rajsbaum, S., Yanagisawa, N.: A characterization of colorless anonymous t-resilient task computability. Technical report, Kyoto University. arXiv:1712.04393v1, December 2017
17. Delporte-Gallet, C., Fauconnier, H., Tielmann, A.: Fault-tolerant consensus in unknown and anonymous networks. In: 29th IEEE International Conference on Distributed Computing Systems (ICDCS 2009), Montreal, Québec, Canada, 22–26 June 2009, pp. 368–375. IEEE Computer Society (2009)
18. Ellen, F., Fatourou, P., Ruppert, E.: The space complexity of unbounded timestamps. Distrib. Comput. **21**(2), 103–115 (2008)
19. Fich, F.E.: How hard is it to take a snapshot? In: Vojtáš, P., Bieliková, M., Charron-Bost, B., Sýkora, O. (eds.) SOFSEM 2005. LNCS, vol. 3381, pp. 28–37. Springer, Heidelberg (2005). https://doi.org/10.1007/978-3-540-30577-4_3
20. Guerraoui, R., Ruppert, E.: Anonymous and fault-tolerant shared-memory computing. Distrib. Comput. **20**(3), 165–177 (2007)
21. Herlihy, M.: Wait-free synchronization. ACM Trans. Program. Lang. Syst. **13**(1), 124–149 (1991)
22. Herlihy, M.P., Wing, J.M.: Linearizability: a correctness condition for concurrent objects. ACM Trans. Program. Lang. Syst. **12**(3), 463–492 (1990)

23. Imbs, D., Raynal, M.: Help when needed, but no more: efficient read/write partial snapshot. J. Parallel Distrib. Comput. **72**(1), 1–12 (2012)
24. Inoue, M., Masuzawa, T., Chen, W., Tokura, N.: Linear-time snapshot using multi-writer multi-reader registers. In: Tel, G., Vitányi, P. (eds.) WDAG 1994. LNCS, vol. 857, pp. 130–140. Springer, Heidelberg (1994). https://doi.org/10.1007/BFb0020429
25. Johnson, R.E., Schneider, F.B.: Symmetry and similarity in distributed systems. In: Malcolm, M.A., Strong, H.R. (eds.) Proceedings of the Fourth Annual ACM Symposium on Principles of Distributed Computing, Minaki, Ontario, Canada, 5–7 August 1985, pp. 13–22. ACM (1985)
26. Lamport, L.: On interprocess communication-part i: basic formalism, part ii: algorithms. Distrib. Comput. **2**, 77–101 (1986)
27. Yanagisawa, N.: Wait-free solvability of colorless tasks in anonymous shared-memory model. Theory Comput. Syst. 1–18 (2017). https://doi.org/10.1007/s00224-017-9819-0

# Efficient Means of Achieving Composability Using Object Based Semantics in Transactional Memory Systems

Sathya Peri$^{(\boxtimes)}$, Ajay Singh$^{(\boxtimes)}$, and Archit Somani$^{(\boxtimes)}$

Department of Computer Science and Engineering, IIT Hyderabad, Hyderabad, India
{sathya_p,cs15mtech01001,cs15resch01001}@iith.ac.in

**Abstract.** Composing together the individual atomic methods of concurrent data-structures (*cds*) pose multiple design and consistency challenges. In this context composition provided by transactions in software transaction memory (STM) can be handy. However, most of the STMs offer read/write primitives to access shared *cds*. These read/write primitives result in unnecessary aborts. Instead, semantically rich higher-level methods of the underlying *cds* like lookup, insert or delete (in case of hash-table or lists) aid in ignoring unimportant lower level read/write conflicts and allow better concurrency.

In this paper, we adapt transaction tree model in databases to propose OSTM which enables efficient composition in *cds*. We extend the traditional notion of conflicts and legality to higher level methods of *cds* using STMs and lay down detailed correctness proof to show that it is co-opaque. We implement OSTM with concurrent closed addressed hash-table (*HT-OSTM*) and list (*list-OSTM*) which exports the higher-level operations as transaction interface.

In our experiments with varying workloads and randomly generated transaction operations, *HT-OSTM* shows speedup of 3 to 6 times and w.r.t aborts *HT-OSTM* is 3 to 7 times better than ESTM and read/write based STM, respectively. Where as, *list-OSTM* outperforms state of the art lock-free transactional list, NOrec STM list and boosted list by 30% to 80% across all workloads and scenarios. Further, *list-OSTM* incurred negligible aborts in comparison to other techniques considered in the paper.

**Keywords:** Concurrent data structures · Composability
Software transactional memory · Opacity · Co-opacity

A preliminary version of this work was accepted in AADDA 2017 as work in progress. Author sequence follows lexical order of last names.

A. Podelski and F. Taïani (Eds.): NETYS 2018, LNCS 11028, pp. 157–174, 2019.
https://doi.org/10.1007/978-3-030-05529-5_11

# 1   Introduction

Software Transaction Memory Systems (*STMs*) are a convenient programming interface for a programmer to access shared memory without worrying about concurrency issues [1,2] and are natural choice for achieving composability [3].

Most of the *STMs* proposed in the literature are specifically based on read-/write primitive operations (or methods) on memory buffers (or memory registers). These *STMs* typically export the following methods: *STM_begin* which begins a transaction, *t_read* which reads from a buffer, *t_write* which writes onto a buffer, *tryC* which validates the operations of the transaction and tries to commit. We refer to these as *Read-Write STMs or RWSTMs*. As a part of the validation, the STMs typically check for *conflicts* among the operations. Two operations are said to be conflicting if at least one of them is a write (or update) operation. Normally, the order of two conflicting operations cannot be commutated. On the other hand, *Object STMs or OSTMs* operate on higher level objects rather than read & write operations on memory locations. They include more semantically rich operations such as enq/deq on queue objects, push/pop on stack objects and insert/lookup/delete on sets, trees or `hash-table` objects depending upon the underlying data structure used to implement OSTM.

It was shown in databases that object-level systems provide greater concurrency than read/write systems [4, Chap. 6]. Along the same lines, we propose a model to achieve composability with greater concurrency for *STMs* by considering higher-level objects which leverage the richer semantics of object level methods. We motivate this with an interesting example.

Consider an *OSTM* operating on the `hash-table` object called as *Hash-table Object STM* or *HT-OSTM* which exports the following methods - *STM_begin*which begins a transaction (same as in *RWSTMs*); *STM_insert* which inserts a value for a given key; *STM_delete* which deletes the value associated with the given key; *STM_lookup* which looks up the value associated with the given key and *STM_tryC* which validates the operations of the transaction.

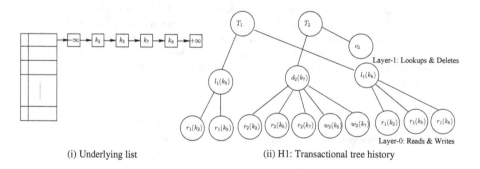

(i) Underlying list                    (ii) H1: Transactional tree history

**Fig. 1.** Motivational example for OSTMs

A simple way to implement the concurrent *HT-OSTM* is using a list (a single bucket) where each element of the list stores the ⟨key, value⟩ pair. The elements of the list are sorted by their keys similar to the set implementations discussed in [5, Chap. 9]. It can be seen that the underlying list is a concurrent data-structure manipulated by multiple transactions. So, we may use the lazy-list based concurrent set [6] to implement the operations of the list denoted as: *list_insert*, *list_del* and *list_lookup*. Thus, when a transaction invokes *STM_insert*(shortened as i), *STM_delete*(shortened as d) and *STM_lookup*(shortened as l) methods, the STM internally invokes the *list_insert*, *list_del* and *list_lookup* methods respectively.

Consider an instance of list in which the nodes with keys $\langle k_2 \ k_5 \ k_7 \ k_8 \rangle$ are present in the hash-table as shown in Fig. 1(i) and transactions $T_1$ and $T_2$ are concurrently executing $STM\_lookup_1(k_5)$, $STM\_delete_2(k_7)$ and $STM\_lookup_1(k_8)$ as shown in Fig. 1(ii). In this setting, suppose a transaction $T_1$ of *HT-OSTM* invokes methods *STM_lookup* on the keys $k_5, k_8$. This would internally cause the *HT-OSTM* to invoke *list_lookup* method on keys $\langle k_2, k_5 \rangle$ and $\langle k_2, k_5, k_7, k_8 \rangle$ respectively.

Concurrently, suppose transaction $T_2$ invokes the method *STM_delete* on key $k_7$ between the two *STM_lookups* of $T_1$. This would cause, *HT-OSTM* to invoke *list_del* method of list on $k_7$. Since, we are using lazy-list approach on the underlying list, *list_del* involves pointing the next field of element $k_5$ to $k_8$ and marking element $k_7$ as deleted. Thus *list_del* of $k_7$ would execute the following sequence of read/write level operations- $r(k_2)r(k_5)r(k_7)w(k_5)w(k_7)$ where $r(k_5), w(k_5)$ denote read & write on the element $k_5$ with some value respectively. The execution of *HT-OSTM* denoted as a *history* can be represented as a transactional forest as shown in Fig. 1(ii). Here the execution of each transaction is a tree.

In this execution, we denote the read/write operations (leaves) as layer-0 and *STM_lookup*, *STM_delete* methods as layer-1. Consider the history (execution) at layer-0 (while ignoring higher-level operations), denoted as $H0$. It can be verified this history is not opaque [7]. This is because between the two reads of $k_5$ by $T_1$, $T_2$ writes to $k_5$. It can be seen that if history $H0$ is input to a *RWSTMs* one of the transactions among $T_1$ and $T_2$ would be aborted to ensure correctness (in this case opacity [7]). On the other hand consider the history $H1$ at layer-1 consisting of *STM_lookup*, *STM_delete* methods while ignoring the underlying read/write operations. We ignore the underlying read & write operations since they do not overlap (referred to as pruning in [4, Chap. 6]). Since these methods operate on different keys, they are not conflicting and can be re-ordered either way. Thus, we get that $H1$ is opaque [7] with $T_1T_2$ (or $T_2T_1$) being an equivalent serial history.

The important idea in the above argument is that some conflicts at lower-level operations do not matter at higher level operations. Thus, such lower level conflicting operations may be ignored[1]. Harris et al. referred to it as *benign-conflicts* [9]. With object level modeling of histories, we get a higher number of acceptable schedules than read/write model. The history, $H1$ in Fig. 1(ii)

---

[1] While some conflicts of lower level do not matter at higher level, some other conflicts do. An example illustrating this is shown in the technical report [8].

clearly shows the advantage of considering STMs with higher level *STM_insert*, *STM_delete* and *STM_lookup* operations.

The atomic property of transactions helps to correctly compose together several different individual operations. The above examples demonstrate that the concurrency in such STM can be enhanced by considering the object level semantics. To achieve this, in this paper: **(a)** We propose a generic framework for composing higher level objects based on the notion of conflicts for objects in databases [4, Chap. 6]. **(b)** For correctness our framework considers, opacity [7] a popular correctness-criterion for STMs which is different from serializability commonly used in databases. It can be proved that verifying the membership of opacity similar to view-serializability is NP-Complete [10]. Hence, using conflicts we develop a subclass of opacity which is *conflict co-opacity* or *co-opacity* for objects. We then develop polynomial time graph characterization for co-opacity based on conflict-graph acyclicity. The proposed correctness-criterion, co-opacity is similar to the notion of conflict-opacity developed for *RWSTMs* by Kuznetsov and Peri [11]. **(c)** To show the efficacy of this framework, we develop *HT-OSTM* based on the idea of *basic timestamp order (BTO)* scheduler developed in databases [4, Chap. 4]. For showing correctness of *HT-OSTM*, we show that all the methods are linearizabale while the transactions are *co-opaque* by showing that the corresponding conflict graph is acyclic. Although we have considered *HT-OSTM* here, we believe that this notion of conflicts can be extended to other high-level objects such as Stacks, Queues, Tries etc.

A simple modification of *HT-OSTM* gives us a concurrent list based STM or *list-OSTM*. Finally, we compared the performance of *HT-OSTM* against a `hash-table` application built ESTM [12] and BTO [4] based RWSTM. The *list-OSTM* is compared with lock-free transactional list [13], NOrec based RSTM list [14] and boosting list [15]. The results in Sect. 5 represent *HT-OSTM* and *list-OSTM* reduces the number of aborts to minimal and show significant performance gain in comparison to other techniques.

**Related Work:** Our work differs from databases model in with regard to correctness-criterion used for safety. While databases consider CSR. We consider linearizability to prove the correctness of the methods of the transactions and opacity to show the correctness of the transactions. Earliest work of using the semantics of concurrent data structures for object level granularity include that of open nested transactions [16] and transaction boosting of Herlihy et al. [15] which is based on serializability(strict or commit order serializability) of generated schedules as correctness criteria. Herlihy's model is pessimistic and uses undo logs for rollback. Our model is more optimistic in that sense and the underlying data structure is updated only after there is a guarantee that there is no inconsistency due to concurrency. Thus, we do not need to do rollbacks which keeps the log overhead minimal. This also solves the problem of irrevocable operations being executed during a transaction which might abort later otherwise.

Hassan et al. [17] have proposed optimistic transactional boosting (OTB) that extends original transactional boosting methodology by optimizing and making it more adaptable to STMs. Although there seem similarities between their work and our implementation, we differ w.r.t the correctness-criterion which is co-opacity a subclass of opacity [11] in our case. They did not prove opacity for OTB however, their work extensively talks of linearizability. Furthermore, we also differ in the development of the conflict-based theoretical framework which can be adapted to build other object based STMs. Spiegelman et al. [18] try to build a transactional data structure library from existing concurrent data structure library. Their work is much of a mechanism than a methodology.

Zhang et al. [13] recently propose a method to transform lockfree *cds* to transactional lockfree linked *cds* and base the correctness on *strict serializability*. Fraser et. al. [19] proposed OSTM based on shadow copy mechanism, which involves a level of indirection to access the shared objects through *OSTMOpenForReading* and *OSTMOpenForWriting* as exported methods. The exported methods in Fraser et.al's OSTM may allow *OSTMOpenForReading* to see the inconsistent state of the shared objects but our OSTM model precludes this possibility by validating the access during execution of rv_method (i.e. the methods which do not modify the underlying objects and only return some value by performing a search on them). Thus, we can say our motivation and implementation is different from Fraser OSTM [19] and only the name happens to coincide.

**Roadmap.** We explain the system model in Sect. 2. In Sect. 3, we build the notion of legality, conflicts to describe opacity, co-opacity and the graph characterization. Based on the model we demonstrate the *HT-OSTM* design in Sect. 4. In Sect. 5 we show the evaluation results. Finally, we conclude in Sect. 6.

## 2    Building System Model

In this paper, we assume that our system consists finite number of $n$ threads that run in a completely asynchronous manner and communicate using shared objects. The threads communicate with each other by invoking higher-level methods on the shared objects and getting corresponding responses. Consequently, we make no assumption about the relative speeds of the threads. We also assume that none of these processors and threads fail or crash abruptly.

*Events and Methods:* We assume that the threads execute atomic *events*. We assume that these events by different threads are (1) read/write on shared/local memory objects, (2) method invocations (or *inv*) event and responses (or *rsp*) event on higher level shared-memory objects.

Within a transaction, a process can invoke layer-1 methods (or operations) on a *hash-table* transaction object. A hash-table($ht$) consists of multiple key-value pairs of the form $\langle k, v \rangle$. The keys and values are respectively from sets $\mathscr{K}$ and $\mathscr{V}$. The methods that a transaction $T_i$ can invoke are: (1) $STM\_begin_i()$: Begins a transaction and returns an unique id to the invoking thread (2) $STM\_insert_i(ht, k, v)$: Inserts a value $v$ onto key $k$ in hash-table $ht$ (3) $STM\_delete_i(ht, k, v)$: Deletes the key $k$ from the hash-table $ht$ & returns the current value $v$ (4) $STM\_lookup_i(ht, k, v)$: returns the current value $v$ for key

$k$ in $ht$ (5) $tryC_i()$ which tries to commit all the operations of $T_i$ and (6) $tryA_i()$ aborts $T_i$. We assume that each method consists of an $inv$ and $rsp$ event.

We denote $STM\_insert$ and $STM\_delete$ as $update$ methods (or $upd\_method$) since both of these change the underlying data-structure. We denote $STM\_delete$ and $STM\_lookup$ as $return\text{-}value$ $methods$ $(or$ $rv\_method)$ as these operations return values from $ht$. A method may return $ok$ if successful or $\mathscr{A}$(abort) if it sees inconsistent state of $ht$.

**Transactions:** Following the notations used in database multi-level transactions [4], we model a transaction as a two-level tree. The $layer\text{-}0$ consist of read/write events and $layer\text{-}1$ of the tree consists of methods invoked by transaction.

Having informally explained a transaction, we formally define a transaction $T$ as the tuple $\langle evts(T), <_T \rangle$. Here $evts(T)$ are all the read/write events at $layer\text{-}0$ of the transaction. $<_T$ is a total order among all the events of the transaction.

We denote the first and last events of a transaction $T_i$ as $T_i.firstEvt$ and $T_i.lastEvt$. Given any other read/write event $rw$ in $T_i$, we assume that $T_i.firstEvt <_{T_i} rw <_{T_i} T_i.lastEvt$. All the methods of $T_i$ are denoted as $methods(T_i)$.

**Histories:** A $history$ is a sequence of events belonging to different transactions. The collection of events is denoted as $evts(H)$. Similar to a transaction, we denote a history $H$ as tuple $\langle evts(H), <_H \rangle$ where all the events are totally ordered by $<_H$. The set of methods that are in $H$ is denoted by $methods(H)$. A method $m$ is $incomplete$ if $inv(m)$ is in $evts(H)$ but not its corresponding response event. Otherwise $m$ is $complete$ in $H$.

Coming to transactions in $H$, the set of transactions in $H$ are denoted as $txns(H)$. The set of committed (resp., aborted) transactions in $H$ is denoted by $committed(H)$ (resp., $aborted(H)$). The set of $live$ transactions in $H$ are those which are neither committed nor aborted. On the other hand, the set of $terminated$ transactions are those which have either committed or aborted.

We denote two histories $H1, H2$ as $equivalent$ if their events are the same, i.e., $evts(H1) = evts(H2)$. A history $H$ is qualified to be $well\text{-}formed$ if: (1) all the methods of a transaction $T_i$ in $H$ are totally ordered, i.e. a transaction invokes a method only after it receives a response of the previous method invoked by it (2) $T_i$ does not invoke any other method after it received an $\mathscr{A}$ response or after $tryC(ok)$ method. We only consider $well\text{-}formed$ histories for $HT\text{-}OSTM$.

A method $m_{ij}$ ($j^{th}$ method of a transaction $T_i$) in a history $H$ is said to be $isolated$ or $atomic$ if for any other event $e_{pqr}$ belonging to some other method $m_{pq}$ (of transaction $T_p$) either $e_{pqr}$ occurs before $inv(m_{ij})$ or after $rsp(m_{ij})$. Here, $e_{pqr}$ stands for $r^{th}$ event of $m_{pq}$.

**Sequential Histories:** A history $H$ is said to be $sequential$ (term used in [11, 20]) if all the methods in it are complete and isolated. From now on wards, most of our discussion would relate to sequential histories.

Since in sequential histories all the methods are isolated, we treat each method as whole without referring to its $inv$ and $rsp$ events. For a sequential history $H$, we construct the *completion* of $H$, denoted $\overline{H}$, by inserting $tryA_k(\mathscr{A})$ immediately after the last method of every transaction $T_k \in live(H)$. Since all the methods in a sequential history are complete, this definition only has to take care of completed transactions. Consider a sequential history $H$. Let $m_{ij}(ht, k, v/NULL)$ be the first method of $T_i$ in $H$ operating on the key $k$ as $H.firstKeyMth(\langle ht, k\rangle, T_i)$. For a method $m_{ix}(ht, k, v)$ which is not the first method on $\langle ht, k\rangle$ of $T_i$ in $H$, we denote its previous method on $k$ of $T_i$ as $m_{ij}(ht, k, v) = H.prevKeyMth(m_{ix}, T_i)$.

**Real-time Order and Serial Histories:** Given a history $H$, $<_H$ orders all the events in $H$. For two complete methods $m_{ij}, m_{pq}$ in $methods(H)$, we denote $m_{ij} \prec_H^{MR} m_{pq}$ if $rsp(m_{ij}) <_H inv(m_{pq})$. Here MR stands for method real-time order. It must be noted that all the methods of the same transaction are ordered. Similarly, for two transactions $T_i, T_p$ in $term(H)$, we denote $(T_i \prec_H^{TR} T_p)$ if $(T_i.lastEvt <_H T_p.firstEvt)$. Here TR stands for transactional real-time order.

We define a history $H$ as *serial* [10] or *t-sequential* [20] if all the transactions in $H$ have terminated and can be totally ordered w.r.t $\prec_{TR}$, i.e. all the transactions execute one after the other without any interleaving. Intuitively, a history $H$ is serial if all its transactions can be isolated. Formally, $\langle (H \text{ is serial}) \implies (\forall T_i \in txns(H) : (T_i \in term(H)) \wedge (\forall T_i, T_p \in txns(H) : (T_i \prec_H^{TR} T_p) \vee (T_p \prec_H^{TR} T_i)))\rangle$. Since all the methods within a transaction are ordered, a serial history is also sequential.

# 3 Correctness of *HT-OSTM*: Opacity and Conflict Opacity

In this section, we define the correctness of *HT-OSTM* by extending opacity [7]. We then define a tractable subclass of opacity, co-opacity which is defined using conflict like CSR [4] in databases. We start with legality and opacity.

## 3.1 Legal Histories and Opacity

In this subsection, we start with defining legal histories. To simplify our analysis, we assume that there exists an initial transaction $T_0$ that invokes *STM_delete* method on all the keys of all the hash-tables used by any transaction.

We define *legality* of rv_methods (*STM_delete* & *STM_lookup*) on sequential histories which we later use to define correctness criterion. Consider a sequential history $H$ having a rv_method $rvm_{ij}(ht, k, v)$ (with $v \neq NULL$) belonging to transaction $T_i$. We define this *rvm* method to be *legal* if:

LR1 If the $rvm_{ij}$ is not first method of $T_i$ to operate on $\langle ht, k\rangle$ and $m_{ix}$ is the previous method of $T_i$ on $\langle ht, k\rangle$. Formally, $rvm_{ij} \neq H.firstKeyMth(\langle ht, k\rangle, T_i) \wedge (m_{ix}(ht, k, v') = H.prevKeyMth(\langle ht, k\rangle, T_i))$ (where $v'$ could be NULL). Then,
(a) If $m_{ix}(ht, k, v')$ is a *STM_insert* method then $v = v'$.
(b) If $m_{ix}(ht, k, v')$ is a *STM_lookup* method then $v = v'$.

(c) If $m_{ix}(ht, k, v')$ is a *STM_delete* method then $v = NULL$.

In this case, we denote $m_{ix}$ as the last update method of $rvm_{ij}$, i.e., $m_{ix}(ht, k, v') = H.lastUpdt(rvm_{ij}(ht, k, v))$.

LR2 If $rvm_{ij}$ is the first method of $T_i$ to operate on $\langle ht, k \rangle$ and $v$ is not NULL. Formally, $rvm_{ij}(ht, k, v) = H.firstKeyMth(\langle ht, k \rangle, T_i) \wedge (v \neq NULL)$. Then,

(a) There is a *STM_insert* method $STM\_insert_{pq}(ht, k, v)$ in $methods(H)$ such that $T_p$ committed before $rvm_{ij}$. Formally, $\langle \exists STM\_insert_{pq}(ht, k, v) \in methods(H) : tryC_p \prec_H^{MR} rvm_{ij} \rangle$.

(b) There is no other update method $up_{xy}$ of a transaction $T_x$ operating on $\langle ht, k \rangle$ in $methods(H)$ such that $T_x$ committed after $T_p$ but before $rvm_{ij}$. Formally, $\langle \nexists up_{xy}(ht, k, v'') \in methods(H) : tryC_p \prec_H^{MR} tryC_x \prec_H^{MR} rvm_{ij} \rangle$.

In this case, we denote $tryC_p$ as the last update method of $rvm_{ij}$, i.e., $tryC_p(ht, k, v) = H.lastUpdt(rvm_{ij}(ht, k, v))$.

LR3 If $rvm_{ij}$ is the first method of $T_i$ to operate on $\langle ht, k \rangle$ and $v$ is NULL. Formally, $rvm_{ij}(ht, k, v) = H.firstKeyMth(\langle ht, k \rangle, T_i) \wedge (v = NULL)$. Then,

(a) There is *STM_delete* method $STM\_delete_{pq}(ht, k, v')$ in $methods(H)$ such that $T_p$ (which could be $T_0$ as well) committed before $rvm_{ij}$. Formally, $\langle \exists STM\_delete_{pq}(ht, k, v') \in methods(H) : tryC_p \prec_H^{MR} rvm_{ij} \rangle$. Here $v'$ could be NULL.

(b) There is no other update method $up_{xy}$ of a transaction $T_x$ operating on $\langle ht, k \rangle$ in $methods(H)$ such that $T_x$ committed after $T_p$ but before $rvm_{ij}$. Formally, $\langle \nexists up_{xy}(ht, k, v'') \in methods(H) : tryC_p \prec_H^{MR} tryC_x \prec_H^{MR} rvm_{ij} \rangle$.

In this case similar to step 3.1, we denote $tryC_p$ as the last update method of $rvm_{ij}$, i.e., $tryC_p(ht, k, v) = H.lastUpdt(rvm_{ij}(ht, k, v))$.

We assume that when a transaction $T_i$ operates on key $k$ of a `hash-table` $ht$, the result of this method is stored in *local logs* of $T_i$ for later methods to reuse. Thus, only the first rv_method operating on $\langle ht, k \rangle$ of $T_i$ accesses the shared-memory. The other rv_methods of $T_i$ operating on $\langle ht, k \rangle$ do not access the shared-memory and they see the effect of the previous method from the *local logs*. This idea is utilized in LR1. With reference to LR2 and LR3, it is possible that $T_x$ could have aborted before $rvm_{ij}$. For LR3, since we are assuming that transaction $T_0$ has invoked a *STM_delete* method on all the keys used of all `hash-table` objects, there exists at least one *STM_delete* method for every rv_method on $k$ of $ht$. We formally prove legality in technical report [8] and then we finally show that *HT-OSTM* histories are co-opaque [11].

Coming to *STM_insert* methods, since a *STM_insert* method always returns *ok* as they overwrite the node if already present therefore they always take effect on the $ht$. Thus, we denote all *STM_insert* methods as legal and only give legality definition for rv_method. We denote a sequential history $H$ as *legal* or *linearized* [21] if all its *rvm* methods are legal.

*Correctness-Criteria and Opacity:* A *correctness-criterion* is a set of histories. A history $H$ satisfying a correctness-criterion has some desirable properties. A popular correctness-criterion is *opacity* [7]. A sequential history $H$ is opaque if there exists a serial history $S$ such that: (1) $S$ is equivalent to $\overline{H}$, i.e., $evts(\overline{H}) = evts(S)$ (2) $S$ is legal and (3) $S$ respects the transactional real-time order of $H$, i.e., $\prec_H^{TR} \subseteq \prec_S^{TR}$.

## 3.2   Conflict Notion and Conflict-Opacity

Opacity is a popular correctness-criterion for STMs. But, as observed in Sect. 1, it can be proved that verifying the membership of opacity similar to view-serializability (VSR) in databases is NP-Complete [10]. To circumvent this issue, researchers in databases have identified an efficient sub-class of VSR, called conflict-serializability or CSR, based on the notion of conflicts. The membership of CSR can be verified in polynomial time using conflict graph characterization. Along the same lines, we develop the notion of conflicts for *HT-OSTM* and identify a sub-class of opacity, co-opacity. The proposed correctness-criterion is extension of the notion of conflict-opacity developed for *RWSTMs* by Kuznetsov and Peri [11].

We say two transactions $T_i, T_j$ of a sequential history $H$ for *HT-OSTM* are in *conflict* if atleast one of the following conflicts holds:

- **tryC-tryC** conflict:(1) $T_i$ & $T_j$ are committed and (2) $T_i$ & $T_j$ update the same key $k$ of the **hash-table**, $ht$, i.e., $((\langle ht, k \rangle \in updtSet(T_i)) \wedge ((\langle ht, k \rangle \in updtSet(T_j))$, where $updtSet(T_i)$ is update set of $T_i$. (3) $T_i$'s *tryC* completed before $T_j$'s *tryC*, i.e., $tryC_i \prec_H^{MR} tryC_j$.
- **tryC-rv** conflict:(1) $T_i$ is committed (2) $T_i$ updates the key $k$ of **hash-table**, $ht$. $T_j$ invokes a rv_method $rvm_{jy}$ on the key same $k$ of **hash-table** $ht$ which is the first method on $\langle ht, k \rangle$. Thus, $((\langle ht, k \rangle \in updtSet(T_i)) \wedge (rvm_{jy}(ht, k, v) \in rvSet(T_j)) \wedge (rvm_{jy}(ht, k, v) = H.firstKeyMth(\langle ht, k \rangle, T_j))$, where $rvSet(T_j)$ is return value set of $T_j$. (3) $T_i$'s *tryC* completed before $T_j$'s *rvm*, i.e., $tryC_i \prec_H^{MR} rvm_{jy}$.
- **rv-tryC** conflict:(1) $T_j$ is committed (2) $T_i$ invokes a rv_method on the key same $k$ of **hash-table** $ht$ which is the first method on $\langle ht, k \rangle$. $T_j$ updates the key $k$ of the **hash-table**, $ht$. Thus, $(rvm_{ix}(ht, k, v) \in rvSet(T_i)) \wedge (rvm_{ix}(ht, k, v) = H.firstKeyMth(\langle ht, k \rangle, T_i)) \wedge ((\langle ht, k \rangle \in updtSet(T_j))$ (3) $T_i$'s *rvm* completed before $T_j$'s *tryC*, i.e., $rvm_{ix} \prec_H^{MR} tryC_j$.

A rv_method $rvm_{ij}$ conflicts with a *tryC* method only if $rvm_{ij}$ is the first method of $T_i$ that operates on **hash-table** with a given key. Thus the conflict notion is defined only by the methods that access the shared memory. $(tryC_i, tryC_j)$, $(tryC_i, STM\_lookup_j)$, $(STM\_lookup_i, tryC_j)$, $(tryC_i, STM\_delete_j)$ and $(STM\_delete_i, tryC_j)$ can be the possible conflicting methods. For example, consider the history $H5 : l_1(ht, k_1, NULL)l_2(ht, k_2 , NULL)i_2(ht, k_1, v_1)i_1(ht, k_4, v_1)c_1 i_3(ht, k_3, v_3)c_3 d_2(ht, k_4, v_1)c_2 l_4(ht, k_4, NULL) i_4(ht, k_2, v_4)c_4$ in Fig. 2. $(l_1(ht, k_1, NULL), i_3(ht, k_1, v_1))$ and $(l_2(ht, k_2 ,$

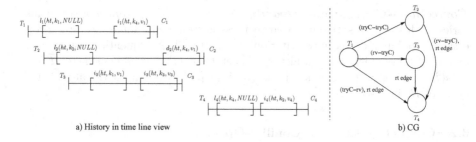

**Fig. 2.** Graph characterization of history $H5$

$NULL), i_4$ $(ht, k_2, v_4))$ are a conflict of type $rv\text{-}tryC$. Conflict type of $(i_1(ht, k_4, v_1), d_2(ht, k_4, v_1))$ and $(i_1(ht, k_4, v_1), l_4(ht, k_4, NULL))$ are $tryC\text{-}tryC$ and $tryC\text{-}rv$ respectively.

**Conflict Opacity:** Using this conflict notion, we can now define co-opacity. A sequential history $H$ is conflict-opaque (or co-opaque) if there exists a serial history $S$ such that: (1) $S$ is equivalent to $\overline{H}$, i.e. , $evts(\overline{H}) = evts(S)$ (2) $S$ is legal and (3) $S$ respects the transactional real-time order of $H$, i.e., $\prec_H^{TR} \subseteq \prec_S^{TR}$ and (4) S preserves conflicts (i.e. $\prec_H^{CO} \subseteq \prec_S^{CO}$).

Thus from the above definition, it can be seen that any history that is co-opaque is also opaque.

**Graph Characterization:** We now develop a graph characterization of co-opacity. For a sequential history $H$, we define *conflict-graph* of $H$, $CG(H)$ as the pair $(V, E)$ where $V$ is the set of $txns(H)$ and $E$ can be of following types: (a) *conflict edges:* $\{(T_i, T_j) : (T_i, T_j) \in \text{conflict(H)}\}$ where, conflict(H) is an ordered pair of transactions such that the transactions have one of the above pair of conflicts. (b) *real-time edge(or rt edge):* $\{(T_i, T_j)$: Transaction $T_i$ precedes $T_j$ in real-time, i.e., $T_i \prec_H^{TR} T_j\}$. Now, we have the following theorem which explains how graph characterization is useful.

**Theorem 1.** *A legal HT-OSTM history $H$ is co-opaque iff $CG(H)$ is acyclic.*

Using this framework, we next develop *HT-OSTM* using the notion of BTO. We show the transactional level correctness of the proposed algorithm by showing that all conflict graph of the histories generated by it are acyclic in the accompanying report [8].

## 4    *HT-OSTM*

We design *HT-OSTM* a concurrent closed addressed `hash-table` using above explained legality and conflict notion. The *HT-OSTM* exports *STM_begin()*, *STM_insert()*, *STM_delete()*, *STM_lookup()* and *STM_tryC()* and has $m$ number of buckets, which we refer to as size of the `hash-table`. The main part of interest from concurrency perspective is each bucket of the `hash-table` implemented as lazyrb-list (lazy red-blue list), the shared memory data structure.

**Lazyrb-list:** It is a linked structure with immutable *head* and *tail* sentinel nodes of the form of a tuple ⟨*key, value, lock, marked, max_ts, rl, bl*⟩ representing a node. The *key* represents unique id of the node so that a transaction could differentiate between two nodes. The *key* values may range from $-\infty$ (key of head node) to $+\infty$ (key of tail node). The *value* field may accommodate any type ranging from a basic integer to a complex class type. The *marked* field is to have lazy deletion as popular in lazylists [5,6] and *lock* to implement exclusive access to the node.

Lazyrb-list node have two links - *bl* (blue links) and *rl* (red links). First, the nodes which are not marked (not deleted) are reachable by bl from the head. Second, the nodes which are marked (i.e. logically deleted) and are only reached by *rl*. Thus, the name lazyrb-list. All marked nodes are reachable via *rl* and all the unmarked nodes are reachable via *bl* & *rl* from the head. Thus nodes reachable by *bl* are the subset of the nodes reachable by *rl*. Every node of lazyrb-list is in increasing order of its key.

Furthermore, every lazyrb-list node also has a *time-stamp* field (*max_ts*) to record the ids of the transaction which most recently executed some method. Augmenting the underlying shared data structure with time-stamps help in identifying conflicts which can cause a cycle in the execution and hence violate co-opacity [11]. This is captured by the graph characterization of a generated history as discussed in Fig. 2 which implies that cyclic conflicts leads to non co-opaque execution.

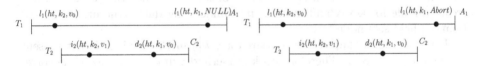

**Fig. 3.** History H is not co-opaque      **Fig. 4.** Co-opaque History H1 (Color figure online)

Now, we explain why we need to maintain deleted nodes through Figs. 3 and 4. History H shown in Fig. 3 is not co-opaque because there is no serial execution of T1 & T2 that can be shown co-opaque. In order to make it co-opaque $l_1(ht, k_1, NULL)$ needs to be aborted. And $l_1(ht, k_1, NULL)$ can only be aborted if *HT-OSTM* scheduler knows that a conflicting operation $d_2(ht, k_1, v_0)$ has already been scheduled and thus violating co-opacity. One way to have this information is that if the node represented by $k_1$ records the time-stamp of the delete method so that the scheduler realizes the violation of the time-order [4] and aborts $l_1(ht, k_1, NULL)$ to ensure co-opacity.

Thus, to ensure correctness, we need to maintain information about the nodes deleted from the `hash-table`. This can be achieved by only marking node deleted from the list of `hash-table`. But do not unlink it such that the marked node is still part of the list. This way, the information from deleted nodes can be used for ensuring co-opacity. In this case, after aborting $l_1(ht, k_1)$, we get that the history is co-opaque with $T1$ & $T2$ being the equivalent serial history as shown in Fig. 4. The deleted keys (nodes with marked field set) can be reused if another transaction comes & inserts the same key back.

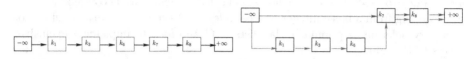

**Fig. 5.** Searching $k_8$ over lazylist (Color figure online)

**Fig. 6.** Searching $k_8$ over lazyrb-list (Color figure online)

But, the major hindrance in maintaining the deleted nodes as part of the ordinary lazy-list is that it would reduce search efficiency of the data structure. For example, in Fig. 5 searching $k_8$ would unnecessary cause traversal over marked (marked for lazy deletion) nodes represented by $k_1, k_3$ and $k_6$. We solve this problem in lazyrb-list by using two pointers. (1) bl (blue link): used to traverse over the actual inserted nodes and (2) rl (red link) used to traverse over the deleted nodes. Hence, in Fig. 6 to search for $k_8$ we can directly use bl saving significant search computations. A question may arise that how would we maintain the time-stamp of a node which has not yet been inserted? Such a case arises when *STM_lookup()* or *STM_delete()* is invoked from *rv_method*, and node corresponding to the key, say $k$ is not present in *bl* and *rl*. Then the *rv_method* will create a node for key $k$ and insert it into underlying data structure as deleted (marked field set) node.

For example, lookup wants to search key $k_{10}$ in Fig. 6 which is not present in the *bl* as well as *rl*. Therefore, lookup method will create a new node corresponding to the key $k_{10}$ and insert it into *rl* (refer the Fig. 7). So, we discuss in detail the invariants and properties of the lazyrb-list and ensure that no duplicate nodes are inserted while proving the method level correctness in technical report [8].

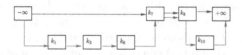

**Fig. 7.** Execution under lazyrb-list. $k_{10}$ is added in lazyrb-list if not present. (Color figure online)

**Transaction Log.** Each transaction maintains local log called *txlog*. It stores transaction id and status: live, commit or abort signifying that transaction is executing, has committed or has aborted due to some method failing the validation, respectively.

Each entry of the *txlog* is called *log_entry* (shortened as *le*) stores the meta information of each method a transaction encounters as $updtSet()$ and $rvSet()$ as formalized in Sect. 3.2. The *le* is a tuple of type $\langle key, value, status, preds, currs \rangle$. A method may have $OK$ and $FAIL$ as it's status. The *preds* and *currs* are the array of nodes in rl and bl identified during the traversal over the lazyrb-list by each method. It depicts the location over the lazyrb-list where the method would take effect.

### *HT-OSTM* Methodology:

In this section, we provide the working idea of the methods exported to transactions of the *HT-OSTM* and detailed algorithms are provided in the accompanying report [8]. Execution of every transaction $T_i$ can be categorized into *rv_method execution* phase and *upd_method execution* phase.

### rv_method execution phase:

1. $\forall\ m_{ij}(k) \in \{STM\_lookup(),\ STM\_delete()\}$
   (a) If legality rule 3.1 is applicable.
      i. update the *txlog* and return.
   (b) If legality rule 3.2 & 3.3 is applicable.
      i. Traverse the *cds* to identify pred and curr nodes for both the rl and bl as done in lazy-lists or skip lists. Then, acquire ordered locks on the nodes.
      ii. *Validate.* If the *Validate()* returns $\mathscr{A}$, the $m_{ij}(k)$ aborts and subsequently $T_i$ is aborted. Otherwise, if *Validate()* returns *retry* then $m_{ij}(k)$ is retried from step 1.(b).
      iii. If validation succeeds, create a new *le* in *txlog* & update the *le*. And, insert a node in rl if the node is not present in lazyrb-list as explained in Fig. 7.
      iv Release locks and return.
2. If $m_{ij}(k) \in \{STM\_insert()\}$
   (a) Update the *txlog* and return.

We validate *STM_lookup()* immediately and do not validate again in *STM_tryC()* unlike the implementation of OTB by Hassan et. al [17]. This is required to ensure that the execution is opaque.

### Validate():

1. First the current operation validates for any possible interference due to concurrent transactions through method validation.
   **methodValidation rule:** If the preds are marked and the next node of pred is not curr, implies a conflicting concurrent operation has also made changes. Thus, the current operation has to *retry*. Otherwise method validation is said to succeed.
2. Time order validation is performed when method validation succeeds.
   **time orderValidation rule** [4, Chap. 4]: If a transaction $T_i$ with time-stamp $i$ want to access a node $n$. Also, Let $T_j$ be a conflicting transaction with time-stamp j which accessed $n$ previously. Now, If $i < j$ then $T_i$ is aborted. Else this method returns *ok*.

3. Return *abort* or *retry* or *ok*.

*STM_delete()* in *rv_method execution* phase behaves as *STM_lookup()* but it is validated twice. First, in *rv_method execution* similar to *STM_lookup()* and secondly in *upd_method execution* to ensure co-opacity. We adopt lazy delete approach for *STM_delete()*. Thus, nodes are marked for deletion and not physically deleted for *STM_delete()* method. In the current work we assume that a garbage collection mechanism is present and we do not worry about it.

**upd_method execution phase.** During this phase a transaction executes *STM_tryC()*. It begins by ordering the *txlog* in increasing order of the keys. This way locks can be acquired in increasing order of keys to avoid deadlock. We re-validate upd_method in *txlog* to ensure that the *pred & curr* for the methods has not changed since the point they were logged during *rv_method execution* phase. Please note that *txlog* only contains the log entry (*le*) for upd_method. Because we do not validate the lookup and failed delete again in *STM_tryC()*.

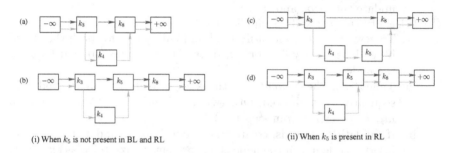

(i) When $k_5$ is not present in BL and RL            (ii) When $k_5$ is present in RL

**Fig. 8.** Insert of $k_5$ in *STM_tryC()*. (i) bl & rl of $k_5$ is set to $K_8$ then bl of $k_3$ linked to $K_5$ & rl of $k_4$ is linked to $k_5$. (ii) Only bl of $k_5$ is set to $K_8$ then bl of $k_3$ linked to $K_5$. (Color figure online)

Now after successful validation, we update the shared lazyrb-list using the log entries (*le*) of the *txlog* one by one. There may be two cases when a node is inserted into lazyrb-list by the *STM_insert()*. First, the node is not reachable by both rl and bl (not present in *cds*). Figure 8(i) represents this case when $k_5$ is neither reachable by *bl* and nor in *rl*. It adds $k_5$ to lazyrb-list at location $preds\langle k_3, k_4\rangle$ and $currs\langle k_8, k_8\rangle$ (in the notation, first and second index is the key reachable by bl & rl, respectively). Figure 8(i)(a) is lazyrb-list before addition of $k_5$ and Fig. 8(i)(b) is lazyrb-list state post addition. Second, if the node is reached only by rl. Figure 8(ii) represents this case where $k_5$ is reached only by *rl*. It adds $k_5$ to lazyrb-list at location $pred\langle k_3, k_4\rangle$ and $curr\langle k_5, k_8\rangle$. Figure 8(i)(c) is lazyrb-list before addition of $k_5$ with bl and Fig. 8(i)(d) is lazyrb-list state post addition.

During *STM_delete()* if a node to be removed is reachable with bl then its marked field is set and the links are modified such that it is not reachable by bl. Figure 9 shows a case where a node $k_5$ needs to be deleted from the lazyrb-list in Fig. 9(i). So, here the node $k_5$ sets its marked field and then is detached from the bl (Fig. 9(ii)).

**Fig. 9.** Delete of $k_5$ in $STM\_tryC()$. $k_5$ is unlinked from bl by linking bl of $k_1$ to $\infty$. (Color figure online)

**Correctness:** In object based STM techniques like *HT-OSTM* where methods are intervals, proving that its methods can be partially ordered or linearized is complex. But, proving the correctness of *cds* requires taking into account the semantics and implementation details as asserted by work of Hassan et al. [17]. We establish that all methods can be linearized at *method level* before arguing about the co-opacity of *HT-OSTM* history at *transaction level* using graph characterization. The accompanying technical report [8] provides detailed proof, here we only state the major theorem which contributes to proving that *HT-OSTM* is co-opaque.

**Theorem 2.** *Consider a history H generated by HT-OSTM. Then there exists a sequential & legal history H' equivalent to H such that the conflict-graph of H' is acyclic.*

## 5   Evaluation

We performed all the experiments on Intel(R) Xeon(R) CPU E5-2690 v4 @ 2.60GHz machine with 56 CPUs and 32K L1 data cache and 32 GB memory. Each thread spawns 10 transactions each of which randomly generate up to 5 methods of *HT-OSTM*. We assume that the `hash-table` of *HT-OSTM* has 5 buckets and each of the bucket (or list in case of *list-OSTM*) can have maximum size of 1K keys. We ran the experiments to calculate two parameters: (1) time taken for a transaction to commit. Upon abort, a transaction is retried until it commits. (2) Number of aborts incurred until all the transactions commit.

We compare *HT-OSTM* with the ESTM [12] based `hash-table` and the transactional `hash-table` application built using RWSTM which is synchronised by basic time stamp ordering protocol [4, Chap. 4]. Further, we evaluate *list-OSTM* with the state of the art lock-free transactional list (LFT) [13], NOrec STM list (NTM) [14] and boosting list (BST) [15]. All these implementations are directly taken from the TLDS framework[2]. The experiments were performed under two kinds of workloads. Update intensive(lookup:50%, insert:25%, delete:25%) and lookup intensive(lookup:70%, insert:10%, delete:20%). Here,

---

[2] https://ucf-cs.github.io/tlds/.

upto 70% lookups *HT-OSTM* performs better but with more than 70% of lookups ESTM shows better performance when contention is higher. The evaluation is done by varying threads from 2 to 64 in power of 2. Before each application is run there is a initialization phase where the data structure is populated randomly with nodes of half its maximum size.

**HT-OSTM.**[3] Figure 10a shows that w.r.t. time taken *HT-OSTM* outperforms ESTM [12] and RWSTM on an average by 3 times for lookup intensive workload. Plus, for update intensive workload *HT-OSTM* on average is 6 times better than ESTM & RWSTM. Similarly, in terms of aborts, *HT-OSTM* has 3 & 2 times lesser aborts than ESTM and RWSTM for lookup intensive workload, respectively. Also for update intensive load *HT-OSTM* has 7 and 8 times lesser aborts with ESTM and RWSTM respectively, as can be seen in Fig. 10b.

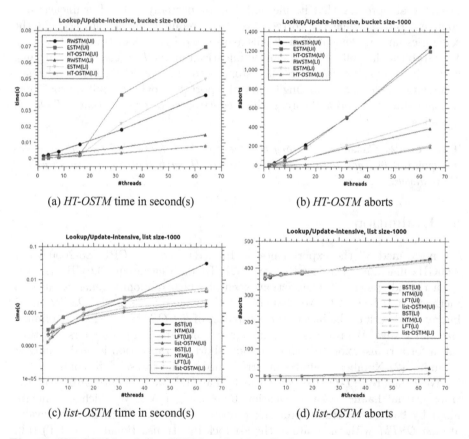

(a) *HT-OSTM* time in second(s)

(b) *HT-OSTM* aborts

(c) *list-OSTM* time in second(s)

(d) *list-OSTM* aborts

**Fig. 10.** *HT-OSTM* and *list-OSTM* evaluation. Each curve is named as technique name(workload type). LI/UI denotes lookup intensive/ update intensive.

---

[3] lib source code link: https://github.com/PDCRL/ht-ostm.

***list-OSTM.*** The average aborts for *list-OSTM* never go beyond 30 in magnitude while that of other techniques (in Fig. 10d) are of 388 in the magnitude for both types of workloads. While time taken is 76%, 89% and 33% (with lookup intensive) and 77%, 77% and 154% (with update intensive) better than LFT, NTM and BST respectively (as shown in Fig. 10c).

## 6    Conclusion and Future Work

In this paper, we build a model for building highly concurrent and composable data structures using object based transactional memory. We use the observation that higher concurrency can be obtained by considering OSTMs as compared to traditional *RWSTMs* by leveraging richer object-level semantics. To achieve this, we propose comprehensive theoretical model based on legality semantics and conflict notions for `hash-table` based OSTM. Using these notions we extend the definition of opacity and co-opacity for *HT-OSTMs* in Sect. 3. Then, based on this model, we develop a practical implementation of `hash-table` based object STM, *HT-OSTM*. We then perform some extensive experiments to verify the gains achieved as demonstrated in Sect. 5. As a part of future work, we plan to develop multi-version object STMs similar to multi-version STMs & databases.

**Acknowledgment.** We extend our thanks to Dr. Roy Friedman and anonymous reviewers for careful reading of the draft and suggestions. This research is partially supported by the grant from Board of Research in Nuclear Sciences (BRNS), India with project number- 36(3)/14/19/2016-BRNS/36019.

## References

1. Herlihy, M., Moss, J.E.B.: Transactional memory: architectural support for lock-free data structures. SIGARCH Comput. Archit. News **21**(2), 289–300 (1993)
2. Shavit, N., Touitou, D.: Software transactional memory. In: PODC, pp. 204–213 (1995)
3. Harris, T., Marlow, S., Peyton-Jones, S., Herlihy, M.: Composable memory transactions. In: PPOPP, New York, NY, USA, pp. 48–60. ACM (2005)
4. Weikum, G., Vossen, G.: Transactional Information Systems: Theory, Algorithms, and the Practice of Concurrency Control and Recovery. Morgan Kaufmann, Burlington (2002)
5. Herlihy, M., Shavit, N.: The Art of Multiprocessor Programming. Elsevier Science, Amsterdam (2012)
6. Heller, S., Herlihy, M., Luchangco, V., Moir, M., Scherer, W.N., Shavit, N.: A lazy concurrent list-based set algorithm. Parallel Process. Lett. **17**(4), 411–424 (2007)
7. Guerraoui, R., Kapalka, M.: On the correctness of transactional memory. In: PPOPP, pp. 175–184. ACM (2008)
8. Peri, S., Singh, A., Somani, A.: Efficient means of achieving composability using transactional memory. CoRR abs/1709.00681 (2017)
9. Harris, T., et al.: Abstract nested transactions (2007)
10. Papadimitriou, C.H.: The serializability of concurrent database updates. J. ACM **26**(4), 631–653 (1979)

11. Kuznetsov, P., Peri, S.: Non-interference and local correctness in transactional memory. Theory Comput. Sci. **688**, 103–116 (2017)

12. Felber, P., Gramoli, V., Guerraoui, R.: Elastic transactions. J. Parallel Distrib. Comput. **100**(C), 103–127 (2017)

13. Zhang, D., Dechev, D.: Lock-free transactions without rollbacks for linked data structures. In: SPAA 2016, New York, NY, USA, pp. 325–336. ACM (2016)

14. Dalessandro, L., Spear, M.F., Scott, M.L.: NOrec: streamlining STM by abolishing ownership records. In: Govindarajan, R., Padua, D.A., Hall, M.W., (eds.) PPOPP, pp. 67–78. ACM (2010)

15. Herlihy, M., Koskinen, E.: Transactional boosting: a methodology for highly-concurrent transactional objects. In: PPOPP, pp. 207–216. ACM (2008)

16. Ni, Y., et al.: Open nesting in software transactional memory. In: PPOPP. ACM (2007)

17. Hassan, A., Palmieri, R., Ravindran, B.: Optimistic transactional boosting. In: Moreira, J.E., Larus, J.R. (eds.) PPOPP, pp. 387–388. ACM (2014)

18. Spiegelman, A., Golan-Gueta, G., Keidar, I.: Transactional data structure libraries. In: PLDI, pp. 682–696. ACM (2016)

19. Fraser, K., Harris, T.: Concurrent programming without locks. ACM Trans. Comput. Syst. **25**(2), 5 (2007)

20. Kuznetsov, P., Ravi, S.: On the cost of concurrency in transactional memory. In: Fernàndez Anta, A., Lipari, G., Roy, M. (eds.) OPODIS 2011. LNCS, vol. 7109, pp. 112–127. Springer, Heidelberg (2011). https://doi.org/10.1007/978-3-642-25873-2_9

21. Herlihy, M.P., Wing, J.M.: Linearizability: a correctness condition for concurrent objects. ACM Trans. Program. Lang. Syst. **12**(3), 463–492 (1990)

# Unleashing and Speeding Up Readers in Atomic Object Implementations

Chryssis Georgiou[1], Theophanis Hadjistasi[2(✉)], Nicolas Nicolaou[3,4], and Alexander A. Schwarzmann[2]

[1] Department of Computer Science, University of Cyprus, Nicosia, Cyprus
chryssis@cs.ucy.ac.cy
[2] University of Connecticut, Storrs, CT, USA
{theo,aas}@uconn.edu
[3] KIOS Research and Innovation Center of Excellence,
University of Cyprus, Nicosia, Cyprus
nicolasn@cs.ucy.ac.cy
[4] Algolysis Ltd., Nicosia, Cyprus

**Abstract.** Providing efficient emulations of atomic read/write objects in asynchronous, crash-prone, message-passing systems is an important problem in distributed computing. Communication latency is a factor that typically dominates the performance of message-passing systems, consequently the efficiency of algorithms implementing atomic objects is measured in terms of the number of communication exchanges involved in each read and write operation. The seminal result of Attiya, Bar-Noy, and Dolev established that two pairs of communication exchanges, or equivalently two round-trip communications, are sufficient. Subsequent research examined the possibility of implementations that involve less than four exchanges. The work of Dutta et al. showed that for single-writer/multiple-reader (SWMR) settings two exchanges are sufficient, provided that the number of readers is severely constrained with respect to the number of object replicas in the system and the number of replica failures, and also showed that no two-exchange implementations of multiple-writer/multiple-reader (MWMR) objects are possible. Later research focused on providing implementations that remove the constraint on the number of readers, while having read and write operations that use variable number of communication exchanges, specifically two, three, or four exchanges.

This work presents two advances in the state-of-the-art in this area. Specifically, for SWMR and MWMR systems algorithms are given in which read operations take *two or three* exchanges. This improves on prior works where read operations took either (*a*) three exchanges, or (*b*) two or four exchanges. The number of readers in the new algorithms is *unconstrained*, and write operations take the same number of exchanges as in prior work (two for SWMR and four for MWMR settings). The correctness of algorithms is rigorously argued. The paper presents an empirical study using the NS3 simulator that compares the performance of relevant algorithms, demonstrates the practicality of the new algorithms, and identifies settings in which their performance is clearly superior.

© Springer Nature Switzerland AG 2019
A. Podelski and F. Taïani (Eds.): NETYS 2018, LNCS 11028, pp. 175–190, 2019.
https://doi.org/10.1007/978-3-030-05529-5_12

# 1    Introduction

Emulating atomic [11] (or linearizable [10]) read/write objects in asynchronous, message-passing environments with crash-prone processors is a fundamental problem in distributed computing. To cope with processor failures, distributed object implementations use *redundancy* by replicating the object at multiple network locations. Replication masks failures, however it introduces the problem of consistency because operations may access different object replicas possibly containing obsolete values. Atomicity is the most intuitive consistency semantic as it provides the illusion of a single-copy object that serializes all accesses such that each read operation returns the value of the latest preceding write operation.

**Background and Prior Work.** The seminal work of Attiya et al. [2] provided an algorithm, colloquially referred to as ABD, that implements SWMR (Single Writer, Multiple Reader) atomic objects in message-passing crash-prone asynchronous environments. Operations are ordered using logical *timestamps* associated with each value. Operations terminate provided some majority of replica servers does not crash. Writes involve a single communication round-trip involving *two* communication exchanges. Each read operation takes two rounds involving in *four* communication exchanges. Subsequently, Lynch et al. [13] showed how to implement MWMR (Multi-Writer, Multi-Reader) atomic memory where both read and write operations take two communication round trips, for a total of *four* exchanges.

Dutta et al. [3] introduced a *fast* SWMR implementation where both reads and writes involve *two* exchanges (such operations are called 'fast'). It was shown that this is possible only when the number of readers $r$ is constrained with respect to the number of servers $s$ and the number of server failures $f$, viz. $r < \frac{s}{f} - 2$. Other works focused on relaxing the bound on the number of readers in the service by proposing hybrid approaches where some operations complete in *one* and others in *two* rounds, e.g., [4].

Georgiou et al. [6] introduced Quorum Views, client-side tools that examine the distribution of the latest value among the replicas in order to enable fast read operations (two exchanges). A SWMR algorithm, called SLIQ, was given that requires at least one single slow read per write operation, and where all writes are fast. A later work [5] generalized the client-side decision tools and presented a MWMR algorithm, called CWFR, that allows fast read operations.

Previous works considered only client-server communication round-trips. Recently, Hadjistasi et al. [9] showed that atomic operations do not necessarily require complete communication round trips, by introducing server-to-server communication. They presented a SWMR algorithm, called OHSAM, where reads take *three* exchanges: two of these are between clients and servers, and one is among servers; their MWMR algorithm, called OHMAM, uses a similar approach. These algorithms do not impose constrains on reader participation and perform a modest amount of local computation, resulting in negligible computation overhead.

**Table 1.** Summary of communication exchanges and communication complexities.

| Model | Algorithm | Read exch. | Write exch. | Read comm. | Write comm. |
|-------|-----------|------------|-------------|------------|-------------|
| SWMR | ABD [2] | 4 | 2 | $4\|S\|$ | $2\|S\|$ |
| SWMR | OhSam [9] | 3 | 2 | $\|S\|^2 + 2\|S\|$ | $2\|S\|$ |
| SWMR | Sliq [6] | 2 or 4 | 2 | $4\|S\|$ | $2\|S\|$ |
| SWMR | Erato | 2 or 3 | 2 | $\|S\|^2 + 3\|S\|$ | $2\|S\|$ |
| MWMR | ABD-mw [2,13] | 4 | 4 | $4\|S\|$ | $4\|S\|$ |
| MWMR | OhMam [9] | 3 | 4 | $\|S\|^2 + 2\|S\|$ | $4\|S\|$ |
| MWMR | CwFr [5] | 2 or 4 | 4 | $4\|S\|$ | $4\|S\|$ |
| MWMR | Erato-mw | 2 or 3 | 4 | $\|S\|^2 + 3\|S\|$ | $4\|S\|$ |

**Contributions.** We focus on the gap between one-round and two-round algorithms by presenting atomic memory algorithms where read operations can take *at most* "one and a half rounds," i.e., complete in either *two* or *three* exchanges. Complexity results are shown in Table 1, additional details are as follows.

**1.** We present ERATO,[1] *Efficient Reads for ATomic Objects*, a SWMR algorithm for atomic objects in the asynchronous message-passing model with processor crashes. We improve the *three*-exchange read protocol of OHSAM [9] to allow reads to terminate in either *two* or *three* exchanges using client-side tools, Quorum Views, from algorithm SLIQ [6]. During the second exchange, based on the distribution of the timestamps, the reader may be able to complete the read. If not, it awaits for "enough" messages from the third exchange to complete. A key idea is that when the reader is "slow" it returns the value associated with the *minimum* timestamp, i.e., the value of the previous write that is guaranteed to be complete (cf. [9] and [3]). Read operations are optimal in terms of exchanges in light of [8]. Similarly to ABD, writes take *two* exchanges (Sect. 3).

**2.** Using the SWMR algorithm as the basis, we develop a MWMR algorithm, ERATO-MW. The algorithm supports *three*-exchange read protocol based on [9] in combination with the iterative technique using quorum views as in [5]. Reads take either *two* or *three* exchanges. Writes are similar to ABD-MW and take *four* communication exchanges (cf. [13]) (Sect. 4).

**3.** We simulate the algorithms using the NS3 simulator and assess their performance under practical considerations by varying the number of participants, frequency of operations, and network topologies (Sect. 5).

Improvements in latency are obtained in a trade-off for communication complexity. Simulation results suggest that in practical settings, such as data centers with well-connected servers, the communication overhead is not prohibitive.

## 2   Models and Definitions

We now present the model, definitions, and notations used in the paper. The system is a collection of crash-prone, asynchronous processors with unique

---

[1]   $E\rho\alpha\tau\dot{\omega}$ is a Greek Muse, and the authors thank the lovely muse for her inspiration.

identifiers (ids). The ids are from a totally-ordered set $\mathcal{I}$ that is composed of three disjoint sets, set $\mathcal{W}$ of writer ids, set $\mathcal{R}$ of reader ids, and set $\mathcal{S}$ of replica server ids. Each *server* maintains a copy of the object.

Processors communicate by exchanging messages via asynchronous point-to-point reliable channels; messages may be reordered. We use the term *broadcast* as a shorthand denoting sending point-to-point messages to multiple destinations.

A quorum system over a set is a collection of subsets, called quorums, such that every pair of quorums intersects. We define a quorum system $\mathbb{Q}$ over the set of server ids $\mathcal{S}$ as $\mathbb{Q} = \{Q_i : Q_i \subseteq \mathcal{S}\}$; it follows that for any $Q_i, Q_j \in \mathbb{Q}$ we have $Q_i \cap Q_i \neq \emptyset$. We assume that every process in the system is aware of $\mathbb{Q}$.

**Executions.** An algorithm $A$ is a collection of processes, where process $A_p$ is assigned to processor $p \in \mathcal{I}$. The *state* of processor $p$ is determined over a set of state variables, and the state of $A$ is a vector that contains the state of each process. Algorithm $A$ performs a *step*, when some process $p$ (i) receives a message, (ii) performs local computation, (iii) sends a message. Each such action causes the state at $p$ to change. An *execution* is an alternating sequence of states and actions of $A$ starting with the initial state and ending in a state.

**Failure Model.** A process may crash at any point in an execution. If it crashes, then it stops taking steps; otherwise, the process is *correct*. Any subset of readers and writers may crash. A quorum $Q \in \mathbb{Q}$ is non-faulty if $\forall p \in Q$, $p$ is correct. Otherwise, $Q$ is faulty. Any server may crash as long one quorum is non-faulty.

**Efficiency and Message Exchanges.** Efficiency of implementations is assessed in terms of *operation latency* and *message complexity*. Latency of an operation is determined by *computation time* and the *communication delays*. Computation time accounts for all local computation within an operation. Communication delays are measured in terms of *communication exchanges*. The protocol implementing each operation involves a collection of sends (or broadcasts) of typed messages and the corresponding receives. As defined in [9], a *communication exchange* within an execution of an operation is the set of sends and receives for the specific message type. Traditional implementations in the style of ABD [2] are structured in terms of *rounds*, each consisting of two exchanges, the first, a broadcast, is initiated by the process executing an operation, and the second, a convergecast, consists of responses to the initiator. The number of messages that a process expects during a convergecast depends on the implementation. *Message complexity* measures the worst-case total number of messages exchanged.

**Atomicity.** An implementation of a read or a write operation contains an *invocation* action and a *response* action. An operation $\pi$ is *complete* in an execution, if it contains both the invocation and the *matching* response actions for $\pi$; otherwise $\pi$ is *incomplete*. An execution is *well formed* if any process invokes one operation at a time. We say that an operation $\pi$ *precedes* an operation $\pi'$ in an execution $\xi$, denoted by $\pi \rightarrow \pi'$, if the response step of $\pi$ appears before the invocation step in $\pi'$ in $\xi$. Two operations are *concurrent* if neither precedes the other. The correctness of an atomic read/write object implementation is defined in terms of *atomicity* (safety) and *termination* (liveness) properties. Termination requires that any operation invoked by a correct process eventually completes. Atomicity is defined following [12]. For any execution $\xi$, if $\Pi$ is the set of all completed read and write operations in $\xi$, then there exists a partial order $\prec$ on the operations in $\Pi$, s.t. the following properties are satisfied:

**A1** For any $\pi_1, \pi_2 \in \Pi$ such that $\pi_1 \rightarrow \pi_2$, it cannot be that $\pi_2 \prec \pi_1$.
**A2** For any write $\omega \in \Pi$ and any operation $\pi \in \Pi$, then either $\omega \prec \pi$ or $\pi \prec \omega$.
**A3** Every read operation returns the value of the last write preceding it according to $\prec$ (or the initial value if there is no such write).

**Timestamps and Quorum Views.** Atomic object implementations typically use logical timestamps (or tags) associated with the written values to impose a partial order on operations that satisfies the properties A1, A2, and A3.

A *quorum view* [6] refers to the distribution of the highest timestamp among the servers, $maxTS$, that a read operation witnesses during a communication exchange, and can be used as a tool to determine the state of a write operation i.e., whether it is complete or incomplete. Suppose that during an exchange, a read $\rho$ strictly receives timestamp and value pairs $\langle s.ts, v \rangle$ from each server $s \in Q_i$. As presented in [6], $\rho$ can distinguish three different quorum views:

- QV(1): $\forall s \in Q_i : s.ts = maxTS$
- QV(2): $\forall Q_j \in \mathbb{Q}, i \neq j, \exists A \subseteq Q_i \cap Q_j$, s.t. $A \neq \emptyset$ and $\forall s \in A : s.ts < maxTS$
- QV(3): $\exists s' \in Q_i : s'.ts < maxTS$ and $\exists Q_j \in \mathbb{Q}, i \neq j$ s.t. $\forall s \in Q_i \cap Q_j : s.ts = maxTS$.

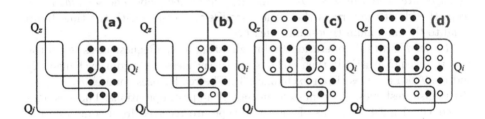

**Fig. 1.** (a) QV(1), (b) QV(2), (c) QV(3) incomplete write, (d) QV(3) complete write

For example, in Fig. 1 dark circles represent servers that contain the $maxTS$, and light ones any older timestamp. The quorum system $\mathbb{Q}$ consists of three quorums, $\{Q_i, Q_j, Q_z\}$. If QV(1) is observed, Fig. 1(a), it means that only one timestamp is received, thus the write associated with $maxTS$ has potentially been completed. If QV(2) is observed, Fig. 1(b), this indicates that the write associated with $maxTS$ is still in progress (because older timestamps are detected in the intersections of quorums). Lastly, if QV(3) is observed, the distribution of timestamps does not provide sufficient information for the state of the write. This, because there are two possibilities as shown in Fig. 1(c) and (d). In Fig. 1(c) the write is incomplete while in Fig. 1(d) the write completes in quorum $Q_z$, however, in both executions every server in the intersection of $Q_z \cap Q_i$ replies with $maxTS$. We use quorum views as a design element in our algorithms.

# 3  SWMR Algorithm ERATO

We now present and analyze the SWMR algorithm ERATO.

## 3.1  Algorithm Description

In ERATO reads take either *two* or *three* exchanges. This is achieved by combining the *three* exchange read protocol of [9] with the use of Quorum Views of [6]. The read protocol design aims to return the value associated with the timestamp of the last complete write operation. We refer to the three exchanges of the read protocol as E1, E2, and E3. Exchange E1 is initiated by the reader, and exchanges E2 and E3 are conducted by the servers. When the reader receive messages during E2, it analyses the timestamps to determine whether to terminate or wait for the conclusion of E3. Due to asynchrony it is possible for the message from E3 to arrive at the reader before messages from E2. In this case the reader still terminates in *three* exchanges. Similarly to ABD, writes take *two* exchanges. The code is given in Algorithm 1. We now give the details of the protocols; in referring to the numbered lines of code we use the prefix "L" to stand for "line".

***Reader Protocol.*** Each reader $r$ maintain several temporary variables. Key variable include $minTS$ and $maxTS$ hold the minimum and the maximum timestamps discovered during the read operation. Sets $RR$ and $RA$ hold the received readRelay and readAck messages respectively. The ids of servers that sent these messages are stored in sets $RRsrv$ and $RAsrv$ respectively. The set $maxTSrv$ keeps the ids of the servers that sent a readRelay message with the timestamp equal to the maximum timestamp $maxTS$.

Reader $r$ starts its operation by broadcasting a readRequest message to the servers (exchange E1). It then collects readRelay messages (from exchange E2) and readAck messages (from exchange E3). The reader uses counter $read\_op$ to distinguish fresh message from stale message from prior operations. The messages are collected until messages of the same type are received from some quorum $Q$ of servers (L7–11). If readRelay messages are received from quorum $Q$ then the reader examines the timestamps to determine what quorum view is observed (recall Sect. 2). If QV(1) is observed, then all timestamps are the same, meaning that the write operation associated with the timestamp is complete, and it is safe to return the value associated with it without exchange E3. (L24–25). If QV(2) is observed, then the write associated with the maximum timestamp $maxTS$ is not complete. But because there is a sole writer, it is safe to return the value associated with timestamp $maxTS$-1, i.e., the value of the preceding complete write, again without exchange E3 (L34–37). If QV(3) is observed, then the write associated with the maximum timestamp $maxTS$ is in progress or complete. Since the reader is unable to decide which case applies, it waits for the exchange E3 readAck messages from some quorum $Q$. The reader here returns the value associated with the *minimum* timestamp observed (L27–33). It is possible, due to asynchrony, that messages from E3 arrive from a quorum before enough messages from E2 are gathered. Here the reader decides as above for E3 (L12–16).

**Writer Protocol.** Writer $w$ increments its local timestamp $ts$ and broadcasts a writeRequest message to all servers. It completes once writeAck messages are received from some quorum $Q$ (L52–56).

**Server Protocol.** Server $s$ stores the value of the replica $v$ and its associated timestamp $ts$. The *relays* array is used to store sets of processes that relayed to $s$ regarding a read operation. Destinations set $D$ is initialized to set containing all servers from every quorum that contains $s$. It is used for sending relay messages during exchange E2.

---

**Algorithm 1.** Reader, Writer, and Server Protocols for SWMR algorithm ERATO

---

1: At each reader $r$
2: **Variables:**
3: $minTS, maxTS \in \mathbb{N}; read\_op \in \mathbb{N}$ init 0
4: $RR, RA, maxACK \subseteq S \times M$
5: $v \in V; RRsrv, RAsrv, maxTSrv \subseteq S$
6: **function** READ
7:   $read\_op \leftarrow read\_op + 1$
8:   $(RR, RA, RRsrv, RAsrv) \leftarrow (\emptyset, \emptyset, \emptyset, \emptyset)$
9:   **bcast** ($\langle$readRequest, $r, read\_op\rangle$) to $S$
10:   **wait until** $\exists Q \in \mathbb{Q} : Q \subseteq RRsrv$
11:     $\lor Q \subseteq RAsrv$
12:   **if** $(\exists Q \in \mathbb{Q} : Q \subseteq RAsrv)$ **then**
13:     $minTS \leftarrow \min\{(m.ts) : (s,m) \in RA$
14:       $\land s \in Q\}$
15:     **return**($m.v$ s.t. $(s,m) \in RA$
16:       $\land m.ts = minTS$)
17:   **else if** $(\exists Q \in \mathbb{Q} : Q \subseteq RRsrv)$ **then**
18:     $maxTS \leftarrow \max(\{(m.ts) :$
19:       $(s,m) \in RR \land s \in Q\})$
20:     $maxACK \leftarrow \{(s,m) \in RR :$
21:       $s \in Q \land m.ts = maxTS\}$
22:     $maxTSrv \leftarrow \{s \in Q :$
23:       $(s,m) \in maxACK\}$
24:     **if** $Q \subseteq maxTSrv$ **then**//**Qview1**//
25:       **return**($m.v$ s.t. $(s,m) \in maxACK$)
26:     **if** $\exists Q' \in \mathbb{Q}, Q' \neq Q$
27:       s.t. $Q' \cap Q \subseteq maxTSrv$ **then**
28:       // ** Qview3** //
29:       **wait until** $\exists Q \in \mathbb{Q} : Q \subseteq RAsrv$
30:       $minTS \leftarrow \min(\{(m.ts) :$
31:         $(s,m) \in RA \land s \in Q\})$
32:       **return**($m.v$ s.t. $(s,m) \in RA$
33:         $\land s \in Q \land m.ts = minTS$)
34:     **else** // ** Qview2** //
35:       $maxACK \leftarrow \{(s,m) \in RR :$
36:         $s \in Q \land m.ts = maxTS - 1\}$
37:       **return**($m.v$ s.t. $(s,m) \in maxACK$)
38: **Upon receive** $m$ from $s$
39:   **if** $m.read\_op = read\_op$ **then**
40:     **if** $m.type = $ readRelay **then**
41:       $RR \leftarrow RR \cup \{(s,m)\}$
42:       $RRsrv \leftarrow RRsrv \cup \{s\}$
43:     **else** // readAck //
44:       $RA \leftarrow RA \cup \{(s,m)\}$
45:       $RAsrv \leftarrow RAsrv \cup \{s\}$

46: At writer $w$
47: **Variables:**
48: $ts \in \mathbb{N}^+, v \in V, wAck \subseteq S$
49: **Initialization:**
50: $ts \leftarrow 0, v \leftarrow \bot, wAck \leftarrow \emptyset$
51: **function** WRITE($val : input$)
52:   $(ts, v) \leftarrow (ts + 1, val)$
53:   $wAck \leftarrow \emptyset$
54:   **bcast** ($\langle$writeRequest, $ts, v, w\rangle$) to $S$
55:   **wait until** $(\exists Q \in \mathbb{Q} : Q \subseteq wAck)$
56:   **return**()
57: **Upon receive** $m$ from $s$
58: **if** $m.ts = ts$ **then**
59:   $wAck \leftarrow wAck \cup \{s\}$

60: At server $s$
61: **Variables:**
62: $ts \in \mathbb{N}$ init 0 ; $v \in V$ init $\bot$
63: $D \subseteq S$ init $\{s' : Q \in \mathbb{Q} \land (s, s') \in Q\}$
64: $operations : \mathcal{R} \rightarrow \mathbb{N}$ init $0^{|\mathcal{R}|}$
65: $relays : \mathcal{R} \rightarrow 2^S$ init $0^{|\mathcal{R}|}$
66: **Upon receive**($\langle$readRequest, $r, read\_op\rangle$)
67: **bcast**($\langle$readRelay, $ts, v, r, read\_op, s\rangle$)
68:   to $D \cup r$
69: **Upon receive**($\langle$writeRequest, $ts', v', w\rangle$)
70: **if** $(ts < ts')$ **then**
71:   $(ts, v) \leftarrow (ts', v')$
72: **send** ($\langle$writeAck, $ts, s\rangle$) to $w$
73: **Upon receive**
74:   $(\langle$readRelay, $ts', v', r, read\_op, s\rangle)$
75: **if** $(ts < ts')$ **then**
76:   $(ts, v, vp) \leftarrow (ts', v')$
77: **if** $(operations[r] < read\_op)$ **then**
78:   $operations[r] \leftarrow read\_op$
79:   $relays[r] \leftarrow \emptyset.$
80: **if** $(operations[r] = read\_op)$ **then**
81:   $relays[r] \leftarrow relays[r] \cup \{s\}$
82: **if** $(\exists Q \in \mathbb{Q} : Q \subseteq relays[r_i])$ **then**
83:   **send** ($\langle$readAck, $ts, v, read\_op, s\rangle$)
84:     to $r$

In exchange E1 of a read, upon receiving message $\langle$readRequest, $r$, $read\_op\rangle$, the server creates a readRelay message, containing its $ts$, $v$, and $s$, and broadcasts it in exchange E2 to destinations in $D$ and reader $r$ (L66–68).

In exchange E2, upon receiving message $\langle$readRelay, $ts'$, $v'$, $r$, $read\_op\rangle$ $s$ compares its local timestamp $ts$ with $ts'$. If $ts < ts'$, then $s$ sets its local value and timestamp to those enclosed in the message (L75–76). Next, $s$ checks if the received readRelay marks a new read by $r$, i.e., $read\_op > operations[r]$. If so, then $s$: (a) sets its local counter for $r$ to the enclosed one, $operations[r] = read\_op$; and (b) re-initializes the relay set for $r$ to an empty set, $relays[r] = \emptyset$ (L77–79). It then adds the sender of the readRelay message to the set of servers that informed it regarding the read invoked by $r$ (L80–81). Once readRelay messages are received from a quorum $Q$, $s$ creates a readAck message and sends it to $r$ in exchange E3 of the read (L82–84).

Within a write operation, upon receiving message $\langle$writeRequest, $ts'$, $v'$, $w\rangle$, $s$ compares its $ts$ to the received one. If $ts < ts'$, then $s$ sets its local timestamp and value to those received, and sends acknowledgment to the writer (L69–72).

## 3.2   Correctness and Complexity

Here we prove correctness of algorithm ERATO. Termination (liveness) is satisfied with respect to our failure model: at least one quorum $Q$ is non-faulty and each operation waits for messages from a single quorum.

To prove atomicity we order the operations with respect to the timestamps associated with the written values. For each execution of the algorithm there must exist a partial order $\prec$ on the operations that satisfy conditions A1, A2, and A3 given in Sect. 2. Let $ts_\pi$ be the timestamp at the completion of $\pi$ when $\pi$ is a write, and the timestamp associated with the returned value when $\pi$ is a read. We now define the partial order as follows. For two operations $\pi_1$ and $\pi_2$, when $\pi_1$ is any operation and $\pi_2$ is a write, we let $\pi_1 \prec \pi_2$ if $ts_{\pi_1} < ts_{\pi_2}$. For two operations $\pi_1$ and $\pi_2$, when $\pi_1$ is a write and $\pi_2$ is a read we let $\pi_1 \prec \pi_2$ if $ts_{\pi_1} \leq ts_{\pi_2}$. The rest of the order is established by transitivity, without ordering the reads with the same timestamps. We now state the following lemmas (detailed proofs are given in the full paper [7]).

**Lemma 1.** *In any execution $\xi$ of ERATO, if a read $\rho$ succeeds a write operation $\omega$ that writes timestamp $ts$, i.e. $\omega \to \rho$, and returns a timestamp $ts'$, then $ts' \geq ts$.*

**Lemma 2.** *In any execution $\xi$ of ERATO, if $\rho_1$ and $\rho_2$ are two read operations such that $\rho_1$ precedes $\rho_2$, i.e., $\rho_1 \to \rho_2$, and $\rho_1$ returns timestamp $ts_1$, then $\rho_2$ returns a timestamp $ts_2$, s.t. $ts_2 \geq ts_1$.*

**Theorem 1.** *Algorithm ERATO implements an atomic SWMR object.*

*Proof.* We now use the lemmas above and the partial order definition to reason about each of the three conditions A1, A2 and A3.

**A1** For any $\pi_1, \pi_2 \in \Pi$ such that $\pi_1 \to \pi_2$, it cannot be that $\pi_2 \prec \pi_1$.

When the two operations $\pi_1$ and $\pi_2$ are reads and $\pi_1 \to \pi_2$ holds, then from Lemma 2 it follows that the timestamp of $\pi_2$ is no less than the one rof $\pi_1$, $ts_{\pi_2} \geq ts_{\pi_1}$. If $ts_{\pi_2} > ts_{\pi_1}$ then by the ordering definition $\pi_1 \prec \pi_2$ is satisfied. When $ts_{\pi_2} = ts_{\pi_1}$ then the ordering is not defined, thus it cannot be the case that $\pi_2 \prec \pi_1$. If $\pi_2$ is a write, the sole writer generates a new timestamp by incrementing the largest timestamp in the system. By well-formedness (see Sect. 2), any timestamp generated in any write operation that precedes $\pi_2$ must be smaller than $ts_{\pi_2}$. Since $\pi_1 \to \pi_2$, then it holds that $ts_{\pi_1} < ts_{\pi_2}$. Hence, by the ordering definition it cannot be the case that $\pi_2 \prec \pi_1$. Lastly, when $\pi_2$ is a read and $\pi_1$ a write and $\pi_1 \to \pi_2$ holds, then from Lemma 1 it follows that $ts_{\pi_2} \geq ts_{\pi_1}$. By the ordering definition, it cannot hold that $\pi_2 \prec \pi_1$ in this case either.

**A2** For any write $\omega \in \Pi$ and any operation $\pi \in \Pi$, then either $\omega \prec \pi$ or $\pi \prec \omega$.

If the timestamp returned from $\omega$ is greater than the one returned from $\pi$, i.e. $ts_\omega > ts_\pi$, then $\pi \prec \omega$ follows directly. Similarly, if $ts_\omega < ts_\pi$ holds, then $\omega \prec \pi$ follows. If $ts_\omega = ts_\pi$, then it must be that $\pi$ is a read and $\pi$ discovered $ts_\omega$ in a quorum view QV1 or QV3. Thus, $\omega \prec \pi$ follows.

**A3** Every read operation returns the value of the last write preceding it according to $\prec$ (or the initial value if there is no such write).

Let $\omega$ be the last write preceding read $\rho$. From our definition it follows that $ts_\rho \geq ts_\omega$. If $ts_\rho = ts_\omega$, then $\rho$ returns the value conveyed by $\omega$ to some servers in a quorum $Q$, satisfying either QV1 or QV3. If $ts_\rho > ts_\omega$, then $\rho$ obtains a larger timestamp, but such a timestamp can only be created by a write that succeeds $\omega$, thus $\omega$ does not precede the read and this cannot be the case. Lastly, if $ts_\rho = 0$, no preceding writes exist, and $\rho$ returns the initial value.□

**Communication and Message Complexity.** By inspection of the code, write operations take 2 exchanges and read operations take either 2 or 3 exchanges. The message complexity of write operations is $2|\mathcal{S}|$ and of read operations is $|\mathcal{S}|^2 + 2|\mathcal{S}|$, as follows from the structure of the algorithm.

## 4    Algorithm ERATO-MW

We now aim for a MWMR algorithm that involves *two* or *three* communications exchanges per read operation and *four* exchanges per write operation. The read protocol of algorithm ERATO relies on the fact of the sole writer in the system: based on the distribution of the timestamp in a quorum $Q$, if the reader knows that the write operation is not complete, then any previous write is complete (by well-formedness). In the MWMR setting this does not hold due to the possibility of concurrent writes. Consequently, algorithm ERATO-MW, in order to allow operations to terminate in either *two* or *three* communication exchanges, adapts the read protocol from algorithm OHMAM in combination with the iterative technique using quorum views of CWFR. The latter approach not only predicts the completion status of a write operation, but also detects the last potentially complete write operation. The code is given in Algorithm 2.

**Algorithm 2.** Reader, Writer and Server Protocols for MWMR algorithm ERATO-MW

```
 1: At each reader r
 2: Variables:
 3:   v ∈ V; read_op ∈ ℕ; minTAG, maxTAG ∈ T
 4:   RR, RA, maxACK ⊆ S × M init ∅
 5:   RRsrv, RAsrv, maxTGsrv ⊆ S init ∅
 6: Initialization:
 7:   minTAG ← ⟨0, 0⟩, maxTAG ← ⟨0, 0⟩
 8:   v ←⊥, read_op ← 0
 9: function READ
10:   read_op ← read_op + 1
11:   (RR, RA, maxACK) ← (∅, ∅, ∅)
12:   (RRsrv, RAsrv, maxTGsrv) ← (∅, ∅, ∅)
13:   bcast (⟨readRequest, r, read_op⟩) to S
14:   wait until ∃Q ∈ ℚ : Q ⊆ RRsrv ∨ Q ⊆ RAsrv
15:   if (∃Q ∈ ℚ : Q ⊆ RAsrv) then
16:     minTAG ← min({(m.ts, m.id) :
17:               (s, m) ∈ RA ∧ s ∈ Q})
18:     return(m.v s.t. (s, m) ∈ RA ∧ s ∈ Q
19:            ∧ (m.ts, m.id) = minTAG)
20:   else if (∃Q ∈ ℚ : Q ⊆ RRsrv) then
21:     while (Q ≠ ∅) do
22:       maxTAG ← max{(m.ts, m.id) :
23:                 (s, m) ∈ RA ∧ s ∈ Q}
24:       maxACK ← {(s, m) ∈ RR : s ∈ Q∧
25:                 (m.ts, m.id) = maxTAG}
26:       maxTGsrv ← {s ∈ Q :
27:                 (s, m) ∈ maxACK}
28:       if Q ⊆ maxTGsrv then
29:         //** Qview1**//
30:         return(m.v s.t. (s, m) ∈ maxACK}
31:       if ∃Q' ∈ ℚ, Q' ≠ Q : Q' ∩ Q
32:         ⊆ maxTGsr then //**Qview3**//
33:         wait until
34:           ∃Q'' ∈ ℚ : Q'' ⊆ RAsrv
35:         minTAG ← min{(m.ts, m.id) :
36:                   (s, m) ∈ RA ∧ s ∈ Q''}
37:         return(m.v s.t., (s, m) ∈RA ∧ s ∈ Q''
38:              ∧ (m.ts, m.id) = minTAG)
39:       else //** Qview2**//
40:         Q ← Q − maxTGsrv
41: Upon receive m from s
42: if m.read_op = read_op then
43:   if m.type = readRelay then
44:     RR ← RR ∪ {(s, m)}
45:     RRsrv ← RRsrv ∪ {s}
46:   else // readAck //
47:     RA ← RA ∪ {(s, m)}
48:     RAsrv ← RAsrv ∪ {s}
```

```
49: At each writer w
50: Variables:
51:   ts ∈ ℕ, v ∈ V, write_op ∈ ℕ, maxTS ∈ ℕ
52:   Acks ⊆ S × M init ∅ ; AcksSrv ⊆ S init ∅
53: Initialization:
54:   ts ← 0, v ←⊥, write_op ← 0, maxTS ← 0
55: function WRITE(val : input)
56:   write_op ← write_op + 1
57:   (Acks, AcksSrv) ← (∅, ∅)
58:   bcast (⟨writeDiscover, write_op, w⟩) to S
59:   wait until (∃Q ∈ ℚ : Q ⊆ AcksSrv)
60:   maxTS ← max{(m.ts) :
61:             (s, m) ∈ Acks ∧ s ∈ Q}
62:   (ts, id, v) ← (maxTS + 1, i, val)
63:   write_op ← write_op + 1
64:   (Acks, AcksSrv) ← (∅, ∅)
65:   bcast (⟨writeRequest, ts, v, w, write_op⟩) to S
66:   wait until (∃Q ∈ ℚ : Q ⊆ AcksSrv)
67:   return()
68: Upon receive m from s
69: if m.write_op = write_op then
70:   Acks ← Acks ∪ {(s, m)}
71:   AcksSrv ← AcksSrv ∪ {s}

72: At server s
73: Variables and Initialization:
74:   ts ∈ ℕ init 0; id ∈ 𝒲 init ⊥; v ∈ V init ⊥
75:   operations : ℛ → ℕ init 0^|ℛ|
76:   write_ops : 𝒲 → ℕ init 0^|𝒲|
77:   relays : ℛ → 2^S init ∅^|ℛ|
78:   D ⊆ S init {s : (∃Q ∈ ℚ), (s, sᵢ) ∈ Q)}
79: Upon receive(⟨writeDiscover, write_op, w⟩)
80: send (⟨discoverAck, ts, id, sᵢ⟩) to w
81: Upon receive
82:   (⟨writeRequest, ts', v', id', write_op, w⟩)
83: if write_ops[w] < write_op then
84:   write_ops[w] ← write_op
85:   if (ts < ts') ∨ (ts = ts' ∧ id < id') then
86:     (ts, id, v) ← (ts', id', v')
87: send (⟨writeAck, write_op, s⟩) to w
88: Upon receive(⟨readRequest, r, read_op⟩)
89: bcast⟨readRelay, ts, id, v, r, read_op, s⟩ to D ∪ r
90: Upon receive(⟨readRelay, ts', id', v', r, read_op, s⟩)
91: if (ts < ts') ∨ (ts = ts' ∧ id < id') then
92:   (ts, id, v) ← (ts', id', v')
93: if (operations[r] < read_op) then
94:   operations[rᵢ] ← read_op ; relays[r] ← ∅.
95: if (operations[r] = read_op) then
96:   relays[r] ← relays[r] ∪ {s}
97: if (∃Q ∈ ℚ : Q ⊆ relays[r]) then
98:   send (⟨readAck, ts, id, v, read_op, s⟩) to r
```

## 4.1 Detailed Algorithm Description

To impose an ordering on the values written by the writers we associate each value with a tag $tg$ defined as the pair $(ts, id)$, where $ts$ is a timestamp and $id$ the identifier of a writer. Tags are ordered lexicographically (cf. [13]).

**Reader Protocol.** Readers use state variables similarly to algorithm ERATO. Reader $r$ broadcasts a readRequest message to all servers, then awaits either (a) readRelay messages from some quorum, or (b) readAck messages from some quorum (L10–14). The key departure here is in how the reader handles case (a) when QV(2) is detected, which indicates that the write associated with the *maximum* tag is not complete. Here the reader considers past history and discovers the tag associated with the last complete write. This is accomplished in an iterative manner, by removing the servers that respond with the maximum tag in the responding quorum $Q$ and repeating the analysis (L21–40). During the iterative process, if $r$ detects QV(1) it returns the value associated with the *maximum* tag discovered during the current iteration. If no iteration yields QV(1), then eventually $r$ observes QV(3). In the last case, QV(3) is detected when a single server remains in some intersection of $Q$. If so, the reader waits readAck messages to arrive from some quorum, and returns the value associated with the *minimum* tag. If case (b) happens before case (a), then $r$ proceeds identically as in the case where QV(3) is detected (L15–19).

**Writer Protocol.** Similarly to the four-exchange implementation [13], a writer broadcasts a writeDiscover message to all servers, and awaits "fresh" discoverAck messages from some quorum $Q$ (L56–59). Among these responses the writer finds the *maximum* timestamp, $maxTS$, increments it, and associates it and its own id with the new value by broadcasting the new timestamp, its id, and the new value in a writeRequest message to all servers. The write completes when writeAck messages are received from some quorum $Q$ (L61–66).

**Server Protocol.** Servers react to messages from readers exactly as in Algorithm 1. We now describe how the messages from writers are handled.

(1) Upon receiving message $\langle \text{writeDiscover}, write\_op, w \rangle$, server $s$ replies with a discoverAck message containing its local tag and value. (L79–80).
(2) Upon receiving message $\langle \text{writeRequest}, ts', id', v', write\_op, w \rangle$, server $s$ compares lexicographically its local tag with the received one. If $(ts, id) < (ts', id')$, then $s$ updates its local information and replies using writeAck message (L82–87).

## 4.2 Correctness and Complexity

Termination of algorithm ERATO-MW is satisfied with respect to our failure model. Atomicity (safety) is reasoned about as in Sect. 3.2, except using *tags* instead of timestamps. (Complete proofs are given in the the full paper [7]).

**Lemma 3.** *In any execution $\xi$ of ERATO-MW, if a write $\omega$ writes tag $tg'$ and succeeds a read operation $\rho$ that returns a tag $tg$, i.e., $\rho \to \omega$, then $tg' > tg$.*

**Lemma 4.** *In any execution $\xi$ of ERATO-MW, if a write $\omega_1$ writes tag $tg_1$ and precedes a write $\omega_2$ that writes tag $tg_2$, i.e., $\omega_1 \to \omega_2$, then $tg_2 > tg_1$.*

**Lemma 5.** *In any execution $\xi$ of ERATO-MW, if a read $\rho$ succeeds a write operation $\omega$ that writes tag $tg$, i.e. $\omega \to \rho$, and returns a tag $tg'$, then $tg' \geq tg$.*

**Lemma 6.** *In any execution $\xi$ of* ERATO-MW, *if $\rho_1$ and $\rho_2$ are two read operations s.t. $\rho_1$ precedes $\rho_2$, i.e., $\rho_1 \to \rho_2$, and $\rho_1$ returns tag $tg_1$, then $\rho_2$ returns a tag $tg_2$, s.t. $tg_2 \geq tg_1$.*

**Theorem 2.** *Algorithm* ERATO-MW *implements an atomic MWMR object.*

*Proof.* We use the above lemmas and the operations order definition to reason about each of the three atomicity conditions A1, A2 and A3.

**A1** For any $\pi_1, \pi_2 \in \Pi$ such that $\pi_1 \to \pi_2$, it cannot be that $\pi_2 \prec \pi_1$.

If both $\pi_1$ and $\pi_2$ are writes and $\pi_1 \to \pi_2$ holds, then from Lemma 4 it follows that $tg_{\pi_2} > tg_{\pi_1}$. From the definition of order $\prec$ we have $\pi_1 \prec \pi_2$. When $\pi_1$ is a write, $\pi_2$ a read and $\pi_1 \to \pi_2$ holds, then from Lemma 5 it follows that $tg_{\pi_2} \geq tg_{\pi_1}$. By definition $\pi_1 \prec \pi_2$ holds. If $\pi_1$ is a read, $\pi_2$ is a write and $\pi_1 \to \pi_2$ holds, then from Lemma 3 it follows that $\pi_2$ returns a tag $tg_{\pi_2}$ s.t. $tg_{\pi_2} > tg_{\pi_1}$. By the order definition $\pi_1 \prec \pi_2$ is satisfied. If both $\pi_1$ and $\pi_2$ are reads and $\pi_1 \to \pi_2$ holds, then from Lemma 6 it follows that $tg_{\pi_2} \geq tg_{\pi_1}$. If $tg_{\pi_2} > tg_{\pi_1}$, then by the ordering definition $\pi_1 \prec \pi_2$ holds. When $tg_{\pi_2} = tg_{\pi_1}$ then the ordering is not defined, thus it cannot be that $\pi_2 \prec \pi_1$.

**A2** For any write $\omega \in \Pi$ and any operation $\pi \in \Pi$, then either $\omega \prec \pi$ or $\pi \prec \omega$.

If $tg_\omega > tg_\pi$, then $\pi \prec \omega$ follows directly. If $tg_\omega < tg_\pi$ holds, then it follows that $\omega \prec \pi$. When $ts_\omega = ts_\pi$ holds, then because all writer tags are unique (each server increments timestamps monotonically, and the server ids disambiguate among servers) $\pi$ can only be a read. Since $\pi$ is a read and the distribution of the tag written by $\omega$ satisfies either QV(1) or QV(3), it follows that $\omega \prec \pi$.

**A3** Every read operation returns the value of the last write preceding it according to $\prec$ (or the initial value if there is no such write).

Let $\omega$ be the last write preceding read $\rho$. From our definition it follows that $tg_\rho \geq tg_\omega$. If $tg_\rho = tg_\omega$, then $\rho$ returned a value written by $\omega$ in some servers in a quorum $Q$. Read $\rho$ either was *fast* and during the iterative analysis it noticed a distribution of the tags in $Q$ that satisfied QV(1) or $\rho$ was *slow* and waited for readAck messages from a full quorum $Q$. In the latter, the intersection properties of quorums ensure that $\omega$ was the last complete write. If $tg_\rho > tg_\omega$ holds, it must be the case that there is a write $\omega'$ that wrote $tg_\rho$ and by definition it must hold that $\omega \prec \omega' \prec \rho$. Thus, $\omega$ is not the preceding write and this cannot be the case. Lastly, if $tg_\rho = 0$, no preceding writes exist, and $\rho$ returns the initial value. $\square$

**Communication and Message Complexity.** Writes take 4 exchanges and reads either 2 or 3 exchanges. Message complexity of writes is $4|\mathcal{S}|$ and of reads $|\mathcal{S}|^2 + 2|\mathcal{S}|$. This follows from the structure of the algorithm.

# 5 Empirical Evaluations

We now compare the algorithms using the NS3 discrete event simulator [1]. The following SWMR algorithms ERATO, ABD [2], OHSAM [9], and SLIQ [6], and the corresponding MWMR algorithms: ERATO-MW, ABD-MW [13], OHMAM [9], and

CwFR [5] were simulated. For comparison, we implemented benchmark LB that mimics the minimum message requirements: LB does two exchanges for reads and writes, and neither performs any computation nor ensures consistency.

We developed two topologies that use the same array of routers, but differ in the deployment of server and client nodes. Clients are connected to routers over 5 Mbps links with 4 ms delay and the routers over 10 Mpbs links with 6 ms delay. In *Series* topology, Fig. 2(a), a server is connected to each router over 10 Mbps bandwidth with 2 ms delay, modeling a network where servers are separated and appear to be in different networks. In *Star* topology, Fig. 2(b), servers are connected to a single router over 50 Mbps links with 2 ms delay, modeling a network where servers are in close proximity and well-connected, e.g., a datacenter. Clients are located uniformly with respect to the routers.

**Performance.** We assess algorithms in terms of *operation latency* that depends on communication delays and local computation time. For operation latency we combine two clocks: the simulation clock to measure communication delays, and a real time clock for computation delays. The sum of the two yields latency.

**Experimentation Setup.** To subject the system to high communication traffic, no failures are assumed (ironically, crashes reduce network traffic). Communication is via point-to-point bidirectional links implemented with a DropTail queue.

**Scenarios.** The scenarios are designed to test $(i)$ the scalability of the algorithms as the number of readers, writers, and servers increases; $(ii)$ the contention effect on efficiency, and $(iii)$ the effects of chosen topologies on the efficiency. For scalability we test with the number of readers $|\mathcal{R}|$ from the set $\{10, 20, 40, 80\}$ and the number of servers $|\mathcal{S}|$ from the set $\{9, 16, 25, 36\}$. Algorithms are evaluated with matrix quorums (unions of rows and columns). For the MWMR setting we range the number of writers $|\mathcal{W}|$ over the set $\{10, 20, 40\}$. We issue reads (and writes) every $rInt$ (and $wInt$ respectively) from the

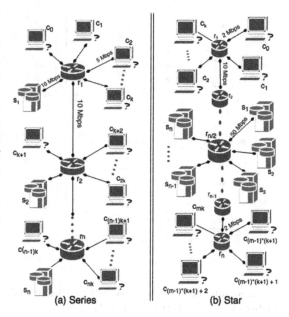

**Fig. 2.** Simulated topologies.

set of $\{2, 4\}$ seconds. To test contention we define two invocation schemes: *fixed* and *stochastic*. In the *fixed* scheme all operations are scheduled periodically at

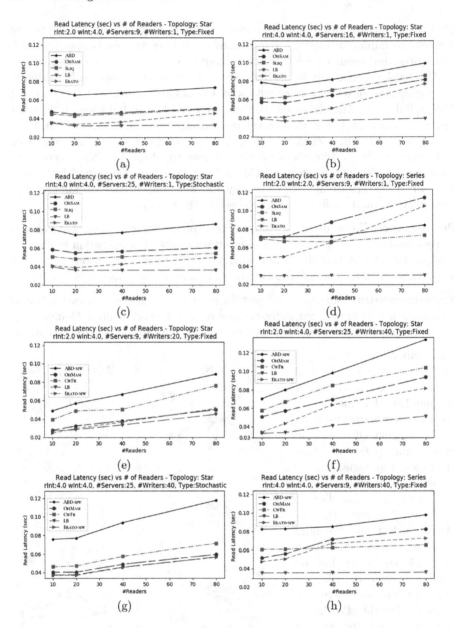

**Fig. 3.** Simulation results for SWMR (a–d) and MWMR (e–g). Horizontal axis is the number of readers. Vertical axis is latency.

a constant interval. In the *stochastic* scheme reads are scheduled randomly from the intervals $[1...rInt]$ and write operations from the intervals $[1...wInt]$.

**Results.** We note that generally the new algorithms outperform the competition. A closer examination yields the following observations.

*Scalability:* Increased number of readers and servers increases latency in both settings. Observe Fig. 3(a), (b) for SWMR and Fig. 3(e), (f) for MWMR algorithms. Not surprisingly, latency is better for smaller numbers of readers, writers, and servers. However, the relative performance of the algorithms remains the same.

*Contention:* The efficiency of the algorithms is examined under different concurrency schemes. We notice that in the *stochastic* scheme reads complete faster than in the *fixed* scheme – Fig. 3(b) and (c) for the SWMR and Fig. 3(f) and (g) for the MWMR setting. This outcome is expected as the *fixed* scheme causes congestion. For the *stochastic* scheme the invocation time intervals are distributed uniformly (randomness prevents the operations from being invoked simultaneously), and this reduces congestion in the network and improves latency.

*Topology:* Topology substantially impacts performance and the behavior of the algorithms. This can be seen in Figs. 3(b) and (d) for the SWMR setting, and Figs. 3(f) and (h) for the MWMR setting. The results show clearly that the proposed algorithms outperform the competition in the *Star* topology, where servers are well-connected using high bandwidth links.

# 6    Conclusions

We focused on the problem of emulating atomic read/write shared objects in the asynchronous, crash-prone, message-passing settings with the goal of synthesizing algorithms where read operations can *always* terminate in *less* than two communication round-trips. We presented such algorithms for the SWMR and MWMR models. We rigorously reasoned about the correctness of our algorithms. The algorithms impose no constraints on the number of readers, and no constraints on the number of writers (in the MWMR model). The algorithms are shown to be optimal in terms of *communication exchanges* with unconstrained participation. The empirical study demonstrates the practicality of the new algorithms, and identifies settings in which their performance is clearly superior.

# References

1. NS3 network simulator. https://www.nsnam.org/
2. Attiya, H., Bar-Noy, A., Dolev, D.: Sharing memory robustly in message passing systems. J. ACM **42**(1), 124–142 (1996)
3. Dutta, P., Guerraoui, R., Levy, R.R., Chakraborty, A.: How fast can a distributed atomic read be? In: Proceedings of PODC 2004, pp. 236–245 (2004)
4. Englert, B., Georgiou, C., Musial, P.M., Nicolaou, N., Shvartsman, A.A.: On the efficiency of atomic multi-reader, multi-writer distributed memory. In: Abdelzaher, T., Raynal, M., Santoro, N. (eds.) OPODIS 2009. LNCS, vol. 5923, pp. 240–254. Springer, Heidelberg (2009). https://doi.org/10.1007/978-3-642-10877-8_20
5. Georgiou, C., Nicolaou, N., Russell, A., Shvartsman, A.A.: Towards feasible implementations of low-latency multi-writer atomic registers. In: Proceedings of NCA 2011, pp. 75–82 (2011)

6. Georgiou, C., Nicolaou, N.C., Shvartsman, A.A.: On the robustness of (semi) fast quorum-based implementations of atomic shared memory. In: Taubenfeld, G. (ed.) DISC 2008. LNCS, vol. 5218, pp. 289–304. Springer, Heidelberg (2008). https://doi.org/10.1007/978-3-540-87779-0_20

7. Georgiou, C., Hadjistasi, T., Nicolaou, N., Schwarzmann, A.A.: Unleashing and speading up readers in atomic object implementations. https://arxiv.org/abs/1803.11211 (2018)

8. Hadjistasi, T., Nicolaou, N., Schwarzmann, A.A.: On the impossibility of one-and-a-half round atomic memory. https://arxiv.org/abs/1610.08373 (2016)

9. Hadjistasi, T., Nicolaou, N., Schwarzmann, A.A.: Oh-RAM! One and a half round atomic memory. In: El Abbadi, A., Garbinato, B. (eds.) NETYS 2017. LNCS, vol. 10299, pp. 117–132. Springer, Cham (2017). https://doi.org/10.1007/978-3-319-59647-1_10

10. Herlihy, M.P., Wing, J.M.: Linearizability: a correctness condition for concurrent objects. ACM Trans. Prog. Lang. Syst. 12(3), 463–492 (1990)

11. Lamport, L.: How to make a multiprocessor computer that correctly executes multiprocess progranm. IEEE Trans. Comput. 28(9), 690–691 (1979)

12. Lynch, N.: Distributed Algorithms. Morgan Kaufmann Publishers, Burlington (1996)

13. Lynch, N.A., Shvartsman, A.A.: Robust emulation of shared memory using dynamic quorum-acknowledged broadcasts. In: Proceedings of FTCS 1997, pp. 272–281 (1997)

# Optimal Recoverable Mutual Exclusion Using only FASAS

Prasad Jayanti[1], Siddhartha Jayanti[2], and Anup Joshi[1($\boxtimes$)]

[1] Dartmouth College, Hanover, NH 03755, USA
anupj@cs.dartmouth.edu
[2] Massachusetts Institute of Technology, Cambridge, MA 02139, USA

**Abstract.** Recent research has focused on designing concurrent algorithms that are resilient to process crashes. The idea is to leverage non-volatile memory so that processes can recover from crashes with as little disruption to the normal behavior of the system as possible. We present the first Recoverable Mutual Exclusion algorithm whose Remote Memory Reference (RMR) complexity is optimal for both Cache-Coherent (CC) and Distributed Shared Memory (DSM) machines. If a process fails $f$ times during its attempt to acquire the Critical Section, our algorithm ensures that the process incurs $O(1)$ RMRs on a DSM machine and $O(f)$ RMRs on a CC machine, which we prove is an optimal bound. Our algorithm improves on a recent algorithm by Golab and Hendler in three ways: It has a provably optimal RMR complexity, has a wait-free Exit section, and less reliance on instructions that are not commonly supported on multiprocessors. In particular, Golab and Hendler's algorithm relies on hardware support for both Fetch-And-Store-And-Store (FASAS) and Double-Word Compare-And-Swap (DCAS), while our algorithm relies only on FASAS. (If $X$ and $Y$ are shared variables and $v$ is a value, FASAS($X, Y, v$) writes $X$'s value in $Y$ and writes $v$ in $X$, all in a single atomic action.)

**Keywords:** Concurrent algorithm · Synchronization
Mutual exclusion · Recovery · Fault tolerance
Non-volatile main memory · Shared memory · Multi-core algorithms

## 1 Introduction

Traditionally a locking algorithm, also known as a mutual exclusion algorithm [1], is designed on the assumption that processes do not crash while acquiring, holding, or releasing a lock. Accordingly, such an algorithm is modeled as follows.

The first author is grateful to the Frank family and Dartmouth College for their support through James Frank Family Professorship of Computer Science.
The second author is grateful for the support of Department of Defense (DoD) through the National Defense Science & Engineering Graduate Fellowship (NDSEG) Program.
The third author is grateful for the support of Dartmouth Fellowship.

A. Podelski and F. Taïani (Eds.): NETYS 2018, LNCS 11028, pp. 191–206, 2019.
https://doi.org/10.1007/978-3-030-05529-5_13

Each process in a system of asynchronous processes repeatedly cycles through four sections called the *Remainder section, Try section, Critical section (CS)*, and *Exit section*. A process can stay in the Remainder section for any length of time, including possibly forever. The algorithm specifies the code for the Try and Exit sections so that the following properties are satisfied:

- <u>Mutual Exclusion</u>: At most one process is in the CS at any time.
- <u>Wait-free Exit</u>: A process in the Exit section completes the Exit section in a bounded number of its own steps, regardless of the relative speeds of other processes.
- <u>Starvation Freedom</u>: If no process stays in the CS forever and no process crashes while in the Try or Exit sections, every process in the Try section eventually enters the CS.
- <u>First Come First Served (FCFS)</u>: There is a constant $b$ such that if a process $p$ executes $b$ steps of the Try section before a process $q$ enters the Try section, then $q$ does not enter the CS before $p$.

Recent research has moved from this traditional model to a more challenging model where processes can crash anytime and anywhere, including in the Try, CS, and Exit sections [2–5], and subsequently restart. This model assumes that the system's memory is partitioned into volatile and nonvolatile memory. When a process $p$ crashes, all its registers and any variables stored in the volatile memory lose their contents, and $p$'s program counter is reset to the the Remainder section. When $p$ eventually restarts after a crash, it moves from Remainder to a certain section of code called the Recover section, regardless of where it was when it last crashed. It is the responsibility of the algorithm designer to write the Recover section so that $p$ can restore the essential part of its lost state by reading the contents of the nonvolatile memory. It is normally assumed that all shared variables of a program are stored in the nonvolatile memory, and hence survive the crash. The CPU registers and the local variables of a process are volatile, and are lost when the process crashes.

The mutual exclusion problem, reimagined for this new model where processes may crash anywhere and subsequently restart from the Recover section, is called a *Recoverable Mutual Exclusion* (RME) problem, and was first formulated by Golab and Ramaraju [3]. An RME algorithm specifies the code for the Recover section, besides specifying the code for the Try and Exit sections. The various properties listed above are still important, but as described in the Sect. 2, their formulations are suitably revised to make sense for the new model.

## 1.1   Remote Memory Reference (RMR) Complexity

For a concurrent algorithm to perform well on a multiprocessor, it is generally agreed that processes should generate as few remote memory references as possible. An operation by a process $p$ on a shared variable $X$ is considered a Remote Memory Reference (RMR) if it involves traversing the processor-memory interconnect. On a Cache-Coherent (CC) machine, a read of $X$ by $p$ counts as an RMR if $X$ was not in $p$'s cache (in which case the read brings $X$ into $p$'s cache), and a non-read operation on $X$ by $p$ always counts as an RMR as it might update or invalidate copies of $X$ from all caches (not every non-read might incur an RMR if the underlying cache coherence protocol uses a write-back strategy, but by counting every non-read as an RMR, the RMR complexity bound we prove for an algorithm will apply to all CC machines, regardless of how their underlying cache-coherence protocols are implemented). When a process crashes during an execution, the contents of that process' cache are potentially lost. Therefore, if $X$ was in $p$'s cache prior to a crash, $p$'s read of $X$ just after the crash would count as an RMR. On a Distributed Shared Memory (DSM) machine, shared memory is partitioned and each process hosts a partition. An operation by $p$ on $X$, whether a read or a non-read, is counted as an RMR if and only if $X$ is not in $p$'s partition.

The *RMR complexity* of a mutual exclusion algorithm is the worst case number of RMRs that a process incurs during a single attempt, which lasts from the time the process enters the Try section from Remainder to the earliest subsequent time when the process completes Exit and moves back to Remainder. In a traditional mutual exclusion algorithm, a process executes each of Try and Exit sections exactly once in an attempt, and the algorithm's RMR complexity is in general a function of $n$, the maximum number of processes that may execute the algorithm concurrently. In contrast, in a recoverable mutual exclusion algorithm, because of possibly repeatedly crashing, a process may execute each of Try, Exit, and Recover sections many times. Therefore, the RMR complexity of a recoverable algorithm is in general a function of both $n$ and $f$, the number of times a process crashes during its attempt.

## 1.2   State of the Art

Ideally, we would want to design an algorithm that relies only on operations supported by real architectures and still guarantees optimal RMR complexity on both CC and DSM machines. For the traditional mutual exclusion problem, this ideal is achievable: the MCS algorithm [9] has $O(1)$ RMR complexity for both CC and DSM and uses only the commonly supported Fetch-And-Store (FAS) and Compare-And-Swap (CAS) operations, while its variant, due to Craig [6], needs only FAS. Recently, Golab and Hendler investigated whether such an ideal algorithm is also possible for *recoverable* mutual exclusion [2], and presented a recoverable algorithm of small RMR complexity of $O(f)$ for both CC and DSM models. They do not address whether their algorithm achieves optimal RMR complexity. Moreover, their algorithm has two drawbacks: (i) its Exit section is not wait-free, and (ii) it relies on two instructions that are not commonly supported on real multiprocessors, namely, Fetch-And-Store-And-Store (FASAS) and Double-word Campare-And-Swap (DCAS). (If $X$ and $Y$ are shared variables and $v$ is a value, FASAS$(X, Y, v)$ writes $X$'s value in $Y$ and writes $v$ in $X$, all in a single atomic action.)

### 1.3   Our Result

We present the first Recoverable Mutual Exclusion algorithm whose RMR complexity is provably optimal for both CC and DSM machines. Our algorithm has an RMR complexity of $O(1)$ for the DSM model and $O(f)$ for the CC model, which matches a lower bound of $\Omega(f)$ that we prove for the CC model. Our algorithm improves on Golab and Hendler's in two more ways: it has a wait-free Exit section and eliminates the need for DCAS (so our algorithm requires support for only FASAS).

To design a recoverable lock, one typically enhances an existing non-recoverable algorithm to turn it into a recoverable algorithm. Golab and Hendler built their recoverable lock from the MCS lock [9], thereby inheriting its dual weaknesses of non-wait-free Exit section and reliance on more than one synchronization primitive (MCS lock relies on FAS and CAS, and correspondingly Golab and Hendler's recoverable lock relies on FASAS and DCAS). We are able to improve on Golab and Hendler's lock primarily because we have built our recoverable lock from variants of the MCS lock [6,7] that are free of MCS' shortcomings.

### 1.4   Organization

The rest of this paper is organized as follows. We describe our model in Sect. 2 and explain where our model differs from the original model of Golab and Ramaraju. We state some more related work in Sect. 3. We prove the RMR lower bound of $\Omega(f)$ for the CC model in Sect. 4, and finally present our algorithm that has optimal RMR complexity for both CC and DSM models in Sect. 5.

## 2   The Model and the Problem Specification

In this section we describe our model, which shares a lot of features with the model from the first work on recoverable mutual exclusion by Golab and Ramaraju [3]. There are also important differences between our models, which we discuss at the end of the section.

### 2.1   Model

The system consists of asynchronous processes that communicate by applying atomic operations on shared variables. Each process has five sections of code—Remainder, Recover, Try, CS, and Exit. A *recoverable mutual exclusion algorithm* specifies the code for Recover, Try, and Exit sections of all processes, and the initial values for all local and shared variables. We make no assumptions about the Remainder section and CS other than that none of the shared and local variables of the mutual exclusion algorithm are modified in these sections. All processes are initially in the Remainder section. If $X$ and $Y$ are any shared variables and $v$ is a value, the following operations are allowed: $read(X)$, $write(X, v)$, and

$FASAS(X, Y, v)$, where the semantics of the first two operations are well known and of third are explained already in the Introduction.

A *configuration* of the system is specified by the values of all shared variables and the states of all the processes, where the state of a process $p$ is in turn specified by the value of $PC_p$ ($p$'s program counter) and the values of $p$'s local variables. The configuration changes when a process executes a step. There are two types of steps that a process can execute: *normal step* and *crash step*. A normal step by a process $p$ from a configuration $C$ causes $p$ to perform the instruction that $PC_p$ points to in $C$, including some bounded local computation. A *crash step* by $p$ sets $PC_p$ to the Remainder section, sets all the local variables of $p$ to arbitrary values, and invalidates the contents of $p$'s cache. (In Golab and Ramaraju's model [3] and in [2], when $p$ crashes, its local variables are set to initial values instead of being set to arbitrary values. This difference is minor since it is straightforward to transform an algorithm designed for one model to work in the other model.)

From the above, we see that a step is determined by which process takes the step and whether the step is normal or crash. A *schedule* is any finite or infinite sequence of steps. An *execution* corresponding to a schedule $\sigma = s_1, s_2, \ldots$ is $C_0, s_1, C_1, s_2, C_2, \ldots$, where $C_0$ is the initial configuration specified by the algorithm, $C_1$ is the configuration after step $s_1$, $C_2$ is the configuration after steps $s_1$ and $s_2$, and so on.

Let $E$ be an execution and $s$ be a step by a process $p$ from a configuration $C$ in $E$. We say $p$ *initiates an attempt in step $s$* if $p$ is in the Remainder section in $C$ and either $s$ is $p$'s first step in $E$ or $p$'s latest step in $E$ before $s$ is a normal step. We say $p$ *completes an attempt in step $s'$* if $s'$ is a normal step by $p$ that moves $p$ to the Remainder section. An *attempt* by $p$ in $E$ is a fragment of $E$ that starts with an attempt initiation step $s$ by $p$ and ends with $p$'s earliest attempt completion step $s'$ that follows $s$. We say $p$ *is active in a configuration $C$* if $C$ occurs in an attempt by $p$. It is important to note that $p$ might visit the Remainder section multiple times during an attempt because of its crash steps; thus, $p$ can be active even when it is in the Remainder section.

## 2.2  Problem Specification

The *recoverable mutual exclusion problem* is to design an algorithm that satisfies the following properties:

P1.  Mutual Exclusion: At most one process is in the CS at any time.

P2.  Well-formedness: Let $s$ be a normal step by $p$ in which $p$ completes the Recover section, and $s'$ be the latest step by $p$ before $s$ in which $p$ initiates an attempt or $p$ crashes outside of the Recover section in Try, CS, or Exit. *Well-formedness* stipulates where the control moves to after step $s$, as follows:

- If $s'$ is an attempt initiation step, then $s$ moves control to Try section or CS.

- If $s'$ is a crash step while $p$ is in Try section, then $s$ moves control to Try section or CS.
- If $s'$ is a crash step while $p$ is in CS, then $s$ moves control to CS.
- If $s'$ is a crash step while $p$ is in Exit, then $s$ moves control to CS, Exit section, or Remainder section.

P3.  Starvation-Freedom: An execution is *fair* if, for all processes $p$, we have: (i) if $p$ is in the CS and does not crash while there, then $p$ subsequently enters the Exit section, (ii) $p$ has only a finite number of crash steps in any one attempt, and (iii) if $p$ initiates an attempt, then either $p$ completes that attempt or $p$ has an infinite number of normal steps.

*Starvation-Freedom* stipulates that in every fair execution every process that initiates an attempt enters the CS in that attempt and completes that attempt.

P4.  Critical Section Reentry [3]: If a process $p$ crashes inside the CS, then no other process enters the CS before $p$ reenters the CS.

P5.  Wait-free Exit: There is a bound $b$ such that, if $p$ is in the Exit section and the subsequent steps of $p$ are all normal steps, then $p$ moves to the Remainder section in at most $b$ of its own steps, regardless of the relative speeds and crashes of other processes.

P6.  Wait-Free Recovery to CS: There is a bound $b$ such that if a process crashes while in the CS, then the process reenters the CS before completing $b$ consecutive normal steps in the future, regardless of the relative speeds and crashes of other processes.

(As observed in [4], this property, together with Mutual Exclusion, implies the Critical Section Reentry property.)

P7.  Wait-Free Recovery to Exit: There is a bound $b$ such that if a process crashes while in the Exit section, then the process enters either the CS or the Exit section before completing $b$ consecutive normal steps in the future, regardless of the relative speeds and crashes of other processes.

An additional desirable property, which might be considered optional, is the FCFS property that was first formulated by Lamport [8] for the traditional mutual exclusion problem. Its adaptation to recoverable mutual exclusion, stated below, is taken from [4].

P8.  First Come First Served (FCFS): There is a bound $b$ such that, for all attempts $A$ and $A'$ in any execution, if $A$ is an attempt by a process $p$, $A'$ is an attempt by a process $p'$, and $p$ performs $b$ consecutive normal steps in attempt $A$ before $p'$ initiates attempt $A'$, then $p'$ does not enter the CS in attempt $A'$ before $p$ first enters the CS in attempt $A$.

### 2.3  Differences with Golab and Ramaraju's Model

Our model differs from the model of Golab and Ramaraju [3] and Golab and Hendler [2] in two important ways. First, in their model, following a crash, when a process $p$ restarts and executes the Recover section, the Recover section puts

$p$ in the Try section, *regardless* of where in the algorithm $p$ was at the time of its crash. Thus, even if $p$ completed the CS and crashed while in the Exit, upon restart Recover puts it in Try section, thereby forcing it to enter the CS once more. In contrast, our well-formedness property (P2) allows the Recover section to send $p$ back to the Exit section, if $p$ had crashed while in the Exit section. We introduced this change in the model because while it is important to ensure that a process enters the CS and leaves the CS normally at least once, we see no reason to insist that, within the same attempt, a process should enter the CS after every crash.

A second and a significant difference is our insistence on Wait-Free Recovery to CS (P6) and Wait-Free Recovery to Exit (P7). If a process $p$ crashes while in the CS, the Critical Section Reentry (CSR) property of Golab and Ramaraju insists that, until $p$ restarts and enters the CS once again, no other process enters the CS. Thus, CSR prevents other processes from entering the CS until $p$ enters the CS. This being the case, it is clearly undesirable if other processes are allowed to block or delay $p$ from entering the CS. Hence, our insistence on the *Wait-Free Recovery to CS*. Similarly, if $p$ crashes while in the Exit section, when $p$ subsequently restarts, to remain true to the spirit of Wait-Free Exit, it is clearly desirable that $p$ should be able to exit the protocol without being blocked or delayed by other processes. Hence, our insistence on the *Wait-Free Recovery to Exit*.

In our earlier paper [4], we required the Recover section to be wait-free, which implies *Wait-Free Recovery to CS* and *Wait-Free Recovery to Exit*, but we have dropped this requirement now because "Wait-Free Recovery to *Try*" is pointless given that a process waits in the Try section anyway. (We note however that the algorithm presented in this paper has a wait-free Recover section.)

## 3    Related Work

Golab and Ramaraju specified the recoverable mutual exclusion problem and gave several algorithms, including one of $O(f + \log n)$ RMR complexity, using only read and write operations [3]. Ramaraju gave the first FCFS recoverable algorithm, but it uses FASAS besides CAS [5]. Jayanti and Joshi gave the first FCFS algorithm that uses only the commonly supported CAS operation [4]. Golab and Hendler [2] gave two algorithms, the first of which is closely related to our work here and was discussed in detail in Sect. 1. Their second algorithm has $O(f \log n / \log \log n)$ RMR complexity on CC machines and uses only FAS and CAS.

## 4    RMR Lower Bound for CC Machines

In this section we prove that the RMR complexity of any algorithm is $\Omega(f)$ on a CC machine. To make this lower bound as strong as possible, we prove that this bound holds even if (i) the algorithm is "one shot", where a process executes at most one attempt in the entire run, (ii) the algorithm is executed by only two processes, and (iii) Mutual Exclusion, Well-Formedness, and the following weak Solo-Termination condition are the only properties that the algorithm satisfies.

- <u>Solo-Termination</u>: If all processes except $p$ are in the Remainder section and are not active, and $p$ is in the Try or the Recover section, and $p$ alone keeps taking steps and $p$ does not crash, then $p$ eventually completes that section.

**Lemma 1.** *Let $\mathcal{A}$ be any one-shot recoverable mutual exclusion algorithm for two processes that satisfies Mutual Exclusion and Well-Formedness. On a CC machine, each time a process executes the Recover section following a crash in Try, Critical, or Exit section, if the process executes the Recover section to completion without crashing, the process incurs at least one RMR during that execution of the Recover section.*

*Proof Sketch:* Suppose that, for a contradiction, there is a scenario $S$ where some process $p$ crashes while in Try, Critical, or Exit section, $p$'s crash sets its local variables to $\perp$, $p$ subsequently restarts and executes the Recover section to completion without failing and without incurring any RMR. Since $p$'s cache lost its contents at crash, the fact that $p$ did not incur any RMR during the Recover section implies that $p$ did not perform any operation on any of the shared variables during the Recover section. We consider two other scenarios $S'$ and $S''$, described as follows. Let $p$ and $q$ be the two processes for which the algorithm is designed.

- In Scenario $S'$, $q$ is not active (and is in Remainder), $p$ is in the CS, $p$ crashes, and the crash sets $p$'s local variables to $\perp$. Process $p$ then restarts and executes the Recover section without crashing.
- In Scenario $S''$, $q$ is in the CS, and $p$ is in the Try section, $p$ crashes, and the crash sets $p$'s local variables to $\perp$. Process $p$ then restarts and executes the Recover section without crashing.

In the following we derive a contradiction by observing that scenarios $S$ and $S'$ are indistinguishable to $p$, and that $S'$ and $S''$ are also indistinguishable to $p$.

Since $p$'s local variables contain $\perp$ at the start of the Recover section in both $S$ and $S'$, the two scenarios are indistinguishable to $p$ at the start of the Recover section. Further, since $p$ completes the Recover section without performing any operation on any of the shared variables in Scenario $S$, it follows that $p$ completes the Recover section without performing any operation on any of the shared variables in Scenario $S'$ as well. It follows from the Well-Formedness property (P2) that, upon completion of the Recover section, $p$ enters the CS.

Since $p$'s local variables contain $\perp$ at the start of the Recover section in both $S'$ and $S''$, the two scenarios are indistinguishable to $p$ at the start of the Recover section. Further, since $p$ completes the Recover section without performing any operation on any of the shared variables in Scenario $S'$, it follows that $p$ completes the Recover section without performing any operation on any of the shared variables in Scenario $S''$ as well. Thus, $S'$ and $S''$ remain indistinguishable to $p$ all the way until it completes the Recover section. Since $p$ enters the CS upon completing the Recover section in scenario $S'$, it follows that $p$ enters the CS upon completing the Recover section in scenario $S''$ as well. Since $q$ is already in the CS in scenario $S''$, mutual exclusion is violated in $S''$. Hence, we have the lemma.                                                                                                    □

**Theorem 1.** *Let $\mathcal{A}$ be any one-shot recoverable mutual exclusion algorithm for two processes that satisfies Mutual Exclusion, Well-Formedness, and Solo-Termination. The RMR complexity of $\mathcal{A}$ on a CC machine is $\Omega(f)$, where $f$ is the maximum number of failures of a process within an attempt.*

*Proof.* Let $p$ and $q$ be the two processes for which the algorithm is designed. Suppose that $q$ is not active (and is in Remainder), and $p$ is in the CS. Suppose that the following sequence of events repeats $f$ times:

- $p$ crashes while in the CS.
- $p$ restarts, executes the Recover section to completion without crashing, and returns to CS (by well-formedness).

By Lemma 1, $p$ incurs at least one RMR during the Recover section following each crash. So, $p$ incurs at least $\Omega(f)$ RMRs in its attempt. Hence, we have the theorem.                                                                                            □

The above argument does not apply to DSM machines because, when executing the Recover section, without incurring any RMRs a process can read from shared variables stored in its own memory module and use this information to distinguish various scenarios. In fact we exploit this feature in the next section to design an algorithm that incurs only $O(1)$ RMRs per attempt on DSM machines.

## 5   An Optimal RMR Complexity Algorithm for CC and DSM Machines

Our optimal RMR complexity recoverable mutual exclusion algorithm is presented in Fig. 1. This algorithm is designed to handle an arbitrary and unknown number of processes, and ensures that a process incurs at most $O(1)$ RMRs per attempt on DSM machines and $O(f)$ RMRs per attempt on CC machines, where $f$ is the number of times a process crashes during the attempt. We assume that all the shared variables of the algorithm are stored in the non-volatile memory.

### 5.1   Shared Variables and Their Purpose

The role played by each shared variable is as described below.

TAIL: This variable, like in the MCS lock [9], stores the address of the last node in the queue.

$\text{CUR}_{p_i}$: This variable stores the address of the node that a process uses during its attempt. In DSM machines this variable is stored in $p_i$'s memory module.

**Types**

Node = **record** ADDR is a reference to a memory word **end**

**Shared objects (Stored in NVMM)**

SPECIALNODE is a Node instance, initialized to (NIL) and
initially not assigned to any process.

**Shared variables (Stored in NVMM)**

TAIL is a reference to a Node, initially &SPECIALNODE.

$CUR_p$ is a reference to a Node, initialized to a new Node instance: (NIL).

$GO_p$ is a reference to a memory word, initially &TAIL.

$PREV_p$ is a reference to a Node, initially same as $CUR_p$.

$X_p$ is a reference to a memory word, initially &$PREV_p$.

<u>Recover Section</u>

1. $cur_p \leftarrow CUR_p$
2. $prev_p \leftarrow PREV_p$
3. $x_p \leftarrow X_p$
   **if** $cur_p == prev_p$ **then**
       **go to** Line 4
   **else if** $x_p ==$ &TAIL **then**
       **go to** Line 15
   **else if** $x_p \notin \{$&$PREV_p, prev_p, NIL\}$ **then**
       **go to** Line 13
   **else if** $x_p \in \{prev_p, NIL\}$ **then**
       **go to** Line 10
   **else go to** Line 9

<u>Try Section</u>

4. $X_p \leftarrow$ &$PREV_p$
5. $cur_p$.ADDR $\leftarrow cur_p$
6. $GO_p \leftarrow$ &TAIL
7. FASAS(&TAIL, &$PREV_p, cur_p$)
8. $prev_p \leftarrow PREV_p$
9. FASAS(&($prev_p$.ADDR), &$X_p$, &$GO_p$)
10. **if** $X_p \neq$ NIL **then**
11.     **wait till** $GO_p \neq$ &TAIL

<u>Exit Section</u>

12. FASAS(&($cur_p$.ADDR), &$X_p$, NIL)
13. $x_p \leftarrow X_p$
    **if** $x_p \neq cur_p$ **then**
14.     FASAS($x_p$, &$X_p$, &$CUR_p$)
15. $CUR_p \leftarrow prev_p$

**Fig. 1.** Recoverable mutual exclusion lock using FASAS. Algorithm for process $p$.

$PREV_{p_i}$: This variable stores the address of a node that appears before a process's own node inside the queue. In DSM machines this variable is stored in $p_i$'s memory module.

$X_{p_i}$: This variable is used for checkpointing purposes. Inside the Recover section a process uses the value stored in this variable to identify the location it might have crashed during its attempt. In DSM machines this variable is stored in $p_i$'s memory module.

$GO_{p_i}$: This is a flag variable that process $p_i$ busywaits on before entering the CS. The variable is set to point to the address of TAIL at the start of an attempt, and $p_i$ is released from its busywait when the variable is set to point to some other location. $GO_{p_i}$ is allocated to $p_i$'s memory module to achieve local-spin property. In DSM machines this variable is stored in $p_i$'s memory module.

## 5.2   Informal Description

The symbol & is prefixed to a shared variable in the code to obtain the address of that shared variable. When a local variable is supposed to supply the address of a shared variable, we do not prefix it with an & (e.g., Line 14). The symbol "." (dot) dereferences a pointer and accesses a field from the record pointed to by that pointer. Un-numbered lines in the code perform local computation as part of the latest numbered line preceding that line (e.g., the **if** ... **then** ... **else** ladder in Recover section is part of the local execution of Line 3). We assume that a process $p_i$ is in the Remainder section when $PC_{p_i} = 1$ and is in the CS when $PC_{p_i} = 12$. The code is described informally as follows.

When a process $p_i$ wants to enter the CS from the Remainder section, it executes an attempt initiation step (i.e. executing the first instruction of Recover and initializing local variable $cur_{p_i}$ to the value of $\text{CUR}_{p_i}$). Recover doesn't put the process in any other section before execution of Line 3, therefore the process initializes $prev_{p_i}$ to $\text{PREV}_{p_i}$ (Line 2). In Line 3, the process initializes $x_{p_i}$ and finds that it has just initiated an attempt (because $cur_{p_i} == prev_{p_i}$), hence the process proceeds to Line 4 in the Try section. In the Try section the process first initializes variable $\text{X}_{p_i}$ (Line 4) that it uses for checkpointing, then it initializes its own node (Line 5), and also initializes its local-spin variable $\text{GO}_{p_i}$ (Line 6). It then puts itself in the queue by performing a FASAS on the TAIL variable (Line 7), which puts the previous value of TAIL into $\text{PREV}_{p_i}$. The process then attempts to inform the process before itself in the queue that it is waiting to enter the CS (Lines 8, 9). It does so with a FASAS that puts the address of its $\text{GO}_{p_i}$ variable into the node of its predecessor, and atomically $\text{X}_{p_i}$ gets the value previously held by the ADDR pointer in the predecessor's node. The process then checks the value held by the ADDR pointer in the predecessor's node (Line 10), if the predecessor has already left a token (a NIL value), then the CS is empty and the process is free to go to the CS. Otherwise, the process busywaits on Line 11 until it is informed that it is free to go to the CS. In the Exit section the process first performs a FASAS on the ADDR pointer of its own node (Line 12). This way it atomically leaves a token for a successor in its own node and also learns the address of the GO variable of a successor into $\text{X}_{p_i}$, if there is one. At Line 13 it checks if a successor did inform $p_i$ of its GO variable by checking if the previous value of $\text{CUR}_{p_i}$.ADDR has departed from the initial value of $\text{CUR}_{p_i}$. If it has, then the process lets its successor into the CS by writing into their GO variable (Line 14). Otherwise, it takes the free node left by its predecessor for a future attempt, and leaves its own node for a successor (Line 15), thus ending the current attempt.

After a crash occurs during an attempt, the process executes the Recover section as described above reading the values of $\text{CUR}_{p_i}$, $\text{PREV}_{p_i}$, and $\text{X}_{p_i}$ (Lines 1, 2, and 3). It then decides where to jump on reading the shared state as follows. If $\text{CUR}_{p_i} == \text{PREV}_{p_i}$, then the process has just began the attempt, hence it jumps to the start of the Try section. If $\text{X}_{p_i} ==\&$ TAIL, then the process has already performed a FASAS at Line 14 and it is free to jump into the Exit section to end the attempt. If $\text{X}_{p_i}$ has taken any of the values other than the ones it takes in the Try section (and & TAIL), then the process crashed after performing the FASAS at Line 12, hence the process jumps to Line 13. Otherwise, the process is in the queue and there are only two cases remaining where the process could have crashed. If the $X_{p_i}$ points to any of $PREV_{p_i}$ or NIL, then the process performed the FASAS at Line 9 and crashed after that, hence it jumps to Line 10. Or it is yet to perform the FASAS but has put itself in the queue, hence it jumps to Line 9.

# 6   Proof of Correctness

In this section we present a proof of correctness for the algorithm presented in Fig. 1. Our recoverable mutex algorithm is complex enough so that a rigorous proof is required to convince about its correctness. We do this by giving an invariant for the algorithm and then proving correctness using the invariant. Figure 2 gives the invariant satisfied by the algorithm.

We begin with some notation used in the proof and the invariant. A process may crash several times during its attempt, at which point all its local variables get wiped out and the program counter is reset to 1 (i.e. first instruction of Recover). In order to prove correctness we maintain a hidden program counter which we call *shadow program counter*, whose value mirrors the Program Counter so long as the process is in the Try, CS, or Exit section. The shadow program counter is denoted by $\widehat{PC_p}$. The shadow program counter does not change when the process is taking steps inside the Recover section. Intuitively, a shadow program counter helps in capturing the current state of a process in the Try, CS, or Exit section, or the state it will recover to from a crash if it is in the Recover section.

We say that a process is in the CS if and only if $\widehat{PC_p} = 12$. If $p$ is not active and is in the Remainder section, $\widehat{PC_p} = 4$. We assume that initially all the local variables take arbitrary values.

**Lemma 2 (Mutual Exclusion).** *At most one process is in the CS in every configuration of every execution.*

*Proof.* Suppose there are two processes $p_i$ and $p_j$ in the queue, such that both of them are in the CS in some configuration $C$. Therefore, $\widehat{PC_{p_i}} = 12$ and $\widehat{PC_{p_j}} = 12$ in $C$. By Condition 3 of the invariant, one of the two processes is not $p_1$ in the ordering of processes in $Q$, without loss of generality let $p_j$ be that process. Therefore, by Condition 3(e)iii, $\widehat{PC_{p_j}} \in [8, 11]$, a contradiction.     □

**Lemma 3 (First Come First Served).** *There exists a bound $b$ such that, for all executions $E$ and for all attempts $A$ and $A'$ in $E$, if $A$ is an attempt by $p$, $A'$ is an attempt by $p'$, and $p$ performs $b$ consecutive normal steps in attempt $A$ before $p'$ initiates attempt $A'$, then $p'$ does not enter the CS in attempt $A'$ before $p$ first enters the CS in attempt $A$.*

**Definitions**

$\mathcal{P}$ is a set of all processes.

$\mathcal{N}$ is a set of $|\mathcal{P}| + 1$ distinct nodes.

$\mathcal{Q} = \{p \in \mathcal{P} \mid \widehat{PC_p} \in [8, 12] \cup \{14\} \vee (\widehat{PC_p} = 13 \wedge X_p \neq \text{CUR}_p)\}$
    is a set of queued processes.

$mynode_p = \begin{cases} \text{PREV}_p, & \text{if } (\widehat{PC_p} = 13 \wedge X_p = \text{CUR}_p) \vee \widehat{PC_p} = 15 \\ \text{CUR}_p, & \text{otherwise} \end{cases}$

**Conditions**

1. $\forall p, q \in \mathcal{P}, mynode_p \in \mathcal{N} \wedge (p \neq q \Rightarrow mynode_p \neq mynode_q)$
   **Observation:** $\mathcal{N} - \{mynode_p \mid p \in \mathcal{P}\}$ is a singleton set.
   Let $freenode$ denote the element of this singleton set.
2. $|\mathcal{Q}| = 0$ if and only if $\text{TAIL} = freenode \wedge freenode.\text{ADDR} = \text{NIL}$.
3. If $|\mathcal{Q}| = k > 0$, then there is an order $p_1, p_2, \ldots, p_k$ of processes in $\mathcal{Q}$ such that:
   (a) $\text{PREV}_{p_1} = freenode$
   (b) $(\widehat{PC_{p_1}} = [12, 14]) \vee (\widehat{PC_{p_1}} = 11 \wedge \text{GO}_{p_1} \neq \&\text{TAIL})$
       $\vee (\widehat{PC_{p_1}} = 10 \wedge (X_{p_1} = \text{NIL} \vee (X_{p_1} = \text{PREV}_{p_1} \wedge \text{GO}_{p_1} \neq \&\text{TAIL})))$
       $\vee (\widehat{PC_{p_1}} \in [8, 9] \wedge \text{PREV}_{p_1}.\text{ADDR} = \text{NIL})$
   (c) $\widehat{PC_{p_1}} = 14 \vee (\widehat{PC_{p_1}} = 13 \wedge X_{p_1} \neq \text{CUR}_{p_1}) \Rightarrow$
       $k \geq 2 \wedge \widehat{PC_{p_2}} \in [10, 11] \wedge X_{p_2} = \text{PREV}_{p_2} \wedge X_{p_1} = \&\text{GO}_{p_2}$
   (d) $k \geq 2 \wedge X_{p_2} = \text{PREV}_{p_2} \Rightarrow$
       $\widehat{PC_{p_1}} = 14 \vee (\widehat{PC_{p_1}} = 13 \wedge X_{p_1} \neq \text{CUR}_{p_1})$
       $\vee (\widehat{PC_{p_1}} \notin [13, 14] \wedge \text{CUR}_{p_1}.\text{ADDR} = \&\text{GO}_{p_2})$
   (e) $\forall i \in [2, k]$
       i. $\text{PREV}_{p_i} = \text{CUR}_{p_{i-1}}$
       ii. $\text{GO}_{p_i} = \&\text{TAIL}$
       iii. $\widehat{PC_{p_i}} \in [8, 11]$
       iv. $\widehat{PC_{p_i}} \in [8, 9] \Rightarrow \text{CUR}_{p_{i-1}}.\text{ADDR} = \text{CUR}_{p_{i-1}}$
       v. $\widehat{PC_{p_i}} \in [10, 11] \Rightarrow X_{p_i} = \text{PREV}_{p_i}$
       vi. $(i > 2 \wedge \widehat{PC_{p_i}} \in [10, 11] \Rightarrow \text{CUR}_{p_{i-1}}.\text{ADDR} = \&\text{GO}_{p_i})$
           $\wedge ((k \geq 2 \wedge \widehat{PC_{p_1}} \notin [13, 14] \wedge \widehat{PC_{p_2}} \in [10, 11]) \Rightarrow$
           $\text{CUR}_{p_1}.\text{ADDR} = \&\text{GO}_{p_2})$
   (f) $\text{CUR}_{p_k}.\text{ADDR} = \text{CUR}_{p_k}$
   (g) $\text{TAIL} = \text{CUR}_{p_k}$
4. For each process $p$, the conjunction of the following conditions is true:
   (a) $\widehat{PC_p} \in [5, 9] \Rightarrow X_p = \&\text{PREV}_p$
   (b) $\widehat{PC_p} \in [10, 12] \Leftrightarrow X_p \in \{\text{PREV}_p, \text{NIL}\}$
   (c) $(\widehat{PC_p} \in [13, 14] \Rightarrow X_p \notin \{\&\text{PREV}_p, \text{PREV}_p, \&\text{TAIL}, \text{NIL}\}) \wedge (PC_p = 14 \Rightarrow x_p = X_p)$
   (d) $\widehat{PC_p} = 15 \Rightarrow X_p \in \{\&\text{TAIL}, \text{CUR}_p\}$
5. For each process $p$, the conjunction of the following conditions is true:
   (a) $PC_p \in [2, 15] \Rightarrow cur_p = \text{CUR}_p$
   (b) $PC_p \in [3, 7] \cup [9, 15] \Rightarrow prev_p = \text{PREV}_p$
   (c) $\widehat{PC_p} \in [4, 7] \Leftrightarrow \text{PREV}_p = \text{CUR}_p$
   (d) $\widehat{PC_p} \in [6, 7] \Rightarrow \text{CUR}_p.\text{ADDR} = \text{CUR}_p$
   (e) $\widehat{PC_p} \in [7, 8] \Rightarrow \text{GO}_p = \&\text{TAIL}$
   (f) $\widehat{PC_p} \in [8, 12] \Rightarrow (\text{CUR}_p.\text{ADDR} = \text{CUR}_p \vee \exists r \in \mathcal{P}, (\widehat{PC_r} \in [10, 11] \wedge \text{PREV}_r = \text{CUR}_p))$

**Fig. 2.** Invariant of the recoverable mutual exclusion lock from Fig. 1.

*Proof.* For the purpose of this algorithm, we require that the bound be $b = 7$, hence, a process would be at Line 8 if it executed 7 consecutive normal steps starting from the attempt initiation step (or after a crash step).

To prove FCFS we need the following claim first:

**Claim**: A process executes Line 7 exactly once during an attempt.

*Proof:* We argue that a process executes Line 7 at least once as follows. Suppose a process $p$ executes seven consecutive normal steps after its attempt initiation step. On the seventh step the process executes Line 7. Suppose it crashes in between before executing the seven consecutive normal steps, then it crashes when $\widehat{PC_p} \in [4, 7]$. Therefore by Case 2 of the proof for Well-formedness as argued above, $p$ goes back to Line 4. Hence it eventually executes Line 7.

We now argue that a process executes Line 7 at most once as follows. Suppose $p$ goes past Line 7, i.e., $\widehat{PC_p} \in [8, 15]$ and $p$ has executed Line 7 once. On a scenario where no crashes occur, $p$ continues normal execution and never executes Line 7 again. Suppose a crash happens somewhere when $\widehat{PC_p} \in [8, 15]$. Then by Cases 3, 4, 5, 6, 7 of the proof for Well-formedness as argued above, $p$ will jump back to either Line 9 or somewhere after that. Therefore $p$ will never execute Line 7 one more time.

Hence we have that a process executes Line 7 exactly once during an attempt. □

We now give an additional invariant satisfied by the algorithm that helps us in arguing FCFS, but before that we give the following definition:

**Definition:** Let $p$ and $q$ be any two active processes during a configuration $C$ and $A_p$ and $A_q$ be their respective attempts. We say $p$ *precedes* $q$ in $C$, denoted symbolically as $p \prec q$, if $p$ executes Line 7 in $A_p$ before $q$ executes Line 7 in $A_q$.

**Invariant:** Let $p_1, p_2, \ldots, p_k$ be an ordering of processes in the queue $\mathcal{Q}$ given by Condition 3 of the invariant in Fig. 2. We have $p_1 \prec p_2 \prec \cdots \prec p_k$.

*Proof:* The correctness of the invariant is affected only when a process executes Line 7. As argued above, any process executes Line 7 exactly once in its attempt, therefore the proof is by induction as follows. The induction is on the number of processes in the queue $\mathcal{Q}$.

Let $|\mathcal{Q}| = 0$. If process $p$ executes Line 7 in a step, $|\mathcal{Q}| = 1$ after the step. Therefore the Invariant holds since $p$ is the only process in the queue.

Assume there is a configuration $C$ in which $|\mathcal{Q}| = k$, for $k \geq 1$, and there is an ordering $p_1, p_2, \ldots, p_k$ of processes in $\mathcal{Q}$ such that $p_1 \prec p_2 \prec \cdots \prec p_k$ by the invariant. Suppose $p$ is the earliest process to execute Line 7 after $C$ and let $C'$ be the configuration immediately after $p$ executes Line 7. By our assumption $p_k$ has executed Line 7 before $p$, and by transitivity, $p_i$, for $i = 1 \ldots k - 1$, has executed Line 7 before $p$. Hence, $p_1 \prec p_2 \prec \cdots \prec p_k \prec p$ in $C'$. Therefore the invariant holds in $C'$. □

Now we are poised to prove the FCFS property as follows. Suppose an arbitrary process $p$ is in the Critical section in a configuration $C$. By Condition 3, $p$ is the first process in the ordering of processes in $\mathcal{Q}$. By the invariant above, $p$ precedes all other processes in $\mathcal{Q}$. Hence, when $p$ is in the Critical section, no other process in $\mathcal{Q}$ precedes $p$ and therefore no other process in $\mathcal{Q}$ has completed $b = 7$ consecutive steps before $p$ initiated its attempt. Hence we have the claim. □

Due to space constraints we skip the proof for the Starvation Freedom and Well-formedness property. From an inspection of the Recover and Exit sections of the algorithm it is obvious that the algorithm satisfies Wait-Free Recovery to CS, Wait-Free Recovery to Exit, and Wait-free Exit. The variables $\text{CUR}_p$, $\text{PREV}_p$, and $\text{X}_p$ reside in $p$'s memory module in the DSM model, therefore $p$ does not incur an RMR when it reads these variables in the Recover section.

Putting all of the above together, we obtain the main result of the paper summarized as follows.

**Theorem 2.** *The algorithm in Fig. 1 solves the recoverable mutual exclusion problem for an arbitrary and unknown number of processes, satisfying properties P1-P8 stated in Sect. 2.2. The algorithm uses read, write and FASAS operations. It has an optimal RMR complexity of $O(f)$ on CC machines and $O(1)$ on DSM machines, where $f$ is the maximum number of failures of a process within an attempt.*

An interesting open question is whether $O(1)$, or even $O(f)$, RMR complexity is achievable using only commonly supported operations such as FAS, CAS, and Fetch&Add, on CC and DSM machines.

**Acknowledgment.** We are grateful to the anonymous reviewers for their careful and detailed reviews.

# References

1. Dijkstra, E.W.: Solution of a problem in concurrent programming control. Commun. ACM **8**(9), 569 (1965)
2. Golab, W., Hendler, D.: Recoverable mutual exclusion in sub-logarithmic time. In: Proceedings of the ACM Symposium on Principles of Distributed Computing. PODC 2017, pp. 211–220. ACM, New York (2017)
3. Golab, W., Ramaraju, A.: Recoverable mutual exclusion: [extended abstract]. In: Proceedings of the 2016 ACM Symposium on Principles of Distributed Computing. PODC 2016, pp. 65–74. ACM, New York (2016)
4. Jayanti, P., Joshi, A.: Recoverable FCFS mutual exclusion with wait-free recovery. In: 31st International Symposium on Distributed Computing. DISC, pp. 30:1–30:15 (2017)
5. Ramaraju, A.: RGLock: Recoverable mutual exclusion for non-volatile main memory systems. Master's thesis. University of Waterloo (2015)

6. Craig, T.S.: Building FIFO and Priority-Queuing Spin Locks from Atomic Swap. Technical report TR-93-02-02, Department of Computer Science, University of Washington, February 1993
7. Dvir, R., Taubenfeld, G.: Mutual exclusion algorithms with constant RMR complexity and wait-free exit code. In: Proceedings of The 21st International Conference on Principles of Distributed Systems, OPODIS 2017 (2017)
8. Lamport, L.: A new solution of Dijkstra's concurrent programming problem. Commun. ACM **17**(8), 453–455 (1974)
9. Mellor-Crummey, J.M., Scott, M.L.: Algorithms for scalable synchronization on shared-memory multiprocessors. ACM Trans. Comput. Syst. **9**(1), 21–65 (1991)

# Verification

# Declarative Parameterized Verification of Topology-Sensitive Distributed Protocols

Sylvain Conchon[1], Giorgio Delzanno[2(✉)], and Angelo Ferrando[2(✉)]

[1] LRI, Université Paris-Sud, Orsay, France
sylvain.conchon@lri.fr
[2] DIBRIS, University of Genova, Genoa, Italy
{giorgio.delzanno,angelo.ferrando}@unige.it

**Abstract.** We show that Cubicle [9], an SMT-based infinite-state model checker, can be applied as a verification engine for GLog, a logic-based specification language for topology-sensitive distributed protocols with asynchronous communication. Existential coverability queries in GLog can be translated into verification judgements in Cubicle by encoding relational updates rules as unbounded array transitions. We apply the resulting framework to automatically verify a distributed version of the Dining Philosopher mutual exclusion protocol formulated for an arbitrary number of nodes and communication buffers.

## 1 Introduction

Automated verification of distributed systems is a difficult task for standard model checkers [7,8]. Protocols designed to operate in distributed systems are often defined for an arbitrary number of nodes, arbitrary connection topology, and asynchronous communication. protocol rules typically depend on the current network configuration (e.g., presence of a communication link, state of all connections, etc.). Several formal languages have been proposed to specify this class of systems, e.g., communicating state machines, automata, process algebraic languages, (graph) rewriting, etc. In this setting safety properties can be nicely formulated by lifting decision problems based on reachability and coverability, in which the initial configuration is typically fixed a priory, to formulations that are existentially quantified over an infinite set of initial configurations. Existentially quantified coverability problems have been considered in [5,6,14–16] in order to reason on parameterized formulation of distributed protocols with broadcast communication. The coverability decision problem [1] is typically used to formulate reachability of bad configurations independently from the number of components of a system. Therefore, a constructive way to solve an existentially quantified coverability problem for a formal specification of a distributed algorithm provides a characterization of initial configurations from which it is possible to reach a bad configuration (e.g. an anomaly in the protocol). Existentially quantified coverability problems turn out to be undecidable

A. Podelski and F. Taïani (Eds.): NETYS 2018, LNCS 11028, pp. 209–224, 2019.
https://doi.org/10.1007/978-3-030-05529-5_14

even for systems with a static communication topology and very basic interaction primitives like atomic broadcast communication [1,7,13–15]. As mentioned before, communicating state machine (automata), adopted e.g. in [11,14–16], and graph rewriting, adopted in [5], are two examples of formal description languages for this kind of systems. communicating state machines can be considered a standard design and protocol specification language adopted in several verification tools like Uppaal and Spin. Graph rewriting systems are well-suited for representing topology-sensitive rules as shown by the examples of the Groove tool suite. In several case-studies, protocol rules require complex guards that require the inspection of the state of nodes, links, paths, vicinity etc. and tables to store information collected during the execution of protocol phases. The combination of these features seems to require more general specification formalisms. To this aim, in [12] we proposed to adopt a logic-based declarative language, named GLog, a fragment of both DCDCs [12] and MSR [23]. GLog can be viewed as a logic-based presentation of graph update rules with global conditions expressed using quantified first order formulas. GLog is based on a quantified predicate logic in a finite relational signature with no function symbols. Configurations are represented here as sets of ground atomic formulas (instances of unary and binary predicates). Update rules consist of a guard and two sets of first order predicates that define resp. deletion and addition of state components. Differently from specification languages based on extension of Petri nets like transfer and broadcast protocols, guards are checked atomically but update transitions have only local effect. In other words, we forbid simultaneously update of the state of all nodes in a graph. Update rules can be applied to update a global configuration node by node and to operate on the vicinity of a node by restricting updates to given predicates. Termination of an update subprotocol can then be checked via a global condition. Similar specification patterns have been applied to model non-atomic consistency protocol and mutual exclusion protocols with non-atomic global conditions. GLog has been applied to manually analyze distributed protocols in [12]. In the present paper we show that Cubicle [9,18], an SMT-based infinite-state model checker based on previous work by Ghilardi et al. [3], can be applied as automated verification engine for existentially quantified coverability queries in GLog. In Cubicle parameterized systems can be specified as unbounded arrays in which individual components can be referred to via an array index. The Cubicle verification engine performs a symbolic backward reachability analysis using an SMT solver for computing intermediate steps (preimage computation, entailment and termination test) and applies overapproximates predecessors using upward closed sets as in monotone abstractions [2]. A peculiar feature of Cubicle w.r.t. MCMT [3] is that the tool can handle unbounded matrices. This is particularly relevant when modeling topology-sensitive protocols as done in GLog using binary relations defined over component identifiers. Furthermore, existentially quantified coverability decision problems in GLog can directly be mapped into Cubicle. More specifically, the encoding transforms GLog update rules into array-based update formulas in Cubicle. Classes of initial configurations are specified by using partial specifications of initial configurations in Cubicle verification judgements. Infinite sets of bad configurations can be expressed using unsafe configurations in Cubicle verification judgements.

As a case-study, we consider the distributed version of the Dining Philosopher mutual exclusion protocol (DDP) recently studied in [12,17,20]. The protocol deals with an arbitrary, finite number of nodes and buffers that act as single-place communication channels, and arbitrary link topology between nodes and buffers. Ownership of buffers is specified using asynchronous rules. Global conditions over linked buffers are used as enabling conditions for acquiring access to resources shared among neighbors. The GLog formal specification of DDP is mapped to a Cubicle verification problem in a natural way. In our preliminary experiments, Cubicle verified the correctness of the protocols in negligible time. Furthermore, as expected it reports potential error traces when introducing network reconfiguration rules (e.g. dynamic link creation and deletion) unrelated to the state of the corresponding involved nodes. The application of declarative specification languages and SMT-based engine seems a very promising research line for dealing for a larger class of distributed algorithms.

*Contents.* The paper is organized as follows: we first present the GLog declarative language and, in that context, the existential coverabiliity problem; we then introduce Cubicle and exhibit a general encoding of existential coverability into Cubicle; we then discuss the experimental evaluation on the DDP case-study, and, finally, discuss other examples and future directions.

## 2   GLog

GLog [12] formulas are based on a simple relational calculus that can be used to express updates of sets of ground atoms. A set of ground atoms can be interpreted as the current state or configuration of the system we are modeling. Update rules contain a formula working as a condition and deletion and addition sets that specify ground atoms to be deleted and added to the current state. More formally, let $P$ be a finite set of names of (unary and binary) predicate names, $\mathcal{N}$ a denumerable set of node identifiers equipped with a total order $<$, $V$ be a denumerable set of variables. Predicates in $P$ are used to model current configurations. In addition to predicates in $P$, we interpret the binary relation $lt$ as the total order $<$ in our model. Our logic has no function symbols but can be instantiated with elements from $\mathcal{N}$. An atomic formula is either a formula $p(x)$, $lt(x, y)$ or $p(x, y)$, where $p \in P$, $x, y \in V \cup \mathcal{N}$ A ground atom is a either a $p(n)$, $lt(n, m)$, or $p(n, m)$, where $n, m \in \mathcal{N}$. A literal is either an atomic formula or the negation $\neg A$ of an atomic formula $A$. A formula is a first order formula built on literals, namely, any literal is a formula, conjunctions, disjunctions, universally and existentially quantified formulas are still formulas. Multiple occurrences of the same variable implicitly model equality constraints. The set of free variables of a formula $F$, namely, $FV(F)$, is the minimal set satisfying $FV(p(x, y)) = \{x, y\}$, $FV(A \vee B) = FV(A) \cup FV(B)$,

$FV(A \wedge B) = FV(A) \cap FV(B)$, $FV(\neg A) = FV(A)$, $FV(\forall v.A) = FV(A) \setminus \{v\}$, and $FV(\exists v.A) = FV(A) \setminus \{v\}$. Given $S = \{F_1, \ldots, F_n\}$, we define $FV(S) = FV(F_1) \cup \ldots \cup FV(F_n)$. Quantified formulas we will be used as application conditions of rules.

**Configurations, Interpretations and Update Rules.** As mentioned before a set of ground atoms will be used to model a configuration. Formally, a configuration is a finite set $\Delta$ of ground atomic formulas with predicates in $P$. A configuration implicitly defines a graph in which directed edges are represented by atomic formulas whose predicate name acts as edge label. Configurations can also be viewed as models in which to evaluate a conditions. An interpretation is a mapping $\sigma$ from $V$ to $\mathcal{N}$. We use here a fixed interpretation of variables. The interpretation domain however consists of a denumerable set of node identifiers. For a formula $F$ we use $F\sigma$ as an abbreviation for $\hat{\sigma}(F)$, where $\hat{\sigma}$ is the natural extension of $\sigma$ to terms. For a set $S = \{A_1, \ldots, A_n\}$, we use $S\sigma$ to denote the set $\{A_1\sigma, \ldots, A_n\sigma\}$. Update rules consists of conditions defined by quantified formulas with no function symbols, a deletion and an addition set. The deletion (resp. addition) set defines the set of ground atoms that have to be cancelled from (resp. added to) the current configuration. A rule has the following form $\langle C, D, A \rangle$, where $C$ is a quantified formula, $D$ and $A$ are two sets of atomic formulas with variables in $V$ and predicates in $P$, and such that $FV(A) \cup FV(D) \subseteq FV(C)$. A protocol $\mathcal{P}$ is defined as a set of rules.

**Operational Semantics.** To fix an operational semantics for our language we need a support for the interpretation of relations and variables. We use $\Delta \models A$ to define the satisfiability relation of a quantified formula $A$ s.t. $FV(A) = \emptyset$. Let $A[n/X]$ denote the formula obtained by replacing each free occurrence of $X$ with $n$. The relation is defined by induction as follows. $\Delta \models p(n)$, if $p(n) \in \Delta$, $\Delta \models lt(n, m)$, if $n < m$, $\Delta \models p(n, m)$ for $p \in P$, if $p(n, m) \in \Delta$, $\Delta \models A \wedge B$, if $\Delta \models A$ and $\Delta \models B$, $\Delta \models \neg A$, if $\Delta \not\models A$, $\Delta \models \forall X.A$, if $\Delta \models A[n/X]$ for each $n \in \mathcal{N}$, and $\Delta \models \exists X.A$, if $\Delta \models A[n/X]$ for some $n \in \mathcal{N}$. Given a configuration $\Delta$, we say that the quantified formula $A$ is satisfied in $\Delta$, if there exists an interpretation $\sigma$ s.t. $A\sigma$ is satisfiable. In order to apply a rule $\langle C, D, A \rangle$ to $\Delta$, there must be an interpretation $\sigma$ that satisfies the quantified formula $C$. The same interpretation $\sigma$ is then applied to the atomic formulas in $D$ and $A$. The resulting sets of atoms, say $D'$ and $A'$ respectively, are deleted from and added to $\Delta$, respectively.

The operational semantics of a protocol $\mathcal{P}$ is given by a transition system $T_\mathcal{P} = \langle \mathcal{C}, \rightarrow \rangle$, where $\mathcal{C}$ is the set of possible configurations, i.e., finite subsets of ground atoms with predicates in $P$, and $\rightarrow \subseteq \mathcal{C} \times \mathcal{C}$ is a relation defined as follows. For $\Delta, \Delta' \in \mathcal{C}$ and a rule $\langle C, D, A \rangle \in \mathcal{P}$, $\Delta \rightarrow \Delta'$ if there exists $\sigma$ s.t. $\Delta \models C\sigma$ and $\Delta' = (\Delta \setminus D\sigma) \cup A\sigma$. A computation is a sequence of configurations $\Delta_0 \Delta_1 \ldots$ s.t. $\Delta_i \rightarrow \Delta_{i+1}$ for $i \geq 0$. We use $\rightarrow^*$ to denote the reflexive and transitive closure of $\rightarrow$. In a single step of the operational semantics a rule is evaluated in the current configuration by taking a sort of closed-world assumption, i.e., ground atomic formulas that do not occur in a configuration are evaluated to false. Furthermore, ground atomic formulas that are not deleted are transferred from the current to the successor configuration. The latter property can be viewed then as a sort of frame axiom. It is important to notice that, in general, a configuration $\Delta$ has several possible successors. Indeed, depending of the chosen interpretation of free variables the same rule can be applied to different subsets of ground atoms contained in the same configuration. Furthermore, the choice of the rules to be applied at a given step is non-deterministic.

As an example, we consider possible application of GLog to the specification of distributed protocols. The key ingredient of the specification language is the combination of complex conditions and update rules to reason on graphs in which predicates can be viewed as labels of links between agents and communication buffers. We have shown that we can also add labels to individual agents and buffers, e.g., to represent their current state. Update rules can be used to dynamically reconfigure the graph, i.e., change labels, topology and add or delete agents. The separation between agents and buffers is convenient to model asynchronous communication. For instance, let us consider a protocol in which two agents need to establish a connection via a shared buffer.

- An agent $n_1$ of type $A$ connects to a buffer $e_1$ in idle state (the buffer is free) and sets the state of the buffer to *ready*.
- An agent $n_2$ of type $B$ connects to $e_1$ in state *ready* and changes the state to *ack*.
- Agent $n_1$ sends message $m$ by changing the state of $e_1$ to $msg_m$.
- Agent $n_2$ receives message $m$ and updates the state of the channel to *ack* for further communications.

The protocol can be specified as follows. We use unary predicates to associate states to edges. *send* messages are non-deterministically generated. An initial configuration has the form $idle(b_1), \ldots, idle(b_k)$, where $b_i < b_j$ for $i \neq j$, $i, j : 1, \ldots, k$. For the sake of simplicity, we do not model the state of agents but only their capabilities (req, rec, send).

| R | C | D | A |
|---|---|---|---|
| 1 | $idle(B) \wedge \neg req(A, B)$ | $\{idle(B)\}$ | $\{ready(B), req(A, B)\}$ |
| 2 | $ready(B) \wedge \neg rec(A, B)$ | $\{ready(B)\}$ | $\{ack(B), rec(A, B)\}$ |
| 3 | $true$ | $\{\}$ | $\{send(A, B, M)\}$ |
| 4 | $ack(B) \wedge send(A, B)$ | $\{ack(B), send(A, B)\}$ | $\{msg(B, M)\}$ |
| 5 | $msg(B, M) \wedge rec(A, B)$ | $\{msg(B, M), rec(A, B)\}$ | $\{idle(B)\}$ |

In rule 1 a buffer $B$ is locked by a non-deterministically generated request $req(A, B)$ from sender agent $A$ (a variable). In rule 2 a buffer $B$ is locked by a non-deterministically generated request $rec(A, B)$ from receiver agent $A$ (a variable). Rule 3 nondeterministically generates a send action from agent $A$.

Rule 4 synchronizes a send action from agent $A$ with a buffer locked by the same agent. The (non deterministically generated) message $M$ is stored in the buffer. Rule 5 synchronizes and consumes a message in the buffer with the receiver agent, releasing the buffer.

The model provides other form of interactions. For instance, we can model ordered buffers by forming lists of messages attached to a given edge as in the representation of the tape of the Turing machine.

We can also model synchronous communication as in the following example

| C | $link(A, B) \wedge s_1(A) \wedge link(E, B) \wedge s_2(E)$ |
|---|---|
| D | $\{s_1(A), link(A, B), link(E, B), s_2(E)\}$ |
| A | $\{link(A, B), s_1'(A), link(E, B), s_2'(E)\}$ |

Here $s(A)$ and $s'(A)$ denote agent $A$ resp. in state $s$ and $s'$, $s_1(E)$ and $s_1'(E)$ denote agent $E$ resp. in state $s_1$ and $s_1'$, and $link(A, B)$ and $link(Y, B)$ denote links to a common buffer $B$.

## 2.1    Existential Coverability

We consider here decision problems that generalize the standard notion of reachability between configurations. The key point is to reason about an infinite set of initial configurations in order to prove properties for protocol instances with an arbitrary number of nodes. For a set $S$ of configurations, we first define the *Post* and *Pre* operators as follows $Post(S) = \{\Delta' \mid \exists \Delta \in S, \ \Delta \to \Delta'\}$ and $Pre(S) = \{\Delta' \mid \exists \Delta \in S, \ \Delta' \to \Delta\}$. We use $Post^*(S)$ (resp. $Pre^*(S)$) to denote the reflexive-transitive closure of $Post$ (resp. $Pre$).

We now introduce the ∃-coverability problem as follows.

**Definition 1 (∃-coverability).** *Given a protocol $\mathcal{P}$, a set of target configurations $T$ and a possibly infinite set of initial configurations $I$, ∃-coverability is satisfied for $\mathcal{P}$, $I$ and $T$, written $\exists Reach(\mathcal{P}, I, T)$, if there exists $\Delta \in T$ and a configuration $\Delta_1$ s.t. $\Delta_1 \in Post^*(I)$ and $\Delta \subseteq \Delta_1$.*

By expanding the definition of $Post^*$, $\exists Reach(\mathcal{P}, I, T)$ holds if there exists a configuration $\Delta_0 \in I$ s.t. $\Delta_0 \to^* \Delta_1$ and $\Delta \subseteq \Delta_1$ for some $\Delta \in T$. The target $T$ can be interpreted as a pattern to match or avoid in computations starting from initial configurations. If the set $I$ consists of configurations consisting of an arbitrary, finite number of components than ∃-coverability formally describes a parameterized verification decision problem for specifications given in GLog. The ∃-coverability problem turns out to be undecidable [12].

## 3   From GLog to Cubicle

Cubicle is a model checker that can be applied to verify safety properties of array-based systems, a syntactically restricted class of parametrized transition systems with states represented as arrays indexed by an arbitrary number of processes [9,18]. Cache coherence protocols and mutual exclusion algorithms are typical examples of such systems. Cubicle model-checks by a symbolic backward reachability analysis on infinite sets of states represented by specific simple formulas, called cubes. Cubicle is written in OCaml. The SMT solver is a tightly integrated, lightweight and enhanced version of Alt-Ergo [21]; and its parallel implementation relies on the Functory library [22]. Cubicle input language is a typed version of Murphi similar to the one of Uclid. A system is described in Cubicle by: (1) a set of type, variable, and array declarations; (2) a formula for the initial states; and (3) a set of transitions. It is parametrized by a set of process identifiers, denoted by the built-in type proc. Standard types int, real, and bool are also built in. Additionally, the user can specify abstract types and enumerations with simple declarations like type data and type msg = Empty | Req | Ack. As an example consider the following declaration.

```
var Turn : proc
array Want[proc] : bool
array Crit[proc] : bool

init (z) { Want[z] = False && Crit[z] = False }

unsafe (x y) {
   Crit[x] = True && Crit[y] = True }
```

The system state is defined by a set of global variables and arrays. The initial states are defined by a universal conjunction of literals characterizing the values for some variables and array entries.

```
init (z) { Want[z] = False && Crit[z] = False }
```

A state of our example consists of a process identifier Turn and two boolean arrays Want and Crit; a state is initial iff every cell of both arrays are set to false Transitions are given in the usual guard/action form and may be parameterized by (one or more) process identifiers. Guards are expressed via required expressions. They are quantified formulas. Quantification is defined only over variables of type *proc*. As an example, consider the following rule.

```
transition req (i)
requires { Want[i] = False }
            { Want[j] := case
              | i = j : True
              | _: Want[j]  }
```

The transition req(i) is enabled if there exists index i (a process) such that Want[i]=false. Its effect is to set Want to true for index i and leave the array unchanged in all other positions. A system execution is defined by an infinite loop that at each iteration: (1) non-deterministically chooses a transition instance whose guard is true in the current state; and (2) updates state variables according to the action of the fired transition instance.

Infinite sets of unsafe states (bad configurations) are defined by using *unsafe* constraints. For instance, the judgement

```
unsafe (x y) {
    Crit[x] = True && Crit[y] = True }
```

specifies the infinite set of arrays $Crit$ (with any size) in which there exist two cells with value $True$.

The Cubicle verification engine is based on symbolic backward exploration. Cubicle operates over sets of existentially quantified formulas called cubes. Formulas containing universally quantified formulas (generated during the computation of predecessors) are over-approximated by existentially quantified formulas. The class of formulas manipulated by the backward reachability loop of Cubicle in not closed by pre-image in presence of universally quantified guards. To handle such formulas, Cubicle implements a safe but over-approximate pre-image computation. Given a cube $\exists \bar{i}.\Phi$ and a guard $G$ of the form $\forall \bar{j}.\Psi(\bar{j})$, the pre-image replaces $G$ by the conjunction $\bigwedge_{\sigma \in \Sigma(\bar{j}, \bar{i})} \Psi(\bar{j})\sigma$ of instances over the permutation of $\Sigma(\bar{j}, \bar{i})$. In other words, in order to handle universally quantified guards, Cubicle applies monotone abstraction [2] and over-approximates predecessors via upward-closed sets of configurations. The search procedure maintains a set $V$ and a priority queue $Q$ resp. of visited and unvisited cubes. Initially, let $V$ be empty and let $Q$ contain the cubes representing bad states. At each iteration, the procedure selects the highest-priority cube $\Phi$ from $Q$ and checks for intersection with the formula denoting the initial configurations (satisfiability of conjunction of $\Phi$ and formulas in the initial conditions). If the test fails, it terminates reporting a possibile error trace. If the test passes, the procedure proceeds to the subsumption check, i.e., implication between formulas. If subsumption fails, then add $\Phi$ to $V$, compute all cubes in $pred_t$ (for every $t$), add them to $Q$, and move on to the next iteration. If the subsumption check succeeds, then drop $\Phi$ from consideration and move on. The algorithm terminates when a safety check fails or $Q$ becomes empty. When an unsafe cube is found, Cubicle actually produces a counterexample trace. Safety checks, being ground satisfiability queries, are easy for SMT solvers. The challenge is in the subsumption check because of their size and the existential implies existential logical form. Cubicle applies the heuristics described in [9] to handle subsumption. The BRAB algorithm introduce in [10] automatically computes over-approximations of backward reachable states that are checked to be unreachable in a finite instance of the system (using Murφ). The resulting approximations (candidate invariants) are model checked together with the original safety properties. Completeness of the approach is ensured by a mechanism for backtracking on spurious traces introduced by too coarse approximations.

**Encoding GLog in Cubicle**

In this section we present an encoding of GLog into an array-based specification language. The encoding is quite natural. The interpretation domain of variables is that of process indexes. For each unary predicate $p \in P$, we introduce a corresponding Boolean array variable array p.

```
array p[proc] : bool
```

For each binary predicate $q$, we introduce a two-dimensional Boolean array q

```
array q[proc,proc] : bool
```

Encoding of guards is straightforward. Free variables occurring in GLog update rules become parameters of transition definitions. A literal $q(x, y)$ [resp. $q(x)$] is mapped to the formula $q(x, y) = true$ [resp. $q(x) = true$]. A literal $\neg q(x, y)$ [resp. $\neg q(x)$] is mapped to the formula $q(x, y) = false$ [resp. $q(x) = false$]. Compound/quantified require conditions are mapped to compound/quantified formulas over literals.

Some care has to be taken in the encoding of GLog update rules. Transitions in Cubicle operate simultaneously on every cell of an array to provide support for global operations like reset and transfer. This kind of operations are not provided in GLog since the focus is on asynchronous behavior, i.e., we assume that global operations are split into several asynchronous operations equipped with guards that can be used to check for the current state of the protocol phase under consideration.

To encode a deletion rule, operating on the atomic formula $A(x, y)$, we use auxiliary variables $u, t$ and a case analysis on indexes: for the case $x = u, y = t$ we add the action $A[x, y] := false$, and $A[x, y] := A[x, y]$ in all other cases. To encode an addition rule, operating on the atomic formula $A(x, y)$, we use again auxiliary variables $u, t$ and a case analysis on indexes: for $x = u, y = t$ we add the action $A[x, y] := true$, and $A[x, y] := A[x, y]$ in all other cases.

To encode $\exists$-coverability, we also need to specify initial and unsafe configurations. Unsafe configurations can be described as in Cubicle using an existentially quantified formula over array cells. To select classes of initial states, we can use init declarations in which we specify only partial conditions on array cells.

## 4    Case Study: Distributed Dining Philosophers

We consider here a distributed version of the dining philosopher mutual exclusion problem presented in [19]. Agents are distributed on an arbitrary graph and communicate asynchronously via point-to-point channels. Channels are viewed as buffers with state. Distributed Dining Philosophers (DDP) is defined as follows. The goal is to ensure that agents can access a resource shared in common with their neighbors in mutual exclusion. The protocol from the perspective a single agent consists of the following steps:

– Initially, all agents are in *idle* state.

- When an agent $A$ wants to get a resource, $A$ has to acquire the control of each buffer shared with his/her neighbors.
- To acquire a channel, $A$ marks the channel with its identifier. If the channel is already marked, $A$ has to wait.
- $A$ acquires the resources when all channels shared with neighbors are marked with his/her identifier.
- To release a resource, $A$ first resets each buffer. When all buffers are reset, $A$ moves back to idle state.

In a statically defined topology, agent $A$ gets access to a resource when all neighbors are either idle or are waiting for acquiring some channel. Communication between two neighbors is asynchronous. Indeed, they interact by reading and writing on the shared channel. The protocol should guarantee that two agents that share the same channel cannot acquire and use a resource simultaneously. The protocol should be robust under dynamic reconfigurations of the network.

### 4.1  Formal Specification of DDP

In this section we present a formal specification of the DDP protocol. Network configurations are expressed as GLog configurations. The dynamics in a protocol interaction is expressed via a finite set of update rules. We use a predicate *link* to represent connections from an agent to a possibly shared buffer. We model buffers with states using unary predicates. Asynchronous communication is modeled as in the previous example, i.e., agents interact only via a common buffer. Communication between two agents is not atomic. Instead of modeling identifiers and buffers with data, we introduce a special relation *own* that is used to model ownership of a given buffer to which a agent is linked. Ownership is normed in the same way as the labeling of buffers in the original protocol, i.e., an agent can acquire ownership only if the buffer is not owned by other agents. Ownership can be released when in *idle* state. We also model non-deterministic creation (in *idle* state) and deletion of links. We model this behavior using the following predicates and rules (rules have the form $(C_i, D_i, A_i)$ for $i : 1, \ldots, 6$):

| R | C | D | A |
|---|---|---|---|
| *getE* | $link(X, E) \wedge \forall Z.\neg own(Z, E)$ | $\emptyset$ | $\{own(X, E)\}$ |
| *relE* | $\{idle(X), own(X, E)\}$ | $\{own(X, E)\}$ | $\emptyset$ |
| *acquire* | $idle(X) \wedge \forall E.(link(X, E) \supset own(X, E))$ | $\{idle(X)\}$ | $\{busy(X)\}$ |
| *release* | $\{busy(X)\}$ | $\{busy(X)\}$ | $\{idle(X)\}$ |

An initial state configuration has the following form $idle(n_1), \ldots, idle(n_k)$, where $n_i \neq n_j$ for $i \neq j$, $i, j : 1, \ldots, k$ and $k \geq 1$.

## 4.2   Encoding in Cubicle

Following the encoding rules specified for GLog, we can now obtain a Cubicle specification for DDP. To simplify a little bit the specification, we introduce an enumeration type `state` over node states.

```
type state = Idle | Busy
```

This way, we can use a single array `State` with cell type `state` instead of two Boolean arrays. We also need a `link` array and a `own` array to specify link and ownership relations between nodes and buffers.

```
array State[proc]    : state
array Link[proc,proc] : bool
array Own[proc,proc] : bool
```

The initial configuration consists of all possible topologies in which nodes are in idle state. We also enforce the ownership relation to be false for each pair of node and buffer.

```
init (n m) {
  State[n] = Idle &&
  Own[n,m] = False }
```

This way we do not put any constraints on link topology. The bad configuration are defined by graphs of the following form.

```
unsafe (n m e) {
  State[n]  = Busy && State[m]  = Busy &&
  Link[n,e] = True && Link[m,e] = True
}
```

Two node are in mutex state while pointing to at the same buffer. The transitions are obtained via the encoding of the GLog specification into Cubicle input language shown in Appendix A. When applying Cubicle to the above described problem, the tool proves the model correct in few seconds without need to apply multicore optimizations via the Functory library. More specifically, Cubicle visits 19 nodes with at most 3 process indexes, 529 fixpoint checks, and 176 calls to the Alter-Ego SMT solver. Since Cubicle operates over unbounded arrays, the above result provides a formal correctness proof of the considered model for any number of nodes and links and any topology. The proof certificate can be obtained by taking the set of assertions (formulas) collected during the fixpoint computation. By applying the BRAB algorithm with parameter 3, the number of visited nodes reduces to 10 with 312 fixpoint tests, and 88 calls to the Alter-Ego solver. Furthermore, the BRAB algorithm infers the invariant $\neg(Own[\#1, \#3] = True \wedge Own[\#2, \#3] = True)$.

| R | C | D | A |
|---|---|---|---|
| *Link* | $\neg link(X, E)$ | $\emptyset$ | $\{link(X, E)\}$ |
| *Unlink* | $link(X, E)$ | $\{link(X, E)\}$ | $\emptyset$ |

### 4.3    Dynamic Reconfiguration

To model dynamic reconfigurations, we can non-deterministically add and remove *link* predicates between pairs of agents and buffers. We first consider the non-deterministic rules *link* and *unlink* defined below.

When the model extended with the above rules is checked with Cubicle (see Appendix B), the tool reports the error trace $acquire(\#1) \rightarrow link(\#1, \#3) \rightarrow get(\#2, \#3) \rightarrow acquire(\#2) \rightarrow unsafe[1]$. This trace is a real error trace. Indeed, process $p_1$ can acquire ownership when there are no links to buffer $b_3$. Since the *link* rule has no condition on $p_1$, a link can then be added from $p_1$ to $b_3$. However, Process $p_2$ can now become owner of $b_3$ and then move to state *Busy*. Two processes are linked to the same buffer $b_3$ while in state *Busy*.

| Model | dfs | brab(3) | V | F | S | M | D | I | C |
|---|---|---|---|---|---|---|---|---|---|
| DPP | | | 19 | 529 | 176 | 3 | 0 | 0 | Yes |
| ” | √ | | 19 | 529 | 176 | 3 | 0 | 0 | Yes |
| ” | | √ | 10 | 312 | 88 | 3 | 0 | 1 | Yes |
| DPP+Link+Unlink | | | 38 | 379 | 528 | 3 | 10 | 0 | No |
| ” | √ | | 63 | 2660 | 961 | 3 | 12 | 0 | No |
| ” | | √ | 33 | 365 | 617 | 3 | 9 | 1 | No |
| DPP+iLink+Unlink | | | 28 | 1449 | 261 | 3 | 6 | 0 | Yes |
| ” | √ | | 39 | 1996 | 414 | 3 | 6 | 0 | Yes |
| ” | | √ | 14 | 735 | 153 | 3 | 2 | 1 | Yes |

**Fig. 1.** Experimental results: **V** = visited nodes, **F** = fixpoint tests, **S** = solver calls, **M** = max process number, **D** = deleted node, **I** = number of invariants (brab), **C** = property checked (Yes/No).

We can modify the model and restrict addition of new link connected to node $X$ only when $X$ is in state *Idle* as follows.

| R | C | D | A |
|---|---|---|---|
| *iLink* | $idle(X), \neg link(X, E)$ | $\emptyset$ | $\{link(X, E)\}$ |
| *Unlink* | $link(X, E)$ | $\{link(X, E)\}$ | $\emptyset$ |

In this model we assume that nodes have some form of control over connections with buffers (i.e. a new link is detected by a node in state *Idle*).

When the model extended with the *link'* and *unlink* rules is checked with Cubicle (see Appendix B), the tool verifies correctness by visiting 28 nodes with at most 3 process indexes, invoking 261 times the SMT solver, performs 1449 fixpoint tests, and deletes 6 redundant nodes. The above result provides a formal correctness proof of the considered model for any number of nodes and links and any topology. Using dfs search, the tool verifies the property but the number of visited nodes is 39 with 414 calls to the SMT solver and 1996 fixpoint checks. Using the BRAB algorithm with parameter 3, the number of visited nodes reduces to 14 with 735 fixpoint tests, and 153 calls to the Alter-Ego solver. As for static topologies, the BRAB algorithm infers the invariant $\neg(Own[\#1, \#3] = True \wedge Own[\#2, \#3] = True)$. A summary of the results with the considered models and heuristics are shown in Fig. 1.

## 5   Conclusions

We have studied a possible application of SMT-based infinite-state model checker to the verification of topology-sensitive distributed protocols, i.e., protocols defined over network graphs and in which rules have guards and effects that depend on communication links. Starting from a logic-based presentation of distributed protocols based on the GLog relational update language, we have shown how to encode existential coverability queries in GLog as Cubicle verification judgements. As a case-study, we have shown that the declarative approach supported by GLog + Cubicle provides a very effective way to verify protocols operating on graphs. For instance, in previous work DDP required complex verification methodologies like assume-guarantee reasoning or ad hoc algorithms for graph rewriting systems. In the present paper DDP is verified using a very simple declarative specification and a general purpose model checker. Cubicle verifies correctness in negligible execution time (without need of multicore optimizations via the Functory library).

   The proposed methodology can be applied to other types of distributed protocols. More specifically, we are currently studying how to deal with routing protocols for arbitrary topologies and hierarchical protocols for reference counting (e.g. garbage collections disciplines etc.). Another interesting direction is related to the possible application of Cubicle for verification of protocol specifications in parameterized multi-agent systems [4].

## A   DDP in Cubicle

```
transition get(n e)
requires {
  Link[n,e] = True  &&   forall_other m.   (Own[m,e] = False)
}
{
Own[m,f] := case   | m=n && f=e : True  |  _ : Own[m,f];
}
```

```
transition rel(n e)
requires {
 State[n] = Idle  && Own[n,e] = True
}
{
Own[m,f] := case  | m=n && f=e : False  | _ : Own[m,f];
 }


transition acquire (n)
requires {
  State[n] = Idle
  &&
  forall_other g.
    (Link[n,g] = False || Link[n,g] = True && Own[n,g] = True)
}
{
State[m] := case  | m=n : Busy  | _ : State[m];
 }
```

## B    Dynamic Reconfiguration in Cubicle

```
transition unlink(n m)
requires {
 Link[n,m] = True
}
{
Link[p,q] := case  | p=n && q=m : False  | _ : Link[p,q];
 }


transition link(n m)
requires {
 Link[n,m] = False
}
{
Link[p,q] := case  | p=n && q=m : True  | _ : Link[p,q];
 }


transition iLink(n m)
requires {
 State[n] = Idle  && Link[n,m] = False
}
{
Link[p,q] := case  | p=n && q=m : True  | _ : Link[p,q];
 }
```

# References

1. Abdulla, P.A., Delzanno, G.: Parameterized verification. STTT **18**(5), 469–473 (2016)
2. Abdulla, P.A., Delzanno, G., Ben Henda, N., Rezine, A.: Monotonic abstraction: on efficient verification of parameterized systems. Int. J. Found. Comput. Sci. **20**(5), 779–801 (2009)
3. Alberti, F., Ghilardi, S., Sharygina, N.: A framework for the verification of parameterized infinite-state systems. Fundam. Inform. **150**(1), 1–24 (2017)
4. Ancona, D., Ferrando, A., Mascardi, V.: Parametric runtime verification of multiagent systems. In: Proceedings of the 16th Conference on Autonomous Agents and MultiAgent Systems, AAMAS 2017, São Paulo, Brazil, 8–12 May 2017, pp. 1457–1459 (2017)
5. Bertrand, N., Delzanno, G., König, B., Sangnier, A., Stückrath, J.: On the decidability status of reachability and coverability in graph transformation systems. In: RTA 2012, Volume 15 of LIPIcs, pp. 101–116. Schloss Dagstuhl - Leibniz-Zentrum fuer Informatik (2012)
6. Bertrand, N., Fournier, P., Sangnier, A.: Distributed local strategies in broadcast networks. In: 26th International Conference on Concurrency Theory, CONCUR 2015, Madrid, Spain, 1–4 September 2015, pp. 44–57 (2015)
7. Bloem, R., et al.: Decidability of Parameterized Verification. Synthesis Lectures on Distributed Computing Theory. Morgan & Claypool Publishers, San Rafael (2015)
8. Bloem, R., et al.: Decidability in parameterized verification. SIGACT News **47**(2), 53–64 (2016)
9. Conchon, S., Goel, A., Krstić, S., Mebsout, A., Zaïdi, F.: Cubicle: a parallel SMT-based model checker for parameterized systems. In: Madhusudan, P., Seshia, S.A. (eds.) CAV 2012. LNCS, vol. 7358, pp. 718–724. Springer, Heidelberg (2012). https://doi.org/10.1007/978-3-642-31424-7_55
10. Conchon, S., Goel, A., Krstic, S., Mebsout, A., Zaïdi, F.: Invariants for finite instances and beyond. In: Formal Methods in Computer-Aided Design, FMCAD 2013, Portland, OR, USA, 20–23 October 2013, pp. 61–68 (2013)
11. Delzanno, G.: Constraint-based verification of parameterized cache coherence protocols. Form. Methods Syst. Des. **23**(3), 257–301 (2003)
12. Delzanno, G.: A logic-based approach to verify distributed protocols. In: Proceedings of the 31st Italian Conference on Computational Logic, Milano, Italy, 20–22 June 2016, pp. 86–101 (2016)
13. Delzanno, G.: A unified view of parameterized verification of abstract models of broadcast communication. STTT **18**(5), 475–493 (2016)
14. Delzanno, G., Sangnier, A., Zavattaro, G.: Parameterized verification of Ad Hoc networks. In: Gastin, P., Laroussinie, F. (eds.) CONCUR 2010. LNCS, vol. 6269, pp. 313–327. Springer, Heidelberg (2010). https://doi.org/10.1007/978-3-642-15375-4_22
15. Delzanno, G., Sangnier, A., Zavattaro, G.: On the power of cliques in the parameterized verification of Ad Hoc networks. In: Hofmann, M. (ed.) FoSSaCS 2011. LNCS, vol. 6604, pp. 441–455. Springer, Heidelberg (2011). https://doi.org/10.1007/978-3-642-19805-2_30
16. Delzanno, G., Sangnier, A., Zavattaro, G.: Verification of Ad Hoc networks with node and communication failures. In: Giese, H., Rosu, G. (eds.) FMOODS/FORTE -2012. LNCS, vol. 7273, pp. 235–250. Springer, Heidelberg (2012). https://doi.org/10.1007/978-3-642-30793-5_15

17. Delzanno, G., Stückrath, J.: Parameterized verification of graph transformation systems with whole neighbourhood operations. In: Ouaknine, J., Potapov, I., Worrell, J. (eds.) RP 2014. LNCS, vol. 8762, pp. 72–84. Springer, Cham (2014). https://doi.org/10.1007/978-3-319-11439-2_6

18. Mebsout, A.: Inférence d'invariants pour le model checking de systèmes paramétrés (Invariants inference for model checking of parameterized systems). PhD thesis, University of Paris-Sud, Orsay, France (2014)

19. Namjoshi, K.S., Trefler, R.J.: Uncovering symmetries in irregular process networks. In: Giacobazzi, R., Berdine, J., Mastroeni, I. (eds.) VMCAI 2013. LNCS, vol. 7737, pp. 496–514. Springer, Heidelberg (2013). https://doi.org/10.1007/978-3-642-35873-9_29

20. Namjoshi, K.S., Trefler, R.J.: Analysis of dynamic process networks. In: Baier, C., Tinelli, C. (eds.) TACAS 2015. LNCS, vol. 9035, pp. 164–178. Springer, Heidelberg (2015). https://doi.org/10.1007/978-3-662-46681-0_11

21. http://alt-ergo.lri.fr

22. http://functory.lri.fr/

23. http://www.disi.unige.it/person/DelzannoG/MSR/

# On Verifying TSO Robustness
# for Event-Driven Asynchronous Programs

Ahmed Bouajjani[1], Constantin Enea[1(✉)], Madhavan Mukund[2],
and Rajarshi Roy[2]

[1] IRIF, University Paris Diderot, Paris, France
cenea@irif.fr
[2] Chennai Mathematical Institute, Chennai, India

**Abstract.** We present a method for checking whether an event-driven asynchronous program running under the Total Store Ordering (TSO) memory model is robust, i.e., all its TSO computations are equivalent to computations under the Sequential Consistency (SC) semantics. We show that this verification problem can be reduced in polynomial time to a reachability problem in a program with two threads, provided that the original program satisfies a criterion called robustness against concurrency, introduced recently in the literature. This result allows to avoid explicit handling of all concurrent executions in the analysis, which leads to an important gain in complexity.

## 1 Introduction

Asynchronous event-driven programming allows procedures to be executed asynchronously (after their invocation), e.g., as callbacks handling the occurrences of external events. In particular, modern user interface (UI) frameworks in Android, iOS, and Javascript, are instances of asynchronous event-driven programming. These frameworks dedicate a distinguished main thread, called UI thread, to handling user interface events. Since responsiveness to user events is a key concern, common practice is to let the UI thread perform only short-running work in response to each event, delegating to asynchronous tasks the more computationally demanding part of the work. These asynchronous tasks are in general executed in parallel on different background threads, depending on the computational resources offered by the execution platform. The apparent simplicity of UI programming models is somewhat deceptive. The difficulty of writing safe programs given the concurrency of the underlying execution platform is still all there.

Bouajjani et al. [6] have proposed a correctness criterion for such programs which requires that their standard (multi-thread) semantics is a *refinement* of

This work is supported in part by the European Research Council (ERC) under the European Union's Horizon 2020 research and innovation programme (grant agreement No. 678177), and the Franco-Indian CNRS-DST/CEFIPRA collaborative project AVECSO.

© Springer Nature Switzerland AG 2019
A. Podelski and F. Taïani (Eds.): NETYS 2018, LNCS 11028, pp. 225–239, 2019.
https://doi.org/10.1007/978-3-030-05529-5_15

a single-thread semantics where user events are executed until completion in a serial manner, one after the other, and the asynchronous tasks created by an event handler (and recursively, by its callee) are executed asynchronously (once the execution of the creator finishes), but serially and in the order of their invocation. The multi-thread semantics being a refinement of the single-thread implies that the sets of observable reachable states of the program w.r.t. both semantics are exactly the same (see Sect. 4 for the exact definition). While the multi-thread semantics provides greater performance and responsiveness, the single-thread semantics is simpler to apprehend. The inherent non-determinism due to concurrency and asynchronous task dispatching from the multi-thread semantics is not present in the context of the single-thread one. A program that satisfies this refinement condition is said to be *robust against concurrency*. The same work has shown that violations of this criterion correspond in practice to undesirable behaviors, and that this criterion can be checked efficiently (in polynomial time for Boolean programs), using a linear time reduction to the state reachability problem in *sequential programs*.

Robustness against concurrency assumes that the programs are executed under Sequential Consistency [15] (SC), where the actions of different threads are interleaved while the program order between actions of each thread is preserved. For performance reasons, modern multiprocessors implement weaker memory models, e.g., Total Store Ordering (TSO) [18] in x86 machines, which relax the program order. For instance, the main feature of TSO is the write-to-read relaxation, which allows reads to overtake writes. This relaxation reflects the fact that writes are buffered before being flushed non-deterministically to the main memory. In this work, we consider asynchronous event-driven programs that are executed under TSO, and investigate the relationship between robustness against concurrency and *robustness against TSO* [3,7–9], which requires that a TSO program admits the same behaviors as if it was run under SC.

We first show that robustness against concurrency (which concerns only the SC semantics) doesn't imply robustness against TSO (see Sect. 2), i.e., even if the SC semantics doesn't allow interference between events and asynchronous invocations (they can be seen as atomic), the TSO semantics can still introduce new behaviors which are not possible under SC (therefore, breaking the atomicity of the events and asynchronous invocations). However, we show that checking robustness against TSO for programs satisfying robustness against concurrency is more efficient than in the general case. Using the approach in [5], we show that such a program is not robust against TSO iff it admits a robustness violation which can be simulated using just *two* threads. This implies that checking robustness against TSO for a program with an unbounded number of threads (that is robust against concurrency) can be reduced in polynomial time to the problem of checking TSO robustness for a program with just two threads. The latter has been proved to be polynomial time for Boolean programs in [5].

Our work leads in particular to an efficient approach for the verification of functional correctness of event-driven asynchronous programs running under TSO that consists in solving three separate problems: (1) showing that the program is functionally correct w.r.t the single-thread semantics, (2) showing that the program is robust against concurrency, and (3) showing that the program is robust against TSO. These problems can be solved efficiently by considering only particular types of computations captured by sequential or two thread programs.

**Related Work.** The weakest correctness criterion that enables SC reasoning for proving invariants of programs running under TSO is *state-robustness against TSO* i.e., the reachable set of states is the same under both SC and TSO. However, this problem has high complexity (at least non-primitive recursive for programs with a finite number of threads and a finite data domain [4]). Therefore, it is difficult to come up with an efficient and precise solution. A symbolic decision procedure is presented in [1] and over-approximate analyses are proposed in [13,14]. Due to the high complexity of state-robustness, stronger correctness criteria with lower complexity have been proposed. Trace-robustness (that we call simply robustness against TSO in our paper) is one of the most studied criteria in the literature. Trace-robustness is PSPACE-complete for a finite number of threads and a finite data domain [7] and EXPSPACE-complete for an unbounded number of threads. Besides trace-robustness, there are other correctness criteria like triangular race freedom (TRF) and persistence that are stronger than state-robustness. Persistence [2] is incomparable to trace-robustness and TRF [16] is stronger than both trace-robustness and persistence. Our work considers the specific case of event-driven asynchronous programs and shows that checking trace-robustness has a much lower complexity (polynomial time), provided the programs are robust against concurrency.

The works in [10–12,17] target exploring interesting subsets of executions and schedules for asynchronous programs running under SC, that offer a large coverage of the execution space. This is orthogonal to the focus of our paper which is to analyze behaviors of these programs running under TSO.

```
// Event 1                              class SearchTask extends AsyncTask {
void searchForNews(String key) {            List result = null;
    new SearchTask.execute(key);            void doInBackground(String key) {
    new SaveTask.execute(key); }                result = ...
                                            // get from the network
// Event 2                                  }
void showDetail(int id) {                   void onPostExecute() {
    // show detail of the idth news             list = result;
    new DownloadTask.execute(id); }             // display the list of titles } }

class SaveTask extends AsyncTask {      class DownloadTask extends AsyncTask {
    void doInBackground(String key) {       String content = null;
        // write key to the database } }    void doInBackground(int id) {
                                                content = ... // get from the network
                                            }
                                            void onPostExecute() {
                                                // display the content } }
```

**Fig. 1.** Program which is robust against concurrency.

## 2    Motivation

We briefly discuss the relevance of robustness against concurrency using the program in Fig. 1, which is extracted from an Android application (we assume it is executed under SC). This program has two event handlers searchForNews and showDetail which can be invoked by the user to search for news containing a keyword and to display the details of a selected news respectively. Robustness against concurrency can be characterized as the conjunction of *event-serializability* and *event determinism*, which are variants of the classical notions of serializability and determinism, adapted to our context. Intuitively, since the single-thread semantics defines a unique execution, given a set of external events (partially ordered w.r.t. some causality relation imposed by the environment), then (1) the executions of the event handlers must be serializable (to an order compatible with their causality relation), i.e., the execution of each event handler and its subtasks can be seen as an atomic transaction, and (2) the execution of each event handler is deterministic, i.e., it always leads to the same state, for any possible scheduling of its parallel subtasks.

The procedure searchForNews creates two AsyncTask objects SearchTask and SaveTask whose execute method will invoke asynchronously doInBackground followed by onPostExecute, in the case of the former. Under the multi-thread semantics, doInBackground is invoked on a new thread and onPostExecute is invoked on the main thread. When the user input to search for news is triggered, the invocation doInBackground of searchTask connects to the network, searches for the keyword and fetches the list of resulting news titles. Then, the invocation onPostExecute displays the list of titles to the user. SaveTask saves the keyword to a database representing the search history in the background. The background tasks SearchTask.doInBackground and SaveTask.doInBackground might interfere but any interleaving produces the same result, i.e., it can be assumed searchForNews is deterministic.

The second event, to show the details of a title, can be triggered once the list of titles are displayed on the screen. It invokes an asynchronous task to download the contents of the news in the background and then displays it. In this case, the tasks are executed in a fixed order and the event is trivially deterministic.

Concerning serializability, the invocation of SaveTask in the first event and the second event might interleave (under the concrete semantics). However, assuming that the second event is triggered once the results are displayed, any such interleaving results in the same state as a serial execution of these events.

To show that robustness against concurrency doesn't imply robustness against TSO consider the two programs in Fig. 2. The program on the left of Fig. 2 consists of a single event which is deterministic, but it is not robust against TSO. The TSO memory model admits a computation where both a and b are 0 at the end of the program which is not possible under SC. The program on the right of Fig. 2 consists of $n$ events $e_i$ with $1 \leq i \leq n$, which are all deterministic and serializable (therefore the program is robust against concurrency) but its semantics under TSO admits a computation where all the $a_i$ variables are 0 at the end of the program (which is again not possible under SC).

```
                                    // for every 1 ≤ i ≤ n
                                    procedure eᵢ() {
     procedure e₁() {                 if (y_{i−1}=1)
       x:=1;                             async[any] pᵢ();
       a:=y;                         }
       async[any] p();              procedure pᵢ() {
     }                                 xᵢ:=1;
     procedure p() {                   aᵢ:=x_{(i+1) mod n};
       y:=1;                           async[any] qᵢ();
       b:=x;                         }
     }                              procedure qᵢ() {
                                      yᵢ:=1;
                                    }
```

**Fig. 2.** Asynchronous programs which are not robust against TSO. All variables are initially set to 0 except for $y_0$ in the second program which is set to 1.

## 3 Programs

In order to give a generic definition of robustness, which doesn't depend on any particular asynchronous-programming platform or syntax, we frame our discussion around the abstract notion of programs defined in Sect. 3.1. Two alternative *multi-thread* and *single-thread* semantics to programs *under the SC memory model* are given in Sects. 3.2 and 3.4. A version of the multi-threaded semantics *under the TSO memory model* is given in Sect. 3.3.

### 3.1 Asynchronous Event-Driven Programs

We define an event handler as a procedure which is invoked in response to a user or a system input. For simplicity, we assume that inputs can arrive in any order. Event handlers may have some asynchronous invocations of other procedures, to be executed later on the same thread or on a background thread.

We fix sets $G$ and $L$ of global and local program states. Local states $\ell \in L$ represent the code and data of an asynchronous procedure or event-handler invocation, including the code and data of all nested synchronous procedure calls. A program is defined as a mapping between pairs of global and local states which gives the semantics of each statement in the code of a procedure (the association between threads, local states, and procedure invocations is defined in Sects. 3.2 and 3.4). To formalize the notions of robustness, this mapping associates with each statement a label called *program action* that records the set of accessed global variables and the asynchronous invocations in that statement. An *event set* $E \subset L$ is a set of local states; each $e \in E$ represents the code and data for a single event handler invocation (called event for short).

Formally, a *program* $P : G \times L \rightarrow G \times L \times B$ maps global states $g \in G$ and local states $\ell \in L$ to new states and program actions; each $P(g, \ell)$ represents a single program transition. Supposing that the global states $g \in G$ are maps from program variables $x$ to values $g(x)$, and that local states $\ell \in L$ map program variables $a$ to values $\ell(a)$ and a program counter variable pc to program statements $\ell(\text{pc})$, we give an interpretation to the standard program syntax listed in Fig. 3.

$$x := a \quad a := x \quad a := expr \quad \texttt{call } p(\boldsymbol{y}) \quad \texttt{async}[w] \, p(\boldsymbol{y}) \quad \texttt{return}$$

**Fig. 3.** Basic statements. The metavariables $x$ and $a$ range over global and local variable names, respectively, $expr$ is an expression over local variables, $p$ ranges over procedure names, and $w$ over the symbols "main" and "any."

Besides assignments and synchronous procedure calls, $\texttt{async}[w] \, p(\boldsymbol{y})$ represents an asynchronous invocation of $p(\boldsymbol{y})$ run on a distinguished main thread when $w = \text{main}$, and on an arbitrary thread when $w = \text{any}$. For instance, writing $\ell^+$ to denote $\ell[\text{pc} \mapsto \ell(\text{pc})+1]$, then $P(g, \ell)$ is

- $\langle g[x \mapsto \ell(a)], \ell^+, \text{wr}(x, \ell(a)) \rangle$ when $\ell(\text{pc})$ is a global-variable write $x := a$,
- $\langle g, \ell^+[a \mapsto g(x)], \text{rd}(x, g(x)) \rangle$ when $\ell(\text{pc})$ is a global-variable read $a := x$,
- $\langle g, \ell^+[a \mapsto \ell(expr)], \epsilon \rangle$ when $\ell(\text{pc})$ is a local computation $a := expr$ (here, $\ell(expr)$ is the standard extension of $\ell$ to expressions $expr$ over local variables),
- $\langle g, \ell^+, \text{invoke}(\ell', w) \rangle$ when $\ell(\text{pc})$ is an asynchronous invocation $\texttt{async}[w] \, p(\boldsymbol{y})$, where $\ell'$ maps the parameters of procedure $p$ to the invocation arguments $\boldsymbol{y}$ and pc to the initial statement of $p$, and
- $\langle g, \ell, \text{return} \rangle$ when $\ell(\text{pc})$ is the $\texttt{return}$ statement.

The semantics of other statements, including synchronous procedure calls $\texttt{call } p(\boldsymbol{y})$, if-then-else conditionals, while loops, or goto statements, etc., is standard, and yield the empty program action $\varepsilon$.

An event is called *sequential* when its code doesn't contain asynchronous invocations $\texttt{async}[w] \, p(\boldsymbol{y})$. Also, a program $P$ with event set $E$ is called *sequential* when every event $e \in E$ is sequential. Otherwise, $P$ is called *concurrent*.

## 3.2   SC Multi-thread Asynchronous Semantics

A *task* $u = \langle \ell, i, j, k \rangle$ is a local state $\ell \in L$ along with invocation, event and thread identifiers $i, j, k \in \mathbb{N}$, and $U$ denotes the set of tasks. We write $\text{invoc}(u)$, $\text{event}(u)$, and $\text{thread}(u)$ to refer to $i$, $j$, and $k$, respectively. A *configuration* $c = \langle g, t, q \rangle$ is a global state $g \in G$ along with sets $t, q \subseteq U$ of running and waiting tasks such that: (1) invocation identifiers are unique, i.e., $\text{invoc}(u_1) \neq \text{invoc}(u_2)$ for all $u_1 \neq u_2 \in t \cup q$, and (2) threads run one task at a time, i.e., $\text{thread}(u_1) \neq \text{thread}(u_2)$ for all $u_1 \neq u_2 \in t$. The set of configurations is denoted by $C_m$. We say that a thread $k$ is *idle* in $c$ when $k \notin \{\text{thread}(u) : u \in t\}$, and that an identifier $i, j, k$ is *fresh* when $i, j, k \notin \{\alpha(u) : u \in (t \cup q)\}$ for $\alpha \in \{\text{invoc}, \text{event}, \text{thread}\}$, respectively. A configuration is *idle* when all threads are *idle*.

To define robustness against concurrency, we expose the following set $A$ of actions in execution traces:

$$A = \{\text{start}(j), \text{end}(j) : j \in \mathbb{N}\} \cup B \cup \{\text{invoke}(i), \text{begin}(i), \text{return}(i) : i \in \mathbb{N}\}$$

By convention, we denote asynchronous procedure invocation, event, and thread identifiers, respectively, with the symbols $i, j, k$. The $\text{start}(j)$ and $\text{end}(j)$ actions represent the start and end of event $j$; the invoke($i$), begin($i$), and return($i$) actions represent an asynchronous procedure invocation (when it is added to the queue of pending invocations), the start of $i$'s execution (when it is removed from the queue), and return of $i$, respectively. The set $X$ of memory accesses is defined as in the program actions of Sect. 3.1.

The transition function $\rightarrow$ in Fig. 4 is determined by a program $P$ and event set $E$, and maps a configuration $c_1 \in C_m$ and thread identifier $k \in \mathbb{N}$ to another configuration $c_2 \in C_m$ and label $\lambda = \langle k, i, j, a \rangle$ where $i$ and $j$ are invocation and event identifiers, and $a \in A$ is an action—we write thread($\lambda$), invoc($\lambda$), event($\lambda$), and act($\lambda$) to refer to $k$, $i$, $j$, and $a$, respectively. Let $\Lambda_{SC}$ denote the set of such transition labels $\lambda$. EVENT transitions mark the beginnings of events. We assume that all events are initiated on thread 0, which is also referred to as the *main* thread. Also, for simplicity, we assume that events can be initiated arbitrarily at any time. Adding causality constraints between events, e.g., one event can be initiated only when a certain action has been executed, is possible but tedious. ASYNC transitions create pending asynchronous invocations, DISPATCH transitions begin the execution of pending invocations, and RETURN transitions signal their end (the condition in the right ensures that this is not a return from an event). END EVENT transitions mark the end of an event and by an abuse of notation, they map $c_1$ and $k$ to a configuration $c_2$ and two labels, return($i$) denoting the end of the asynchronous invocation and end($j$) denoting the end of the event. All other transitions are LOCAL.

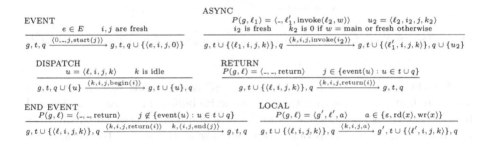

**Fig. 4.** The multi-thread transition function $\rightarrow$ for a program $P$ with event set $E$.

An *execution* of a program $P$ under the SC multi-thread semantics with event set $E$ to configuration $c_n$ is a configuration sequence $c_0 c_1 \ldots c_n$ such that $c_m \xrightarrow{\lambda_{m+1}} c_{m+1}$ for $0 \leq m < n$. We call the sequence $\lambda_1 \ldots \lambda_n$ the *trace* of $c_0 c_1 \ldots c_n$. The set of traces of $P$ with $E$ under the SC multi-thread semantics is denoted by $[\![P, E]\!]_m^{SC}$. We may omit $P$ when it is understood from the context.

The *call tree* of a trace $\tau$ is a ranked tree $CallTree_\tau = \langle V, E, O \rangle$ where $V$ are the invocation identifiers in $\tau$, and the set of edges $E$ contains an edge from $i_1$ to $i_2$ whenever $i_2$ is invoked by $i_1$, i.e., $\tau$ contains a label $\langle i_1, \_, \text{invoke}(i_2) \rangle$. The function $O : E \rightarrow \mathbb{N}$ labels each edge $(i_1, i_2)$ with an integer $n$ whenever $i_2$ is the $n$th invocation made by $i_1$, i.e., $\langle i_1, \_, \mathrm{invoke}(i_2)\rangle$ is the $n$th label of the form $\langle i_1, \_, \mathrm{invoke}(\_)\rangle$ occurring in $\tau$ (reading $\tau$ from left to right).

### 3.3   TSO Multi-thread Asynchronous Semantics

The extension of the SC multi-thread semantics of Sect. 3.2 to the TSO memory model is obtained by adding write buffers to each thread, such that each write on a global variable is first stored in a write buffer before being flushed non-deterministically to the global memory, and each read takes a value from the write buffer, if a write on the corresponding global variable exists, or the global memory, otherwise. To deal with TSO memory effects, we also extend the program syntax of Sect. 3.1 by adding a statement fence which ensures that all the writes in the buffer have been flushed to the global memory.

WRITE ISSUE
$$\frac{P(g,\ell) = \langle g',\ell',\mathrm{wr}(x)\rangle}{g,t \cup \{\langle \ell,i,j,k\rangle\}, q, b \xrightarrow{\langle k,i,j,\mathrm{issue}(x,g'(x))\rangle} g, t \cup \{\langle \ell',i,j,k\rangle\}, q, b[k \mapsto b[k] \cdot \mathrm{wr}(x,g'(x))]}$$

WRITE COMMIT
$$\frac{}{g,t,q,b[k \mapsto \mathrm{wr}(x,v) \cdot \sigma] \xrightarrow{\langle k,i,j,\mathrm{wr}(x,v)\rangle} g[x \mapsto v], t, q, b[k \mapsto \sigma]}$$

FENCE
$$\frac{b[k] = \epsilon}{g,t,q,b \xrightarrow{\langle k,i,j,\mathrm{fence}\rangle} g,t,q,b}$$

READ
$$\frac{P(g',\ell) = \langle g',\ell',\mathrm{rd}(x)\rangle}{g' = g[x \mapsto v] \text{ if the latest write on } x \text{ in } b[k] \text{ is } \mathrm{wr}(x,v), \text{ and } g' = g, \text{ otherwise}}$$
$$g,t \cup \{\langle \ell,i,j,k\rangle\}, q, b \xrightarrow{\langle k,i,j,\mathrm{rd}(x,v)\rangle} g, t \cup \{\langle \ell',i,j,k\rangle\}, q, b$$

**Fig. 5.** The TSO multi-thread transition function $\to$ for a program $P$ with event set $E$.

A configuration $c = \langle g,t,q,b\rangle$ extends an SC configuration $\langle g,t,q\rangle$ with a set $b$ of write buffers, one for each thread. The write buffer of a thread $k$ is denoted by $b[k]$. The transition function $\to$ for local actions that access global variables is given in Fig. 5 (the transitions corresponding to the rest of the actions are defined exactly as in the SC case). WRITE ISSUE adds a global variable write to a write buffer, WRITE COMMIT executes the oldest write in a buffer on the global memory, READ and FENCE give the semantics of global variable read and fence statements. Let $\Lambda_{TSO}$ be the set of transition labels in the TSO semantics, i.e., the union of $\Lambda_{SC}$ and all labels $\langle k,i,j,\mathrm{issue}(x,v)\rangle$ and $\langle k,i,j,\mathrm{fence}\rangle$ representing write issue and fence transitions, respectively.

The set of traces of $P$ with $E$ under the TSO multi-thread semantics is denoted by $[\![P,E]\!]_m^{TSO}$.

### 3.4   Single-Thread Asynchronous Semantics

Conversely to the multi-thread semantics of Sect. 3.2, our single-thread semantics minimizes the set of possible program behaviors by executing all events and asynchronous invocations on the main thread, the asynchronous procedure invocations being executed in a *fixed* order (in this context, the memory model is not important since SC and TSO produce the same behaviors on a single thread).

We explain the order in which asynchronous invocations are executed using the event handler `searchForNews` in Fig. 1. This event handler is supposed to add the keyword to the search history only after the fetching of the news containing that keyword succeeds. This expectation corresponds to executing the asynchronous procedures according to the DFS traversal of the call tree. In general, this traversal is relevant because it preserves causality constraints which are imprinted in the structure of the code, like in the case of standard synchronous procedure calls. Note however that this semantics is not equivalent to interpreting asynchronous invocations as synchronous, since the caller finishes before the callee starts. In the formalization of this semantics, the DFS traversal is modeled using a stack of FIFO queues for storing the pending invocations.

The formalization of the single-thread semantics reuses the notions of task and label in Sect. 3.2. Let $U_0$ be the set of tasks $u = \langle \ell, i, j, 0 \rangle$ executing on thread 0. We overload the term *configuration* which in this context is a tuple $c = \langle g, u, q \rangle$ where $g \in G$, $u \in (U_0 \cup \{\bot\})$ is a possibly-empty task placeholder (at most one task is running at any moment), and $q \in (\mathsf{Tuples}(U_0))^*$ is a sequence of tuples of tasks (a tuple, resp., a sequence, denotes a FIFO queue, resp., a stack). $C_s$ is the set of configurations of the single-thread semantics. We call $c \in C_s$ *idle* if $u = \bot$.

The transition function $\Rightarrow$ in Fig. 6 is essentially a restriction of $\rightarrow$ where all the procedures run on the main thread, an event begins when there are no pending invocations, and the rules ASYNC and DISPATCH use a stack of FIFO queues for storing pending invocations. The effect of pushing/popping a queue to the stack or enqueuing/dequeueing a task to a queue is represented using the concatenation operation $\cdot$, resp., $\circ$, for sequences, resp., tuples. Every task created by ASYNC is posted to the *main* thread and it is enqueued in the queue on the top of the stack $q$. DISPATCH dequeues a pending task from the queue $f$ on the top of $q$, and pushes a new *empty* queue to $q$ (for storing the tasks created during the newly started invocation) if $f$ doesn't become empty. Moreover, the rules RETURN and END EVENT pop the queue on the top of $q$ if it is empty.

An *execution* of a program $P$ under the single-thread semantics with event set $E$ to configuration $c_n$ is a sequence $c_0 c_1 \ldots c_n$ s.t. $c_m \xrightarrow{0, \lambda_{m+1}} c_{m+1}$ for $0 \le m < n$. We call the sequence $\lambda_1 \ldots \lambda_n$ the *trace* of $c_0 c_1 \ldots c_n$.

The set of traces of $P$ with $E$ under the single-thread semantics is denoted by $[\![P, E]\!]_s$ ($P$ may be omitted when it is understood from the context).

## 4   Robustness Criteria

We introduce the notions of robustness against concurrency [6] and robustness against TSO [3,7–9] which imply that every "final"[1] state of a program $P$ reachable under a weak semantics, the SC multi-thread semantics and respectively,

---

[1] Here, "final" means that there are no pending invocations.

EVENT

$$\frac{e \in E \qquad i,j \text{ are fresh}}{g, \bot, \varepsilon \xrightarrow{\langle 0, \_, j, \text{start}(j) \rangle} g, \bot, \langle e, i, j, 0 \rangle}$$

END EVENT

$$\frac{P(g, \ell) = \langle \_, \_, \text{return} \rangle}{g, \langle \ell, i, j, k \rangle, \varepsilon \xrightarrow{\langle 0, i, j, \text{return}(i) \rangle} k, \langle i, j, \text{end}(j) \rangle} g, \bot, \varepsilon}$$

ASYNC

$$\frac{P(g, \ell_1) = \langle \_, \ell_1', \text{invoke}(\ell_2, w) \rangle \qquad u_2 = \langle \ell_2, i_2, j, 0 \rangle \qquad i_2 \text{ is fresh}}{g, \langle \ell_1, i, j, k \rangle, q \cdot f \xrightarrow{\langle 0, i, j, \text{invoke}(i_2) \rangle} g, \langle \ell_1', i, j, k \rangle, q \cdot (f \circ i_2)}$$

DISPATCH

$$\frac{u = \langle \ell, i, j, k \rangle \qquad f = u \circ f' \qquad q' \text{ is } \langle \rangle \text{ if } f' = \langle \rangle \text{ or } f' \cdot \langle \rangle, \text{ otherwise}}{g, \bot, q \cdot f \xrightarrow{\langle 0, i, j, \text{begin}(i) \rangle} g, u, q \cdot q'}$$

RETURN

$$\frac{P(g, \ell) = \langle \_, \_, \text{return} \rangle \qquad j \in \{\text{event}(u) : u \in q\}}{g, \langle \ell, i, j, k \rangle, q \xrightarrow{\langle 0, i, j, \text{return}(i) \rangle} g, \bot, \overline{q}}$$

LOCAL

$$\frac{P(g, \ell) = \langle g', \ell', a \rangle \qquad a \in \{\varepsilon, \text{rd}(x), \text{wr}(x)\}}{g, \langle \ell, i, j, k \rangle, q \xrightarrow{\langle 0, i, j, a \rangle} g', \langle \ell', i, j, k \rangle, q}$$

**Fig. 6.** The single-thread transition function $\Rightarrow$ for a program $P$ with events $E$ ($\varepsilon$ and $\langle \rangle$ are the empty sequence and tuple, resp.,). Also, $f$ and $f'$ are tuples, and $\overline{q}$ is obtained by popping a queue from $q$ if this queue is empty, or $\overline{q} = q$, otherwise.

the TSO multi-thread semantics, is also reachable in $P$ under a strong semantics, the single-thread semantics and respectively, the SC multi-thread semantics. Since reasoning about sets of reachable states is difficult in general, these robustness notions are defined on traces and require that roughly, every trace of the weak semantics is "equivalent" to a trace of the same program under the strong semantics. A trace is equivalent to another if it is a permutation that preserves the order between "conflicting" labels, e.g., accesses to the same global variable.

Let $\prec \subseteq \Lambda_{TSO} \times \Lambda_{TSO}$ be a *conflict relation* defined by

$$\lambda_1 \prec \lambda_2 \text{ iff } act(\lambda_1), act(\lambda_2) \in \{\text{wr}(x, v), \text{rd}(x, v')\} \text{ for some } x, v, v', \text{and}$$
$$act(\lambda_1) = \text{wr}(x, v) \text{ or } act(\lambda_2) = \text{wr}(x, v)$$
$$\text{or}$$
$$\text{thread}(\lambda_1) = \text{thread}(\lambda_2)$$

that relates any two labels accessing the same variable, one of them being a write (commit), or any two labels associated to the same thread. Given a trace $\tau = \tau_1 \cdot \lambda_1 \cdot \lambda_2 \cdot \tau_2$, we say that the trace $\tau' = \tau_1 \cdot \lambda_2 \cdot \lambda_1 \cdot \tau_2$ is derived from $\tau$ by a $\prec$-*valid swap* iff $\lambda_1 \not\prec \lambda_2$. A permutation $\tau'$ of a trace $\tau$ is *conflict-preserving* when $\tau'$ can be derived from $\tau$ through a sequence of $\prec$-valid swaps.

Robustness against concurrency states that every trace of the SC multi-thread semantics of a program $P$ with event set $E$ has a conflict-preserving permutation where events and asynchronous invocations don't interleave (they are executed serially, but maybe not until completion) and asynchronous invocations execute according to the DFS traversal of the call tree. Such conflict-preserving permutations can be simulated by a sequential program $\text{seq}(P)$ where asynchronous invocations are rewritten to regular procedure calls which however, are not necessarily executed until completion. Incomplete executions of the procedures are simulated by adding a boolean flag skip to each procedure, which is non-deterministically turned to `false` (it is initially `true`) and which guards every statement in the original program (i.e., the statement can be executed only if `skip` is `true`). Since asynchronous invocations are rewritten to regular procedure calls, different events cannot interleave and invocations execute according to the DFS traversal of the call tree exactly as in the single-thread semantics (the latter requires that asynchronous invocations are not followed by accesses to global variables; see Bouajjani et al. [6] for more details.). Therefore, the SC multi-thread semantics of $\mathsf{seq}(P, E)$ coincides with its single-thread semantics. By an abuse of terminology, we say that a trace $\tau$ belongs to the single-thread semantics $[\![\mathsf{seq}(P), E]\!]_s$ even if the trace $\tau$ involves multiple threads, but substituting every thread id with 0 results in a trace in $[\![\mathsf{seq}(P), E]\!]_s$.

**Definition 1.** *A program $P$ with event set $E$ is* robust *against concurrency if there is a conflict preserving permutation $\tau' \in [\![\mathsf{seq}(P), E]\!]_s$ for every trace $\tau \in [\![P, E]\!]_m^{SC}$.*

The following theorem shows that the problem of checking robustness against concurrency is polynomial time for boolean programs. It is a consequence of the fact that this problem can be reduced in linear time to a reachability problem in sequential programs (even for infinite-state programs).

**Theorem 1 ([6]).** *Checking robustness against concurrency for a program $P$ with event set $E$, a fixed number of variables which are all boolean, and a fixed number of procedures, each procedure containing a fixed number of asynchronous invocations, is polynomial time decidable.*

While robustness against concurrency shows that there is no interference between events and asynchronous invocations under an SC semantics, robustness against TSO holds when the *non-atomic* writes allowed by the TSO memory model (that can be delayed and executed later on the global memory) introduce no behavior which is not also possible under the SC semantics. To simplify the exposition, we say that a trace $\tau \in [\![P, E]\!]_m^{TSO}$ (under the TSO memory model) belongs to the SC semantics $[\![P, E]\!]_m^{SC}$ of a program $P$ with event set $E$ even if the trace $\tau$ contains write issue and fence transition labels, but every write issue $\langle k, i, j, \mathsf{issue}(x, v) \rangle$ is immediately followed by the corresponding write commit $\langle k, i, j, \mathsf{wr}(x, v) \rangle$ and removing all the write issue and fence transition labels results in a trace in $[\![P, E]\!]_m^{SC}$.

**Definition 2.** *A program $P$ with event set $E$ is* robust *against TSO if there is a conflict preserving permutation $\tau' \in [\![P, E]\!]_m^{SC}$ for every trace $\tau \in [\![P, E]\!]_m^{TSO}$.*

Bouajjani et al. [5] have shown that checking robustness against TSO is EXPSPACE-complete. The upper bound relies on a polynomial time reduction to a reachability problem in a concurrent program running under SC.

## 5    Checking Robustness Against TSO

While Sect. 2 shows that robustness against concurrency doesn't imply robustness against TSO, we show however that for programs which are robust against concurrency, the problem of checking robustness against TSO can be solved more efficiently than in the general case. More precisely, we show that the latter can be reduced in polynomial time to the problem of checking robustness against TSO for a program with only two threads, which is itself polynomial time for boolean programs (since by the results of Bouajjani et al. [5], it can be reduced to a reachability problem in a boolean program with 2 threads).

Let $P$ be a program with event set $E$ that is robust against concurrency. We show that all its *minimal* TSO robustness violations, if any, can be simulated by a program 2-threads($P$) similar to seq($P$) except that exactly one invocation which was asynchronous in $P$ remains asynchronous in 2-threads($P$) as well (this asynchronous invocation is chosen non-deterministically).

Following the results in [5], if $P$ is not robust against TSO, then there exists a *minimal* TSO robustness violation which is a trace of the form

$$\tau = \tau_1 \cdot \langle k, i, j, \mathrm{issue}(x, v) \rangle \cdot \tau_2 \cdot \lambda \cdot \langle k, i, j, \mathrm{wr}(x, v) \rangle \text{ where}$$

1. the writes of only one thread $k$ are delayed (i.e., not flushed from the write buffer immediately after the write issue) and all the other threads behave like in the SC semantics (i.e., for all the other threads, the write issue is followed immediately by the corresponding write commit),
2. $\langle k, i, j, \mathrm{wr}(x, v) \rangle$ is the first write of thread $k$ which is delayed, i.e., $\tau_2$ doesn't contain any write commit action of thread $k$,
3. $\tau_2$ contains a transition label $\lambda_1$ which conflicts with $\langle k, i, j, \mathrm{issue}(x, v) \rangle$ (necessarily, a read of thread $k$) such that every label following $\lambda_1$ conflicts with its predecessor and the last action of $\tau_2$ conflicts with $\lambda$, i.e., there exists a suffix of $\tau_2$ of the form $\lambda_1 \cdot \ldots \cdot \lambda_n$ such that $\langle k, i, j, \mathrm{issue}(x, v) \rangle \prec \lambda_1$, $\lambda_m \prec \lambda_{m+1}$ for every $1 \leq m < n$, and $\lambda_n \prec \lambda$, and
4. the label $\lambda$ conflicts with the last write commit in $\tau$, i.e., $\lambda \prec \langle k, i, j, \mathrm{wr}(x, v) \rangle$ (which together with the above, implies that $\tau$ doesn't have a conflict-preserving permutation admitted by the SC semantics), and
5. the trace $\tau$ without the last write commit is a *minimal* trace satisfying the above conditions, i.e., extending $\tau_1 \cdot \langle k, i, j, \mathrm{issue}(x, v) \rangle \cdot \tau_2$ with all the write commits corresponding to write issues of thread $k$ has a conflict-preserving permutation admitted by the SC semantics.

We show that such a trace $\tau$ has a conflict-preserving permutation that is admitted by a program with only two threads. For simplicity, assume that $k$ is not the main thread. By the minimality assumption (5) and since $P$ is robust against concurrency, the trace $\tau_1 \cdot \langle k, i, j, \mathrm{issue}(x, v) \rangle \cdot \tau_2 \cdot \tau_3$, where $\tau_3$ contains a write commit action for every write issue of thread $k$ in $\tau_2$, has a conflict-preserving permutation $\tau'$ which belongs to $[\![\mathrm{seq}(P), E]\!]_s$. Let $\tau''$ be a trace obtained from $\tau'$ by removing again all the write commit actions that were present in $\tau_3$. This trace is admitted by the TSO multi-thread semantics since the values written by the write-commits in $\tau_3$ are not read. Since $\tau''$ preserves the order between conflicting labels in the original trace $\tau$, the trace $\tau'' \cdot \lambda \cdot \langle k, i, j, \mathrm{wr}(x, v) \rangle$ still satisfies properties (1–5). Also, since $\tau'$ was a trace of the sequential program seq($P$), all the transitions which are not performed by thread $k$ can be executed by the main thread (they belong to events and invocations which don't interleave). The transitions of thread $k$, the reads in particular, cannot be executed on the main thread since they can access the values of the writes of thread $k$ which are only issued but not committed. These values are not visible to other threads. Therefore, the trace obtained from $\tau'' \cdot \lambda \cdot \langle k, i, j, \mathrm{wr}(x, v) \rangle$ by substituting every thread id $k' \neq k$ with 0 (the id of the main thread) is admitted by the TSO multi-thread semantics of $P$. This trace can be simulated by a program 2-threads($P$) obtained from $P$ by replacing every asynchronous invocation async[any] $p(\boldsymbol{y})$ with the following code:

```
if ( * & fork )
    async[any] p(y);
    fork = false;
else
    if (PID == 0)
        call p(y);
    else
        async[main] p(y);
```

where fork is a global boolean flag which is initially set to true. The code above can invoke a procedure $p(\boldsymbol{y})$ either asynchronously, provided that flag is still true, or synchronously, or on the main thread if it is invoked from another thread (the test PID $== 0$ checks whether the executing thread is the main thread). Note that exactly one invocation of $P$ is asynchronous (since after the first asynchronous invocation, fork is turned to false) and that this invocation is chosen non-deterministically (the expression $*$ returns a randomly-chosen Boolean value). Also, since any thread different from the main thread executes a single invocation (in the multi-thread semantics), any invocation made during the asynchronous invocation is on the main thread (it cannot be transformed to a regular procedure call since it will be executed on the same thread).

The following theorem states the correctness of the construction.

**Theorem 2.** *Let $P$ be a program with event set $E$. If $P$ is robust against concurrency, then $P$ is robust against TSO iff* 2-threads($P$) *is robust against TSO.*

As a corollary of the results in [5] which state that checking TSO robustness for a program with $N$ threads can be reduced to a reachability problem in a program with $N$ threads under the SC semantics, we get that checking TSO robustness for Boolean programs which are already robust against concurrency is polynomial time.

**Corollary 1.** *Checking robustness against TSO for a program $P$ with event set $E$, a fixed number of variables which are all boolean, and a fixed number of procedures, each procedure containing a fixed number of asynchronous invocations, is polynomial time decidable, provided that $P$ is robust against concurrency.*

## 6   Conclusions

We have presented an approach for checking robustness against TSO for event-driven asynchronous programs (with an unbounded number of threads), that avoids explicit handling of all concurrent executions. This approach reduces TSO robustness checking to a reachability problem in a program with only two threads, provided that the original program is robust against concurrency. Besides yielding an important gain in asymptotic complexity, leading to a polynomial-time TSO robustness checking procedure (for boolean programs), our reduction enables the use of existing safety-verification tools for TSO robustness checking.

# References

1. Abdulla, P.A., Atig, M.F., Chen, Y.-F., Leonardsson, C., Rezine, A.: Counter-example guided fence insertion under TSO. In: Flanagan, C., König, B. (eds.) TACAS 2012. LNCS, vol. 7214, pp. 204–219. Springer, Heidelberg (2012). https://doi.org/10.1007/978-3-642-28756-5_15
2. Abdulla, P.A., Atig, M.F., Ngo, T.-P.: The best of both worlds: trading efficiency and optimality in fence insertion for TSO. In: Vitek, J. (ed.) ESOP 2015. LNCS, vol. 9032, pp. 308–332. Springer, Heidelberg (2015). https://doi.org/10.1007/978-3-662-46669-8_13
3. Alglave, J., Maranget, L.: Stability in weak memory models. In: Gopalakrishnan, G., Qadeer, S. (eds.) CAV 2011. LNCS, vol. 6806, pp. 50–66. Springer, Heidelberg (2011). https://doi.org/10.1007/978-3-642-22110-1_6
4. Atig, M.F., Bouajjani, A., Burckhardt, S., Musuvathi, M.: On the verification problem for weak memory models. ACM Sigplan Not. **45**(1), 7–18 (2010)
5. Bouajjani, A., Derevenetc, E., Meyer, R.: Checking and enforcing robustness against TSO. In: Felleisen, M., Gardner, P. (eds.) ESOP 2013. LNCS, vol. 7792, pp. 533–553. Springer, Heidelberg (2013). https://doi.org/10.1007/978-3-642-37036-6_29
6. Bouajjani, A., Emmi, M., Enea, C., Ozkan, B.K., Tasiran, S.: Verifying robustness of event-driven asynchronous programs against concurrency. In: Yang, H. (ed.) ESOP 2017. LNCS, vol. 10201, pp. 170–200. Springer, Heidelberg (2017). https://doi.org/10.1007/978-3-662-54434-1_7
7. Bouajjani, A., Meyer, R., Möhlmann, E.: Deciding robustness against total store ordering. In: Aceto, L., Henzinger, M., Sgall, J. (eds.) ICALP 2011. LNCS, vol. 6756, pp. 428–440. Springer, Heidelberg (2011). https://doi.org/10.1007/978-3-642-22012-8_34
8. Burckhardt, S., Musuvathi, M.: Effective program verification for relaxed memory models. In: Gupta, A., Malik, S. (eds.) CAV 2008. LNCS, vol. 5123, pp. 107–120. Springer, Heidelberg (2008). https://doi.org/10.1007/978-3-540-70545-1_12
9. Burnim, J., Sen, K., Stergiou, C.: Sound and complete monitoring of sequential consistency for relaxed memory models. In: Abdulla, P.A., Leino, K.R.M. (eds.) TACAS 2011. LNCS, vol. 6605, pp. 11–25. Springer, Heidelberg (2011). https://doi.org/10.1007/978-3-642-19835-9_3
10. Emmi, M., Lal, A., Qadeer, S.: Asynchronous programs with prioritized task-buffers. In: Proceedings of the International Symposium on Foundations of Software Engineering, FSE 2012, pp. 48:1–48:11. ACM (2012)
11. Emmi, M., Ozkan, B.K., Tasiran, S.: Exploiting synchronization in the analysis of shared-memory asynchronous programs. In: Proceedings of the International SPIN Symposium on Model Checking of Software, pp. 20–29. ACM (2014)

12. Emmi, M., Qadeer, S., Rakamarić, Z.: Delay-bounded scheduling. SIGPLAN Not. **46**(1), 411–422 (2011)
13. Kuperstein, M., Vechev, M., Yahav, E.: Partial-coherence abstractions for relaxed memory models. In: ACM SIGPLAN Notices, vol. 46, pp. 187–198. ACM (2011)
14. Kuperstein, M., Vechev, M., Yahav, E.: Automatic inference of memory fences. ACM SIGACT News **43**(2), 108–123 (2012)
15. Lamport, L.: How to make a multiprocessor computer that correctly executes multiprocess programs. IEEE Trans. Comput. **100**(9), 690–691 (1979)
16. Owens, S.: Reasoning about the implementation of concurrency abstractions on x86-TSO. In: D'Hondt, T. (ed.) ECOOP 2010. LNCS, vol. 6183, pp. 478–503. Springer, Heidelberg (2010). https://doi.org/10.1007/978-3-642-14107-2_23
17. Ozkan, B.K., Emmi, M., Tasiran, S.: Systematic asynchrony bug exploration for android apps. In: Kroening, D., Păsăreanu, C.S. (eds.) CAV 2015. LNCS, vol. 9206, pp. 455–461. Springer, Cham (2015). https://doi.org/10.1007/978-3-319-21690-4_28
18. Sewell, P., Sarkar, S., Owens, S., Nardelli, F.Z., Myreen, M.O.: x86-TSO: a rigorous and usable programmer's model for x86 multiprocessors. Commun. ACM **53**(7), 89–97 (2010)

# Model Checking Dynamic Pushdown Networks with Locks and Priorities

Marcio Diaz[1]([✉]) and Tayssir Touili[2]

[1] LIPN and University Paris Diderot, Paris, France
diaz@lipn.univ-paris13.fr
[2] LIPN, CNRS and University Paris 13, Villetaneuse, France
touili@lipn.univ-paris13.fr

**Abstract.** A dynamic pushdown network (DPN) is a set of pushdown systems (PDSs) where each process can dynamically create new instances of PDSs. DPNs are a natural model of multi-threaded programs with (possibly recursive) procedure calls and thread creation. A PL-DPN is an extension of DPNs that allows threads to synchronize using locks and priorities. Transitions in a PL-DPN can have different priorities and acquire/release locks. We consider in this work model checking PL-DPNs against single-indexed LTL properties. We show that this model checking problem is decidable. We propose automata-based approaches for computing the set of configurations of a PL-DPN that satisfy the corresponding single-indexed LTL formula.

## 1 Introduction

Writing multi-threaded programs is notoriously difficult, as concurrency related bugs are hard to find and reproduce. This difficulty is increased if we consider that several software systems consist of different components that react to the environment and use resources like CPU or memory according to a real time need. For instance, in systems that control automobiles we can have a component in charge of the music sub-system and another component in charge of the braking sub-system. Obviously, the braking sub-system should have a higher priority access to the resources needed, since a delay in the action of the brakes can cost lives.

The programming model used in the vast majority of these software systems, used from automobiles to spacecrafts, defines a set of threads that respond to events. Each thread is typically assigned a priority and are scheduled by a priority round-robin preemptive scheduler: if a thread with a higher static priority becomes ready to run, the currently running thread will be preempted and returned to the wait list for its priority level. The round-robin scheduling policy allows each thread to run only for a fixed amount of time before it must yield its processing slot to another thread of the same priority.

The use of threads with different priorities and other synchronization primitives, like locks, can easily lead to a large number of undesirable behaviors. Consider for example the control flow graph of Fig. 1. It consists of three threads:

A. Podelski and F. Taïani (Eds.): NETYS 2018, LNCS 11028, pp. 240–251, 2019.
https://doi.org/10.1007/978-3-030-05529-5_16

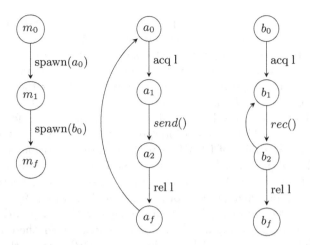

**Fig. 1.** Control-flow graph of a main thread starting at $m_0$ that creates two child threads starting at $a_0$ and $b_0$. The threads child execute a loop and use a lock $l$.

a main thread $M$ starting at control location $m_0$ that creates two threads $A$ and $B$. The thread $A$ takes and releases (uses) a lock $l$ inside a loop, and the thread $B$ loops while holding the lock $l$ (between $b_1$ and $b_2$). Suppose that $A$ and $B$ should act like daemon threads, continuously running in the background reacting to events. This means that the LTL formula $G\ F\ a_1 \wedge G\ F\ b_1$, saying that $a_1$ *is executed frequently often and $b_1$ is executed frequently often*, should be valid for all executions.

But this is not the case in the program of Fig. 1: once thread $B$ starts executing its loop and holding lock $l$, thread $A$ is going to starve since it cannot take the lock until it is released. A similar problem occurs if threads A and B have different priority of execution, the thread with lower priority will starve. The program of Fig. 1 shows that there is a real need for formal methods to find automatic verification techniques for checking *liveness properties* in *multi-threaded programs with locks and priorities*. Indeed, starvation or absence of livelocks are among the most crucial properties that need to be checked for multi-threaded programs.

Dynamic pushdown networks (DPNs) [1] are a natural model for multi-threaded programs with (possibly recursive) procedure calls and thread creation. A DPN consists of a finite set of pushdown systems (PDSs), each of them models a sequential program that can dynamically create new instances of PDSs. The model-checking problems of DPNs against Linear Temporal Logic (LTL), Computation Tree Logic (CTL) and reachability properties are well studied in the literature [1–5,16].

However, DPNs cannot model communication between processes. Previous works [6–9,16] extended DPNs with locks (and priorities). A DPN with locks and priorities is called PL-DPN. This allows to model multi-threaded programs where threads communicate via locks and where each thread can have a different priority. Indeed, locks and priorities are frequently used in multithreaded programs as synchronization primitives. However, only reachability properties are studied for PL-DPNs, with some restricted lock and priority usages (due to undecidability) [9].

In general, the model checking problem of DPNs against unrestricted LTL formulas (where atomic propositions can be interpreted over the control states of two or more threads) is undecidable. In [2] it is shown that this problem becomes decidable if we consider single-indexed LTL properties (formulas of the form $\bigwedge f_i$ s.t. $f_i$ is a LTL formula interpreted over the PDS $i$). On the other hand, pairwise reachability of PL-DPNs without thread creation is undecidable in the general case [9,10]. It becomes decidable if locks are accessed in a well-nested style [10], where each thread can only releases the latest acquired lock, and a thread does not change its priority while holding a lock [9].

In this work, we combine these ideas and show that model-checking single indexed LTL properties is decidable for PL-DPNs under these restrictions. It is non-trivial to do LTL model checking for PL-DPNs, since the number of instances of PDSs can be unbounded. Checking independently whether all the different PDSs satisfy the corresponding subformula $f_i$ is not correct. Indeed, we do not need to check whether an instance of a PDS $j$ satisfies $f_j$ if this instance is not created during a run. The approach of [2] cannot be directly applied to perform single-indexed LTL model-checking for PL-DPNs due to locks and priorities. Indeed, we have to consider communication between each instance of PDSs running in parallel in the network. To overcome this problem, we will reduce single-indexed LTL model-checking for PL-DPNs to the membership problem of DPNs with Büchi acceptance condition.

In [9] we presented an approach for checking pairwise reachability of PL-DPNs using priority-lock structures, an extension of acquisition structures introduced in [7]. This structure is used to get rid of locks and priorities in PL-DPNs, such that pairwise reachability of PL-DPNs can be reduced to constrained pairwise reachability on DPNs. It works by keeping track of the locks and priorities used in a run. For pairwise reachability, we only need to consider finite runs, as a configuration of a PL-DPN reaches another configuration only using finite steps. However, we have to consider infinite runs of PL-DPNs when we study LTL model checking.

In this work, we adapted the priority-lock structures to keep track also of the infinitely used locks and priorities. Indeed, we need to assure that a finally acquired lock, a lock that will not be released in the run, cannot be infinitely used, and that an infinitely used priority does not block other threads.

After getting rid of locks and priorities using this extended priority-lock structure, we construct Büchi dynamic PDSs which are a synchronization of a PDS $i$ and the corresponding LTL formula $f_i$. The language accepted by a Büchi dynamic PDS corresponds to the configurations that satisfy the formula $f_i$. This language is computed by the automata-based approach for standard LTL model checking for PDSs [2].

Thus, the main contribution of this paper is an algorithm for single-indexed LTL Model Checking for PL-DPNs, developed in Sect. 5.

## 2    Model Definition

Let $L$ be the set of all locks and $I$ be the set of all priorities. A PL-DPN can be seen as a collection of threads running in parallel, each of them having a set of acquired locks and a priority. They are able to:

1. Perform pushdown operations. This can be used to model calls and returns from (possible recursive) functions.
2. Change its priority if its set of acquired locks is empty. Removing this constraint leads to undecidability [9].
3. Acquire a lock that does not belong to any set of acquired locks (between the running threads).
4. Release a lock belonging to its set of acquired locks.
5. Create a new thread with any (initial) priority and an empty set of acquired locks.

**Definition 1.** *A Dynamic Pushdown System with Locks and Priorities (PL-DPDS) is a tuple $\mathcal{P} = (P, \Gamma, \Delta, \eta_p, \eta_l)$, where $P$ is a finite set of control states, $\Gamma$ is a finite stack alphabet, $\eta_p$ is a function from control states to priorities, $\eta_l$ is a function from control states to set of locks, $\Delta$ is a finite set of transition rules of the following forms:*

1. *$p\gamma \xrightarrow{\tau} q\omega$, with $\eta_p(q) = \eta_p(p)$ and $\eta_l(q) = \eta_l(p)$;*
2. *$p\gamma \xrightarrow{ch(x)} q\omega$, with $\eta_p(q) = x$ and $\eta_l(q) = \eta_l(p) = \emptyset$;*
3. *$p\gamma \xrightarrow{acq\ l} q\omega$, with $\eta_p(q) = \eta_p(p)$, $\eta_l(q) = \eta_l(p) \cup \{l\}$ and $l \notin \eta_l(p)$;*
4. *$p\gamma \xrightarrow{rel\ l} q\omega$, with $\eta_p(q) = \eta_p(p)$, $\eta_l(q) = \eta_l(p) \setminus \{l\}$ and $l \in \eta_l(p)$;*
5. *$p\gamma \xrightarrow{\tau} q_1\omega_1 \rhd q_2\omega_2$, with $\eta_p(q_1) = \eta_p(p)$, $\eta_l(q_1) = \eta_l(p)$ and $\eta_l(q_2) = \emptyset$;*

*where $p, q_1, q_2 \in P, \gamma \in \Gamma, w, w_1, w_2 \in \Gamma^*, l \in L, x \in I$. A Dynamic Pushdown System (DPDS) can be seen as a PL-DPDS where $\eta_p(p) = 0$ and $\eta_l(p) = \emptyset$, for all control state $p$.*

A *local configuration* $p\omega \in P\Gamma^*$, of a PL-DPDS $\mathcal{P} = (P, \Gamma, \Delta, \eta_p, \eta_l)$, represents the state of a thread. The state of a thread consists of a priority, a set of acquired locks and a stack. The priority of a thread and the set of acquired locks are represented by the control state $p$ and can be retrieved from it by using the functions $\eta_p$ and $\eta_l$, respectively. The stack of a thread is represented by the sequence of stack letters $\omega \in \Gamma^*$.

The function $\eta_p$ assigns a priority to each control state. Intuitively, this means that a thread can be in configurations with different priorities. The function $\eta_l$ assigns a set of locks to each control state. This set of locks represents the locks held (acquired but not yet released) by the thread at such configuration.

**Definition 2.** *A Dynamic Pushdown Network with Priorities and Locks (PL-DPN) is a tuple $(Act, L, I, \mathcal{P}_1, \ldots, \mathcal{P}_n)$, such that $L$ is a set of locks, $I$ is set of priorities (natural numbers), $Act$ is a finite set of actions $\{acq(l), rel(l) \mid l \in$*

$L\} \cup \{ch(x) \mid x \in I\} \cup \{\tau\}$, *where the action* $acq(l)$ *(resp.* $rel(l))$ *for every* $l \in L$ *denotes the* acquisition *(resp.* release) *of the lock* $l$, *the action* $ch(x)$ *denotes the* change to priority $x$ *and the action* $\tau$ *denotes a pushdown action. For every* $i \in \{1, \ldots, n\}$, $P_i$ *is a PL-DPDS. A Dynamic Pushdown Network (DPN) can be seen as a PL-DPN with* $L = \emptyset$ *and* $I = \{0\}$. *A DPN can be represented as a tuple* $(P_1, \ldots, P_n)$, *where each* $P_i$ *is a DPDS.*

A *global configuration* is a sequence of local configurations, each of them corresponding to the configuration of one of the threads running in parallel on the system. Let $Conf_M$ be the set of all global configurations of a PL-DPN $M$.

Following previous works, we assume that locks are used in a well-nested fashion, i.e. a process has to release locks in the opposite order of acquisition, an assumption that is often satisfied in practice. Note that for non-well-nested locks even simple reachability problems are undecidable [11].

### 2.1   Example

The PL-DPN modeling the program of Fig. 1 can be defined as follows: $M = (\{acq\ l, rel\ l, ch\ l, \tau\}, \{l\}, \{1\}, P_1, P_2, P_3)$, where

- $P_1 = (\{p_1\}, \{m_0, m_1, m_f\}, \{p_1 m_0 \overset{\tau}{\hookrightarrow} p_1 m_1 \triangleright p_1 a_0, p_1 m_1 \overset{\tau}{\hookrightarrow} p_1 m_f \triangleright p_1 b_0\}, \eta_p, \eta_l)$ such that $\eta_p(p_1) = 1$ and $\eta_l(p_1) = \emptyset$.
- $P_2 = (\{p_1, p_{1,l}\}, \{a_0, a_1, a_2, a_f\}, \{p_1 a_0 \xrightarrow{acq\ l} p_{1,l} a_1, p_{1,l} a_1 \overset{\tau}{\hookrightarrow} p_{1,l} a_2, p_{1,l} a_2 \overset{\tau}{\hookrightarrow} p_1 a_f, p_1 a_f \overset{\tau}{\hookrightarrow} p_1 a_0\}, \eta_p, \eta_l)$ such that $\eta_p(p_1) = \eta_p(p_{1,l}) = 1$ and $\eta_l(p_1) = \emptyset, \eta_l(p_{1,l}) = \{l\}$.
- $P_3 = (\{p_1, p_{1,l}\}, \{b_0, b_1, b_2, b_f\}, \{p_1 b_0 \xrightarrow{acq\ l} p_{1,l} b_1, p_{1,l} b_1 \overset{\tau}{\hookrightarrow} p_{1,l} b_2, p_{1,l} b_2 \xrightarrow{rel\ l} p_1 b_f, p_{1,l} b_2 \overset{\tau}{\hookrightarrow} p_{1,l} b_1\}, \eta_p, \eta_l)$ such that $\eta_p(p_1) = \eta_p(p_{1,l}) = 1$ and $\eta_l(p_1) = \emptyset, \eta_l(p_{1,l}) = \{l\}$.

Note that the initial configuration of this PL-DPN $M$ is $p_1 m_0$.

## 3   Semantics of the Model

The semantics of PL-DPNs is defined such that:

- Transitions of threads with highest priority should be executed first.
- Transitions that manipulate locks should follow the locking rules:
  - A transition attempting to acquire a lock can only be executed if the lock is free, i.e. does not belong to any set of acquired locks.
  - A transition attempting to release a lock can only be executed if the lock is in possession of the corresponding thread, i.e. in its set of acquired locks.

We overload the functions $\eta_p$ and $\eta_l$ to global configurations as follows: for all $c = p_1 \omega_1 \ldots p_n \omega_n \in Conf_M$, $\eta_p(p_1 \omega_1 \ldots p_n \omega_n) := max(\eta_p(p_1), \ldots, \eta_p(p_n))$ and $\eta_l(p_1 \omega_1 \ldots p_n \omega_n) := \eta_l(p_1) \cup \cdots \cup \eta_l(p_n)$.

**Definition 3.** *The transition relation* $\longrightarrow_M$ *is defined as the smallest relation in* $Conf_M \times Conf_M$ *such that* $\forall c_1, c_2 \in Conf_M$:

1. $c_1\ p\gamma r\ c_2 \longrightarrow_M c_1\ q\omega r\ c_2$,
   *if* $\eta_p(p) = \eta_p(c_1\ p\gamma r\ c_2)$, $p\gamma \xrightarrow{act} q\omega \in \Delta$, $act \in \{\tau, rel\ l\} \cup \{ch(x) \mid x \in I\}$;
2. $c_1\ p\gamma r\ c_2 \longrightarrow_M c_1\ q\omega r\ c_2$,
   *if* $\eta_p(p) = \eta_p(c_1\ p\gamma r\ c_2)$, $l \notin \eta_l(c_1\ p\gamma r\ c_2)$ *and* $p\gamma \xrightarrow{acq\ l} q\omega \in \Delta$;
3. $c_1\ p\gamma r\ c_2 \longrightarrow_M c_1\ q_2\omega_2\ q_1\omega_1 r\ c_2$,
   *if* $\eta_p(p) = \eta_p(c_1\ p\gamma r\ c_2)$ *and* $p\gamma \xrightarrow{\tau} q_1\omega_1 \triangleright q_2\omega_2 \in \Delta$;

*where* $p, q, q_1, q_2 \in P, \gamma \in \Gamma, \omega, \omega_1, \omega_2, r \in \Gamma^*, l \in L$.

The semantics above says that:

1. A thread in a local configuration with control state $p$ and top of stack $\gamma$, can move to a local configuration with control state $q$, replacing the top of its stack $\gamma$ by $\omega$, if there is a $\tau$, $ch(x)$ or *release* rule $p\gamma \hookrightarrow q\omega \in \Delta$ and its priority ($\eta_p(p)$) is equal to the highest priority among all the threads ($\eta_p(c_1\ p\gamma r\ c_2)$);
2. A thread in a local configuration with control state $p$ and top of stack $\gamma$, can move to a local configuration with control state $q$, replacing the top of its stack $\gamma$ by $\omega$, if there is an *acquire* rule $p\gamma \xrightarrow{acq\ l} q\omega \in \Delta$, the lock that the rule attempts to take is free ($l \notin \eta_l(c_1\ p\gamma r\ c_2)$), and its priority ($\eta_p(p)$) is equal to the highest priority among all the threads ($\eta_p(c_1\ p\gamma r\ c_2)$);
3. A thread in a local configuration with control state $p$ and top of stack $\gamma$ can move to a local configuration with control state $q_1$, replacing the top of its stack $\gamma$ by $\omega_1$ and create another thread in control state $q_2$ with stack $\omega_2$, if there is a rule $p\gamma \xrightarrow{\tau} q_1\omega_1 \triangleright q_2\omega_2 \in \Delta$ and its priority ($\eta_p(p)$) is equal to the highest priority among all the threads ($\eta_p(c_1\ p\gamma r\ c_2)$).

Note that the semantics of locks corresponds to the one of spin-locks, found in most of the libraries for threads (like Pthreads). Spin-locks are similar to mutexes, but they might have lower overhead for very short-term blocking. When the calling thread requests a spin-lock that is already held by another thread, the calling thread spins in a loop to test if the lock has become available. This means that if a thread with lower priority, holding a lock l, is interrupted by a thread with higher priority, attempting to acquire the same lock, then the program becomes blocked (assuming there is only one CPU). In this paper we assume that programs are free of deadlocks since they can be detected using the technique of our previous work [9].

We call *DPN semantics* to the semantics resulting from dropping the lock and priority constraints from the PL-DPN semantics. A *run* of a PL-DPN (or DPN) is the sequence of configurations resulting from the application of the corresponding semantics rules. Given a configuration $c$, the set of immediate predecessors of $c$ in a PL-DPN $M$ is defined as $pre_M(c) = \{c' \in Conf_M : c' \longrightarrow_M c\}$. This notation can be generalized straightforwardly to sets of configurations. Let $pre_M^*$ denote the reflexive-transitive closure of $pre_M$. For the rest of this paper, we assume that we have fixed a PL-DPN $M = (Act, L, I, \mathcal{P}_1, \ldots, \mathcal{P}_n)$.

## 4   Priority-Lock Structures

**Definition 4** *(From [9]).* *A priority-lock structure of a global run $R$, of a PL-DPN under DPN semantics (dropping lock and priority constraints), is defined as either a tuple $[\![x, y, g_r, g_a, la]\!]$ or the symbol $\bot$.*

In [9] is given an algorithm to compute a priority-lock structure from a finite global run $R$ such that: we get $\bot$ if the run is not valid under PL-DPN semantics, or we get the tuple $[\![x, y, g_r, g_a, la]\!]$ otherwise, where:

- $x$ is the lowest transition priority, between the control states visited during the run;
- $y$ is the highest final priority, between the control states of the final configuration;
- $g_r$ is a set of dependencies, between lock *usages* (acquire and release of a lock) and *final releases* (release without acquisition) of a lock;
- $g_a$ is a set of dependencies, between lock usages and *initial acquisitions* (acquisition of a lock without the corresponding release) of a lock;
- $la$ is the set with all lock actions in the run, and their corresponding priorities.

In this work, we just need to know that given a PL-DPN $M$ and a regular set of configurations $S$, we can construct a DPN $M'$ ([9]), with priority-lock structures embedded in the control states, such that the predecessor configurations of $S$ over $M$ are the predecessor configurations of $S$ over $M'$ with a priority-lock structure not equal to $\bot$. Formally, from [9]:

**Theorem 1.** $pre_M^*(S) = \{p\omega \mid (p, s)\omega \in pre_{M'}^*(S \times [\![\infty, 0, \emptyset, \emptyset, \emptyset]\!]) \wedge s \neq \bot\}.$

Using the previous theorem we can reduce LTL model checking on the PL-DPN $M$ to a series of $pre^*$ queries over a DPN $M'$. In order to keep the queries consistent with each other, taking in account the priorities and locks, we need to inspect the priority-lock structure stored in the configurations. For this reason, given a control state $p$ in the DPN $M'$, we define $X(p)$, $U(p)$ and $A(p)$, to be the lowest transition priority, the set of usages and the set of final acquisitions, respectively, embedded in the control state $p$.

### 4.1   Example

The PL-DPN $M$ of Example 2.1 can be reduced to the DPN $M' = (\{\tau\}, \mathcal{P}_1', \mathcal{P}_2', \mathcal{P}_3')$, using the algorithm from [9], where:

- $\mathcal{P}_1' = (\{p_0' = (p_1, [\![1, 1, \emptyset, \emptyset, \emptyset]\!]), p_1' = (p_1, [\![1, 1, \emptyset, \emptyset, \{(l, usg, 1, 1)\}]\!]),$
  $p_2' = (p_1, [\![1, 1, \emptyset, \emptyset, \{(l, acq, 1, 1)\}]\!]),$
  $p_3' = (p_1, [\![1, 1, \emptyset, \emptyset, \{(l, acq, 1, 1), (l, usg, 1, 1)\}]\!]), p_4' = (p_1, \bot), \}, \{m_0, m_1,$
  $m_f\},$
  $\{p_1'm_0 \overset{\tau}{\hookrightarrow} p_1'm_1 \triangleright p_1'a_0, p_3'm_0 \overset{\tau}{\hookrightarrow} p_1'm_1 \triangleright p_2'a_0, p_3'm_0 \overset{\tau}{\hookrightarrow} p_2'm_1 \triangleright p_1'a_0,$
  $p_4'm_0 \overset{\tau}{\hookrightarrow} p_2'm_1 \triangleright p_2'a_0, p_2'm_0 \overset{\tau}{\hookrightarrow} p_0'm_f \triangleright p_2'b_0, p_1'm_0 \overset{\tau}{\hookrightarrow} p_0'm_f \triangleright p_1'b_0, \})$
- $\mathcal{P}_2'$ and $\mathcal{P}_3'$ are defined in a similar way.

Here we abbreviate *usage* with *usg*.

# 5   Single-Indexed LTL Model Checking for PL-DPNs

## 5.1   Linear Temporal Logic (LTL) and Büchi Automata

From now on, we fix a finite set of atomic propositions $AP$.

**Definition 5.** *The set of LTL formulas is given by (where $q \in AP$):*

$$\varphi ::= q \mid \varphi_1 \wedge \varphi_2 \mid \neg\varphi \mid X\varphi \mid F\varphi \mid G\varphi \mid \varphi_1 \, U \, \varphi_2$$

Given an $\omega$-word $\alpha = \alpha_0\alpha_1 \dots$ over $2^{AP}$, let $\alpha^k$ denote the suffix of $\alpha$ starting from $\alpha_k$. The notation $\alpha \models \varphi$ indicates that $\alpha$ satisfies $\varphi$, where $\models$ is inductively defined as follows: $\alpha \models q$ if $q \in \alpha_0$; $\alpha \models \neg\varphi$ if $\alpha\neg \models \varphi$; $\alpha \models \varphi_1 \wedge \varphi_2$ if $\alpha \models \varphi_1$ and $\alpha \models \varphi_2$; $\alpha \models X\varphi$ if $\alpha^1 \models \varphi$; $\alpha \models \varphi_1 U \varphi_2$ if there exists $k \geq 0$ such that $\alpha^k \models \varphi_2$ and for every $j : 1 \leq j < k$, $\alpha_j \models \varphi_1$. The temporal operators $F$ and $G$ can be defined using the following equivalences: $F\varphi \equiv true \, U\varphi$, $G\varphi \equiv \neg F \neg\varphi$.

**Definition 6.** *A Büchi automaton (BA) $\mathcal{B}$ is a tuple $(G, \Sigma, \theta, g^0, F)$, where $G$ is a finite set of states, $\Sigma$ is the input alphabet, $\theta \subseteq G \times \Sigma \times G$ is a finite set of transitions, $g^0 \in G$ is the initial state and $F \subseteq G$ is a finite set of accepting states.*

A run of $\mathcal{B}$ over an $\omega$-word $\alpha_0\alpha_1 \dots$ is a sequence of states $q_0 q_1 \dots$ s.t. $q_0 = g^0$ and $(q_i, \alpha_i, q_{i+1}) \in \theta$ for every $i \geq 0$. A run is accepting iff it infinitely often visits some states in $F$.

**Theorem 2** *(From [15]). Given a LTL formula $f$ we can construct a BA $\mathcal{B}_f$ recognizing all the $\omega$-words that satisfy $f$.*

## 5.2   The Model Checking Problem

The model checking problem of PL-DPNs against double-indexed LTL formulas, where the validity of atomic propositions depends on two or more PDSs, is undecidable [10].

In this work, in order to obtain decidability results, we consider the model-checking problem of PL-DPNs against single-indexed LTL properties of the form $f = \bigwedge_{i=1}^n f_i$, where $f_i$ is interpreted over the PL-DPDS $\mathcal{P}_i$.

Let $\lambda$ be a labeling function $\lambda : \bigcup_i P_i \to 2^{AP}$, that assigns to each control state of the PL-DPN $M$ a set of atomic propositions.

**Definition 7.** *Given a labeling function $\lambda$, a local run $r = p_0\omega_0 p_1\omega_1 \dots$ of a PL-DPDS $\mathcal{P}$ satisfies a LTL formula $f$, denoted by $r \models f$, iff the $\omega$-word $\lambda(p_0)\lambda(p_1) \dots$ satisfies $f$.*

**Definition 8.** *A global run $R$ satisfies a single-indexed LTL formula $f = \bigwedge_i f_i$, denoted by $R \models f$, iff all local runs of each instance of each PL-DPDS $\mathcal{P}_i$, running in parallel in $R$, satisfy the corresponding formula $f_i$.*

**Definition 9.** *A PL-DPN $M$, with initial configuration $p_0\gamma_0$, satisfies the single-indexed LTL formula $f = \bigwedge_i f_i$, iff all global runs starting with $p_0\gamma_0$ satisfy $f$, denoted by $M \models f$.*

These definitions are extended to DPNs and multiple initial configurations in a straightforwardly way. From now on, we fix a single-indexed LTL formula $f = \bigwedge_{i=1}^{n} f_i$.

## 5.3 The Model-Checking Approach

In this section, we assume having the DPN $M'$, of Sect. 4, and we extend its DPDSs with a Büchi acceptance condition.

**Definition 10.** *A Büchi DPDS (BDPDS) is a tuple $\mathcal{BP} = (P, \Gamma, \Delta, F)$, where $(P, \Gamma, \Delta)$ is a DPDS and $F \subseteq P$ is a finite set of accepting control states.*

For $i \in \{1, \ldots, n\}$, given $\mathcal{B}_i = (G_i, \Sigma_i, \theta_i, g_i^0, F_i)$ the Büchi automata recognizing the $\omega$-words that satisfy the LTL formula $f_i$ and the DPDSs $\mathcal{P}_i = (P_i, \Gamma_i, \Delta_i)$, we create the Büchi DPDS as follows:

**Definition 11.** *The BDPDSs $\mathcal{BP}_i$ are defined as $((P_i \times G_i) \times (2^L \times I), \Gamma_i, \Delta_i', F_i')$ where $F_i' = \{((p, g), (U(p), X(p))) \mid (p, g) \in P_i \times F_i\}$. The rules in $\Delta_i'$ are computed such that for every $(g_1, \lambda(p), g_2) \in \theta_i$, $a \in Act$, $x, x_1, x_2 \in I$, $u, u_1, u_2 \in 2^L$, $g_1, g_2 \in F_i$, $g_j^0 \in F_j$ and $(p_2, s_2)\omega_2 \in P_j \times \Gamma_j^*$ we have:*

1. *$((p, g_1), (u, x))\gamma \overset{a}{\hookrightarrow} ((p_1, g_2), (u, x))\omega_1 \in \Delta_i'$, if $p\gamma \overset{a}{\hookrightarrow} p_1\omega_1 \in \Delta_i$,*
2. *for all $p\gamma \overset{a}{\hookrightarrow} p_1\omega_1 \rhd p_2\omega_2 \in \Delta_i$,*
   *$((p, g_1), s_1 \oplus s_2)\gamma \overset{a}{\hookrightarrow} ((p_1, g_2), s_1)\omega_1 \rhd ((p_2, g_j^0), s_2)\omega_2 \in \Delta_i'$,*
   *where $s_1 \oplus s_2 = (u_1 \cup u_2, x_1)$ if $s_1 \neq \bot$, $s_2 \neq \bot$, $A(p_1) \cap u_1 = A(p_2) \cap u_2 = \emptyset$ and $x_1 = x_2$; or $s_1 \oplus s_2 = \bot$, otherwise. Similar for a non-spawning rule.*

Intuitively, the BDPDS $\mathcal{BP}_i$ synchronizes the DPDS $\mathcal{P}_i$ with the formula $f_i$. In this definition, we introduce a new kind of priority-lock structure, the tuple $(u, x)$, where $u$ is the set of locks and $x$ is the lowest priority used an infinite number of times in the run. We initialize them in the definition of the set of final states, obtaining the value from the control state, and we propagate them towards the beginning of the run using the transition rules. This tuple is necessary to detect the cases where we use an infinite number of times a lock that was acquired but not released in another thread. This cases create livelocks, and are detected because the priority-lock structure of the initial configurations of these runs are marked by $\bot$.

Let $L(\mathcal{BP}_i)$ be the set of all the tuples $(((p, g_i^0), (u, x))\gamma, D)$, such that $\mathcal{BP}_i$ has an accepting run starting from the configuration $((p, g_i^0), (u, x))\gamma$, using infinitely the lowest priority $x$, the set of locks $u$ and spawning the set of configurations $D$. We can compute the language of $\mathcal{BP}_i$ using the algorithm from [2]:

**Theorem 3** *(From [2]). For every BDPDS $\mathcal{BP}_i = (P_i, \Gamma_i, \Delta_i, F_i)$, we can construct a finite automaton $A_i$ such that $L(A_i) = L(\mathcal{BP}_i)$.*

**Theorem 4.** *Given a DPDS* $P_i = (P_i, \Gamma_i, \Delta_i)$ *and a LTL formula* $f_i$ *we can compute an BDPDS* $\mathcal{B}P_i$ *such that* $p\omega \models_D f_i$ *iff* $((p, s)\omega, D) \in L(\mathcal{B}P_i)$ *and* $s \neq \perp$.

This theorem says that, when $s \neq \perp$, the runs of other threads starting from configurations in $D$ do not create livelocks.

### 5.4   Main Algorithm

Given a PL-DPN $M = (Act, L, I, \mathcal{P}_1, \ldots, \mathcal{P}_n)$, with starting configuration $p_0\gamma_0$, and a single-indexed LTL formula $f = \bigwedge_i f_i$, in order to check if $M \models f$, we proceed as follows:

1. Create the DPN $M' = (\mathcal{P}'_1, \ldots, \mathcal{P}'_n)$.
2. Create Büchi automata $\mathcal{B}_i^{\neg}$ satisfying the formulas $\neg f_i$.
3. Construct BDPDSs $\mathcal{B}_i^{\neg}\mathcal{P}'_i$ from the DPN $M'$ and the Büchi automata $\mathcal{B}^{\neg}$ of (2), as in Definition 11.
4. If an initial configuration $((p'_0, g_0), (u, x))\gamma_0$ is in $X$ (the set of configurations that satisfy the formula $\neg f$), with some set of locks $u$ and priority $x$, then $M \not\models f$. Otherwise, we continue to the next step, to be sure there are no livelocks.
5. Create Büchi automata $\mathcal{B}_i$ satisfying the formulas $f_i$.
6. Construct BDPDSs $\mathcal{B}_i\mathcal{P}'_i$ from them the DPN $M'$ and the Büchi automata $\mathcal{B}_i$ of (5), as in Definition 11.
7. If an initial configuration $((p'_0, g_0), \perp)\gamma_0$ is in $Y$ (the set of of configurations that satisfy the formula $f$), then there is a livelock and $M \not\models f$. Otherwise $M \not\models f$.

We can construct the set $X$ in the following iterative way:

1. $X' = \bigcup_i L(\mathcal{B}_i^{\neg}\mathcal{P}'_i)$.
2. $X = \{p\gamma \mid (p\gamma, D) \in Z \wedge D \cap X' \neq \emptyset\}$.
3. If $X \neq X'$, set $X' = X$ and go to 2. Otherwise return $X$.

The set $Z$, is the language of initial configurations of all infinite paths in each DPDS $\mathcal{P}'_i$. We can construct the set $Y$ in the following iterative way:

1. $Y' = \bigcup_i L(\mathcal{B}_i\mathcal{P}'_i)$.
2. $Y = \{(p\gamma, D) \in Y' \mid \forall p'\gamma' \in D \; \exists D' \subseteq Conf_{M'} \; s.t. \; (p'\gamma', D') \in Y'\}$.
3. If $Y \neq Y'$, set $Y' = Y$ and go to 2. Otherwise return $Y$.

**Theorem 5.** *A PL-DPN $M$ satisfies a single-indexed LTL formula $f$ $(M \models f)$ iff there is not initial configuration in $X$ with non-bottom priority-lock structure and there is not initial configuration in $Y$ with bottom priority-lock structure.*

## 5.5   Example

We want to check if the single-indexed LTL formula $f = f_1 \wedge f_2 \wedge f_3$, where $f_1 = true$, $f_2 = GF\ a_1$ and $f_3 = GF\ b_1$, is satisfied by the PL-DPN $M = (Act, \mathcal{P}_1, \mathcal{P}_2, \mathcal{P}_2)$ of Example 2.1.

The first step is to create the DPN $M' = (\mathcal{P}'_1, \mathcal{P}'_2, \mathcal{P}'_3)$ as in Example 4.1. The second step is to create Büchi automata $\mathcal{B}_1^-$, $\mathcal{B}_2^-$ and $\mathcal{B}_3^-$ recognizing the $\omega$-words that satisfy the formulas $\neg f_1 = false$, $\neg f_2 = FG\ \neg a_1$ and $\neg f_3 = FG\ \neg b_1$, respectively. Then we create the BDPDSs $\mathcal{B}_1^-\mathcal{P}'_1$, $\mathcal{B}_2^-\mathcal{P}'_2$ and $\mathcal{B}_2^-\mathcal{P}'_3$ using Definition 11. The next step is to construct the set of configurations $X$, we get:

1. $X' = L(\mathcal{B}^-\mathcal{P}_1) \cup L(\mathcal{B}^-\mathcal{P}_2) \cup L(\mathcal{B}^-\mathcal{P}_3) = \emptyset \cup \emptyset \cup \emptyset = \emptyset$.
2. $X = \{p\gamma \mid (p\gamma, D) \in Z) \wedge D \cap \emptyset \neq \emptyset\} = \emptyset$.

We have that $X = \emptyset$, this means that the negation of $f$ is not satisfied, but still can be the case that we have a livelock. Thus, we continue calculating $Y$. The algorithm proceeds as follows:

1. $L(\mathcal{BP}'_1) = \{(((p'_3, g_0), \bot)m_0, \{((p'_1, g_0), (\{l\}, 1))a_0, ((p'_2, g_0), (\emptyset, 1))b_0\}), \dots \}$.
2. $L(\mathcal{BP}'_2) = \{((p'_1, g_0), (\{l\}, 1))a_0, \emptyset)\}$ with $A(p'_1) = \emptyset$.
3. $L(\mathcal{BP}'_3) = \{((p'_2, g_0), (\emptyset, 1))b_0, \emptyset)\}$ with $A(p'_2) = \{l\}$.
4. $Y' = L(\mathcal{BP}'_1) \cup L(\mathcal{BP}'_2) \cup L(\mathcal{BP}'_3)$.
5. $Y = \{(((p'_3, g_0), \bot)m_0, \{((p'_1, g_0), (\{l\}, 1))a_0, ((p'_2, g_0), (\emptyset, 1))b_0\})\}$.

We can observe that $Y$ has the initial configuration $((p'_3, g_0), \bot)m_0$. This configuration has a $\bot$ priority-lock structure, since the child corresponding to thread A infinitely uses lock $l$ and the child corresponding to thread B acquire lock $l$ without releasing it (see the rules of Definition 11). This means that there is a livelock and then the formula $f$ is not always satisfied int the PL-DPN $M$.

# References

1. Bouajjani, A., Müller-Olm, M., Touili, T.: Regular symbolic analysis of dynamic networks of pushdown systems. In: Abadi, M., de Alfaro, L. (eds.) CONCUR 2005. LNCS, vol. 3653, pp. 473–487. Springer, Heidelberg (2005). https://doi.org/10.1007/11539452_36
2. Song, F., Touili, T.: Model checking dynamic pushdown networks. In: Shan, C. (ed.) APLAS 2013. LNCS, vol. 8301, pp. 33–49. Springer, Cham (2013). https://doi.org/10.1007/978-3-319-03542-0_3
3. Wenner, A.: Weighted dynamic pushdown networks. In: Gordon, A.D. (ed.) ESOP 2010. LNCS, vol. 6012, pp. 590–609. Springer, Heidelberg (2010). https://doi.org/10.1007/978-3-642-11957-6_31
4. Lammich, P., Müller-Olm, M.: Precise fixpoint-based analysis of programs with thread-creation and procedures. In: Caires, L., Vasconcelos, V.T. (eds.) CONCUR 2007. LNCS, vol. 4703, pp. 287–302. Springer, Heidelberg (2007). https://doi.org/10.1007/978-3-540-74407-8_20

5. Gawlitza, T.M., Lammich, P., Müller-Olm, M., Seidl, H., Wenner, A.: Join-lock-sensitive forward reachability analysis for concurrent programs with dynamic process creation. In: Jhala, R., Schmidt, D. (eds.) VMCAI 2011. LNCS, vol. 6538, pp. 199–213. Springer, Heidelberg (2011). https://doi.org/10.1007/978-3-642-18275-4_15

6. Lammich, P., Müller-Olm, M., Seidl, H., Wenner, A.: Contextual locking for dynamic pushdown networks. In: Logozzo, F., Fähndrich, M. (eds.) SAS 2013. LNCS, vol. 7935, pp. 477–498. Springer, Heidelberg (2013). https://doi.org/10.1007/978-3-642-38856-9_25

7. Lammich, P., Müller-Olm, M., Wenner, A.: Predecessor sets of dynamic pushdown networks with tree-regular constraints. In: Bouajjani, A., Maler, O. (eds.) CAV 2009. LNCS, vol. 5643, pp. 525–539. Springer, Heidelberg (2009). https://doi.org/10.1007/978-3-642-02658-4_39

8. Diaz, M., Touili, T.: Reachability analysis of dynamic pushdown networks with priorities. In: El Abbadi, A., Garbinato, B. (eds.) NETYS 2017. LNCS, vol. 10299, pp. 288–303. Springer, Cham (2017). https://doi.org/10.1007/978-3-319-59647-1_22

9. Diaz, M., Touili, T.: Dealing with priorities and locks for concurrent programs. In: D'Souza, D., Narayan Kumar, K. (eds.) ATVA 2017. LNCS, vol. 10482, pp. 208–224. Springer, Cham (2017). https://doi.org/10.1007/978-3-319-68167-2_15

10. Kahlon, V., Gupta, A.: An automata-theoretic approach for model checking threads for LTL properties. In: LICS, pp. 101–110 (2006)

11. Kahlon, V., Ivančić, F., Gupta, A.: Reasoning about threads communicating via locks. In: Etessami, K., Rajamani, S.K. (eds.) CAV 2005. LNCS, vol. 3576, pp. 505–518. Springer, Heidelberg (2005). https://doi.org/10.1007/11513988_49

12. Gawlitza, T.M., Lammich, P., Müller-Olm, M., Seidl, H., Wenner, A.: Join-lock-sensitive forward reachability analysis for concurrent programs with dynamic process creation. In: Jhala, R., Schmidt, D. (eds.) VMCAI 2011. LNCS, vol. 6538, pp. 199–213. Springer, Heidelberg (2011). https://doi.org/10.1007/978-3-642-18275-4_15

13. Wenner, A.: Weighted dynamic pushdown networks. In: Gordon, A.D. (ed.) ESOP 2010. LNCS, vol. 6012, pp. 590–609. Springer, Heidelberg (2010). https://doi.org/10.1007/978-3-642-11957-6_31

14. Bouajjani, A., Esparza, J., Maler, O.: Reachability analysis of pushdown automata: application to model-checking. In: Mazurkiewicz, A., Winkowski, J. (eds.) CONCUR 1997. LNCS, vol. 1243, pp. 135–150. Springer, Heidelberg (1997). https://doi.org/10.1007/3-540-63141-0_10

15. Vardi, M.Y., Wolper, P.: Automata-theoretic techniques for modal logics of programs. J. Comput. Syst. Sci. **32**(2), 183–221 (1986)

16. Song, F., Touili, T.: LTL Model-Checking for Dynamic Pushdown Networks Communicating via Locks. CoRR abs/1611.02528 (2016). https://urldefense.proofpoint.com/v2/url?u=https-3A__arxiv.org_abs_1611.02528&d=DwIDaQ&c=vh6FgFnduejNhPPD0fl_yRaSfZy8CWbWnIf4XJhSqx8&r=GalGWerTTF2ligrwh4CynzfQm8fWDVChT5-vICkuj3o&m=qj6Xi8h5_C7JOPqLTcI2Qo4EXwln0lud_bqODYUoH94&s=l_zvBDEuLa3uVKQFR9-k2pvG86J7bA6ERo9QLcaNipc&e=

# Networking

# OSM-GKM Optimal Shared Multicast-Based Solution for Group Key Management in Mobile IPv6

Youssef Baddi[1](✉) and Mohamed Dafir Ech-cherif El Kettani[2]

[1] ESTSB, UCD University, El Jadida, Morocco
Baddi.y@ucd.ac.ma
[2] ENSIAS Mohammed V University, Rabat, Morocco
dafir@um5s.net.ma

**Abstract.** In the last few years, multicasting is increasingly used as an efficient communication mechanism for group-oriented applications in the Internet. This progress has motivated Internet research community to propose many multicast routing protocols to support efficiently multimedia applications such as IPTV, videoconferencing, group games. However, these multicast routing protocols doesn't designed for mobile members and sources, and has not tested in wireless and mobile environment since they were introduced for multicast parties whose members and sources are topologically stationary. In addition, multicast applications require confidentiality for transmitted data. Traffic encryption key is used to assure this confidentiality and has to be changed and distributed to all valid members whenever a membership change (join or leave) occurs in the group and members move from one network to another. Our goal aims to support secure group communications in mobile environments. This paper presents OSM-GKM a new scheme to secure a transparent multicast communication in mobile environment based on Optimal Shared Multicast tree protocol. Its contribution is twofold: first, we evoke transparent multicast routing in mobile IPv6. Second, we present an architecture topology to transmit keys to multicast members. The paper is concluded with simulation studies, which show that our architecture achieves better performance in terms of delay, variation delay and tree cost for rekeying process.

**Keywords:** Multicast IP · Mobile IP · Key management · PIM-SM

## 1 Introduction

The phenomenal growth of the Internet in the last few years, the increase of bandwidth in today networks and the progress of network multimedia technology has provided both inspiration and motivation for the development of new group-oriented applications and services, with the promise of reaching the millions of users on the Internet. To support group-oriented communication more and more applications are relying on an underlying IP facility to disseminate information to several receivers simultaneously with minimum overheads. This progress has also motivated Internet research community to propose many multicast routing protocols to support efficiently many

© Springer Nature Switzerland AG 2019
A. Podelski and F. Taïani (Eds.): NETYS 2018, LNCS 11028, pp. 255–269, 2019.
https://doi.org/10.1007/978-3-030-05529-5_17

important new emerging distributed real-time and multimedia applications, such as IPTV, video on demand (VoD), audio- and video-conferencing, e-learning, group games, database replication, software distribution, collaborative environments and distributed interactive simulation. As well as non-real-time services such as database replication, and software updates or distribution.

In other side, mobility is considered a key technology of the next generation Internet and has been standardised within the IETF. The extension of group communication to the mobile environment remains a great challenge, more difficult and complex in key management protocols, fewer efforts have been spent in the specific problems of mobile members and sources. Mobile devices typically suffer from such primary constraints as mobiles members' move from attachment point in one sub-network to another one to another sub-network, which is challenging. Additionally, Mobile devices suffer of bandwidth limitation, low computation power, and low capacity storage [19, 33].

In a multicast environment that needs access control, it is unfeasible to deploy mobility without reliable mechanisms of mobile source and receiver's identification and authorisation. OSM-GKM approach aims to support secure group communications in mobile environments. In this paper, we describe the security issues in multicasting IP in mobile environment and propose a decentralised secure multicast group key management architecture in mobile IP environments where the group is organised into clusters of areas, and areas of the same clusters use a common set of keys. The proposed architecture and schemes match the key management tree to the mobile multicast environment for best focusing the delivery of the rekeying messages, reducing the communication costs, and solving the handoff problem in mobile member area. We conducted several simulations of the proposed protocol and the obtained results show that our architecture solution is efficient and achieves better performance trade-offs compared to other schemes while reducing the overall overhead and the number of re-keying messages and has no security failures.

The rest of this paper is organised as follows: Sect. 2 gives an overview of multicast IP, Mobile Ipv6 and group key management in mobile IP. In Sect. 3, we overview proposed group key management protocols and architecture for mobile environment in the literature. In Sect. 4, we present our architecture for group key management in mobile environments and our re-keying strategy. In Sect. 5, we give our simulation model and results. Finally, Sect. 6 concludes the paper.

## 2    Terminology

### 2.1    Multicast IP

The IP and IP Multicast protocols are standardised by the Internet Engineering Task Force (IETF). In 1991 Deering [13] is the first to propose a technique called Multicast IP in his thesis work to support Group based applications. IP multicast is emerging to be the future vehicle of delivery for multimedia on the Internet, with the promise of reaching the millions of users on the Internet. One crucial architecture component to this future vision is the multicast routing protocol that delivers multicast data packets (data stream) to group members, following the basic IP multicast model proposed in [13]. Multicast IP is a routing approach to ensure one-to-multiple and multiples-to-multiple communication. Multicast IP duplicates IP packets at routers level and delivers them to the intended receivers. Multicasting aims to deliver data to a set of selected receivers in an effective way: application sender needs to send just one single copy of each packet and address it to the group of involved computers; the network takes care of message duplication to the receivers of the group. Consequently, IP Multicast avoids processing overheads associated with replication at the source and saves the network bandwidth.

## 2.2   Mobile IP (MIP)

The most widely employed network protocol IP (IPv6 and IPv4) is not designed to handle natively the issues of mobility. For this purpose, NEMO working group in Internet Engineering Task Force (IETF) develops a new protocol as an enhancement to the existing Internet Protocol called Mobile IP (MIP) [X] of IPv4 (MIPv4) and IPv6 (MIPv6). The main objective of IP mobility support is to propose a set of network-based mobility management protocols and mechanisms to support mobile nodes (MNs) for IP with mobility. Mobile IP enable a mobile host to change its point of attachment to the Internet while still maintaining connectivity with its Correspondent Nodes (CNs) during its movement at the transport layer (i.e., TCP/UDP), which usually assumes that a host address is permanent [30].

An operational overview of MIP as presented in RFC 3775 [22]. Mobile IP addresses the problem by introducing two IP addresses for mobile hosts: regardless of its location on the Internet, the host is always identified by its permanent static home address, which it is known globally across the network, when attached to different networks other than its home network so-called foreign network, the host obtains a temporary transient CoA. This address acquired through either two mechanisms [35], stateless [21] or state-full auto-configuration [28] mechanisms.

## 2.3   Multicast Mobile IPv6 (MMIPv6)

Multicast routing protocols doesn't designed for mobile members, and has not tested in wireless and mobile environment since they were introduced for multicast parties whose members and sources are topologically stationary. In particular, seamless support for mobile multicast senders requires efforts significantly exceeding unicast mobility management schemes.

Multicast IP is known by highly dynamic multicast group membership join and leave. This dynamism can rapidly affect quality of both routing protocol scheme and multicast tree used. Studying and solving multicast issues in the stationary multicast infrastructure has been largely studied in the literature. However, fewer efforts have been spent in the specific problems of mobile members and sources caused by the frequent change of membership and point of attachment. The scenario of hand-over where a mobile source moves from attachment point in one sub-network to another one in another sub-network is challenging. Multicast source is identified by a Home Address HoA, but the mobile IP protocol implies acquisition of a new topologically

Care-of-Address CoA at each handoff resulting in a change of identity of the multicast source, however, the established multicast routing states are always based on the home address of the mobile source. Mobile IPv6 introduces two basic methods, known as bi-directional tunnelling and remote subscription [22].

## 2.4    Key Management in Multicast Mobile IPv6

After this presentation of multicast IP and mobile IP, the main three functional areas are multicast data handling, group key management, and the multicast security policies. Multicast security and group key management issues may be considered as two main aspects: the first being end-to-end security (i.e. protection of the multicast traffic content). The second being multicast infrastructure security (i.e. security issues in the multicast delivery tree, the delivery tree comprising multicast routers in charge of transmitting and receiving multicast traffic from sources and receivers, and other nodes connected there between). For successfully deploying many multicast service in the mobile environment, security infrastructure must be developed that manage the keys needed to provide access control to content.

Many measures to address the second problem are known in that it is sufficient to secure the control messages of multicast routing protocols to ensure that the multicast tree has been correctly built as proposed for MOSPF (Multicast Open Shortest Path First), PIM-SM (Protocol Independent Multicast-Sparse Mode), and CBT (Core Based Tree). However, securing multicast routing protocols is not sufficient to protect the multicast distribution tree since it only ensures that the group membership subscription information maintained in the edge multicast routers are populated correctly. They do not have the ability to check whether a particular host is authorised to join a particular group, or whether a given host is authorised to send its traffic over the tree towards group receivers.

# 3    State of Art

The article illustrates a survey of existing group key management schemes that specifically consider the host mobility issue in securing group communication in mobile environments. A brief citation of existing static group key management schemes are presented especially extended schemes with mobility.

There are many research works to secure multicast communications, many group key management protocols and architectures have been conducted in the literature to address the security issue in group communication [20]. Several survey studies are published, to cite this group key management protocols and architectures [4, 26, 31, 32]. These survey papers categorise these existing secure multicast protocols into multiple categories, such as flat scheme and the hierarchical scheme [14], or centralised, decentralised and distributed. These categories are deduced from the mechanism, which is used for generating the traffic encryption key. Either a single or multiple entities or the collaboration of the group members can generate the TEK.

Logical Key Hierarchy (LKH) protocol proposed at same time by Wong et al. [36] and Wallner et al. [12] is one of the most widely used group key management schemes.

In the LKH scheme, a hierarchy of keys is used to reduce the required number of TEK update messages induced by re-keying after membership changes to the order of log (n). The Iolus scheme, proposed by Mittra in [27], is designed as a framework of a hierarchy of multicast subgroups, each subgroup is managed by a Group Security Agent (GSA), which is responsible for key management inside the subgroup. To manages all Group Security Agents (GSAs) of all subgroups, Iolus [27] uses a main controller called the Group Security Controller (GSC). When a membership change occurs in a subgroup, only conserned subgroup is involved in a rekey process. This way, Iolus scales to large groups and mitigates 1-affects-n phenomenon. In the Balade scheme, proposed by [9], authors uses a decentralised architecture with the common TEK, which decomposes dynamically a group into a number of clusters. A local manager is responsible to manage each cluster. A common key is shared between the cluster manager and the members residing in the cluster.

While the problem of developing efficient group key management protocols is difficult, the problem becomes more difficult and complex when we consider member mobility [6]. Few efforts have been done to explicitly address the mobility issue of members from one area to another one while remaining in the session with a transparent key management. This section gives an overview on proposed solutions in details.

To reduce the 1-affects-n phenomenon, Kamat et al. proposed Micro-grouped IOLUS (M-Iolus) scheme [23], which is version of Iolus, that supports members mobility. To reduce the 1-affects-n phenomenon, M-Iolus [23] divides subgroups into micro-subgroups. M-Iolus [23] introduced a subgroup manager, called GSA, responsible to form dynamically a number of micro groups. This design reduces the communication overhead of updating keying materials on any changes. A micro key is shared among all members belonging to the same micro group, which is used for protecting all controlling messages transmitted.

Key management scheme to Secure Group Communication in Mobile Environments KMGM, proposed by [17], adopted a decentralised approach with the independent TEK, ASGK [10], as the main group key management scheme. KMGM [17] authors proposed organizing the group into a hierarchy of administrative areas, this hierarchy of areas is partitioned into clusters of areas. Where an Area Key Distributor (AKD) manages each are: this management include its responsibility for the key management process inside the area under its control and is considered as a member in its area and in its parent area. The scheme introduce null rekeying for intra move between areas of the same cluster. Consequently, the communication overhead and 1-affects-n overhead using KMGM [17] is lower than the other similar schemes. The main drawback of this scheme: the backward secrecy is breached as the mobile member may access to the security information of visited area, which is valid, prior the mobile member joined the group.

Kiah and Martin [24, 25] proposed a decentralised key management protocol GKMW where they address the mobility issue of members. Kiah et al. [25] employed a decentralised approach with a common TEK and proposed a group key management scheme that facilitates the host mobility in wireless mobile environment using a list as part of the protocol. In this protocol the group key managers including two types of agents: Domain key Manager DKM and Area Key Manager AKM. The Domain key

Manager DKM is the main key manager of a domain and AKM (Area Key Manager) is the key manager of one area inside a domain.

# 4 Proposed Solution

In this section, the detailed architecture of the proposed secure group key management models for mobile services are described.

## 4.1 Overview

Multicast security issues may take in consideration two main parts: the first part end-to-end security including secure end-to-end multicast traffic content; the second part multicast infrastructure and signaling security including security issues in the Multicast Delivery Tree. Multicast infrastructure may comprise multicast routers in charge of transmitting and receiving multicast traffic from sources and receivers (sources DR and receivers DR), and other nodes connected there between forming the multicast tree. Multicast signaling may comprise all signaling messages used to maintain multicast tress and group membership management (i.e. MLD). The Multicast Delivery Tree incorporate all multicast routers in charge of transmitting and receiving multicast traffic from sources and receivers, and including other nodes connected there between.

## 4.2 Mathematic Modeling and Notations

A computer network is modeled as a simple directed and connected graph $G = (N, E)$, where N is a finite set of nodes and E is the set of edges (or links) connecting the nodes. Let $|N|$ be the number of network nodes and $|E|$ the number of network links. An edge e $\in$ E connecting two adjacent nodes $u \in N$ and $v \in N$ will be denoted by $e(u, v)$, the fact that the graph is directional, implies the existence of a link $e(v, u)$ between v and u. Each edge is associated with two positive real value: a cost function $C(e) = C(e(u, v))$ represents link utilization (may be either monetary cost or any measure of resource utilization), and a delay function $D(e) = D(e(u, v))$ represents the delay that the packet experiences through passing that link including switching, queuing, transmission and propagation delays. We associate for each path $P(v_0, v_n) = (e(v_0, v_1), e(v_1, v_2),\ldots, e(v_{n-1}, v_n))$ in the network two metrics:

$$C(P(v_0, v_n)) = \sum_0^{n-1} C(e(v_i, v_{i+1})) \text{ And } D(P(v_0, v_n)) = \sum_0^{n-1} D(e(v_i, v_{i+1}))$$

A multicast tree $T_M(S, C, D)$ is a sub-graph of G spanning the set of sources node S $\subset$ N and the set of destination nodes $D \subset N$ with a selected Core router C. Let $|S|$ be the number of multicast destination nodes and $|D|$ is the number of multicast destination nodes. In Protocols using Shared multicast Tree, all sources node needs to transmit the multicast information to selected Core C via unicast routing, then it will be forwarded to all receptors in the shared tree, to model the existence of these two parts separated by Core C router, we use both cost function and delay following:

$$C(T_M(S, C, D)) = \sum_{s \in S} C(P(s, C)) + \sum_{d \in D} C(P(C, d)) \tag{3}$$

$$And \quad D(T_M(S, C, D)) = \sum_{s \in S} D(P(s, C)) + \sum_{d \in D} D(P(C, d)) \tag{4}$$

We also introduce a Delay Variation (7) function defined as the difference between the Maximum (5) and minimum (6) end-to-end delays along the multicast tree from the source to all destination nodes and is calculated as follows:

$$Max_{Delay} = Max(D(T_M(S, C, D))) \tag{5}$$

$$Min_{Delay} = Min(D(T_M(S, C, D))) \tag{6}$$

$$DelayVariation = Max_{Delay} - Min_{Delay} \tag{7}$$

Rendezvous Point RP selection problem tries to find an optimal node RP in the network with an optimal function Opt_F by minimizing in the first time the cost function $C(T_M(S, RP, D))$ and in the second a Delay and delay variation bound as follows:

$$Opt\_F(RP, T_M) \begin{cases} Min\ C(T_M(S, RP, D)) \\ Delay < \alpha \\ DelayVariation < \beta \end{cases} \tag{8}$$

### 4.3 Multicast Based Key Management

Existing protocol implementations for multicast routing, like PIM-SM [15], or enhanced route optimization for MIPv6 [1] can easily be adapted, since all processing functions are already available

Our proposal uses a multicast routing protocol based in Shared Multicast Tree SMT (or core based tree CBT), such as the Protocol Independent Multicast – Sparse Mode protocol (PIM-SM) [15] or Core-Based Tree (CBT) [7] protocol, to deliver keys between Mobile Multicast Group Members and Multicast Routing Tree. Our SMT choice is motivated by its scalability and dynamism; In general, SMT based protocols are designed for the larger and sparser groups encountered on the Internet. Without any dependence to unicast protocol and infrastructure topology, SMT based protocols uses soft state mechanisms to adapt to underlying topology-gathering protocol to develop a routing table.

### 4.4 Core Based Key Management

We can note, that SMT based protocol has several interesting characteristics. First, the transition property; that is, it transmits from the shared tree to source-based tree. For example, PIM-SM [15] is a multicast routing protocol based by default initially in Shared Rendezvous Point Tree SRPT [2, 5] to forward multicast packets. This kind of tree separate the concept of source from receivers, Joining and leaving a group member is achieves explicitly in a hop-to-hop way along the shortest path from the local router to core router resulting in less control overhead, efficient management of multicast path in changing group memberships, scalability and performance [8, 15]. After the receiver receives the multicast packets from the RP through the shared tree, it gets the other multicast packets directly from the source through the source-based tree if this tree is shorter.

RP is the core router of PIM-SM; all the senders report their existence to one or more RPs, and PIM-SM maintains the traditional IP multicast service model of receiver-initiated membership, the receivers find the multicast session by querying explicitly RPs. Furthermore, routers member of the multicast delivery tree join the PIM-SM tree through explicit message when there are downstream receivers.

All this characteristics combining flexibility and scaling make PIM-SM more suitable for those groups where members are dynamic and distributed sparsely across a wide area. The solution proposed to secure key distribution makes use of the fact that the Rendezvous Point (RP) is a good decision-point for access control and that the group-key management event can be extended to facilitate receiver access control.

As described in literature [20] and in PIM Working Group IETF specifications [15] as an introduction to secure PIM protocol, when security is enabled, all PIM version 2 messages will carry an IPsec authentication header (AH) [29].

## 4.5    Architecture

First, we show that partitioning the group into clusters of subgroups that use independent traffic encryption keys can be formulated as tree partitioning problem. In other words, it is possible that each subgroup members in the key tree is in the different area. When the membership changes, the rekeying messages are generated per each subgroup. In our work, we propose an architecture to solve the problem with respect to the application requirements and membership behaviour, consequently, the key management tree that matches the mobile multicast topology. Note that in this proposed solution, the routers within the main multicast distribution tree and temporary multicast distribution tree exchange key management signaling massages and do not maintain any host-identification information. Hence, the solution still promotes the "anonymous-receiver" approach underlying the IP multicast model [29], first proposed by Deering [13] in ASM and style respected in SSM communication mode.

Our proposition is based in One-to-many multicat model independent on the network topology. One-to-many multicast covers such scenarios where the multicast group has only one sender and multiple receivers. Only one sender can transmit the data and the transmission is unidirectional from the sender to other group members. The sender is the producer of the data and the receivers are the passive consumers of the data.

Some examples of this multicast application include video-on-demand, Internet TV and other applications such as broadasting of stock quotes and news.

Our architecture is based on PIM-SM [15] multicast protocol with a simultaneously active, independent cores Shared Tree to manager the multicast mobile receivers and sources as defined by [6]. We choose the PIM-SM [15] multicast protocol as an example of multicast protocol because of his efficiency join/leave manager by using a Rendezvous Point RP router to store multicast routing state.

Each domain contains two type of networks: network with mobile nodes and network with fixed nodes. There are, also, two types of specialized controllers, that control, manage, generate and distribute the keys. They are Domain Controller and Area Controller. All the members (mobiles or fixes) in the service belong to the domain controlled by a Domain controller. Based on the administrative regions and connected sub-network, the domain is divided into areas. Each area is controlled and managed by area controller called Mobile Area Key Distribtor MAKD.

As specified in [6], The primary multicast tree can be constructed by any multicast routing protocol, such as, DVMRP, CBT, and PIM, our architecture is independent on used routing protocol (Fig. 1).

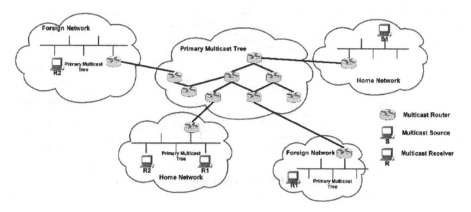

**Fig. 1.** Architectural topology

In the Multicast delivery temporary tree, the whole group of a specific HoA can be organised in a multicast hierarchy Shared Tree having as a root the selected RP where traffic source is connected. Therefore, mobile group members in the Multicast delivery temporary key tree could not neighbour each other. In other words, it is possible that each mobile group member in the Multicast delivery temporary key tree be in the different area. Multi-domain multicast routing need to use another protocol to manage multicast source, such as PIM-SM with Multicast Source Discovery Protocol (MSDP) [16]. Currently, no specific security measures are incorporated into MSDP [16] that interconnects multiple inter-domains Rendezvous Points (RPs) within PIM-SM.

### 4.6   Cluster Presentation

The construction of clusters can be done using different heuristics and algorithms presented in state of art section and in many previous works [10, 11, 18]. Each domain contains two type of networks (nodes): network with mobile nodes and network with fixed nodes.

Contrary to cited solution in the state of the art section, which the rekeying message of one subgroup or cluster is duplicated several times and delivered to each different region, our architecture create independent clusters. The principle of our approach is based on merging in the same cluster subgroups having homogeneous membership dynamism based in mobility.

Each cluster is composed of a set of subgroups that share the same TEK. These subgroups are called area. Initially all multicast group members constitute a single cluster and use the same keys encryption (TEK). In Fig. (2) for example, subgroups belonging to the Cluster 3 use the same traffic encryption key TEK3, which is different from TEK2, the traffic encryption key of Cluster 2.

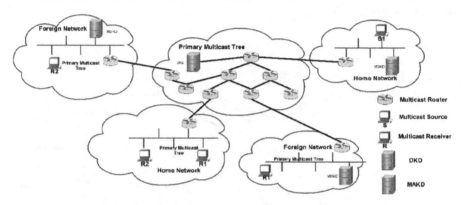

**Fig. 2.**  OSM-GKM with DKD and MAKDs agents

## 4.7   Area Presentation

Our approach is logically hierarchical organization into subgroups. The partitioning of group members into subgroups aims to reduce the 1-affects-n phenomenon and to to find a hierarchic clusters of subgroups with similar membership change frequencies which minimizes delays in transmission.

The group key management domain is organised into multiple areas. An area represents an autonomous system which can be a corporate network, a multicast domain (e.g. PIM domain) with its own multicast group address. An area can also be any wireless LAN with an access router and many access points in Mobile IPv6 environment. This separation allow managing separately wired and wireless area.

Each time a member moves to a new area, it receive the KEK key of that area. Member's mobility does not compromise group secrecy and does not require any rekeying operations. While this seems to be challenging given that there is no inter-action between the AKDs for mobility events, we will show that using a conditional and self-generation technique of encryption keys for mobile member we achieve the expectations with reduced costs.

Areas belonging to the same domain or corporate network are organised into clusters where each cluster is controlled by a group controller/key server called Domain Key Distributor (DKD) which manages MAKDs of cluster's areas.

To each cluster Ci, we associate a cost C(Ci), Delay(Ci) and Delay Variation (Ci) that evaluates the different overheads induced by subgroups and areas of this cluster.

## 4.8    Agents

Our solution is based in Shared Multicast Tree SMT which use a special router named Core router (RP router in PIM-SM protocol [15]) to manage multicast traffic. Shared Multicast Tree SMT is designed with facilities to allow the Core router to be aided by other network entities (e.g. servers) in its task of verifying join-requests and deciding access control.

Each HoA is member in two type of subgroups: its own sub-group and all sub-groups of his mobile members. Thus, each HoAi knows two set of TEKs, its TEK and set of TEKs of subgroups of his mobile members ({TEKHoA,{TEKHoA,TEKHoA, ....,TEKHoA}}.

DKD is responsible for authenticating the multicast member, generating and se-curely distributing keys to members, managing the key tree, and administrating the multicast tree router members. Domain Key Distributor (DKD), which is a key trust server for the domain, distributes each DR's secret key via secure channels in the domain separately.

We introduce a security entity called the Mobile Area Key Distributor (MDKD) which has a number of roles in the foreign domain, one of which is to be a key-server for the mobile members in the domain.

The mobile area key distributor MAKD is a security entity that is responsible for managing mobile multicast groups' members in the foreign network. The MAKD represents the first point of contact for host-members wishing to join a multicast group, it performs the rekey procedure locally to reduce the communication cost and can also disseminates The group members access control information (source and receiver). The mission of an MAKD is the key management within the area for which it is responsible and the exchange of well-specified messages with the other HoAs of mobile mem-bers visiting this area. Each MAKD is a member in two groups (zones), the zone it controls, and the parent zone in the hierarchy related to HoA with group mobile members.

All MAKDs share the symmetric key SEK which is known only by AKDs. We assume that this key is generated by the MAKD where the traffic source is connected at session setup, and distributed securely to other MAKDs. Both the multicast designed router DR and the mobile member MM (source or receiver) know the MAKD (e.g. MAKD's certificate is trusted by both the MM and the DRr). In practice the MAKD can be implemented by several servers for reliability and availability reasons. Any such server must be implemented with the strongest security protection available due to their sensitivity.

# 5    Simulation

In this section, we present simulation results to demonstrate the effectiveness of the designed architecture.

## 5.1   Overview and Topology

To study the performance of our propose architecture, we perform simulations with the Network Simulator NS3 [38]. NS3 is an open source discrete-event network simulator for Internet systems, targeted primarily for research and educational use. NS3 is free software, distributed under the GNU GPL v2 license, and is publicly available for research, development, and use. NS3 is the successor of NS-2 and is intended as an eventual replacement for the popular NS2 simulator once most popular open source simulator among research groups. The project acronym "nsnam" derives historically from the concatenation of ns (network simulator) and nam (network animator).

IPv4/IPv6 and TCP/UDP models are provided in NS3 Simulator. Also, a user can define its own physical and application layer models. Because its source code is open, it is possible to modify existing models. To simulate PIM-SM and Mobile IPv6 we extend NS3 simulator by adding [3] extension.

Network topology is generated with BRITE [34] module, for this, we adopt Waxman [37] as the graph model. Where n vertices are placed randomly in a rectangular coordinate grid by generating uniformly distributed values for their x and y coordinates. The edge probability is given by $P(u, v) = k\,e^{-d(u;v)/LD}$. Where d(u, v) is the distance from node u to v, D is the maximum distance between two nodes, and K and L are parameters in the interval [0; 1]. It is noted that increasing L increases the number of connections between far off nodes and increasing K increases the degree of each node. The values of K = 0:2 and L = 0:2 were used to generate networks with an average degree between 3 and 4 in the mathematical model of Waxman. We simulate each algorithm with the variation of network size from 10 to 160 with 25% of nodes are mobile multicast group members. Our simulation studies were performed on a set of 100 random networks.

To demonstrate the performance of our proposal architecture, Optimal Shared Multicast-based solution for group key management OSM-GKM is compared in the same simulation environment to existing ones, such as M-Iolus [23], KMGM [17] and GKMW [25] solutions.

## 5.2   Simulation Metrics and Results

Group key management is totally influenced by group membership information. Hence, To estimate and evaluate our scheme, we implement simulation based in several criteria for examining group key management solution in mobile environment such as scalability, join/leave secrecy, number of keys with a controller, number of keys (with each group members, in each area and cluster), processing time for key management. Many other metrics related to mobile and multicast IP are studded, simulation results show that good performance is achieved in terms of handoff latency, end-to-end delay, tree construction delay and others metrics. In this section, we describe some numerical results that can be used for comparing the performances of the proposed algorithm.

We consider delay as the required time to transmit multicast packets from source node to the furthest receiver node in the multicast group after group key management processes is established. Figure 3 shows that OSM-GKM is the best among all the algorithms, with M-Iolus [23] and KMGM [17] following it, and GKMW [25] is the worst. The good performance of OSM-GKM is attributed by the fact that it searches the optimal Shared Based Tree in the network topology with a delay and delay variation based fitness function.

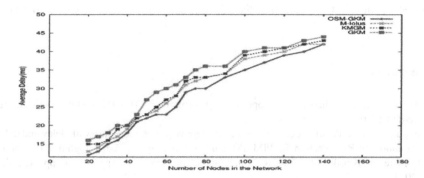

**Fig. 3.** Number of network size with delay

Delay Variation is the difference between the first time of the reception of a multicast packet by a receiver of the multicast group and the last reception of the same multicast packet by another receiver. This metric present if the architecture supports reel time application and the group key management process chose an optimal multicast tree. In Fig. 4 the Delay Variation is plotted as a function of the number of nodes in the network topology, it shows that OSM-GKM decrease more the delay variation to transmit multicast packet to all multicast group, this reduction is caused by the selection of an optimal Core router in each temporary Shared tree, followed by others algorithms.

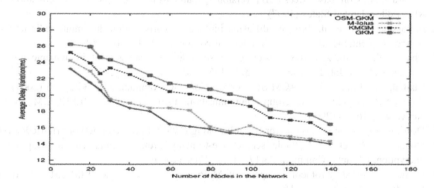

**Fig. 4.** Number of network size with delay variation

# 6  Conclusion

Current Group Key Management protocol doesn't take into consideration the mo-bile multicast group members. Therefore, these protocols fail generally to find the optimal rekeying process in any mobile or multicast membership change (move, join, leave).

To solve these problems, OSM-GKM architecture is proposed based on Opti-mal Shared multicast tree protocol. Simulation results indicate that this architecture has good performance in multicast cost, delay, delay variation and other aspects. Our future work is focused on extending this architecture to support multiple QOS criteria imposed by multicast source across the network and a distributed execution to reduce new entities charge used.

# References

1. Arkko, J., et al.: Enhanced route optimization for mobile IPv6 (2007). http://www.ietf.org/rfc/rfc4866.txt
2. Baddi, Y., et al.: Parallel greedy randomized adaptive search procedure with delay and delay variation for RP selection in PIM-SM multicast routing. In: 2013 Eighth International Conference Broadband Wireless Computing Communication Application, pp. 481–487 (2013)
3. Baddi, Y.: ybaddi/ns3-dev-pimsm dev (2018). https://doi.org/10.5281/zenodo.1173320
4. Baddi, Y., Ech-Cherif El Kettani, M.D.: Key management for secure multicast communication: a survey. In: 2013 National Security Days (JNS3), pp. 1–6. IEEE (2013)
5. Baddi, Y., Ech-Cherif El Kettani, M.D.: Parallel GRASP algorithm with delay and delay variation for core selection in shared tree based multicast routing protocols. In: Third International Conference on Innovative Computing Technology (INTECH 2013), pp. 227–232. IEEE (2013)
6. Baddi, Y., Security, I.: A fast dynamic multicast tree adjustment protocol for mobile IPv6 (2014)
7. Ballardie, A.: Core based trees (CBT) multicast routing architecture (1997). http://www.ietf.org/rfc/rfc2201.txt
8. Ballardie, A.: Core based trees (CBT version 2) multicast routing – protocol specification –. RFC Editor, United States (1997)
9. Bouassida, M.S., et al.: Balade : diffusion multicast sécurisée d'un flux multimédia multi-sources séquentielles dans un environnement ad hoc, pp. 531–546 (2005)
10. Challal, Y., et al.: Adaptive clustering for scalable key management in dynamic group communications. Int. J. Secur Netw. **3, 2**, 133 (2008)
11. Challal, Y., et al.: SAKM. ACM SIGCOMM Comput. Commun. Rev. **34**(2), 55 (2004)
12. Wong, C.K., et al.: Secure group communications using key graphs. IEEE/ACM Trans. Netw. **8**(1), 16–30 (2000)
13. Deering, S.E.: Host extensions for IP multicasting (1986). http://www.ietf.org/rfc/rfc988.txt
14. Dondeti, L.R., et al.: Scalable secure one-to-many group communication using dual encryption. Comput. Commun. **23**(17), 1681–1701 (2000)
15. Fenner, B., et al.: Protocol Independent Multicast - Sparse Mode (PIM-SM): Protocol Specification (Revised). (2016)
16. Fenner, B., Meyer, D.: Multicast Source Discovery Protocol (MSDP), IETF (2003)
17. Gharout, S., et al.: Adaptive group key management protocol for wireless communications. J. Univers. Comput. Sci. **18**(6), 874–899 (2012)
18. Gharout, S., et al.: Scalable delay-constrained multicast group key management. Int. J. Netw. Secur. **7**(2), 142–156 (2008)
19. Gupta, A.K., Gupta, A.K.: Challenges of mobile computing. In: Proceedings 2nd National Conference on Challenges and Opportunities in Information (COIT-2008), RIMT-IET, Mandi Gobindgarh, 29 March, p. 86 (2008)

20. Hardjono, T.: Router-assistance for receiver access control in PIM-SM. In: Proceedings Fifth IEEE Symposium on Computers and Communications ISCC 2000, pp. 687–692. IEEE Computer Society (2000)

21. Jelger, C., Noël, T.: Supporting mobile SSM sources for IPv6. In: Globecom 2002 IEEE Global Communication, vol. 2, pp. 1693–1697 (2002)

22. Johnson, D., et al.: RFC 3775: Mobility support in IPv6 (2004)

23. Kamat, S., et al.: Reduction in control overhead for a secure, scalable framework for mobile multicast. In: IEEE International Conference on Communications ICC 2003, pp. 98–103. IEEE (2003)

24. Kiah, M.L.M., Martin, K.M.: Host mobility protocol for secure group communication in wireless mobile environments. In: Future Generation Communication and Networking (FGCN 2007), pp. 100–107. IEEE (2007)

25. Kiah, M.L.M., et al.: Host mobility protocol for secure group communication in wireless mobile environments. Int. J. Secur. Appl. **2**, 1 (2008)

26. Mapoka, T.T.: Group key management protocols for secure mobile multicast communication: a comprehensive survey. Int. J. Comput. Appl. **84**(12), 975–8887 (2013)

27. Mittra, S.: Iolus: a framework for scalable secure multicasting. In: Proceedings of the ACM SIGCOMM 1997 Conference on Applications, Technologies, Architectures, and Protocols for Computer Communication - SIGCOMM 1997, pp. 277–288. ACM Press, New York (1997)

28. O'Neill, A.: Mobility management and IP multicast (2002)

29. Perkins, C., et al.: Mobility support in IPv6 (2011). http://www.ietf.org/rfc/rfc6275.txt

30. Romdhani, I., et al.: IP mobile multicast: challenges and solutions. IEEE Commun. Surv. Tutorials **6**(1), 18–41 (2004)

31. Salma, U., Lawrence, B.A.A.: A survey of group key management protocols in wireless mobile. Int. J. Innov. Res. Adv. Eng. **2**(2), 2163–2349 (2015)

32. Seetha, R., Saravanan, R.: A Survey on Group Key Management Schemes. Cybern. Inf. Technol. **15**(3), 3–25 (2015)

33. Shin, Y., et al.: Video multicast over WLANs: power saving and reliability perspectives. IEEE Netw. **27**(2), 40–46 (2013)

34. Tangmunarunkit, H., et al.: Network topologies, power laws, and hierarchy (2001)

35. Thomson, S., et al.: IPv6 Stateless Address Autoconfiguration. Fremont, CA, USA (2007)

36. Wallner, D., et al.: Key management for multicast: issues and architectures (1999). http://www.ietf.org/rfc/rfc2627.txt

37. Waxman, B.M.: Routing of multipoint connections. Sel. Areas Commun. IEEE J. **6**(9), 1617–1622 (2002)

38. ns-3 reference manual. https://www.nsnam.org/docs/release/3.9/manual.pdf

# A Game-Theoretic Approach for the Internet Content Distribution Chain

Driss Ait Omar$^{(\boxtimes)}$ , Mohamed El Amrani, Mohamed Baslam,
and Mohamed Fakir

Information Processing and Decision Support Laboratory,
Faculty of Sciences and Technics, University of Sultan Moulay Slimane,
Beni Mellal, Morocco
aitomard@gmail.com, med.el.amran@gmail.com, baslam.med@gmail.com,
fakfad@yahoo.fr

**Abstract.** Currently, commercial $CDN$ providers have become major
actors in the Internet content distribution chain. They serve a large portion of the Internet traffic since they allow an efficient user-perceived
response time and availability of content. In this paper, we consider an
ecosystem that contains content providers $CPs$ as customers of content
distribution network providers $CDNs$. The content distribution network
seeks to attract more content providers by offering them prices to save
and distribute their contents to end users with better QoS. Thus, the
quality and price of the content, which are considered in this study as
decision parameters for content providers have an indirect impact on the
revenue of the $CDN$. Once the content of a $CP$ is stored in the $CDN$
content replication servers, the CDN is the delivery manager of this content to all end users' requests; for this another common parameter is
added to our modeling and it determines the share of the $CDN$ that
the $CP$ wins requests from users on this content. After formulating non-
cooperative games, we have demonstrated the existence and uniqueness
of the Nash equilibrium and used the best response dynamic algorithm
to make a numerical analysis to the problems. We were able to learn
that when the game between the $CDNs$ is socially optimal, the $CPs$ win
more and vice versa in the case where the game becomes a monopoly.

**Keywords:** Content delivery · CDN · Content provider
Non-cooperative game · Nash equilibrium · Price of anarchy

## 1 Introduction

Content distribution and congestion limitation in the Internet network are the
subject of much research in the field of telecommunication networks. This problem of congestion occurs when a content stored in the original server of the
content provider is the subject of a very large number of requests. These studies
are concentrated in order to reduce the response time (Latency) and thus ensure

© Springer Nature Switzerland AG 2019
A. Podelski and F. Taïani (Eds.): NETYS 2018, LNCS 11028, pp. 270–285, 2019.
https://doi.org/10.1007/978-3-030-05529-5_18

the content distribution with a better QoS to the end users, which surrounds the problem of traffic congestion in the network [13]. Among the most effective solutions is the use of content distribution networks as important actors in the content distribution chain. These networks consist of an original server connected to the other servers of content replication to hide the content requested by the population they cover. The basic operation mechanism of a Content Distribution Network ($CDN$) is the fact that first request on a content is served by the original server and immediately this content will be transferred to the content replication server that is in the area of the request coverage to serve future requests on the same content and it reduces the problem of congestion, that recurs in the network "backhaul" and improves the user QoS.

According to [11], the content distribution networks' $CDN$ customers are the end user, the content provider $CP$, the Internet service providers, the mobile operators, ...etc. The end user is the entity that consumes the content (e.g. video, web page, music, ... ) of the content provider. The content provider (for example: YouTube, Hulu, Dailymotion, ... ) is the entity that owns the content or has obtained the rights to sell it. The CDN provider (for example: Akamai, Azure, Level 3, ... ) is the entity that has replication servers in strategic locations and provides content delivery services to the content providers. Existing relationships between these actors are business relationships such as the purchase of content from a content provider $CP$ by an end user. The costs of hosting the content by the $CDN$ provider are paid by the content provider. These relationships have forced them to seek more satisfying services with moderately acceptable prices to earn profits to survive. This requires many studies in this area and our contribution falls within this framework.

In the papers [4,6,8,16], the authors questioned the concept of Internet neutrality and its implication on the different levels of the content distribution chain taking into account the participation of several like the CDNs in this process. They studied the system with a single CDN actor who seeks to maximize his income that model mathematically according to parameters such as service, transport and storage prices. This diversity of actors leads to a strong competition between them, the point which is not studied in these works. The authors in work [14] have discussed the different parameters that could influence the usefulness of a CDN like the pricing policy it follows, the popularity of the content it stores in the servers of the content replication (that is to say the demand of the content) and the QoS it offers to these customers (CP, Users, ... ). In the paper [7] the authors discussed the case of an ecosystem where we have users want to benefit from the content offered by a content provider and access to the service is through two ISPs taking into consideration three cases for the delivery of the content. The first case, without using CDN, means that the delivery will be done directly via the origin server of the CP. The second case entails distribution using an independent CDN. The third case is when the CDN becomes an integrated entity in one of the Internet Service Providers (Hosting CDN). The authors of this paper concluded that users are satisfied with the use of CDNs.

However, when it comes to ISPs, it would be better to operate an independent CDN so as not to lose too much by adding fees for installing a hosting CDN.

Diffusing acceleration of the diversified content on the Internet and offering quality of performances is one the major objects in the content distribution chain. For this purpose the authors of the work [15] have described the strength of the implementation of CDNs and their very important place in the problem of content distribution. So, they discussed the different architectures of $CDN$s and their implications for interconnection markets. They concluded as reported by Cisco [1] that 70% of Internet traffic will go through CDN by 2021, up from 52% in 2016.

Previous works have studied relationships between actors in the Internet content distribution chain. But the ecosystems analyzed each time resulted in the existence of a single content distribution network provider $CDN$. This is strongly not the casebecause we currently notice the new several commercial $CDN$s and what represents a competitive environment since each one of them seeks to maximize its profit. Profit optimization is related to the strategy that each $CDN$ provider seeks to achieve its objective. This depends on the price it offers content providers. The aim is to distribute their content and the QoS that is based on the size of the caches and the number of content replication servers exploited which meant the rate of coverage of user requests in different regions of the world. However, our contribution is to study and analyze an ecosystem where we have several content providers $CP$s who will select the most appropriate $CDN$ providers and those who meet their objectives in the content distribution chain. The choice is an outpouring of their own strategies and those of the $CDN$ providers. A $CDN$ provider may serve one or more content providers $CP$s.

The instead of this paper is structured as follows: In Sect. 2, we present the problem formulation by modeling the interaction existing in different level of the pseudo-ecosystem studied. Next, we present the theoretical analysis of the non-cooperative games considered in this study in Sect. 3 and we describe in Sect. 4 the method used for learning a Nash Equilibrium Point. Finally, we give a numerical analysis obtained on the models proposed in this work to validate what was obtained in the theoretical analysis in Sect. 5 and we conclude this paper with perspectives in Sect. 6.

## 2    Problem Modeling

In this section, we proceed to the modelling of the problem by considering the actors that can be contributed in the various levels of the Internet content distribution chain. Content Providers ($CP$s) that provide content to end users with a certain price $P^c$ and quality of content $q^c$. Content Distribution Network Providers ($CDN$s) are entities that store the contents of $CP$ in server caches placed near end users. These servers allow the loading and downloading of content with a satisfactory QoS and a price $P$ that the $CP$ has to pay to $CDN$. Service providers $SP$s allow end users access to content with fees that are not taken into consideration in this study and the end users which are the purpose of the content distribution chain. The Fig. 1 represents the different actors used in the content delivery chain. Our contribution focuses on a restricted model that analyzes the interaction between CDNs providers and CPs providers. We consider a system with $N$ $CDN$ providers and $M$ $CP$ providers. $p_i$ and $q_i^s$ represent respectively the price and QoS guaranteed by $CDN_i$ $\forall i \in \{1, \ldots, N\}$. $p_j^c$ and $q_j^c$ represents the content access price and the quality of content assured by $CP_j$ $\forall j \in \{1, \ldots, M\}$.

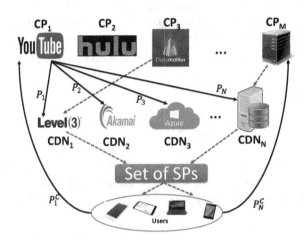

**Fig. 1.** Representation of relations between the actors of the Internet Content delivery chain. The plain arrows depict monetary transactions. The dotted arrows present data delivery from the CP via CDN to the end-users.

## 2.1  Demand Model

Modeling the demand of an actor in telecommunication networks is a kind of representation on his part of the customers who are registered in their services. For simplicity, the demand $D_{ij}$ of $CDN_i$ and $CP_j$ is written as a function that depends on the decision parameters and is assumed to be linear (like the procedure followed by the author of the paper [3]) with respect to the price $p_i$, the promised QoS $q_i^s$, the price of content $p_j^c$ and the quality of content $q_j^c$. This demand function depends also on prices $\mathbf{p}_{-i}$, QoS $\mathbf{q}_{-i}^s$, price of content $\mathbf{p}_{-j}^c$ and quality of content $\mathbf{q}_{-j}^c$ set by the competitors. Eventually, $D_{ij}$ is decreasing with respect to $p_i$, $p_j^c$ and increasing with respect to $p_n$, $n \neq i$,$p_k^c$, $k \neq j$. Whereas it is increasing with respect to $q_i^s$, $q_j^c$ and decreasing with respect to $q_n^s$,$n \neq i$, $q_k^c$, $k \neq j$.

Then, the demand functions with respect to services of $CDN_i$ and $CP_j$ can be written as follows:

$$D_{ij}(\mathbf{p}, \mathbf{q^s}, \mathbf{p^c}, \mathbf{q^c}) = d_i^0 - \alpha_i^i p_i + \beta_i^i q_i^s - \lambda_j^j p_j^c + \gamma_j^j q_j^c + \sum_{n, n \neq i} (\alpha_i^n p_n - \beta_i^n q_n^s)$$

$$+ \sum_{k, k \neq j} (\lambda_j^k p_k^c - \gamma_j^k q_k^c), \quad \forall n \in \{1, \ldots, N\}, \; \forall k \in \{1, \ldots, M\} \quad (1)$$

where $d_i^0$ is a positive constant used to insure non-negative demands over the feasible region. While $\alpha_i^n$ and $\beta_i^n$ are positive constants representing respectively the sensitivity of CDN provider $i$ to price and QoS of CDN provider $n$. $\lambda_j^k$ and $\gamma_j^k$ are positive constants representing respectively the sensitivity of content provider $j$ to the price of content and quality of content of content provider $k$.

The constraints on the coefficients presented in the demand function are as follows: $\sum_{n=1}^{N} \alpha_i^n = 1, \sum_{n=1}^{N} \beta_i^n = 1 \; \forall i \in \{1, \ldots, N\}; \; \sum_{k=1}^{M} \lambda_j^k = 1, \sum_{k=1}^{M} \gamma_j^k = 1 \; \forall j \in \{1, \ldots, M\}$

**Assumption 1**

$$\alpha_i^i \geq \sum_{n, n \neq i} \alpha_i^n, \forall n, i = 1, \ldots, N \quad (2)$$

*Will be necessary to ensure the uniqueness of the Nash equilibrium. This Assumption 1 means that the influence of the price decided by $CDN_i$ on its demand is greater than the sum of the influences of prices decided by $CDN_{-i}$ competitors on its demand.*

## 2.2   CDN Demand Model

$CDN_i$'s demand is the sum of all the $CPs$ demand it served to end-users, and is expressed as follows:

$$D_{CDN_i} = \sum_{j=1}^{M} D_{ij} \quad (3)$$

## 2.3   CP Demand Model

The $CP_j$'s demand is the sum of their demands served by each $CDN_i$ $\forall i \in \{1, \ldots, N\}$, it is expressed by:

$$D_{CP_j} = \sum_{i=1}^{N} D_{ij} \quad (4)$$

## 2.4   CDN Utiliy Model

The usefulness (net profit) of a commercial $CDN_i$ is the difference between the total revenue and the investment costs, the aim of which is to ensure satisfactory QoS for the end users. It represents his intervention to improve bandwidth $\Phi$ of $SPs$ by putting content to servers close to users and not forgetting the size of the dedicated storage space to cache the content of $CPs$.

The total revenue $R_i$ of $CDN_i$ is based on the price it offers $CP$s for the delivery of their content and on its demand $D_{CDN_i}$ as well as its share of the $CP$s revenue related to the price of the content they offer to users. It is expressed as follows:

$$R_i = p_i.D_{CDN_i} + \sum_{j=1}^{M} f_{ij}.p_j^c.D_{ij} \tag{5}$$

with $f_{ij} \in [0, 1]$ is a percentage that represents the share of the $CDN_i$ through the income of the request of the $CP_j$ delivered by the $CDN_i$.

**Assumption 2**

$$\sum_{i=1}^{N} f_{ij} < 1, \quad \forall j \in \mathcal{M} \tag{6}$$

*This condition is often realistic because: if $\sum_{i=1}^{N} f_{ij} = 1$ then $U_{CP_j} < 0$ which means that $CP_j$ shared everything it earns with the $CDN$s and strongly this is not the case.*

The cost of a $CDN$ is related to the size of the cache provided to store the contents of the $CP$s and the number of replication servers used to keep the content close to the end users. These opportunities that the $CDN$ offer $CP$s have a goal to improve the QoS perceived by users limiting the problems of congestion, especially if it's a query on a live video (video-streaming). Hence the cost $C_i$ is formulated in this form:

$$C_i = \vartheta_i.(q_i^s)^2 \tag{7}$$

with $\vartheta_i$ is a positive constant that represents the cost per unit of the cache size used.

So from the Eq. 5 and the Eq. 7, we can conclude that the utility of a $CDN_i$ is the following:

$$U_{CDN_i}(\mathbf{p}, \mathbf{q^s}, \mathbf{p^c}, \mathbf{q^c}) = p_i.D_{CDN_i} + \sum_{j=1}^{M} f_{ij}.p_j^c.D_{ij} - \vartheta_i.(q_i^s)^2 \tag{8}$$

## 2.5   CP Utiliy Model

The total revenue of $CP_j$ is $p_j^c.D_{CP_j}(\mathbf{p}, \mathbf{q^s}, \mathbf{p^c}, \mathbf{q^c})$. Its cost is that relating to the establishment of a quality of content $q_j^c$ and the share of $CDN$s that it uses for the delivery and storage of its contents. the utility of a $CP_j$ is the following:

$$U_{CP_j}(\mathbf{p}, \mathbf{q^s}, \mathbf{p^c}, \mathbf{q^c}) = p_j^c.D_{CP_j} - \sum_{i=1}^{N} f_{ij}.p_j^c.D_{ij} - c_j.(q_j^c)^2 \tag{9}$$

with $c_j$ is a positive constant that represents the cost per unit of the established content quality.

# 3    A Non-cooperative Game Formulation

In game theory, the formulation of a non-cooperative game in a precise manner requires the following points:

– Determine the number of players involved in the system.
– Define all available actions for each player: this is to specify to each player his own space of strategies.
– Model the objective function of each player it tries to optimize.

We formulate two non-cooperative games, the first one (**G1**) studies the interactions between the commercial $CDNs$ and the second (**G2**) it will be a modeling of the competition between the CPs.

Let $\mathbf{G1} = [\mathcal{N}, \{P_i, Q_i^s\}, \{U_{CDN_i}(.)\}]$ denote the non-cooperative price and QoS game (NPQG), where $\mathcal{N} = \{1, \ldots, N\}$ is the index set identifying the $CDNs$ provider, $P_i$ is the price strategy set of $CDN_i$, $Q_i^s$ is the QoS strategy set of $CDN_i$, and $U_{CDN_i}(.)$ is the utility function. Each $CDN_i$ selects a price $p_i \in P_i$ and a QoS measure $q_i^s \in Q_i^s$. Let the price vector $\mathbf{p} = (p_1, \ldots, p_N)^T \in P_N = P_1 \times P_2 \times \ldots \times P_N$, QoS vector $\mathbf{q}^s = (q_1^s, \ldots, q_N^s)^T \in Q_N^s = Q_1^s \times Q_2^s \times \ldots \times Q_N^s$ (where T represents the transpose operator). The utility of $CDN_i$ when it decides the strategy price $p_i$ to allocate the QoS $q_i^s$ is given in Eq. (8). We assume that the strategy spaces $P_i$ and $Q_i^s$ of each CDN are compact and convex sets with maximum and minimum constraints. For any given $CDN_i$ we consider strategy spaces the closed intervals $P_i = [\underline{p_i}, \overline{p_i}]$ and $Q_i^s = [\underline{q_i^s}, \overline{q_i^s}]$. In order to maximize their utilities, each $CDN_i$ decides a price $P_i$ and $\overline{Q}$oS $q_i^s$. Formally, the NPQG problem can be expressed as:

$$\max_{p_i \in P_i, q_i^s \in Q_i^s} U_{CDN_i}(\mathbf{p}, \mathbf{q}^s), \forall i \in \mathcal{N}$$

Let $\mathbf{G2} = [\mathcal{M}, \{P_j^c, Q_j^c\}, \{U_{CP_j}(.)\}]$ denote the non-cooperative price and quality of content game (NPQG), where $\mathcal{M} = \{1, .., M\}$ is the index set identifying the $CPs$ provider, $P_j^c$ is the price of content strategy set of $CP_j$, $Q_j^c$ is the Quality of content strategy set of $CP_j$, and $U_{CP_j}(.)$ is the utility function. Each $CP_j$ selects a price $p_j^c \in P_j^c$ and a quality of content measure $q_j^c \in Q_j^c$. Let the price vector $\mathbf{p}^c = (p_1^c, \ldots, p_M^c)^T \in P_N^c = P_1^c \times P_2^c \times \ldots \times P_N^c$, quality of content vector $\mathbf{q}^c = (q_1^c, \ldots, q_M^c)^T \in Q_M^c = Q_1^c \times Q_2^c \times \ldots \times Q_N^c$ (where T represents the transpose operator). The utility of $CP_j$ when it decides the strategy price $p_j^c$ to allocate the quality of content $q_j^c$ is given in Eq. (9). We assume that the strategy spaces $P_j^c$ and $Q_j^c$ of each CP are compact and convex sets with maximum and minimum constraints. For any given $CP_j$ we consider strategy spaces the closed intervals $P_j^c = [\underline{p_j^c}, \overline{p_j^c}]$ and $Q_j^c = [\underline{q_j^c}, \overline{q_j^c}]$. In order to maximize their utilities, each $CP_j$ decides a price $P_j^c$ and QoS $q_j^c$. Formally, the NPQG problem can be expressed as:

$$\max_{p_j^c \in P_j^c, q_j^c \in Q_j^c} U_{CP_j}(\mathbf{p}^c, \mathbf{q}^c), \forall j \in \mathcal{M}$$

### 3.1   Game with Fixed QoS of CDN

**Definition 1.** *A price vector $\mathbf{p}^* = (p_1^*, \ldots, p_N^*)$ is the Nash equilibrium price of the game $G1 = [\mathcal{N}, \{P_i, Q_i^s\}, \{U_{CDN_i}(.)\}]$ if:*

$$\forall (i, p_i) \in (\mathcal{N}, P_i), U_{CDN_i}(p_i^*, \mathbf{p}_{-i}^*) \geq U_{CDN_i}(p_i, \mathbf{p}_{-i}^*)$$

**Theorem 1.** *A Nash equilibrium price for the game $G1 = [\mathcal{N}, \{P_i, Q_i^s\}, \{U_{CDN_i}(.)\}]$ exists and is unique.*

*Proof.* To prove existence, we note that each CDN's strategy space $P_i$ is defined by all prices in the closed interval bounded by the minimum and maximum prices. Thus, the joint strategy space $P$ is a non empty, convex, and compact subset of the Euclidean space $\mathbb{R}^N$. In addition, the utility functions are concave with respect to prices as can be seen from the second derivative test:

$$\frac{\partial U_{CDN_i}(p_i, \mathbf{P}_{-i})}{\partial p_i} = D_{CDN_i} - M p_i \alpha_i^i - \sum_{j=1}^{M} f_{ij} p_j^c \alpha_i^i, \forall i \in \mathcal{N}$$

thus

$$\frac{\partial^2 U_{CDN_i}(p_i, \mathbf{P}_{-i})}{\partial p_i^2} = -2 M \alpha_i^i, \forall i \in \mathcal{N}$$

then

$$\frac{\partial^2 U_{CDN_i}(p_i, \mathbf{P}_{-i})}{\partial p_i^2} < 0, \forall i \in \mathcal{N}$$

which shows the existence of a Nash equilibrium price.

The most common method to show uniqueness is the following condition of Rosen [12]. Moulin [10], (see, for example, [9]):

we have

$$\frac{\partial^2 U_{CDN_i}(p_i, \mathbf{P}_{-i})}{\partial p_i^2} = -2 M \alpha_i^i, \forall i \in \mathcal{N}$$

and

$$\frac{\partial^2 U_{CDN_i}(p_i, \mathbf{P}_{-i})}{\partial p_i \partial p_n} = M \alpha_i^n, \forall i, n \in \mathcal{N} \text{ and } n \neq i$$

which means that:

$$\sum_{n, n \neq i} \left| \frac{\partial^2 U_{CDN_i}(p_i, \mathbf{P}_{-i})}{\partial p_i \partial p_n} \right| = M \sum_{n, n \neq i} \alpha_i^n, \forall i, n \in \mathcal{N} \text{ and } n \neq i$$

Using Assumption 1, we conclude that:

$$\frac{\partial^2 \Pi_i}{\partial p_i^2} + \sum_{n, n \neq i} \left| \frac{\partial^2 \Pi_i}{\partial p_i \partial p_n} \right| < 0.$$

Finally, the Nash Equilibrium price is unique and is given by:

$$p_i^* \in \operatorname*{argmax}_{p_i \in P_i} U_{CDN_i}(p_i, \mathbf{P}_{-i}), \forall i \in \mathcal{N}$$

## 3.2   Game with Fixed Price of CDN

**Definition 2.** *A price vector $q^{s*} = (q_1^{s*}, \ldots, q_N^{s*})$ is the Nash equilibrium QoS of the game $G1 = [\mathcal{N}, \{P_i, Q_i^s\}, \{U_{CDN_i}(.)\}]$ if:*

$$\forall (i, q_i^s) \in (\mathcal{N}, Q_i^s), U_{CDN_i}(q_i^{s*}, \mathbf{q_{-i}^{s}}^*) \geq U_{CDN_i}(q_i^s, \mathbf{q_{-i}^{s}}^*)$$

**Theorem 2.** *A Nash equilibrium QoS for the game $G1 = [\mathcal{N}, \{P_i, Q_i^s\}, \{U_{CDN_i}(.)\}]$ exists and is unique.*

*Proof.* To prove existence, we note that each CDN's strategy space $Q_i^s$ is defined by all prices in the closed interval bounded by the minimum and maximum QoS. Thus, the joint strategy space $Q^s$ is a non empty, convex, and compact subset of the Euclidean space $\mathbb{R}^N$. In addition, the utility functions are concave with respect to QoS as can be seen from the second derivative test:

$$\frac{\partial U_{CDN_i}(q_i^s, \mathbf{q}_{-i}^s)}{\partial q_i^s} = Mp_i\beta_i^i + \sum_{j=1}^{M} f_{ij} p_j^c \beta_i^i - 2\vartheta_i q_i^s, \forall i \in \mathcal{N}$$

thus

$$\frac{\partial^2 U_{CDN_i}(q_i^s, \mathbf{q}_{-i}^s)}{\partial (q_i^s)^2} = -2\vartheta_i, \forall i \in \mathcal{N}$$

then

$$\frac{\partial^2 U_{CDN_i}(q_i^s, \mathbf{q}_{-i}^s)}{\partial (q_i^s)^2} < 0, \forall i \in \mathcal{N}$$

which shows the existence of a Nash equilibrium QoS.

In order to prove uniqueness Nash equilibrium QoS and according to [12], in a concave game the Nash equilibrium exists if the joint strategy space is compact and convex, and the objective function that a player in the system seeks to maximize is concave in his own strategy and and continues at each point in the product strategy space. Formally, if the weighted sum of the utility works with non-negative weights:

$$\Psi = \sum_{i=1} x_i U_i, \ \forall i$$

is diagonally strictly concave, which implies that the Nash equilibrium point is unique. The notion of strict diagonal concavity means that an individual user has more control over its utility function than other users, and is proven using the pseudo-gradient of the weighted sum of utility functions.

For that we define the weighted sum of user utility functions to demonstrate the uniqueness of Nash equilibrium QoS, as follow:

$$\Psi(\mathbf{q^s}, \mathbf{x}) = \sum_{i=1}^{N} x_i U_{CDN_i}(q_i^s, \mathbf{q}_{-i}^s), \tag{10}$$

The pseudo-gradient of (10) is given by :

$$pg(\mathbf{q^s}, \mathbf{x}) = [x_1 \nabla U_{CDN_1}(q_1^s, q_{-1}^s), \ldots, x_N \nabla U_{CDN_N}(q_N^s, q_{-N}^s)]^T$$

The Jacobian matrix $\mathbf{J}_{pg}$ of the pseudo-gradient (with respect to $\mathbf{q}^s$) is written

$$
J_{pg} = \begin{pmatrix}
x_1 \dfrac{\partial^2 U_{CDN_1}(q_1^s,\mathbf{q}_{-1}^s)}{\partial (q_1^s)^2} & x_1 \dfrac{\partial^2 U_{CDN_1}(q_1^s,\mathbf{q}_{-1}^s)}{\partial q_1^s \partial q_2^s} & \cdots & x_1 \dfrac{\partial^2 U_{CDN_1}(q_1^s,\mathbf{q}_{-1}^s)}{\partial q_1^s \partial q_N^s} \\[2ex]
x_2 \dfrac{\partial^2 U_{CDN_2}(q_2^s,\mathbf{q}_{-2}^s)}{\partial q_2^s \partial q_1^s} & x_2 \dfrac{\partial^2 U_{CDN_2}(q_2^s,\mathbf{q}_{-2}^s)}{\partial (q_2^s)^2} & \cdots & x_2 \dfrac{\partial^2 U_{CDN_2}(q_2^s,\mathbf{q}_{-2}^s)}{\partial q_2^s \partial q_N^s} \\[2ex]
\vdots & \vdots & \ddots & \vdots \\[2ex]
x_N \dfrac{\partial^2 U_{CDN_N}(q_N^s,\mathbf{q}_{-N}^s)}{\partial q_N^s \partial q_1^s} & x_N \dfrac{\partial^2 U_{CDN_N}(q_N^s,\mathbf{q}_{-N}^s)}{\partial q_N^s \partial q_2^s} & \cdots & x_N \dfrac{\partial^2 U_{CDN_N}(q_N^s,\mathbf{q}_{-N}^s)}{\partial (q_N^s)^2}
\end{pmatrix}
$$

By calculating the different derivatives, we find that:

$$
J_{pg} = \begin{pmatrix}
-2x_1\vartheta_1 & 0 & \cdots & 0 \\
0 & -2x_2\vartheta_2 & \cdots & 0 \\
\vdots & \vdots & \ddots & \vdots \\
0 & 0 & \cdots & -2x_N\vartheta_N
\end{pmatrix}
$$

From this matrix we can conclude that $J_{pg}$ is a diagonal matrix with negative diagonal elements. This implies that $J_{pg}$ is negative definite. Henceforth $[J_{pg}+J_{pg}^T]$ is also negative definite, and according to Theorem (6) in, [12], the weighted sum of the utility functions $\Psi(\mathbf{q}^s,x)$ is diagonally strictly concave. Thus the fixed-price Nash equilibrium point

$$
q_i^{s*} \in \operatorname*{argmax}_{q_i^s \in Q_i^s} U_{CDN_i}(q_i^s,\mathbf{q}_{-i}^s), \forall i \in \mathcal{N}
$$

is unique.

### 3.3   Game with Fixed QoContent of CP

**Definition 3.** *A price vector $\mathbf{p}^{c*} = (p_1^{c*},\ldots,p_M^{c*})$ is the Nash equilibrium price of the game $G2 = [\mathcal{M}, \{P_j^c, Q_j^c\}, \{U_{CP_j}(.)\}]$ if:*

$$
\forall(j,p_j^c) \in (\mathcal{M}, P_j^c), U_{CP_j}(p_j^{c*},\mathbf{p}_{-j}^{c*}) \geq U_{CP_j}(p_j^c, \mathbf{p}_{-j}^{c*})
$$

**Theorem 3.** *A Nash equilibrium price for the game $G2 = [\mathcal{M}, \{P_j^c, Q_j^c\}, \{U_{CP_j}(.)\}]$ exists and is unique.*

*Proof.* To prove existence, we note that each CP's strategy space $P_j^c \in \mathbb{R}^M$ is defined by all prices in the closed interval bounded by the minimum and maximum prices of content and we proceed in the same way with what we did to demonstrate the existence and uniqueness of the price equilibrium for $CDNs$.

$$
\frac{\partial U_{CP_j}(p_j^c,\mathbf{p}_{-j}^c)}{\partial p_j^c} = D_{CP_j} - N\lambda_j^j p_j^c - \sum_{i=1}^{N}(-f_{ij}\lambda_j^j p_j^c + f_{ij}D_{ij}), \quad \forall j \in \mathcal{M}
$$

thus

$$
\frac{\partial^2 U_{CP_j}(p_j^c,\mathbf{p}_{-j}^c)}{\partial^2 p_j^c} = -2N\lambda_j^j + 2\lambda_j^j \sum_{i=1}^{N} f_{ij}, \quad \forall j \in \mathcal{M}
$$

then
$$\frac{\partial^2 U_{CP_j}(p_j^c, \mathbf{p}_{-j}^c)}{\partial^2 p_j^c} < 0, \quad \forall j \in \mathcal{M} \tag{11}$$

which shows the existence of a Nash equilibrium price.

Similarly, we have

$$\frac{\partial^2 U_{CP_j}(p_j^c, \mathbf{p}_{-j}^c)}{\partial^2 p_j^c} = -2N\lambda_j^j + 2\lambda_j^j \sum_{i=1}^{N} f_{ij}, \quad \forall j \in \mathcal{M}$$

and

$$\frac{\partial^2 U_{CP_j}(p_j^c, \mathbf{p}_{-j}^c)}{\partial p_j^c \partial p_m^c} = N\lambda_j^m - \lambda_j^m \sum_{i=1}^{N} f_{ij} > 0, \quad \forall j, m \in \mathcal{M} \text{ and } m \neq j$$

which means that:

$$\sum_{m,m\neq j} \left| \frac{\partial^2 U_{CP_j}(p_j^c, \mathbf{p}_{-j}^c)}{\partial p_j^c \partial p_m^c} \right| = N \sum_{m,m\neq j} \lambda_j^m - \sum_{m,m\neq j} \sum_{i=1}^{N} \lambda_j^m f_{ij}, \quad \forall j, m \in \mathcal{M} \text{ and } m \neq j$$

hence

$$\frac{\partial^2 U_{CP_j}(p_j^c, \mathbf{p}_{-j}^c)}{\partial^2 p_j^c} + \sum_{m,m\neq j} \left| \frac{\partial^2 U_{CP_j}(p_j^c, \mathbf{p}_{-j}^c)}{\partial p_j^c \partial p_m^c} \right| = -2N\lambda_j^j + 2\lambda_j^j \sum_{i=1}^{N} f_{ij} + N \sum_{m,m\neq j} \lambda_j^m$$

$$- \sum_{m,m\neq j} \sum_{i=1}^{N} \lambda_j^m f_{ij}, \quad \forall j, m \in \mathcal{M} \text{ and } m \neq j$$

Taking into consideration Assumption 2, we have:

$$\sum_{i=1}^{N} f_{ij} < 1 < N, \quad \forall j \in \mathcal{M}$$

then

$$\sum_{m,m\neq j} \sum_{i=1}^{N} \lambda_j^m f_{ij} < N \sum_{m,m\neq j} \lambda_j^m, \quad \forall j \in \mathcal{M}$$

$$\frac{\partial^2 U_{CP_j}(p_j^c, \mathbf{p}_{-j}^c)}{\partial^2 p_j^c} + \sum_{m,m\neq j} \left| \frac{\partial^2 U_{CP_j}(p_j^c, \mathbf{p}_{-j}^c)}{\partial p_j^c \partial p_m^c} \right| < -2N\lambda_j^j + 2\lambda_j^j \sum_{i=1}^{N} f_{ij}, \quad \forall j \in \mathcal{M}$$

From what we have already shown in the Eq. (11), we have:

$$\frac{\partial^2 U_{CP_j}(p_j^c, \mathbf{p}_{-j}^c)}{\partial^2 p_j^c} + \sum_{n,n\neq i} \left| \frac{\partial^2 U_{CP_j}(p_j^c, \mathbf{p}_{-j}^c)}{\partial p_j^c \partial p_m^c} \right| < 0.$$

Finally, the Nash Equilibrium price of $CP$ is unique and is given by:

$$p_j^{c^*} \in \operatorname*{argmax}_{p_j^c \in P_j^c} U_{CP_j}(p_j^c, \mathbf{p}_{-j}^c), \quad \forall j \in \mathcal{M}$$

### 3.4   Game with Fixed Content Price of CP

**Definition 4.** *A quality of content (QoContent) vector $\boldsymbol{q}^* = (q_1^{c*}, \ldots, q_M^{c*})$ is the Nash equilibrium QoContent of the game $G2 = [\mathcal{M}, \{P_j^c, Q_j^c\}, \{U_{CP_j}(.)\}]$ if:*

$$\forall (j, q_j^c) \in (\mathcal{M}, Q_j^c), U_{CP_j}(q_j^{c*}, \mathbf{q}_{-\mathbf{j}}^{\mathbf{c}*}) \geq U_{CP_j}(q_j^c, \mathbf{q}_{-\mathbf{j}}^{\mathbf{c}*})$$

**Theorem 4.** *A Nash equilibrium QoContent for the game $G2 = [\mathcal{N}, \{P_j^c, Q_j^c\}, \{U_{CP_j}(.)\}]$ exists and is unique.*

*Proof.* To prove existence, we note that each CP's strategy space $Q_j^c \in \mathbb{R}^M$ is defined by all quality of contents in the closed interval bounded by the minimum and maximum QoContents and we proceed in the same way with what we did to demonstrate the existence and uniqueness of the QoS equilibrium for $CDNs$ in previous section.

$$\frac{\partial U_{CP_j}(q_j^c, \mathbf{q}_{-j}^c)}{\partial q_j^c} = N p_j^c \gamma_j^j - \sum_{i=1}^{N} f_{ij} p_j^c \gamma_j^j - 2c_j q_j^c, \forall j \in \mathcal{M}$$

thus

$$\frac{\partial^2 U_{CP_j}(q_j^c, \mathbf{q}_{-j}^c)}{\partial^2 q_j^c} = -2c_j, \forall j \in \mathcal{M}$$

then

$$\frac{\partial^2 U_{CP_j}(q_j^c, \mathbf{q}_{-j}^c)}{\partial^2 q_j^c} < 0, \forall j \in \mathcal{M}$$

which shows the existence of a Nash equilibrium QoContent of the game.

We define the weighted sum of user utility functions to demonstrate the uniqueness of Nash equilibrium QoContent, as follow:

$$\Psi(\mathbf{q^c}, \mathbf{y}) = \sum_{j=1}^{M} y_j U_{CP_j}(q_j^c, \mathbf{q}_{-\mathbf{j}}^{\mathbf{c}}), \tag{12}$$

The pseudo-gradient of (12) is given by :

$$pg(\mathbf{q^c}, \mathbf{y}) = [y_1 \nabla U_{CP_1}(q_1^c, q_{-1}^c), \ldots, y_M \nabla U_{CP_M}(q_M^c, q_{-M}^c)]^T$$

The Jacobian matrix $\mathbf{J}_{pg}$ of the pseudo-gradient (with respect to $\mathbf{q}^c$) is:

$$\mathbf{J}_{pg} = \begin{pmatrix} -2y_1 c_1 & 0 & \cdots & 0 \\ 0 & -2y_2 c_2 & \cdots & 0 \\ \vdots & \vdots & \ddots & \vdots \\ 0 & 0 & \cdots & -2y_M c_M \end{pmatrix}$$

The elements of the diagonal of the matrix $J_{pg}$ are negative. This implies that $J_{pg}$ is negative definite. Henceforth $[J_{pg} + J_{pg}^T]$ is also negative definite, and according to Theorem (6) in, [12], the weighted sum of the utility functions

$\Psi(\mathbf{q}^c, y)$ is diagonally strictly concave. Thus the fixed-price of content Nash equilibrium point

$$q_j{}^{c*} \in \underset{q_j^c \in Q_j^c}{\operatorname{argmax}}\ U_{CP_j}(q_j^c, \mathbf{q}^c_{-j}), \forall j \in \mathcal{M}$$

is unique.

## 4   Learning Nash Equilibrium

### 4.1   Best Response Dynamic

The best response of a player is defined as his optimal strategy which makes him an optimal gain taking into account the strategies of adversaries. The best response dynamic of a player, as the name suggests, is to adapt his strategy with the recent strategies of others and without taking into account the effect of the current strategies of all players on the future game in the game.

---

**Algorithm 1.** Best Response Algorithm Dynamics

---

1: **Initialize** vectors $\mathbf{a} = [a_1, \ldots, a_n]$ to be an arbitrary action profile.
2: **While** There exists $i$ such that $a_i \notin \underset{a \in A_i}{\operatorname{argmax}}(U_i(a, \mathbf{a}_{-i}))$ **do**

   **Set** $a_i = \underset{a \in A_i}{\operatorname{argmax}}(U_i(a, \mathbf{a}_{-i}))$.

   **End While**
3: **Halt** and return $\mathbf{a}$.

---

Where $\mathbf{a}$ denotes the vector $\mathbf{p}$, $\mathbf{q^s}$, $\mathbf{p^c}$ and $\mathbf{q^c}$. $A_i$ denotes the policy profile price $P_i$, policy profile QoS $Q_i^s$, policy profile price of content $P_i^C$ and policy profile QoContent $Q_i^c$.

### 4.2   Price of Anarchy

The concept of the price of anarchy is a measure intruded by Koutsoupias and Papadimitriou [5] to quantify the ineffectiveness of the Nash equilibrium which is caused by the selfish behavior of actors in the system. This measure is defined as the worst-case ratio between the cost of a Nash equilibrium and the cost of an optimal system. The latter is defined as the maximum of the sum of the utilities of all the actors in the systems:

$$PoA = \frac{\min_{a_i, \mathbf{a}_{-i}} W_{NE}(a_i, \mathbf{a}_{-i})}{\max_{a_i, \mathbf{a}_{-i}} W(a_i, \mathbf{a}_{-i})} \tag{13}$$

where $W(a_i, \mathbf{a_{-i}}) = \sum\limits_{i=1}^{N} U_i(a_i, \mathbf{a_{-i}})$ is a function of welfare and $W_{NE}(a_i, \mathbf{a_{-i}}) = \sum\limits_{i=1}^{N} U_i(a_i^*, \mathbf{a_{-i}})$ is a sum of utilities of all actors in the Nash equilibrium.

## 5   Numerical Investigation

In this section, we present a numerical study of games taking into account the previous expressions of utilities. As an illustration, we consider two content providers $CP$s and two $CDN$ s providers.

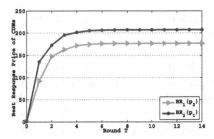

**Fig. 2.** Convergence to the Price Nash equilibrium for the game G1

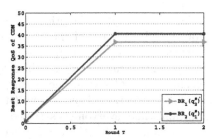

**Fig. 3.** Convergence to the QoS Nash equilibrium for the game G1

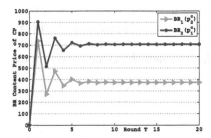

**Fig. 4.** Convergence to the Content Price Nash equilibrium for the game G2

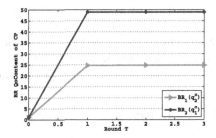

**Fig. 5.** Convergence to the QoContent Nash equilibrium for the game G2

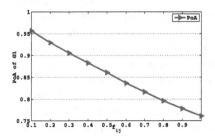

**Fig. 6.** Price of anarchy as a function of $f_{ij}$ in the game G1.

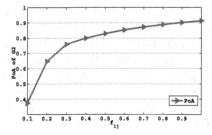

**Fig. 7.** Price of anarchy as a function of $f_{ij}$ in the game G2.

Figures 2, 3, 4 and 5 respectively represent the convergence towards the Nash equilibrium for the price, the QoS of the $CDN$s, the price and the quality of the contents of the $CP$s. The convergence to a Nash equilibrium is a situation in which all actors have a satisfaction and each one can not make such a decision all alone without taking into consideration what happens to his opponents. This strengthens what we found in the theoretical study presented in the previous sections.

Using the concept of the price of anarchy which is a measure to give information on the effectiveness of the Nash equilibrium, Fig. 6 represents the anarchy price evolution according to $f_{ij}$ parameter in the game $G1$; we notice that when $CDN$s providers take smaller values for $f_{ij}$, the price of anarchy tends to 1 which shows that $CDN$s are not selfish and each seeks to gain an optimal profit based on the situation of the system (strategies of others) to converge to a Nash equilibrium where everyone is satisfied in terms of gain. Whereas, for the higher choices of values of $f_{ij}$, the $CDN$s become selfish and each one tries to maximize its profit without taking into account the strategies of the adversaries. It is confused with the reality seen when $f_{ij}$ tends to 1, this means that the $CP$ will lose if it uses the $CDN$s for the distribution of its content. Which leads it to look for other solutions to do so. Therefore, the game of $CDN$s converge to situation of the monopoly where everyone tries to convince the $CP$ by using other motivating strategies. Conversely, Fig. 7 represents the curve of the price of anarchy in the game G2, we see that when $f_{ij}$ tends to 0, the game between the $CP$ s becomes monopoly and cons when $f_{ij}$ increases the game converges to the point that makes it socially optimal.

## 6   Conclusion

In this paper, we have modeled and analyzed the interactions that may exist between the main players in the Internet content distribution chain. This study of this ecosystem led us to design two non-cooperative games, one between the content providers and the other between the Internet content distribution network providers. After demonstrating the existence and uniqueness of Nash equilibrium for both games, we used the dynamic best response algorithm to learn Nash equilibrium, and thus we showed numerically the convergence towards this point of equilibrium. We have concluded that the marginalization of a common parameter such as $f_{ij}$ converges the game to a monopoly situation where everyone tries to maximize their profit without taking into account the decision-making strategies of their opponents. The bargaining tools will therefore be one of the solutions to fight against such aggressive behavior by one of the actors compared to others in telecommunication networks.

In future work, we also propose to study this system with a more complex topology by introducing other actors (users, mobile operators, ... ) in our study. Thus, we think to integrate the notion of bounded rationality [2] to know what is its implication for the studied system.

# References

1. Cisco Visual Networking Index: Forecast and Methodology, 20162021. Technical report (2017)
2. Ait Omar, D., Outanoute, M., Baslam, M., Fakir, M., Bouikhalne, B.: Joint price and QoS competition with bounded rational customers. In: El Abbadi, A., Garbinato, B. (eds.) NETYS 2017. LNCS, vol. 10299, pp. 457–471. Springer, Cham (2017). https://doi.org/10.1007/978-3-319-59647-1_33
3. Baslam, M., El-Azouzi, R., Sabir, E., Echabbi, L.: Market share game with adversarial access providers: a neutral and a non-neutral network analysis. In: 2011 5th International Conference on Network Games, Control and Optimization (NetG-CooP), pp. 1–6. IEEE (2011)
4. Gourdin, E., Maill, P., Simon, G., Tuffin, B.: The economics of CDNs and Their impact on service fairness. IEEE Trans. Netw. and Ser. Manag. **14**(1), 22–33 (2017). https://doi.org/10.1109/TNSM.2017.2649045
5. Koutsoupias, E., Papadimitriou, C.: Worst-case equilibria. Comput. Sci. Rev. **3**(2), 65–69 (2009)
6. Maille, P., Simon, G., Tuffin, B.: Toward a net neutrality debate that conforms to the 2010s. IEEE Commun. Mag. **54**(3), 94–99 (2016)
7. Maille, P., Simon, G., Tuffin, B.: Vertical integration of CDN and network operator: model and analysis, pp. 189–195. IEEE, Sepember 2016. https://doi.org/10.1109/MASCOTS.2016.24
8. Maillé, P., Tuffin, B.: How do content delivery networks affect the economy of the internet and the network neutrality debate? In: Altmann, J., Vanmechelen, K., Rana, O.F. (eds.) GECON 2014. LNCS, vol. 8914, pp. 222–230. Springer, Cham (2014). https://doi.org/10.1007/978-3-319-14609-6_15
9. Milgrom, P., Roberts, J.: Rationalizability, learning, and equilibrium in games with strategic complementarities. Econometrica **58**(6), 1255–1277 (1990)
10. Moulin, H.: On the uniqueness and stability of Nash equilibrium in non-cooperative games. In: Benoussan, A., Kleindorfer, P.R., Tapiero, C.S. (eds.) Applied Stochastic Control in Econometrics and Management Science, p. 271. North-Holland Publishing Company, Amsterdam (1980)
11. Pathan, A.M.K., Buyya, R.: A taxonomy and survey of content delivery networks. Technical Report 4, Grid Computing and Distributed Systems Laboratory, University of Melbourne (2007)
12. Rosen, J.B.: Existence and uniqueness of equilibrium points for concave N-person games. Econometrica **33**(3), 520–534 (1965). https://doi.org/10.2307/1911749
13. Sahoo, J., Salahuddin, M., Glitho, R., Elbiaze, H., Ajib, W.: A survey on replica server placement algorithms for content delivery networks. IEEE Commun. Surv. Tutor. **19**, 1002–1026 (2016)
14. Stamos, K., Pallis, G., Vakali, A., Dikaiakos, M.D.: Evaluating the utility of content delivery networks. In: Proceedings of the 4th Edition of the UPGRADE-CN Workshop on Use of P2P, GRID and Agents for the Development of Content Networks, pp. 11–20. ACM (2009)
15. Stocker, V., Smaragdakis, G., Lehr, W., Bauer, S.: The growing complexity of content delivery networks: challenges and implications for the Internet ecosystem. Telecommun. Policy **41**(10), 1003–1016 (2017). https://doi.org/10.1016/j.telpol.2017.02.004
16. Tuffin, B.: Network neutrality: modeling and challenges and its impact on clouds. In: Pham, C., Altmann, J., Bañares, J.Á. (eds.) GECON 2017. LNCS, vol. 10537, pp. 277–280. Springer, Cham (2017). https://doi.org/10.1007/978-3-319-68066-8_21

# New Competition-Based Approach for Caching Popular Content in ICN

Hamid Garmani[1]([⊠]) [ID], M'hamed Outanoute[2], Mohamed Baslam[1], and Mostafa Jourhmane[1]

[1] Information Processing and Decision Support Laboratory,
Faculty of Sciences and Technics, Sultan Moulay Slimane University,
Beni Mellal, Morocco
garmani.hamid@gmail.com,baslam.med@gmail.com,jourhman@hotmail.com
[2] Interdisciplinary Laboratory of Research in Sciences and Technologies,
Faculty of Sciences and Technics, Sultan Moulay Slimane University,
Beni Mellal, Morocco
mhamed.outanoute@gmail.com

**Abstract.** Improving the performance of the Internet, as part of the new generations networks, requires support for caching and multicast content delivery on each network cable. This new concept is called Information Centric Networking (ICN). In present paper, we consider a duopoly model of rational internet Service providers competing in ICN model where each ISP is motivated to cache content. Using a generalized Zipf distribution to model content popularity, we devise a game theoretic approach to determine caching and pricing strategies for each ISP. In turn, the subscribers' demand for the service of an ISP depends not only on the price and QoS of that ISP but also upon those proposed by all of its competitors. Through rigorous mathematical analysis, we prove existence and uniqueness of the Nash equilibrium. An iterative and distributed algorithm based on best response dynamics are proposed to achieve the equilibrium point. Finally, extensive simulations show convergence of a proposed scheme to the Nash equilibrium and give some insights on how the game parameters may vary the price and QoS at Nash equilibrium.

**Keywords:** Information centric networking (ICN) · ISP · Pricing
QoS · Cache · Game theory · Nash equilibrium

## 1 Introduction

Internet traffic is rapidly increasing, due to the proliferation of video sites like YouTube, Dailymotion, etc. This high increase in demand for content on the internet and the need of new approaches that controls the large volume of information have motivated the development of new approach called Information Centric Network ICN. This last (ICN) is a new communication paradigm aims

© Springer Nature Switzerland AG 2019
A. Podelski and F. Taïani (Eds.): NETYS 2018, LNCS 11028, pp. 286–300, 2019.
https://doi.org/10.1007/978-3-030-05529-5_19

to reflect current and future needs better than the existing Internet architecture. By naming information at the network layer, ICN favors the deployment of in-network caching and multicast mechanisms, thus facilitating the efficient and timely delivery of information to the users. The main idea in ICN: content is located by name instead of by location and every node can cache and serve the content, which means that users do not care where the content comes from, but are only interested in what the content is. The advantages motivating the ICN approach Scalable, Persistent, Security, Mobility, etc [2]. To fulfill that purpose, several architectures have been proposed for ICN: CCN [14], DONA [17], PSIRP [15], 4WardNetInf [1], XIA [13].

Several works have been done to address the problem of the economic implications of caching [9,11,12,16,19]. However, there has been little discussion about ISP caching with regard to the competition between the ISPs and CPs in ICN. A pricing model proposed in [20] to study the economic incentive for caching and sharing content in ICN, where ICN consists of access ICN, transit ICN and CP. Therefore, a unique Nash Equilibrium (NE) exists in a non-cooperative pricing caching game. The result of this work shows the case where caching investment is profitable for access ISP. In [16] the authors considered a non-cooperative game between CP and ISP in ICN, where CP and ISP playing with their pricing strategies and fixing the caching strategies. Depending on the caching cost, the ISP may be incentivized to cache content in ICN. The authors in [11] analyzed the impact of caching cost in joint caching and pricing strategies in ICN with one CP, tow access ICN, one transit ICN. Competition between entities modeled as a non-cooperative game and observes that caching strategy depending on the caching cost and price at the transit ICN. In [12] the authors developed game theoretic models to evaluate joint caching and pricing strategies among access networks, transit networks and content providers in an ICN with the notion of content popularity. In [19] the authors studied a non-cooperative game between one CP and one ISP in ICN, where ISP cache content. It shows that caching investment is beneficial for ISP and CP. The authors in [9] modeled the caching game between CP and ISP as a cooperative game, where ISP cache a fraction of content. Then, CP and ISP share both the cost of caching and profit of caching. Also, a competition between CPs modeled as a non-cooperative game to capture the negative impact on demand when the ISP cache content of other CPs.

In this paper, we investigate caching, pricing and QoS strategies of the ISPs based on content popularity. We study Nash strategies for a non-cooperative game among the above entities using a probabilistic model by assuming that users' requests generally follow the generalized Zipf distribution. We analytically prove the existence and uniqueness of Nash equilibrium in non-cooperative game between ISPs, which means that there exists a stable state where all ISPs do not have an incentive to change their strategies. So, our model provides economic incentives for caching content, and ensures the existence of an equilibrium for keeping the economy stable and achieving economic growth. We complement our analysis with numerical results show that both the ISPs and end-users can receive benefit from caching investment.

The remainder of the paper is organized as follows: In Sect. 2 we describe the system model and we introduce a new demand and utility functions. In Sect. 3 we formulate a non-cooperative game, and we proof the existence and uniqueness of Nash equilibrium solution. Section 4 presents numerical results, and we conclude in Sect. 5.

## 2   Problem Modeling

We consider a simplified networking market with one CP, two ISP and large number of users is considered. All end users can access the contents of the CP only through the network infrastructure provided by the ISP while CP provides the content for the users. Figure 1 shows the monetary flow among different entities with various prices. The network economy depends on three effective factors pricing, caching and quality of service QoS. Under the assumption that each ISP can have access to all content, it can decide to either cache the entire or portion of the requested content. Let H, the number of items that the CP sells. The caching strategy adopted by each ISP is denoted by $k_{jh}$ that take value 1 if the $ISP_j$ decide to cache item $h$ and take value 0 if the $ISP_j$ decide to not cache item $h$. Each $ISP_j$ sets two different prices: (1) the network price per unit data $p_{s_j}$ for transporting the content to end users; and (2) the price per unit data $p_j$ for providing content from its cache. Each $ISP_j$ allocates a Bandwidth $B_j$ and advertises to users a quality of service QoS $q_{s_j}$. To model the behavior of users, we have considered content demand at each ISPs to be a linear function of the strategies of all ISPs.

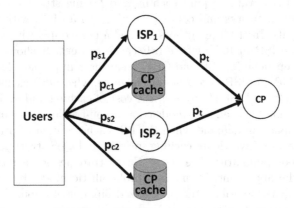

**Fig. 1.** ICN architecture.

### 2.1   Content Popularity

Let $H$ the number of items that any of the users under consideration might want to access it, each item has a measure of popularity reflected by the probability of requests for it. We consider a model where the popularity of content is the same for all users. As in previous works (e.g., [8,10,22]), in this paper the probability of requests follows generalized Zipf distribution function as:

$$\phi_h = A^{-1}h^{-\eta} \tag{1}$$

Where $A = \sum_{h=1}^{H} h^{-\eta}$, $h^\eta$ the rank of item h, $\eta$ is a fixed parameter determines the skewness of the popularity distribution. If $\eta = 0$ the distribution is uniform and all item have the same popularity, while in the case of high value of $\eta$, there are only a few popular item, while the other have very low probability to be requested, whereas the case of $\eta = 1$ the content popularity distribution following classic Zipf law. The item ranked in order of their popularity where item h is the h most popular item, i.e: $h = 1$ is the most popular item, $h = H$ is the least popular item.

## 2.2   Caching Cost

We present an explicit formula of the caching cost $c_{jh}$ of item h as a function of the content popularity that has been proposed in [12]; the authors assume that: for a finite cache, the caching costs of item h by $ISP_j$ is defined to be inversely proportional to the content popularity as follows:

$$c_{jh} = \frac{C_j}{\phi_h} \tag{2}$$

where, $C_j$ is a fixed initial caching cost at $ISP_j$.

## 2.3   Demand Model

The demand of $ISP_j$ is linear function with respect to the network access price $p_{s_j}$, price to access to the content in cache $p_{c_j}$ and quality of service QoS $q_{s_j}$, see [5–7]. This demand depends also on the price $p_{s_{-j}}$, price $p_{c_{-j}}$, quality of service QoS $q_{s_{-j}}$. set by the competitors. Namely, the demand function of $ISP_j$ depends on $p_s = [p_{s_1}, p_{s_2}]$, $p_c = [p_{c_1}, p_{c_2}]$ and $q_s = [q_{s_1}, q_{s_2}]$. The demand function of $ISP_j$ can be write as follows:

$$D_j(\mathbf{p_s}, \mathbf{q_s}, \mathbf{p_c}) = \max\left\{0, \ d_j - \alpha_j^j p_{s_j} + \beta_j^j q_{s_j} - \gamma_j^j p_{c_j} + \alpha_j^i p_{s_i} - \beta_j^i q_{s_i} + \gamma_j^i p_{c_i}\right\}, \ j \neq i. \tag{3}$$

The parameter $d_j$ reflects the total potential demand of users. $\alpha_j^m$, $\beta_j^i$ and $\gamma_j^i$ denote the responsiveness of demand the $ISP_j$ to price $p_{s_i}$, QoS $q_{s_i}$ and price $p_{c_i}$ (note that in economics, we also call the parameter $\alpha_j^m$ as price elasticity of demand or price sensitivity of demand). The meaning of Eq. 3 can be interpreted as this way: $D_j$ decreasing w.r.t $p_{s_j}$, $p_{c_j}$ and increasing w.r.t $p_{s_i}$, $p_{c_i}$. $D_j$ increasing w.r.t $q_{s_j}$ and decreasing w.r.t $q_{s_i}$.

$$\sum_{i=1}^{2} \alpha_j^i = 1, \ \sum_{i=1}^{2} \beta_j^i = 1, \ \sum_{i=1}^{2} \gamma_j^i = 1, \ \sum_{i=1}^{2} \sigma_j^i = 1, \ j = 1, 2.$$

*Assumption 1.* The sensitivity mutual $\alpha$ satisfy:

$$\alpha_j^j \geq \alpha_j^i, \quad \forall j \neq i \in \{1, 2\} \tag{4}$$

The sensitivity mutual sensitivity $\beta$ satisfy:

$$\beta_j^j \geq \beta_j^i, \quad \forall j \neq i \in \{1, 2\} \tag{5}$$

The sensitivity mutual sensitivity $\sigma$ satisfy

$$\sigma_j^j \geq \sigma_j^i, \quad \forall j \neq i \in \{1, 2\} \tag{6}$$

Assumption 1 will be needed to ensure the uniqueness of the resulting equilibrium. The Assumption 1 means that the influence of price (resp Qos) the ISP on its demand is greater than the influence of the prices (resp Qos) of its opponents on its demand.

## 2.4   Utility Model

Each ISP can cache the content or just forward the request to CP based on the utility that it gain. The utility function of each ISP is defined as the utility received by providing the network or content for users. Therefore, the utility function of each ISP is the difference between the total revenue and the fee:

$$U_j = \sum_{h=1}^{H} \phi_h \left\{ (p_{s_j} - p_t) D_j(\mathbf{p}_s, \mathbf{q}_s, \mathbf{p}_c)(1 - k_{jh}) + (p_{s_j} + p_{c_j} - c_j) k_{jh} D_j(\mathbf{p}_s, \mathbf{q}_s, \mathbf{p}_c) \right\}$$

$$- v_j (H - \sum_{h=1}^{H} k_{jh}) B_j \tag{7}$$

Where $p_{s_j}$ denote the price that $ISP_j$ charges users for access to network. $p_{c_j}$ the price that users pay the $ISP_j$ for access to content of their cache. $q_{s_j}$ the QoS guaranteed by $ISP_j$. $p_t$ is the price that the ISP pays the CP when requesting content from it (transmission fee or side payment), because the polarity of the side-payment (from the ISP to the CP) in an ICN is basically different from that in the current Internet model (i.e. host-centric communication model). $c_{jh}$ the caching costs of item $h$. $c_{jh} k_{jh} \phi_h D_j$ the fee of $ISP_j$ by serving the requested demand $k_{jh} \phi_h D_j$ of item $h$ from its cache. $(p_{s_j} + p_{c_j} - c_{jh}) \phi_h k_j D_j$ is the revenue of the $ISP_j$ by serving the requested demand $\phi_h k_{jh} D_j$ of item $h$ from its cache. The revenue of the $ISP_j$ is $(p_{s_j} - p_t) \phi_h D_j(1 - k_{jh})$ when the $ISP_j$ fulfils an amount of content request $\phi_h D_j(1 - k_j)$ of item $h$ by retrieving content from the CP. $v_j$ unit backhaul bandwidth cost. $B_j$ Backhaul bandwidth needed to serve the demand $D_j$. $B_j$ is the backhaul bandwidth required by the ISP. It is increasing function w.r.t $D_j$ and QoS $q_{s_j}$ because a larger demand or higher QoS usually require a larger backhaul bandwidth. The quality of service $q_{s_j}$ can be defined by various metrics such as latency, jitter, or bandwidth. Latency is a measure of the delay that the traffic experiences as it traverses a network, and jitter is defined as the variation in that delay. Bandwidth is measured as the amount of data that can pass through a point in a network over time. Here, we define the QoS as the "expected delay". The expected delay is computed by the Kleinrock function that corresponds to the delay of M/M/1 queue with FIFO discipline or M/G/1 queue under processor sharing [4]. Similar to [4], instead of using the actual delay, we consider the reciprocal of its square root.

$$q_{s_j} = \frac{1}{\sqrt{Delay}} = \sqrt{B_j(D_j, q_{s_j}) - D_j(\mathbf{p}_s, \mathbf{q}_s, \mathbf{p}_c)} \tag{8}$$

it means that:

$$B_j = q_{s_j}^2 + D_j(\mathbf{p}_s, \mathbf{q}_s, \mathbf{p}_c) \tag{9}$$

Then, the utility function of the $ISP_j$ given by the following formula:

$$U_j = \sum_{h=1}^{H} \phi_h \left\{ (p_{s_j} - p_t)D_j(\mathbf{p}_s, \mathbf{q}_s, \mathbf{p}_c)(1 - k_{jh}) + (p_{s_j} + p_{c_j} - c_j)k_{jh}D_j(\mathbf{p}_s, \mathbf{q}_s, \mathbf{p}_c) \right\}$$

$$- v_j(H - \sum_{h=1}^{H} k_{jh})(q_{s_j}^2 + D_j(\mathbf{p}_s, \mathbf{q}_s, \mathbf{p}_c) \tag{10}$$

The $ISP_j$ cache item $h$ under the condition defined as follow:

$$k_{jh} = \begin{cases} 1 & \text{if } \phi_h(p_{c_j} - c_j)D_j \geqslant -\phi_h p_t D_j - v_j B_j \\ 0 & \text{otherwise} \end{cases} \tag{11}$$

where $\phi_h(p_{c_j} - c_j)D_j$ is the revenue of $ISP_j$ by serving requested demand $\phi_h D_j$ of item $h$ from the $ISP_j$ cache. $(-\phi_h p_t D_j - v_j B_j)$ is the cost when $ISP_j$ forwards the requested demand of item $h$ to the CP. $k_{jh} = 1$ means that $ISP_j$ decides to caches item $h$, because the revenue of $ISP_j$ by serving the requested demand of item $h$ from the ISP cache is larger than cost of forwards the request demand of item $h$ to the CP. $k_{jh} = 0$ means that $ISP$ not cache item $h$.

## 3    A Non-cooperative Game Formulation

For a precise formulation of a non-cooperative game, we have to specify (i) the number of players, (ii) the possible actions available to each player, and any constraints that may be imposed on them, (iii) the objective function of each player which she attempts to optimize. Here we will consider formulation of games where items (i)–(iii) above are relevant.

Let $G = [\mathscr{M}, \{P_{s_j}, Q_{s_j}, P_{c_j}\}, \{U_i(.)\}]$ denote the non-cooperative price QoS price game (NPQPG), where $\mathscr{M} = \{1,2\}$ is the index set identifying the ISPs. $P_{s_j}$ is the network access price strategy set of $ISP_j$, $Q_{s_j}$ is the QoS strategy set of $ISP_j$, $P_{c_j}$ is the content access price strategy set of $ISP_j$. $U_j(.)$ is the utility function of $ISP_j$ defined in 10. We assume that the strategy spaces $P_{s_j}$, $Q_{s_j}$,

$P_{c_i}$ of each $ISP_j$ are compact and convex sets with maximum and minimum constraints. Thus, for each $ISP_j$ we consider as respective strategy spaces the closed intervals: $P_{s_j} = \left[ \underline{p}_{s_j}, \overline{p}_{s_j} \right]$, $Q_{s_j} = \left[ \underline{q}_{s_j}, \overline{q}_{s_j} \right]$ and $P_{c_j} = \left[ \underline{p}_{c_j}, \overline{p}_{c_j} \right]$. Let the price vector $\mathbf{p}_s = (p_{s_1}, p_{s_2})^T \in P_s = P_{s_1} \times P_{s_2}$, QoS vector $\mathbf{q}_s = (q_{s_1}, q_{s_2})^T \in Q_s = Q_{s_1} \times Q_{s_2}$, price vector $\mathbf{p}_c = (p_{c_1}, p_{c_2})^T \in P_c = P_{c_1} \times P_{c_2}$. (where T represents the transpose operator).

In order to maximize their utilities, each $ISP_j$ decides a price $p_{s_j}$, QoS $q_{s_j}$, price $p_{c_j}$. Formally, the NPQCG problem can be expressed as:

$$\max_{p_{s_j} \in P_{s_j}, q_{s_j} \in Q_{s_j}, p_{c_j} \in P_{c_j}} U_j(\mathbf{p}_s, \mathbf{q}_s, \mathbf{p}_c), \quad \forall j \in \mathcal{M}. \tag{12}$$

### 3.1   The Nash Equilibrium

Nash Equilibrium (NE) is the most well-known solution to the non-cooperative games. Nash equilibrium is a fixed point of a non-cooperative game where no player can increase the value of its utility function through individual action.

According to, [21], a Nash equilibrium exists in a concave game if the joint strategy space is compact and convex, and the utility function that any given player seeks to maximize is concave in its own strategy and continuous at every point in the product strategy space. Formally, if the weighted sum of the utility functions with nonnegative weights:

$$\psi = \sum_{j=1} x_j U_j, \quad x_j > 0 \ \forall j. \tag{13}$$

is diagonally strictly concave, this implies that the Nash equilibrium point is unique. Also, according to, [18] a Nash equilibrium is unique in a concave game, if the game satisfies the dominance solvability condition.

**Joint price $P_s$ Game.** A NPQPG in network access price is defined for fixed $\mathbf{q}_s \in Q_s$, $\mathbf{p}_c \in P_C$ as $G(\mathbf{q}_s, \mathbf{p}_c) = [\mathcal{M}, \{P_{s_j}\}, \{U_j(., \mathbf{q}_s, \mathbf{p}_c)\}]$.

**Definition 1.** *A price vector $\mathbf{p}_s^* = (p_{s_1}^*, p_{s_2}^*)$ is a Nash equilibrium of the NPQPG $G(\mathbf{q}_s, \mathbf{p}_c)$ if for every $j \in \mathcal{M}$, $U_j(p_{s_j}^*, p_{s_i}^*, \mathbf{q}_s, \mathbf{p}_c) \geq U_j(p_{s_j}, p_{s_i}^*, \mathbf{q}_s, \mathbf{p}_c)$ for all $p_{s_j} \in P_{s_j}$.*

**Theorem 1.** *For each $\mathbf{q}_s \in Q_s$, $\mathbf{p}_c \in P_c$, the game $[\mathcal{M}, \{P_{s_j}\}, \{U_j(., \mathbf{q}_s, \mathbf{p}_c)\}]$ admits a unique Nash equilibrium.*

*Proof.* To prove existence, we note that each ISPs strategy space $P_{s_j}$ is defined by all prices in the closed interval bounded by the minimum and maximum prices. Thus, the joint strategy space $P_s$ a nonempty, convex, and compact subset of the Euclidean space $R^N$. In addition, the utility functions are concave with respect to prices as can be seen from the second derivative test:

$$\frac{\partial U_j}{\partial p_{s_j}} = \sum_{h=1}^{H} \phi_h \{(D_j(\mathbf{p}_s, \mathbf{p}_c, \mathbf{q}_s) - \alpha_j^j(p_{s_j} - p_t))(1 - k_{jh}) + D_j(\mathbf{p}_s, \mathbf{p}_c, \mathbf{q}_s)k_{jh}$$

$$- \alpha_i^i(p_{s_j} + p_{c_j} - c_j)k_{jh}\} + v_j(H - \sum_{h=1}^{H} k_{jh})\alpha_j^j$$

then,

$$\frac{\partial^2 U_j}{\partial p_{s_j}^2} = -2\alpha_j^j \leq 0$$

which ensures existence of a Nash equilibrium.

We use the following proposition that holds for a concave game [18]: If a concave game satisfies the dominance solvability condition:

$$-\frac{\partial^2 U_j}{\partial p_{s_j}^2} \geq \sum_{i=1, i \neq j}^{M} \left| \frac{\partial^2 U_j}{\partial p_{s_j} \partial p_{s_i}} \right|$$

then the game G admits a unique NE.

in duopoly model:

$$\sum_{i=1, i \neq j}^{M} \left| \frac{\partial^2 U_j}{\partial p_{s_j} \partial p_{s_i}} \right| = \left| \frac{\partial^2 U_j}{\partial p_{s_j} \partial p_{s_i}} \right|$$

The mixed partial is written as:

$$\frac{\partial^2 U_j}{\partial p_{s_j} \partial p_{s_i}} = \alpha_j^i$$

Then,

$$-\frac{\partial^2 U_j}{\partial p_{s_j}^2} - \left| \frac{\partial^2 U_j}{\partial p_{s_j} \partial p_{s_i}} \right| = \left(2\alpha_j^j - \alpha_j^i\right) \geq 0$$

Thus, the Nash equilibrium point is unique.    □

**Joint price $P_c$ Game.** A NPQPG in content access price is defined for fixed $\mathbf{p}_s \in P_s$, $\mathbf{q}_s \in Q_s$ as $G(\mathbf{p}_s, \mathbf{q}_s) = [\mathcal{M}, \{P_{c_j}\}, \{U_j(\mathbf{p}_s, \mathbf{q}_s, .)\}]$.

**Definition 2.** *A price vector $\mathbf{p}_c^* = (p_{c_1}^*, p_{c_2}^*)$ is a Nash equilibrium of the NPQPG $G(\mathbf{p}_s, \mathbf{q}_s)$ if for every $j \in \mathcal{M}$, $U_j(\mathbf{p}_s, \mathbf{q}_s, p_{c_j}^*, p_{c_i}^*) \geq U_j(\mathbf{p}_s, \mathbf{q}_s, p_{c_j}, p_{c_i}^*)$ for all $p_{c_j} \in P_{c_j}$.*

**Theorem 2.** *For each $\mathbf{p}_s \in P_s$, $\mathbf{q}_s \in Q_s$, the game $[\mathcal{M}, \{P_{c_j}\}, \{U_j(\mathbf{p}_s, \mathbf{q}_s, .)\}]$ admits a unique Nash equilibrium.*

*Proof.* To prove existence, we note that each ISPs strategy space $P_{c_j}$ is defined by all prices in the closed interval bounded by the minimum and maximum prices. Thus, the joint strategy space $P_c$ a nonempty, convex, and compact subset of the Euclidean space $R^N$. In addition, the utility functions are concave with respect to prices as can be seen from the second derivative test:

$$\frac{\partial U_j}{\partial p_{c_j}} = \sum_{h=1}^{H} \phi_h \left\{ -\gamma_j^j(p_{s_j} - p_t)(1 - k_{jh}) + D_j(\mathbf{p}_s, \mathbf{p}_c, \mathbf{q}_s)k_{jh} - \gamma_j^j(p_{s_j} + p_{c_j} - c_j)k_{jh} \right\}$$

$$+ v_j(H - \sum_{h=1}^{H} k_{jh})\gamma_j^j$$

then,

$$\frac{\partial^2 U_j}{\partial p_{c_j}^2} = -2\gamma_j^j \sum_{h=1}^{H} \phi_h k_{jh} \leq 0$$

which ensures existence of a Nash equilibrium.

We use the following proposition that holds for a concave game [18]: If a concave game satisfies the dominance solvability condition:

$$-\frac{\partial^2 U_j}{\partial p_{c_j}^2} \geq \left| \frac{\partial^2 U_j}{\partial p_{c_j} \partial p_{c_i}} \right|$$

then the game G admits a unique NE.

The mixed partial is written as:

$$\frac{\partial^2 U_j}{\partial p_{c_j} \partial p_{c_i}} = \gamma_j^i \sum_{h=1}^{H} \phi_h k_{jh}$$

Then,

$$-\frac{\partial^2 U_j}{\partial p_{c_j}^2} - \left| \frac{\partial^2 U_j}{\partial p_{c_j} \partial p_{c_i}} \right| = \left( 2\gamma_j^j - \gamma_j^i \right) \sum_{h=1}^{H} \phi_h k_{jh} \geq 0$$

thus, the Nash equilibrium point is unique.                                □

**Joint QoS Game.** A NPQPG in QoS is defined for fixed $\mathbf{p}_s \in P_s$, $\mathbf{p}_c \in P_c$ as $G(\mathbf{p}_s, \mathbf{p}_c) = [\mathcal{M}, \{Q_{s_j}\}, \{U_j(\mathbf{p}_s, ., \mathbf{p}_c)\}]$.

**Definition 3.** *A QoS vector $\mathbf{q}_s^* = (q_{s_1}^*, q_{s_2}^*)$ is a Nash equilibrium of the NPQPG $G(\mathbf{p}_s, \mathbf{p}_c)$ if for every $j \in \mathcal{M}$, $U_j(\mathbf{p}_s, q_{s_j}^*, q_{s_i}^*, \mathbf{p}_c) \geq U_j(\mathbf{p}_s, q_{s_j}, q_{s_i}^*, \mathbf{p}_c)$ for all $q_{s_j} \in Q_{s_j}$.*

**Theorem 3.** *For each $\mathbf{p}_s \in P_s$, $\mathbf{p}_c \in P_c$, the game $[\mathcal{M}, \{Q_{s_j}\}, \{U_j(\mathbf{p}_s, ., \mathbf{p}_c)\}]$ admits a unique Nash equilibrium.*

*Proof.* To prove existence, we note that each ISPs strategy space $Q_{s_j}$ is defined by all QoSs in the closed interval bounded by the minimum and maximum QoSs. Thus, the joint strategy space $Q_s$ a nonempty, convex, and compact subset of the Euclidean space $R^M$. In addition, the utility functions are concave with respect to QoSs as can be seen from the second derivative test:

$$\frac{\partial U_j}{\partial q_{s_j}} = \sum_{h=1}^{H} \phi_h \left\{ \beta_j^j (p_{s_j} - p_t)(1 - k_{jh}) + \beta_i^i (p_{s_j} + p_{c_j} - c_j) k_{jh} \right\}$$

$$+ v_j (H - \sum_{h=1}^{H} k_{jh})(\beta_j^j - 2q_{s_j})$$

then,

$$\frac{\partial^2 U_j}{\partial q_{s_j}^2} = -2v_j(H - \sum_{h=1}^{H} k_{jh}) \leq 0$$

which ensures existence of a Nash equilibrium.
In order to prove uniqueness, we follow, [21], and define the weighted sum of user utility functions.

$$\psi(\mathbf{q}_s, \mathbf{x}) = \sum_{j=1}^{2} x_j U_j(q_{s_j}, \mathbf{q}_{s-j}) \tag{14}$$

The pseudo-gradient of 14 is given by:

$$v(\mathbf{q}_s, x) = [x_1 \nabla U_1(q_{s_1}, q_{s_2}), x_2 \nabla U_2(q_{s_2}, q_{s_1})]^T \tag{15}$$

The Jacobian matrix J of the pseudo-gradient (w.r.t.q) is written:

$$J = \begin{pmatrix} x_1 \frac{\partial^2 U_1}{\partial q_{s_1}^2} & x_1 \frac{\partial^2 U_1}{\partial q_{s_1} \partial q_{s_2}} \\ x_2 \frac{\partial^2 U_2}{\partial q_{s_2} \partial q_{s_1}} & x_2 \frac{\partial^2 U_2}{\partial p_{q_2}^2} \end{pmatrix}$$

$$= \begin{pmatrix} -2x_1 v_1 (H - \sum_{h=1}^{H} k_{1h}) & 0 \\ 0 & -2x_2 v_2 (H - \sum_{h=1}^{H} k_{2h}) \end{pmatrix}$$

Thus, J is a diagonal matrix with negative diagonal elements. This implies that J is negative definite. Henceforth $[J+J^T]$ is also negative definite, and according to Theorem (6) in, [21], the weighted sum of the utility functions $\psi(q_s, x)$ is diagonally strictly concave. Thus, the Nash equilibrium point is unique.    □

**Learning Nash Equilibrium.** The section mentioned above show clearly that the Nash equilibrium is unique. Now, we turn to develop a fully algorithms that converge quickly to Nash equilibrium. However, we assume that each ISP has a perfect information on strategies of its competitors. Each ISP fixes its desirable strategies in order to maximize its own profit. Then, each ISP can observe the policy taken by its competitors in previous rounds and input them in its decision process to update its policy. Therefore, the best response algorithm will converge a to unique equilibrium. The best response algorithm is summarized in Algorithm 1.

---

**Algorithm 1.** Best response Algorithm

---

1: Initialize vectors $x(0) = [x_1(0), ..., x_M(0)]$ randomly;
2: Each $ISP_j$ $j \in \mathcal{M}$ at time instant $t$ computes:

    a) $x_j(t+1) = \underset{x_j \in X_j}{\operatorname{argmax}} (U_j(x(t)))$.

3: If $ISP_j$ $|x_j(t+1) - x_j(t)| < \epsilon$, then STOP.
4: Else, make t=t+1 and go to step (2)

---

Where x denotes the vector $p_s$, vector $q_s$, vector $p_c$. $X_j$ denotes the policy profile price $P_{s_j}$, policy profile QoS $Q_{s_j}$, policy profile price $P_{c_j}$.

## 4    Numerical Investigations

So far, we have complete all theoretical analyses and in this section, we propose to numerically study the gaming market taking account of previous expression of utility of the ISPs. For illustrative purpose, we consider two homogeneous ISPs seeking to maximize their earnings.

The Figs. 2, 3, 4 present respectively curves of the convergence to Nash equilibrium prices and QoS. It is clear that the best response algorithm converges to the unique Nash equilibrium prices and QoS. We also remark that the speed of convergence is relatively high, so in this simulation Algorithm 1 is capable of efficiently converging to Nash equilibrium prices and QoS.

Figure 5 shows price $p_c$ as function of $\eta$. $p_c$ decrease as $\eta$ gets higher. The reason is that as $\eta$ increase, the caching cost of more popular content at ISP cache getting lower. Then, each ISP is incentive to cache popular content. In fact, when the amount of content requested from ISP cache Increase, then the transmission fee decrease and the cost bandwidth decrease, this introduces the increase in the ISPs's revenues. As a result, the ISPs decreases the price $p_c$ to further incentivize greater user demand for popular content.

In Fig. 6 we plot price $p_s$ as a function of cost $C$. Price $p_s$ increase with respect to cost $C$. When $C$ increase, the caching cost of ISPs is getting higher and they do not have an incentive to cache content. Therefore, at this point, the CP start to serve more content then before and the ISPs forwards requests to the CP, which increase the transmission fee and cost of bandwidth. Thus, the ISPs needs to slightly increase its price $p_s$ to compensate the increase in transmission fee and cost of bandwidth.

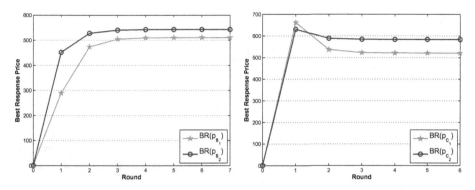

**Fig. 2.** Price $p_s$ game: convergence to the $p_s$ at Nash equilibrium.

**Fig. 3.** Price $p_c$ game: convergence to the $p_c$ at Nash equilibrium.

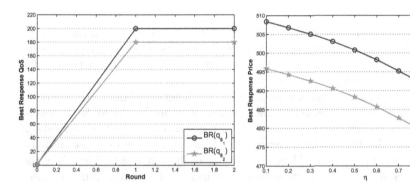

**Fig. 4.** QoS game: convergence to the QoS $q_s$ at Nash equilibrium.

**Fig. 5.** Equilibrium price $p_c$ as a function of Zipfs factor $\eta$.

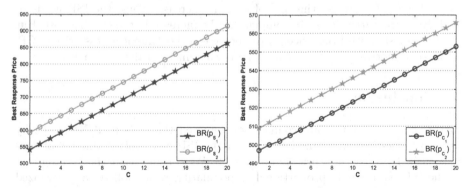

**Fig. 6.** Equilibrium price $p_s$ as a function of cost $C$.

**Fig. 7.** Equilibrium price $p_c$ as a function of cost $C$.

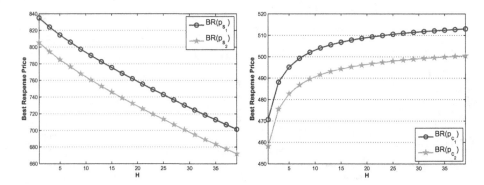

**Fig. 8.** Equilibrium price $p_s$ as a function of number's cached items $H$.

**Fig. 9.** Equilibrium price $p_c$ as a function of number's cached items $H$.

Figure 7 represent the impact of the cost $C$ on price $p_c$. $p_c$ increase with respect to $C$. When $C$ increases, each ISPs increase its prices $p_c$ to compensate the increase in the caching cost. Thus, the access ICN needs to cache popular content in order to decrease caching cost.

In Fig. 8 we plot network access price $p_s$ as a function of number's items $H$. price $p_s$ decreases with respect to the number of items $H$. When $H$ increases, the number of cached item increase. Then, the fraction of content requests js satisfied from the ISP cache increases, the transmission fee decrease and the cost of bandwidth decreases. Thus, the revenue of ISPs increases. Therefore, the ISP decreases its price $p_s$ in order to induce increased demand from the users (see the relationship between price $p_s$ and demand in Eq. 3).

Figure 9 shows the price to access to the content in the cache as a function of the number of items $H$. From the figure we note that $p_c$ increases with respect to $H$. When $H$ increase, the cost of caching increase. Thus, the ISP needs to slightly increase its price $p_c$ to compensate the increase in the caching cost. But the ISPs must control the price $p_c$, to not exceed the content access price of CP, in order to motivate users to request more content from the ISP cache.

## 5    Conclusion

In this paper, we formulate competition between the ISPs in ICNs model by using a game-theoretical model in which the ISP can control amount of content cached, adjust their prices and its QoS. We consider that the caching cost of the ISPs is inversely proportional to popularity, which follows a generalized Zipf distribution. Each ISPs caches item $h$ if the revenue of ISP by serving the requested demand of item $h$ from ISP cache is larger than cost of forwards the request demand of item $h$ to the CP. We have demonstrated the existence and uniqueness of the Nash equilibrium, then we applied the Best response Algorithm for learning Nash equilibrium. Finally, using numerical results we showed that caching investment is beneficial for the ISPs and users.

Possible extensions of our results include the more detailed analysis taking into account competition among multiple ISPs and multiple CPs. Modeling customer behavior by using the Luce probabilistic model that incorporates bounded rational choice of customers [3].

# References

1. Ahlgren, B., et al.: Design considerations for a network of information. In: Proceedings of the 2008 ACM CoNEXT Conference, p. 66. ACM (2008)
2. Ahlgren, B., Dannewitz, C., Imbrenda, C., Kutscher, D., Ohlman, B.: A survey of information-centric networking. IEEE Commun. Mag. **50**(7), 26–36 (2012)
3. Ait Omar, D., Outanoute, M., Baslam, M., Fakir, M., Bouikhalne, B.: Joint price and QoS competition with bounded rational customers. In: El Abbadi, A., Garbinato, B. (eds.) NETYS 2017. LNCS, vol. 10299, pp. 457–471. Springer, Cham (2017). https://doi.org/10.1007/978-3-319-59647-1_33
4. Azouzi, R.E., Altman, E., Wynter, L.: Telecommunications network equilibrium with price and quality-of-service characteristics. In: Charzinski, J., Lehnert, R., Tran-Gia, P. (eds.) Providing Quality of Service in Heterogeneous Environments, Proceedings of the 18th International Teletraffic Congress - ITC-18, Teletraffic Science and Engineering, vol. 5, pp. 369–378. Elsevier (2003)
5. Baslam, M., Echabbi, L., El-Azouzi, R., Sabir, E.: Joint price and QoS market share game with adversarial service providers and migrating customers. In: Jain, R., Kannan, R. (eds.) GameNets 2011. LNICST, vol. 75, pp. 642–657. Springer, Heidelberg (2012). https://doi.org/10.1007/978-3-642-30373-9_44
6. Baslam, M., El-Azouzi, R., Sabir, E., Echabbi, L.: Market share game with adversarial access providers: a neutral and a non-neutral network analysis. In: 2011 5th International Conference on Network Games, Control and Optimization (NetG-CooP), pp. 1–6. IEEE (2011)
7. Bernstein, F., Federgruen, A.: A general equilibrium model for industries with price and service competition. Oper. Res. **52**(6), 868–886 (2004)
8. Cha, M., Kwak, H., Rodriguez, P., Ahn, Y.Y., Moon, S.: I tube, you tube, everybody tubes: analyzing the world's largest user generated content video system. In: Proceedings of the 7th ACM SIGCOMM Conference on Internet Measurement, pp. 1–14. ACM (2007)
9. Douros, V.G., Elayoubi, S.E., Altman, E., Hayel, Y.: Caching games between Content Providers and Internet Service Providers. Perform. Eval. **113**, 13–25 (2017)
10. Fricker, C., Robert, P., Roberts, J., Sbihi, N.: Impact of traffic mix on caching performance in a content-centric network. In: 2012 IEEE Conference on Computer Communications Workshops (INFOCOM WKSHPS), pp. 310–315. IEEE (2012)
11. Hajimirsadeghi, M., Mandayam, N.B., Reznik, A.: Joint caching and pricing strategies for information centric networks. In: Global Communications Conference (GLOBECOM), 2015 IEEE, pp. 1–6. IEEE (2015)
12. Hajimirsadeghi, M., Mandayam, N.B., Reznik, A.: Joint caching and pricing strategies for popular content in information centric networks. IEEE J. Sel. Areas Commun. **35**(3), 654–667 (2017)
13. Han, D., et al.: XIA: efficient support for evolvable internetworking. In: NSDI 2012, p. 23 (2012)

14. Jacobson, V., Smetters, D.K., Thornton, J.D., Plass, M.F., Briggs, N.H., Braynard, R.L.: Networking named content. In: Proceedings of the 5th International Conference on Emerging Networking Experiments and Technologies, pp. 1–12. ACM (2009)
15. Jokela, P., Zahemszky, A., Esteve Rothenberg, C., Arianfar, S., Nikander, P.: LIPSIN: line speed publish/subscribe inter-networking. ACM SIGCOMM Comput. Commun. Rev. **39**(4), 195–206 (2009)
16. Kocak, F., Kesidis, G., Pham, T.M., Fdida, S.: The effect of caching on a model of content and access provider revenues in information-centric networks, pp. 45–50. IEEE, September 2013
17. Koponen, T., et al.: A data-oriented (and beyond) network architecture. In: ACM SIGCOMM Computer Communication Review, vol. 37, pp. 181–192. ACM (2007)
18. Lasaulce, S., Debbah, M., Altman, E.: Methodologies for analyzing equilibria in wireless games. IEEE Signal Process. Mag. **26**(5), 41–52 (2009)
19. Pham, T.M.: Analysis of ISP caching in information-centric networks. In: 2015 IEEE RIVF International Conference on Computing & Communication Technologies-Research, Innovation, and Vision for the Future (RIVF), pp. 151–156. IEEE (2015)
20. Pham, T.M., Fdida, S., Antoniadis, P.: Pricing in information-centric network interconnection. In: IFIP Networking Conference, pp. 1–9. IEEE (2013)
21. Rosen, J.B.: Existence and uniqueness of equilibrium points for concave N-person games. Econometrica **33**(3), 520 (1965)
22. Vanichpun, S., Makowski, A.M.: The output of a cache under the independent reference model: where did the locality of reference go? In: ACM SIGMETRICS Performance Evaluation Review, vol. 32, pp. 295–306. ACM (2004)

# Self-Stabilization

# Churn Possibilities and Impossibilities

Dianne Foreback[1]($\boxtimes$), Mikhail Nesterenko[1], and Sébastien Tixeuil[2]

[1] Kent State University, Kent, OH, USA
`dforeback@kent.edu`, `mikhail@cs.kent.edu`
[2] Sorbonne Université, CNRS, LIP6, 75005 Paris, France

**Abstract.** Churn is processes joining or leaving the peer-to-peer overlay network. We study handling of various churn variants. Cooperative churn requires leaving processes to participate in the churn algorithm while adversarial churn allows the processes to just quit. Infinite churn considers unbounded number of churning processes throughout a single computation. Unlimited churn does not place a bound on the number of concurrently churning processes. Fair churn handling requires that each churn request is eventually satisfied. A local solution involves only a limited part of the network in handing a churn request.

We prove that it is impossible to handle adversarial unlimited churn. We sketch a global solution to all variants of cooperative churn and focus on local churn handling. We prove that a local fair solution to infinite churn, whether limited or unlimited, is impossible. On the constructive side, we present an algorithm that maintains a linear topology and handles the least restrictive unfair churn: infinite and unlimited. We extend this solution to a 1-2 skip list, describe enhancements for generalized skip lists and skip graphs.

## 1 Introduction

In a peer-to-peer overlay network, each member maintains the identifiers of its overlay neighbors in its memory while leaving message routing to the underlay. Such a network is inherently decentralized and scales well. Peer-to-peer overlays are well suited for distributed content storage and delivery. Their recent applications range from internet telephony [8] to digital cryptocurrencies [29]. Due to the lack of central authority and the volunteer nature of overlay network participation, *churn*, or joining and leaving of peers, is a particularly vexing problem. Churn may be cooperative, if departing processes execute a prescribed departure algorithm; or adversarial, if they just quit.

**Infinite and Unlimited Churn.** Every peer-to-peer overlay network has to handle churn. Usually, while the topological changes in the overlay required by the churn request occur, the primary services of the overlay, such as content retrieval, are either suspended or disregarded altogether. In other words, the churn is considered finite and the overlay network users have to wait till

---

Preliminary fragments of this work appeared in [17].

© Springer Nature Switzerland AG 2019
A. Podelski and F. Taïani (Eds.): NETYS 2018, LNCS 11028, pp. 303–317, 2019.
https://doi.org/10.1007/978-3-030-05529-5_20

join/leave requests stop coming. Then, the overlay network recovers and restores services. This may be tolerable if churn is infrequent since the overlay network is available most of the time. However, at the scales that peer-to-peer overlay networks achieve, churn is frequent if not continuous. In this case, churn related service degradation may become unacceptable. It is, therefore, necessary to consider *infinite churn* under which the overlay network has to maintain services while handling it.

One way to handle churn is to engineer sufficient redundancy in the overlay network topology so that if peers leave or join, there are enough alternative paths for the operation of the network to proceed uninterrupted. In this approach, the amount of redundancy necessarily places a limit on the number of processes that churn concurrently: the churning processes must not sever all redundant paths. If this limit is breached due to extensive churn, the network may collapse and partition itself. To prevent such an outcome, the redundancy has to be extensive. However, in the absence of heavy churn, this redundancy wastes resources. In this paper, we consider *unlimited churn* with no bound on the number of concurrently joining or leaving processes.

**Unfair and Local Churn.** In cooperative churn, the joining or leaving peer submits a request to the churn handling algorithm. Such an algorithm is *fair* if it eventually satisfies every such request. A fair algorithm may not always be possible or efficient. An *unfair* churn handling algorithm may guarantee progress by satisfying some requests but denying others indefinitely. A *global* churn handling algorithm may designate a single process to handle all churn requests. Although such a serial request handling solution may be simple, it may not be practical as it creates a performance bottleneck and a single point of failure. In contrast, a *local* solution only involves processes in the vicinity of the churning process. In this paper, we study fairness and locality of churn solutions.

**Topologies.** An ad hoc peer-to-peer network forms haphazardly. A structured peer-to-peer network maintains a particular topology to optimize its performance. Most structured networks start with peer linearization [19] and then add skip-links for search acceleration [1,5,34,37]. A skip-list and skip-graph [13,24,30] are examples of a structured network built in this manner. Handling churn in a skip-list extends to other similarly built structured networks in a straightforward manner.

| | | finite<br>limited or unlimited | infinite<br>limited or unlimited |
|---|---|---|---|
| global | | possible, Proposition 1 | |
| local | unfair | possible, Theorems 3 and 4 | |
| | fair | | impossible, Theorem 2 |

**Fig. 1.** Cooperative churn solutions summary.

**Our Contribution.** We consider the problem of churn in structured peer-to-peer overlay networks in the asynchronous message passing system model. We first prove that there does not exist an algorithm that can handle unlimited adversarial churn. We then focus on cooperative unlimited churn. Our results are summarized in Fig. 1. We outline the solution to global unlimited churn and focus on local solutions. We distinguish fair and unfair types of the problem. We prove that there is no local solution to the Fair Infinite Churn Problem regardless of whether it is limited or unlimited. We then present an algorithm that solves the unfair version of the problem while maintaining a linear topology, i.e. topological sort. This solution immediately applies to fair and finite churn. We extend our algorithm to handle churn in a more efficient structure of a 1-2 skip list. We describe solutions for generalized skip lists and skip graphs.

To the best of our knowledge, this paper is one of the first to focus specifically on churn and is the first systematic study of unlimited infinite churn.

**Related Work.** Independently of peer-to-peer overlay networks, several papers [25,28,38] address determination of the rate of churn, which is a difficult task itself. Churn is studied for some fundamental problems in distributed computing such as Agreement [3,4,21]. Churn can potentially be addressed by the solution to the Group Membership Problem [11] or an implementation of a perfect failure detector [12]. However, the studied problems are inherently global, which makes them unsuitable for peer-to-peer network use.

Peer-to-peer overlay networks are often designed to have redundant links so that they can withstand limited churn [5–7,20]. Many papers address repairing the topology after determining a process unexpectedly left the overlay network [1, 4,15,22,34,35]. Others limit churn to maintain overlay services while adjusting the network [2,27].

An alternative approach is to self-stabilize from churn. Self-stabilization allows the peer-to-peer network to recover from an arbitrary state once the disruptions cease [9,10,14,16,19,23,24,26,30,31,33,36]. Using oracles allows a peer-to-peer network to recover from an initial incorrect state, even disconnection [16,31]. A general framework of dealing with node departures is discussed [9,26]. These approaches address finite churn.

Thus, previously, studies focused on limited or finite churn, while this paper focuses on unlimited and infinite churn.

## 2   Model and Problem Statement

**Peer-to-Peer Overlay Networks, Topology.** A peer-to-peer overlay network consists of a set of processes with unique identifiers. When it is clear from the context, we refer to processes and their identifiers interchangeably. Processes communicate by message passing. A process stores identifiers of other processes in its memory. Process $a$ is a *neighbor* of process $b$ if $b$ stores the identifier of $a$. Note that $b$ is not necessarily a neighbor of $a$. A process may send a message to any of its neighbors. Message routing from the sender to the receiver is carried out by the underlying network. A process may send a message only to the receiver with a specific id, i.e. we do not consider broadcasts or multicasts. Communication channels are FIFO with unlimited message capacity. A *structured* peer-to-peer overlay network maintains a particular topology. One of the basic topologies is *linear*, or a topological sort, where each process $b$ has two neighbors $a < b$ and $b < c$ such that $a$ is the highest id in the overlay network that is less than $b$ and $c$ is the lowest id greater than $b$.

Consider a particular topology. A *cut-set* is a (proper) subset of processes of the network such that the removal of these processes and their incident edges disconnects the network. It is known that if a network topology is not a complete graph, it has a cut-set. Since a peer-to-peer overlay network maintains its connectivity by storing identifiers in the memory of other processes, once disconnected it may not re-connect. Hence, a peer-to-peer overlay network must not become disconnected either through the actions of the algorithm or through churn actions.

**Searching, Joining and Leaving the Overlay Network.** The primary use of a peer-to-peer overlay network is to determine whether a certain identifier is present in the network. A search request message bearing the identifier of interest may appear in the incoming channel of any process that has already joined the overlay network. The request is routed until either the identifier is found or its absence is determined.

A process may request to join the overlay network. We abstract bootstrapping by assuming that a join request, bearing the joining process identifier, appears in an incoming channel of any process that has already joined the overlay network. A process that joined the overlay network may leave it in two ways. In *adversarial churn* a leaving process just exits the overlay network without participating in further algorithm actions. In *cooperative churn* a leaving process sends a request to leave the overlay network; the leaving process exits only after it is allowed to do so by the algorithm. A process may join the overlay network and then leave. However, a process that left the overlay network may not join it again with the same identifier. A join or leave request is a *churn request* and the corresponding join or leave message is a *churn message*. When a leaving process exits the overlay network, the messages in its incoming channels are lost. However, the messages sent from this process before exiting remain in the incoming channel of the receiving process.

**Churn Algorithm.** A churn algorithm handles churn requests in cooperative churn. For each process, an algorithm specifies a set of variables and actions. An *action* is of the form ⟨*label*⟩ : ⟨*guard*⟩ ⟶ ⟨*command*⟩ where *label* differentiates actions, *guard* is a predicate over local variables, and *command* is a sequence of statements that are executed *atomically*. The execution of an action transitions the overlay network from one state to another. An algorithm *computation* is an infinite fair sequence of such states. We assume two kinds of fairness of computation: weak fairness of action execution and fair message receipt. *Weak fairness* of action execution means that if an action is enabled in all but finitely many states of the computation then this action is executed infinitely often. *Fair* *message receipt* means that if the computation contains a state where there is a message in a channel, this computation also contains a later state where this message is not present in the channel, i.e. there is no message loss and the message is received. We place no bounds on message propagation delay or relative process execution speeds, i.e. we consider fully asynchronous computations.

**Algorithm Locality.** A churn request may potentially be far, i.e. a large number of hops, from the place where the topology maintenance operation needs to occur. *Place of join* for a join request of process $x$, is the pair of processes $y$ and $z$ that already joined the overlay network, such that $y$ has the greatest identifier less than $x$ and $z$ has the smallest identifier greater than $x$. In every particular state of the overlay network, for any join request, there is a unique place of join. Note that as the algorithm progresses and other processes join or leave the overlay network, the place of join may change. *Place of leave* for a leave request of process $x$ is defined similarly. *Place of churn* is a place of join or leave.

A network topology is *expansive* if there exists a constant $m$ independent of the network size such that for every pair of processes $x$ and $y$ where the distance between $x$ and $y$ is greater than $m$, a finite number of processes may be added $m$ hops away from $x$ and the same number of processes may be removed from the network such the distance between $x$ and $y$ is increased by at least one. This constant $m$ is the *expansion vicinity* of the topology. In other words, in an expansive topology, every pair of processes far enough away may be further separated by adding processes to the network while removing processes elsewhere. Note that a completely connected topology is not expansive since the distance between any pair of processes is always one. However, a lot of practical peer-to-peer overlay network topologies are expansive. For example, a linear topology is expansive with expansion vicinity of 1 since the distance between any pair of processes at least two hops away may be increased by one if a process is added outside the neighborhood of one member of the pair.

A churn algorithm is *local* if there exists a constant $l$ independent of the overlay network size, such that only processes within $l$ hops from the place of churn need to take steps to satisfy this churn request. The maximum such constant $l$ is the *locality* of the algorithm. Note that a local algorithm may maintain only an expansive topology, and that the expansive vicinity of this topology must not be greater than the locality of the algorithm.

**Orthogonality of Infinite and Unlimited Churn.** A churn algorithm is designed to handle particular churn. Churn is *infinite* if the number of churn requests in a computation is not bounded by a constant either known or unknown to the algorithm. To prevent the degenerate case of an indefinitely expanding network, we assume that the difference between the number of join and leave requests is still bounded. Churn is *unlimited* if the number of concurrent churn requests in the overlay network is not bounded by a constant either known or unknown to the algorithm. Observe that unlimited churn allows, for example, that all process of the network request to leave. For limited churn, we assume that there is a number $k > 1$ such that in any computation, the number of concurrent requests is no more than $k$.

Note that these pairs of conditions are orthogonal. For example, churn may be finite but unlimited: all processes may request to leave but no more join or leave requests are forthcoming. Alternatively, in infinite limited churn, there may be an infinite total number of join or leave requests but only, for example, five of them in any given state.

**The Problem Statements.** A *link* is the state of channels between a pair of neighbor processes. As a churn algorithm services requests, it may temporarily violate the overlay network topology that is being maintained. A *transitional link* violates the overlay network topology while a *stable link* conforms to it. An algorithm that solves a particular churn problem conforms to the following properties.

*request progress:* if there is a churn request in the overlay network, some churn request is eventually satisfied;

*fair request:* if there is a churn request in the overlay network, this churn request is eventually satisfied;

*terminating transition:* every transitional link eventually becomes stable;

*message progress:* a message in a stable link is either delivered or forwarded closer to the destination;

*message safety:* a message in a transitional link is not lost.

Note that the fair request property implies the request progress property. The converse is not necessarily true. The following combinations of properties are of particular interest.

**Definition 1.** *A solution to the* Unfair Churn Problem *satisfies the combination of request progress, terminating transition, message progress and message safety properties.*

**Definition 2.** *A solution to the* Fair Churn Problem *satisfies the combination of fair request, terminating transition, message progress and message safety properties.*

In other words, a solution to the Fair Churn Problem guarantees that every churn request is eventually satisfied while a solution to the Unfair Churn Problem does not. An algorithm may satisfy these properties while handling finite or infinite, limited or unlimited churn. Note that if a solution is proven impossible under more restrictive churn conditions, it is also impossible under less restrictive conditions. For example, if the solution to the Fair Churn Problem cannot handle limited churn, it cannot handle unlimited churn either. Conversely, if a solution is proven to handle less restrictive conditions, it is guaranteed to handle more restrictive conditions. For example, if the solution to the Unfair Churn Problem handles infinite unlimited churn, it also handles limited and finite churn.

# 3   Impossibilities and Global Solutions

## Adversarial Churn

**Theorem 1.** *There does not exist a solution for unlimited adversarial churn if the maintained topology is not fully connected.*

Formal proofs are in the full version of the paper [18]. Intuitively, the reason for the negative result of Theorem 1 is as follows. So long as the network is not completely connected, there is a subset of nodes whose abrupt departure may disconnect the network. For the rest of the paper, we are focusing on cooperative churn.

**Theorem 2.** *There does not exist a local solution to the Fair Churn Problem that can handle infinite limited or unlimited churn for an expansive overlay network topology.*

The intuition for Theorem 2 is that, in an expansive overlay network topology, the requests may arrive to produce a "treadmill effect" for a particular churn request $r$: the satisfaction of inopportune requests by a local algorithm extends the topology such that $r$ never reaches its place of churn. Hence, no fairness.

## Global Churn Handling

**Proposition 1.** *There exists a global Fair Churn Algorithm that can handle infinite unlimited cooperative churn.*

Let us sketch the global solution. The algorithm chooses the coordinator, for example the process with the highest id, to handle churn requests. All processes know this coordinator and forward their requests to it. The coordinator serializes the requests handling. For each request, the coordinator sends the topology updates to the churning process and its neighbors. The coordinator waits for the process acknowledgements before starting the next request. If the coordinator $x$ itself requests to leave, it stops handling other churn requests, selects the next coordinator $y$, forwards the incoming requests to $y$. The new coordinator $y$ does not start handling requests until it gets the permission from $x$. Meanwhile, $x$ informs all processes of the coordinator change, waits for their acknowledgements, forwards the permission for $y$ to start handling requests and then leaves. This algorithm satisfies all the properties of the Fair Churn Algorithm.

Note that the outlined algorithm handles the least restrictive churn: infinite and unlimited. Therefore, this algorithm also handles infinite limited and finite limited and unlimited, see Fig. 1. We now focus on local algorithms.

# 4   Linear Topology Churn Handling

**Linear Topology Under Churn.** In a linear topology, each process $p$ maintains two identifiers: *left*, where it stores the largest identifier less than $p$ and *right*, where it stores the smallest identifier greater than $p$. Processes are thus joined in a chain. For ease of exposition, we consider the chain laid out horizontally with higher-id processes to the right and lower-id processes to the left. The largest process stores positive infinity in its *right* variable; the smallest process stores negative infinity in *left*. A *left end* of a link is the smaller-id neighbor process. A *right end* is the greater-id process.

As a process joins or leaves the overlay network, it may change the values of its own or its neighbors variables thus transitioning the link from one state to another. In a linear topology, a link is *transitional* if its left end is not a neighbor of its right end or vice versa. The link is *stable* otherwise. The largest and smallest processes may not leave. The links to the right of the largest process and to the left of the smallest processes are always stable. A process may leave the overlay network only after it has joined. We assume that in the initial state of the overlay network, all links are stable.

```
constant p // process identifier
variables
    left, right: ids of left and right neighbors,
        ⊥ if undefined
    leaving: boolean, initially false, read only,
        application request
    busy: boolean, initially false; true when
        servicing a join/leave request
        or when joining
    C: incoming channel

actions
joinRequest:
    join ∈ C ⟶
        receive join (reqId)
        if (p < reqId < right) and not leaving
        and not busy then
            send sua(right) to reqId
            busy := true
        else
            if reqId < p then
                send join(reqId) to left
            else
                send join(reqId) to right

leaveRequest:
    leave ∈ C ⟶
        receive leave(reqId, q)
        if reqId = right and not leaving
        and not busy then
            send sua(⊥) to q
            busy := true
        else
            if p <= reqId then
                send leave(reqId, q) to left
            else
                send leave(reqId, q) to right
```

```
setUpA:
    sua ∈ C ⟶
        receive sua(reqId) from q
        if reqId ≠ ⊥ then // Join 1.1 received
            right := reqId
            left := q
            send sua(⊥) to right
        else // Join 1.2 or Leave 1 received
            left := q
            send sub to left

setUpB:
    sub ∈ C ⟶
        receive sub from q
        if q ≠ right then // Join 2.2 or Leave 2 received
            send tda to right
            right := q
        else // Join 2.1 received
            send sub to left

tearDownA:
    tda ∈ C ⟶
        receive tda from q
        if q ≠ left then // Join 3 or Leave 3.2 received
            send tdb to q
        else // Leave 3.1 received
            send tda to right

tearDownB:
    tdb ∈ C ⟶
        receive tdb from q
        if q ≠ right then // Join 4 or Leave 4.2 received
            send ftd to q
            busy := false
        else // Leave 4.1 received
            send tdb to left

tranDone:
    ftd ∈ C ⟶
        receive ftd from q
        if leaving then // Leave 5 received, p may exit
            right = ⊥
            left = ⊥
        else
            busy := false // Join 5 received
```

**Fig. 2.** Algorithm $\mathcal{CL}$ for process $p$.

**Algorithm Description.** We present a local algorithm *Unfair Infinite Unlimited Churn* ($\mathcal{CL}$) that satisfies the four properties of the Unfair Churn Problem while handling unfair unlimited churn and maintaining a linear topology. The basic idea of the algorithm is to have the *handler* process with the smaller identifier of the place of join coordinate churn requests to its immediate right. This handler considers one such request at a time. This serializes request processing and guarantees the accepted request's eventual completion.

The algorithm is shown in Fig. 2. To maintain the topology, each process $p$ has two variables: *left* and *right* with respective domains less than $p$ and greater than $p$. Read-only variable *leaving* is set to **true** by the environment once the joined process wishes to leave the overlay network. Variable *busy* is used by the handler process to indicate whether it currently coordinates a churn request, or is initialized to **true** for a joining process. The incoming channel for process $p$ is variable $C$. Processes do not accept churn requests when *busy* is **true**.

The request is sent in the form of a single *join* or *leave* message. We assume that a *join* and, for symmetry, a *leave* message is inserted into an incoming channel of an arbitrary joined process in the overlay network.

Message *join* carries the identifier of the process wishing to join the overlay network. Message *leave* carries the identifier of the leaving process as well as the identifier of the process immediately to its right. Actions *joinRequest* and *leaveRequest* describe the processing of the two types of requests. If the receiver realizes that it is to the immediate left of the place of join or leave, and the receiver is not currently handling another request, i.e. *busy* $\neq$ **true**, and it does not want to leave, it starts handling the arrived request. Otherwise, the recipient process forwards the request to its left or right.

Request handling is illustrated in Fig. 3. It is similar for join and leave and is divided into five stages. The first two stages are *setup* stages: they set up the channels for the links of the joining process or for the processes that are the neighbors of the leaving process. The third and forth stages are *teardown* stages: they remove the channels of the links being replaced. The last stage informs either the leaving process that it may exit, or the joining process that it may start coordinating its own churn requests. In the case of join, links between two pairs of neighbors need to be set up, hence the setup stages are divided into two substages 1.1, 1.2, 2.1 and 2.2, and links between one pair of neighbors are tore down in stages 3 and 4. Similarly, in the case of leave, link setup stages 1 and 2 establish links between a pair of neighbors, followed by the teardown stages substages 3.1, 3.2, 4.1 and 4.2 to tear down links between two pairs of neighbors, then stage 5. We include the stage and substage numbers in the comments of Fig. 2. The messages transmitted during corresponding stages are 1. set up A **sua**, 2. set up B **sub**, 3. tear down A **tda**, 4. tear down B **tdb** and 5. finish teardown **ftd**.

$\mathcal{CL}$ **Correctness Proof.** The formal proof is here [18] but the idea is as follows. We denote message **tda** or **tdb** as **td\***. Similarly, **su\*** is **sua** or **sub**. We show that in $\mathcal{CL}$, a teardown **td\*** message is the last in the channel being torn down. Similar **su\*** is the first message in a channel to be set up. The processes locally

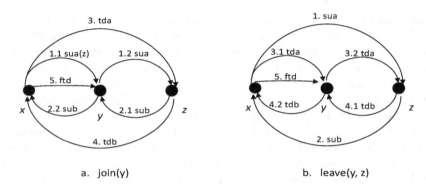

Fig. 3. $\mathcal{CL}$ join and leave request handling.

handle churn request sequentially. Thus, no regular messages are lost in the transition process. Moreover, the messages are eventually received and forwarded correctly, which leads to some churn request eventually being handled. Hence the below theorem.

**Theorem 3.** $\mathcal{CL}$ *is a local Unfair Churn Algorithm that handles infinite unlimited churn and maintains the linear topology.*

Since finite churn limits the number of requests in a computation, it follows that $\mathcal{CL}$ handles finite unlimited churn and maintains the linear topology.

## 5    Skip List Churn Handling

In this section, we describe the algorithm $\mathcal{CSL}$ that handles unlimited infinite churn to maintain a deterministic 1-2 skip list. The advantage of a skip list over linear topology is that data search and churn request processing takes $O(\log N)$ steps compared to the linear search complexity. A *skip list* [32] consists of $n$ levels with each level sorted in ascending order. The bottom level 0 contains all processes in the overlay network. In a 1-2 deterministic skip list, processes at level $i + 1 > 0$ skip over one or two processes at level $i$. Algorithm $\mathcal{CSL}$ derives from $\mathcal{CL}$. Therefore, instead of presenting the code for the algorithm, we describe its operation. We use the same system model defined in Sect. 2.

**Variables.** Similar to the $\mathcal{CL}$ algorithm, variable *leaving* indicates if a process wishes to leave. At every level $i$, each process uses the *busy* variable to block itself at that level. Also, at every level $i$, each process $x$ stores 1-hop and 2-hop neighbor identifiers. The first hop are *conversational* links that are used to exchange messages. The variables $x.i.l$ and $x.i.r$ store 1-hop left and right conversational neighbors. The second hop are *informational* links that do not contain messages but are used by the algorithm to make decisions. Variables $x.i.2l$ and $x.i.2r$ store 2-hop informational neighbors. Boolean variable $x.i.up$

indicates whether the process $x$ exists at level $i + 1$. If $x.i.up = \textbf{true}$, process $x$ is *up* at level $i$, it is *down* otherwise. The smallest and largest id processes never leave and are present at every level of the skip list. The smallest process stores negative infinity in its $i.l$ and $i.2l$ variables. The largest process stores positive infinity in its $i.r$ and $i.2r$ variables.

**Phases of Operation.** We use two phases to construct a 1-2 skip list: permission and construction. The *permission phase* gathers all necessary permissions and blocks all processes involved in a particular churn request from accepting additional churn requests. Once all permissions are gathered and the required processes are blocked by setting *busy* to **true** at each required level, the *construction phase* carries out the topology modification related to the churn request.

**Permission Phase.** The permission phase proceeds recursively from level 0. At each level $i$, the handler considers the churn request. If it is not *busy* handling another churn request or wishing to leave, it blocks itself from considering any other requests, gathers the necessary permissions for the request at this level and, if necessary, submits the request to level $i+1$ and awaits level $i+1$'s permission. Once level $i$ is secured, the permission is submitted to the lower level handler. If permission is not secured, a rejection is sent to the lower level handler.

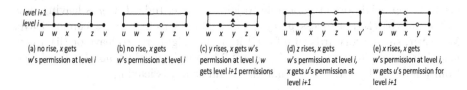

**Fig. 4.** The cases of process $x$ coordinating $y$'s joining.

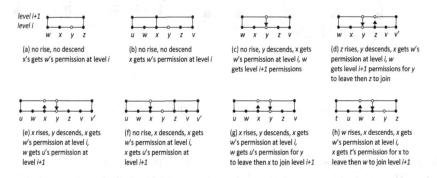

**Fig. 5.** The cases of process $x$ coordinating $y$'s leaving.

To determine the necessary permissions required for the join request from process $y$ at level $i$, the handler process $x$ considers the five cases shown in

Fig. 4. Similarly, for leaving, $x$ considers the eight cases in Fig. 5. For all cases, handler $x$ at level $i$ requests permission from its left neighbor $w$. Once $x$ gets the permission from $w$, if necessary, $x$ requests permission from its left neighbor at level $i+1$. Before $w$ replies to $x$, it may need to get permission from its left neighbor at level $i$, if further necessary, $w$ requests permission from level $i+1$ becoming the handler at level $i+1$.

To determine the processes that must rise or descend, handler $x$ requires 2-hop information, as opposed to only 1-hop information per the $\mathcal{CL}$ algorithm. Let's consider join Case e in Fig. 4 in more detail. Process $x$ is the handler and $y$ is requesting to join. A hollow circle indicates a process whose status is changing at the corresponding level. At level $i$, $w$ and $x$ are *down* while $u$ and $z$ are *up*. When handler $x$ accepts $y$'s join request at level $i$, $x$ examines its 2-hop neighborhood status and determines that it must rise and join level $i+1$ and that $y$'s status must change to be *down*. Process $x$ first requests $w$'s permission at level $i$. If $w$ is not blocked handling another request, $w$ blocks itself. Then, $w$ sends to $u$ a request for $x$ to join level $i+1$. Process $u$ becomes the handler of the request at level $i+1$. If the necessary permissions are obtained at this and higher levels, $w$ sends the permission to $x$ and $x$ sends it further downward. If the request is rejected, the process unblocks itself and sends the rejection downward.

Once the permission phase for a certain churning process $y$ ends, the appropriate 2-hop neighbors are not able to join or leave. Indeed, if $y$ is leaving, $y, x$ and $w$ are blocked. Process $y$ rejects all requests from $z$, so $z$ cannot leave. Moreover, since $z$ forwards to $y$ for (i) its right neighbor $v$ to leave or (ii) a new neighbor $z'$ to join, where $z < z' < v$, $y$'s 2-hop right neighborhood is precluded from joining or leaving. The situation is similar if $y$ is leaving.

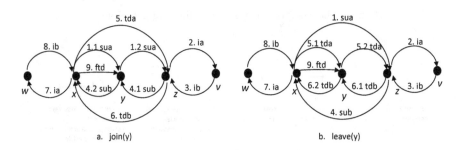

**Fig. 6.** $\mathcal{CSL}$ join and leave request handling.

**Construction Phase.** The construction phase proceeds from the top level down. At each level, the construction phase operates similar to $\mathcal{CL}$ algorithm. See Fig. 6. The setup and tear down messages, **sua, sub, tda** and **tdb**, setup and tear down 1-hop conversational links. The informational messages, **ia** and **ib**, are added to maintain the informational 2-hop right and 2-hop left neighbor links and status, and to unblock $y$'s 2-hop left neighborhood.

**Correctness Proof.** The formal proof of $\mathcal{CSL}$ correctness is here [18]. The basic operation of the algorithm is similar to that of $\mathcal{CL}$, the major additions are the multi-level permission and construction phases. We show that for each request, the phases eventually end. Indeed, since the difference between the number of join and leave requests is bounded, the number of levels in a skip list is bounded also. The number of steps at each level is finite. Hence, eventually, the permission phase either returns the permission or rejection. The only way it can return a rejection is if some other request succeeds. Once all permissions are gathered, the construction phase proceeds in a similar manner. The correctness proof result is summarized in the below theorem.

**Theorem 4.** $\mathcal{CSL}$ *is a local Unfair Churn Algorithm that handles infinite unlimited churn and maintains a 1-2 skip list.*

Since finite churn limits the number of requests in a computation, it follows that $\mathcal{CSL}$ handles finite unlimited churn and maintains a 1-2 skip list.

## 6  Extensions and Future Work

Our solution for a 1-2 skip list can be extended to generalized skip lists and skip graphs. Notice, the locality of a 1-2 skip list is 2 and the permission phase blocked, whether explicitly or implicitly, the 2-hop neighborhood of the churning process. For a 2-3 skip list, the locality is 3, and the permission phase should block the 3-hop neighborhood. In general, the permission phase should block the specific neighborhood of the churning process. The construction phase should be modified to include the serialization of additional information messages, **ia\*** and **ib\***, to reach the specific neighborhood. For a 2-3 skip list, the informational messages are sent to the 2-hop and 3-hop neighbors of the churning process. The set up and tear down message patterns remain the same for the 1-hop neighborhood covering the conversational links.

As further research, it is interesting to consider extensions of $\mathcal{CL}$ to ring structures such as Chord [37] or Hyperring [5]. Another important area of inquiry is addition of limited adversarial churn.

## References

1. Andersen, D., Balakrishnan, H., Kaashoek, F., Morris, R.: Resilient overlay networks. In: SOSP, pp. 131–145. ACM, New York (2001)
2. Augustine, J., Molla, A.R., Morsy, E., Pandurangan, G., Robinson, P., Upfal, E.: Storage and search in dynamic peer-to-peer networks. In: Proceedings of the Twenty-Fifth Annual ACM Symposium on Parallelism in Algorithms and Architectures, pp. 53–62. ACM (2013)
3. Augustine, J., Pandurangan, G., Robinson, P.: Fast byzantine agreement in dynamic networks. In: Proceedings of the 2013 ACM Symposium on Principles of Distributed Computing, pp. 74–83. ACM (2013)

4. Augustine, J., Pandurangan, G., Robinson, P., Roche, S., Upfal, E.: Enabling robust and efficient distributed computation in dynamic peer-to-peer networks. In: 2015 IEEE 56th Annual Symposium on Foundations of Computer Science, pp. 350–369. IEEE (2015)

5. Awerbuch, B., Scheideler, C.: The hyperring: a low-congestion deterministic data structure for distributed environments. In: SODA, pp. 318–327. Society for Industrial and Applied Mathematics, Philadelphia (2004)

6. Awerbuch, B., Scheideler, C.: Towards scalable and robust overlay networks. In: IPTPS (2007)

7. Awerbuch, B., Scheideler, C.: Towards a scalable and robust DHT. Theory Comput. Syst. **45**(2), 234–260 (2009)

8. Baset, S.A., Schulzrinne, H.: An analysis of the skype peer-to-peer internet telephony protocol. arXiv preprint arxiv:cs/0412017 (2004)

9. Berns, A., Ghosh, S., Pemmaraju, S.V.: Building self-stabilizing overlay networks with the transitive closure framework. In: Défago, X., Petit, F., Villain, V. (eds.) SSS 2011. LNCS, vol. 6976, pp. 62–76. Springer, Heidelberg (2011). https://doi.org/10.1007/978-3-642-24550-3_7

10. Caron, E., Desprez, F., Petit, F., Tedeschi, C.: Snap-stabilizing prefix tree for peer-to-peer systems. Parallel Process. Lett. **20**(1), 15–30 (2010)

11. Chandra, T.D., Hadzilacos, V., Toueg, S., Charron-Bost, B.: On the impossibility of group membership. In: Proceedings of the Fifteenth Annual ACM Symposium on Principles of Distributed Computing, pp. 322–330. ACM (1996)

12. Chandra, T.D., Toueg, S.: Unreliable failure detectors for reliable distributed systems. J. ACM **43**(2), 225–267 (1996)

13. Clouser, T., Nesterenko, M., Scheideler, C.: Tiara: a self-stabilizing deterministic skip list and skip graph. Theor. Comput. Sci. **428**, 18–35 (2012)

14. Dolev, S., Kat, R.I.: Hypertree for self-stabilizing peer-to-peer systems. In: NCA, pp. 25–32 (2004)

15. Drees, M., Gmyr, R., Scheideler, C.: Churn-and dos-resistant overlay networks based on network reconfiguration. In: Proceedings of the 28th ACM Symposium on Parallelism in Algorithms and Architectures (SPAA), California, USA, pp. 417–427. ACM (2016)

16. Foreback, D., Koutsopoulos, A., Nesterenko, M., Scheideler, C., Strothmann, T.: On stabilizing departures in overlay networks. In: Felber, P., Garg, V. (eds.) SSS 2014. LNCS, vol. 8756, pp. 48–62. Springer, Cham (2014). https://doi.org/10.1007/978-3-319-11764-5_4

17. Foreback, D., Nesterenko, M., Tixeuil, S.: Infinite unlimited churn (short paper). In: Bonakdarpour, B., Petit, F. (eds.) SSS 2016. LNCS, vol. 10083, pp. 148–153. Springer, Cham (2016). https://doi.org/10.1007/978-3-319-49259-9_12

18. Foreback, D., Nesterenko, M., Tixeuil, S.: Churn possibilities and impossibilities. Technical report hal-01753397, HAL (2018)

19. Gall, D., Jacob, R., Richa, A., Scheideler, C., Schmid, S., Täubig, H.: Time complexity of distributed topological self-stabilization: the case of graph linearization. In: López-Ortiz, A. (ed.) LATIN 2010. LNCS, vol. 6034, pp. 294–305. Springer, Heidelberg (2010). https://doi.org/10.1007/978-3-642-12200-2_27

20. Gambs, S., Guerraoui, R., Harkous, H., Huc, F., Kermarrec, A.-M.: Scalable and secure polling in dynamic distributed networks. In: 31st Symposium on Reliable Distributed Systems (SRDS), pp. 181–190. IEEE (2012)

21. Guerraoui, R., Huc, F., Kermarrec, A.-M.: Highly dynamic distributed computing with byzantine failures. In: PODC, pp. 176–183. ACM (2013)

22. Hayes, T.P., Saia, J., Trehan, A.: The forgiving graph: a distributed data structure for low stretch under adversarial attack. Distrib. Comput. **25**(4), 261–278 (2012)

23. Jacob, R., Richa, A., Scheideler, C., Schmid, S., Täaubig, H.: A distributed polylogarithmic time algorithm for self-stabilizing skip graphs. In: PODC, pp. 131–140 (2009)

24. Jacob, R., Richa, A., Scheideler, C., Schmid, S., Täubig, H.: Skip+: a self-stabilizing skip graph. J. ACM (JACM) **61**(6), 36 (2014)

25. Ko, S.Y., Hoque, I., Gupta, I.: Using tractable and realistic churn models to analyze quiescence behavior of distributed protocols. In: SRDS, pp. 259–268 (2008)

26. Koutsopoulos, A., Scheideler, C., Strothmann, T.: Towards a universal approach for the finite departure problem in overlay networks. In: Pelc, A., Schwarzmann, A.A. (eds.) SSS 2015. LNCS, vol. 9212, pp. 201–216. Springer, Cham (2015). https://doi.org/10.1007/978-3-319-21741-3_14

27. Kuhn, F., Schmid, S., Wattenhofer, R.: Towards worst-case churn resistant peer-to-peer systems. Distrib. Comput. **22**(4), 249–267 (2010)

28. Mega, G., Montresor, A., Picco, G.P.: On churn and communication delays in social overlays. In: 2012 IEEE 12th International Conference on Peer-to-Peer Computing (P2P), pp. 214–224. IEEE (2012)

29. Nakamoto, S.: Bitcoin: a peer-to-peer electronic cash system. Consulted **1**(2012), 28 (2008)

30. Nor, R.M., Nesterenko, M., Scheideler, C.: Corona: a stabilizing deterministic message-passing skip list. In: 13th International Symposium on Stabilization, Safety, and Security of Distributed Systems (SSS), Grenoble, France, pp. 356–370, October 2011

31. Nor, R.M., Nesterenko, M., Tixeuil, S.: Linearizing peer-to-peer systems with oracles. In: Higashino, T., Katayama, Y., Masuzawa, T., Potop-Butucaru, M., Yamashita, M. (eds.) SSS 2013. LNCS, vol. 8255, pp. 221–236. Springer, Cham (2013). https://doi.org/10.1007/978-3-319-03089-0_16

32. Pugh, W.: Skip lists: a probabilistic alternative to balanced trees. Commun. ACM **33**(6), 668–676 (1990)

33. Rickmann, C., Wagner, C., Nestmann, U., Schmid, S.: Topological self-stabilization with name-passing process calculi. In: Desharnaisand, J., Jagadeesan, R., (eds.), 27th International Conference on Concurrency Theory (CONCUR 2016), volume 59 of Leibniz International Proceedings in Informatics (LIPIcs), Dagstuhl, Germany, pp. 19:1–19:15 (2016). SchlossDagstuhl–Leibniz-Zentrum fuer Informatik

34. Rowstron, A., Druschel, P.: Pastry: scalable, decentralized object location, and routing for large-scale peer-to-peer systems. In: Guerraoui, R. (ed.) Middleware 2001. LNCS, vol. 2218, pp. 329–350. Springer, Heidelberg (2001). https://doi.org/10.1007/3-540-45518-3_18

35. Saia, J., Trehan, A.: Picking up the pieces: self-healing in reconfigurable networks. In: 2008 IEEE International Symposium on Parallel and Distributed Processing, IPDPS 2008, pp. 1–12. IEEE (2008)

36. Shaker, A., Reeves, D.S.: Self-stabilizing structured ring topology P2P systems. In: Fifth International Conference on Peer-to-Peer Computing (P2P), pp. 39–46. IEEE (2005)

37. Stoica, I., et al.: Chord: a scalable peer-to-peer lookup protocol for Internet applications. IEEE/ACM Trans. Netw. **11**(1), 17–32 (2003)

38. Stutzbach, D., Rejaie, R.: Understanding churn in peer-to-peer networks. In: IMC, pp. 189–202, October 2006

# Practically-Self-stabilizing Vector Clocks in the Absence of Execution Fairness

Iosif Salem[✉] and Elad Michael Schiller

Chalmers University of Technology, Gothenburg, Sweden
{iosif,elad}@chalmers.se

**Abstract.** Vector clock algorithms are basic wait-free building blocks that facilitate causal ordering of events. As wait-free algorithms, they are guaranteed to complete their operations within a finite number of steps. Stabilizing algorithms allow the system to recover after the occurrence of transient faults, such as soft errors and arbitrary violations of the assumptions according to which the system was designed to behave.

We present the first, to the best of our knowledge, stabilizing vector clock algorithm for asynchronous crash-prone message-passing systems that can recover in a *wait-free manner* after the occurrence of transient faults (as well as communication and crash failures) in the absence of execution fairness. We use bounded message and storage sizes and do not rely on any means of synchronization.

The proposed algorithm provides bounded time recovery during fair executions that follow the last transient fault. The novelty is for the case of more challenging settings that consider no execution fairness. The proposed algorithm guarantees a bound on the number of times in which the system might violate safety (while existing algorithms might block forever due to the presence of both transient faults and crash failures).

## 1 Introduction

Vector clocks allow reasoning about causality among events in distributed systems, for example, when constructing distributed snapshots. This paper presents the design of a highly fault-tolerant decentralized algorithm for vector clocks, in large-scale asynchronous message-passing systems that use no synchronization and do not assume fair scheduling.

**Fault Model.** The message-passing system is asynchronous and prone to: (a) crash failures (b) failing nodes may perform an undetectable restart [1], and (c) packet failures, such as omission, duplication, and reordering. In addition to these benign failures, we consider *transient faults*, i.e., any temporary violation of assumptions according to which the system was designed to behave. We assume that these transient faults arbitrarily change the system state in unpredictable manners (while keeping the program code intact). Since these faults are rare, our model assumes that they occur before the system run starts.

**Design Criteria.** Dijkstra [2] requires self-stabilizing systems, which may start in an arbitrary state, to return to correct behavior within a bounded period.

© Springer Nature Switzerland AG 2019
A. Podelski and F. Taïani (Eds.): NETYS 2018, LNCS 11028, pp. 318–333, 2019.
https://doi.org/10.1007/978-3-030-05529-5_21

Asynchronous systems (with bounded memory and channel capacity) can indefinitely hide stale information that transient faults introduce. At any time, this corrupted data can cause the system to violate safety. This is true for any system, and in particular, for Dijkstra's self-stabilizing systems [2], which are required to remove, within a bounded time, all stale information whenever they appear. Here, the scheduler acts as an adversary that has a bounded number of opportunities to disrupt the system. However, this adversary never reveals *when* it will disrupt the system. Against such unfair adversaries, systems cannot specify the time it would take to remove all stale information.

*Pseudo-self-stabilization* [3] deals with the above inability by bounding the number of times in which the system violates safety. We consider the newer criteria of *practically-self-stabilizing systems* [4–7] that can address additional challenges. For example, any transient fault can cause a bounded counter to reach its maximum value and yet the system might need to increment the counter for an unbounded number of times after that overflow event. This challenge is greater when there is no elegant way to maintain an order among the different counter values, say, by wrapping around to zero upon counter overflow. Existing attempts to address this challenge use non-blocking resets in the absence of faults, as described in [8]. In case faults occur, the system recovery requires the use of a synchronization mechanism that, at best, blocks the system until the scheduler becomes fair. This contradicts our liveness requirements.

Without fair scheduling, a system that takes an extraordinary (or even an infinite) number of steps is bound to break any ordering constraint, because unfair schedulers can arbitrarily suspend node operations and defer message arrivals until such violations occur. Having feasible systems in mind, we consider this number of (sequential) steps to be no more than *practically infinite* [5,7], say, $2^{64}$. Practically-self-stabilizing systems [4,6,7] require a bounded number of safety violations during any practically infinite period. (*Practically*-self-stabilizing systems are named by the concept of *practically* infinite executions [5].)

To the end of providing safety (and independently of the practically-self-stabilizing algorithm), the application can use a synchronization mechanism (similar to [4,6,7]). The advantage here is that the application can selectively use synchronization only when needed (without requiring the entire system to be synchronous or blocking after the occurrence of transient faults).

**Vector Clocks.**    A common (non-self-stabilizing and unbounded) way for implementing vector clocks is to maintain local copies of the vector $V[]$, such that each of the $N$ system nodes has a component, e.g., $V[i]$ is the component of node $p_i$. Upon the occurrence of a local event, $p_i$ *increments* $V_i[i]$, and sends an update message $m = \langle V[] \rangle$. Upon $m$'s arrival to node $p_j$, the latter *merges* the events counted in $V[]$ and $m.V[]$ by assigning $V[j] \leftarrow \max(V[j], m.V[j])$ for each component $V[j]$. The partial order $\leq_C$ can show causality between two events by checking if the corresponding vector clocks are comparable in $\leq_C$, where $V$ and $W$ are $N$-size integer vectors and $(V \leq_C W) \iff (\forall x \in \{1, \ldots, N\}, V[x] \leq W[x])$ [9].

**Related Work.**    There exist bounded but non-stabilizing solutions [10,11]. Self-stabilizing resettable vector clocks [8] use a *blocking* global reset (after the occurrence of transient faults) that requires crash-free fair scheduling. Our solution never uses blocking operations. There are practically-stabilizing algorithms for solving agreement [5,6], state-machine replication [6,7], and shared memory emulation [12]. They all rely on synchronization mechanisms. We solve a different problem than [5–7,12] and never use synchronization mechanisms.

**Our Contributions.** We present an important building block for dependable large-scale decentralized systems that need to reason about event causality. In particular, we provide a practically-self-stabilizing algorithm for vector clocks that does not require synchrony assumptions or synchronization mechanisms. Concretely, we present, to the best of our knowledge, the first solution that: (i) Deals with a wide range of failures in asynchronous systems that are prone to crash failures (possibly followed by undetectable restarts) and communication failures, such as packet omission, duplication, and reordering. (ii) Uses bounded storage and message size (of $3N$ integers and two labels per vector, where $N$ is the number of nodes and each label has $\mathcal{O}(N^3)$ bits [7]). (iii) Deals with transient faults and unfair scheduling. We prove wait-free recovery within $\mathcal{O}(N^8 \mathcal{C})$ safety violations after the occurrence of transient faults, which is the complexity measure for practically-stabilizing systems, where $\mathcal{C}$ is an upper bound on the channel capacity. Due to the page limit, some of the proof details appear in [13].

# 2   System Settings, Problem Definition, Solution Outline

The system includes a set of processors $P = \{p_1, \ldots, p_N\}$, which are computing and communicating entities that we model as finite-state machines. Processor $p_i$ has an identifier, $i$, that is unique in $P$. Any pair of active processors can communicate directly with each other via their bidirectional communication channels (of bounded capacity per direction, $\mathcal{C} \in \mathbb{N}$). That is, the network's topology is a fully-connected graph and each $p_i \in P$ has a buffer of finite capacity $\mathcal{C}$ that stores incoming messages from $p_j$, where $p_j \in P \setminus \{p_i\}$. Note that [14,15] present a self-stabilizing reliable FIFO message delivery protocol that tolerates packet omissions, reordering, and duplication over the system's non-FIFO channels. We assume that if $p_i$ sends a packet infinitely often to $p_j$, processor $p_j$ receives that packet infinitely often, i.e., the communication channels are fair.

**The Interleaving Model.** The processor's program is a sequence of *(atomic) steps*. Each *step* starts with an internal computation and finishes with a single communication operation, i.e., packet *send* or *receive*. We assume the interleaving model, where steps are executed atomically; one step at a time. Input events refer to packet receptions or a periodic timer that can, for example, trigger the processor to broadcast a message. Note that the system is asynchronous and the algorithm that each processor is running is oblivious to the timer rate.

The *state*, $s_i$, of $p_i \in P$ includes all of $p_i$'s variables as well as the set of all messages in $p_i$'s incoming communication channels. Note that $p_i$'s step can change $s_i$ as well as remove a message from $channel_{j,i}$ (upon message arrival) or queue a message in $channel_{i,j}$ (when a message is sent). The term *system state* refers to a tuple of the form $c = (s_1, s_2, \cdots, s_N)$, where each $s_i$ is $p_i$'s state (including messages in transit to $p_i$). We define an *execution (or run)* $R = c_0, a_0, c_1, a_1, \ldots$ as an alternating sequence of system states $c_x$ and steps $a_x$, such that each system state $c_{x+1}$, except for the initial system state $c_0$, is obtained from the preceding system state $c_x$ by the execution of step $a_x$.

**Active Processors, Processor Crashes, and Undetectable Restarts.** At any point and without warning, $p_i$ is prone to a crash failure, which causes $p_i$ to either forever stop taking steps (without the possibility of failure detection by any other processor) or to perform an undetectable restart in a subsequent step [1]. When $p_i$ performs an undetectable restart, it continues to take steps by having the same state as immediately before crashing, but possibly having lost incoming messages between crashing and restarting. Processors know the set $P$, but have no knowledge about the number or the identities of the processors that never crash. We assume that transient faults occur only before the starting system state $c_0$, and thus $c_0$ is arbitrary. Since processors can crash after $c_0$, the executions that we consider are not fair [16]. We say that a processor is active during an execution $R'$ if it takes at least one step in $R'$.

**Execution Length, Practically Infinite, and the $\ll$ (Significantly Less) Relation.** To define the stabilization criteria, we need to compare the number of steps that violate safety in a finite execution $R$ with the length of $R$. The length of a finite execution $R = c_0, a_0, c_1, a_1, \ldots, c_{x-1}, a_{x-1}$ is equal to $x$, denoted by $|R| = x$. We denote with $\sqsubseteq$ the subexecution relation between two executions. Let *MAXINT* be an integer that is considered as a *practically infinite* [5] quantity for a system $\mathcal{S}$ (e.g., the system's lifetime). For example, *MAXINT* can refer to $2^b$ (e.g. $b \geq 64$) sequential system steps. We use $\ll$ as a formal way of referring to the comparison of, say, $N^c$, for a small integer $c$, and *MAXINT*, such that $N^c$ is an insignificant number when compared to *MAXINT*. Let $\mathcal{L}_\mathcal{S}$ be a practically-infinite quantity for a system $\mathcal{S}$. We denote by $x \ll \mathcal{L}_\mathcal{S}$ the fact that $x \in \mathbb{N}$ is significantly less than $\mathcal{L}_\mathcal{S}$. We say that an execution $R$ is *of $\mathcal{L}_\mathcal{S}$-scale*, if there exists an integer $y \ll MAXINT$, such that $|R| = y \cdot MAXINT$ holds.

**The Design Criteria of Practically-Self-stabilizing Systems.** We define the system's *abstract task* $\mathcal{T}$ by a set of variables (of the processor states) and constraints, which we call the *system requirements*, in a way that defines a desired system behavior, but does not consider necessarily all the implementation details. We say that an execution $R$ is a *legal execution* if the requirements of task $\mathcal{T}$ hold for all the processors that take steps during $R$. We denote the set of legal executions with LE. Let $f_R$ be the number of deviations from the abstract task in an execution $R$. Definition 1 specifies our stabilization criteria.

**Definition 1 (Practically-self-stabilizing System).** *For every infinite execution $R$, and for every $\mathcal{L}_\mathcal{S}$-scale subexecution $R'$ of $R$, $f_{R'} \ll |R'|$ holds.*

**Problem Definition (task requirement).** We assume that each processor $p_i$ is recording the occurrence of a new local event by incrementing the $i$-th entry of its vector clock. For the vector clock abstract task, we require that the processors count all the events occurring in the system, despite the (possibly concurrent) wrap around events. Hence, we require that the vector clock element of each (active) processor records all the increments done by that processor (Requirement 1). We assume that each processor can always query the value of its local vector clock. We say that the task requirement holds in an execution $R^*$, if Requirement 1 holds for all processors that are active in $R^*$ (hence $R^* \in \mathsf{LE}$).

Let $V$ and $V'$ be two vector clocks, and $causalPrecedence(V, V')$ be a query that is true, if and only if, $V$ causally precedes $V'$, i.e., $V'$ records all the events that appear in $V$ [9]. Then, $V$ and $V'$ are concurrent when $\neg causalPrecedence(V, V') \wedge \neg causalPrecedence(V', V)$ holds. Note that if Requirement 1 holds, then it is possible to compare how many events occurred in a single processor between two states, and hence compute correctly $causalPrecedence()$.

**Requirement 1 (Counting all events).** *Let $R$ be an execution, $p_i$ be an active processor, and $V_i^k$ be $p_i$'s vector clock in $c_k \in R$. The number of $p_i$'s counter increments between the states $c_k$ and $c_\ell \in R$ is $V_i^\ell[i] - V_i^k[i]$, where $k < \ell$.*

**Solution Outline.** To the end of designing a system in which Requirement 1 holds, we introduce the *vector clock pairs* in Sect. 4, which is a novel data structure that represents vector clocks. A vector clock pair consists of a bounded vector clock to which we associate static metadata consisting of two labels and two $N$-size vectors. In Sect. 3 we detail the labeling scheme which we associate with vector clock pairs. In Sect. 4 we present vector clock pairs and their invariants, as well as the methods for incrementing, merging, and handling exhausted vector clock counters. Then, in Sect. 5 we present Algorithm 1, which includes the procedures that each processor runs to guarantee the vector clock pair invariants, to handle counter exhaustions and reception of vector clock pairs from other processors. Upon violation of invariants (which transient faults can cause), a processor running Algorithm 1 *resets* its local vector clock to the zero vector, possibly violating Requirement 1. Thus, in Sect. 6 we prove that Algorithm 1 is practically-self-stabilizing (Definition 1) with respect to Requirement 1.

## 3   Practically-Self-stabilizing Labeling Schemes

In this section we give an overview of labeling schemes that can be used for designing an algorithm that guarantees Requirement 1. A solution for comparing vector clock elements that overflow can be based on associating each vector clock element with a timestamp (or label, or epoch). This way, even if a vector clock element overflows, it is possible to maintain order by comparing the timestamps.

A first approach for providing these timestamps could rely on an integer counter, $cn$. Any system has memory limitations, thus a single transient fault can cause the counter to quickly reach the memory limit, say $MAXINT$. A counter overflow event occurs when a processor increments the counter $cn$, causing $cn$

to encode the maximum value $MAXINT$. In this case, the solution often is that $cn$ wraps around to zero. Thus, this approach faces the same ordering challenges with the vector clock elements.

Existing solutions associate counters with *epochs* $\ell$, which mark the period between two counter overflow events. The order among the counters is simply the lexicographic order among the pairs $\langle \ell, cn \rangle$. Alon et al. [4] and Dolev et al. [7] present practically-self-stabilizing bounded-size (epoch) labels, that tolerate concurrent overflow events, transient faults, and the absence of execution fairness. Whenever a counter $cn$ reaches $MAXINT$, the algorithms by Alon et al. [4] and Dolev et al. [7] replace the current label $\ell$ with $\ell'$, which at the moment of this replacement is greater than any label that appears in the system state.

**The Case of No Concurrent Overflow Events.**    Alon et al. [4] address the challenge of always being able to introduce a globally maximum label. Their algorithm eventually discovers the labels that appeared in the arbitrary starting system state, and produces a globally maximum label. A label component $\ell = (sting, Antistings)$ is a pair, where $sting \in D$, $D = \{1, \ldots, k^2 + 1\}$, $Antistings \subset D$, $|Antistings| = k$, and $k > 1$ is an integer (this terminology was introduced in [4]). The order among label components is defined by the relation $\prec_b$, where $\ell_i \prec_b \ell_j \iff (\ell_i.sting \in \ell_j.Antistings) \wedge (\ell_j.sting \notin \ell_i.Antistings)$. The function $Next_b(L)$ takes a set $L = \{\ell_1, \ldots, \ell_\kappa\}$ of (up to) $\kappa \in \mathbb{N}$ label components, and returns a newly created label component, $\ell_j = \langle s, A \rangle$, such that $\forall \ell_i \in L : \ell_i \prec_b \ell_j$, where $s \in D \setminus \cup_{i=1}^{\kappa} A_i$ and $A = \{s_1, \ldots, s_\kappa\}$, possibly augmented by arbitrary elements of $D \setminus A$ when $|A| < k$. Alon et al. [4] use the order $\prec_b$ for which, during the period of recovery from transient faults, it can happen that $\ell_1$, $\ell_2$, and $\ell_3$ appear in the system and $\ell_1 \prec_b \ell_2 \prec_b \ell_3 \prec_b \ell_1$ holds (label cycle). The algorithm breaks such cycles by *canceling* these label components.

**The Case of Concurrent Overflow Events.**    Alon et al. [4]'s labels allow, once a single label (epoch) $\ell$ is established, to order the system events using the counter $(\ell, cn)$. Dolev et al. [7] extend Alon et al. [4] to support concurrent $cn$ overflow events, by including the label creator identity. This information facilitates symmetry breaking, and decisions about which label is the most recent one, even upon concurrent label creations. The algorithm guarantees label cycle breaking by logging all observed labels in bounded local histories (of size $\mathcal{O}(N^3)$).

Dolev et al. [7] extend Alon et al.'s label component to $(creator, sting, Antistings)$, where $creator$ is the identity of the label creating processor, and $sting$ as well as $Antistings$ are as in [4]. They use $=_{lb}$ to denote that two labels, $\ell_i$ and $\ell_j$, are identical and define the relation $\ell_i \prec_{lb} \ell_j \iff (\ell_i.creator < \ell_j.creator) \vee (\ell_i.creator = \ell_j.creator \wedge ((\ell_i.sting \in \ell_j.Antistings) \wedge (\ell_j.sting \notin \ell_i.Antistings)))$. The labels $\ell_i$ and $\ell_j$ are *incomparable* when $\ell_i \nprec_{lb} \ell_j \wedge \ell_j \nprec_{lb} \ell_i$ (and comparable otherwise). Dolev et al. consider label $\ell$ to be obsolete when there exists another label $\ell' \nprec_{lb} \ell$ of the same creator. In detail, $\ell_i$ cancels $\ell_j$, if and only if, $\ell_i$ and $\ell_j$ are incomparable, or if $\ell_i.creator = \ell_j.creator \wedge \ell_i.sting \in \ell_j.Antistings \wedge \ell_j.sting \notin \ell_i.Antistings$, i.e., $\ell_i$ and $\ell_j$ have the same creator but $\ell_j$ is greater than $\ell_i$ according to the $\prec_b$ order.

**Interface to Practically-Self-stabilizing Labeling Schemes.** We present a set of functions that consist an interface to a practically-self-stabilizing labeling scheme. Any algorithm that needs to rely on such labeling schemes can be composed with a practically-self-stabilizing labeling algorithm via this interface. Note that these functions are implemented in the algorithms of Dolev et al. [7].

(i) *labelBookkeeping()*: when called without arguments, this function lets the labeling algorithm take a step [7, Algorithm 2, lines 21–28]. When calling *labelBookkeeping(m, j)* the labeling algorithm processes the labels included in a message $m$ that was received from a processor $p_j$ [7, Algorithm 2, lines 19–28].
(ii) *isStored($\ell$)* and *isCanceled($\ell$)*: these predicates are true if a label $\ell$ is stored in the local history, and respectively, if $\ell$ is cancelled [7, Algorithm 2, line 6].
(iii) *getLabel()*: returns the local maximal label [7, Algorithm 2, lines 27–28].
(iv) *legitMsg()*: the predicate *legitMsg(m, $\ell$)* returns true if and only if the label $\ell$ is the maximal label that appears in the message $m$.
(v) *cancel()*: $\ell.cancel(\ell')$ marks $\ell$ as canceled by $\ell'$ [7, Algorithm 3, line 10].
(vi) *encapsulate()*: Let $labelPart = \langle maxLabel, \bullet \rangle$ be the outgoing message of the labeling algorithm and $m_{alg}$ be the outgoing message of the algorithm that is composed with the labeling algorithm. Here, $\bullet$ denotes the labeling algorithm's metadata, but we will also use it to denote any finite sequence of values. Then, *encapsulate($m_{alg}$)* returns the outgoing message of the compound algorithm, $m = \langle \langle maxLabel, \bullet \rangle, m_{alg} \rangle$.

## 4    Vector Clock Pairs: Invariants, Operations, Counting

In this section we define a (vector clock) pair, which is a construction for emulating a vector clock that can tolerate counter overflows and the absence of execution fairness. We define pair invariants (for Requirement 1) and operations, as well as how to merge two pairs and compute the predicate *causalPrecedence()*.

**The (Vector Clock) Pair.** We say that $I = \langle \ell, m, o \rangle$ is a *(vector clock) item*, where $\ell$ is a label from a practically-self-stabilizing labeling scheme (such as the one by Dolev et al. [7] – Sect. 3), $m$ (main) is an $N$-size vector of integers that holds the processor increments, and $o$ (offset) is an $N$-size vector of integers that the algorithm uses as a reference to $m$'s value upon $\ell$'s creation. We use $(I.m - I.o)(\text{mod } MAXINT)$ for retrieving $I$'s vector clock value. We define a *(vector clock) pair* as the tuple $Z = \langle curr, prev \rangle$, where both $curr$ and $prev$ are vector clock items, such that $Z.curr.o = Z.prev.m$, i.e., two variable names that refer to the same storage (memory cell).

We use $VC(Z) := (Z.curr.m - Z.curr.o)(\text{mod } MAXINT)$ for retrieving the vector clock of a pair $Z$. We assume that each processor $p_i$ stores a vector clock pair $local_i$ and we explain below how $p_i$ uses $local_i$ for counting local events as well as events that it receives from other processors, even when counter overflows occur. We require that *labelsOrdered(Z)* holds for each pair, where $labelsOrdered(Z) \iff ((Z.prev.\ell \prec_{lb} Z.curr.\ell \wedge isCanceled(Z.prev.\ell)) \vee (Z.prev.\ell = Z.curr.\ell \wedge \neg isCanceled(Z.curr.\ell))$.

**Starting a (Vector Clock) Pair.** The first value of a pair $Z$ is $\langle\langle\ell, zrs, zrs\rangle, \langle\ell, zrs, zrs\rangle\rangle$, where $\ell := getLabel()$ is the local maximal label and $zrs := (0, \ldots, 0)$ is the zero vector. Hence, $VC(Z) = zrs$ holds.

**Pair Exhaustion.** We say that a pair $Z$ is *exhausted* when $exhausted(Z)$ holds, where $exhausted(Z) \Longleftrightarrow \Sigma_{k=1}^{N}(Z.curr.m[k] - Z.curr.o[k]) \geq MAXINT - 1$. We define exhaustion when the sum of the elements of the vector clock's value $VC(Z)$ is at least $MAXINT - 1$. Defining exhaustion according to the sum of vector clock values reduces the exhaustion events, in comparison to defining exhaustion per vector clock element, hence we can use two labels per pair (instead of $N$). This linear improvement is significant, since the label size in existing practically-self-stabilizing labeling schemes is in $\Theta(N^2)$ [4] and $\Theta(N^3)$ [7].

**Reviving a (Vector Clock) Pair.** When the (vector clock) pair $Z$ is exhausted, $p_i$ *revives* $Z$ by (i) canceling the labels of $Z$, i.e., $Z.curr.\ell$ and $Z.prev.\ell$, and (ii) replacing $Z$ with $Z' = \langle\langle getLabel(), Z.curr.m, Z.curr.m\rangle, Z.curr\rangle$. Hence, the value of the new vector clock, $Z'$, is an $N$-sized vector of zeros, i.e., $VC(Z') = Z.curr.m - Z.curr.m = (0, \ldots, 0)$. The fact that $Z'.prev$ equals $Z.curr$ will allow us to tolerate concurrent exhaustions when merging two pairs.

**Incrementing Vector Clock Values.** Processor $p_i \in P$ increments its (vector clock) pair, $Z$, by incrementing the $i^{th}$ entry of $Z$'s current item, i.e., it increments $Z.curr.m[i]$ by 1( mod $MAXINT$). In case that increment leads to exhaustion, $p_i$ has to revive the pair $Z$. We assume that a processor calls $increment()$ only before it starts the computations of a step that ends with a send operation, to ensure that increments are immediately propagated.

**Merging Two Pairs.** We present the invariants and the procedure of merging two pairs, which is based on finding a common *reference* item between the pairs.

We define the relations $=_{\ell,o}$ and $<_{\ell,o}$ to be able to compare vector clock items. Let $\langle\ell, m, o\rangle =_{\ell,o} \langle\ell', m', o'\rangle \Longleftrightarrow \ell = \ell' \wedge o = o'$. We say that two (vector clock) items $z$ and $z'$ *match (in label and offset)*, if and only if, $z =_{\ell,o} z'$. We use the order $\langle\ell_1, m_1, o_1\rangle <_{\ell,o} \langle\ell_2, m_2, o_2\rangle \Longleftrightarrow \ell_1 \prec_{lb} \ell_2 \vee (\ell_1 = \ell_2 \wedge o_1 <_{lex} o_2)$, where $m_1, o_1, m_2, o_2$ are $N$-size vectors with elements in $\mathbb{N}$, $\prec_{lb}$ is the label order of the labeling scheme, and $<_{lex}$ is the lexicographic order.

Condition 1 tests the feasibility of merging the pairs $Z$ and $Z'$, and is true when: (a) $Z$ and $Z'$ match (in label and offset) in their *curr* and *prev*, i.e., $Z.itm =_{\ell,o} Z'.itm$, for $itm \in \{curr, prev\}$ (Fig. 1a), or (b) the label and offset in the *prev* of one equals the label and offset in the *curr* of the other one, i.e., $Z.curr =_{\ell,o} Z'.prev \vee Z.prev =_{\ell,o} Z'.curr$ (Fig. 1b), or (c) $Z$ and $Z'$ match in their *prev*, i.e., $Z.prev =_{\ell,o} Z'.prev$ (Fig. 1c). We refer to the common item (in label and offset) between $Z$ and $Z'$ as the *pivot* item.

$$existsPivot(Z, Z') \Leftrightarrow Z.prev =_{\ell,o} Z'.prev \vee Z.curr =_{\ell,o} Z'.prev \vee Z.prev =_{\ell,o} Z'.curr$$

$$(1)$$

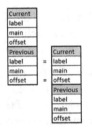

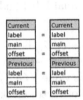

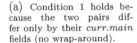

(a) Condition 1 holds because the two pairs differ only by their *curr.main* fields (no wrap-around).

(b) Condition 1 holds because *Z.prev* and *Z'.curr* differ only by their main filed (*Z* wrapped-around).

(c) Condition 1 holds because the two pairs match in their *prev* item (concurrent wrap-around).

**Fig. 1.** Conditions for merging two given pairs; $Z$ (left) and $Z'$ (right).

Two vector clocks $Z$ and $Z'$ can be merged when there exists a pivot item, i.e., $existsPivot(Z, Z')$ holds (Fig. 1). The $<_{\ell,o}$-maximum pivot item, $pivot$, in $Z$ and $Z'$, provides a reference point when merging $Z$ and $Z'$, because it refers to a point in time from which both $Z$ and $Z'$ had started counting their events. We merge $Z$ and $Z'$ to the pair $output$ in two steps; one for initialization and another for aggregation. We initialize $output$ to the pair with the $<_{\ell,o}$-maximum item between $Z$ and $Z'$ (Fig. 1), and choose $Z$ (the first input argument) when symmetry exists (Figs. 1a and 1c). In order to distinguish when we treat numbers and operations in $\mathbb{N}$ or in $\mathbb{Z}_{MAXINT}$, we denote by $x +_{\mathbb{N}} y$ the result of adding two numbers $x, y \in \mathbb{Z}_{MAXINT}$ in $\mathbb{N}$ ($x +_{\mathbb{N}} y$ can be possibly larger than $MAXINT$) and $x|_{\mathbb{N}}$ denotes that $x \in \mathbb{Z}_{MAXINT}$ is treated as a number in $\mathbb{N}$.

For every $i \in \{1, \ldots, N\}$, let $newEvents(X, pivot)[i]$ be the number of new events that the pair $X \in \{Z, Z'\}$ counts since the $pivot$ item. In Eq. 2 we compute $newEvents(X, pivot)[i]$ depending on whether $pivot$ matches $X.curr$ or $X.prev$. In the former case, we count the number of events in $X.curr.m[i]$ since the offset $X.curr.o[i]$. In the latter case, we also add the number of events in $X.prev.m[i]$ since the offset $X.prev.o[i]$, because $X.prev.o$ is the common offset of $Z$ and $Z'$. The aggregation step sets $output.curr.m[i] = \max\{newEvents(X, pivot)[i] \mid X \in \{Z, Z'\}\} + pivot[i](\text{mod } MAXINT)$, for every $i \in \{1, \ldots, N\}$.

$$newEvents(X, pivot)[i] = \begin{cases} (X.curr.m[i] - X.curr.o[i](\text{mod } MAXINT))|_{\mathbb{N}}, \\ \qquad \text{if } pivot =_{\ell,o} X.curr, \\ \\ (X.curr.m[i] - X.curr.o[i](\text{mod } MAXINT))|_{\mathbb{N}} +_{\mathbb{N}} \\ (X.prev.m[i] - X.prev.o[i](\text{mod } MAXINT))|_{\mathbb{N}}, \\ \qquad \text{if } pivot =_{\ell,o} X.prev \end{cases} \qquad (2)$$

**Event Counting and Causal Precedence.** Let $V_i^k[i]$ be the $i^{th}$ entry of $p_i$'s vector clock $V_i$ in state $c_k$, $k \in \{x, y\}$. Requirement 1 implies that in a legal execution, the query $V_i^y[i] - V_i^x[i]$ returns the number of events that occurred in $p_i$ between the states $c_x$ and $c_y$, where $c_x$ precedes $c_y$. Let $local_i^k$ be the value of $local_i$ in state $c_k$. As we show in Sect. 6, if there are two or more steps in which $p_i$ revives $local_i$ between $c_x$ and $c_x$, then there is no pivot between $local_i^x$ and $local_i^y$. Thus, the response to the query $V_i^y[i] - V_i^x[i]$ is: (i) $VC(local_i^y)[i] - VC(local_i^x)[i]$, if $local_i^x$ and $local_i^y$ differ only on the field $curr.m$ (cf. Fig. 1a), (ii) $newEvents(local_i^y, local_i^y.prev)[i]$, if $local_i^x.curr =_{\ell,o} local_i^y.prev$ (cf. Fig. 1b), and (iii) $\bot$, otherwise. Similarly, we compute the query $causalPrecedence(Z, Z')$ (Sect. 2) as follows: $causalPrecedence(Z, Z') \Leftrightarrow existsPivot(Z, Z') \wedge (\forall_{i \in \{1,...,N\}} newEvents (Z, pivot)[i] \le newEvents(Z', pivot)[i] \wedge \exists_{j \in \{1,...,N\}} newEvents(Z, pivot)[j] < newEvents(Z', pivot)[j])$.

# 5   Practically-Self-stabilizing Vector Clock Algorithm

We propose Algorithm 1 as a practically-self-stabilizing vector clock algorithm that fulfills Requirement 1 (Sect. 2). It includes procedures for (i) vector clock increments, (ii) checking the invariants of the local pair, the pair exhaustion condition, and sending the local pair of a processor to its neighbors (do-forever loop procedure), and (iii) merging an incoming pair with the local one.

**Local Variables (Line 2).** Processor $p_i \in P$ maintains a local pair, $local_i$, such that for any state, $p_i$'s vector clock value is $VC(local_i)$ (cf. Section 4). Whenever the invariants for $local_i$ do not hold in the do-forever loop or in the message arrival procedures of Algorithm 1, $p_i$ sets $local_i$ to its initial value via $restartLocal()$ (line 9 and Sect. 4). Processor $p_i$ can call the function $increment()$ (lines 15–17) to increment its vector clock pair (cf. Section 4).

**The Function revive() (Lines 13–14).** When the pair $Z$ is exhausted, a call to $revive(Z)$ lets $Z$ to wrap around and return its new version (Sect. 4). That is, $p_i$ cancels $Z$'s labels, $Z.curr.\ell$ and $Z.prev.\ell$, by calling the labeling algorithm (function $cancelPairLabels()$, lines 11-12), and then sets $Z$ to $\langle\langle getLabel(), Z.curr.m, Z.curr.m\rangle, Z.curr\rangle$.

**Token Passing Mechanism.** Algorithm 1 uses a token passing mechanism for sending and receiving $local$, which is independent of the computations on $local$. This mechanism ensures that for every two processors $p_i, p_j \in P$, $p_j$ processes a message from $p_i$ only if $p_i$ has received the latest value of $local_j$, and hence we avoid having unbounded number of steps in which the latter does not hold. To that end, each processor $p_i$ maintains an $N$-size vector of pairs, $pairs_i[]$, where $pairs_i[j]$, for $j \ne i$, is the last value of $local_j$ that $p_i$ received (from $p_j$), and $pairs_i[i]$ stores $p_i$'s pair, i.e., $local_i$ is an alias for $pairs_i[i]$. Processor $p_i$ sends $\langle local_i, pairs_i[j]\rangle$ to a processor $p_j$ by calling $encapsulate(\langle local_i, pairs_i[j]\rangle)$ in line 29. Hence, a message sent by $p_j$ and received by $p_i$ has the form $m_j = \langle \bullet, \langle arriving_j, rcvdLocal_j\rangle\rangle$ (line 30). Processor $p_i$ stores $arriving_j$ in $pairs_i[j]$ (line 32), in order to ensure that $p_i$ has received the latest value of $local_j$, and processes the message $m_j$ if the pairs $local_i$ and $rcvdLocal_j$ differ only on their $curr.m$, since the merging conditions (Sect. 4) do not depend on $curr.m$.

---

**Algorithm 1.** Practically-self-stabilizing vector-clock algorithm, code for $p_i$

---

1 **Constants:** $zrs := (0, \ldots, 0)$: the $N$-size vector of zeros, $idV(i)$: $N$-size vector, where $idV(i)[i] = 1$ and $idV(i)[j] = 0$, for $j \neq i$;

2 **Variables:** $pairs[]$: $N$-size vector of pairs: $pairs[i]$ is the local vector clock pair, i.e., $local$ is an alias to $pairs[i]$, and $pairs[j]$, $j \neq i$, is the latest value of $p_j$'s $local$ that $p_i$ received.

3 **Interface:** $isStored()$, $getLabel()$, $legitMsg()$, $encapsulate()$, $labelBookkeeping()$, $cancel()$ (Section 3).

4 **Macros:** $labelsOrdered()$, $exhausted()$, $existsPivot()$, $newEvents()$ (Section 4), as well as:

5 $mirroredLocalLabels() := isStored(local.prev.\ell) \wedge local.curr.\ell = getLabel()$;

6 $pairInv(X) := \neg exhausted(X) \wedge (X.prev.\ell \preceq_{lb} X.curr.\ell)$;

7 $comparableLabels(\mathcal{X}) := \forall \ell, \ell' \in \{X.curr.\ell, X.prev.\ell \mid X \in \mathcal{X}\}, \ell \preceq_{lb} \ell' \vee \ell' \preceq_{lb} \ell$;

8 $legitPairs(X, Y) := comparableLabels(\{X, Y\}) \wedge existsPivot(X, Y)$ (Condition 1);

9 $restartLocal() := \{local \leftarrow \langle y, y \rangle\}$, where $y = \langle getLabel(), zrs, zrs \rangle$;

10 $eqlStatic(X, Y) := (X.curr.\ell = Y.curr.\ell \wedge X.curr.o = Y.curr.o \wedge X.prev = Y.prev)$;

11 **procedure** $cancelPairLabels(Z)$ **begin**

12 | **foreach** $\ell \in \{Z.curr.\ell, Z.prev.\ell\}$ **do** $\ell.cancel(\ell)$; $labelBookkeeping()$;

13 **function** $revive(Z)$ **begin**

14 | $cancelPairLabels(Z)$; **return** $\langle\langle getLabel(), Z.curr.m, Z.curr.m \rangle, Z.curr \rangle$;

15 **procedure** $increment()$ **begin**

16 | **let** $local =$
$\langle\langle local.curr.\ell, (local.curr.m + idV(i))(\mod MAXINT), local.curr.o \rangle, local.prev \rangle$;

17 | **if** $exhausted(local)$ **then** $local \leftarrow revive(local)$;

18 **function** $merge(loc, arr)$ **begin**

19 | **if** $\exists_{x \in \{curr, prev\}} loc.curr =_{\ell,o} arr.x$ **then let** $pivot := loc.curr.o$ **else let** $pivot := loc.prev.o$;

20 | **if** $arr.curr \leq_{\ell,o} loc.curr$ **then let** $output := loc$ **else let** $output := arr$;

21 | **foreach** $k \in \{1, \ldots, N\}$ **do**

22 | | **let** $maxNewEvents = \max\{newEvents(Z, pivot)[k] \mid Z \in \{loc, arr\}\}$;

23 | | $output.curr.m[k] \leftarrow (pivot[k] + maxNewEvents)(\mod MAXINT)$ ;

24 | **return** $output$;

25 **do forever begin**

26 | $labelBookkeeping()$;

27 | **if** $\neg(mirroredLocalLabels() \wedge labelsOrdered(local))$ **then** $restartLocal()$;

28 | **if** $exhausted(local)$ **then** $local \leftarrow revive(local)$;

29 | **foreach** $p_k \in P \setminus \{p_i\}$ **do send** $encapsulate(\langle local, pairs[k] \rangle)$ **to** $p_k$;

30 **upon message** $m = \langle \bullet, \langle arriving, rcvdLocal \rangle \rangle$ **arrival from** $p_j$ **begin**

31 | $labelBookkeeping(m, j)$;

32 | $pairs[j] \leftarrow arriving$;

33 | **if** $eqlStatic(local, rcvdLocal) \wedge legitMsg(m, arriving.curr.\ell) \wedge pairInv(arriving)$ **then**

34 | | **if** $\neg legitPairs(local, arriving)$ **then** $restartLocal()$;

35 | | **else**

36 | | | $local \leftarrow merge(local, arriving)$;

37 | | | **if** $exhausted(local)$ **then** $local \leftarrow revive(local)$;

---

**The Do-Forever Loop Procedure (Lines 25–29).** The do-forever loop starts by letting the labeling algorithm take a step in line 26. Algorithm 1 calls $restartLocal()$ in line 27, in case one of the following does not hold: (i) $local.curr.\ell$ is not the local maximal label or $local.prev.\ell$ is not stored in the labeling algorithm's storage, i.e., if $mirroredLocalLabels()$ is false (line 5), or (ii) $labelsOrdered(local)$ is false (cf. Section 4). In line 28, the algorithm checks if $local$ is exhausted and in the positive case, $p_i$ calls $revive(local)$ (cf. line 9). In line 29 the processor sends $local$ to every other processor in the system.

**The Message Arrival Procedure (Lines 30–37).** Upon arrival of a message $m = \langle \bullet, \langle arriving, rcvdLocal \rangle \rangle$ from processor $p_j$ the labeling algorithm processes its own part of $m$ by the call to $labelBookkeeping(m, j)$ in line 31. In line 32 the algorithm stores $arriving$ to $pairs[j]$. Algorithm 1 processes $arriving$ only if $eqlStatic(local, rcvdLocal) \land legitMsg(m, arriving.curr.\ell) \land pairInv(arriving)$ holds (line 33), where $rcvdLocal$ is the pair that $p_j$ had received from $p_i$ immediately before sending $m$ to $p_i$. In case $legitPairs(local, arriving)$ is false, the algorithm calls $restartLocal(local)$ (line 34), since merging must be possible in a legal execution. Otherwise, the algorithm lets $local$ to have the output value of $merge(local, arriving)$ (line 36) and checks that output for exhaustion (line 37).

## 6    Correctness Proof

We show that Algorithm 1 is practically-self-stabilizing. For the vector clock abstract task, $f_R$ denotes the number of system states in an execution $R$, in which Requirement 1 does not hold, with respect to the active processors in $R$. Theorem 1 shows that for any $\mathcal{L}_S$-scale execution $R$, $f_R \ll |R|$ holds (cf. Sect. 2). Due to the page limit, some of the proof details appear in [13].

**Theorem 1 (Algorithm 1 is practically-self-stabilizing).** *For every infinite execution $R$ of Algorithm 1, and for every $\mathcal{L}_S$-scale subexecution $R' \sqsubseteq R$, $f_{R'} \ll |R'|$ holds.*

**Notation.** We refer to the values of variable $X$ at processor $p_i$ as $X_i$. Similarly, $f_i()$ refers to the returned value of function $f()$ that processor $p_i$ executes. Let $M = \mathcal{C}N(N - 1)$ be the maximum number of messages, and hence pairs, that can exist in the communication channels in any system state, i.e., $N(N - 1)/2$ links, where each link is a bidirectional communication channel of capacity $\mathcal{C}$ in each direction. When referring to a value $Z_x$ that a variable takes, e.g., $local_i$, we treat $Z_x$ as an (immutable) value that does not change. For a pair $Z = \langle \langle \ell, m, o \rangle, \langle \ell', m', o' \rangle \rangle$, we say that $\langle \langle \ell, \bot, o \rangle, \langle \ell', m', o' \rangle \rangle$ is $Z$'s *static part*, i.e., all the elements of the pair except for $curr.m$.

**Proof Outline.** We study the invariants that determine if an execution is legal. We define the predicate $localInvariants(i)$ (Definition 2), which gives the local invariants for $local_i$ of a processor $p_i$. That is, if $localInvariants(i)$ is false in line 27, then processor $p_i$ calls $restartLocal_i()$. Lemma 1 shows that $localInvariants(i)$ holds for the outputs of all the functions of Algorithm 1. Lemma 2 shows that if, during an execution $R$, there are no steps that include a call to $restartLocal()$ and every active processor calls $revive()$ at most once, then Requirement 1 holds during $R$. Lemma 3 shows that for every execution $R'$, where $|R'| \leq MAXINT$, the number of steps that include a call to either $restartLocal()$ or $revive()$ is significantly less than $|R'|$. Corollary 1 combines the above to prove Theorem 1.

**Definition 2 ($localInvariants()$).** *Let $R$ be an execution, $c \in R$ be a system state, and $p_i \in P$. We say that the local invariants hold for $p_i$ in $c$, if and only if $localInvariants(i) := mirroredLocalLabels_i() \land labelsOrdered_i(local_i)$ holds.*

**Lemma 1.** *Let $R$ be an execution, $p_i, p_j \in P$, and $c_k \in R$ be a system state, followed by a step $a_k$ in which $p_i$ calls $revive_i(local_i)$, or $increment_i()$, or $merge_i(local_i, arriving_j)$. If $localInvariants(i)$ holds in $c_k$, then $localInvariants(i)$ holds also in $c_{k+1}$. Also, if $p_i$ calls $restartLocal_i()$ in $a_k$, then $localInvariants(i)$ holds in $c_{k+1}$.*

*Proof (sketch).* Observe that immediately after $p_i$ calls $labelBookkeeping_i()$ in lines 26 or 31, the function $getLabel_i()$ returns the local maximal label. The lemma follows due to the predicates in the if-statements in lines 27 and 34 ($restartLocal_i()$), 27 and 28 ($revive_i()$ calls in lines 17 and 28), 33 and 34 ($merge_i()$ and $revive_i()$ calls in message reception procedure), as well as due to the definitions of $restartLocal()$, $revive()$, $merge()$, and $increment()$.   □

**Lemma 2.** *Let $R$ be an $\mathcal{L}_S$-scale execution. For every subexecution $R^*$ of $R$, such that (i) there is no step in $R^*$ in which a processor calls $restartLocal()$, and (ii) for every processor $p_i$ there exists at most one step $a_x \in R^*$ in which $p_i$ calls $revive()$ in $a_x$, it holds that $R^* \in \mathsf{LE}$, i.e., $R^*$ is a legal execution.*

*Proof (sketch).* We show that if either (i) or (ii) does not hold, then $R^* \notin \mathsf{LE}$ holds. The lemma follows by observing that if both (i) and (ii) hold during $R^*$, then since $restartLocal()$ is never called, all pairs of active processors can be merged (there is always a pivot between them) and none of them is deleted.

**A Call to** $restartLocal()$ **Breaks Requirement** 1. It is possible that Requirement 1 does not hold immediately after the execution of $restartLocal()$ (lines 27 and 34). Since after executing $restartLocal()$ all values in the main and offset of $local_i.curr$ and $local_i.prev$ are set to zero, it is possible to miscount events when comparing two pairs in the states of active processors, except for the case when $local_i$ remains the same before and after the call to $restartLocal_i()$.

**Two Calls to** $revive()$ **by the Same Processor Break Requirement** 1. Let $p_i$ be a processor, and $c_x, c_y$ be two states, such that there exist at least two steps between $c_x$ and $c_y$ in which $p_i$ called $revive_i$. It is not possible to compute correctly the events that occurred between $c_x$ and $c_y$ by comparing $local_i^x$ and $local_i^y$, where $local_i^k$ is the value of $local_i$ in state $c_k$. To demonstrate the latter let $local_i^a = \langle item_1, item_2 \rangle$ be the value of $local_i$ immediately before the first call to $revive_i()$ and $local_i^b = \langle item_3, item_4 \rangle$ be the value of $local_i$ immediately after the first call to $revive_i()$. Assume that the static part of $local_i^b$ stays intact until the second call to $revive_i()$, and $local_i^c = \langle item_5, item_6 \rangle$ is $local_i$'s value immediately after the second call to $revive_i()$ (cf. Sect. 4). These assumptions imply that $item_u =_{\ell,o} item_{u+1}$ holds for $u \in \{2, 4\}$ and that $item_v =_{\ell,o} item_{v+1}$ does not hold for $v \in \{3, 5\}$. Hence, there is no pivot item between $local_i^a$ and $local_i^c$ in order to compute query $V_i^c[i] - V_i^a[i]$ (cf. Sect. 4), i.e., we cannot count the local events in $p_i$ by comparing $local_i^a$ and $local_i^c$.   □

**Lemma 3.** *Let $R$ be an execution of Algorithm 1 and $R'$ be a subexecution of $R$, such that $|R'| \leq MAXINT$. Then, the number of steps in which a processor calls either $revive()$ or $restartLocal()$ in $R'$ is significantly less than $MAXINT$.*

*Proof (sketch).* We first bound the number of calls to *revive*(), and then use this bound for the case of *restartLocal*().

**Bounding the Number of Calls to** *revive*() **in** $R'$. Since $|R| \leq MAXINT$, there can be at most $MAXINT$ steps that include a call to *increment*() and thus each processor can exhaust its vector clock pair at most once. Each pair $local_k$ in a processor $p_k$ that is close to exhaustion can be merged to every neighboring processor $p_j$, and then cause the exhaustion of $local_j$. There are at most $N$ choices for $p_k$ and $p_j$, so there can be at most $N^2$ steps that include a call to *revive*(), due to processors that exhaust their pairs. In addition, to the bound of $N^2$, pairs that appeared in the starting system state can be very close to exhaustion. There are at most $N + M$ pairs in the starting system state, and each of them can cause the exhaustion of all processors' pairs, hence at most $N(N + M)$ in total. Combining the two bounds, there can be at most $V := N^2 + N(N + M) = 2N^2 + NM \in O(\mathcal{C}N^3)$ calls to *revive*() in $R'$.

**Bounding the Number of Calls to** *restartLocal*() **in** $R'$. A processor can call *restartLocal*() either in line 27 or 34. The condition in line 27 can be false due to stale information that resided in the processor's state in the starting system state, $c_0$. By Lemma 1, for any function that changes *local*, it holds that the condition in line 27 is false for the returned value of *local*. Hence, there can be at most one call per processor to *restartLocal*() during any execution due to line 27 and at most $N$ such calls during $R'$. Calls to *restartLocal*() in line 34 can occur due to the recovery of the link-layer algorithm and the token-passing mechanism (Sect. 5), as well as due to incomparability of an incoming pair with the local one (Condition 1 is false). The maximum number of steps that include a call to *restartLocal*() in line 34 during $R'$ is $f_{link} + f_{token} + f_{incomp}$.

   Since the link-layer algorithm recovers within $2\mathcal{C} + 1$ message receptions [15] and there are at most $N^2$ links, there can be at most $f_{link} := (2\mathcal{C} + 1)N^2$ calls to *restartLocal*() due to the link-layer algorithm. Also, there can be at most $f_{token} := M$ messages in the starting system state that were not sent by any processor and yet can cause the condition in line 33 to be true, and a subsequent call to *restartLocal*(). We note that at most $L := V + (4N^2 + 4NM - 4N - 2M) \in \mathcal{O}(\mathcal{C}N^3)$ labels can appear in $R'$. That is, there can be at most $V$ new labels due to the at most $V$ number of calls to *revive*() and the remaining part of the bound corresponds to the number of labels that the labeling scheme requires to stabilize [7] (the two labels per pair imply an extra factor of 2 in the bound).

   Let $Y$ be the maximum number of pair static parts that appear in $R'$ and $X$ be the maximum number of times that each processor can generate a static part. Then, $f_{incomp} \leq X \cdot Y$ holds. There can be at most $N + M$ pair static parts in the starting system state, at most $L$ pair static parts of the form $\langle\langle \ell, \bullet, zrs \rangle, \langle \ell, zrs, zrs \rangle\rangle$ due to calls to *restartLocal*(), and at most $2V$ pair static parts due to calls to *revive*() (the factor of 2 is because each of these $V$ pair static parts can be an input to *restartLocal*()). Hence, $Y = N + M + L + 2V$.

   Finally, each pair static part can be recycled at most $X = 2N^2L$ times, since (i) for every two processors $p_i$ and $p_j$, a pair static part in $p_i$ can cause at most two calls to *restartLocal*$_j$() at $p_j$ before $p_j$ stores a $local_j$ with a different static part, due to the token passing mechanism (there are $N$ choices for $p_i$ and $N$ for $p_j$, hence the $2N^2$ factor), and (ii) each pair of the form $Z(\ell) := \langle\langle \ell, \bullet, zrs\rangle, \langle \ell, zrs, zrs\rangle\rangle$ can be recycled by a processor $p_k$ at most $L$ times. The latter holds since $p_k$ might use a label $\ell'$ that is larger than $\ell$ in $local_k = Z(\ell')$ without canceling $\ell$, cancel $\ell'$ in a subsequent step, and then create a $local_k$ such that its static part equals to the one of $Z(\ell)$ (recycling).

By the arguments above, we have that there can be at most $N + f_{link} + f_{token} + 2N^2L \cdot (N + M + L + 2V) \in O(N^8\mathcal{C})$ calls to $restartLocal()$ in $R'$. $\square$

**Corollary 1.** *Let $R$ be an $\mathcal{L}_\mathcal{S}$-scale execution of Algorithm 1. By the definition of $\mathcal{L}_\mathcal{S}$-scale (Sect. 2), there exists an integer $x \ll MAXINT$, such that $|R| = x \cdot MAXINT$ holds. By Lemma 3 the number of steps in which a processor calls $restartLocal()$ or $revive()$ in every $MAXINT$-segment $R'$ of $R$ is significantly less than $|R'| = MAXINT$. Hence, since $x \ll MAXINT$, the number of steps in which a processor calls $restartLocal()$ or $revive()$ in $R$ is also significantly less than $|R|$. Therefore, by Lemma 2 the number of states in $R$ in which Requirement 1 does not hold is significantly less than $|R|$, and thus (by Definition 1) Algorithm 1 is practically-self-stabilizing.*

## 7   Conclusion

Self-stabilization often requires, within a bounded recovery period, the complete absence of stale information. This paper studies stabilization criteria that are less restrictive than self-stabilization. The design criteria that we consider allow recovery after the occurrence of transient faults (without considering fair execution) and still tolerate crash failures, which we do not model as transient faults. We present an elegant technique for dealing with concurrent overflow events. We believe that the proposed algorithm and its proof techniques (e.g., the counting arguments) can be the basis of other practically-self-stabilizing algorithms.

## References

1. Georgiou, C., Shvartsman, A.A.: Cooperative task-oriented computing: algorithms and complexity. Synth. Lect. Distrib. Comput. Theory **2**(2), 1–167 (2011)
2. Dijkstra, E.W.: Self-stabilizing systems in spite of distributed control. Commun. ACM **17**(11), 643–644 (1974)
3. Burns, J.E., Gouda, M.G., Miller, R.E.: Stabilization and pseudo-stabilization. Distrib. Comput. **7**(1), 35–42 (1993)
4. Alon, N., Attiya, H., Dolev, S., Dubois, S., Potop-Butucaru, M., Tixeuil, S.: Practically stabilizing SWMR atomic memory in message-passing systems. J. Comput. Syst. Sci. **81**(4), 692–701 (2015)
5. Dolev, S., Kat, R.I., Schiller, E.M.: When consensus meets self-stabilization. J. Comput. Syst. Sci. **76**(8), 884–900 (2010)
6. Blanchard, P., Dolev, S., Beauquier, J., Delaët, S.: Practically self-stabilizing paxos replicated state-machine. In: Noubir, G., Raynal, M. (eds.) NETYS 2014. LNCS, vol. 8593, pp. 99–121. Springer, Cham (2014). https://doi.org/10.1007/978-3-319-09581-3_8

7. Dolev, S., Georgiou, C., Marcoullis, I., Schiller, E.M.: Practically stabilizing virtual synchrony. In: Stabilization, Safety, and Security of Distributed Systems, SSS (2015)
8. Arora, A., Kulkarni, S.S., Demirbas, M.: Resettable vector clocks. J. Parallel Distrib. Comput. **66**(2), 221–237 (2006)
9. Tanenbaum, A.S., Van Steen, M.: Distributed Systems: Principles and Paradigms. Prentice-Hall, Upper Saddle River (2007)
10. Almeida, J.B., Almeida, P.S., Baquero, C.: Bounded version vectors. In: Guerraoui, R. (ed.) DISC 2004. LNCS, vol. 3274, pp. 102–116. Springer, Heidelberg (2004). https://doi.org/10.1007/978-3-540-30186-8_8
11. Malkhi, D., Terry, D.B.: Concise version vectors in WinFS. Distrib. Comput. **20**(3), 209–219 (2007)
12. Bonomi, S., Dolev, S., Potop-Butucaru, M., Raynal, M.: Stabilizing server-based storage in Byzantine asynchronous message-passing systems. In: Symposium on Principles of. Distributed Computing, PODC, pp. 471–479. ACM(2015)
13. Salem, I., Schiller, E.M.: Practically-self-stabilizing vector clocks in the absence of execution fairness. CoRR abs/1712.08205 (2017)
14. Dolev, S., Dubois, S., Potop-Butucaru, M., Tixeuil, S.: Stabilizing data-link over non-FIFO channels with optimal fault-resilience. Inf. Process. Lett. **111**(18), 912–920 (2011)
15. Dolev, S., Hanemann, A., Schiller, E.M., Sharma, S.: Self-stabilizing End-to-end communication in (bounded capacity, omitting, duplicating and non-FIFO) dynamic networks. In: Richa, A.W., Scheideler, C. (eds.) SSS 2012. LNCS, vol. 7596, pp. 133–147. Springer, Heidelberg (2012). https://doi.org/10.1007/978-3-642-33536-5_14
16. Dolev, S.: Self-Stabilization. MIT Press, Cambridge (2000)

# Short Paper: Tight Bounds for Universal and Cautious Self-stabilizing 1-Maximal Matching

Michiko Inoue[1]([⊠]) and Sébastien Tixeuil[2]

[1] Nara Institute of Science and Technology, Ikoma, Nara 630-0192, Japan
kounoe@is.naist.jp
[2] Sorbonne Universités, LIP6 CNRS 7606 and IUF, Paris, France

**Abstract.** We consider the problem of constructing a matching in an $n$-nodes graph in a distributed and self-stabilizing manner. We prove that there exists a lower bound in space of $\Omega(n \log n)$ bits for universal *maximal* matching algorithms, and a lower bound in time of $\Omega(e)$ moves for universal and cautious *1-maximal* matching algorithms. A side contribution of our result is the optimality in both time and space of the self-stabilizing 1-maximal matching algorithm of Inoue et al. [8].

## 1 Introduction

*Self-Stabilization* [4] is a versatile technique to withstand any kind of transient failure that may occur in computer networks, *e.g.*, caused by memory corruption, erroneous initialization, or topology change.

A *matching* is a set of pairs of adjacent nodes in a network such that any node belongs to at most one pair. A matching is *maximal* if no proper superset of it is a matching as well, and it is *maximum* if its cardinality is the largest among all matchings. A matching $M$ is 1-maximal if, for any $e \in M$, no matching can be produced by removing $e$ from $M$ and adding two edges to $M - \{e\}$. A 1-maximal matching is a $\frac{2}{3}$-approximation of the maximum matching, while a *maximal matching* is a $\frac{1}{2}$-approximation (but not a $\frac{2}{3}$-approximation) of the maximum matching. Table 1 summarizes the results that are related to 1-maximal matching in the context of self-stabilization, where $n$ and $e$ denote the numbers of nodes and edges, respectively.

We prove that there exists a lower bound in space of $\Omega(n \log n)$ bits for universal *maximal* matching algorithms, and a lower bound in time of $\Omega(e)$ moves for universal and cautious *1-maximal* matching algorithms. Algorithms are universal if they may output any valid solution and algorithms are cautious if they can improve the current configuration locally. To our knowledge, this is the first time this notion of universality is used to establish lower bounds in a self-stabilizing context, and we believe this concept can be useful to establish other lower bounds for a variety of other problems. An important byproduct of our results is the observation that the best known algorithm for the 1-maximal

© Springer Nature Switzerland AG 2019
A. Podelski and F. Taïani (Eds.): NETYS 2018, LNCS 11028, pp. 334–339, 2019.
https://doi.org/10.1007/978-3-030-05529-5_22

**Table 1.** Self-stabilizing 1-maximal matching algorithms. $n$ denotes the number of nodes, $e$ denotes the number of edges, $\delta$ denotes the maximum degree, and $k$ is a positive integer.

| Reference | Topology | Structural info | Daemon | Complexity |
|-----------|----------|-----------------|--------|------------|
| [9] | Arbitrary* | Global ID | Distributed | $O(2^n \delta n)$ moves |
| [3] | Arbitrary* | Global ID | Distributed | $O(n^3)$ moves |
| [5] | Tree, cycle (no $3k$) | Local ID | Central | $O(n^4)$ moves |
| [1] | No $3k$ cycle | Local ID | Central | $O(e)$ moves |
| [6] | No $3k$ cycle | Local ID | Distributed | $O(e)$ moves |
| [8] | Arbitrary | Local ID | Distributed | $O(e)$ moves |

\* An underlying existing maximal matching is supposed.

matching problem [8] provides matching upper bounds. As this algorithm is universal and cautious, our developed lower bounds are tight for the considered problem.

## 2  Preliminaries

A distributed system consists of multiple asynchronous processes. Its topology is represented by an undirected connected graph $G = (V, E)$ where a node in $V$ represents a process, and an edge in $E$ represents the possibility of communication between processes. A node may have an identifier, where each identifier may be unique in a whole graph or just locally unique (that is, unique within some distance $k$). We consider *state-reading model* and an *unfair distributed daemon*. A distributed unfair daemon chooses any non empty set of nodes among privileged nodes at one time, and the selected nodes *move* simultaneously. For more detailed definitions, readers can refer related works including [8].

A static problem $\mathcal{P}$ is specified by its correct output configurations. An output configuration is obtained from a configuration with a mapping function, that maps the state of any node $u$ and its neighbors into an output state for $u$. To represent a matching, a node state includes information on whether a node is *matched* (incident to some matching edge) or *free* (otherwise) and one neighboring node with which the node is matched in case of matched. An edge $(u, v)$ is in a matching if both nodes $u$ and $v$ are matched with each other.

A self-stabilizing algorithm is *silent* if the system reaches a terminal configuration where no node can move. A silent self-stabilizing algorithm $\mathcal{A}$ is *universal* if for every solution $p$ to its problem specification $\mathcal{P}$, there exists a terminal configuration of $\mathcal{A}$ that maps to $p$.

For an odd integer $q$, a $q$-augmenting path is a path of $q + 1$ consecutive nodes $v_1, v_2, \cdots, v_{q+1}$, such that $v_1$ and $v_{q+1}$ are free and $v_{2i}$ and $v_{2i+1}$ $(1 \leq i \leq (q-1)/2)$ are matched with each other. If an output configuration does not have 1-augmenting path or 3-augmenting path, it is a 1-maximal matching. For configuration $C$, let $U_C$ denote a set of nodes that belong to some

1-augmenting path or 3-augmenting path. A silent self-stabilizing 1-maximal matching algorithm $\mathcal{A}$ is *cautious* if from any configuration $C$, there exists an execution that reaches a terminal configuration that maps to a 1-maximal matching such that moves of nodes in $U_C$ are solely determined by states of nodes in $U_C$, and only nodes in $U_C$ change their matches.

## 3   Lower Bound for Space

If the algorithm is *universal*, then lower bounding the number of possible solutions yields a memory lower bound for the entire distributed algorithm, regardless of how bits of memory are distributed across the network.

**Theorem 1.** *Every self-stabilizing universal maximal matching algorithm requires* $n \log n$ *bits in a* $n$*-sized network.*

*Proof.* For a $2k$-sized clique, for some integer $k > 1$, it is known [2] that the number of *perfect* matchings (that is, matchings of size exactly $k$) is equal to $(2k-1)!!$, and therefore, $\log_2((2k-1)!!)$ bits are required, where $x!!$ denotes the double factorial of $x$. By Stirling formula of $n! \approx \sqrt{2\pi n} \times \left(\frac{n}{e}\right)^n$, we can derive

$$\log_2((2k-1)!!) > \frac{1}{3} \times (2k-1) \log_2(2k-1) = \Omega(k \log_2 k)$$

## 4   Lower Bound for Time

A time lower bound is shown by considering several families of graphs.

For any integer $k > 0$, we define $A_k$ as a graph with $6k$ nodes where $A_k$ has 6 groups of nodes $V_j = \{p_{1,j}, p_{2,j}, \cdots, p_{k,j}\}$ for $j = 1, \cdots 6$ and edges between $p_{i,1}$ and $p_{i,2}$, $p_{i,3}$ and $p_{i,4}$, $p_{i,5}$ and $p_{i,6}$, $p_{i,2}$ and nodes in $V_3$, and $p_{i,4}$ and nodes in $V_5$, for $i = 1, \cdots, k$. From universality, there is a terminal configuration for $A_k$ where nodes $p_{i,1}$ and $p_{i,2}$, nodes $p_{i,3}$ and $p_{i,4}$, and nodes $p_{i,5}$ and $p_{i,6}$ are matched with each other, for $i = 1, \cdots, k$. Let $C_0^{A_k}$ denote a such terminal configuration (Fig. 1(a)), where thick edges denote edges that belong to the matching, and grey nodes denote matched nodes.

For any integers $k > 0$ and $l > 0$, we define $B_{k,l}$ as a graph obtained from $A_k$ by deleting nodes $p_{1,1}, p_{2,1}, \cdots, p_{l,1}$, and nodes $p_{1,6}, p_{2,6}, \cdots, p_{l,6}$. Let $C_0^{B_{k,1}}$ and $C_0^{B_{k,k}}$ be configurations of graphs $B_{k,1}$ and $B_{k,k}$ where each node has the same state as its corresponding node in $C_0^{A_k}$ in graph $A_k$ (Fig. 1(b) and (c)).

We show that there exists an execution starting from $C_0^{B_{k,1}}$, such that only nodes $p_{1,2}$ and $p_{1,5}$ move until becoming unprivileged ($C_1^{B_{k,1}}$ (Fig. 2(a))), at least one node in each $(p_{i,3}, p_{i,4})$ $(i = 1, 2, \cdots, k)$ moves, and then one match between $p_{i,3}$ and $p_{i,4}$ for some $i$ in $C_0^{B_{k,1}}$ is replaced with two new matches between $p_{1,2}$ and $p_{i,3}$, and between $p_{i,4}$ and $p_{1,5}$ ($C_2^{B_{k,1}}$ (Fig. 2(c))). In the execution, one node in each $(p_{i,3}, p_{i,4})$ $(i = 1, 2, \cdots, k)$ moves in $C_1^{B_{k,1}}$ since, for example, $p_{1,3}$ and $p_{1,4}$ could not distinguish $C_1^{B_{k,1}}$ and $C_1^{D_{k,1}}$ as shown in Fig. 2(b) where $p_{1,3}$ or $p_{1,4}$ can move under the cautiousness. That derives the following lemma.

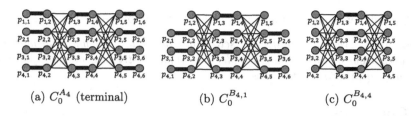

(a) $C_0^{A_4}$ (terminal)          (b) $C_0^{B_4,1}$          (c) $C_0^{B_4,4}$

**Fig. 1.** Graphs $A_k$, $B_{k,1}$, and $B_{k,k}$ ($k = 4$)

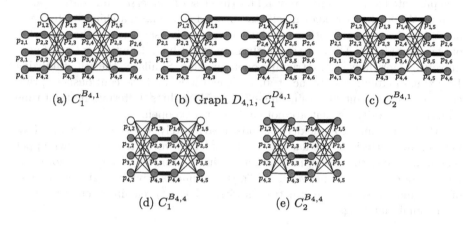

(a) $C_1^{B_4,1}$          (b) Graph $D_{4,1}$, $C_1^{D_4,1}$          (c) $C_2^{B_4,1}$

(d) $C_1^{B_4,4}$          (e) $C_2^{B_4,4}$

**Fig. 2.** Configurations in graphs $B_{4,1}$, $B_{4,4}$, $D_{4,1}$

**Lemma 1.** *For every integer $k > 0$, there exists an execution from $C_0^{B_k,1}$ to $C_2^{B_k,1}$ that includes at least $k$ moves.*

The similar execution from configuration $C_0^{B_k,k}$ to configuration $C_2^{B_k,k}$ via configuration $C_1^{B_k,k}$ is possible under the unfair distributed daemon (Figs. 1(c), 2(d) and (e)).

**Lemma 2.** *For every integer $k > 0$, there exists an execution from $C_0^{B_k,k}$ to $C_2^{B_k,k}$ that includes at least $k$ moves.*

In $C_2^{B_k,k}$ in graph $B_{k,k}$, nodes $p_{i,j}$ (for $i \in \{2, 3, \cdots, k\}$ and $j \in \{2, 3, 4, 5\}$) belong to 3-augmenting paths. Therefore, these nodes can reach a terminal configuration even though other nodes (that is, $p_{1,2}, p_{1,3}, p_{1,4}, p_{1,5}$) do not move. Now, nodes $p_{i,j}$ (for $i \in \{2, 3, \cdots, k\}$ and $j \in \{2, 3, 4, 5\}$) induce a graph $B_{k-1,k-1}$ with $4(k - 1)$ nodes. Therefore, the following lemma holds.

**Lemma 3.** *For every integer $k > 0$, there exists an execution including at least $k - 1$ moves from $C_2^{B_k,k}$ to some configuration where one match $(p_{i,3}, p_{i,4})$ is replaced with two matches $(p_{2,2}, p_{i,3})$, and $(p_{i,4}, p_{2,5})$, for some $i \in \{2, 3, \cdots, k\}$ in graph $B_{k,k}$.*

By applying Lemma 3 repeatedly, we obtain the following theorem.

**Theorem 2.** *Any silent universal self-stabilizing cautious 1-maximal matching algorithm requires $\Omega(n^2)$ moves under the unfair distributed daemon for some class of graphs with $\Omega(n^2)$ edges.*

## 5   Conclusion

The presented lower bounds are valid for the class of *universal* and *cautious* algorithms. While the best known self-stabilizing 1-maximal matching by Inoue et al. [7] is universal, some other solutions are not universal (such as the algorithm of Manne et al. [9]). The question of obtaining tight bounds in the context of non-universal algorithms is an intriguing open question. Similarly, the self-stabilizing 1-maximal matching by Inoue et al. [7] is cautious, and the cautiousness property seems important to obtain time-efficient algorithms. Determining tight time bounds for algorithms that are not cautious is also open.

Also, our time complexity bounds heavily rely on the existence of 3-augmenting paths in particular classes of graphs. However, the best known upper bound in time in the case of maximal matching is also $O(e)$, where $e$ denotes the number of edges in the network. While this bound is trivially tight in the case of rings and trees, the case of networks with $e = \Omega(n^2)$ remains open in the case of maximal matchings.

## References

1. Asada, Y., Ooshita, F., Inoue, M.: An efficient silent self-stabilizing 1-maximal matching algorithm in anonymous networks. J. Graph Algorithms Appl. **20**(1), 59–78 (2016). https://doi.org/10.7155/jgaa.00384
2. Callan, D.: A combinatorial survey of identities for the double factorial. arXiv preprint arXiv:0906.1317 (2009)
3. Cohen, J., Maâmra, K., Manoussakis, G., Pilard, L.: Polynomial self-stabilizing maximal matching algorithm with approximation ratio 2/3. In: International Conference on Principles of Distributed Systems (2016)
4. Dijkstra, E.W.: Self-stabilizing systems in spite of distributed control. Commun. ACM **17**(11), 643–644 (1974). https://doi.org/10.1145/361179.361202
5. Goddard, W., Hedetniemi, S.T., Shi, Z., et al.: An anonymous self-stabilizing algorithm for 1-maximal matching in trees. In: Proceedings of International Conference on Parallel and Distributed Processing Techniques and Applications, pp. 797–803 (2006)
6. Inoue, M., Ooshita, F., Tixeuil, S.: An efficient silent self-stabilizing 1-maximal matching algorithm under distributed daemon without global identifiers. In: Bonakdarpour, B., Petit, F. (eds.) SSS 2016. LNCS, vol. 10083, pp. 195–212. Springer, Cham (2016). https://doi.org/10.1007/978-3-319-49259-9_17
7. Inoue, M., Ooshita, F., Tixeuil, S.: Brief announcement: efficient self-stabilizing 1-maximal matching algorithm for arbitrary networks. In: Proceedings of the ACM Symposium on Principles of Distributed Computing, PODC 2017, Washington, DC, USA, 25–27 July 2017, pp. 411–413. ACM (2017).https://doi.org/10.1145/3087801.3087840

8. Inoue, M., Ooshita, F., Tixeuil, S.: An efficient silent self-stabilizing 1-maximal matching algorithm under distributed daemon for arbitrary networks. In: Spirakis, P., Tsigas, P. (eds.) SSS 2017. LNCS, vol. 10616, pp. 93–108. Springer, Cham (2017). https://doi.org/10.1007/978-3-319-69084-1_7
9. Manne, F., Mjelde, M., Pilard, L., Tixeuil, S.: A self-stabilizing 2/3-approximation algorithm for the maximum matching problem. Theor. Comput. Sci. **412**(40), 5515–5526 (2011). https://doi.org/10.1016/j.tcs.2011.05.019

# Security

# Automata-Based Bottom-Up Design of Conflict-Free Security Policies Specified as Policy Expressions

Ahmed Khoumsi[1(✉)] and Mohammed Erradi[2]

[1] Department of Electrical and Computer Engineering, University of Sherbrooke,
Sherbrooke, Canada
`Ahmed.Khoumsi@USherbrooke.ca`
[2] ENSIAS, University Mohammed V in Rabat, Rabat, Morocco
`mohamed.erradi@gmail.com`

**Abstract.** Security policies (or more briefly: policies) are used to filter accesses to computing resources. A policy is usually specified by a table of rules, where each rule specifies conditions to accept or reject an access request. Since the acceptance of malicious requests or the rejection of legitimate requests may lead to serious consequences, the correct design of policies is very important. The present paper is inspired by two works: the first one uses an automata-based method to design policies, while the second one suggests a bottom-up design method of policies specified as policy expressions. A policy expression looks like a boolean expression, where policies are composed using three operators: $\neg$, $\wedge$, $\vee$. In this paper, we generalize the automata-based method for the bottom-up design of policies specified as policy expressions. In our context, designing a policy specified as a policy expression $PE$ amounts to constructing an automaton $\Gamma_{PE}$ that models the access control specified in $PE$. To respect the essence of bottom-up design, the automaton $\Gamma_{PE}$ is constructed incrementally, by first constructing the automata that model the basic policies that compose $PE$, and then constructing incrementally the automata that model the subexpressions that compose $PE$, until we obtain $\Gamma_{PE}$. Then we show how to use $\Gamma_{PE}$ to determine whether $PE$ verifies several properties, namely adequacy, implication, and equivalence. Also, we study the problem of conflicting rules, i.e. policy rules that do not agree on whether some request must be accepted or rejected. We show that our bottom-up design supports any strategy of conflict resolution.

## 1 Introduction

Security policies (or more briefly: policies) are used to filter accesses to computing resources; firewalls are the most known example of policies. A policy is usually specified by a table of rules, where each rule specifies conditions to accept or reject an access request (or more briefly: a request). A badly designed policy may lead to the acceptance of malicious requests or the rejection of legitimate

© Springer Nature Switzerland AG 2019
A. Podelski and F. Taïani (Eds.): NETYS 2018, LNCS 11028, pp. 343–357, 2019.
https://doi.org/10.1007/978-3-030-05529-5_23

requests. Therefore, the correct design and analysis of policies is very important and has been addressed by many researchers, e.g. [1–6,8–10,12–16,18–29].

The two works that most inspired this paper are [26] and [14] (less complete versions of [14] can be found in [15,16]). The authors of [14] suggest an automata-based method to design and analyze policies. The authors of [26] suggest a bottom-up design method of policies specified as policy expressions. A policy expression looks like a boolean expression, where policies are composed using three operators: ¬, ∧, ∨. In the present paper, we generalize the automata-based method of [14] for the bottom-up design of policies specified as policy expressions.

The rest of the paper is organized as follows: Preliminaries on policies are given in Sect. 2. Section 3 presents the automata-based method of [14] to design and analyze policies. In Sect. 4, we present policy expressions of [26]. In Sect. 5, we present an incremental construction of an automaton that describes a given policy expression: given an automaton describing a policy expression $PE$, we show how to obtain an automaton that describes $\neg(PE)$; and given two automata describing respectively two policy expressions $PE_1$ and $PE_2$, we show how to obtain automata that describe $PE_1 \wedge PE_2$ and $PE_1 \vee PE_2$. In Sect. 6, we show how the automaton describing a policy expression $PE$ is used to determine whether $PE$ verifies several properties. In Sect. 7, we present related work and recapitulate our contributions. Finally, a conclusion is given in Sect. 8.

## 2    Preliminaries About Policies

A policy is a set of rules specifying whether access requests to a resource must be accepted or rejected. A rule $R$ is defined by a pair (*Condition*, *Action*) which means: if *Condition* is satisfied by a request $rq$, then *Action* (which may be Accept or Reject) must be applied to $rq$. More precisely:

- *Condition* is specified by several (say $m$) filtering fields $F^1, \cdots, F^m$, where each $F^j$ is a set of values. Every request $rq$ has several headers $H^1, \cdots, H^m$, where each $H^j$ is a value. *Condition* is satisfied for $rq$ (which is termed as: $rq$ matches $R$, or $R$ matches $rq$), if for each $j = 1, \cdots m$: $H^j$ belongs to $F^j$.
- *Action* may be Accept or Reject.

Accept-rule (resp. Reject-rule) denotes a rule whose action is Accept (resp. Reject).

For illustration purpose, let us consider Table 1 that represents a toy example of a firewall policy. The requests correspond to packets arriving at the firewall. The condition of each rule is defined by the four fields IPsrc, IPdst, Port and Protocol. The symbol ∗ in the column of $F^j$ means any value of the domain of $F^j$. The expression a.b.c.0/x represents the set of 32-bit addresses obtained by giving all the possible values to the 32−x last bits in the 32-bit value a.b.c.0. The expression not(80.15.15.0/24) denotes the set of 32-bit addresses that are not in 80.15.15.0/24. A request $rq$ matches a rule $R_i$ if it comes from and is destined to addresses belonging to IPsrc and IPdst respectively, and is transmitted through a port belonging to Port by a protocol belonging to Protocol. For example, a packet with the headers $(190.170.15.10), (82.15.15.11), (25)$, (UDP), is a packet that comes from $190.170.15.10$, is destined to $82.15.15.11$, and is transmitted through the port 25 by the protocol UDP. This packet is rejected by the firewall, because the only rule that matches it is the Reject-rule $R_3$.

**Table 1.** Example of policy $\mathcal{F}_1$

| Rule | IPsrc | IPdst | Port | Protocol | Action |
|------|-------|-------|------|----------|--------|
| $R_1$ | * | 80.15.15.0/24 | * | * | Accept |
| $R_2$ | 190.170.15.0/24 | 80.15.15.0/24 | 25, 81 | TCP | Reject |
| $R_3$ | * | not(80.15.15.0/24) | * | * | Reject |

## 3   Automata-Based Design and Analysis of Policies

This section introduces the method of [14] that receives as input a policy $\mathcal{F}$ described by a table of several (say $n$) rules $R_1, \cdots, R_n$, and generates automata $\Gamma_{\mathcal{F}}^*$ and $\Gamma_{\mathcal{F}}$ that model $\mathcal{F}$. The basic principle of the method is as follows: (1) every rule $R_i$ of $\mathcal{F}$ is modeled by an automaton $\Gamma_{R_i}$, (2) an automaton $\Gamma_{\mathcal{F}}^*$ is generated by composing all automata $(\Gamma_{R_i})_{i=1,\cdots,n}$, and (3) $\Gamma_{\mathcal{F}}^*$ is analyzed and transformed into an anomaly-free automaton $\Gamma_{\mathcal{F}}$ if anomalies are detected in $\Gamma_{\mathcal{F}}^*$. The relevance of this automata-based method is that:

1. $\Gamma_{\mathcal{F}}^*$ can be used to determine efficiently the rules of $\mathcal{F}$ that match a request $rq$ (see Sect. 3.1).
2. $\Gamma_{\mathcal{F}}^*$ can be used to detect and resolve efficiently several types of anomalies of $\mathcal{F}$ (see Sect. 3.2).
3. $\Gamma_{\mathcal{F}}$ can be used to determine efficiently if a request is accepted or rejected by $\mathcal{F}$ (see Sect. 3.2).
4. $\Gamma_{\mathcal{F}}$ can be used to determine if $\mathcal{F}$ verifies several properties, such as adequacy, implication, and equivalence. This point is studied in Sect. 6.

The automaton construction is explained in detail in [14]. This section explains the intuition and utility of $\Gamma_{\mathcal{F}}^*$ and $\Gamma_{\mathcal{F}}$. For example, for the policy $\mathcal{F}_1$ of Table 1, we obtain the automaton $\Gamma_{\mathcal{F}_1}^*$ of Fig. 1. $\Gamma_{\mathcal{F}_1}^*$ has 5 state levels (0 to 4) and 4 transition levels (1 to 4), where transitions of level $j$ relate states of levels $j-1$ and $j$. The number of transition levels is the number $m$ of fields, which is 4 in the example: transitions of levels 1 to 4 correspond to the 4 fields IPsrc, IPdst, Port and Protocol of $\mathcal{F}_1$, respectively. Each transition of level $j$ is labelled by a set of values of field $F^j$. The states of the last level (i.e. state level 4) are called *final* states. Each state is defined by its level and a 3-tuple ($n$-tuple in the general case) whose 3 components correspond respectively to the 3 rules of

$\mathcal{F}_1$. Each of the 3 components is "a", "r", or "*". The label "All ports" denotes
the set of all port numbers, and not$(25, 81)$ denotes the set of all port numbers
except 25 and 81. If $X$ is a set of IP addresses, not$(X)$ denotes the set of all IP
addresses, except the IP addresses of $X$. For the sake of clarity, henceforth we
use the index $i$ for rules and the index $j$ for fields.

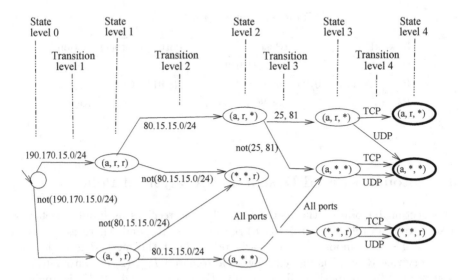

**Fig. 1.** Automaton $\Gamma^*_{\mathcal{F}_1}$ obtained from the policy $\mathcal{F}_1$ of Table 1.

### 3.1   Determining the Rules that Match a Request

Let us explain how the automaton $\Gamma^*_{\mathcal{F}}$ can be used for the above point 1, i.e. to
determine the rules of $\mathcal{F}$ that match a request $rq$, i.e. to determine the rules that
accept and the rules that reject $rq$. We illustrate our explanation by the policy
$\mathcal{F}_1$ of Table 1, and its corresponding automaton $\Gamma^*_{\mathcal{F}_1}$ of Fig. 1.

Consider a request $rq$ whose 4 headers are values $H^1$ to $H^4$ corresponding
to the 4 fields IPsrc, IPdst, Port, and Protocol, respectively. We start in the
initial state of $\Gamma^*_{\mathcal{F}_1}$ and execute the sequence of 4 transitions labeled respectively
$\ell_1, \ell_2, \ell_3, \ell_4$, such that each $H^j$ (which is a value of field $F^j$) belongs to $\ell_j$ (which
is a set of values of $F^j$). Hence, the executed 4-transition path (from the initial
state to a final state) depends on the considered request $rq$. Let us consider the
reached final state and explain how its 3-tuple is interpreted. For each position
$i$ ($i = 1, 2, 3$) in the 3-tuple: if the $i$th component is "a" (resp. "r"), this means
that rule $R_i$ accepts (resp. rejects) $rq$; if the $i$th component is "*", this means
that rule $R_i$ does not match $rq$.

Let us consider the intermediate states (of levels 1, 2, 3) that have been
crossed before reaching the final state. When a state of level $j$ ($j = 1, 2, 3$) is

reached: if its $i$th component is "a" (resp. "r"), this means that the Accept-rule (resp. Reject-rule) $R_i$ is still matching the request $rq$ after considering the first $j$ fields; if its $i$th component is "∗", this means that $R_i$ does not match $rq$ anymore after considering the first $j$ fields.

Consider for example a request $rq$ whose headers $H^1$ to $H^4$ are (190.170.15.12), (80.15.15.20), (23) and (TCP), respectively. Hence, we first execute the transition labeled 190.170.15.0/24 (containing $H^1$) and reach $\langle a, r, r \rangle$ of level 1. Then, we execute the transition labeled 80.15.15.0/24 (containing $H^2$) and reach $\langle a, r, ∗ \rangle$ of level 2. Then, we execute the transition labeled not(25, 81) (containing $H^3$) and reach $\langle a, ∗, ∗ \rangle$ of level 3. Finally, we execute the transition labeled (TCP) (containing $H^4$) and reach the second final state $\langle a, ∗, ∗ \rangle$. Therefore, the Accept-rule $R_1$ matches $rq$, and rules $R_2$ and $R_3$ do not match $rq$. The final decision is to accept $rq$, because it is accepted by the unique rule that matches it.

## 3.2   Anomaly Detection and Resolution

Let us discuss how the automaton $\Gamma_{\mathcal{F}}^*$ of a policy $\mathcal{F}$ can be used for the above point 2, i.e. to detect and resolve anomalies in $\mathcal{F}$. A first type of anomaly is *incompleteness*: $\mathcal{F}$ is said to be incomplete if there exists at least one request that matches no rule of $\mathcal{F}$. On the contrary, $\mathcal{F}$ is said to be complete if every request matches at least one rule of $\mathcal{F}$. The authors of [14] show that $\mathcal{F}$ is incomplete if and only if $\Gamma_{\mathcal{F}}^*$ contains the final state whose all components are ∗, which is called NoAction-state. The requests that match no rule of $\mathcal{F}$ lead to such a NoAction-state. For example, the policy $\mathcal{F}_1$ of Table 1 is complete, because $\Gamma_{\mathcal{F}_1}^*$ of Fig. 1 does not contain the NoAction-state.

Another type of anomaly is *conflict*: rules $R_{i_1}$ and $R_{i_2}$ are conflicting if they have different actions and there exists at least one request $rq$ that matches both rules. That is, $R_{i_1}$ and $R_{i_2}$ do not agree on whether a request should be accepted of rejected. The authors of [14] show that a policy $\mathcal{F}$ has conflicting rules if and only if $\Gamma_{\mathcal{F}}^*$ contains final states with at least one component "a" and one component "r". Components "∗" in a final state $q$ are not taken into account, because they correspond to rules that do not match the requests leading to $q$. Consider for example $\Gamma_{\mathcal{F}_1}^*$ of Fig. 1 that has three final states:

- The final state $\langle a, r, ∗ \rangle$ represents a conflict. Intuitively, every request $rq$ that leads to this state is accepted by $R_1$ and rejected by $R_2$.
- The final state $\langle a, ∗, ∗ \rangle$ does not represent any conflict, because there is no component "r". Intuitively, every request $rq$ that leads to this state is accepted by $R_1$ and is not rejected by any rule.
- The final state $\langle ∗, ∗, r \rangle$ does not represent any conflict, because there is no component "a". Intuitively, every request $rq$ that leads to this state is rejected by $R_3$ and is not accepted by any rule.

Consider a conflicting state, i.e. a final state that has both components "a" and "r". Resolving such conflict consists in using some strategy that determines which action Accept or Reject to select. Several strategies have been proposed in the literature to resolve detected conflicts. Conflict resolution is not the main topic of the present work, however it is worth noting that our automata-based modeling supports any resolution strategy, which is used as an interchangeable module that receives a conflicting state as input and generates an action Accept or Reject as output. For illustration purpose, here are three simple strategies to resolve a conflict between two or more rules $R_{i_1}, R_{i_2}, \cdots$ ($i_1 < i_2 < \cdots$) that have different actions and match a request $rq$:

- *Decreasing priority order* (DPO) strategy: the action of $R_{i_1}$ is selected.
- *Permissive* strategy: priority is given to Accept over Reject, i.e. the action Accept is selected.
- *Anti-permissive* strategy: priority is given to Reject over Accept.

Conflict resolution in $\Gamma_{\mathcal{F}}^*$ has therefore the effect of replacing each $n$-tuple in a final state by a unique action. Let $\Gamma_{\mathcal{F}}$ denotes the automaton obtained from $\Gamma_{\mathcal{F}}^*$ after conflict resolution. Note that the intermediate (i.e. non-final) states of $\Gamma_{\mathcal{F}}^*$ and $\Gamma_{\mathcal{F}}$ can be renamed by any identifier, because their tuples were useful only during the procedure of construction of $\Gamma_{\mathcal{F}}^*$. Once $\Gamma_{\mathcal{F}}^*$ is constructed, these tuples are no longer useful.

For the automaton $\Gamma_{\mathcal{F}_1}^*$ of Fig. 1, $\Gamma_{\mathcal{F}_1}$ is obtained by replacing each 3-tuple in a final state by Accept or Reject. If for example, we apply the anti-permissive conflict resolution, we obtain the automaton $\Gamma_{\mathcal{F}_1}$ of Fig. 2.

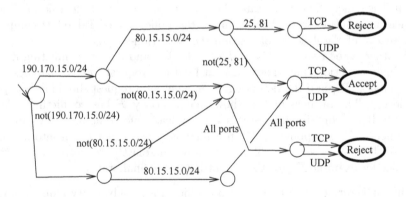

**Fig. 2.** Automaton $\Gamma_{\mathcal{F}_1}$ obtained from $\Gamma_{\mathcal{F}_1}^*$ of Fig. 1 using the anti-permissive conflict resolution.

## 4   Policy Expressions

In this section, we present the policy expressions of [26].

### 4.1   Syntax of Policy Expressions

A policy expression consists of several policies that are combined using operators $\wedge$, $\vee$, and $\neg$. The syntax of policy expressions is similar to boolean expressions. Formally, it is defined inductively as one of the following four options, where $\mathcal{F}$ denotes a policy, and $PE$, $PE_1$ and $PE_2$ denote policy expressions:

$\mathcal{F}$

$\neg(PE)$

$PE_1 \wedge PE_2$

$PE_1 \vee PE_2$

### 4.2   Action Expressions

Before specifying the semantics of policy expressions, we need to define action expressions. Syntactically, action expressions have the same form as policy expressions, but their operands are actions Accept and Reject (instead of policies). The evaluation (or semantics) of an action expression is defined inductively using the following rules, where "$A = B$" means "$A$ evaluates to $B$" (hence $A$ can be replaced by $B$):

$\neg(\text{Accept}) = \text{Reject}$

$\neg(\text{Reject}) = \text{Accept}$

$\text{Accept} \wedge \text{Accept} = \text{Accept}$

$\text{Reject} \wedge \text{Reject} = \text{Reject}$

$\text{Accept} \wedge \text{Reject} = \text{Reject}$

$\text{Reject} \wedge \text{Accept} = \text{Reject}$

$\text{Accept} \vee \text{Accept} = \text{Accept}$

$\text{Reject} \vee \text{Reject} = \text{Reject}$

$\text{Accept} \vee \text{Reject} = \text{Accept}$

$\text{Reject} \vee \text{Accept} = \text{Accept}$

### 4.3   Semantics of Policy Expressions

The semantics of a policy expression $PE$ determines the action (Accept or Reject) of $PE$ for every request. The action of $PE$ for a given request $rq$ can be determined as follows:

- Determine the action of every policy of $PE$ on $rq$.
- Construct the action expression $AE$ obtained from $PE$ by replacing every policy by its action.
- Evaluate $AE$.

## 5   Incremental Construction of an Automaton Describing a Policy Expression

The authors of [26] proposed policy expressions as a framework for bottom-up design of policies. Consider for example the policy expression $\mathcal{F}_1 \wedge (\neg(\mathcal{F}_2) \vee \mathcal{F}_3)$

constructed from policies $\mathcal{F}_1, \mathcal{F}_2, \mathcal{F}_3$. The principle of bottom-up design is to proceed in the following order: (1) design policies $\mathcal{F}_1$, $\mathcal{F}_2$ and $\mathcal{F}_3$; (2) design a policy equivalent to $PE_1 = \neg(\mathcal{F}_2)$; (3) design a policy equivalent to $PE_2 = PE_1 \vee \mathcal{F}_3$; and (4) design a policy equivalent to $PE = \mathcal{F}_1 \wedge PE_2$.

A more formal way to specify the above order is to represent the policy expression $PE$ as an abstract syntax tree (AST) $AST_{PE}$ where each leaf corresponds to a policy in $PE$, and each node corresponds to an operator $\neg$, $\wedge$ or $\vee$. A node "$\neg$" has one child, and a node "$\wedge$" or "$\vee$" has two children. Each subtree of the AST represents a subexpression of $PE$. For example, the AST of $\mathcal{F}_1 \wedge (\neg(\mathcal{F}_2) \vee \mathcal{F}_3)$ is represented in Fig. 3.

The order of bottom-up design is then specified as follows:

– Before designing a policy represented by a subtree of $AST_{PE}$ whose root $X$ is a node "$\neg$", we must design the policy represented by the subtree whose root is the child of $X$.
– Before designing a policy represented by a subtree of $AST_{PE}$ whose root $Y$ is a node "$\wedge$" or "$\vee$", we must design the two policies represented by the subtrees whose roots are the two children of $Y$.

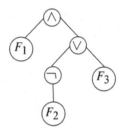

**Fig. 3.** AST of $\mathcal{F}_1 \wedge (\neg(\mathcal{F}_2) \vee \mathcal{F}_3)$.

In Sect. 3, we showed how from a policy $\mathcal{F}$ given as a table of rules, one can construct an automaton $\Gamma_\mathcal{F}$ that models $\mathcal{F}$. To use a bottom-up design with that automata-based approach, we must develop a method to construct incrementally an automaton describing a policy expression $PE$ from the automata that model the policies that compose $PE$. For example, to design a policy described by the policy expression $\mathcal{F}_1 \wedge (\neg(\mathcal{F}_2) \vee \mathcal{F}_3)$, we should proceed in the following order, where $\Gamma_{PE}$ denotes an automata modeling a policy expression $PE$:

– From the tables of $\mathcal{F}_1$, $\mathcal{F}_2$ and $\mathcal{F}_3$, construct and analyze $\Gamma_{\mathcal{F}_1}$, $\Gamma_{\mathcal{F}_2}$ and $\Gamma_{\mathcal{F}_3}$ (as shown in Sect. 3).
– From $\Gamma_{\mathcal{F}_2}$, construct and analyze $\Gamma_{PE_1}$, where $PE_1$ denotes $\neg(\mathcal{F}_2)$.
– From $\Gamma_{PE_1}$ and $\Gamma_{\mathcal{F}_3}$, construct and analyze $\Gamma_{PE_2}$, where $PE_2$ denotes $PE_1 \vee \mathcal{F}_3$.
– From $\Gamma_{\mathcal{F}_1}$ and $\Gamma_{PE_2}$, construct and analyze $\Gamma_{PE_3}$, where $PE_3$ denotes $\mathcal{F}_1 \wedge PE_2$.

For that purpose, we must develop procedures that make the following constructions, where $PE, PE_1, PE_2$ are policy expressions:

1. Construct $\Gamma_{\neg(PE)}$ from $\Gamma_{PE}$
2. Construct $\Gamma_{PE_1 \wedge PE_2}$ and $\Gamma_{PE_1 \vee PE_2}$ from $\Gamma_{PE_1}$ and $\Gamma_{PE_2}$

Point 1 is straightforward: $\Gamma_{\neg(PE)}$ is obtained by interchanging actions Accept and Reject in every final state of $\Gamma_{PE}$. Let us see how to proceed for point 2. As mentioned in Sect. 3, the basic principle to construct the automaton $\Gamma_{\mathcal{F}}$ of a policy $\mathcal{F}$ is to: first model each rule $R_i$ of $\mathcal{F}$ by an automaton $\Gamma_{R_i}$, and then compose automata $(\Gamma_{R_i})_{i=1,\cdots,n}$ into a single automaton $\Gamma_{\mathcal{F}}^*$ that is then analyzed and transformed into $\Gamma_{\mathcal{F}}$. For the above point 2, we adopt a quite similar method by composing $\Gamma_{PE_1}$ and $\Gamma_{PE_2}$ into a single automaton noted $\Gamma_{(PE_1, PE_2)}$. Since each final state of $\Gamma_{PE_1}$ and $\Gamma_{PE_2}$ is defined by an action, then every final state of $\Gamma_{(PE_1, PE_2)}$ is defined by a pair of actions. Then, $\Gamma_{PE_1 \wedge PE_2}$ (resp. $\Gamma_{PE_1 \vee PE_2}$) is constructed from $\Gamma_{(PE_1, PE_2)}$ by treating every final state $q$ as follows, where $a_1$ and $a_2$ denote the two actions of $q$:

– $a_1 \wedge a_2$ (resp. $a_1 \vee a_2$) is evaluated as shown in Sect. 4.3, and the resulting action is associated to $q$.

Consider for example the policies $\mathcal{F}_1$ and $\mathcal{F}_2$ of Tables 1 and 2 and show how to construct the automaton $\Gamma_{(\mathcal{F}_1 \wedge \neg(\mathcal{F}_2))}$. For $\mathcal{F}_1$, we have already constructed $\Gamma_{\mathcal{F}_1}$ of Fig. 2. For $\mathcal{F}_2$, we obtain $\Gamma_{\mathcal{F}_2}$ of Fig. 4, if we apply the anti-permissive conflict resolution. Then, we obtain $\Gamma_{\neg(\mathcal{F}_2)}$ by just interchanging the decisions Accept and Reject of $\Gamma_{\mathcal{F}_2}$ in Fig. 4. If we compose $\Gamma_{\mathcal{F}_1}$ and $\Gamma_{\neg(\mathcal{F}_2)}$, we obtain the automaton $\Gamma_{(\mathcal{F}_1, \neg \mathcal{F}_2)}$ of Fig. 5. Then, we obtain $\Gamma_{(\mathcal{F}_1 \wedge \neg(\mathcal{F}_2))}$ of Fig. 6 by applying the operator $\wedge$ to every pair of decisions in the $\Gamma_{(\mathcal{F}_1, \neg \mathcal{F}_2)}$ of Fig. 5.

**Table 2.** Policy $\mathcal{F}_2$

| Rule | IPsrc | IPdst | Port | Protocol | Action |
|------|-------|-------|------|----------|--------|
| $R_1$ | 190.170.15.0/24 | 80.15.15.0/24 | 25, 83 | * | Reject |
| $R_2$ | * | * | * | * | Accept |

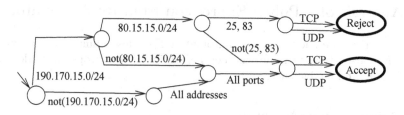

**Fig. 4.** Automaton $\Gamma_{\mathcal{F}_2}$ obtained from $\mathcal{F}_2$ of Table 2 using the anti-permissive conflict resolution.

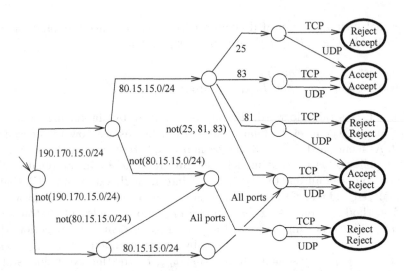

**Fig. 5.** Automaton $\Gamma_{(\mathcal{F}_1, \neg \mathcal{F}_2)}$ obtained from $\Gamma_{\mathcal{F}_1}$ and $\Gamma_{\mathcal{F}_2}$ of Figs. 2 and 4.

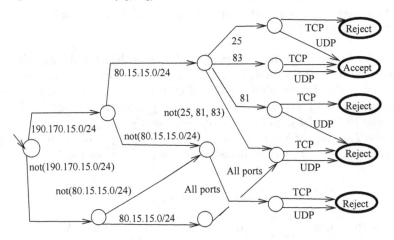

**Fig. 6.** Automaton $\Gamma_{(\mathcal{F}_1 \wedge \neg(\mathcal{F}_2))}$ obtained from $\Gamma_{(\mathcal{F}_1, \neg \mathcal{F}_2)}$ of Fig. 5.

## 6   Analysis of a Policy Expression from Its Automaton

In this section, we show how the automaton $\Gamma_{PE}$ describing a policy expression $PE$ is used to determine whether $PE$ verifies three properties: adequacy, implication, and equivalence.

### 6.1   Verification of Adequacy

A policy expression $PE$ is said to be adequate if $PE$ accepts at least one request [26]. We have already explained that when a request $rq$ leads to a final state $q$ of $\Gamma_{PE}$, then the action associated to $q$ in $\Gamma_{PE}$ indicates the action specified by $PE$ for $rq$. Therefore:

**Proposition 1.** *A policy expression PE is adequate if and only if the automaton $\Gamma_{PE}$ has at least one final state whose action is* Accept.

For example, with the policies $\mathcal{F}_1$ and $\mathcal{F}_2$ of Tables 1 and 2, the policy expression $(\mathcal{F}_1 \wedge \neg(\mathcal{F}_2))$ is adequate because $\Gamma_{(\mathcal{F}_1 \wedge \neg(\mathcal{F}_2))}$ of Fig. 6 has one final state whose action is Accept.

### 6.2   Verification of Implication

A policy expression $PE_1$ is said to imply a policy expression $PE_2$, if $PE_2$ accepts every request accepted by $PE_1$.

**Proposition 2.** *A policy expression $PE_1$ implies a policy expression $PE_2$ if and only if the policy expression $(PE_1 \wedge \neg(PE_2))$ is not adequate.*

Proposition 2 can be intuitively explained by the fact that if $PE_2$ accepts all the requests accepted by $PE_1$, then the complementary of $PE_2$ (which is $\neg(PE_2)$) does not accept any requests that are accepted by $PE_1$. Determining whether $PE_1$ implies $PE_2$ can therefore be done by determining whether the policy expression $(PE_1 \wedge \neg(PE_2))$ is not adequate.

Consider for example the policies $\mathcal{F}_1$ and $\mathcal{F}_2$ of Tables 1 and 2. $\mathcal{F}_1$ does not imply $\mathcal{F}_2$, because we have seen in Sect. 6.1 that the policy expression $(\mathcal{F}_1 \wedge \neg(\mathcal{F}_2))$ is adequate.

Note that our definition of implication is different from, but equivalent to, the definition of [26] where Proposition 2 is used as a definition of implication.

### 6.3   Verification of Equivalence

Two policy expressions $PE_1$ and $PE_2$ are said to be equivalent, if $PE_1$ implies $PE_2$ and $PE_2$ implies $PE_1$ [26].

**Proposition 3.** *Two policy expressions $PE_1$ and $PE_2$ are equivalent if and only if none of $(PE_1 \wedge \neg(PE_2))$ and $(\neg(PE_1) \wedge PE_2)$ is adequate.*

Determining whether $PE_1$ and $PE_2$ are equivalent can therefore be done by determining whether $PE_1$ implies $PE_2$ and whether $PE_1$ implies $PE_2$.

Consider for example the policies $\mathcal{F}_1$ and $\mathcal{F}_2$ of Tables 1 and 2. We have seen in Sect. 6.2 that $\mathcal{F}_1$ does not imply $\mathcal{F}_2$, and hence $\mathcal{F}_1$ and $\mathcal{F}_2$ are not equivalent.

## 7   Related Work and Contributions

There exist several methods that provide practical algorithms of logical analysis of policies, for example for testing [10], configuration error analysis [28] and vulnerability detection [12]. Other more fundamental methods provide analysis algorithms with estimations of time complexities, such as [2,3,5,18,19]. The authors of [7] show that the analyses of several problems of policies are NP-hard.

There exist several approaches to design and analyze policies, such as those used in [1,18,26,27], which are respectively referred to as "divide-and-conquer", "diverse policy design", "bottom-up design" and "step-wise refinement" in [26].

The authors of [25] propose CONFIDDENT, a model-driven design, development and maintenance framework for firewalls.

The authors of [22] propose a framework to generate test sequences to check the conformance of a policy to a specification. The system behavior is described by an extended automaton [17] and the policy that we wish to apply to this system is described by organization-based access control (OrBAC) [11].

Several methods have been developed to detect anomalies in policies or discrepancies between policies, such as in [4,6,8,9,13,14,18,21]. The authors of [21] define an anomaly in a policy by the existence of at least one request that matches several rules of the policy. The authors of [4,13] present techniques to detect anomalies in a policy, where a policy is specified by a *Policy tree* in [4] and a *Decision tree* in [13]. The authors of [6,9] propose methods to study *stateful* anomalies. The authors of [8] propose mechanisms to detect anomalies in configuration rules of policies. The authors of [18] show how to detect discrepancies between several designs of the same policy, where the policy is modeled by a *Firewall Decision Diagram* (FDD) defined in [20]. [14] is summarized Sect. 3.

Several tools have been developed to analyze and design policies, such as the engines Fireman [29] and Fang [24]. In [23], a tool is proposed to visualize and analyze firewall configurations.

The two works that most inspired this paper are [14] and [26]. As seen in Sect. 3, the authors of [14] propose a method where a policy $\mathcal{F}$ is modeled by an automaton $\Gamma_{\mathcal{F}}$ which is then used to verify several properties of $\mathcal{F}$. The authors of [26] propose a generalization of policies called policy expressions. A policy expression is specified by one or more policies and three policy operators: $\neg$, $\wedge$, $\vee$. They show how to represent each policy expression by a set of special types of policies, called slices. Then they show how to use the slice representation of a policy expression to verify whether that policy expression verifies three properties: adequacy, implication, equivalence.

Our main contribution is that this work generalizes the automata-based design approach of [14] using policy expressions of [26]. Moreover:

- We present automata in a more intuitive way than in [14], which may promote the use of our approach. Indeed, in an automaton that models a policy $\mathcal{F}$, the identifier of each state $q$ indicates the action (Accept or Reject) of every rule of $\mathcal{F}$ that matches any request leading to $q$. In [14], state identifiers are more abstract and less easy to interpret.
- As we have explained in Sect. 3.2, with our method, any conflict resolution strategy can be used as an interchangeable module. We can even apply different resolution strategies for the different policies that constitute a policy

expression. On the contrary, the method of [26] assumes that the rules are ordered in decreasing priority.

As in [26], we humbly suggest our design method to be an element of a library of policy design methods. It is up to the designer to select which design method in this library to use.

## 8  Conclusion

In [14], an automata-based approach is developed to model, design and analyze policies. In [26], a bottom-up design method of policies specified as policy expressions is suggested. A policy expression looks like a boolean expression, where policies are composed using three operators: $\neg$, $\wedge$, $\vee$. In the present paper, we have generalized the automata-based framework of [14] for policy expressions. Our contributions are indicated in detail in Sect. 7.

For future work, we plan:

- To generalize our method to support incomplete policies.
- To evaluate the space and time complexities of our method.
- To investigate the relevance of using policy expressions in concrete examples.

## References

1. Acharya, H., Joshi, A., Gouda, M.: Firewall modules and modular firewalls. In: IEEE International Conference on Network Protocols (ICNP), pp. 174–182 (2010)
2. Acharya, H.B., Gouda, M.G.: Projection and division: linear space verification of firewalls. In: 30th IEEE International Conference on Distributed Computing Systems (ICDCS), Genova, Italy, pp. 736–743, June 2010
3. Acharya, H.B., Gouda, M.G.: Firewall verification and redundancy checking are equivalent. In: 30th IEEE International Conference on Computer Communication (INFOCOM), Shanghai, China, pp. 2123–2128, April 2011
4. Al-Shaer, E., Hamed, H.: Modeling and management of firewall policies. IEEE Trans. Netw. Serv. Manag. 1(1), 2–10 (2004)
5. Al-Shaer, E., Marrero, W., El-Atawy, A., Elbadawi, K.: Network configuration in a box: towards end-to-end verification of networks reachability and security. In: 17th IEEE International Conference on Network Protocols (ICNP), Princeton, NJ, USA, pp. 736–743, October 2009
6. Cuppens, F., Cuppens-Boulahia, N., Garcia-Alfaro, J., Moataz, T., Rimasson, X.: Handling stateful firewall anomalies. In: Gritzalis, D., Furnell, S., Theoharidou, M. (eds.) SEC 2012. IAICT, vol. 376, pp. 174–186. Springer, Heidelberg (2012). https://doi.org/10.1007/978-3-642-30436-1_15
7. Elmallah, E.S., Gouda, M.G.: Hardness of firewall analysis. In: Noubir, G., Raynal, M. (eds.) NETYS 2014. LNCS, vol. 8593, pp. 153–168. Springer, Cham (2014). https://doi.org/10.1007/978-3-319-09581-3_11
8. Garcia-Alfaro, J., Cuppens, F., Cuppens-Boulahia, N.: Complete analysis of configuration rules to guarantee reliable network security policies. Int. J. Inf. Secur. 7(2), 103–122 (2008)

9. Garcia-Alfaro, J., Cuppens, F., Cuppens-Boulahia, N., Perez, S.M., Cabot, J.: Management of stateful firewall misconfiguration. Comput. Secur. **39**, 64–85 (2013)
10. Hoffman, D., Yoo, K.: Blowtorch: a framework for firewall test automation. In: Proceedings of the 20th IEEE/ACM International Conference on Automated Software Engineering (ASE), Long Beach, California, USA, pp. 96–103, November 2005
11. El Kalam, A.A., et al.: Organization based access control. In: IEEE 4th International Workshop on Policies for Distributed Systems and Networks (POLICY), Lake Come, Italy, June 2003
12. Kamara, S., Fahmy, S., Schultz, E., Kerschbaum, F., Frantzen, M.: Analysis of vulnerabilities in internet firewalls. Comput. Secur. **22**(3), 214–232 (2003)
13. Karoui, K., Ftima, F.B., Ghezala, H.B.: Formal specification, verification and correction of security policies based on the decision tree approach. Int. J. Data Netw. Secur. **3**(3), 92–111 (2013)
14. Khoumsi, A., Erradi, M., Krombi, W.: A formal basis for the design and analysis of firewall security policies. J. King Saud Univ.-Comput. Inf. Sci. **30**(1), 51–66 (2018)
15. Khoumsi, A., Krombi, W., Erradi, M.: A formal approach to verify completeness and detect anomalies in firewall security policies. In: Cuppens, F., Garcia-Alfaro, J., Zincir Heywood, N., Fong, P. (eds.) FPS 2014. LNCS, vol. 8930, pp. 221–236. Springer, Cham (2015). https://doi.org/10.1007/978-3-319-17040-4_14
16. Krombi, W., Erradi, M., Khoumsi, A.: Automata-based approach to design and analyze security policies. In: International Conference on Privacy, Security and Trust (PST), Toronto, Canada, July 2014
17. Lee, D., Yannakakis, M.: Principles and methods of testing finite state machines - a survey. Proc. IEEE **84**, 1090–1126 (1996)
18. Liu, A., Gouda, M.: Diverse firewall design. IEEE Trans. Parallel Distrib. Syst. **19**(9), 1237–1251 (2008)
19. Liu, A., Gouda, M.: Complete redundancy removal for packet classifiers in TCAMs. IEEE Trans. Parallel Distrib. Syst. **21**(4), 424–437 (2010)
20. Liu, A.X., Gouda, M.G.: Structured firewall design. Comput. Netw.: Int. J. Comput. Telecommun. Netw. **51**(4), 1106–1120 (2007)
21. Madhuri, M., Rajesh, K.: Systematic detection and resolution of firewall policy anomalies. Int. J. Res. Comput. Commun. Technol. (IJRCCT) **2**(12), 1387–1392 (2013)
22. Mallouli, W., Orset, J., Cavalli, A., Cuppens, N., Cuppens, F.: A formal approach for testing security rules. In: 12th ACM Symposium on Access Control Models and Technologies (SACMAT), Sophia Antipolis, France, June 2007
23. Mansmann, F., Göbel, T., Cheswick, W.: Visual analysis of complex firewall configurations. In: 9th International Symposium on Visualization for Cyber Security (VizSec), pp. 1–8, Seattle, WA, USA, October 2012
24. Mayer, A., Wool, A., Ziskind, E.: Fang: a firewall analysis engine. In: Proceedings of the IEEE Symposium on Security and Privacy, pp. 177–187, Berkeley, California, USA, May 2000
25. Pozo, S., Gasca, R., Reina-Quintero, A., Varela-Vaca, A.: CONFIDDENT: a model-driven consistent and non-redundant layer-3 firewall ACL design, development and maintenance framework. J. Syst. Softw. **85**(2), 425–457 (2012)
26. Reaz, R., Acharya, H.B., Elmallah, E.S., Cobb, J.A., Gouda, M.G.: Policy expressions and the bottom-up design of computing policies. In: El Abbadi, A., Garbinato, B. (eds.) NETYS 2017. LNCS, vol. 10299, pp. 151–165. Springer, Cham (2017). https://doi.org/10.1007/978-3-319-59647-1_12

27. Reaz, R., Ali, M., Gouda, M.G., Heule, M.J.H., Elmallah, E.S.: The implication problem of computing policies. In: Pelc, A., Schwarzmann, A.A. (eds.) SSS 2015. LNCS, vol. 9212, pp. 109–123. Springer, Cham (2015). https://doi.org/10.1007/978-3-319-21741-3_8

28. Wool, A.: A quantitative study of firewall configuration errors. Computer **37**(6), 62–67 (2004)

29. Yuan, L., Mai, J., Su, Z., Chen, H., Chuah, C.-N., Mohapatra, P.: FIREMAN: a toolkit for firewall modeling and analysis. In: IEEE Symposium on Security and Privacy (S&P), Berkeley/Oakland, CA, USA, May 2006

# Short Paper: STRESS-SGX: Load and Stress Your Enclaves for Fun and Profit

Sébastien Vaucher$^{(\boxtimes)}$, Valerio Schiavoni, and Pascal Felber

University of Neuchâtel, Neuchâtel, Switzerland
{sebastien.vaucher,valerio.schiavoni,pascal.felber}@unine.ch

**Abstract.** The latest generation of Intel processors supports Software Guard Extensions (SGX), a set of instructions that implements a Trusted Execution Environment (TEE) right inside the CPU, by means of so-called enclaves. This paper presents STRESS-SGX, an easy-to-use stress-test tool to evaluate the performance of SGX-enabled nodes. We build on top of the popular STRESS-NG tool, while only keeping the workload injectors (*stressors*) that are meaningful in the SGX context. We report on several insights and lessons learned about porting legacy code to run inside an SGX enclave, as well as the limitations introduced by this process. Finally, we use STRESS-SGX to conduct a study comparing the performance of different SGX-enabled machines.

**Keywords:** Intel SGX · Load · Stress · Benchmark

## 1 Introduction

The latest generation of Intel processors (starting from the Skylake microarchitecture) features a new set of instructions: Software Guard Extensions (SGX). This instruction set allows programs to execute securely inside hardware *enclaves*, hence creating a Trusted Execution Environment (TEE). Specifically, SGX enclaves protect the code from external threats, including privileged system software. Given the novelty of the technology (the first compatible CPU was released in August 2015) and the lack of in-depth literature, it is still challenging to validate the performance of code running inside enclaves. It becomes even harder to study the problem under varying conditions, such as different hardware revisions or workloads. Moreover, as we show in this paper, microcode updates issued by CPU vendors can introduce performance degradations that are difficult to promptly detect.

The main contribution of this paper is STRESS-SGX, a stress tool capable of artificially putting SGX enclaves under high load. It supports workloads of different nature, as explained in Sect. 2. As far as we know, STRESS-SGX is the first tool that can be leveraged to induce hybrid workloads (with and without SGX). We believe that many researchers can benefit from using our tool, simplifying design plans for their evaluation settings. STRESS-SGX is GPL-licensed free software[1].

---

[1] https://github.com/sebyx31/stress-sgx.

© Springer Nature Switzerland AG 2019
A. Podelski and F. Taïani (Eds.): NETYS 2018, LNCS 11028, pp. 358–363, 2019.
https://doi.org/10.1007/978-3-030-05529-5_24

**Motivating Scenarios.** We introduce three use-cases for STRESS-SGX and how researchers could leverage this tool. First, there exist several real-world cluster traces readily available for research, such as the ones released by Google Borg [7] or Microsoft Azure [2]. However, these traces do not have the same properties as typical SGX workloads. Due to anonymization, hardware characteristics of the original machines remain undisclosed. Finally, the nature of jobs deployed on these clusters is also confidential. STRESS-SGX allows to directly map behaviors described in such traces onto similar, SGX-specific ones.

A second motivating scenario stems from the availability of a range of SGX-enabled CPUs on the market, each with their own characteristics and associated performance. Apart from the expected differences due to hardware revision, cache size, available instruction sets or frequency, one still needs to hand-craft micro-benchmarks in order to evaluate SGX-specific performance. STRESS-SGX facilitates this process by providing the same interface as STRESS-NG [4] to inject load on a CPU under controlled conditions.

A third motivating scenario directly derives from the necessity to measure the electric energy consumption of code executing inside enclaves, by means of software [1] or hardware power meters. STRESS-SGX offers a common codebase for both SGX and native contexts, making it easier to isolate the energy requirements of SGX-specific workloads.

**Roadmap.** The remainder of the paper is organized as follows: Sect. 2 describes some implementation details and lessons learned. Section 3 presents our preliminary evaluation. Finally, Sect. 4 discusses future work and concludes.

## 2  Implementation

STRESS-SGX is implemented as a fork of STRESS-NG (version 0.09.10). It directly reuses the same compilation and runtime foundations. From a user perspective, SGX-enabled stressors (specific pieces of executable code that exercise a given CPU functionality or low-level operation) are selected by specifying command-line options starting with --sgx. We concentrate on porting CPU stressing methods to run in an enclave in a way that makes both native and SGX versions comparable from a performance standpoint. All features offered by the CPU stressors shipped with STRESS-NG are supported by STRESS-SGX, with the exception of partial load. Specifying a fixed load percentage is not possible (*i.e.*, it is locked to 100%), because this feature is based on precise timing, which is currently not available inside the enclave. Our STRESS-SGX prototype supports 54 enclave-enabled stress methods out of the 68 currently shipped with STRESS-NG. The exhaustive list is presented in Table 1. We note that support for each stressor depends on the availability of its required functionalities within the enclave, as well as their support by the Software Development Kit (SDK).

**Porting CPU Stressors to Run Inside an Enclave.** The Intel SGX SDK is designed in a way that allows existing code to be ported to run in an enclave with reasonable engineering efforts [3]. We take advantage of this fact to port

**Table 1.** List of stressors supported by STRESS-SGX. "✗" indicates a stressor available in STRESS-NG that is not SGX-compatible. f = float, d = double, ld = longdouble.

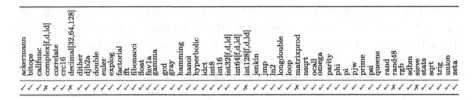

the CPU stressors of STRESS-NG in our own STRESS-SGX fork. We detail here the particular complications that we encountered throughout this porting effort, and the specific adjustments applied to solve each of them.

After creating an enclave using the template given by the SDK, we copy the relevant source code for the CPU stressors in the aforementioned template. STRESS-NG defines several macros in its global header file. It is not possible to include the code *verbatim* as it depends on numerous system-specific features. Our solution is to define the needed symbols on a case-by-case basis.

The next obstacle is the need to split the code in *trusted* and *untrusted* parts. We decompose the code in a way that limits the number of enclave transitions (*i.e.*, entering and exiting the enclave) required to run a stressor. Transitions are costly [6], so it is crucial that none happen while stressing is in progress, to ensure a consistent behavior.

The user can gracefully abort the execution of STRESS-SGX using standard Linux signals such as `SIGINT`. STRESS-NG includes a mechanism to catch the majority of signals and react accordingly for its built-in stressors. We leverage the fact that SGX enclaves can access the *untrusted* memory of their enclosing process to pass a pointer to the `g_keep_stressing_flag` variable to the enclave. This variable is later used to indicate when to stop the execution of stressors. Code running inside the enclave periodically polls the flag, and stops the execution if asked by the user. The same flag is also used to make a stressor run for a given duration. Timekeeping is done outside the enclave, with the indication to stop the execution notified by changing the value of the variable.

**Ensuring Byte-per-Byte Equivalence of Native and SGX Code.** During the initial testing phase of STRESS-SGX, we observed vast differences in performance for the same stressor executed in native and enclave modes. As a matter of fact, while the source code was identical in both instances, the resulting compiled binaries slightly differ. We believe that these slight differences are inevitable, as different linking rules are needed by each execution mode.

Conveniently, an enclave compiled using the official SGX SDK will produce a statically-compiled shared library. We leverage this aspect to guarantee that both native and SGX versions of a stressor execute a perfectly identical binary by dynamically linking this shared object. Choosing this optional approach limits STRESS-SGX to stressors that are available in enclave mode.

**Table 2.** Hardware characteristics of our test machines. All processors are made by Intel.

| Category | Model | Processor | Cores | Freq. [GHz] Base | Max. |
|---|---|---|---|---|---|
| Server | Supermicro 5019S-M2 | Xeon E3-1275 v6 | 4 | 3.8 | 4.2 |
| Desktop | Dell Optiplex 7040 | Core i7-6700 | 4 | 3.4 | 4.0 |
| NUC | Intel NUC7i7BNHX1 | Core i7-7567U | 2 | 3.5 | 4.0 |
| Stick | Intel STK2m3W64CC | Core m3-6Y30 | 2 | 0.9 | 2.2 |

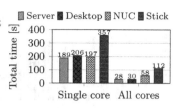

**Fig. 1.** Time needed to perform 100 000 000 enclave transitions.

## 3    Evaluation

This section presents our preliminary evaluation of STRESS-SGX. Table 2 lists the SGX machines used for our experiments. We chose these machines due to their different form factors, hardware features, and widespread market availability. We expect them to represent a meaningful sample of SGX machines that are in use nowadays. These machines are configured to run Ubuntu Linux 17.10, along with v2.0 of the Intel SGX SDK, Platform Software (PSW) and driver.

**Cost of Enclave Transitions.** When programming for SGX, it is important to keep in mind that the cost required to enter and exit an enclave is significant [6]. Figure 1 presents the time needed to perform 100 million enclave transitions on a single core at a time (left) and on all available cores (right). As expected, the server-class machine is consistently faster than the other ones, while the Intel Compute Stick performs the worst. We also observe marginal differences in single-core performance, in which case the processor can run at its maximal turbo frequency. Given the notable price difference between the various machines, the Intel NUC offers the best price-performance ratio.

**Cost of Latest Microcode Update.** The second suite of microbenchmarks highlights a rather surprising effect of a recent microcode update, recently issued by Intel (on 2018-01-08) to mitigate the Spectre attack [5]. To observe the performance impact of this microcode update, we execute all 54 supported stressors before and after the microcode update. Using the previous microcode, all stressors display the same performance in SGX and native modes. Under the updated microcode, on the other hand, we observe a significant difference in SGX *versus* native performance. Figure 2 presents the results for the 27 tests for which SGX performance is affected. We measure slowdowns up to 3.8× (`ackermann` running on a single core). Given the undisclosed nature of microcode updates, it is difficult to identify the root cause of this performance degradation.

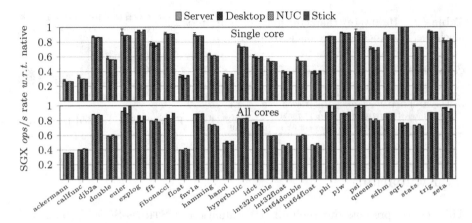

**Fig. 2.** SGX performance compared to native on different types of computers, using January 2018 microcode (previous microcode had performance similar to native).

## 4    Conclusion and Future Work

The expanding availability of SGX-enabled machines calls for new tools to evaluate the performance of *secure clusters*. The current lack of ready-to-deploy SGX applications usually forces researchers to implement single-use workloads. This paper presented STRESS-SGX, an easy-to-use tool capable of stressing SGX enclaves and report on diverse metrics. We plan to extend our prototype along the following directions: first, we intend to evaluate the performance of reading and writing encrypted memory using the memory stressors of STRESS-NG, ported in STRESS-SGX (not presented in this paper due to lack of space). Second, we will integrate these stressors within a large-scale monitoring and performance framework for containerized microservices, to easily monitor performance regressions.

**Acknowledgement.** The research leading to these results has received funding from the European Union's Horizon 2020 research and innovation programme under the LEGaTO Project (legato-project.eu), grant agreement No. 780681.

## References

1. Bourdon, A., Noureddine, A., Rouvoy, R., Seinturier, L.: PowerAPI: a software library to monitor the energy consumed at the process-level. ERCIM News **92**, 43–44 (2013)
2. Cortez, E., Bonde, A., Muzio, A., Russinovich, M., Fontoura, M., Bianchini, R.: Resource central: understanding and predicting workloads for improved resource management in large cloud platforms. In: SOSP 2017, pp. 153–167 (2017)
3. Intel Corporation: Intel Software Guard Extensions SDK Developer Reference for Linux OS, November 2017. https://frama.link/sgx20

4. King, C.I.: Stress-ng. http://kernel.ubuntu.com/~cking/stress-ng/
5. Kocher, P., et al.: Spectre attacks: exploiting speculative execution. arXiv preprint arXiv:1801.01203 (2018)
6. Orenbach, M., Lifshits, P., Minkin, M., Silberstein, M.: Eleos: ExitLess OS services for SGX enclaves. In: EuroSys 2017, pp. 238–253 (2017)
7. Wilkes, J.: More Google cluster data. Google research blog, November 2011. http://googleresearch.blogspot.com/2011/11/more-google-cluster-data.html

# Short Paper: Application of Noisy Attacks on Image Steganography

Ayidh Alharbi[✉] and Tahar M. Kechadi

University College Dublin, Belfield, Dublin 4, Ireland
ayidh.alharbi@ucdconnect.ie, tahar.kechadi@ucd.ie
https://www.insight-centre.org/

**Abstract.** The data hiding techniques have attracted a lot of attention in recent years and mainly with the intensive growth of multimedia and its possibility for covert communication. Steganography is one of the information hiding methods to confirm the ability of a multimedia carrier to exchange secret information between two end-points so that it is imperceptible, thus avoiding the detection of hidden information. The secret information can be embedded in several multimedia carriers, such as image or audio or video files. It works by embedding the message in a source cover which may make the observer feel it is the source cover itself. The type of multimedia carrier here is an image. However, this technique suffers from the problem of the carrier distortion. In this paper, we investigate the impact of some distortion types on the carrier images and discuss the possibility of using distraction images in steganography to protect the stego-image. Furthermore, we highlight the current challenges of image steganography. The experimentations show very interesting results.

**Keywords:** Image · Steganography · Speckle · Poisson · PSNR
Distortion

## 1 Introduction

In the field of information security, the search engines have returned, for cryptography, steganography and watermarking, about 29.6, 1.92 and 101 million results, respectively. This provides evidence for the growing importance of information hiding [1]. Due to the rapid and massive need of multimedia and the widespread of their applications on internet devices, it is important to analyse their potential in dealing with secret information and transformation from different perspectives. An example of that potential is image steganography. Steganography includes a large array of secret communications methods that conceal the message's very existence [2]. Steganography embeds a confidential message into another, more extensive message which serves as a carrier. The goal is to modify the carrier in an imperceptible way, so that it reveals neither the embedding of a message nor the embedded message itself [3]. Images are the

© Springer Nature Switzerland AG 2019
A. Podelski and F. Taïani (Eds.): NETYS 2018, LNCS 11028, pp. 364–368, 2019.
https://doi.org/10.1007/978-3-030-05529-5_25

most common carrier in steganography techniques and their distortion is a critical problem. In this study, we will focus on the distortion attacks against stego images. Various types of noise such as Gaussian noise [4], Poisson noise, Speckle noise [5], Salt&Pepper noise [6], and much more are fundamental noise types in case of digital images. Hence, we present a complete and practical analysis of noise models available on digital images. Furthermore, we study their impact on stego images and their potential to serve the user purposes in various ways as mentioned in Sects. 2 and 3.1, by adding a desired level of noise. Also to acknowledge if they harm the extraction process. Many research on steganography have ignored these possibilities. Their impacts were evaluated by using Peak Signal to Noise Ratio (PSNR) which determine imperceptibility and Mean Square Error (MSE). These metrics are well known in image steganography applications [1].

## 2    Experiment and Results

Several studies have been conducted on the noise models from theory point of view [7,8]. Others explained their effects briefly as part of attacks on steganography [9], and they were reviewed in [4]. However, currently, not much attention has been paid to the possibility of distortion attacks analysis on images either with or without an embedded secret text. Hence, our experiments start with a process of embedding 1000 characters as hidden text on some benchmarks of digital image (Lena) in colour and grayscale versions comparatively. Our steganographic method of embedding and extraction is based on wavelet transform. A result of that is two versions of stego images (a) and (b) shown in Fig. 1. The values of PSNR and MSE for (a) are 74.410, 0.002. Where the same values of (b) are 69.70, 0.007 respectively. The types of simulated noises used in our experiments are: Salt&Pepper, Speckle, Poisson, Gaussian. All the types of noise attacks are applied in 3 levels including their default values to help us estimating the remaining levels with the possibility of increasing or decreasing the level of the attacks. They are computed to measure which attack has the highest effect by measuring the image quality after these noises. Therefore, first, we applied these attacks to their default values (see Fig. 1(a) and (b)). A visualised example of their impact is shown in Fig. 1(c).

(a) Stego-Colour  (b) Stego-Grayscale (c) Stego images after default distortion attacks

**Fig. 1.** Stego-Lena in two versions.

To illustrate the results of stego-Colour (a) and stego-Grayscale (b) after attacks, we calculated their PSNR and MSE as shown in Fig. 2. According to the results, Poisson has the most least impact on imperceptibility value (PSNR), where salt&pepper has the maximum impact, consequently, a reverse visualisation for MSE is shown in Fig. 2(b).

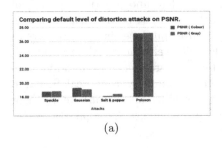

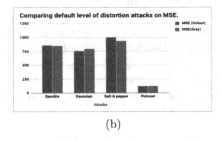

(a)                                      (b)

**Fig. 2.** Values of PSNR (a) and MSE (b) in default noisy-stego images.

In a further experiment, major levels of distortion attacks are studied. The distortion level represents the attack level. We aimed to estimate an upper bound on the noise level from a stego-Lena image and how each noise level can change the imperceptibility value (PSNR) between the stego image and its noisy version. Moreover, their cumulative error difference is based on MSE value. In this context, Poisson can be considered as a constant type of Gaussian attack, while other simulated attacks are not constant such as Speckle, Gaussian, and Salt&pepper. Therefore, they obtain a different consequence on the image feature. We implemented them with levels 0.03, 0.04, and 0.05. Their impacts on PSNR and MSE are shown in Fig. 3(a) and (b) respectively.

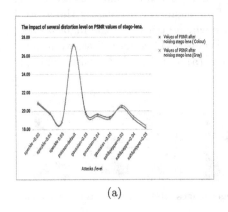

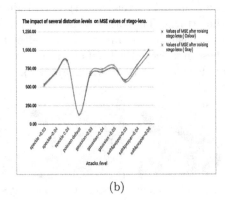

(a)                                      (b)

**Fig. 3.** PSNR and MSE values after several level of attacks

# 3    Summarised Results

Gaussian and Salt&pepper show more variance in their impact on stego image than Speckle and Poisson. In our experiment, the introduction of noise does not affect the secret text extraction process as wavelet transform hides the data in a more robust area.

In default level of attacks, the impact of distortion on PSNR from Low to high order is Poisson, Gaussian, Speckle, and Salt&pepper. Thus, the inverse order is generated for the value of MSE.

Any increasing on the level of distortion attack will be reflected on the image and the corresponding values of PSNR and MSE. It will decrease PSNR and increase MSE simultaneously.

The amount of increasing or decreasing of the image quality after these attacks depend on the type and level of attack and type of image either in grayscale or colour.

Only Gaussian noise shows a less impact on colour image compared to all other attacks, which show a less impact on the grayscale image.

## 3.1    Discussion

This section completes the previous sections on whether it is practically possible to use the distortion for user purpose such as distraction. An example of that possibility is presented in Fig. 4. In stego image, Poisson noise is used because it has the least distortion impact. From the common scenario of Alice, Bob, and the warden Willie. Alice can add a suitable level of noise which does not affect the extraction process so that Bob recognises it as a sign of stego image and the warden Willie will consider it as a normal image with a bad snapshot. We highlight them here as part of the current challenge of image steganography.

**Fig. 4.** Possibility of using noise for distraction

The other side of noisy challenges is shown in Fig. 5. Alice or Bob may add an intensive level of noise which affects the extraction to prevent the warden Willie from an active detection of the secret message. Applying an intensive noise can successfully harm the process of extracting secret message and lead to decoding errors especially with fragile spatial steganographic methods, as they are highly sensitive to noise [10]. A sample of intensive noise is shown in Fig. 5.

**Fig. 5.** Possibility of using noise in destruction

## 4   Conclusion

Typically, there is a possibility that image contains some amount of noise by its nature or by added simulated noise, but denoising the image is not an easy task, mostly because we have no information about which kind of noisy attacks has been used. More importantly, these attacks help to test any image steganographic algorithm efficiency. A suggested future work is to see if the findings are preliminary in constant order under all conditions of stego image. Also, a further study is required about noisy image applications to the end users. In this study, it should take into account the robustness of data hiding algorithm and the type and level of distortion.

## References

1. Al-Korbi, H.A., Al-Ataby, A., Al-Taee, M.A.: Highly efficient image steganography using Haar DWT for hiding miscellaneous data. I(JJCIT) **2**(1), 17–36 (2016)
2. Johnson, N.F., Jajodia, S.: Exploring steganography: seeing the unseen. Computer (1998). https://ieeexplore.ieee.org/Xplore/home.jsp
3. Westfeld, A., Pfitzmann, A.: Attacks on steganographic systems. In: Pfitzmann, A. (ed.) IH 1999. LNCS, vol. 1768, pp. 61–76. Springer, Heidelberg (2000). https://doi.org/10.1007/10719724_5
4. Boyat, A.K., Joshi, B.K.: A review paper: noise models in digital image processing, arXiv preprint arXiv:1505.03489 (2015). arxiv.org
5. Farooque, M.A., Rohankar, J.S.: Survey on various noises and techniques for denoising the color image. J. Appl. Innov. (2013). www.ijaiem.org/
6. Sahin, U., Uguz, S., Sahin, F.: Salt and pepper noise filtering with fuzzy-cellular automata. Comput. Electr. Eng. **40**, 59–69 (2014)
7. Verma, R., Ali, D.J.: A comparative study of various types of image noise and efficient noise removal techniques. International Journal of Advanced (2013). https://www.semanticscholar.org/
8. Yi, Y., Yu, X., Wang, L., Yang, Z.: Image quality assessment based on structural distortion and image definition. In: Computer Science and Software (2008). https://ieeexplore.ieee.org/Xplore/home.jsp
9. Johnson, N.F., Duric, Z., Jajodia, S.: Hiding, Information: Steganography and Watermarking-Attacks and Countermeasures: Steganography and Watermarking: Attacks and Countermeasures. Springer, Heidelberg (2001). https://doi.org/10.1007/978-1-4615-4375-6
10. Bomewar, M., Baraskar, T.: Survey on various LSB (least significant bit) methods. J. Recent. Innov. Trends **2**(6), 1649–1653 (2014)

# Graph

# A Measure for Quantifying
# the Topological Structure
# of Some Networks

Meryam Zeryouh[1][(✉)], Mohamed El Marraki[1], and Mohamed Essalih[2]

[1] LRIT - CNRST URAC 29, Rabat IT Center - Faculty of Sciences,
Mohammed V University in Rabat, B.P 1014, Rabat, Morocco
`zeryouh.meryam@gmail.com, marraki@fsr.ac.ma`
[2] LAPSSII, The Safi's Graduate Shcool of Technology,
Cadi Ayyad University in Marrakesh, Marrakesh, Morocco
`essalih.mohamed@yahoo.fr`

**Abstract.** Determining and quantifying the topological structure of networks is an exciting research topic in theoretical network science. For this purpose, a large amount of topological indices have been studied. They function as effective measures for improving the performance of existing networks and designing new robust networks. In this paper, we focus on a distance-based graph invariant named the Terminal Wiener index. We use this measure to analyze the structure of two well-known hierarchical networks: the Dendrimer tree $\mathcal{T}_{d,h}$ and the Dendrimer graph $\mathcal{D}_{d,h}$. We also investigate two methods of calculation in order to show that the proposed method reduces the computational complexity of the Terminal Wiener index.

**Keywords:** Networks · Topological indices · Terminal Wiener index
Dendrimer tree · Dendrimer graph · Computational complexity

## 1 Introduction

Many complex systems can be modeled as networks and studied using techniques derived from graph theory. Examples include the power grids, communication networks, biological networks, molecular networks, social networks, etc. One of the most fundamental questions arising from the study of networks is to quantify the topological properties of a structure. For this reason, the study of quantitative measures also called topological indices has become a subject of great interest [1]. The concept of topological indices began in 1947, when the physical chemist H. Wiener used the Wiener index for predicting the boiling points of paraffin [2]. Many years after its introduction, the same quantity has been extended to the field of complex systems [3,4]. Due to the success of this graph invariant, a large number of topological indices have been put forward in the literature [1,5].

© Springer Nature Switzerland AG 2019
A. Podelski and F. Taïani (Eds.): NETYS 2018, LNCS 11028, pp. 371–381, 2019.
https://doi.org/10.1007/978-3-030-05529-5_26

In this paper, we focus on some distance-based graph invariants: the Wiener index [2] and the Terminal Wiener index [6]. These two indices can be used as effective measures to evaluate the efficiency of a network and to quantify the communication between people in a social network [7,8]. For a general network $G$, one way for computing the Wiener index or the Terminal Wiener index is to use the definition and compute all the distances between pairs of vertices or pendent vertices, respectively. The complexity of this method is dominated by computing all pairs of shortest paths [9]. Hence, the fundamental task would be to design a fast and an efficient method for calculating any distance-based topological index avoiding computation of all shortest paths. In [10], a powerful method was introduced for computing the Wiener index of networks and showed a linear time complexity especially for hexagonal systems. The main idea of this method is to reduce the original network $G$ into smaller weighted graphs called quotient graphs and then the Wiener index of the original network $G$ is obtained from the quotient graphs. In this work, our aim is to extend this method in the case of the Terminal Wiener index. Then, in order to demonstrate the significance of this technique, we compute the Terminal Wiener index of two hierarchical networks: the Dendrimer tree also called Cayley tree and the Dendrimer graph [11]. For the first network, we apply a re-formula of the Terminal Wiener index, and for the second network, we apply the proposed method.

We proceed as follows: In Sect. 2, we introduce the basic concepts and we prove that the computation of the Terminal Wiener index can be reduced to the computation of the Wiener index of the appropriately weighted quotient graphs. In Sects. 3 and 4, we quantify the topological structure of the Dendrimer tree and the Dendrimer graph by using the two proposed methods. We summarize our findings in the section of concluding remarks.

## 2    Basic Concepts and Methods

Throughout this paper, we use the terms graph and network interchangeably.

Let $G = (V_G, E_G)$ be a graph with $V_G$ is the set of vertices and $E_G$ the set of edges. Let $d_p(k)$ denote the number of all pairs of pendent vertices (vertices of degree 1) of the graph $G$ whose distances $d(u, v)$ is equal to $k$. A weighted graph $(G, \omega)$ is a graph $G$ with a weight function $\omega : V(G) \to \mathbf{R}$ that assigns positive real numbers to the vertices of $G$. The graph $G$ is called a partial cube if its vertices $u$ can be labeled with binary strings $l(u)$ of a fixed length, such that $d(u, v) = H(l(u), l(v))$. The edges $e = xy$ and $f = uv$ are in the relation *Djoković-Winkler* $\theta$ if $d(x, u) + d(y, v) \neq d(x, v) + d(y, u)$. The relation $\theta$ is always reflexive and symmetric, and is transitive on partial cubes. Therefore, $\theta$ partitions the edge set of a partial cube into equivalent classes $F_1, F_2, ..., F_k$, called cuts. The techniques used in this work are presented as follows:

### 2.1    Method Based on a Re-formula of the Terminal Wiener Index

At first, we present the definition of the two topological indices: the Wiener index and the Terminal Wiener index.

**Definition 1.** *Let G be a graph. Then the Wiener index of G is equal to the sum of distances between all pairs of vertices of G.*

$$W(G) = \sum_{\{u,v\} \subseteq V(G)} d(u,v) \tag{1}$$

The Terminal Wiener index is one of the most recent extensions of the Wiener index, that was introduced by Gutman et al. [6].

**Definition 2.** *Let $V_p(G) \subseteq V(G)$ be the set of pendent vertices of the graph G. Then the Terminal Wiener index is defined as the sum of distances between all pairs of pendent vertices of G.*

$$TW(G) = \sum_{\{u,v\} \subseteq V_p(G)} d(u,v) \tag{2}$$

From the above definition, we can rewrite the Terminal Wiener index as follows:

**Lemma 1.** *Let G be a graph with n vertices and $p \geq 2$ pendent vertices. Let $D(G)$ be the diameter of G. Then:*

$$TW(G) = \begin{cases} p(p-1) + d_p(3) + 2d_p(4) + \ldots + (D-2)d_p(D) & \text{if } D(G) > 2, \\ p(p-1) & \text{if } D(G) = 2. \end{cases} \tag{3}$$

*Proof.* The proof of this lemma is obvious, see [12] for illustration.   □

We can observe that Lemma 1 focuses on the calculation of all shortest path between pendent vertices that made the computational complexity of this technique dominated by computing all distances.

## 2.2   Method Based on Edge-Partitions

In this method, we extend the algorithm proposed by Klavžar [10] to the case of the Terminal Wiener index. For this purpose, we need some auxiliary results.

   We start with the definition of the weighted Wiener index of a weighted graph $(G, \omega)$:

**Definition 3** [13]. *Let $(G, \omega)$ be a weighted graph. Then the weighted Wiener index $W(G, \omega)$ of $(G, \omega)$ is defined as:*

$$W(G, \omega) = \sum_{\{u,v\} \subseteq V(G)} \omega(u)\omega(v)d_G(u,v) \tag{4}$$

Let $\theta^*$ be the transitive closure of the relation *Djoković-Winkler* $\theta$. Then, $\theta^*$ partitions the edge set of a graph $G$ into $\theta^*$- equivalent classes. As an example, consider the graph $G$ from Fig. 1. It has two $\theta^*$-classes $F_1$ and $F_2$.

   For describing the proposed method, we need to use the concept of the canonical metric representation of a graph [14].

   Let $\alpha$ be the canonical metric representation of a connected graph $G$:

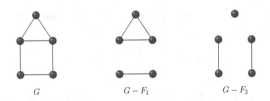

**Fig. 1.** $\theta^*$-equivalent classes of $G$

- Let $G$ be a connected graph and $F_1, ..., F_k$ its $\theta^*$-classes.
- Let $G/F_i$ be the quotient graphs, $i = 1, ..., k$. Its vertices are the connected components of $G - F_i$. Two vertices $u$ and $v$ being adjacent if there exist vertices $x \in u$ and $y \in v$ such that $xy \in F_i$.
- Define $\alpha : G \to \prod_{1 \leq i \leq k} G/F_i$ with $\alpha : u \to (\alpha_1(u), ..., \alpha_k(u))$, where $\alpha_i(u)$ is the connected component of $G - F_i$ that contains the pendent vertex $u$.
- Let $(G/F_i, \omega)$ be a weighted graph, such that, the weight of a vertex of $G/F_i$ is the number of pendent vertices in the corresponding connected components of $G - F_i$. We consider only the pendent vertices that already exist in the original graph $G$.

The computational complexity of the Terminal Wiener index of a graph $G$ can be reduced as follows:

**Theorem 1.** *For any connected graph with $p \geq 2$ pendent vertices, we have:*

$$TW(G) = \sum_{1 \leq i \leq k} W(G/F_i, \omega) \tag{5}$$

*Proof.* Let $C_1^{(i)}, ..., C_{r_i}^{(i)}$ be the connected components of $G - F_i$ with $1 \leq i \leq k$. We denote by $|V_p(C_j^{(i)})|$ the number of pendent vertices in the component $C_j^{(i)}$, and we note that, we should considerate only the number of pendent vertices that already exist in the original graph $G$.

From the above notations of the canonical metric representation $\alpha$, we can see that:

$$TW(G) = \sum_{\{u,v\} \in V_p(G)} d_G(u, v)$$

$$= \sum_{\{u,v\} \in V_p(G)} d_G(\alpha(u), \alpha(v))$$

$$= \sum_{\{u,v\} \in V_p(G)} \sum_{i=1}^{k} d_{G/F_i}(\alpha_i(u), \alpha_i(v))$$

$$= \sum_{i=1}^{k} \sum_{\{u,v\} \in V_p(G)} d_{G/F_i}(\alpha_i(u), \alpha_i(v))$$

$$= \sum_{i=1}^{k} \sum_{1 \le j \le j' \le r_i} d_{G/F_i}\left(C_j^{(i)}, C_{j'}^{(i)}\right) |V_p(C_j^{(i)})| |V_p(C_{j'}^{(i)})|$$

$$= \sum_{i=1}^{k} W(G/F_i, \omega)$$

□

From Theorem 1 we can see that the Terminal Wiener index can be reduced to the computation of the Wiener index of the appropriately weighted quotient graphs. In other words, this method focuses only on counting the number of pendent vertices in the corresponding connected components. From this fact, the main result of this subsection can be useful to design a faster algorithm for computing the Terminal Wiener index avoiding the computation of the distances [9], and it can be implemented to run in linear time if the corresponding quotient graphs of a network $G$ are trees. For more information about linear algorithms for the computation of topological indices of a specific class of graphs we refer to see [15,16]. We note that this technique is also an efficient tool for a hand manipulation, see Sect. 4.

## 3   Quantifying the Topological Structure of the Dendrimer Tree

In this section, we introduce the construction method and some structural properties of the Dendrimer tree $T_{d,h}$. Then, we give the analytical expression of the Terminal Wiener index for this structure by using the first technique, which is based on a re-formula of this index.

### 3.1   Construction Method and Structural Properties

Let $T_{d,h}$ ($d \ge 3, h \ge 0$) be a Dendrimer tree with two additional parameters: fixed maximum degree $d$ and the number of iterations or depth $h$. The Dendrimer tree can be built in the following iterative way. Initially, $T_{d,0}$ consists of only a central vertex that is the core of the Dendrimer tree. $T_{d,1}$ is obtained by attaching $d$ vertices to the central vertex. For any $h > 1$, we obtain $T_{d,h}$ from $T_{d,h-1}$ by attaching $d-1$ new vertices to the pendent vertices of $T_{d,h-1}$. Figure 2 illustrates an example for a Dendrimer tree with $d = 3$ and $h = \{0, 1, 2, 3\}$. Every internal vertex of the Dendrimer tree has degree $d$, and the iteration $h$ denote the distance between all pendent vertices (blue vertices) and the core vertex.

From the construction method of the Dendrimer tree $T_{d,h}$, we can extract the following structural properties:

- The number of pendent vertices of $T_{d,h}$ is:

$$p_h = d(d-1)^{h-1} \qquad with \ h \geq 1 \tag{6}$$

- The number of vertices of $T_{d,h}$ is:

$$N_h = 1 + d\frac{(d-1)^h - 1}{d-2} \tag{7}$$

- The diameter $D_h$ of $T_{d,h}$ is equal to:

$$D_h = 2h \tag{8}$$

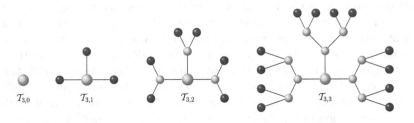

**Fig. 2.** Dendrimer trees $T_{d,h}$ with $d = 3$ and $h = \{0, 1, 2, 3\}$ (Color figure online)

### 3.2  Computation of the Terminal Wiener Index for the Network $T_{d,h}$

In this part, we use the rewrite of the Terminal Wiener index in order to get analytical expression of this index for the structure $T_{d,h}$.

We start with the following lemma, that is defined as follows:

**Lemma 2.** *For any Dendrimer tree* $T_{d,h}$. *The* $d_p(k)$ *for* $k = \{4, 6, 8, ..., D_h\}$ *is given by:*

$$d_p(k) = \begin{cases} \frac{d(d-2)}{2}(d-1)^{\frac{2h+k-4}{2}} & if \ k \leq 2(h-1), \\ \frac{d}{2}(d-1)^{k-1} & if \ k = 2h. \end{cases} \tag{9}$$

*Proof.* We have the distance between pendent vertices of the Dendrimer tree $T_{d,h}$ is always even. In the first iteration, $d$ vertices are attached to the central vertex, and in the next iterations, each pendent vertex $v_i$ is attached to $(d-1)$ vertices. Obviously, with some calculations and due to the symmetry of this structure, we can get the result.                                              □

**Theorem 2.** *Let* $T_{d,h}$ *be a Dendrimer tree with* $h \geq 1$ *and* $d \geq 3$. *Then:*

$$TW(T_{d,h}) = d(d-1)^{h-1}\left[(d-1)^{h-1}\left(hd - \frac{d-1}{d-2}\right) - 1 + \frac{d-1}{d-2}\right] \tag{10}$$

*Proof.* By using Lemmas 1, 2 and the structural properties of $\mathcal{T}_{d,h}$, we get:

$$TW(\mathcal{T}_{d,h}) = p_h(p_h - 1) + 2d_p(4) + 4d_p(6) + \ldots + (D_h - 2)d_p(D_h)$$

$$= d(d-1)^{h-1}[d(d-1)^{h-1} - 1] + \frac{d(d-2)}{2}\sum_{i=1}^{h-2} 2i(d-1)^{h-1+i}$$

$$+ d(h-1)(d-1)^{2h-1}$$

which yields the Eq.(10).                                                        □

**Table 1.** The numerical result of the Terminal Wiener index of the dendrimer tree $\mathcal{T}_{d,h}$

| $TW(\mathcal{T}_{d,h})$ | | | | |
|---|---|---|---|---|
| | $d = 3$ | $d = 4$ | $d = 5$ | $d = 6$ |
| h=1 | 6 | 12 | 20 | 30 |
| h=2 | 54 | 240 | 700 | 1620 |
| h=3 | 348 | 3420 | 17520 | 62850 |
| h=4 | 1944 | 42336 | 382400 | 2133000 |
| h=5 | 10032 | 485676 | 7755520 | 67383750 |

**The Numerical Result:** In Table 1, we present some values of the Terminal Wiener index of the Dendrimer tree $\mathcal{T}_{d,h}$. We can see that the behavior of this measure shows a dominant change with the increasing values of the number of iterations $h$ and the maximum degree $d$.

## 4    Quantifying the Topological Structure of the Dendrimer Graph

In this section, we represent the construction method of the dendrimer graph $\mathcal{D}_{d,h}$, analyze its structural properties and we express the Terminal Wiener index of this structure using the second method.

### 4.1    Construction Method and Structural Properties

Let $\mathcal{D}_{d,h}$ be a Dendrimer graph, where $h$ denote the levels and $d$ the number of vertices added to every vertex in each iteration. The $\mathcal{D}_{d,h}$ can be built in the following iterative way. Initially, the dendrimer graph is composed of a core $\mathcal{D}_0$ that contain a cycle of order $n'$ and $d - 1$ vertices attached to each vertex of the cycle, which gives $p_0$ pendent vertices. $\mathcal{D}_{d,1}$ is obtained from $\mathcal{D}_0$ by adding $d$ vertices to each pendent vertex of $\mathcal{D}_0$. Similarly, we obtain $\mathcal{D}_{d,h}$ from $\mathcal{D}_{d,h-1}$ by attaching $d$ vertices to every pendent vertex of $\mathcal{D}_{d,h-1}$. Figure 3, illustrates some iterations of the Dendrimer graph $\mathcal{D}_{d,h}$. The internal vertices of the network $\mathcal{D}_{d,h}$ have degree equal to $d+1$, and the level $h$ denote the distance between all pendent vertices and terminal vertices of the core.

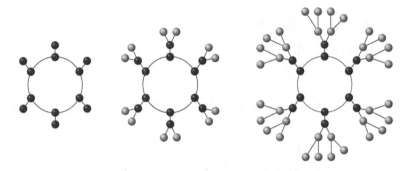

**Fig. 3.** (Left) The core $\mathcal{D}_0$ of the Dendrimer graph, with $n' = 6$ and $p_0 = 6$. (Middle and Right) Dendrimer graphs $\mathcal{D}_{d,h}$, with $d = 2$ and $h = \{1, 2\}$.

From the construction method of the Dendrimer graph $\mathcal{D}_{d,h}$, we can derive some structural properties:

– The number of pendent vertices of the graph $\mathcal{D}_{d,h}$ is equal to:

$$p_h = d^h(d-1)n' \tag{11}$$

– The number of vertices of $\mathcal{D}_{d,h}$ is equal to:

$$N_h = n' + n'(d^{h+1} - 1) \tag{12}$$

– The diameter of this structure $\mathcal{D}_{d,h}$ is equal to:

$$D_h = \lfloor \frac{n'}{2} \rfloor + 2(h+1) \tag{13}$$

## 4.2   Calculation of the Terminal Wiener Index for the Network $\mathcal{D}_{d,h}$

In this section, we apply the technique based on edge partitions in order to obtain the Terminal Wiener index of the structure $\mathcal{D}_{d,h}$.

The following lemma is crucial for the proof of the next theorem.

**Lemma 3.** *Let* $(\mathcal{C}_n, \omega)$ *be a weighted cycle of order* $n$, *such that, all the vertices have the same weight* $\omega$. *Then:*

$$W(\mathcal{C}_n, \omega) = \begin{cases} \frac{1}{8}n^3\omega^2 & \text{if } n \text{ is even,} \\[2mm] \frac{1}{8}(n^3 - n)\omega^2 & \text{if } n \text{ is odd.} \end{cases} \tag{14}$$

*Proof.* Obviously, by using the Definition 3 with identical weights $w(u) = w(v)$.

$\square$

**Theorem 3.** *Let $\mathcal{D}_{d,h}$ be a Dendrimer graph, with $d \geq 2$ and $h \geq 0$. Then:*

*– If $n'$ is even:*

$$TW(\mathcal{D}_{d,h}) = n'd^{2h}\left[(d-1)^2\left(\frac{1}{8}n'^2 + n'(h+1)\right) - d\right] + n'd^h \qquad (15)$$

*– If $n'$ is odd:*

$$TW(\mathcal{D}_{d,h}) = n'd^{2h}\left[(d-1)^2\left(\frac{1}{8}(n'^2 - 1) + n'(h+1)\right) - d\right] + n'd^h \qquad (16)$$

*Proof.* The core $\mathcal{D}_0$ of the Dendrimer graph contains a cycle of order $n'$. In the case of an even $n'$, it is easy to observe that an edge $e$ of the cycle $\mathcal{C}$ of $\mathcal{D}_{d,h}$ is in relation $\theta$ with its antipodal edge on $\mathcal{C}$ and if the order of the cycle is odd, then all the edges will be in the same $\theta^*$-class.

Now, we determine the corresponding weighted graphs of the dendrimer graph $\mathcal{D}_{d,h}$: In category A, we represent the weighted graphs obtained by removing an edge that doesn't belong to the cycle of the core $\mathcal{D}_0$, and category B contains the weighted graphs obtained by removing an edge or all the edges of the cycle of the core $\mathcal{D}_0$.

Category A                           Category B

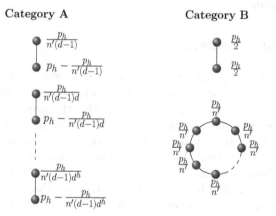

Each weighted graph from the category A is repeated $d^i(d-1)n'$ times with $0 \leq i \leq h$, and if we are in the case of an even cycle, the weighted graph from the category B, that is in the top, is repeated $\frac{n'}{2}$ times.

Then, we apply the Theorem 1 with the above representations, the Lemma 3 and the structural properties of $\mathcal{D}_{d,h}$:

– if $n'$ is even

$$TW(\mathcal{D}_{d,h}) = \frac{n'}{2}\left[\frac{p_h}{2}\frac{p_h}{2}\right] + \sum_{i=0}^{h} d^i(d-1)n'\left[\frac{p_h}{n'(d-1)d^i} * \left(p_h - \frac{p_h}{n'(d-1)d^i}\right)\right]$$

– if $n'$ is odd

$$TW(\mathcal{D}_{d,h}) = \left(\frac{p_h}{n'}\right)^2 \left(\frac{1}{8}n'^3 - \frac{1}{8}n'\right) + \sum_{i=0}^{h} d^i(d-1)n' \left[\frac{p_h}{n'(d-1)d^i}\left(p_h - \frac{p_h}{n'(d-1)d^i}\right)\right]$$

Which yield the Eqs. 15, 16, respectively.                                            □

**Table 2.** The numerical result of the Terminal Wiener index of the dendrimer graph $\mathcal{D}_{d,h}$

| $TW(\mathcal{D}_{d,h})$ for $n' = 3$ | | | | $TW(\mathcal{D}_{d,h})$ for $n' = 4$ | | | |
|---|---|---|---|---|---|---|---|
| | $d=2$ | $d=3$ | $d=4$ | $d=5$ | $d=2$ | $d=3$ | $d=4$ | $d=5$ |
| h=1 | 66 | 684 | 2844 | 8040 | 136 | 1344 | 5520 | 15520 |
| h=2 | 396 | 9018 | 66096 | 290700 | 784 | 17208 | 124992 | 547600 |
| h=3 | 2136 | 107244 | 1388736 | 9516000 | 4128 | 201312 | 2588928 | 17688000 |
| h=4 | 10800 | 1200906 | 27525888 | 294142500 | 20544 | 2231064 | 50856960 | 542190000 |
| h=5 | 52320 | 12932460 | 525339648 | 8759775000 | 98432 | 23856768 | 964694016 | 16005875000 |

**The Numerical Result:** In Table 2, we present some values of the Terminal Wiener index of the Dendrimer graph $\mathcal{D}_{d,h}$. Such that, we take into consideration the parity of $n'$. In general, this measure shows an increasing change by modifying the values of parameters.

## 5   Concluding Remarks

The computation of topological indices is an important task in the study of structural properties of networks. In this paper, we have calculated the Terminal Wiener index of two hierarchical networks: the Dendrimer tree and the Dendrimer graph. In order to show the computational complexity of this index, we have investigated two methods of computation. The first method is based on a re-formula of the Terminal Wiener index and its complexity is dominated by computing all shortest paths at a given distance. The second method is based on the edge-partitions and its efficiency is in the fact that it reduces the original network into smaller components and avoids the computation of all shortest paths.

## References

1. Emmert-Streib, F., Dehmer, M.: Networks for systems biology: conceptual connection of data and function. IET Syst. Biol. **5**(3), 185–207 (2011)
2. Wiener, H.: Structural determination of paraffin boiling points. J. Am. Chem. Soc. **69**, 17–20 (1947)
3. Wuchty, S., Stadler, P.F.: Centers of complex networks. J. Theor. Biol. **223**(1), 45–53 (2003)

4. Estrada, E., Vargas-Estrada, E.: Distance-sum heterogeneity in graphs and complex networks. Appl. Math. Comput. **218**(21), 10393–10405 (2012)
5. Kraus, V., Dehmer, M., Emmert-Streib, F.: Probabilistic inequalities for evaluating structural network measures. Inf. Sci. **288**, 220–245 (2014)
6. Gutman, I., Furtula, B., Petrovic, M.: Terminal Wiener index. J. Math. Chem. **46**, 522–531 (2009)
7. Rodríguez-Velázquez, J.A., Kamišalić, A., Domingo-Ferrer, J.: On reliability indices of communication networks. Comput. Math. Appl. **58**(7), 1433–1440 (2009)
8. Goel, S., Anderson, A., Hofman, J., Watts, D.J.: The structural virality of online diffusion. Manag. Sci. **62**(1), 180–196 (2015)
9. Mohar, B., Pisanski, T.: How to compute the Wiener index of graph. J. Math. Chem. **2**(3), 267–277 (1988)
10. Klavžar, S.: On the canonical metric representation, average distance, and partial Hamming graphs. Eur. J. Comb. **27**(1), 68–73 (2006)
11. Klajnert, B., Bryszewska, M.: Dendrimers: properties and applications (2001)
12. Essalih, M., El Marraki, M., Alhagri, G.: Calculation of some topological indices graph. J. Theor. Appl. Inf. Technol. **30**(2), 122–128 (2011)
13. Klavžar, S., Gutman, I.: Wiener number of vertex-weighted graphs and a chemical application. Discret. Appl. Math. **80**(1), 73–81 (1997)
14. Graham, R.L., Winkler, P.M.: On isometric embeddings of graphs. Trans. Am. Math. Soc. **288**(2), 527–536 (1985)
15. Chepoi, V., Klavžar, S.: The Wiener index and the Szeged index of benzenoid systems in linear time. J. Chem. Inf. Comput. Sci. **37**(4), 752–755 (1997)
16. Črepnjak, M., Tratnik, N.: The Szeged index and the Wiener index of partial cubes with applications to chemical graphs. Appl. Math. Comput. **309**, 324–333 (2017)

# Short Paper: Maintenance of Strongly Connected Component in Shared-Memory Graph

Muktikanta Sa$^{(\boxtimes)}$

Department of Computer Science and Engineering,
Indian Institute of Technology Hyderabad, Hyderabad, India
`cs15resch11012@iith.ac.in`

**Abstract.** In this paper, we present an on-line fully dynamic algorithm for maintaining strongly connected component of a directed graph in a shared memory architecture. The edges and vertices are added or deleted concurrently by fixed number of threads. To the best of our knowledge, this is the first work to propose using linearizable concurrent directed graph and is build using both ordered and unordered list-based set. We provide an empirical comparison against sequential and coarse-grained. The results show our algorithm's throughput is increased between 3 to 6x depending on different workload distributions and applications. We believe that there are huge applications in the on-line graph. Finally, we show how the algorithm can be extended to community detection in on-line graph.

**Keywords:** Concurrent data structure · Directed graph
Strong connected components
Connectivity on directed graphs · Dynamic graph algorithms

## 1 Introduction

Generally the real-world practical graph always dynamically change over time. Dynamic graphs are the one's which are subjected to a sequence of changes like insertion, deletion of vertices and/or edges [1]. Dynamic graph algorithms are used extensively and it has been studied for several decades. Many important results have been achieved for fundamental dynamic graph problems and some of these problems are very challenging i.e, finding cycles, graph coloring, minimum spanning tree, shortest path between a pair of vertices, connectivity, 2-edge & 2-vertex connectivity, transitive closure, strongly connected components, flow network, etc (see, e.g., the survey in [1]).

We have been specifically motivated by largely used problem of fully dynamic evolution *Strongly Connected Components* (SCC). Detection of SCC in dynamically changing graph affects a large community both in the theoretical computer science and the network community. SCC detection on static networks fails to capture the natural phenomena and important dynamics. Discovering SCCs on dynamic graph helps uncover the laws in processes of graph evolution, which

© Springer Nature Switzerland AG 2019
A. Podelski and F. Taïani (Eds.): NETYS 2018, LNCS 11028, pp. 382–387, 2019.
https://doi.org/10.1007/978-3-030-05529-5_27

have been proven necessary to capture essential structural information in on-line social networking platforms (facebook, linkedin, google+, twitter, quora, etc.). SCC often merges or splits because of the changing friendship over time. A common application of SCC on these social graph is to check weather two members belong to the same SCC (or community).

In this paper, we present a new shared-memory algorithm called as *SMSCC* for maintaining SCC in fully dynamic directed graphs. We have not found any comparable concurrent data-structure for solving this strongly connected components problem in shared-memory architecture. Hence we crosscheck against sequential and coarse-grained implementations.

There have been many parallel computing algorithms proposed for computing SCC both in directed and undirected graphs. Hopcroft and Tarjan [4] presented the first algorithm to compute the connected components of a graph using the depth first searches (DFS) approaches. Hirschburg et al. [3] presented a novel parallel algorithm for finding the connected components in an undirected graph. In 1981, Shiloach and Even [7] presented a first decremental algorithm that finds all connected components in dynamic graphs, only edges are deleted. Henzinger and King [2] also proposed a new algorithm that maintains spanning tree for each connected components, which helps them to update the data-structure quickly only when deletion of edge occurs.

None of above proposed algorithms clarify how the internal share-memory access is achieved by the multi-threads/processors and how the memory is synchronized, whether the data-structure is linearizable or not, etc. In this paper we able to address these problems.

## 2   Construction of SCC-Graph

In this section we present the node structures of `vertex`, `edge` and `scc` to construct the SCC-graph. It is implemented as a collection (list) of SCCs, wherein each SCC holds the list of vertex set belongs to it, and each vertex holds the edge list (both incoming and outgoing edges). We represent all incoming edges with negative sign followed by `val` and outgoing edges with the `val`, as shown in the Fig. 1b.

The `Gnode` structure (similar as [5]) is a normal node and has five fields. The `val` field is the actual value of the node, if it is a vertex node, stores the vertex id, if it is an outgoing edge, stores the `val` of the destination vertex and if it is an incoming edge, stores the `-val` of source vertex. The main idea of storing both incoming and outgoing edges for each vertex helps to explore the graph backward and forward manner respectively. And also it helps to trim the SCC-Graph after deleting a vertex, i.e, once a thread successfully deleted a vertex, all its incoming and outgoing edges to be removed quickly instate of iterating over whole SCC-Graph. The vertex and edge nodes are sorted in the `val` order (lower to higher), it provides an efficient way to search when an item is absent. The boolean `marked` field is used to set the node and helps traversal to the target node without lock, we maintain an invariant that every unmarked node is reachable from the sentinel node `Head`. If a node is marked, then that is not logically present in the list. Each node has a `lock` field, that helps to achieve the *fine-grained* concurrency. Each node can be locked by invoking lock() and unlock() methods and helps multiple threads can traverse the list concurrently. The vnext & enext fields are the atomic references to the next vertex node in the vertex list and the next edge node in the edge list of a vertex respectively.

```
unsigned long ccid;
unsigned long ccCount
typedef struct Gnode{
  long val;
  bool marked;
  Lock lock;
  struct Gnode *vnext;
  struct Gnode *enext;
}slist_t;
typedef struct CCnode{
  long ccno;
  bool marked;
  Lock lock;
  struct Gnode* vnext;
  struct CCnode *next;
}cclist_t
class SCC{
  CCnode CCHead, CCTail;
  bool AddVertex(u);
  bool RemoveVertex(u)
  bool AddEdge(u, v);
  bool RemoveEdge(u, v);
  bool checkSCC(u,v);
  int  blongsTo(v);
};
```

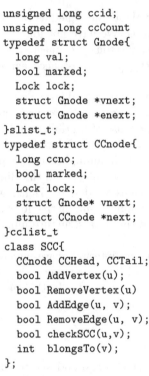

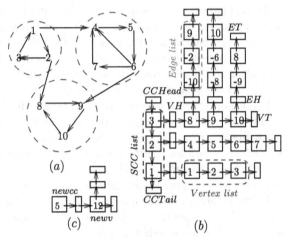

Fig. 1. (a) An example of a directed graph having three SCCs. (b) The SCC-Graph representation of (a), Each SCCs have their own ccno and vertex list, each vertex have their own adjacency vertex (both incoming (−ve) and outgoing) represent in edge list, e.g. vertex 10 present in SCC 3 and it has an incoming edge (-9) and an outgoing edge (8). (c) Structure of a new SCC, whenever a new vertex is added, a new SCC is created with new vertex and then inserted at the beginning of the CCHead in the SCC-Graph.

The CCnode structure is used for holding all vertices belonging to a SCC. Like Gnode, it has five fields. The ccno field is the actual scc key value and unique for each SCC. Once a key assigned to a SCC, same key will never generate again. We assume our system provides sufficient number of unique key and had no upper bound. The boolean marked and lock have same meaning as in the Gnode. The vnext and next fileds are the atomic references to vertex head (VH) and next CCnode. Finally, the SCC class is the actual abstract class, which coordinates all operation activities. This class uses two type of nodes, Gnode and CCnode. The vertex & edge nodes are represent by Gnode and the SCC nodes are represented by CCnode, it also has two sentinel nodes CCHead and CCTail. The SCC class supports four basic graph operations *AddVertex, AddEdge* and *RemoveVertex, RemoveEdge*, and also some application specific methods, *checkSCC, blongsToCommunity*, etc. The detail working and pseudo code is given in the full paper [6]. Apart from above structures and class, we have two atomic variables ccid and ccCount used to hold the unique id for each CCnode and total number of SCCs respectively.

# 3    An Overview of the Algorithm

The SCC class supports some basic operations: AddVertex, RemoveVertex, AddEdge, RemoveEdge, checkSCC, blongsTo, etc. and all of these methods are dead-lock free. The high-level overview of the AddEdge and RemoveEdge methods are given bellow and the technical details of all the methods are in the full paper [6].

**AddEdge (u, v):**
1. Checks the presence of vertices $u$, $v$ and edge$(u, v)$ in the SCC-Graph. If both vertices are present & the edge is not present, adds $v$ in the $u$'s edge list and adds $-u$ in the $v$'s edge list, else returns false.
2. After adding the edge successful, checks the `ccid` of both the vertices.
3. If $u.ccid$ is same as $v.ccid$, returns true, as no changes to the current SCC, else goto step 4.
4. Checks the reachability path from vertex $v$ to $u$, if it is true, goto step 5, else returns true, as no changes to the current SCC.
5. Runs the limited version of Tarjan's algorithm, process the affected SCCs along with its vertices and edges, merge them all to create a new SCC.
   - At first it creates a new scc with any one old vertex, later adds rest of vertices to that newly created SCC and then disconnects from old SCC.

**RemoveEdge (u, v):**
1. Checks the presence of vertex $u$, $v$ and edge$(u, v)$ in the SCC-Graph. If both are present & edge is present, removes $v$ from the $u$'s edge list and removes $-u$ from the $v$'s edge list, else returns false.
2. After successful deleting the edge, checks the `ccid` of both the vertices.
3. if $u.ccid$ is not same as $v.ccid$, returns true, as no changes to the current SCC. Else goto step 4.
4. Runs the forward and backward DFS algorithm (the limited version of Kosaraju's algorithm), process all the affected vertices belongs to that SCC and creates new SCCs.
   - For each new iteration of affected vertices.
     • Creates a new scc with any one of the old vertex belongs to it, later adds rest of vertices to that newly created SCC and then disconnects it from the old SCC.

# 4    Performance Analysis

In this section, we evaluate the performance of our SMSCC algorithm. We ran each experiment for 20 s, and measured the overall number of operations executed by all the threads (starting from 1, 10, 20 to 60). The graphs shown in the Figs. 2 and 3 are the total number of operations executed by all threads. In all the tests, we ran each evaluation 8 times and took the average. The algorithms we compare are, (1) Sequential, (2) Coarse-grained, (3) SMSCC and (4) SMSCC with delete incoming edges. The detail regarding performance analysis, correctness and its proof are given in the full paper [6].

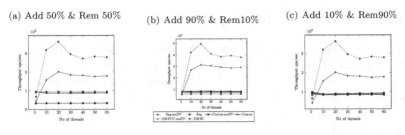

**Fig. 2.** SMSCC execution with different workload distributions

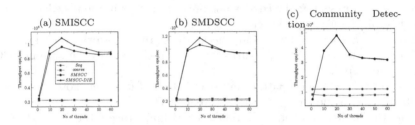

**Fig. 3.** (a) Incremental SCC (100% Add (V+E)), (b) Decremental SCC (100% Rem (V+E) and (c) Community detection (checking 80% + update 20%)

## 5  Conclusion and Future Direction

In this paper, we proposed a fully dynamic algorithm (SMSCC) for maintaining strongly connected component of a directed graph in a shared memory architecture. The edges/vertices are added or deleted concurrently by fixed number of threads. To the best of our knowledge, this is the first work to propose using linearizable concurrent data-structure. We provide an empirical comparison against sequential and coarse-grained, with different workload distributions. Also we compare the result with delete & without delete incoming edges. The throughput is increased between 3 to 6x against coarse-grain. Currently the proposed update algorithms are blocking and deadlock-free. In the future, we plan to explore non-blocking (lock-free & wait-free) variant of all the methods of SCC-Graph.

**Acknowledgement.** I am grateful to Dr. Sathya Peri and Ritambhara Chauhan for their many healpful comments and to MediaLab Asia for funding my scholarship.

## References

1. Demetrescu, C., Eppstein, D., Galil, Z., Italiano, G.F.: Dynamic graph algorithms. In: Atallah, M.J., Blanton, M. (eds.) Algorithms and Theory of Computation Handbook, p. 9. Chapman & Hall/CRC, Boca Raton (2010)
2. Henzinger, M.R., King, V.: Randomized fully dynamic graph algorithms with polylogarithmic time per operation. J. ACM **46**(4), 502–516 (1999)

3. Hirschberg, D.S., Chandra, A.K., Sarwate, D.V.: Computing connected components on parallel computers. Commun. ACM **22**(8), 461–464 (1979)
4. Hopcroft, J., Tarjan, R.: Algorithm 447: efficient algorithms for graph manipulation. Commun. ACM **16**(6), 372–378 (1973)
5. Sathya Peri, M.S., Singhal, N.: Maintaining Acyclicity of Concurrent Graphs CoRR abs/1611.03947 (2016). http://arxiv.org/abs/1611.03947
6. Sa, M.: Maintenance of Strongly Connected Component in Shared-memory Graph CoRR abs/1804.01276 (2018). http://arxiv.org/abs/1804.01276
7. Shiloach, Y., Even, S.: An on-line edge-deletion problem. J. ACM **28**(1), 1–4 (1981)

# Middleware

# Comparative Analysis of Our Association Rules Based Approach and a Genetic Approach for OLAP Partitioning

Khadija Letrache[(✉)], Omar El Beggar, and Mohammed Ramdani

Informatics Department, LIM Laboratory, Faculty of Sciences
and Techniques of Mohammedia, University Hassan II, Casablanca, Morocco
khadijaletrache@gmail.com,elbeggar_omar@yahoo.fr,ramdani@fstm.ac.ma

**Abstract.** OLAP databases remain the first choice of enterprises to store and analyze huge amount of data. Thereby, to further enhance query performances and minimize the maintenance cost, many techniques exist, among which data partitioning is considered as an efficient technique to achieve this purpose. Although most of business intelligence tools support this feature, defining an appropriate partitioning strategy remains a big challenge. Hence, many approaches have been proposed in the literature. Nevertheless, most of them have been evaluated only in relational model. Therefore, we propose in this paper, a comparative study between our partitioning approach based on the association rules algorithm and a genetic based one. The study aims to compare the results of the aforementioned approaches in case of OLAP partitioning.

**Keywords:** Partitioning · OLAP · Data warehouse
Association rules algorithm · Genetic algorithm · Performance

## 1 Introduction

In OLAP databases, partitioning is the operation of breaking up data into small, manageable physical units [1]. Indeed, partitioning divides the OLAP cube into smaller partitions that can be stored in separate physical servers, allowing thus store management. Moreover, partitioning enhances the cube performance by means of improving query response time due to the decreased number of rows that the system has to scan for each user query. Besides, partitioning also enhances the cube refresh time because of reducing the amount of aggregations that the OLAP system recalculates on each data cube update. In addition, partitioning allows integrating parallelism in querying and processing OLAP databases [2]. Hence, given the apparent importance of partitioning in decisional support systems, most of OLAP frameworks support partitioning feature [3]. However, these frameworks do not define the appropriate partitioning strategy which remains the challenged task for BI administrators. Therefore, many approaches have been proposed in the literature aiming to provide partitioning

© Springer Nature Switzerland AG 2019
A. Podelski and F. Taïani (Eds.): NETYS 2018, LNCS 11028, pp. 391–403, 2019.
https://doi.org/10.1007/978-3-030-05529-5_28

strategies and algorithms. However, most of these approaches have been evaluated in relational Data warehouses (DW) only. To deal with this, we propose in this paper a comparative study between two partitioning approaches applied to OLAP cubes. The first one is our approach based on the association rules algorithm (AR). The approach starts by identifying the frequent predicates itemsets from the user queries. Then, the partitioning process is performed using the resulting predicates itemsets. The partitioning algorithm aims to create new partitions that fit with the user requirements until attaining a minimum support parameter. The second approach [4] is based on the genetic algorithm (GA) widely used in optimization problems. It consists on modeling the partitioning problem as a genetic concept with chromosomes and genes and then performing genetic operations (reproduction, mutation etc.) to find the best solution. This approach uses the frequent user queries to select the predicates that will be used in the partitioning process. To carry out the evaluation of our approach in comparison with the genetic one, we implemented the two algorithms and conducted a set of experiments whose results are discussed in this paper.

The reminder of the paper is organized as follows: Sect. 2 presents previous works related to DW partitioning. Section 3 gives a background overview and addresses our partitioning solution as well as the genetic one. Next, the Sect. 4 describes the implementation of the two studied algorithms and the Sect. 5 discusses and analyzes the experiments results of both approaches. Finally, Sect. 6 presents the conclusion and perspectives.

## 2    Related Work

In [4] the authors Bellatreche et al. proposed a genetic based approach for horizontal partitioning of relational data warehouses. The proposal provides a cost model (fitness function) based on the IO cost to identify the best solution. The proposed partitioning algorithm is based on the frequent user queries though it ignores the correlation between predicates. The authors proposed latter two other partitioning approaches based on their GA approach [5], the first one is a hill climbing (HC) approach and the second is a simulated annealing (SA) one. In [6], the authors compared the new algorithms to the GA one, the results show that the GA remains a middle solution between HC and SA in term of query execution time and IO cost. More recently, Amirat et al. proposed in [7] a combined approach of horizontal partitioning and bitmap join index for data warehouse optimization. The proposal aims to classify the query workload on two categories defining the appropriate optimization method to be used. The partitioning is performed using the GA algorithm. Another genetic based approach was proposed by the authors Bouchakri et al. [8] which aims to deal with the query workload evolvement. In fact, the proposal consists on performing new partitioning by merging and splitting partitions when new queries are executed. The approach seems heavy to use in case of OLAP cubes because of time required to reprocess the partitions each time. Another partitioning approach has been proposed by Toumi et al. [9] based on binary particle swarm optimization. The approach consists on calculating the attraction between predicates using the Jaccard index and then clustering the predicates from which the best solution of partitioning is identified by using the particle swarm optimization. In [10] the authors Sun et al. proposed a partitioning framework that consists firstly on analyzing the query workload. Afterwards, constructing predicates vectors which constitute the input of the partitioning algorithm. The proposal includes also storing the partitioning schema in the system catalog to minimize the number of partitions scanned by the users queries. More recently, a data partitioning approach for Hadoop-based data warehouses was proposed by Arres et al. [11]. The proposal consists on partitioning the data warehouse tables vertically and horizontally and then placing dimension tables of frequent predicates in the same cluster or closest according to the user frequent queries. Finally, a vertical data partitioning is given by the authors Kim et al. [12]. Indeed, the authors intended to identify columns that appear together in user queries and then selecting the best partitioning schema according to the storage constraint.

In summary, most of partitioning approaches concern the relational DW. Some of them ignore the correlation between predicates and thereby generate unnecessary partitions. Moreover, some approaches ignore the preprocessing phase of predicates especially the date ones. Furthermore, all of the listed approaches do not integrate any control on the resulting partitions size while the store management is one of the partitioning advantages. Hence, our AR partitioning approach aims firstly to deal with all these problems and also to provide better results in term of cube performance. We notice also that in the several partitioning approaches that have been proposed in the literature, the genetic algorithm is the most used one or is to which, the most other approaches, have been compared. Therefore, we have chosen this algorithm to evaluate and confirm the efficiency of our association rules based approach.

## 3   Partitioning Algorithms

### 3.1   Background Overview

Data warehouse partitioning: refers to the breakup of data into separate physical units that can be handled independently [1]. In OLAP model, a partition is a subset of a cube used for performance or storage reasons. A horizontal partition contains all of the measures and dimensions of its cube. While a vertical partition contains a subset of the measures and dimensions of its cube [13]. Hence, considering a cube C defined by a set of dimensions D and a set of measures M, we can define a partition P by : $P(D_p, M_p, Y_p)$ where $D_p$ is the set of dimensions of P like $D_p \subseteq D$, $M_p$ is the set of measures used by P like $M_p \subseteq M$ and $Y_p$ the set of dimension members (predicates) used to drive P. we can also note simply $P(Y_p)$, if P has the same measures and dimensions as its parent cube.

### 3.2   Preparation of the Partitioning Algorithms Inputs

Both studied partitioning algorithms are based on the user queries predicates. Hence, before performing the partitioning process, we first gather the user queries. Afterwards, a preprocessing step is required that consists on, firstly, replacing date predicates by general formula. Indeed, date predicates are dynamic depending on the query execution date. Thereby, by comparing the date predicate with the query execution date, we can deduce the dynamic formula of the predicate. For instance, considering a date predicate "Sale date", by comparing its query values $\{d_1, d_2, .., d_n\}$ with the query execution time $\{t_1, t_2, .., t_n\}$, we can figure out that all the predicate values correspond to the current day $d_i = t_i$, we replace then $d_1, d_2, .., d_n$ by the MDX (MultiDimensional eXpressions) expression "Now()". The second preprocessing operation is the separation of MDX sets onto multiple tuples which corresponds to an "OR" operator. Given the preprocessing is done, we identify thereafter the most frequent queries from which we extract the list of used predicates for each attribute. We call the list of used predicates of an attribute $A_i$ the selection domain [4] that we note by $SD_i = \{a_1, a_2, .., a_n\}$. The resulting selection domains will constitute the input of the genetic algorithm. On the other hand, from all user queries, we extracted the most frequent predicates itemsets by using the apriori algorithm [14]. We note each resulting predicates itemset $I_i$ by $I_i = \{i_1, i_2, .., i_m\}$. The resulting itemsets, which we sorted by frequency, will be used as input of the AR algorithm.

### 3.3   Our Association Rules Based Approach

Our approach based on the association rules algorithm [15] consists on using the frequent predicates itemsets I=$\{I_1, I_2, .., I_m\}$ sorted by frequency as input and trying to create cube partitions that fit exactly with these itemsets and that satisfies a predefined threshold min_sup. This latter aims to avoid creating too small partitions sizes or huge amount of partitions which will increase the maintenance cost. The algorithm (see Algorithm 1) rolls up the cube partitions (the cube only in the first iteration) and calculates the support of each predicates itemset $I_j$ in each partition $P_i(y_p)$ which formula is $Support(y_p, I_j) = \frac{Count(y_p \bigcup I_j)}{|C|}$ where $|C|$ is the number of records in the cube. Furthermore, by using $I_j$ to partition $P_i$ two new partitions $P_{i_1}$ and $\overline{P_{i_1}}$ will be created like $P_i = P_{i_1} \bigcup \overline{P_{i_1}}$ and $P_{i_1} \bigcap \overline{P_{i_1}} = \emptyset$ (see [Fig. 1]). Hence, to avoid creating small partitions, the support of $\overline{P_{i_1}}$ which verifies the condition $\overline{I_j}$ (the opposite of $I_j$), also must fulfill the threshold min_sup. For instance, considering an itemset $I_j = \{Jewelry, 201803\}$ to be used to divide a partition containing data of Morocco like $P_i(\{Morocco\})$. The two resulting partitions are $P_{i_1}(\{Jewelry, 201803, Morocco\})$ and $\overline{P_{i_1}}(\{Jewelry, 201803, \overline{Morocco}\})$. The supports of these two partitions whose formula are respectively $\frac{count(\{Jewelry, 201803, Morocco\})}{Count(All)}$ and $\frac{Count(\{Jewelry, 201803, \overline{Morocco}\})}{Count(All)}$ must verify the min_sup threshold. Moreover, in case that the support is less than the min_sup, the algorithm, instead of ignoring the itemset, tries to enlarge the scope by going up in the predicates hierarchies. The algorithm thus starts from the last predicate which means from the predicate having the smaller support, then replaces it by its first ancestor and so on, until the fulfillment of the support threshold

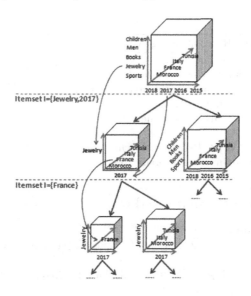

**Fig. 1.** Illustration of our partitioning algorithm

or until attaining the predicate root in which case the predicate will be ignored, and the algorithm skips then to the next predicates etc. as shown in the example of the [Fig. 2].

Finally, in addition to the support, the algorithm calculates the confidence of each itemset $I_j$ whose formula is [14]: $Confidence(y_p, I_j) = \frac{Count(y_p \bigcup I_j)}{Count(y_p)}$ If this latter is equal to 100% hence $y_p \subseteq I_j$, which means that $I_j$ (or its descendants) is already used to obtain $P_i$. $I_j$ is thus ignored. In the example listed above, considering an item $I_k = \{Africa\}$ to be used to partition $P_{i_1}(\{Jewelry, 201803, Morocco\})$. The confidence of the new resulting partition is $\frac{Count(Jewelry,201803,Morocco,Africa)}{Count(Jewelry,201803,Morocco)}$ which is equal to 100% because $\{Jewelry, 201803, Morocco\} \subseteq \{Jewelry, 201803, Morocco, Africa\}$.

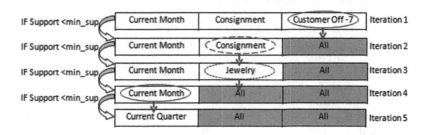

**Fig. 2.** Illustration of the scope enlargement mechanism

---

**Algorithm 1.** The AR partitioning Algorithm

---

**Require:** C cube to partition,
  $min\_sup$ the minimum support threshold
  $Predicates\_Itemsets$ list of frequent predicate itemsets
**Ensure:** P list of resulting partitions
  $P = \{C\}$     // P contains initially the cube
  $P' = P$
  **for all** $I_i = \{i_1, i_2, ., i_n\} \in Predicates\_Itemsets$ **do**
    $j = n$     // n is the number of predicates in $I_i$
    $P = P'$
    **for all** $p_k \begin{cases} D_k \\ M_k \\ Y_k \end{cases} \in P = \{p_1, p_2, ., p_m\}$ **do**
      **while** $j \geq 1$ **do**
        $sup(Y_k, I_i) = \frac{Count(Y_k \bigcup I_i)}{|C|}$     // calculates the frequency of $I_i$ in the Cube
        C
        $conf(Y_k, I_i) = \frac{Count(Y_k \bigcup I_i)}{Count(Y_k)}$     // calculates the frequency of $I_i$ in the partition
        $p_k$
        $sup(Y_k, \overline{I_i}) = \frac{Count(Y_k \bigcup \overline{I_i})}{|C|}$     // calculates the frequency of $\overline{I_i}$ in the Cube
        $conf(Y_k, \overline{I_i}) = \frac{Count(Y_k \bigcup \overline{I_i})}{Count(Y_k)}$ // calculates the frequency of $\overline{I_i}$ in the partition
        $p_k$
        **if** $sup(Y_k, I_i) = 0$ or $sup(Y_k, \overline{I_i}) = 0$ **then**
          $j = 0$     // Go to next partition
        Else
          **if** $sup(Y_k, I_i) \geq min\_sup$ and $sup(Y_k, \overline{I_i}) \geq min\_sup$ **then**
            **if** $conf(Y_k, I_i) = 1$ or $conf(Y_k, \overline{I_i}) = 1$ **then**
              j=0     // Go to next partition
            Else
              //Partition $p_k$ using $I_i$ and add the new partitions to $P'$
              $P'.add(p_k.Partition\_with(I_i))$
              $P'.delete(p_k)$ // delete $p_k$ from $P'$
              $j = 0$ // Go to next partition
          **end if**
          Else     // loop on predicates ancestors
          **while** $A$ is null and $j \geq 1$ **do**
            $A = Ancestor(i_j, 1)$
            **if** A is not null **then**
              $I_i.Replace(i_j, A)$     // replace $i_j$ by its ancestor
            Else
              $j = j - 1$     // Go to next predicate
            **end if**
          **end while**
          **end if**
        **end if**
      **end while**
    **end for**
  **end for**

---

## 3.4   Genetic Algorithm

The genetic algorithm (GA) proposed by Holland in 1960s [16], is an evolutionary based algorithm that uses operators inspired by natural genetic variation and natural selection to solve engineering optimization problems. The genetic algorithm consists on starting with an initial population of chromosomes (individuals) randomly generated and then performing genetic operations, namely selection, mutation and crossover, to get new population (offspring) that might represent the current problem's solution. The selection operation consists on selecting the fittest individuals for reproduction according to a defined fitness function. The crossover exchanges subparts of two chromosomes and the mutation randomly changes the allele values of some locations in the chromosome [16].

Hence, to use the genetic algorithm (GA) for OLAP partitioning, the first step is to model the partitioning problem with genetic concepts. In the solution proposed by Bellatreche et al. [4], each fragmentation schema is represented by a chromosome whose genes are the partitioning attributes, for example, the genes can be the product category, month or customer state etc. Each gene is represented by an array of integers with the same length as the associated selection domain deduced from the queries analysis phase and each allele corresponds to a value from this attribute selection domain, for example, the available values of the gene product category are {Books, Sports, Jewelry, Other categories} as shown in the example in [Fig. 3]. The partitioning solution is thus the Cartesian product of the chromosome genes. The gene alleles having the same value are grouped together. In the example shown in [Fig. 3], the chromosome will result on 3x2x2 fragments corresponding to the Cartesian product of the following items: [{Books, Jewelry},Sports,Other_Categories]x [January,Other_Months]x[IL,{CO,MN,Other_States}]. The second step is to define the selection function that returns the fitness value of each chromosome and allows identifying the best solution. For that, we use a cost function (1) that returns approximately the number of I/O needed to execute a query Q:

| Product category | Books | Sports | Jewelry | Other_Categoies |
|---|---|---|---|---|
| Gene 1 | 1 | 2 | 1 | 3 |
| Month | January | Other_Months | | |
| Gene 2 | 1 | 2 | | |
| Customer state | CO | IL | MN | Other_States |
| Gene 3 | 3 | 2 | 3 | 3 |

**Fig. 3.** Example of chromosome representation

$$Cost(Q) = \sum_{i=1}^{n} \prod_{j=1}^{M_i} \frac{Sel_j \times |F| \times L}{PS}$$ where n is the number of partitions needed to respond to a query Q, $M_i$ is the number of predicates defining a partition $P_i$, $Sel_j$ is the selectivity factor of a partition predicate $y_j$, which corresponds to the frequency of the predicate in the fact table, $|F|$ is the size of the fact table F, L corresponds to record size and PS is the system page size.

## 4  Experimental Study

### 4.1  Experimental Setup Parameters

To conduct our experiments to compare our AR based algorithm and the GA based one, we implemented the two algorithms in C# language using the GAF framework for the GA algorithm and the ADOMD for the AR algorithm. We used the TPC-DS [17] database to create the DW and the associated OLAP cube in SQL Server Analysis Services. The cube contains one fact table named Store Sales with 24M records and four regular dimensions (see [Fig. 4]): Date (73K) which contains the hierarchy date-month-quarter-year, customer (100K) includes the hierarchy customer-city-state-country, item dimension (18K) contains the hierarchy item-brand-class-category, promotion dimension (300) and store dimension (12) which contains the hierarchy store-city-state-country. We also used the TPC-DS query generator to generate a set of 100 queries. Finally, we performed our experiments on an i3 processor machine.

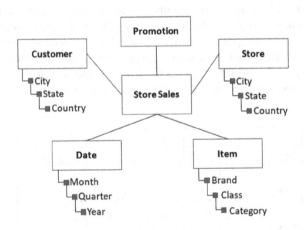

**Fig. 4.** The multidimensional model of our case study

### 4.2  The Association Rules Based Algorithm

As already discussed, the AR algorithm uses the frequent predicates itemsets as input. In our case study, the user queries analysis phase resulted on 24 frequent itemsets sorted by frequency. Giving the fact that the smaller the min_sup is, the more the partitioning algorithm goes up in the predicates hierarchy trying to enlarge the frequent itemsets scope instead of ignoring them, we fixed thus the min_sup threshold to 5% to test this ability. We then performed the partitioning algorithm. In the first iteration, the frequent itemset corresponds to the current month. Nevertheless, the support of this latter is less than the min_sup threshold. The algorithm tries thus to enlarge the scope by replacing the month by its ancestor in the date hierarchy, the quarter. This latter, whose support fulfills the min_sup, is thereby used to partition the cube. The algorithm continues, in this way, rolling up the rest of itemsets and partitioning the cube. At last, we obtained 9 partitions.

### 4.3    The Genetic Based Algorithm

After identifying the frequent queries, we determined the selection domain of each predicate and calculated their selectivity factor. We then performed the genetic algorithm as already described (see Algorithm 2). Therefore, an initial population of 40 chromosomes is generated (as proposed in [4]) by randomly constructing chromosome genes represented by integer arrays, having the same length as the associated SD. The crossover is performed using the parameter 0.7 and double point (as proposed in [4]) and the mutation fixed to 0.1 (in [4] the authors varied the parameter from 0.06 to 0.3). In our case study, the maximum number of resulting partitions is 768 which represent a huge number of partitions to create and manage. We hence add a maximum number of partitions threshold B that we fixed to 15 partitions and we modified the cost function by integrating a penalty function to eliminate solutions with huge amount of partitions, we used then the following function: Cost'(Q)=Cost(Q)$\times \frac{N}{B}$ where N is the number of resulted partitions. The algorithm results thus on 8 partitions for our case study.

## 5    Comparative Analysis

After executing the two studied algorithms as described above, we created the resulted partitions from each approach. Afterwards, we conducted a set of experiments to compare the two approaches. We stared thus by comparing the queries execution time enhancement as shown in the [Fig. 5]. We noted that the AR approach provides better results than the GA one with an average of 26%. Next, we compared the I/O cost for the two approaches which corresponds concretely to the number of memory pages needed to store partitions required to respond to a query Q. we used thus the reel partitions size like: $Cost(Q) = \sum_{i=1}^{n} \frac{|P_i|}{PS}$ where n is the number of partitions needed to respond to Q and $|P_i|$ is the size of a partition $P_i$ and PS is the system page size. The comparison shows that the I/O cost with AR approach is about 51% better than the GA approach (see [Fig. 6]). This can be explained by the fact that, because of the use of the frequent predicates

---

**Algorithm 2.** The GA partitioning Algorithm

---

**Require:** SD : List of attributes selection domains,
   Q : List of frequent queries
   B : Max number of partitions
**Ensure:** chromosome
   //Generate random initial population
   **for** $(i = 0; i < 40; i + +)$ **do**
      chromosome=Create_chromosome()
   **end for**
   **for all** (s in SD) **do**
      a=CreateRandomArray(s.lenght)
      chromosome.genes.add(a)
   **end for**
   population.add(chromosome)
   //Perfom GA operations
   SelectFitest(population, FitnessFunction)
   **while** $(nb\_generation <= 1000)$ **do**
      Crossover(population,0.7,DoublePoint)
      Mutation(population,0.1)
      SelectFittest(population, FitnessFunction)
   **end while**
   chromosome=FitestChromosome(population)
   //Fitness Function
   FitnessFunction(Chromosome c){
   Fragments=ChromosomeToFragments(c);
   **for all** (query in Q) **do**
      **for all** (F in Fragments) **do**
         $Cost+ = CalculateQueryCost(q, F)$
      **end for**
      Return Cost* B/Fragments.count
   **end for**
   }

---

itemsets, the AR approach enhances almost of queries, while the GA approach satisfies the frequent queries only. Besides, due to the Cartesian product of predicates, the GA approach generates unfeasible solution for none frequently asked data, while the AR approach isolates all this data in a separate partition that can be managed alone. The Table 1 provides the detail of the IO cost calculation.

Afterwards, we compared the resulted partitions size from each approach. We noted that the AR approach generates regular partitions (between 8 to 27 MB), as shown in the [Fig. 7], since the min_sup parameter in AR-based algorithm allows controlling the store constraint. Conversely, the GA approach, which controls only the number of partitions, generates irregular partitions size (between 0.08 and 83 MB), as shown in [Fig. 8]. In summary, our AR approach provides better performances in all aspects namely queries response time, IO cost and partitions size regularity as shown in Table 2.

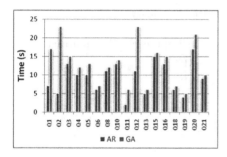

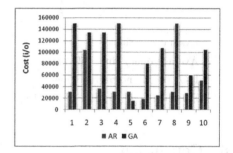

**Fig. 5.** AR and GA query execution time

**Fig. 6.** AR and GA I/O cost

**Table 1.** IO cost results

| Template | Frequency | AR partitions | GA partitions | AR I/O cost | GA I/O cost |
|----------|-----------|---------------|---------------|-------------|-------------|
| Q1 | 10 | P1 | P1+P2+P5+P6 | 3120 | 150073 |
| Q2 | 10 | P2+P3+P5 | P5+P6 | 10419 | 134643 |
| Q3 | 10 | P5 | P5+P6 | 3708 | 134643 |
| Q4 | 10 | P2 | P1+P2+P5+P6 | 3120 | 150073 |
| Q5 | 10 | P2 | P1+P2 | 3120 | 15429 |
| Q6 | 6 | P2 | P5+P6 | 3120 | 80786 |
| Q7 | 8 | P2 | P5+P6 | 3120 | 107714 |
| Q8 | 10 | P2 | P1+P2+P5+P6 | 3120 | 150073 |
| Q10 | 4 | P3+P5 | P1+P2+P5+P6 | 7299 | 60029 |
| Q11 | 7 | P3+P5 | P1+P2+P5+P6 | 7299 | 105051 |
| Q12 | 5 | P4 | P5+P6 | 6660 | 67321 |
| Q13 | 7 | P4 | P5+P6 | 6660 | 94250 |
| Q14 | 4 | P8 | P5+P6 | 5139 | 53857 |
| Total | 101 | 9 | 8 | 65908 | 1303947 |

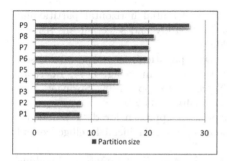

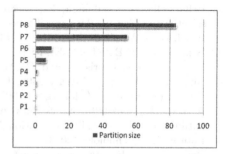

**Fig. 7.** AR resulting partitions size

**Fig. 8.** GA resulting partitions size

Table 2. Approaches evaluation summary

| Evaluation criteria | AR approach | GA approach |
|---|---|---|
| Average query time enhancement | 31% | 8% |
| I/O cost vs. no partitioning | 11% | 30% |
| Partitions size regularity(min size/max size) | 29% | 0.1% |

## 6  Conclusion

In this paper, we presented a comparative study between our partitioning approach based on the association rules algorithm and a genetic approach, one of the well-known optimization approaches, in case of OLAP cube partitioning. The results showed that the AR approach provides better results compared to the GA approach, in term of query execution time as well as IO cost. The results showed also that the AR approach generates partitions with regular size which can help in store management, contrary to the GA approach. For our future works, we intend to adapt and evaluate our AR partitioning approach in big data and unstructured databases.

## References

1. Inmon, W.H.: Building the Data Warehouse. Wiley, Hoboken (2005)
2. Ponniah, P.: Data Warehousing Fundamentals: A Comprehensive Guide for IT Professionals. Wiley, Hobokens (2001)
3. Letrache, K., El Beggar, O., Ramdani, M.: The automatic creation of OLAP cube using an MDA approach. Softw.: Pract. Exp., 117 (2017). https://doi.org/10.1002/spe.2512
4. Bellatreche, L., Boukhalfa, K.: An evolutionary approach to schema partitioning selection in a data warehouse. In: Tjoa, A.M., Trujillo, J. (eds.) DaWaK 2005. LNCS, vol. 3589, pp. 115–125. Springer, Heidelberg (2005). https://doi.org/10.1007/11546849_12
5. Bellatreche, L., Boukhalfa, K., Richard, P.: Referential horizontal partitioning selection problem in data warehouses: hardness study and selection algorithms. Int. J. Data Warehous. Min. 5(4), 1–23 (2009)
6. Bellatreche, L., Boukhalfa, K., Richard, P.: Data partitioning in data warehouses: hardness study, heuristics and ORACLE validation. In: Song, I.-Y., Eder, J., Nguyen, T.M. (eds.) DaWaK 2008. LNCS, vol. 5182, pp. 87–96. Springer, Heidelberg (2008). https://doi.org/10.1007/978-3-540-85836-2_9
7. Amirat, H., Boukhalfa, K.: A data mining-based approach for data warehouse optimisation. In: ICA2IT International Conference on Artificial Intelligence and Information Technology (2014)
8. Bouchakri, R., Bellatreche, L., Faget, Z., Bre, S.: A coding template for handling static and incremental horizontal partitioning in data warehouses. J. Decis. Syst. 23(4), 481–498 (2014)
9. Toumi, L., Moussaoui, A., Ugur, A.: EMeD-part: an efficient methodology for horizontal partitioning in data warehouses. In: ACM IPAC 2015, Batna, Algeria (2015)

10. Sun, L., Krishnan, S., Xin, R.S., Franklin, M.J.: A Partitioning Framework for Aggressive Data Skipping. In: International Conference on Very Large Data Bases, Hangzhou, China (2014)
11. Arres, B., Kabachi, N., Boussaid, O.: A data pre-partitioning and distribution optimization approach for distributed datawarehouses. In: Proceedings of the International Conference on Parallel and Distributed Processing Techniques and Applications (PDPTA), Athens, pp. 454–461 (2015)
12. Kim, J.W., Cho, S.H., Il-Min, K.: Workload-based column partitioning to efficiently process data warehouse query. Int. J. Appl. Eng. Res. **11**(2), 917–921 (2016)
13. Meta Data Coalition Open Information Model Version 1.1, August 1999
14. Han, J., Kamber, M.: Data Mining: Concepts and Techniques, 2nd edn. Elsevier Inc, Amsterdam (2006)
15. Agrawal, R., Imielinski, T., Swami, A.: Mining association rules between sets of items in large databases. In: Proceedings of the 1993 ACM SIG MOD Conference, Washington DC, USA, May 1993 (1993)
16. Mitchell, M.: An Introduction to Genetic Algorithms. A Bradford Book. The MIT Press, Cambridge (1999)
17. TPC-DS database. http://www.tpc.org/tpcds. Accessed 21 Nov 2017

# Short Paper: IoT Context-Driven Architecture: Characterization of the Behavioral Aspect

Radia Belkeziz$^{(\boxtimes)}$ and Zahi Jarir

Cadi Ayyad University, Marrakech, Morocco
radia.belkeziz@ced.uca.ma, jarir@uca.ma

**Abstract.** The contribution of this paper deals with IoT coordination. After a thorough review of the literature, we conclude that the challenge of coordination has not yet been met despite all the contributions already suggested. To address this challenge, we have proposed in a previous work an IoT contextual architecture, while the purpose of this article focuses on the behavior of the proposed multilayer IoT architecture by describing a flood case study. Three aspects are considered: functional aspect, informational aspect and behavioral aspect. When modeling the behavioral aspect, we focus mainly on the control flow throughout the workflow and we put our interest on relative ordering of sub-workflows.

**Keywords:** IoT · IoT architecture · IoT coordination architecture
IoT coordination behavioral · IoT meta-workflow

## 1 Introduction

Internet of Things (IoT) is defined by Gartner research as a network of dedicated physical objects (things) that contain embedded technology to communicate and sense or interact with their internal states or the external environment. Providing better and more resilient IoT services and applications faces unfortunately many challenges such as ease of connectivity, interoperability, scalability, security, coordination, and more. In this paper we focus on IoT coordination that consists of organizing things, objects, information, tasks, functionalities, services, etc. in a network in order to enable them to work together efficiently to attain a required and desired objective. However this organization makes the coordination challenge closely linked to other challenges like heterogeneity, context-awareness, decision-making, discovery and accessibility. Despite the efforts presented in the literature, this challenge remains open.

In [1] we already suggested a flexible multilayered IoT architecture dealing with coordination. This proposed architecture uses a combination of orchestration and choreography as a model of coordination guided by coordination and context policies. The aim of this current contribution deals with behavioral aspect of the proposed multilayered context-driven architecture. To model and formalize IoT coordination behavioral aspect, we use the modeling language proposed by Van Bochmann in [2] that supported a design derivation algorithm having the advantage to support most of the concepts found in UML Activity Diagrams.

The remaining of the paper will be organized as follow: Sect. 2 outlines a related work on coordination models. Section 3 describes the IoT multilayered architecture

© Springer Nature Switzerland AG 2019
A. Podelski and F. Taïani (Eds.): NETYS 2018, LNCS 11028, pp. 404–409, 2019.
https://doi.org/10.1007/978-3-030-05529-5_29

and details its behavior. Section 4 presents a flood case study whereas the Sect. 5 concludes the paper and highlights some future works.

## 2   Related Work

A coordination model offers a framework that considers entities' interactions such as communication, dissemination of actions, time and spatial distribution ... [3]. It can be classified as data-driven model, process-oriented model, control-driven model, or by combining or integrating some elements from each other.

In [4] authors presented a computational model based on events for the automation of team coordination, task and resource allocation. This contribution is dedicated to disaster fields for which the events are generated at run-time. The system supports decision-making, monitoring, inter- and intra-coordination. In [5] authors presented an IoT-based model for smart water management. They defined the requirements and challenges for water management, after they presented an architecture that could handle both ongoing and future requirement about water management. In [6] authors proposed a system architecture for Smart City applications. This system is based on a three-layer architecture that consists of a data layer; a process layer; and a communication layer. Over those layers, there is a coordinator that is responsible for orchestrating the components and monitoring the whole system.

The majority of coordination models suggested is strongly depending on specific application case study, and therefore couldn't be used as a generic architecture to build flexible IoT applications. In addition, we have a particular interest in the work of [4] which introduced the concept of meta-workflow that unfortunately depends on the policies, and the country where the system is used in case of disaster. In our vision a meta-workflow must be a high-level process that defines the overall execution of the system. The tasks to be performed in a normal environment and the overall objective to be achieved by the system are identified as in a natural way. When a problem arises, the system must adapt to changes and finds a solution among those suggested at design-time. Once the alternative is detected, the system continues its execution.

## 3   IoT Context-Driven Multilayered Architecture Behavior

To model efficiently an IoT coordination architecture, we have to address the functional aspect [5, 7], the behavioral aspect, and the informational aspect that aims to provide relevant data on time. So we suggested an IoT context driven coordination architecture as depicted in Fig. 1 where each layer is dedicated to a specific handling [1].

### 3.1   Meta-Workflow Management Layer

A meta-workflow is defined in [4] as a special higher process that involves five control instructions: start; terminate; suspend; resume; wait and suspend. To meet our objective we choose to work with the approach presented by Von Bochmann in [2] thanks to its similarity with the behavior of our architecture. The advantage of this referenced work is its formalization aspect, and the transformation algorithm proposed that has the capability to derive, from a given global behavior, the local behaviors for each of the system components including the exchange of coordination messages for the global synchronization of the activities. In addition our proposed meta-model includes both orchestration and choreography as coordination approaches. Each process is orchestrated and considered as an autonomous system. The choreography is based on the exchange of messages regulated by the policies which supports the global behavior. The application of this meta-model on flood case study is shown in the Fig. 2.

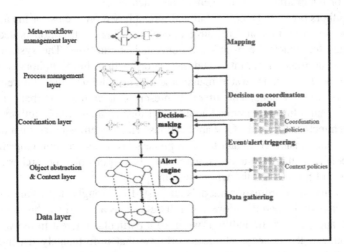

**Fig. 1.** IoT Context-driven multilayered architecture

## 3.2    Process Management Layer

This layer holds specific workflows for concrete scenarios, and is responsible for their management. It has to provide the description of the processes and the logic ordering of their execution. In the literature, we have identified some interesting works [4, 10] that aim to derive a global system behavior to components' behaviors, and assure that the global system behavior is accomplished by coordinating the actions through the exchange of asynchronous messages between these components. However these approaches have a major limitation from our point of view, which is the dynamic coordination adaptation. Thanks to the opted Bochmann work cited in [2] this requirement is taken in consideration. The transformation algorithm of [2] that derives from a global behavior, the local behaviors of each activity of the system, uses some operations such as primitive activity (<action>), invocation of sub-collaboration (<subcol>), strong sequence (;s), weak sequence (;w), choice ([]), strong while loop (*s), concurrency (||), interruption (|>), etc.

### 3.3    Coordination Layer

Generally, to fulfill coordination, two approaches are used: orchestration or choreography. In a previous work, we have presented some related work on orchestration and choreography and classified them according to some criterion [1]. As we presented it before, we use both orchestration and choreography models in accordance with the environment. For our system, in this layer, the decision on which coordination model (orchestration or choreography) to choose is made based on the policies defined. In addition, roles are allocated to components, adequate workflows to be executed are triggered, and their interconnections are established. We apply the translation function TC that determines the behavior of the system component c, for a given global behavior expression C. The component behavior expression is constructed using the same sequencing operators applied for describing the global behavior. Still, since the behavior is performed locally, there is no point in discerning weak and strong sequencing. As presented in [3], we adopt coordination messages between components according to the sequencing operators: Strong sequencing: flow messages (fm(x) or fim (x;i).), choice indication message (cim(y)), and interrupt and interrupt enable messages (im(z) and iem(z)).

## 4    Floods Case Study

In this case study the risk of floods is proportional to the intensity of thunderstorms. The behavior of our whole system is depicted in Fig. 2.

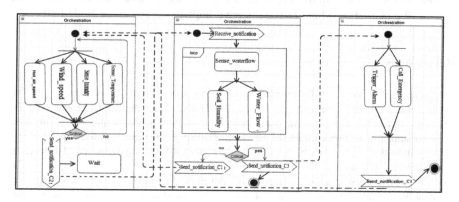

**Fig. 2.** Meta-workflow

Let's take C1 (<Detect_Thunderstorm>). The ordering of its sub-collaborations is defined as follow: the sub-collaborations <Sense_humidity>, <Sense_temperature>, <Wind-speed> and <Hot_air_speed> are executed concurrently followed sequentially by <Send_notification> which in turn is followed sequentially by the execution of

<Wait>.   C1 = (<Sense_humidity> || <Sense_temperature> || <Wind-speed> || <Hot_air_speed>); (<Send_notification>; <Wait>). Then, we define the roles involved in the collaboration. We noted two roles R1 and R2. R2 handles the notification sending while R1 handles all other sub-collaborations. R1 is the starting role; participating roles: R1 and R2. As C1 doesn't have a terminating point, R1 nor R2 aren't terminating roles. Moving to the translation function, it is defined as follow:

$$TR1 (<Detect\_thunderstorm>) = TR1 (<Rate\_humidity>);$$
$$TR1(<Sense\_Temperature>);$$
$$TR1(<Sense\_Wind\_Speed>); \ TR1(<Sense\_Hot\_air\_Speed>)$$
$$TR2 (<Detect\_Thunderstorm>) = TR2(<Send\_notification>).$$

## 5  Conclusion and Perspectives

In this paper, we focus mainly on the behavioral aspect of the proposed IoT multi-layered architecture. The meta-workflow management layer includes the meta-model that represents the overall behavior of the system. The process management layer is responsible for the representation of the processes as well as the management of the various collaborations and sub-collaborations by governing their execution orders and components roles. The coordination layer handles the coordination messages involved in the collaborations' operation based on the decision-making of the overall system.

Our next step is to improve the meta-model in order to make our architecture more generic. We plan also to finalize our system's implementation using Node Red.

## References

1. Belkeziz, R., Jarir, Z.: IoT coordination: designing a context-driven architecture. In: 13th International Conference on Singnal Image Technology & Internet Based Systems (2017)
2. Von Bochmann, G.: Deriving component designs from global requirements. In: 11th International Conference on Model Driven Engineering Languages and Systems (2008)
3. Papadopoulos, G.A., Arbab, F.: Coordination models and languages. In: Advances in Computers, vol. 46, pp. 329–400 (1998)
4. Xhafa, F., Asimakopoulou, E., Bessis, N.: An event-based approach to supporting team coordination and decision making in disaster management scenarios. In: Third International Conference on Intelligent Networking and Collaborative Systems (2011)
5. Robles, T., et al.: An internet of things-based model for smart water management. In: 2th International Conference on Advanced Information Networking and Applications Workshop (2014)
6. Nam, K.G., Rodger L., Blackstock, M., Leung, V.: On building smart city IoT applications: a coordination-based perspective. In: SmartCities (2016)
7. Wesk, M., Vossen, G.: Workflow languages. In: Handbook on Architectures of Information Systems, Chap. 16 (1998)

8. Castejon, H.N., Von Bochmann, G.: On the realizability of collaborative services. Softw. Syst. Model **12**, 597–617 (2013)
9. Bentallah, B., Sheng, Q.Z., Dumas, M.: The Self-serv environment for web services composition. IEEE Internet Comput. **7**(1), 40–48 (2003)
10. Kumar, A., Wainer, J.: Meta workflows as a control and coordination mechanism for exception handling in workflow systems. Decis. Support Syst. **40**, 89–105 (2005)

# Author Index

Printed in the United States
By Bookmasters